ENCYCLOPEDIA
OF THE
AMERICAN THEATRE ORGAN

The 6/51 Barton in the Chicago Stadium was the largest fully unified theatre organ ever built in the "good old days." It is also among the grandest and most thrilling musical instruments on the face of the earth!

ENCYCLOPEDIA
OF THE
AMERICAN THEATRE ORGAN

Volume I

DAVID L. JUNCHEN

SHOWCASE PUBLICATIONS

Pasadena, California

Address all correspondence to:

SHOWCASE PUBLICATIONS
Post Office Box 40165
Pasadena, California 91104

Manufactured in the United States of America

Library of Congress Cataloging in Publication Data

Junchen, David L., 1946-
    Encyclopedia of the American Theatre Organ

        Bibliography: p.
        Includes index.
        1. Organs—United States—Dictionaries. 2. Organ-
builders—United States. I. Title.
ML561.J86   786.6′273′0321   85-51070
ISBN 0-917800-02-8 (v. 1)

ISBN 0-917800-03-6 (set)

This book is dedicated to
the late Kirk Collins and to Steve Adams,
friends with a capital "F";
and to my father, Lawrence Junchen,
without whose love and encouragement
this book would not now be in your hands.

CONTENTS

FOREWORD

by Q. David Bowers

If one were to pick the ideal person to write a history of the theatre pipe organ, no better candidate could be found than David L. Junchen. In one individual he combines knowledge of music theory and arranging, playing ability, scholarship, enthusiasm and the rare attribute of being able to sift the significant from the trivial as well as the interesting from the pedestrian. The reader of Dave's three-volume history is the beneficiary of these abilities.

In the past, published histories of the pipe organ have ranged from enthusiastic (and often inaccurate) articles to a whole panoply of "stuffy" (for want of a better word) technical treatises. Dave Junchen's efforts literally represent the best of both worlds. Here are books which the reader can *enjoy* while at the same time obtaining historical and technical information never before available.

At one time the Wurlitzer company advertised (on signs attached to the back of trolley cars, no less!) that two million people per day listened to Wurlitzer music. Indeed, Wurlitzer was to theatre organs what Ford was to automobiles. While the "Mighty Wurlitzer" justly deserved the worldwide attention received years ago and deserves the enthusiasm lavished by present-day admirers, there were many smaller firms which are deserving of attention and study. Some of these featured complicated roll-playing devices, unusual tonal concepts and other innovations which are fascinating today. Rather than writing from the viewpoint of "my favorite instrument" or "my favorite company" and presenting all others on a lesser plane, Dave Junchen treats each of dozens of different organ builders with the same degree of freshness, enthusiasm and thoroughness. Again the reader is the beneficiary.

The late Farny Wurlitzer, whom the present writer knew well, once related that the Wurlitzer company was so ominpresent in the field that theatre owners would often pay more to obtain a smaller Wurlitzer organ than a larger instrument of another builder simply so that the Wurlitzer name could be featured to patrons. The late Ed Link, also a friend of this writer, once told of the ultimate indignity: a Link theatre organ sold to a New York client was having some small difficulty, whereupon the Link factory was called with the urgent request, "Please come and fix my *Wurlitzer!*"

Each of these gentlemen, Mr. Wurlitzer and Mr. Link, thought his brand of instrument was the best, which is perhaps as it should be. When asked about other organ companies, Farny Wurlitzer said, "Oh yes, we had some competition but it didn't amount to much." He seemed to be totally unaware that Robert-Morton, for example, sold nearly half as many instruments as did Wurlitzer. Such is the myopia of success! On the other hand, when asked about Wurlitzer organs, Ed Link observed that "They made a fine instrument but the tone was rather thin!"

Just as the average car buyer today is not equipped to judge carefully the different technical merits of a Buick compared to a Chrysler, not to mention trying to sort out a proliferation of advertisng claims, years ago the prospective theatre organ purchaser knew little about tibias, wind chests or unification. I found it curious to learn from my conversations with Farny Wurlitzer that only on *rare* occasions did a theatre architect bother to consult with Wurlitzer (or, apparently, with anyone else) concerning the technical specifications of an organ or the features of its installation. Rather, it was the practice to design the theatre and start building it and then, almost after the fact, to select a theatre organ! This haphazard practice, in combination with the fact that acoustics were almost a black art, resulted in varying degrees of musical quality once the finished installation was in place.

In many theatres, as the Wurlitzer (or Robert-Morton, or Artcraft, or Link or whatever) organ helped the locomotive rush toward Pauline or the steamboat come 'round the bend, the audience was really involved. Surrounding the listener completely, and adding almost a fourth dimension, the organ music meant that you were there—right on the railroad tracks or on the shore watching the steamboat. Indeed, the appropriate selection of music combined with novelty sound effects made the moviegoing experience in the silent film days not much different than watching a film with an elaborate sound track today. This may seem difficult for the uninitiated to believe, but anyone who has had the opportunity to hear a good organist in combination with a good film will agree.

After reading the *Encyclopedia of the American Theatre Organ,* the present-day enthusiast will know much more about theatre organs than did the most knowledgeable expert back in the 1920s. Thanks to Dave Junchen's careful research and appropriate commentary, we are provided with a greater than ever potential for enjoying one of man's most fantastic inventions, the theatre organ.

ABOUT THE AUTHOR

Dave Junchen is recognized as *the* authority on theatre pipe organ design, construction, voicing and history. He played his first pipe organ, a two-manual Barton theatre organ, at age ten. By age 15 the pipe organ "bug" had bitten and organs gradually began to displace mechanical musical instruments as his lifelong passion. The first pipe organ he ever worked on was the 3/15 Barton in the Trio Roller Rink in Milan, Illinois, 13 miles from his home town of Sherrard. Thirteen years later he purchased this very instrument, restored it and installed it in a Minneapolis restaurant, one of nine such restaurant installations done by Dave and his late business partner, Kirk Collins.

After receiving a BSEE degree with highest honors from the University of Illinois in 1968, Dave decided to pursue the organ business on a full-time basis. He didn't entirely forsake his electronics training, however; he pioneered the use of solid state relays for pipe organ use and, in fact, wrote the instruction manual for the first commercially available system built by Peterson Electro/Musical Products.

By 1975 Dave's business had grown to such an extent that a major expansion was warranted. He formed the Junchen-Collins Organ Corporation with Kirk Collins and operated that business in Woodstock, Illinois until 1980 when Mr. Collins retired due to ill health. Dave subsequently moved to Pasadena, California where he lives today, specializing in design, consultation, voicing and tonal finishing of theatre and classic pipe organs. Because Dave's career has specialized in theatre organs, many people are unaware of his passion for and competence in the classic organ arena also.

When asked which of his "children" (as Dave fondly refers to his installations) is his favorite, he replies, "That's a difficult choice! My favorite restaurant installation was, I suppose, the Old St. Louis Noodle and Pizza Company. It had a great sound and was one of those instances where the customer could afford an extensive cosmetic treatment. It was really quite a knockout!

"My favorite installation still in service is an easy choice: the 5/28 Foort Moller in the Pasadena Civic Auditorium. That job was a real challenge both mechanically and tonally. In previous installations the organ had acquired a reputation as a 'concert' organ which wasn't

particularly successful at traditional theatre sounds. I was quite complimented when, after the dedication concert, several buffs accused me of replacing large amounts of the organ with Wurlitzer parts. In fact, the tonal transformation was achieved with all the original Moller parts merely by proper design of the winding system and by appropriate tonal finishing."

Dave is a member of the American Institute of Organbuilders and is listed in over a dozen various editions of reference works such as *Who's Who in the West, Who's Who in the World* and *Who's Who in Finance and Industry*. He was a contributor to the *Encyclopedia of Automatic Musical Instruments* and has authored numerous articles for magazines such as *The Console, Theatre Organ* and the *Amica Bulletin*. He is a musician gifted with absolute pitch and is considered by many to be the finest living arranger of rolls for automatic musical instruments. "You don't have to be a musician with perfect pitch to be a good organ man," smiles Dave, "but it doesn't hurt."

ACKNOWLEDGMENTS

The author is grateful to the following individuals who responded to pleas for help. Some shared reminiscences, others loaned photographs and other reference materials; all were gracious and willing to help: Paul Abernethy, George Anderson, Robert Arndt, Lowell Ayars, Robert Balfour, Nelson Barden, David Barnett, S. H. Barrington, William Bartlow, Walter Beaupre, Fred Beeks, Jack Bethards, Bill Biebel, Lawrence Birdsong, Jr., Clealan Blakely, Walter Blanchard III, Ron Bogda, Terry Borne, Q. David Bowers, Harold Bradley, Jim Breneman, Lawrence Broadmoore, Dorothy Bromage, George Brown,

William P. Brown, Ray Brubacher, George Buck, Floyd Bunt, Hugh Burdick, James Burke, Arthur Dean Burnett, Jerome Butera, John M. Chappell, Terry Charles, Paul Chavanne, Robert Clark, Robert Coleberd, Jr., Jim Crank, Jim Crawford, Jerry Critser, E. W. Cunningham, Bruce Davis, Daniel Dawson, Thomas DeLay, Michael Detroy, David Dickson, Robert Dilworth, Ron Downer, Dorothy Dupont, Art Fike, Alan C. Fisher, Charles Fleck, Robert Foley, Randy George, R. E. Giesbrecht, Earl Gilbert, M. Lee Green, Allen Greene, Bill Greenwood, William G. Hale, Richard Harger, Tom Harmon, Tom Hazelton,

Harvey Heck, Dennis Hedberg, Elizabeth Heffer, Richard Heisler, Barry Henry, Fred Hermes, Douglas Hickling, Esther Higgins, John Hill, George Hockmeyer, Clay Holbrook, Henry Hunsicker, W. "Tiny" James, Lance Johnson, Roland Johnson, Robert C. Jones, Lawrence Junchen, Stan Kann, Charles Kegg, Robb Kendall, D. Stuart Kennedy, Gordon Kibbee, Weldon King, Phil Klann, Terry Kleven, Lloyd Klos, Syl Kohler, Eugene Laplante, Robert Letherer, Jim Lewis, Sanford Libman, Alan Lightcap, Hugh Lineback, Robert Longfield, Warren Lubich, George Lufkin, Edgar Lustig, Robert Maes, Harvell Mason, Kay McAbee, Douglas McGee, Dean McNichols, Franklin Mitchell, Ron Mitchell, Edward Mullins, Roger Mumbrue, Don Murphy, Tim Needler, Russell Nelson, Albert Neutel, Buddy Nolan, Robert Oberlander, Mike Ohman, David Olson, Ed Openshaw, Barbara Owen, Bob Pasalich, Harold Pearrell, Lauren Peckham, Stanton Peters, William Pilgermayer, Steven K. Plaggemeyer, Don Rand, Maxine Rash, Arthur Reblitz, Eric Reeve, George Rice, Gary Rickert, Robert Rickett, Scott Rieger, Greg Rister, Albert Robinson, George Robinson, Mel Robinson, Harvey Roehl, Manuel Rosales, Steve Ross, John Schantz, John Schellkopf, Curt Schmitt, Richard Schneider, John Shanahan, Richard Sklenar, Gregory Simanski, Helena Simonton, William T. Singleton, Ewell Stanford, Jr., Dick Starr, John Steele, Don Story, William Taber, Henry Tellers, Dennis Unks, William Van Pelt, Robert Vaughan, Richard Villemin, Randall Wagner, Jack Walden, Judd Walton, Ronald Wehmeier, Tim Wheat, Robert Whiting, David Whitmore, Harvey M. Whitney, Martin Wiegand, Albert Wiggins, Jr., Paul Williamson, David Winges, Edward P. Wood, George Wright and Rodney Yarbrough.

The author is especially grateful to the following individuals who made major contributions in the manner indicated: William Benzeno photocopied all the existing documents in the Midmer-Losh archive pertaining to theatre organs. Earl Beilharz shared much information about the Page Organ Company, of which his father was chief of installations. Homer Blanchard made the Organ Historical Society archive available and encouraged the author in many ways. David Broskowski searched the factory records of the Wangerin and Schaefer companies for theatre organ statistics. Bill Bunch made available the Balcom & Vaughn records and also loaned a number of rare photographs and documents from his personal collection. Alfred "Biff" Buttler and Michael Miller spent hours making additions and corrections to the opus lists of the New York City area. Brother Andrew Corsini and Joseph Duci Bella made available the Theatre Historical Society archive of photographs. Chris Feiereisen and Rosemary Luedtke provided copies of the B. F. Blower Company records. Robert Gilbert, editor of *Theatre Organ*, gave permission to use photographs from that publication. Irvin Glazer provided much information about theatres and organs in the Philadelphia area. W. S. "Stu" Green, editor and publisher of *The Posthorn*, gave the author a complete set of that publication and also recalled his experiences playing Marr & Coltons for the silent screen. Allen Harrah allowed the author complete access to records of the E. M. Skinner and Aeolian-Skinner companies. Robert Hillgreen, Jr. gleaned all the theatre organ statistics from the Hillgreen-Lane contract file. Walter Holtkamp, Jr. provided photocopies of every document in the Holtkamp files pertaining to theatre organs and provided a number of photographs. Bill Lamb made his archive of photographs available for examination and supplied copies of over a hundred of them. Robert Lent searched the files of the United States Pipe Organ Company for theatre organ information and provided many details about that company. Laurence Leonard researched the Estey factory records for theatre organ statistics. David McCain made available a complete file of *The Diapason* and granted permission to use a number of photographs from that magazine. Mr. and Mrs. Gordon Meyer allowed the author to inspect the archive of Jerome B. Meyer & Sons and loaned a number of rare catalogs and documents for reproduction. Allen Miller opened the door for research of the Austin factory records. Max Nagel, former superintendent of the Kilgen factory, made all the Kilgen records available for the author's inspection and graciously loaned some of them for duplication. Ken Rosen and Dr. Alfred Ehrhardt proofread the book. Jay Rosenthal edited the manuscript. Susan Steer, assitant manager of Atlantic City Convention Hall, opened the Convention Hall organs for the author's inspection and arranged for organ curator William Rosser to be on hand for a personally guided tour. Donald Traser, publisher of *The Tracker*, granted permission to use photographs from that publication. Martin Wick and John Sperling allowed the author to examine the Wicks factory archive and also supplied several rare photographs.

The contributions of seven people deserve special recognition. Without their help these volumes would be considerably less complete. The author wishes to convey his extreme gratitude to the following very special people:

★ Steve Adams, consummate friend, assisted in more ways than can be enumerated or remembered. His help can only be described as out of this world.

★ The late Jim Suttie, whose personal files document the locations of thousands of pipe organs, was of inestimable assistance in the preparation of the opus lists.

★ David Hunt and Lester C. Smith of the Spencer Turbine Company allowed the author complete access to that company's files of over 36,000 Spencer Orgoblos. Without their cooperation many of the opus lists would be only fragmentary.

★ Peter Moller Daniels, president of M. P. Moller, Inc., opened the enormous archive of the Moller and Kinetic companies for the author's inspection and entrusted the author with the loan of many rare documents and photographs.

★ Tom B'hend, editor of *The Console*, owns what is undoubtedly the world's largest collection of theatre organ memorabilia. He graciously made his entire archive available to the author.

★ Preston J. Kaufmann is responsible for the excellent layout and graphic design of these volumes. He constantly monitored every step of the publishing process to ensure books of the highest possible quality. When the author would say "Oh, that's good enough," Preston would counter, "No, it's not! We're going to do it *right*."

AUTHOR'S PREFACE

How This Book Came About

My interest in pipe organ history and minutiae is over two decades old. It all started in 1961 when I heard Howard Lane play *Dancing in the Dark* on the 3/14 Barton in the Trio Roller Rink in Milan, Illinois. I'll never forget my reaction to his musicianship and to those gorgeous sounds of solo tibias, diaphonic diapasons and reiterating marimbas. It was love at first hearing! Howard played a recording for me of Richard Purvis performing the Widor *Toccata* on the Aeolian-Skinner organ in San Francisco's Grace Cathedral and that clinched my love for the classical organ, too.

In recent years several people have suggested that I write a book. I didn't give the idea serious thought until recently because I had little time available due to running my own business and I knew how much time a project of this magnitude would require. In late 1981, however, a changing financial picture enabled me to free up some time and I began writing a book which I titled *The Care and Feeding of Theatre Pipe Organs* wherein I intended to share the technical knowledge I had learned about design, restoration and voicing principles.

After writing for a few days it occurred to me that purely technical material might get pretty dry to some readers so I considered adding some spice in the form of interesting historical information. My own collection of ephemera included a great deal of unpublished material and I was particularly intrigued by a few rare opus lists. I decided to use them along with a number of interesting photographs and original documents such as letterheads and contracts.

To make a long story short, I became preoccupied with the historical aspect and the technical writing began to take a back seat. I soon realized that there was enough historical material alone to warrant producing a book. The more I dug, the more leads turned up for further digging. Gradually a format for the book developed, undoubtedly influenced by my experience as an organ builder and by Dave Bowers' *Encyclopedia of Automatic Musical Instruments.* My plan was to include a history of each theatre organ firm together with an opus list for each and whatever interesting photographs and documents I could turn up.

Research for this book has been both fun and rewarding. Nearly everyone from whom I sought information was eager to help and some of the cooooperation was truly extraordinary. Specific acknowledgements have been made on page seven but I'd like to cite several examples of the spirit of helpfulness with which this research has been blessed:

David McCain, editor of *The Diapason*, started the ball rolling by *giving* me a nearly complete file of that publication. This collection is tantamount to a history of American organ building and formed the basis for my research.

Peter Moller Daniels, executive vice-president of M. P. Moller, Inc., allowed me to spend twelve full days examining anything at the Moller factory I wanted to see. I even spent two Saturdays at the factory going through files all by myself with no one around except the night watchman who came by once an hour. Said Pete Daniels, "You may open any file drawer you like. We have no secrets here."

Another example of super cooperation came from Max Nagel, former superintendent of the Kilgen factory, who now operates the St. Louis Pipe Organ Company and has custody of the Kilgen factory records. Mr. Nagel spent nearly two hours telling me much fascinating history about the Kilgen company and when I asked to see the old factory ledgers he replied, "Sure! I have to make some service calls today, but here's a key to the building. You may stay as long as you like." Talk about cooperation!

The Spencer Blower List

One of the major contributions to my research, without which it would be considerably less complete, was the cooperation of the Spencer Turbine Company. This firm has manufactured over 37,000 organ blowers since 1905 and is still making them today, although blowers represent only a fraction of one percent of current business. At one time Spencer maintained a manila file folder for every one of those 37,000 blowers. Each file contained construction details for the machine, the name of the purchaser, the destination, the size and opus number of the organ in some cases and information concerning subsequent changes of location. When the Spencer factory moved from Hartford to Windsor, Connecticut in 1975, these files were considered expendable and were thrown out. As a result, anyone inquiring of the factory about a Spencer Orgoblo in recent years has received a reply saying, "We're sorry but we no longer have that information."[1]

With the hope that some records might still be in existence, I wrote to Spencer President Lester C. Smith and explained the nature of my research. I received a warm letter from Senior Vice-President David Hunt explaining that Mr. Smith had retired in 1971 and that it was indeed true that dozens of filing cabinets had been thrown away. Mr. Hunt dropped a cliffhanger, however, in saying that there were a "few old records" left, "too many to copy," and that I would be welcome to visit the factory to examine them. He included a photocopy of one page of these records and upon seeing it my heart skipped a beat! It was a typewritten page on which were listed fifty consecutive Orgoblo serial numbers together with their destinations and the names of the purchasers.[2] Could the *entire* list of Spencer Orgoblos actually exist after all?

I wasted little time getting to Hartford. I was greeted warmly by David Hunt and also by Lester C. Smith, who came to the factory especially for my visit, one of the few times he had been to the new plant since his retirement. Mr. Smith revealed much fascinating company history and told how he had joined the firm in 1925. He recalled that his first out-of-town assignment was to call on the Wurlitzer factory in North Tonawanda, New York, Spencer's all-time largest Orgoblo customer. He vividly recalled the six *pairs* of 50-horsepower Orgoblos used on the large Wurlitzers. I knew that five 4/36 Wurlitzers had two 50-horsepower Orgoblos each and asked if he didn't

A real benefactor of theatre organ history and a thoroughly nice guy, Pete Daniels allowed the author complete access to files of the Kinetic Engineering Company and M. P. Moller, Inc.

David Hunt, retired senior vice president and Lester C. Smith, retired president of the Spencer Turbine Company are directly responsible for the completeness of this book due to their courtesy in allowing the author to research blower records of the Spencer company.

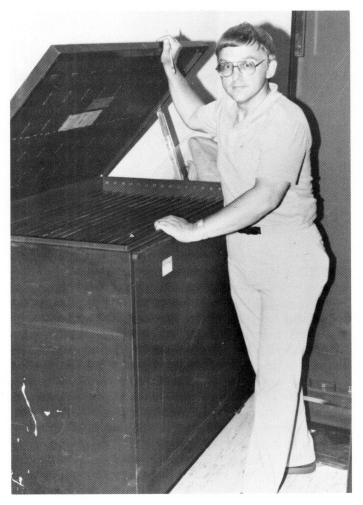

Wurlitzer company official George Buck opens the lid on an ordinary looking olive drab cabinet above to reveal a spectacular cache of theatre organ history—hundreds of gorgeously detailed pen-and-ink linen paper drawings of organs built in the Wurlitzer factory. He also allowed the author to break open locked ledger books (left) to inspect pages which probably hadn't seen the light of day in half a century. Much unknown history of the firm was thus revealed.

19751	Washington Ave. M.E.Church, Parsons, Kansas.	1926(93)
19752	Rudolph Wurlitzer Mfg. Co., North Tonawanda, N.Y.	1926(119)
19753	Harrodsburg Christian Church, Harrodsburg, Kentucky.	1926(36)
19754	First Parish Unitarian Church, Framingham Center, Mass.	1926(40)
19755	St. Andrew's P.E.Church, Richmond, Virginia.	1926 (51)
19756	St. Michael's R.C.Church, New Haven, Conn.	1926 (51)
19757	St. John's Episcopal Church, Hampton, Va.	1926(99)
19758	Omaha Academy of Music, Omaha, Nebraska.	1926(78)
19759	M.E.Church, Cape Vincent, N.Y.	1926(80)
19760	Scottish Rite Temple, San Jose, Calif.	1926 (36)
19761	Academy Theatre, Waukegan, Illinois.	1926(8)
19762	Holy Cross P.E. Church, Brooklyn, N.Y.	1926(119)
19763	Rivoli Theatre, Munie, Ind.	1926(119)
19764	Moline Reformed Church, Moline, Mich.	1926(30)
19765	Rudolph Wurlitzer Mfg. Co., North Tonawanda, N.Y.	1926(119)
19766	Roxy Theatre, Soloist, New York, N.Y.	1927(58)
19767	Roxy Theatre, New York, N.Y.	1927(58)
19768	Roxy Theatre, Broadcasting Studio, New York, N.Y.	1927(58)
19769	Rudolph Wurlitzer Mfg. Co., North Tonawanda, N.Y.	1927(119)
19770	First Presbyterian Church, Springfield, Mass.	1927(35)
19771	St. Trinitatis U.E.Church, Buffalo, N.Y.	1927(117)
19772	First Church of Christ Scientist, Louisville, Ky.	1927(11)
19773	Hon. T.W.Phillips, Butler,Penn.	1927(2)
19774	First Presb. Church, Lewiston, N.Y.	1927(117)
19775	First Presbyterian Church, Augusta, Ga.	1927(1)
19776	Bethel Evangelical Lutheran Church, Milwaukee,Wisc.	1927(51)
19777	Plaza Theatre, Salem, Mass.	1927(40)
19778	Masonic Temple, New Orleans, La.	1927 (58)
19779	Ritz Theatre, Baltimore, Md.	1927(102)
19780	First Church of Christ Scientist, Auburn, N.Y.	1927(36)
19781	Mr. W.F.L.Davis, Fort Washington, L.I.N.Y.	1927(117)
19782	Scottish Rite Cathedral, Galveston, Texas.	1927(117)
19783	Masonic Temple, Willimantic, Conn.	1927(14)
19784	First Methodist Episcopal Church, Ames, N.Y.	1927(30)
19785	St. John's Chapel(Epis), Del Monte, Calif.	1927(11)
19786	Saint Helens R.C.Church, Schenectady, N.Y.	1927(11)
19787	First Church of Christ Scientist, Alhambra, Calif.	1927(30)
19788	First Church of Christ Scientist, Glendale, Calif.	1927(30)
19789	Ardmore Methodist Epis. Church, South, Winston-Salem,N.C.	1927(30)
19790	First Presbyterian Church, Ridgewood, N.J.	1927(30)
19791	Savoy Theatre, Chicago, Ill.	1927(8)
19792	Estey Organ Company, Brattleboro, Vermont.	1927(41)
19793	General Howard S. Borden, Rumson,N.J.	1927(41)
19794	Astor Theatre, 45th St. & Broadway, New York, N.Y.	1927(58)
19795	Tioga Baptist Church, Philadelphia, Penn.	1927(30)
19796	First M.E.Church, Warren, Penn.	1927(11)
19797	A.Dent Theatre, Dallas, Texas.	1927(93)
19798	First M.E.Church, New Bethlehem,Penn.	1927(11)
19799	Mr. E.T.Dyer, Piedmont,Calif.	1927(11)
19800	Albany Theatre, Albany, N.Y.	1927(11)

A sample page from the Spencer blower list. Just imagine the wealth of information contained in 700 such pages! The number in parentheses represents the organ builder to whom the blower was sold. For example, 8 is Barton, 67 is Robert-Morton and 78 is Marr & Colton. The reader should have little difficulty guessing the identity of number 58, the builder who sold three organs to the Roxy Theatre in New York.

mean that five pairs of them were sold. "No, I'm sure there were twelve in all," he said.[3] I didn't think too much more about his response. I've interviewed a number of people who were active in the "good old days" and have found that memories half a century old are frequently not completely accurate as to details. But more about this later.

The time finally came for me to see those "few old records." They were located by Dorothy Dupont, manager of order entry, in an unlabeled file drawer and were about a foot in depth. Once again my heart leapt for joy as the drawer's contents unfolded: it was the complete list of all the Spencer Orgoblos ever built, together with other papers which gave more specific information on some of the machines. Messrs. Hunt and Smith graciously granted permission to photocopy the papers and I stood at their copy machine nearly all day doing so. When I left the office I had over 700 pages with me! When I offered to compensate the company for use of the copying machine, Mr. Hunt said, "Oh, that's all right. Just send us a copy of your book when it's ready."

The Wurlitzer Contribution

From the very beginning of my research I knew that the Wurlitzer chapter would be the largest in the book. After all, Wurlitzer built twice as many theatre organs as their nearest competitor and became literally a household word in the teens and twenties. To this day Wurlitzer and theatre organs go together as do Scotch and tape.

I inquired at Wurlitzer corporate headquarters in DeKalb, Illinois as to the possible existence of any old factory records and received a cordial reception from George Buck, the gentleman who masterminded the installation of the 5/69 "Mightiest Wurlitzer" in the DeKalb headquarters. George proceeded to show me the archive in a dingy basement room. To say that I was overwhelmed is a supreme understatement! It was immediately apparent that the wealth of Wurlitzer information available warranted a book of its own; so the *Encyclopedia of the American Theatre Organ* grew to a third volume.

One of the major "finds" in the Wurlitzer archive was a drawing for the *sixth* 4/36 Fox special. By the way, Spencer Tubine President Lester C. Smith's recollection was absolutely correct: Wurlitzer *did* buy a pair of 50-horsepower Orgoblos for this sixth 4/36.[4] To learn more details you'll just have to buy a copy of Volume III!

Conclusion

I've done my best to be absolutely factual in the statements made in this book. This is important, of course, in any reference work but is especially important in the subject of theatre organ history which for years has been the subject of too much speculation and not enough research. I've done my homework and the sources for my information are indicated in the footnotes which contain references only and may be ignored without missing any textual information. In cases where sources have disagreed on a particular piece of information I have used my intuition to determine which I felt were the most credible and in many instances have omitted data altogether if the supporting material wasn't adequate. My personal speculations are always clearly identified as such. As a result I have a high level of confidence in the accuracy of the historical data in this book.

Likewise, I've attempted to make the opus lists as accurate as possible. Unfortunately, there is room for error here because of the diversity of the sources. In cases where I've been able to examine actual factory records I'm reasonably confident in the reliability of the data. In many instances, however, factory records are either non-existent or fragmentary. To assemble opus lists for these firms requires reliance on trade advertising, blower shipping records, articles in organ magazines and people's memories. None of these sources is infallible. Hopefully the errors which will inevitably creep into the opus lists will be those of omission rather than errors of fact. I will be deeply grateful to readers who offer corrections and/or additions. All such contributions will be included and acknowledged in subsequent editions of this book. Please address correspondence to the author in care of Showcase Publications, Post Office Box 40165, Pasadena, California 91104.

This is one of the author's favorite photos. The spirit and flavor of what the theatre organ is all about have been expertly captured by photographer Bill Lamb as John Muri entertains attendees of the 1967 ATOE convention in the Detroit Fox Theatre. The spotlight projects a beam 160' through the darkened ten-story palace, and with a little imagination one can almost experience the thrill of sitting in that magical atmosphere and of being enthralled by the rolling tibias (all three of them!), the thundering 16' bombardes and the cavernous acoustics.

INTRODUCTION TO THE AMERICAN THEATRE ORGAN

An Historical Perspective

Theatre organs evolved to meet the need for background music to accompany silent films. Pianos were adequate in the smallest theatres but larger houses required orchestras for sufficient volume. Organs were installed so that music could continue while the orchestras took breaks and it was soon discovered that one organist was considerably less expensive than an entire orchestra. Furthermore, a single organist could improvise a more suitable accompaniment in many instances than could an orchestra which was limited to a printed score.

The first organs installed in theatres were identical to church organs of the day and some had tracker action, although Roosevelt and Farrand & Votey theatre instruments as early as 1893 and 1895 featured electric action, nearly a decade before Robert Hope-Jones' arrival in this country. Hope-Jones is frequently dubbed the father of the theatre organ because of his pioneering efforts with high pressures, unification and the use of the tibia clausa. It is ironic, however, that a) Hope-Jones never installed a theatre organ under his own nameplate; b) his concepts of unification are considered poor by today's standards; and c) he used the tibia clausa usually only at 8' pitch as a foundation, rather than a solo stop. In contemporary theatre organs the tibia is the most highly unified rank, often appearing on a dozen or more stops in one instrument.

Nevertheless, the introduction of the Wurlitzer Hope-Jones Unit Orchestra in 1911 paved the way for performance of popular music on the organ. This instrument was, in concept, a simulation of an orchestra and bore faint resemblance to a classical organ. The general public liked the music which could be played on these instruments and they became enormously popular. In fact, theatre pipe organs reached a level of importance second only to the silent film itself. Organ solos became an integral part of the entire entertainment package and organists achieved celebrity status. In promotional advertising the organ was touted as much as the film, often with extravagant claims such as "cost $50,000" or "largest in the state." Many of these claims were pure hyperbole, as will be seen by examining the opus lists in this book.

The organ greatly influenced the design of movie palaces; organ grilles were one of the most important aspects of a theatre's architecture. Conversely, theatre designs affected the organs and many consoles were decorated in Oriental, Mayan, French or Art Deco motifs to meld with theatre interiors. A particularly graphic example of the popularity of the theatre organ is the fact that one of the first phonograph records ever to sell a million copies was *Valencia*, recorded by Jesse Crawford on a Wurlitzer in 1926.

Classical musicians blamed the theatre organ's influence for contributing to the degradation of church organs in the 1920s, many of which were designed along orchestral lines. In retrospect, however, it can be seen that the orchestral organ was evolving long before the need for accompanying silent films came about. In eighteenth- and nineteenth-century America, orchestras were few and far between. Pipe organ design became more and more orchestral to meet the public's desire to hear the great orchestral works in an age long before the radio and phonograph made them readily accessible.

For many years it was fashionable among serious musicians to look askance at theatre organists for catering to popular, vulgar tastes—and for commanding high salaries. A similar case of sour grapes was evidenced by some classical organ builders, probably because they weren't getting their slice of the theatre organ pie. At about the same time that theatre organs were silenced by talking pictures the trend in church organ building began to shift from orchestral to more classical concepts. In many people's eyes the theatre organ became the scapegoat which was blamed for influencing the old, now unacceptable style of organ building. Actually, exactly the opposite was true: the trend towards orchestral organ design is what influenced the theatre organ.

The organ reform movement reached its zenith in the 1960s. Its "screech and shout" tonal concept proved to be as extreme in its direction as were the tubby sounds of some early twentieth-century instruments in their direction. In the 1980s many organists and organ builders have learned that each tonal school of thought fulfills a legitimate musical need. Unlike some of their colleagues of half a century ago, these people recognize that all music is equally legitimate whether it be classical or popular.

Another factor in the contempt which many musicians formerly had for theatre organs was the level of musicianship among theatre organists, which admittedly was not very high in the twenties. The demand for theatre organists grew so fast that there weren't enough qualified musicians to fill the available positions. As a result, many theatre organ performances were mediocre at best and others were downright dreadful. Unfortunately, the blame for these poor performances in many instances was placed on the instruments rather than on the organists where it belonged.

Theatre organ music experienced a renaissance in the 1950s when George Wright at the Mighty Wurlitzer helped usher in the age of modern high fidelity recording. Fortunately for the cause of the theatre organ, George was a superb musician. His excellent performances reached a wide market and went a long way toward legitimizing the music of the theatre organ as a viable art form in its own right.

What Is A Theatre Organ?

Strictly speaking, any organ installed in a theatre qualifies as a theatre organ although in modern usage the term denotes an organ specifically designed to play popular music regardless of where installed. Several criteria have been used in developing the opus lists in this book. First, the instrument must have been primarily an *organ* and not merely a piano with a few short ranks of organ pipes added. Bartolas and Fotoplayers, for example, do not meet this criterion. After fulfilling this requirement, an organ had to meet at least one of the following to be included in the opus lists: a) it must have been installed in a building called a theatre; b) it must have been installed in an auditorium where silent films were shown; or c) it must have been used to play popular music. Under the last category are included organs in some non-theatre locations such as radio stations and private residences.

The author has attempted to reserve use of the term "theatre organ" to denote only organs designed to play popular music. A large percentage of the organs installed in theatres were not very different from church organs of the day and did not perform popular music well. The phrases "theatre instruments" or "organs in a theatre" have been used to refer to such instruments whenever possible.

What really *is* the difference between a church organ and a theatre organ? Church organs are usually designed for the performance of classical organ literature and for accompanying choirs and congregational hymn singing, while theatre organs are designed to play popular music and orchestral works. But many of us have heard, for example, a Kimball theatre organ play a Vierne or Messiaen piece more successfully than could many church organs of the 1920s; and we may also have heard Gershwin and Porter performed more successfully on these same church organs than on the Wurlitzer in the local Bijou. So what *is* the difference? In the first place, not all church organs are *successful* church organs just as not all organs in theatres play popular music well. Furthermore, an unsuccessful church organ does not necessarily make a good theatre organ and vice versa!

There are several factors which are commonly thought to contribute to the difference between church and theatre organs but which, in reality, do not. One common notion is that church organs are voiced on low wind pressures and theatre organs on high pressures. This is generally true but there are some fine theatre organs voiced on 5" pressure and there are a number of church organs voiced on 7½", 10" and 15" wind. Another notion is that church organs are straight and that theatre organs are unified to hundreds of stops; but contrary examples exist. Many church organs are unified—and the Wurlitzer at New York's Radio City Music Hall has a number of straight ranks including two mixtures. By way of definition, a straight rank of pipes is controlled by only one stop key or drawknob and therefore is playable at only one pitch on only one division of the organ. A unified rank is playable at two or more pitches from one or more divisions.

Percussions are commonly thought to be an exclusive province of theatre organs, but in actual fact their use preceded the advent of the theatre organ by several decades in America and even longer in Europe. Stops such as saucer bells, glockenspiels, bass drums, cymbals and thunder pedals were not uncommon on nineteenth-century tracker organs. Some of these old trackers even featured high pressure solo divisions and/or several *unified* stops!

The one factor that distinguishes a good theatre organ is the presence of the tibia clausa, a large-scale stopped flute with a penetrating, hooty quality and a deep tremulant. This voice, more so than any other, is essential for the successful performance of popular music on the organ. A secondary factor in making a successful theatre organ is

An example of the detailed records kept for each blower manufactured by the Spencer Turbine Company. This particular page discloses that Orgoblo #11637 was used on a style 75 (2/4) Robert-Morton theatre organ. Around 10% of these records still exist at the Spencer factory.

that the tremulants on the other ranks be of sufficient depth. Many theatre instruments even without tibia clausas would have been much more successful at performing popular music had their tremulants not been so shallow. It is important to note that tremulant *speed* is not particularly a factor here. *Depth* refers to the degree of change of the amplitude and pitch of the sound wave caused by the tremulant beat.

Understanding The Opus Lists

The opus lists in this book have been gleaned from factory records wherever possible. Unfortunately, records of many firms are either nonexistent or fragmentary. Opus lists for these companies have been assembled with the help of reports from a number of individuals and by researching organ magazines and related trade publications. The greatest assistance has come from records of the Spencer Turbine Company. Inasmuch as Spencer Orgoblos were used on the vast majority of theatre organs sold in this country, the Spencer list is tantamount to an opus list for most of the theatre organs built. It is not so complete or detailed as the records of each organ building firm, of course, but in the absence of such records it is an invaluable resource tool.

There are certain frustrations inherent in using the Spencer list, however. For example, sometimes blowers were shipped to the organ builder's factory and the list failed to disclose their subsequent installations. In some cases a blower may not have represented a new organ by the builder to whom it was sold but may have been a replacement for an old blower or may have been for additions to an existing organ, possiby of a different make. Occasionally the list discloses these ephemera but usually it doesn't. As a result, some entries in the opus lists may not be entered under the proper builder. The fact that a blower was sold to a cerain builder does not necessarily mean that the organ it powered carried that builder's nameplate. Any such errors will hopefully be minimal. In the few cases where entries have been questionable they have been omitted on the theory that a sin of omission would be more acceptable historically than one of commission.

Similar remarks are applicable to the records of the Kinetic Engineering Company, now owned by M. P. Moller, Inc. The Kinetic files are much more detailed than the remaining Spencer files but are more unwieldly for research purposes: they consist of around 60,000 file cards! Needless to say, copying all these records was impractical so the author spent six entire days looking through those cards and recording information relating to theatre instruments. Having built around 23,000 blowers, the Kinetic firm ranks second to Spencer in number of blowers manufactured. The output of these two firms accounts for over 90% of the blowers sold in this country through the 1950s.

Two other firms received a small portion of America's blower business: the Zephyr Electric Organ Blower Company and the B. F. Blower Company. Zephyrs were made by Schantz and were used primarily on Schantz organs although they were also offered to the trade. Schantz kept scant records of the blowers they built;[1] an estimated 1,000 or so may have been sold for use on non-Schantz organs, most of which were small church instruments. The B. F. Blower Company built around 1,300 Simplex blowers, about half of which were sold to Kilgen. Of the others, only a handful were ever used on theatre instruments.[2] Fortunately, records of all but around 200 Simplex blowers have been preserved and were made available through the courtesy of Chris Feiereisen and Rosemary Luedtke. These records of the Spencer, Kinetic and B. F.

companies account for over 99% of the theatre instruments ever built.

The opus lists in this book include blower serial numbers and their horsepower and wind pressure ratings wherever known. There are at least four reasons for including this information. First, the presence of a blower at a theatre certainly helps justify an entry for an organ having been there. Second, the date of blower shipment parallels the date of the organ's installation in most

Above and to the left are samples of the kinds of information found among the 60,000 file cards in the Kinetic Engineering Company records.

cases. Third, the blower size may give a clue as to the size of the organ in instances where the organ organ's size is unknown. Fourth, blower serial numbers may help identify the origins of some errant instruments extant today whose first homes were in theatres.

Serial numbers are identified as follows: Spencer Orgoblos have a four- or five-digit number with no letter prefix. Spencer Turbo blower numbers have the suffix letters TUR in these lists, and Spencer Orgoblo Juniors have the suffix letters JR. On the actual blower nameplate there are no such suffixes, but the nameplates clearly identify whether the machine is an Orgoblo, a Turbo or an Orgoblo Junior.

Kinetic blowers usually have a prefix letter in their serial numbers. Very early Kinetic numbers have four digits without a prefix and in these lists a K suffix has been added to distinguish them from Spencer numbers. Likewise, an S suffix has been added to the Simplex numbers for the same clarification. The Simplex records are unclear as to their numbering system; Simplex numbers appearing in the Kilgen opus list may therefore not be the actual numbers stamped on blower nameplates.

Opus lists of the Austin, Estey, Hillgreen-Lane, Kilgen, and Moller companies are presented in both chronological and alphabetical order. The chronological lists are arranged by opus number and are useful for charting the sales progress of the firms and for understanding how their instruments evolved over the years. These lists contain much more information than the accompanying alphabetical ones, which serve as an index and are pro-

To assist the reader in understanding the opus lists, five sample entries from the Robert-Morton list are given below, with explanations for their interpretation:

CITY/STATE	LOCATION	SIZE	YR	BLWR	HP	WP	REMARKS
1. CALIFORNIA							
Long Beach	Liberty (Roxy) Th.	2/14	1916				Built by California Organ Co.; with 88-note roll player.
2. CONNECTICUT							
New Britain	Lyceum Th.	2/	1925	M1043B	5	10″	Plus 30″ vacuum.
3. MICHIGAN							
Detroit	Riviera Annex Th.	3/13	1926	19334	10		With V'Oleon.
			1927	11560TUR			
4. MISSISSIPPI							
Greenville	People's (Paramount) Th.		1922	13958			
		2/6	1927	19868			
5. PENNSYLVANIA							
Philadelphia	Milgram & Pilch		1925	17906			

1. The original name of this theatre was the Liberty; its name was later changed to Roxy. Every attempt has been made to list theatre names in the order in which they appeared. Tracing theatre history, however, is frequently difficult; one theatre in New York, for example, changed names nine times![3]

In the "remarks" column will be noted that this organ carried the California Organ Company nameplate (a forerunner of the Robert-Morton Company) and contained an unusual feature: a player mechanism using ordinary 88-note rolls. No blower number is listed; this is an example where the blower was shipped to the California Organ Company factory rather than directly to the installation site. As a result, the Kinetic blower records do not disclose its final destination.

2. This organ has a Kinetic blower, as can be determined by the letter prefix in the serial number. The blower had a five horsepower motor and was rated at 10″ wind pressure on one outlet and at 30″ vacuum on the other. The number of ranks in this organ is not known so that information is blank in the entry. However, by exploring the Robert-Morton list, the reader will find a number of similar Kinetic blowers. For many of these the sizes of the organs are known so it is possible to speculate fairly accurately on the size of the Lyceum organ using the theory that similar size organs built by the same company used similar size blowers.

3. This organ used two Spencer blowers: an Orgoblo and a Turbo. In this case, the Turbo supplied vacuum for powering the organ's piano. So far as the author knows, all Spencer Turbos for organ use were used as vacuum sources. The Riviera Annex organ also had the unusual feature of a V'Oleon attachment, as mentioned in the "remarks" column.

4. Two Spencer blowers were shipped to this theatre for reasons not disclosed by the remaining Spencer records. Had the blowers been shipped the same year it would be likely that they were both used in the same organ. One might have been a pressure booster or might have powered a remote division of the organ such as an echo. If the blowers had been shipped only a year apart a likely possibility would be that the first blower proved inadequate and had to be replaced with a larger unit. In this particular example, however, the blowers were shipped five years apart so it is likely that the original organ was enlarged or replaced with a larger one.

5. This entry is an example where the theatre was under construction and had not yet been named when the blower was shipped; Milgram and Pilch were names of the theatre owners. In some cases blower records are even more cryptic and say merely "new theatre."

vided merely for convenience in researching a particular organ. After an opus number is found, complete information on the organ can then be located in the chronological list.

Chronological lists are arranged by opus number, corresponding to the order in which organs were sold. Most entries include the year of installation, which in many cases was not the same year in which the order was placed. This accounts for the fact that entries in the "year" columns sometimes skip back and forth despite the fact that the opus numbers are in consecutive order. These lists may also contain more entries than the alphabetical lists. Consider, for example, a Kilgen organ sold to a theatre which already had a photoplayer. Kilgen would take the photoplayer in on trade and sell it to another theatre, assigning an opus number to the sale. This transaction therefore appears on the chronological list of theatre business conducted by Kilgen but will not appear on the aphabetical index of actual Kilgen organ installations.

Most theatre organs were eventually moved to other locations either because they were being replaced by updated instruments or, in later years, because their usefulness had ended. Susequent locations of these organs are included in these lists wherever known provided that the new locations were theatres or other places where the organs would continue to perform popular music. Chart-

ing contemporary moves of these organs to churches, homes and pizza parlors is beyond the scope of the present volume whose thrust is the "good old days."

How Many Theatre Organs Were Installed?

Exact figures for total production of theatre instruments will never be known, but a very close approximation can be made. The accompanying graph shows the production of the major firms. Totaling the figures for all firms reveals that around 7,000 theatre instruments were manufactured in this country.

Another statistic of interest is the annual number of pipe organs of all types built, according to figures supplied by the United States Census Bureau. It is interesting to compare this graph with comparable statistics of pipe organ production of the Wurlitzer company. Census figures are not available for each year, but by estimating production in the years for which no report is available it can be assumed that a total of 28,000 pipe organs of all types were built in the years 1911-1929. Theatre instruments therefore accounted for 25% of total organ production in these years, so it is readily understandable why the organ industry as a whole took such a beating after the introduction of talking pictures in 1927. The graph clearly shows a sharp decline after 1927, several years before the effects of the Depression of the 1930s.

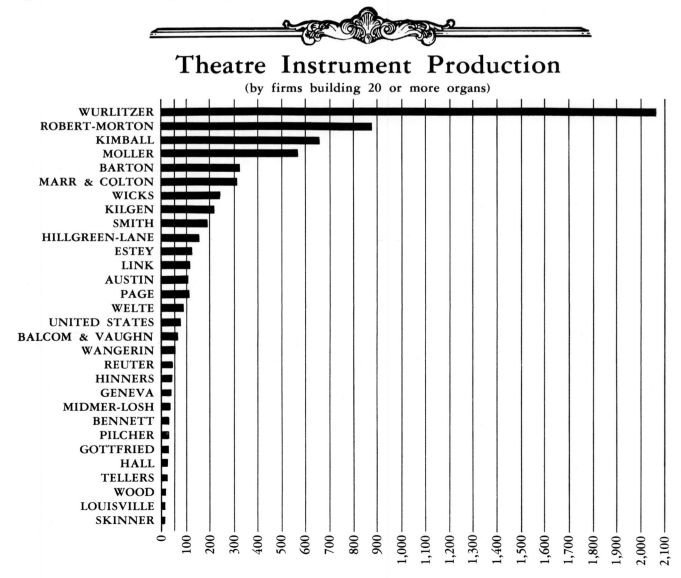

Theatre Instrument Production
(by firms building 20 or more organs)

United States Production Of Pipe Organs Of All Types

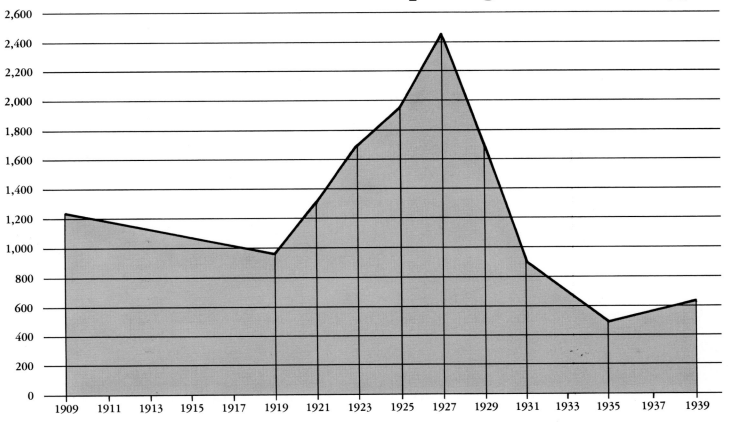

Wurlitzer Pipe Organ Production

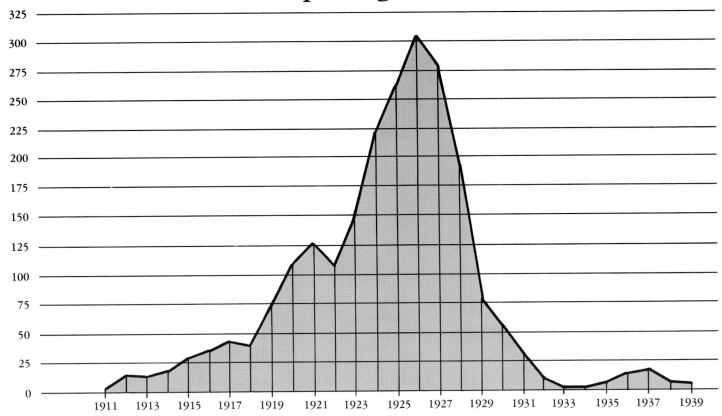

Note the resemblence of Wurlitzer production to the graph of overall United States organ production, reflecting the sizable influence of the theatre organ on the entire organ industry.

The Aeolian Company

PIPE-ORGAN DEPARTMENT

Aeolian Hall New York

Frank Taft Managing Director

Builders of

Aeolian Pipe-Organs

for

Residences

LONDON PARIS

WORKS AEOLIAN NEW JERSEY

The Aeolian Company began its existence in 1878 as the Mechanical Orguinette Company, dealers in player reed organs. The Aeolian name was assumed by 1887. Annual sales reached upwards of $11,000,000 in the years following World War I with 85% of sales coming from roll-operated instruments such as reed organs, pianos and residence pipe organs.[1] Residence organ sales began modestly in the mid-1890s. By 1910 only 300 had been sold[2] but by the end of production in 1931 the opus numbers had reached 1,800.[3] It is remarkable that sales reached this level inasmuch as Aeolians were quite expensive compared to many other makes. At the peak of production, residence organ sales were in excess of $1,000,000 annually.[4]

The Aeolian pipe organ business began in 1893 with the installation of an organ in Aeolian Hall, their New York City showroom. This organ was built by Farrand & Votey of Detroit who continued to build organs sold by Aeolian through the 1890s. In 1897 Farrand & Votey divided into two firms: The Farrand Organ Company made reed organs and the Votey Organ Company made pipe organs. In 1899 the Votey Organ Company merged with Aeolian and manufacturing operations were consolidated at Aeolian's Garwood, New Jersey factory.[5]

Since the Aeolian Company had staked its fortune on automatic musical instruments, profits began to wane as the decade of the 1920s progressed and the radio and phonograph increased in popularity. Aeolian attempted diversification into the fields of phonograph records, speedboats and airplane parts but none of these was financially successful.[6]

In an attempt to diversify their residence organ market, Aeolian hired Robert Pier Elliot in 1927 to head a new church and concert organ division. During the teens and twenties Elliot had been responsible for raising the Kimball company to its eminent position in the organ industry.[7] In 1925 he was hired by the Welte company[8] and in just a short time took it from a small builder of residence organs to one of the leaders in the industry. Aeolian hoped that Mr. Elliot would do the same for them and to a certain extent he did, although sales in the entire organ industry had begun a sharp decline by 1927 (see the graph on page 20). It is interesting that the only theatre organs ever built by Aeolian were sold under R. P. Elliot's leadership. It is not surprising that these bear considerable resemblance to Kimball and Welte designs.

The names of several men in the Aeolian organ division should be mentioned: Frank Taft was general manager and Eugen Braun was chief voicer.[9] Arthur J. Thompson was R. P. Elliot's assistant and had worked for him at Welte.[10] Another Elliot assistant was Nils W. Hillstrom. C. M. "Sandy" Balcom had been in charge of Kimball sales in the Seattle, Washington area and was persuaded by Mr. Elliot to assume a similar position with Aeolian. Sandy sold and installed half of the Aeolian theatre organs that were built.[11]

In 1925 Aeolian signed a contract to construct what would have been the largest organ ever installed in a theatre, a six-manual giant of 141 ranks. The installation was to have been in the Kindt Theatre, the brainchild of Col. B. J. Palmer of Davenport, Iowa, founder of the Palmer School of Chiropractic and already an owner of a small two-manual Aeolian residence organ. Unfortunately, the Kindt Theatre was never built and the Aeolian contract was defaulted after the initial payment. Among the features of this organ were to have been a 64' open wood diapason on the pedal with a low CCCCC pipe 67' long and 3½' square, a Chickering concert grand piano, an orchestral brass division on 25" wind and three military brass trumpets at 16', 8' and 4' pitches on 50" wind.[12]

In January 1932 the organ division of the Aeolian Company merged with the Skinner Organ Company to form the Aeolian-Skinner Organ Company. See the Skinner Organ Company section in *Encyclopedia of the American Theatre Organ*, Volume II for further details of these firms.

Views of the enormous erecting room (121' long, 33' wide, 34' high) in the Aeolian factory at Garwood, New Jersey.

3/11 AEOLIAN PIPE ORGAN
Keswick Theatre, Glenside, Pennsylvania

Note in the following contract for this installation that the specification is virtually identical to Kimball practice of the time, a direct result of R. P. Elliot's influence.

Form No. 26 2-28

MANUFACTURING ORDER and DATA SHEET - THE AEOLIAN COMPANY, NEW YORK

New York, __June 6,__ 192 8   Contract No. __1689__

FACTORY: Please build an organ in accordance with specification No. __28517-2-FG.__ and following data,
compiled by __Geo. B. Lockhart__   __Philadelphia District__
                                                        ~~Duo-Art Division~~ Aeolian-Votey Division.
BUILDING __KESWICK THEATRE__

Address __Keswick Ave. near Easton Road, Glenside, Montgomery County, Penna.__

Owner & Address __Edwin N. Johnson, Easton Road and Wharton Ave., Glenside, Penna.__

Correspond with __same, or Horace F. Case, same office__

Bills to __Edwin N. Johnson__

ARCHITECT __Horace Trumbauer, Land Title Bldg., Phila.__ Att'n __Mr. Milnor or Mr. Cope__

Contractor __Turner Construction Co., 1700 Walnut St., Phila.__ Att'n

Elect. Contr. __Union Electric Co., 2318 Sansom St., Phila.__ *Conduit in our cont? __No__

Metal Contr. __Turner Construction Co.__   *Piping in our cont? __No__

SHIP VIA __P & R Ry.__   To station or track __Glenside Station__

Notify __Edwin N. Johnson__   CL or LCL?

Prepay or collect? __Collect__   If prepaid charge to   Shipping pmt? __Yes__

COMPLETION promised __December 1st, 1928__   Should ship __Nov. 1, 1928.__

Plans to be ready. __6/16__ /192 8   Space to be ready __11/1__ /192 8   Building to be finished __12/1__ /192 8

POWER CURRENT, if AC, volts __220__ cycles __60__ phase __3__ If DC, volts

Lighting current, if AC, volts __110__   If DC, volts   motor h.p. prepared for

Electric Co. & address __Philadelphia Suburban-Counties Gas & Electric Co., Jenkintown, Pa.__

What special local rules apply? __None__

Current data supplied by __Union Electric Co.__   *SWELL BOX __No__

CASE finish   Sample to factory   *Case in contract? __No__

Pipe finish   Sample to factory   *Pipe front in contract? __No__

DRAWING rec'd __6__ /__19__ /192 8   BP to owner /192   and

Checked /192 by   Okd. BP rec'd /192

Final BP to owner /192   O.K. by   rec'd /

Console diagram sent fac. /192 ,   Approved by /192

Scale sheet & pressures /192 by   OK by

1

THE AEOLIAN COMPANY

No. 28517-2-FG.   Page 2

ACCOMPANIMENT   Manual I

Bourdon	16'	pipes
Trumpet	8	
Diapason Phonon	8	
Tibia Clausa	8	
French Horn	8	
Violin I	8	
Violin II	8	
Clarinet	8	
Vox Humana	8	
Kinura	8	
Flute	8	
Viola	8	
Tibia Flute	4	
Violin I	4	
Violin II	4	
Vox Humana	4	
Forest Flute	4	
Viola	4	
Piccolo	2	
Celesta	4	percussions
Xylophone	4	
Glockenspiel	2.	
Snare Drum, roll		traps
Snare Drum, tap		
Muffled Drum		
Chinese Block, roll		
Chinese Block, tap		
Tom Tom		
Castanet		
Tambourine		

4

THE AEOLIAN COMPANY

No. 28517-FG.-2   Page 3

ACCOMPANIMENT (Cont'd)   Manual I

Second Touch	Trumpet	8'	pipes
	Diapason Phonon	8	
	Tibia Clausa	8	
	Cello II	8	
	Clarinet	8	
	Tibia Flute	4	
	Glockenspiel	2	percussions
	Chimes	8	
	Snare Drum, roll		traps
	Chinese Block, roll		
	Triangle		
	Bird		

SOLO   Manual II

First Touch	Trombone	16'	pipes
	Tibia Clausa	16	
	Contre Viole	16	
	Bass Clarinet	16	
	Vox Humana	16	
	Trumpet	8	
	Diapason Phonon	8	
	Tibia Clausa	8	
	French Horn	8	
	Violin I	8	
	Violin II	8	
	Clarinet	8	
	Orchestral Oboe	8	
	Vox Humana	8	
	Kinura	8	

5

Panel 2

AUDITORIUM, dimensions, shape, materials, acoustical information, carpets ? (Send drawings)

Seats, main floor **1576** balcony **None** total **1576** Any stage ? **Yes**

Character of walls **Plaster** Floors **Carpeted** Ceiling **Plaster**

Carpets, cushions, hangings, etc. **As usual**

ORGAN SPACE, dimensions, shape, provision for sound proof chambers (Send drawings. Show largest opening)

See plans

Dist. bet. sections if divided, direct **48' 0"** via cable

CONSOLE, type **Unit, stop keys in colors** dropped music rack Manuals **3** *Mahogany*

Combinations **Recorder board** Wood and finish **Archt. will advise** *Use a satin finish of light walnut*

Bench **Unit console type** Lights **Yes** Inside finish " " " "

Location, etc. **On elevator in orchestra pit** Cable outlet **bottom** *or chestnut brown*

Cable length Add'l. lgth. exposed cable, if movable **#20 extra feet**

DUO-ART **No** Solo 116 Val. or No. of rolls included

Console (s) & Location (s) **No**

CONCERTOLA Location Cabinet

No. of stations Locations

ECHO ! Pld. from Distance direct via cable Separate blower?

BLOWER, location and distance (Send sketch. Show largest opening)

Pressures **Main organ 10#; Diaphone 18"lowe##/pipes on 15"**

*Remote control furnished by **Owner** Starter buttons? **By owner**

RECORD. Organ sold by **Geo. B. Lockhart** Contract price ?

Guarantee ? **Yes** Installed or f.o.b. **installed** Net organ price ?

Service credit $ **330** Effective /192 for **12** mos. Factory cost

Installed by Completed /192 Installation cost $

Inspected by Date /192

Remarks **Will have an new drawing from elevator people for extra cable length.**

*(Extra charge) Please be accurate and thorough. Supplement with letter when necessary.

Panel 3

The Aeolian Company
AEOLIAN HALL, NEW YORK
Specification No. **28517-2-FG.** *for Aeolian-Votey Organ*

Prepared for
689
KESWICK THEATRE
Glenside, Pennsylvania.

* * *

PEDAL

First Touch	Acoustic Bass	32'	pipes
	Diaphone	16	
	String Bass	16	
	Bourdon	16	
	Trumpet	8	
	Diapason	8	
	Tibia Clausa	8	
	Cellos II	8	
	Flute	8	
	Viola	8	
	Cornet	4	
	Violin	4	
	Bass Drum (band)		traps
	Cymbal		
	Bass Drum (orchestra)		
	Snare Drum, roll		
Second Touch	Chimes	8'	percussions
	Chinese Gong		traps
	Bass Drum (band)		
	Cymbal		
	Tympani		

Panel 6

The Aeolian Company
No. **28517-2-FG.** Page 4

	SOLO (Cont'd)		**Manual II**
First Touch	Flute	8'	pipes
	Viola	8	
	Cornet	4	
	Octave	4	
	Tibia Flute	4	
	Violin L	4	
	Violin II	4	
	Forest Flute	4	
	Vox Humana	4	
	Viola	4	
	Nazard	2⅔	
	Fifteenth	2	
	Piccolo	2	
	Tierce	1⅗	
	Celesta	4	percussions
	Xylophone	4	
	Glockenspiel	2	
	Orchestra Bells	2	
Second Touch	Trombone	16'	pipes
	Diapason Phonon	8	

	PERCUSSION		**Manual III**
	Tibia Clausa	8'	pipes
	Solo Piccolo	4	
	Trumpet	8	
	French Horn	8	
	Clarinet	8	
	Kinura	8	
	Vox Humana	8	

Panel 7

The Aeolian Company
No. **28517-2-FG.** Page 5

PERCUSSION (Cont'd)		**Manual III**
Harp	8'	percussions
Celesta	4	
Xylophone	4	
Xylophone	2	
Glockenspiel	2	
Orchestra Bells	2	
Chimes	8	

VIBRATOS

Main, left Main, right
Vox Humana

ADJUSTABLE COMBINATIONS

Five toe pistons affecting pedal.
Seven double touch pistons affecting Accompaniment and Pedal.
Seven double touch pistons affecting Solo and Accompaniment,
Five pistons affecting percussion manual.
Three cancel pistons affecting respective manual groups.
Drum piston; military drums and cymbal, manual and pedal.
Trap cancel pistons.
Vibrato cancel piston.

ADDITIONAL TRAP CONTROLS

Pedals
Chinese Gong; roll, first touch; stroke, second touch.
Grand Crash.

Toe Pistons
Triangle
Two Birds

Push Buttons
Two Birds (duplicating toe pistons)
Two Sleigh Bells, different notes.

ACCESSORIES

Two balanced expression pedals.
Balanced crescendo, affecting entire organ, not moving registers.
Sforzando, affecting entire organ, not moving registers.
Chimes soft pedal.
Chimes dampers pedal.

(concluded on next page)

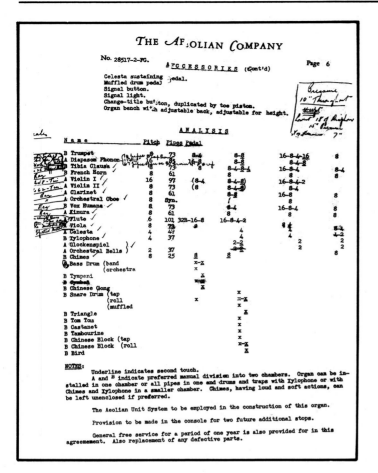

THE AEOLIAN COMPANY

No. 28517-2-FG.   Page 7

GENERAL DETAILS OF CONSTRUCTION

Organ: Manuals, Three compass CC to C⁴ .... 61 notes.
Pedals, compass CCC to G .... 32 notes.
The windchests of the manuals affected by octave couplers to be extended an octave above the compass of the keyboards, to 73 notes.

Console: Type, Unit
Stop control, Stop Keys
Combinations, adjustable at the console, visibly affecting the registers.

Manual keyboards inclined and all keyboards arranged for convenient access to contacts. Pedals A. G. O. pattern, concave and radiating.

Action: Electro-pneumatic throughout. Direct current generator of ample capacity. Contacts of silver. Aeolian high resistance magnets.

Case: No case or screen is embraced in this contract, except console case and bench of Aeolian standard design, built of native hardwood and finished to sample supplied by purchaser.

Pitch: Philharmonic, A—440; C—523.3.

Blower: Electric motor and blower of standard make to furnish an ample and steady supply of wind.

Pipe Work: Exclusively Aeolian manufacture and voicing, scientifically scaled, made and voiced for each organ with full knowledge of the building, organ space and intended use; no "stock" or "piece-work" voicing.

Purchaser Agrees: To furnish drawings and all essential information for the construction of the organ and to make necessary preparations for the organ at his own expense in accordance with directions and information supplied by the organ builder, such to include: the provision of sound-proof chamber or chambers with suitable openings, clean and thoroughly dried out before the organ parts are delivered; suitable room for motor and blower and all wiring, conduit and switches for power current; conduit, if required*, for organ cables and mains; air-tight galvanized iron pipes from blower to organ and console; electric lights in organ chambers, console and blower room; and adequate ventilation and means of keeping the atmosphere in all parts of the organ, console and blower room at a proper temperature and free from dampness, dust or other detrimental conditions. Also to allow such access to and use of the premises as may be necessary and convenient for the proper installation, regulation and tuning of the organ, and to provide necessary light, heat and power therefor.

*NOTE.—Aeolian-Votey organ installations comply with the Code of the National Board of Underwriters which specifies: "The outside covering of organ cables not run in conduit must be either flame-proof or covered with a closely wound fire-proof tape........Conduit may be used, but shall not be required." Aeolian-Votey cables are flame proof and damp proof.

8   9

Factory model of the 6/141 Aeolian console for the Kindt Theatre, Davenport, Iowa. This theatre was never built and the contract for the huge organ was defaulted after the initial payment.

Horace Trumbauer, Architect

AEOLIAN THEATRE ORGAN

KESWICK THEATRE
Glenside, Pennsylvania

❦

ÆOLIAN COMPANY
689 FIFTH AVENUE, NEW YORK, N. Y.

Aeolian boasts about their largest theatre organ in this ad from the July 1929 Diapason.

AEOLIAN OPUS LIST

CITY/STATE	LOCATION	SIZE	OPUS	YR	BLWR	HP	REMARKS
IOWA							
Davenport	Kindt Th.	6/141	1562	1925			Never built.
NEW YORK							
Great Neck	Gallo Th.	2/8	1652	1927		5	Cost $11,500; with 116-note player in console plus separate Duo Art player; repossessed in 1929.
OREGON							
Vernonia	Joy Th.	2/6	1668	1928	21725		
St. Helens	Columbia Th.	2/6	1669	1928	21718	3	Cost $6,000.
PENNSYLVANIA							
Glenside	Keswick Th.	3/11	1689	1928	22382	10	

L. L. ALNETT

The Alnett Company of Los Angeles was a very small builder specializing in residence organs. Alnett is believed to have installed no organs in theatres, but did install a two-manual instrument in radio station KMPC in Beverly Hills, California.

AMERICAN MASTER ORGAN COMPANY

This firm was incorporated in late 1914 with a capitalization of $100,000.[1] In a situation perhaps unique in the organ business, most of the principals of the company were theatre organists. Frank Ross White, president, was organist at the Pitt Theatre, Pittsburgh, the Paris Theatre, Denver and the Century and Vitagraph Theatres in New York. Augustus C. Ely, secretary and general manager, played at the Cort in New York. Other shareholders included Gottfried H. Federlein, organist at the Ethical Cultural Society and Dr. Gustave Widor-Ronfort. All of these gentlemen had experience playing Hope-Jones instruments.[2]

The factory was originally located at Warsaw, New York and after only a year of operation financial trouble was evident. James T. Jordan, a piano dealer from Paterson, New Jersey, headed a group of investors who subscribed an additional $30,000 worth of stock and moved the company to Paterson.[3] The newly organized company also failed to show a profit and finally declared bankruptcy in 1917.[4]

Six American Master theatre installations are defi-

This American Master console in the Rialto Theatre, Butte, Montana had a blind combination action. Lights above each stop key indicated which were activated when a piston was pressed.[8]

Console of
The American Master Organ

| Pipe Organ | Orchestral Instruments | Grand Piano |

The achievement of **Prominent Theatre Organists.**
The **realization** of what you have long sought.

Music of consummate grandeur and refinement
at an expense of one musician.

AMERICAN MASTER ORGAN COMPANY-ING
LAKE VIEW · PATERSON · NEW JERSEY

Drop Card   for Catalogue

nitely known. The Kinetic Engineering Company sold several blowers of 15" wind capacity to American Master for shipment directly to their factory and whose eventual locations are unknown.[5] It is therefore reasonable to assume that the company's total production was around a dozen instruments.

The largest was probably in the Rialto Theatre in Butte, Montana. This organ reportedly cost $25,000 and featured both a four-manual horseshoe console and a two-manual grand piano console, both playable simultaneously and with independent registrations.[6] About thirty years ago Salt Lake City enthusiast Ronald Bishop reported that this organ had a set of 32 tuned steel tympani.[7] If this is true, the author would certainly like to see them!

The American Master organ shown above was self-contained in a large cabinet rather than in the customary organ chamber. At left is another example of the firm's advertising.

AMERICAN MASTER OPUS LIST

CITY/STATE	LOCATION	SIZE	YR	BLWR	HP	WP	REMARKS
MONTANA							
Butte	Rialto Th.	4/	1916	7919			Also had a two-manual grand piano console.
			1916	E607	10"&20"		
NEW JERSEY							
Newark	Goodwin (Globe) Th.		1916				
Ridgewood	Playhouse Th.		1916	7496	5		
West Hoboken	Colonial Th.		1916	7530	5		
			1917	8053			
NEW YORK							
Yonkers	Broadway Th.	2/					Grand piano console.
ONTARIO, CANADA							
Ottawa	Ottawa Th.		1915	D391	3½	15"	

Artcraft Organ Company

Santa Monica, California

The Artcraft Organ Company was formed in 1915[1] and incorporated in 1922 by Clarence E. Haldeman and Charles F. Winder for the purpose of manufacturing and selling pipe and reed organs.[2] Winder had earlier operated an organ business in Richmond, Virginia which went broke in 1915 partly because of the inferior quality of its products (see Winder article in *Encyclopedia of the American Theatre Organ*, Volume II). The name Artcraft also became associated with inferior quality, being referred to by some southern California builders as "artcrap"![3]

The company was first located in Los Angeles and a year later moved to the old Grace Methodist Church building in Santa Monica, California.[4] Haldeman eventually bought out Winder's interest in the company and then sold a third of the stock to Mr. and Mrs. Asa R. Taylor in late 1925.[5] Taylor had been a Pacific Mutual life insurance salesman and was also a salesman at Artcraft. Reminiscing in 1964, Taylor recalled that "people who buy organs don't know much about them and you don't, I found out, have to know much more to sell them!" Taylor's main selling point to potential customers was that since the best lumber for building organs was California sugar pine, it didn't make sense to ship it to some eastern builder, make an organ out of it and then ship it back to California. Apparently this strategy worked because the company sold some 70 organs in its six years of operation, mostly two- and a few three-manuals, many of them to residences and funeral parlors.[6]

After Winder left, Artcraft needed a new person to oversee plant operations. In early 1926 they secured the services of E. G. Beitel for a salary of $50 per week plus 5% of the net operating profits.[7] Beitel for many years had been factory superintendent of Hinners, a very high quality builder.[8] Apparently his arrival at Artcraft came too late to make much of a favorable change in the quality of their products. Leonard Dowling also joined Artcraft in 1926, having been a service man for organs in the Fox West Coast theatre chain. After Artcraft went out of business, Dowling went into partnership with E. A. Spencer in Pasadena, California and went on to become a well known organ service man in southern California.[9]

In January 1927 Artcraft moved into a new building in Santa Monica[10] owned and leased to the firm by Mr. and Mrs. Taylor. Jimmy Bolton, a pipe maker and voicer in Berkeley, California who supplied pipes to Artcraft, was persuaded to move to Santa Monica to set up pipe mak-

ing facilities in the factory, including a metal casting table. Bolton also made pipes for E. A. Spencer and some other firms.[11] In July 1927 Mr. and Mrs. Taylor

An early Artcraft ad in the November 1922 Diapason shows the firm's first address in Los Angeles.

purchased Haldeman's interest in Artcraft for a mere $1,000 and became sole owners.[12] By late 1928 they made a decision to complete work in progress and quietly go out of business, citing the lack of working capital as a principal reason. After this decision was made, the company received a firm contract from a Seattle funeral parlor. Beitel, remembering his old friends, turned the job down and referred the customer to Hinners instead.[13]

This ten roll changer mechanism manufactured by the Automatic Musical Instrument Company of Grand Rapids, Michigan may have been installed in the Artcraft organ at a Barstow, California theatre.

View of an Artcraft chamber. Note the switchstack at center rear, which is out of plumb, and the incorrect 90° mitres on the 8' diapason pipes.

One of Artcraft's last ads appeared in the May 1928 Diapason.

Unidentified men stand at the entrance to the new Artcraft factory on 12th Street in Santa Monica. The firm was in the building only two years before going out of business.

ARTCRAFT OPUS LIST

CITY/STATE	LOCATION	SIZE	YR	BLWR	HP	WP	REMARKS
CALIFORNIA							
Barstow	Wallace Th.	2/4	1926	19122			With roll player.
Bellflower	Bellflower Th.		1925	17004			
Burbank	Victory Th.		1922				
Los Angeles	Glassel Th.	2/5	1926	18706			
	Model Th.		1922	K368	5	10″	
	Vernon Th.		1925	17821			
Pasadena	Washington Th.		1926	19198			
San Diego	Ramona Th.	2/3	1926	19283			

JOHN T. AUSTIN, PRESIDENT.
B.G. AUSTIN, VICE PRESIDENT.
JOHN SPENCER CAMP, TREASURER.

CABLE ADDRESS "ORGANS, HARTFORD"
WESTERN UNION CODE, A.B.C. CODE.

ALL CORRESPONDENCE
SHOULD BE ADDRESSED
TO THE COMPANY

AUSTIN ORGAN COMPANY,

ORGAN DESIGNERS AND BUILDERS CONTROLLING EXCLUSIVELY ALL AUSTIN PATENTS.

HARTFORD, CONN.

HIGHEST AWARD & GOLD MEDALS AT:
JAMESTOWN EXHIBITION 1907.
PANAMA PACIFIC SAN FRANCISCO 1915.
SESQUICENTENNIAL EXPOSITION 1926.

MORMON TABERNACLE, SALT LAKE CITY.
EASTMAN THEATRE, ROCHESTER, N. Y.
MEDINAH TEMPLE, CHICAGO, ILLINOIS.
UNIVERSITY OF COLORADO, BOULDER, COL.
MEMORIAL AUDITORIUM,
   CHATTANOOGA, TENN.
CITY HALL, PORTLAND, MAINE.
CINCINNATI MUSIC HALL, CINCINNATI, O.
FIRST M. E. CHURCH, LOS ANGELES, CAL.
LAKE PLACID CLUB, LAKE PLACID, N. Y.
CHAPEL OF THE INTERCESSION, N. Y. C.
STS. PETER & PAUL R. C. CATHEDRAL, PHILA.
BALBOA PARK, SAN DIEGO, CALIFORNIA.
ST. GEORGES CHURCH, N. Y. C.
   ETC.

John T. Austin started learning organ building at his father's knee in his native England. His father was an amateur who had already built several organs when John T. Austin emigrated to the United States in 1889 at the age of twenty. His first employment was with Farrand & Votey in Detroit. So advanced were his organ building skills that he was made a foreman after only two months.[4] In the early 1890s he invented the famous universal windchest and in 1893 he joined Clough & Warren, also of Detroit, as manager of their pipe organ department, overseeing the manufacture of organs using this new design of chest. While Austin was installing an organ in Hartford, Connecticut in 1898, the Clough & Warren factory was destroyed by fire, paving the way for formation of the Austin Organ Company in Hartford in 1899. John's brother Basil joined the firm in 1900. Basil had worked with his brother at Clough & Warren from 1893-98 but had left to spend two years in Alaska prospecting for gold.[5]

Several prominent men were associated with Austin in its formative years. R. P. Elliot was the first vice-president of the firm, having worked with John T. Austin at Farrand & Votey and also at Clough & Warren. C. C. Michell, a well-known English voicer, joined the firm in 1902, followed by Robert Hope-Jones in 1903.[6] Under Hope-Jones' influence Austin abandoned drawknobs and adopted stop keys as their standard. Hope-Jones' tonal influence *at the time* was minor, however, since Michell was critical of Hope-Jones' ability as a voicer and apparently had greater credibility with John T. Austin. Hope-Jones was permitted to make a number of sample pipes including 16', 8', 4' and 2' wooden diaphonic horns and one "brass diaphone of the new pattern" but a wind pressure of only 5″ was decided upon by the company as their standard.[7]

In 1904 Elliot, Michell and Hope-Jones all left the company, leaving control to the Austin brothers, which they kept until deciding to go out of business in 1935.[8] Early in 1937 the firm of Austin Organs, Inc. was organized by personnel from the old firm: Frederic B. Austin, nephew of the founders, was elected president; Howard A. Walker, general manager for about thirty years, was elected vice president; Basil F. Austin, son of the original firm's vice president, Basil G. Austin, served as secretary; and William Engle, head voicer, acted as assistant secretary.[9]

As of 1983 Austin Organs, Inc. is still a family operated organization, with Donald Austin, son of Frederic B. Austin, as president. Over 2,600 organs bearing the Austin nameplate have been manufactured, including a

John T. Austin
(1869-1948)[3]

Basil G. Austin
(1874-1958)[2]

This building housed the Austin factory until 1937, when the company moved to a smaller structure behind this site.

number of large four-manuals and one five-manual in the Medinah Temple in Chicago. Although the last Austin theatre-type organ was built in 1931, the company has produced some high pressure theatre pipework on special order in recent years under the skillful direction of head voicer Dave Broome. Especially notable are his serpents, *one note* of which can be heard above thirty ranks of Wurlitzer!

The Austin brothers were especially noted for mechanical ingenuity and for original ideas in organ construction. Their designs for chest and console mechanisms were uniquely Austin and were quite unlike anyone else's. They also developed clever labor-saving machines for manufacturing these devices economically.

John T. Austin held nearly forty patents,[10] the most notable of which was for the universal air chest. Chests in most organs are only a few inches deep, but universal

*A power pneumatic like this is used for each note inside an Austin straight chest. Note the **unusual magnet design, unique** to Austin.*

chests were frequently the size of small rooms. The two main advantages of the universal chest were serviceability and steadiness of wind. The chests were large enough that, in most instances, a person could enter them through a double-door airlock to service the mechanism with the wind on!

The wind steadiness of the universal chest was actually a liability in one respect: the wind was so steady that no tremulant could shake it. To provide a tremolo effect Austin used a large motor-driven cardboard vane mounted above the pipes. The effect of the fan tremolo was more of a light flutter than a tremolo but it was more or less acceptable for the requirements of church organs,

A prime example of Austin ingenuity, the remarkable machine on the left transforms solid pieces of wood into pedal unit blocks in fifteen simultaneous sawing and drilling operations. Many similarly clever machines can be found throughout the factory. In the photo below, Allen Miller stands in front of Dave Broome's voicing machine and holds a Wurlitzer brass saxophone pipe and a new Austin non-brass facsimile. Allen was assistant vice president at Austin for a number of years and is responsible for the firm's willingness to voice new theatre pipework on special order. He also made the Austin archives available to the author and supplied several rare photographs.

This ad in the March 1924 Diapason stresses Austin prestige.

Below, the (in)famous Austin fan tremolo.

which were the company's mainstay. When Austin finally began building fully unified theatre organs in the mid-1920s the need for a heavier tremulant was recognized, with the result that many of these later instruments have the more effective Wurlitzer-style tremulants.

Austin theatre consoles, like most of their church brethren, were of the stop key type, with stops in straight or slightly curved rows. The console cases, with a couple of interesting exceptions, were all of the same stock design favored by the company for a couple of decades. The combination actions were entirely electro-mechanical so no air was required in the consoles. So far as is known, the company never built a horseshoe console. Such a design would have necessitated complex mechanical linkages, but had the Austin brothers felt that a horseshoe console were desirable, you can be sure that they would have invented a clever and reliable mechanism for it.

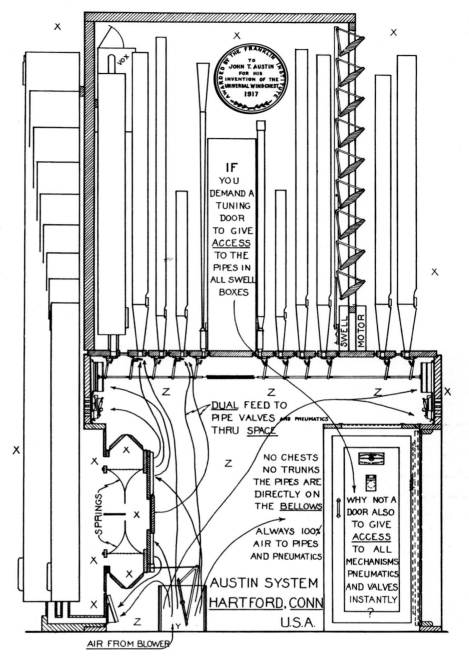

Schematic diagram of an Austin universal windchest. There are actually two entrance doors to the chest, one behind the other. They form an airlock so that the chest can be entered with the wind on. Clever, eh? It is ironic that these chests offer the utmost in ease of serviceability and yet are so reliable that they virtually never need servicing!

LEGEND

X   Atmospheric Pressure
Y   Blower Pressure
Z   Air Chest Pressure

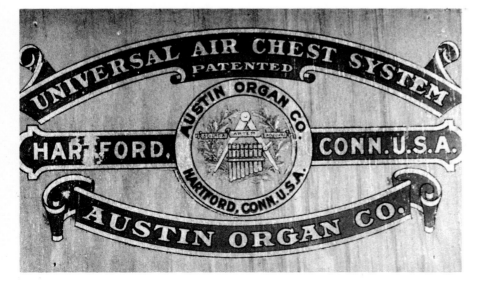

This decal graced the airlock door entrance to Austin chests.

Harry W. Austin, a brother of John and Basil Austin, was in charge of the recording studio and of roll production. He is shown above editing a roll while his son, Frederic B. Austin, operates the quadruplex perforator.

Quadruplex player in the residence of John T. Austin.

Studio at the Austin factory where quadruplex rolls were recorded.

(Right) This Austin ad from the July 1916 Diapason *mentions the Chorophone, their trademark for a 2/4 self-contained cabinet organ. Three Chorophones were sold to theatres, one a "special" containing seven ranks instead of four.*

Austin's famous canceller bars. A touch on the bar cancelled all the stops in that division, enabling the organist to select a solo stop very quickly.

Another remarkable Austin invention was the quadruplex player, so named because it could play three full manuals and pedal simultaneously. The players developed by several other manufacturers could play four divisions independently, too, but only Austin's could record every stop change and every note of three full 61-note manuals and a 32-note pedal clavier. This feat required a roll 21 1/16" wide containing 240 transverse hole positions. Unfortunately, the quadruplex player wasn't marketed until 1925 and only sixteen were ever sold.[11] One of them was on the last Austin theatre-type organ, opus 1788, in Cleveland's WHK radio studios.

Even more remarkable than the player was the recording machine. In most roll recording systems pencil marks corresponding to the notes played by the artist are made on a moving piece of paper, after which the marks are perforated manually, resulting in a playable roll. The Austin brothers invented and built in their own factory a device, operating at an extremely high speed, which would perforate a roll while the artist played. Immediately following the performance this roll could be taken from the machine, inserted into the organ and played back![12]

The Austin brothers, unlike many inventors, were also

skilled businessmen. Profits reached 85-95% per instrument in the teens and twenties,[13] a record rare in the industry. And what they lacked in tonal elegance was made up for in marketing skills. Austin was promotoed as one of the prestige builders and indeed secured a sizable share of the market for large organs. Although some builders built more organs, Austin's sales had a considerable percentage of medium and large three- and four-manual instruments with a smaller proportion of two-manual organs than most builders. Austin's prestige was certainly justified from the standpoint of longevity. A number of their organs from the 1920s were still playing almost perfectly half a century later, much to the consternation of contemporary organists, who had trouble

---

GREAT ORGAN.

Bourdon,	16'	61 notes,	wood.
Open Diapason,	8'	61 "	metal.
Tibia,	8'	61 "	wood.
Concert Flute,	8'	61 "	"
Viole d'Orchestre,	8'	61 "	tin.
Octave,	4'	61 "	metal.
Tibia,	4'	61 "	wood.
Flute,	4'	61 "	"
Viole,	4'	61 "	metal.
Flautino,	2'	61 "	"
Double Oboe,	16'	61 "	reed.
Oboe,	8'	61 "	"
Harp,		61 bars.	
Harp Octave,		49 notes.	

SWELL ORGAN.

Contra Viole, T.C.	16'	49 notes,	metal.
Tibia,	8'	61 "	wood
Concert Flute,	8'	61 "	"
Viole d'Orchestre,	8'	61 "	tin.
Tibia,	4'	61 "	wood.
Flute,	4'	61 "	"
Quintette,	2-2/3'	61 "	"
Viole,	4'	61 "	metal.
Flautino,	2'	61 "	"
Double Oboe,	16'	61 "	reed.
Oboe,	8'	61 "	"
Vox Humana,	8'	61 "	"
Clarion,	4'	61 "	"

CHOIR ORGAN.

Tibia,	8'	61 notes,	wood.
Concert Flute,	8'	61 "	wood.
Viole d'Orchestre,	8'	61 "	tin.
Tibia,	4'	61 "	wood.
Flute,	4'	61 "	"
Viole,	4'	61 "	metal.
Flautino,	2'	61 "	"
Oboe Horn,	16'	61 "	reed.
Oboe,	8'	61 "	"
Vox Humana,	8'	61 "	"

PEDAL ORGAN.

Resultant Bass,	16'	32 notes,	wood.
Bourdon,	16'	32 "	"
Tibia,	8'	32 "	"
Flute,	8'	32 "	"
Viole,	8'	32 "	metal.
Octave,	4'	32 "	"
Flute,	4'	32 "	"
Contra Fagotto,	16'	32 "	reed.
Oboe,	8'	32 "	"

Bass Drum.
Snare Drum.   *Steamboat whistle*
Cymbal.   *Telephone bell*
Chinese Block.
Church Bell.

8 Adjustable pistons to control Great and Pedal
8 Adjustable pistons to control Swell and Pedal.
8 Adjustable pistons to control Choir and Pedal.
4 Adjustable pedals to control Pedal.
8 General pistons controlling entire organ.
Balanced Crescendo & Sforzando Pedal.
Balanced Swell Pedal affecting entire organ.
Tremolo
Three AUSTIN PATENT CANCELER BARS.

****

A typical specification of a late Austin theatre organ (opus 1419) is reproduced here from the original contract. Although this organ is completely unit, notice that it has far fewer stops than would a comparable model of a more popular brand.

Vincent H. Percy plays the 3/15 Austin in Cleveland's WHK radio studios. This 1931 Art Deco design was a rare departure from Austin's norm.

Billy Wright prepares to play a movie at the 3/26 Austin in the Midland Theatre, Hutchinson, Kansas. Most Austins of the teens and twenties had this console style.

3/12 Austin in the Allyn Theatre, Hartford, Connecticut. No, this console wasn't designed in the 1950s: it dates from 1927!

Console of the largest organ ever installed in a theatre: Eastman School of Music, Rochester, New York.

persuading their congregations to consider replacing the tonally dated instruments since they were in nearly perfect shape!

What did Austin theatre organs sound like? Perhaps the most charitable description would be indistinguished. After all, the brothers' forte was mechanical design, not tone. Most of the Austin organs installed in theatres were straight and differed little from the company's church organs of the day, which tended to be loud, tubby, and, well, *indistinguished*. Some of the early ones had traps and percussions but that didn't go far to enhance the droning effect the organs had because of their ineffectual fan tremolos. Austin string voicing was excellent, however, and did help add some zest to the otherwise dull sounds. By the time Austin jumped onto the unit bandwagon in the mid-twenties, other more progressive companies had that market pretty well sewn up with the result that only a couple dozen fully unified Austin theatre organs were sold.

If for no other reason, the name of Austin will be remembered in the annals of theatre organ history for having built the largest organ ever installed in a theatre, the 4/135 in the Eastman Theatre, Rochester, New York. Built in 1923 at a cost of $84,525, this monster's specification was created by Harold Gleason, head of the organ department at the Eastman School of Music. The manuals were primarily straight but there was quite a bit of unification in the pedal. There was a full complement of traps and effects including a vorsetzer for playing a grand piano.

The console was on an elevator in the orchestra pit and chambers were placed on the rear wall of the stage, rather than in the traditional locations flanking the proscenium. This was the novel idea of George Eastman, who felt that music for the silent screen should indeed come from the screen! This placement of the chambers was contrary to the advice of everyone connected with the project but Eastman was, after all, paying the bills and of course had the last word. As a result, the world's largest theatre organ was disappointing in the house because of its virtual entombment although it would curl your hair on stage.[14]

4/135 AUSTIN PIPE ORGAN, OPUS 1010
Eastman Theatre, Rochester, New York

Through the courtesy of Donald Austin, president of Austin Organs, Inc., the contract for the largest theatre organ ever built is herewith reproduced in full. Note the many stringent conditions, such as guarantees of satisfaction with minute details, and the fact that no payments were due until the organ was delivered! These conditions could have been met only by a company which was sure of its abilities and which had enormous financial strength.

CONTRACT

ARTICLE OF AGREEMENT made this 21st day of December, 1920, by and between the Austin Organ Company, Hartford, Connecticut, party of the first part, and the Eastman School of Music, Rochester, New York, party of the second part.

FOR, AND IN CONSIDERATION of the sum of Seventy-eight Thousand, Seven hundred and five ($78,705.00) Dollars, to be paid by the party of the second part to the party of the first part, the said party of the first part agrees to build an organ according to the annexed specifications, in a most thorough and artistic manner, and install it in the Eastman School of Music, Rochester, New York, complete in every detail and fully warranted, on April 1st, 1922, subject, however, to delays from fire, strikes or causes beyond the control of the party of the first part, and especially subject to delays from freight embargos or other railroad interferences.

The party of the second part agrees that during the installation of the said organ, they will keep said building at such reasonable temperature as may be required by the party of the first; that they will provide and allow the use of electric current for tuning and lighting; that they will afford such a condition of quiet within the building as may be needful for the proper tone regulation and tuning of the instrument, and that they will allow suitable convenience and opportunity for the installation and completion of the organ in the said building free from unreasonable interruption, the tuning however to be done at such time as shall not interfere with the use of the Hall.

The party of the second part further agrees to assume all the risk of damage to the organ by fire, lightning, water or tornado while contained in the said building, and to insure the same in good reliable companies for the benefit of the parties hereto as their interests may appear.

- 2 -

The party of the second part agrees to purchase and accept said organ when completed in accordance with these specifications and to pay the party of the first part thereafter the sum of Seventy-eight Thousand, Seven hundred and Five ($78,705.00) Dollars as follows: Two-thirds upon delivery at the building boxed, balance upon completion and acceptance, provided, however, that when said organ is ready for erection and is held up by the inability for any reason of the party of the second part to have the installation proceed the party of the second part to pay interest on the balance for the period of delay.

All verbal agreements and understandings are merged in this contract, and the specifications and details of construction attached hereto, which comprise the entire contract, and no changes, alteration or modification made verbally or in any other way, will be binding upon the party of the first part, unless the same be made in writing signed by an executive officer of the said party of the first part,

IN WITNESS WHEREOF, the parties have hereunto set their hands and seals this 21st day of December, 1920.

Austin Organ Co
John T Austin Pres

Eastman School of Music
by Geo Eastman

SPECIFICATIONS OF AN ORGAN
FOR THE
EASTMAN SCHOOL OF MUSIC, ROCHESTER, NEW YORK,
MOTION PICTURE THEATRE
PREPARED BY HAROLD GLEASON, ORGAN ARCHITECT.

****

GREAT ORGAN: 7" wind

First Enclosed Section:

		PIPES
16' Contra Gamba 37-	Metal	73
8' Second Diapason 46-43	"	73
8' First	"	73
4' Octave 55	"	73

Second Enclosed Section: 7" wind

		PIPES
16' Quintaten	Wood & Metal	73
8' Gemshorn 55 taper		73
8' Claribel Flute	Wood & Metal	73
8' Cello 55		73
8' Cello Celeste 55		73
8' Harmonic Flute #0 with open metal bass	Wood & Metal	73
8' Great Flute		73
8' Third Diapason -46	Metal	73
4' Forest Flute - 4' melodia scale	wood	73
4' Fugara -61		61
2' Fifteenth -70		61
2-2/3 Twelfth usual		61
1-3/5 Tierce usual		61
Mixture - 4 Ranks		244
16' Ophicleide 7½'	Wood & Metal	73
8' Trumpet 5" scale bright		73
4' Clarion 3" trumpet scale		73
Tremolo		
Harp 8' (Choir)	Carillons (Orchestral)	
Harp 4' (Choir)	Chimes (Echo)	

SWELL ORGAN: 7" wind

		PIPES
16' Bourdon	Wood & Metal	73
16' Dulciana -46		73
8' Spitz Flute } 49 taper soft		73
8' Flute Celeste } 49 taper		61
8' Salicional } 61		73
8' Voix Celeste } 61		73
8' Stopped Flute usual scale	Wood & Metal	73
8' Claribella		73
8' Viol d'Gamba } 55 wind		73
8' Gamba Celeste } 55		73
8' Harmonic Flute #3 with open bass		73
8' Geigen Principal 49-46		73
8' Diapason 43-40		73
4' Unda Maris - 2 Ranks		146
4' Harmonic Flute #3		61

SWELL ORGAN: CONTINUED:

		PIPES
4' Violina 64 not too sharp	Metal	61
4' Octave 58		61
2' Flageolet usual		61
2-2/3 Twelfth (From Mixture)		61
1-3/5 Seventeenth (From Mixture)		61
5 Rank Mixture (12th, 15th, 17th)		61
16' Oboe Horn 4" full - like english horn		73
8' Vox Humana very soft		73
8' Oboe usual sh.		73
8' Solo Vox Humana usual		73
8' Cornopean 4½" smooth		73
8' Trumpet 4½" French trumpet fiery		73
4' Clarion 4"		73
Tremolo		
Harp 8' (Choir)	Carillons (Orchestral)	
Harp 4' (Choir)	Chimes (Echo)	

CHOIR ORGAN: 7" wind Big in tone

		PIPES
16' Bourdon Great Bourdon scale	Wood	73
16' Dulciana 55 not too soft	Metal	61
8' Unda Maris 55		73
8' Concert Flute melodia scale	Wood & Metal	73
8' Wood Celeste		61
8' Solo Quintadena 55 - strings		73
8' Viol d'Amour 49 taper bright		73
8' Viol Celeste		73
8' Diapason 46-43	Wood & Metal	73
4' Flute D'Amour usual		73
4' Gemshorn 61 taper voice full		61
2' Flautine usual		73
8' Corno di Bassetto old largest scale		73
8' Muted Trumpet capped Horn not harmonic		73
4' Clarion 4' oboe scale		61
8' Harp (Playable from all Manuals)		
Tremolo (p-ff) with dampers		
Chimes (Echo)		
Carillons (Orchestral)		

SOLO ORGAN: 10" wind

		PIPES
8' Tibia Clausa scale	Wood & Metal	73
8' Gamba 55	Metal	73
8' Gamba Celeste 55		73
8' open flute	Wood & Metal	73
8' Stentorphone 40-37 open flute wood		73
8' Concert Piccolo #0 scale open flute		61
16' Tuba Profunda 7½"	Wood & Metal	73
8' Tuba Mirabilis 5½" big FFFF		73
8' tuba 5"		73
4' Tuba Clarion usual tuba scale		73
8' French Horn from Orch.		
8' English		
8' Clarinet		
8' Musette		
8' Orchestral Oboe		
8' Basseen		
Tremolo		
Chimes (Echo)		
Harp 8' (Choir)		
Harp 4' (Choir)		
Carillons (Orchestral)		

ORCHESTRAL ORGAN: To be available from all manuals.
Operated by Tablets

			PIPES
16' Bass Clarinet			
16' Contra Basse 55	Metal		73
8' Muted Viol 70	"		73
8' Muted Viol Celeste 70	"		61
8' Chimney Flute	"		73
8' Viola 2 Rks	"		73
8' Orchestral Flute imitative	wood		73
8' Viol d'Orchestre #2	metal		73
8' Viol Celeste #2	"		73
5-1/3 Quint	"		61
4' Viol Celeste - 2 Ranks #2 viol scale	"		146
4' Traverse Flute usual scale	wood?		73
2-2/3 Nazard	"		61
2' Orchestral Piccolo usual	"		61
1-3/5 Tierce	"		61
16' Fagotto 5" not too raspy	"		73
8' English Horn usual	"		73
8' Vox Humana usual with body	"		73
8' Bassoon usual	"		73
8' Orchestral Oboe large scale	"		73
8' Clarinet new small scale characteristic	"		73
8' French Horn capped type	"		73
8' Musette usual not too fiery	"		73
Carillons (Church Bells) big scale			37
Tremolo			
(Playable from all Manuals)			
8' Oriental reed (p-ff) with dampers	reed		73 pipes

ECHO ORGAN:

		PIPES
8' Etherial Celeste (2 Ranks) soft	Metal	146
8' Night Horn 49 taper round		73
8' Flute Celeste 49		73
8' Viol d'Orchestre #1		73
8' Viol Celeste #1		73
8' Harmonic Flute #0 scale		73
8' Flute		73
4' Flautine		61
8' Vox Humana		73
8' Forest Horn capped		73
4' Harp (p-ff) with dampers		61
8' Chimes (p-ff)		37
Tremolo		
Chimes Duplexed to Solo & Choir, Great; Swell & Pedal.		

PEDAL ORGAN: Augmented:

		PIPES
32' Bourdon usual	Wood	12
16' usual pedal Bourdon		32
10-2/3 Quinte		12
8' Bourdon	Wood & Metal	12
2' Bourdon	Metal	12

Valves to cut off wind to sections

PEDAL ORGAN: Augmented: Continued:

			PIPES
16' Contra Viol 43	Metal		32
8' 55			12
4'	Wood		12
16' Open Flute #1 open scale	Wood		32
8'			12
4'	Metal		12
16' Violone usual	Wood & Metal		32
8'	Metal		12
32' Resultant	Wood		
16' Open Diapason #3			32
8'			12
4'	Metal		12
32' Bombarde 12"	Wood & Metal		12
16' Bass Tuba	Metal		32
8' Tuba			12
4' Clarion			12
16' Trombone 9'	Wood & Metal		32
8' Tromba	Metal		12
8' Rank Mixture (Synthetic)			
16' Dulciana (Choir)			
16' Soft Bourdon (Swell)	Wood		
16' Contra Basse (Orch.) Celeste	Wood & Metal		
8' Violin Cello			
16' Quintaten (Great)			
16' Horn (Swell)			
16' Fagotto	}Orchestral		
8' Fagotto Bassoon			
Carillons (Orch.)			
Chimes (Echo)			
Quint Coupler ??			
16' Bass Clarinet (Orch)			

STRING ORGAN:

Ranks in Independent Expression Box available from all manuals. Controlled by Expression Pedal of Manual on which it is drawn or may be put on any expression pedal by thumb pistons over Solo. Operated by tablets in left key cheeks of each manual or by registers. To be divided into three two Ranks on Swell & Choir, Solo & Great.

ACCESSORIES:

Balanced Crescendo Pedal Adjustable, not moving registers.
"   Great & Orchestral Pedal
"   Swell Pedal
"   Choir Pedal
"   Solo & Echo Pedal
Sforzando Pedal, Reversible (adjustable)
Great to Pedal Reversible
Solo to Pedal "
"   Great "
32' Bourdon "
Swell to Pedal "
32' Bombarde "
8 Adjustable Composition Pistons to Control Solo Stops

8	"	"	"	"	"	"	Swell
8	"	"	"	"	"	"	Great
8	"	"	"	"	"	"	Choir
8	"	"	"	"	"	"	Pedal Stops
8	"	"	"	"	"	"	Entire Organ including couplers.
8	"	"	"	"	"	"	Couplers
4	"	"	"	"	"	"	Echo Organ
8	"	"	"	"	"	"	Orchestral Organ

Necessary number of pedal pistons for control of manual stops and couplers and pedal stops as mutually agreed upon.

Necessary number of pistons not moving registers to include:

8 Pistons to control entire organ

1 "   " Take off all 16' manual stops

1 "   " "   "   " 16' Pedal stops

1 "   " "   "   " 16' Couplers.

A complete set of couplers suboctave, unison and superoctave between manuals and manuals to pedal including choir to pedal 5th and Pedal to Solo 8'.

Suboctave, unison and super-octave couplers each organ on itself to work on all duplexed and augmented stops.

The Austin Organ Company agrees to provide the following percussion instruments installed with proper manual and pedal pistons for their control at the prices specified. Any or all of these percussion instruments may be selected at the prices given:

		Price $		
	Deep Bell		400.00	
	Oriental Gong		200.00	
	Triangle		100.00	10% Off
One	Tympani (Strike)		350.00	
Drum	Tympani (Roll)		80.00	
	Xylophone		1,200.00	
	Thunder Pedal		150.00	

All percussion instruments to be playable from p-ff and in addition enclosed in a swell box operated by the Solo or Orchestral pedal as desired.

The following items are to be given especial attention and made entirely satisfactory to the Eastman School of Music.

1 - A more gradual crescendo & diminuendo from Swell Boxes.

2 - Metallic sound of piston action in console.

3 - Noises from pneumatics, valves or from other causes noticeable in organ when keys are depressed with no stops drawn or when the softest stops are played.

4 - Noises of swell shutters when closed quickly.

5 - Tremolos to be of valve type unless otherwise specified.

DETAILS

Great (First Enclosed Section): will be coupled to Great Pedal or may be left open by two pistons over Solo Manual.

Great (Second Enclosed Section): will be coupled to Great Expression Pedal.

String Organ: Will be coupled to Expression Pedal of Manual on which drawn or may be coupled to Orchestral only by one piston.

Pedal Organ: To be entirely enclosed and controlled by any or all expression pedals as desired.

The Builders shall warrant the action and construction in all particulars and shall agree to make good and repair any defects in the materials, workmanship or methods of construction which may develop within five years.

The Builders shall warrant the wind pressure to be unvarying under all conditions of use.

Organ Blower Plant: Installed so as to be noiseless from the auditorium.

Orgoblo or Kinetic Blower: to be installed, to be 20% above ample capacity and power to supply wind at proper pressure under all conditions. Switches at console. Electric generator for organ action. (Selection of blower to be approved by the Eastman School of Music).

The Action: to be electric or electro-pneumatic having practically instantaneous attack and repetition.

All parts to be easily accessible for readjustments and repairs, and constructed of the best materials for the purpose.

The Swell Boxes will be of brick or hollow tile and lined with a suitable cement as a reflecting surface. Air space will be left between outer wall of building and boxes.

All Expression Pedals to be operated from Choir Expression Pedal. Great Swell and Choir Expression Pedals to be operated from Choir Pedal by two pistons.

A perfectly regular crescendo and diminuendo including instantaneous and noiseless closing must be secured to the full satisfaction of the architect.

ALL SWELL BOXES to be ample in size and convenient for tuning.

The Voicing is to represent the best of the organ builders art. No Pipes are to be forced and the wind pressures are to be adjusted to give refinement and delicacy in the softer stops. Orchestral stops are to be of their characteristic timber.

The louder stops to be rich, full and sonorous. The ensemble to be given particular attention and made as nearly perfect as possible and all stops except those to be designated are to be voiced with that end in view.

Detailed description of each stop will be furnished by the Organ Architect.

Deagan Harp (aeolian type) and first quality chimes.

The Console: The console is to be located in the Orchestra pit on a movable platform which can be raised to the stage level and console moved onto the stage for concert purposes. Detailed specifications for console will be submitted.

Pipes: No stopped basses in any open stop; no grooving of basses.

Wood Pipes: To be made of clear white pine properly treated and suitable hard wood to be used where necessary to secure the most perfect results.

Metal Pipes: To be made of the best materials and of ample thickness. The Diapasons to be especially heavy.

The Keyboards: To be of 61 notes, best ivory with ebony sharps. Solo and swell manuals to be dipped slightly.

Pedal Boards: Radiating, concave and, if practical, adjustable within distance of two inches. (Dimensions to be specified by Architect). Hard wood to be used. Sharps capped with solid ebony.

Organists Bench: Heavy construction and adjustable.

A complete layout of the organ shall be submitted to the Architect for approval.

The organ to be erected in the Eastman School of Music, tuned and left ready for use on or before April 1st, 1922.

All workmanship and material to be of the best and the entire organ to represent the highest perfection tonally and mechanically that can be produced to the full satisfaction of the Eastman School of Music.

No Case Work:

During the erection of the organ, any stops in the organ, which are not satisfactory to the Eastman School of Music or the Builders will be exchanged, until satisfactory, at the expense of the party of the first part.

The action of the entire organ and blowing mechanism to be noiseless from any seat in the auditorium.

The Eastman School of Music will provide:

1 - Room for blowing plant.

2 - Concrete or brick swell boxes according to Builders and Architects specifications.

3 - All cutting of floors necessary for installation. All wiring to meter. Electric current for lighting interior to be furnished at one point in each swell box where designated by the party of the first part.

4 - Elevator or movable platform for console.

For a period of one year after the acceptance of the organ the party of the first part agrees to make any changes, repairs or alterations which are made necessary by their failure or neglect to carry out the specifications in spirit or letter.

AGREEMENT made this 23rd day of March, 1922, by and between the Austin Organ Company, of Hartford, Connecticut, party of the first part, and the Eastman School of Music, of Rochester, New York, party of the second part.

First: This Agreement is supplemental to and amendatory of an Agreement made on the 21st day of December, 1920, between the parties hereto, for the installation of an organ.

Second: It is hereby mutually agreed that the provision set forth on page 8 of said Agreement of December 21, 1920, whereby the party of the second part is given the right to purchase the percussion instruments therein designated at the specified prices, be and hereby is, together with all rights and obligations thereunder, terminated. In lieu of said provision, the party of the first part hereby agrees to provide and install in connection with the organ contracted for, and the party of the second part agrees to purchase at the net prices specified, the following traps:-

Piano. Player to attach to Grand with cables and air pipe, playable from four manuals and Pedal with expression.	$1,750.00
Bass Drum (Strike and Roll)	250.00
Crash Cymbal (Strike and Roll)	145.00
Snare Drum (Strike and Roll)	75.00
Tambourines	35.00
Castenets	30.00
Chinese Block	30.00
Sleigh Bells (25 Notes)	450.00
Xylophone (49 Notes)	750.00
Triangle	35.00
Bird Effect	25.00
Auto Horn	55.00
Fire Gong	45.00
Steam Boat Whistle	15.00
Horse Hoofs	135.00
Tom Tom	45.00

3870

IN WITNESS WHEREOF, the parties have hereunto set their hands and seals this 23rd day of March, 1922.

AUSTIN ORGAN COMPANY
By *John T. Austin, Pres.*

EASTMAN SCHOOL OF MUSIC
By *Geo. Eastman*

EDWIN S. GORDON, A.I.A.   WILLIAM G. KAELBER, A.I.A.

GORDON AND KAELBER
ARCHITECTS
125 SIBLEY BLOCK
ROCHESTER, N.Y.

May 9, 1922.

Austin Organ Co.,
Hartford, Conn.

Gentlemen:-   RE. EASTMAN SCHOOL OF MUSIC

We have been instructed by Mr. George Eastman to order from you the additional equipment mentioned in your letter of April 24th to Mr. Harold Gleason and as follows:

Duplicate Blower $1500.00 including complete installation
"   Starter installed complete $350.00.
"   Generator installed complete $100.00.

Very truly yours,
Gordon and Kaelber, Architects.

WGK/IAV   PER *Wm. G. Kaelber*

AUSTIN OPUS LIST

Following is a complete list of this firm's theatre-type installations. An alphabetical index appears first, enabling one to locate instruments on a city/state/installation site basis, with a corresponding opus number shown adjoining. This number can be used to find an organ in the accompanying chronological list. Statistics on each organ are shown only in the latter list.

CITY/STATE	LOCATION	OPUS
ALABAMA (AL)		
Montgomery	Strand Th.	814
Selma	Academy of Music	810
Tuscaloosa	Belvedere Th.	1334
CALIFORNIA (CA)		
Los Angeles	Temple Auditorium (Clune's)	156
CONNECTICUT (CT)		
Ansonia	Tremont Th.	1485
Hartford	Allyn Th.	1512
	Horace Bushnell Memorial Hall	1627
	Lenox Th.	1419
	Lyric Th.	1379
	Regal Th.	1630
	Rivoli Th.	1433
	Strand Th.	491
Manchester	Circle Th.	1459
New Britain	Palace (Palmer) Th.	1458
	Strand Th.	1457
New Haven	Howard Th.	1605

CITY/STATE	LOCATION	OPUS
New Haven	Whalley Th.	1474
Willimantic	Gem Th.	1421
DISTRICT OF COLUMBIA		
Washington	Rialto Th.	796
FLORIDA (FL)		
Orlando	Beacham Th.	1034
Pensacola	Isis Th.	493
GEORGIA (GA)		
Atlanta	Criterion Th.	850
ILLINOIS (IL)		
Chicago	WIBO Radio	1419
IOWA (IA)		
Council Bluffs	Strand Th.	892
KANSAS (KS)		
Hutchinson	Midland Th.	902
Wichita	Palace Th.	610

CITY/STATE	LOCATION	OPUS
KENTUCKY (KY)		
Covington	Liberty Th.	1140
LOUISIANA (LA)		
New Orleans	Globe Th.	651
MAINE (ME)		
Portland	Nickel Th.	538
	Strand Th.	538
MASSACHUSETTS (MA)		
Beverly	Lacom Th.	661
	Ware Th.	876
Boston	Park Th.	539, 708
Everett	Capitol Th.	1463
Lawrence	Star Th.	867
Lowell	Strand Th.	725
Lynn	Strand Th.	580
New Bedford	New Bedford Th.	772
Peabody	Strand Th.	661
Springfield	Capitol Th.	891
Worcester	Strand Th.	662
MISSOURI (MO)		
Kansas City	Liberty (Princess) Th.	765
	Newman Th.	828
	Willis-Wood Th.	528
NEW JERSEY (NJ)		
Atlantic City	Virginia Th.	627
Newark	Newark Th.	682
	Rialto Th.	855
Upper Montclair	Bellevue Th.	1027
NEW YORK (NY)		
Albany	Strand Th.	888
Astoria, L.I.	Astoria Th.	901
Brooklyn	Academy of Music	211
	Academy Opera House	232
	Beacon Th.	486
	Farragut Th.	914
	Kingsway Th.	958
	Mayfair (Horneck) Th.	1453
	Marine Th.	1454
	Rialto Th.	970
	Strand Th.	819
Buffalo	New Victoria Th.	476
	Palace Th.	547
	Regent Th.	513
	Victoria Th.	546
Corona, L.I.	Plaza Th.	1552
Far Rockaway	Strand Th.	852
Flushing	Prospect Th.	1452
Freeport	Freeport Th.	1451
Huntington, L.I.	Huntington Th.	1511
Jamaica, L.I.	Merrick Th.	927
Mount Vernon	Mt. Vernon Th.	1307

CITY/STATE	LOCATION	OPUS
New York City	Broadway Th.	872
	Marvin Th.	386
	New Amsterdam Th.	345
	Rialto Th., 42nd St. & 7th Ave.	611
	St. Nicholas Th.	426
	Sheridan Th.	1007
	Strand Th.	481
	Triumph Th.	709
Port Jervis	Strand Th.	901
Port Washington, L.I.	Beacon Th.	1551
Queens Village	Queens Village Th.	1569
Rochester	Eastman Th.	1010
Syracuse	Strand Th.	545
	Syracuse (Regent) Th.	485
Troy	Mark Strand Th.	1065
Watertown	Olympic Th.	703
Woodhaven, L.I.	Willard Th.	1281
OHIO (OH)		
Cincinnati	Hollywood Th.	1303
Cleveland	Alhambra Th.	667
	Doan (Loew's Euclid) Th.	824
	Keith's 105th Street Th.	1025
	Lower Mall Th.	668
	Stillman Th.	630
	Upper Mall Th.	669
	WHK Radio	1788
OKLAHOMA (OK)		
Oklahoma City	Criterion (Cooper) Th.	966
Okmulgee	Cook Th.	874
OREGON (OR)		
Portland	Globe Th.	408
Salem	Circuit Th.	412
PENNSYLVANIA (PA)		
Allentown	Rialto Th.	915
Harrisburg	Regent Th.	1032
Philadelphia	Broadway Th.	795
	Great Northern Th.	636
	Palace Th.	624
	Rialto Th.	711
	Savoy Th.	716
	Stanton (Stanley) Th.	605
Pittsburgh	East Liberty Th.	593
	Henry Shenk Co. Recreation Hall and Theatre	990
Reading	Rajah Th.	1068
Wilkes-Barre	Theis Orpheum Th.	559
UTAH (UT)		
Salt Lake City	American Th.	609
WEST VIRGINIA (WV)		
Charleston	Kearse Th.	1102

OPUS	LOCATION/CITY/STATE	SIZE	YR	PRICE	BLWR	HP	WP	REMARKS
156	Temple Auditorium (Clune's), Los Angeles, CA	4/63	1906	$ 12,500				
			1948		26784	15	6"&11"&16"	
211	Academy of Music, Brooklyn, NY	4/	1908	$ 12,000				Moving cost; moved from Jamestown Exposition, Norfolk, Virginia. Probably not an Austin organ.
232	Academy Opera House, Brooklyn, NY	3/						
345	New Amsterdam Th., New York City, NY	2/15	1911	$ 5,000	3552	7½		
386	Marvin Th., New York City, NY	2/5	1912	$ 2,500	4322			
408	Globe Th., Portland, OR	2/9	1912	$ 4,150				With echo.
412	Circuit Th., Salem, OR	2/9	1912	$ 3,900				
426	St. Nicholas Th., New York City, NY	3/23	1913	$ 8,000				
476	New Victoria Th., Buffalo, NY	2/7	1913	$ 3,000				See opus 546.
481	Strand Th., New York City, NY	3/24	1914	$ 10,000	5316			
		3/34	1917	$ 3,000	7975			Additions: 10-rank stage organ.
			1926	$ 2,500				Additions: traps.
485	Syracuse (Regent) Th., Syracuse, NY	2/12	1914					

OPUS	LOCATION/CITY/STATE	SIZE	YR	PRICE	BLWR	HP	WP	REMARKS
486	Beacon Th., Brooklyn, NY	2/7	1914	$ 3,900				
491	Strand Th., Hartford, CT	3/22	1914	$ 8,025			5	
493	Isis Th., Pensacola, FL	2/7	1914	$ 3,450				
513	Regent Th., Buffalo, NY	2/7	1914	$ 3,500				
528	Willis-Wood Th., Kansas City, MO	3/16	1914	$ 7,000	5755	5		
538	Nickel Th., Portland, ME	2/12	1914	$ 5,500				With echo.
538	Strand Th., Portland, ME	3/15	1917	$ 3,000				Moved from Nickel Th., Portland, Maine; additions: 3 ranks and three-manual console.
539	Park Th., Boston, MA	2/8	1914	$ 4,000				
		3/12	1914	$ 3,500				Additions: 4 ranks and xylophone.
545	Strand Th., Syracuse, NY	2/11	1915	$ 4,000				
546	Victoria Th., Buffalo, NY	2/14	1915	$ 2,000	6017			Rebuild of opus 476.
547	Palace Th., Buffalo, NY	2/11	1915	$ 4,000	6002			
559	Theis Orpheum Th., Wilkes-Barre, PA	2/12	1915	$ 4,800	6214			
580	Strand Th., Lynn, MA	2/13	1915	$ 4,400				
593	East Liberty Th., Pittsburgh, PA	3/20	1915	$ 10,500	6636			With echo.
605	Stanley (Stanton) Th., Philadelphia, PA	3/28	1916	$ 10,000	6651	10		With echo.
609	American Th., Salt Lake City, UT	3/47	1916	$ 10,000	6793			With echo.
610	Palace Th., Wichita, KS	3/15	1916	$ 6,000	6646			
			1918	$ 2,900	9143			Additions: 8 ranks.
					9429			
611	Rialto Th., New York City, NY	3/32	1915	$ 14,000		10		With traps; located at 42nd St. & 7th Ave.
624	Palace Th., Philadelphia, PA	2/13	1916	$ 5,350	6932	5		
627	Virginia Th., Atlantic City, NJ	2/13	1916	$ 5,350	6962	5		
628	Piccadilly Th., Rochester, NY	3/27		$ 10,000				Never built.
630	Stillman Th., Cleveland, OH	3/23	1916	$ 7,500	7335	10		
636	Great Northern Th., Philadelphia, PA	2/13	1916	$ 5,350		7½		
651	Globe Th., New Orleans, LA	2/8	1917	$ 5,221	7509			Unified.
661	Lacom Th., Beverly, MA	2/8	1916	$ 4,600	7320			Unified.
		3/11	1917	$ 2,000				Additions.
			19??					Moved to Strand Th., Peabody, Mass.
662	Strand Th., Worcester, MA	2/13	1916	$ 4,400	7538	5		
667	Alhambra Th., Cleveland, OH	2/15	1916	$ 16,000	8671			Package price for 3 organs.
668	Lower Mall Th., Cleveland, OH	2/15	1916		7580	5		
669	Upper Mall Th., Cleveland, OH	2/15	1916		7597	5		
682	Newark Th., Newark, NJ	2/13	1917	$ 4,400	7825	5		
		2/18	1927	$ 7,000				Additions: 5 ranks and traps.
703	Olympic Th., Watertown, NY	3/17	1917	$ 6,750				
708	Park Th., Boston, MA	3/16	1917	$ 3,500				
709	Triumph Th., New York City, NY	4/33	1917	$ 30,000				
711	Rialto Th., Philadelphia, PA	2/11	1917	$ 4,500	8163	5		
		2/15	1919					Additions: 4 ranks and harp.
716	Savoy Th., Philadelphia, PA	2/18	1917	$ 7,800	8103	5		
725	Strand Th., Lowell, MA	3/19	1917	$ 8,750	8331	10		
765	Liberty (Princess) Th., Kansas City, MO	3/26	1918	$ 10,000	8701	7½		With echo.
772	New Bedford Th., New Bedford, MA	2/4	1917	$ 2,180	8350			Chorophone.
795	Broadway Th., Philadelphia, PA	3/16	1918	$ 8,500	9137	5		
796	Rialto Th., Washington, D.C.	2/13	1918	$ 6,000		5		
810	Academy of Music, Selma, AL	2/14	1919	$ 6,350	9493			Voiced on 10" wp.
814	Strand Th., Montgomery, AL	3/19	1918	$ 8,300	9239	10		Voiced on 10" wp.
819	Strand Th., Brooklyn, NY	3/22	1919	$ 10,000	9841	7½		
					9842	7½		
824	Doan (Loew's Euclid) Th., Cleveland, OH	3/16	1919	$ 8,200	9494			
828	Newman Th., Kansas City, MO	4/42	1918	$ 20,000		15		
850	Criterion Th., Atlanta, GA	3/17	1919	$ 8,030		5		
		3/19	1920	$ 920				Additions: 2 ranks.
852	Strand Th., Far Rockaway, NY	3/12	1919	$ 5,500	9862	5		
855	Rialto Th., Newark, NJ	3/12	1920	$ 6,000	10770			
		3/12	1922	$ 490				New console.
867	Star Th., Lawrence, MA	2/4	1919	$ 2,490	9882			Chorophone.
872	Broadway Th., New York City, NY	3/16	1919	$ 9,350		5		Less $2,350 credit for old organ.
874	Cook Th., Okmulgee, OK	3/16	1920	$ 8,800	10633			
876	Ware Th., Beverly, MA	3/22	1920	$ 10,990	11071	7½		
888	Strand Th., Albany, NY	3/12	1920	$ 5,800	10819			
		3/16	1926	$ 2,190				Additions: 4 ranks.
891	Capitol Th., Springfield, MA	3/14	1920	$ 8,950	10665	5		
892	Strand Th., Council Bluffs, IA	2/12	1920	$ 8,250				Unified great, straight swell.
		4/12	1923					Totally unified; 3 swell ranks changed to tibia, kinura and post horn.
901	Astoria Th., Astoria, L.I., NY	3/14	1920	$ 7,000	11364			Moved to Strand Th., Port Jervis, N.Y., by M. P. Moller in 1926, with blower 0905B, 3hp, 7"wp.
902	Midland Th., Hutchinson, KS	3/26	1920	$ 8,970	10667			
914	Farragut Th., Brooklyn, NY	3/16	1920	$ 8,850	10584			With echo.
915	Rialto Th., Allentown, PA	3/13	1921	$ 7,400	11977			
927	Merrick Th., Jamaica, L.I., NY	3/19	1920	$ 10,900	11387			With echo.
		3/19	1926	$ 2,500				Additions: traps.
958	Kingsway Th., Brooklyn, NY	3/17	1920	$ 10,250	12064			With echo.
		3/17	1926	$ 2,500				Additions: traps.

OPUS	LOCATION/CITY/STATE	SIZE	YR	PRICE	BLWR	HP	WP	REMARKS
966	Criterion (Cooper) Th., Oklahoma City, OK	3/22	1920	$ 15,000	11746			
970	Rialto Th., Brooklyn, NY	3/15	1920	$ 11,850				
990	Henry Shenk Co. Recreation Hall and Theatre, Pittsburgh, PA	3/15	1921	$ 17,900				With roll player.
1007	Sheridan Th., New York City, NY	3/13	1921	$ 9,400	12432			
1010	Eastman Th., Rochester, NY	4/135	1923	$ 84,525	13207	40		
					13212	40		
1025	Keith's 105th Street Th., Cleveland, OH	3/18	1921	$ 18,350	12466	7½		
1027	Belevue Th., Upper Montclair, NJ	3/12	1922	$ 10,000	12822			
1032	Regent Th., Harrisburg, PA	3/25	1921	$ 15,000		7½		
1034	Beacham Th., Orlando, FL	3/17	1921	$ 12,800	12631	5	7"	
1065	Mark Strand Th., Troy, NY	3/15	1922	$ 6,500	13903			
1068	Rajah Th., Reading, PA	4/32	1922	$ 25,000		10	7"	
1102	Kearse Th., Charleston, WV	3/18	1922	$ 15,000		7½		
1140	Liberty Th., Covington, KY	3/20	1923	$ 14,500	14379			
1281	Willard Th., Woodhaven, L.I., NY	3/10	1924	$ 11,900	16160			
1303	Hollywood Th., Cincinnati, OH	2/7	1925	$ 5,500				Special Chorophone.
1307	Mt. Vernon Th., Mount Vernon, NY	3/13	1925	$ 14,300	16813			
1334	Belvedere Th., Tuscaloosa, AL	2/7	1925	$ 6,300	17332			
1379	Lyric Th., Hartford, CT	3/7	1926	$ 7,000	18044			
1419	WIBO Radio, Chicago, IL	3/7	1926	$ 6,500	18554			Installed but never paid for; contract said "to be paid for in full after approval by 3 organ experts".
1419	Lenox Th., Hartford, CT	3/8	1926	$ 5,000	18554			Tibia added; price reduced.
1421	Gem Th., Willimantic, CT	3/7	1926	$ 7,000	18478			
1433	Rivoli Th., Hartford, CT	3/8	1926	$ 10,000	19048			
1451	Freeport Th., Freeport, L.I., NY	3/11	1927	$ 13,500	19839			
1452	Prospect Th., Flsuhing, L.I., NY	3/13	1926	$ 14,500	19659			
1453	Mayfair (Horneck) Th., Brooklyn, NY	3/10	1926	$ 12,500	19194			
1454	Marine Th., Brooklyn, NY	3/10	1926	$ 12,500	19223			
1457	Strand Th., New Britain, CT	3/13	1926	$ 14,500	19166			
1458	Palace (Palmer) Th., New Britain, CT	3/8	1926	$ 8,950	19066			
1459	Circle Th., Manchester, CT	3/7	1926	$ 7,000	19036			
1463	Capitol Th., Everett, MA	2/9	1926	$ 9,000	19108			
1474	Whalley Th., New Haven, CT	3/7	1926	$ 7,400	19481			
1485	Tremont Th., Ansonia, CT	2/4	1926	$ 4,000	19545			
1511	Huntington Th., Huntington, L.I., NY	3/11	1927	$ 13,500	20047			
1512	Allyn Th., Hartford, CT	3/12	1927	$ 15,487	19957			
1551	Beacon Th., Port Washington, L.I., NY	3/11	1927	$ 13,500	20617			
1552	Plaza Th., Corona, L.I., NY	3/11	1927	$ 14,500	20814			
1569	Queens Village Th., Queens Village, L.I., NY	3/9	1927	$ 13,500				
1605	Howard Th., New Haven, CT	3/7	1928	$ 9,250	22174			
1627	Horace Bushnell Memorial Hall, Hartford, CT	4/75	1930	$ 45,000				
1630	Regal Th., Hartford, CT	3/8	1928	$ 10,000	22219			
1788	WHK Radio, Cleveland, OH	3/15	1931	$ 16,500				With roll player.

BALCOM & VAUGHN

In 1914 Clyde M. "Sandy" Balcom, then a lad of 15, went to work for Eilers Music Company, one of San Francisco's leading music retailers. Their product line included everything from sheet music to pipe organs, the latter being installed for the firm by Leo Schoenstein, eldest son of noted San Francisco organ builder Felix Schoenstein. Sandy Balcom learned the organ business from Leo Schoenstein during his apprenticeship in the years 1916-1921.[1]

In late 1921 the Sherman-Clay music retailing chain offered Sandy the position of head of their organ department to be headquartered in Seattle. His duties were to include selling and installing instruments as well as establishing regional service organizations. It was in the latter capacity that Sandy met Ernest LeRoy "Pop" Vaughn, one of the west coast's finest piano technicians, who was employed at the Tacoma, Washington Sherman-Clay store. Sandy Balcom taught Pop Vaughn to service organs and a warm friendship developed.[2] The two men dreamed of establishing their own business, but Mr. Vaughn was unable to do so for several years.[3]

Part of Sandy Balcom's impetus for establishing his own business had to do with Sherman-Clay's business practices. They would sell a Robert-Morton organ to a customer, but the organ would arrive from Highland, Illinois and would be in fact a Wicks with a Robert-Morton nameplate. Sandy didn't think this was fair to the customer. He was also outraged by the markup charged by Sherman-Clay. In one instance they sold a 2/4 Robert-Morton to a theatre for $12,000 and when the organ arrived from Highland, Sandy saw its invoice: its cost was $1,978 including freight![4]

Because Pop Vaughn couldn't join Sandy Balcom in a partnership right away, he suggested that his nephew, Lloyd Provorse, join Sandy for a few years. This partnership was known as Balcom & Provorse. By the mid-1920s Pop Vaughn was able to free himself from the Sherman-Clay organization and the Balcom & Vaughn firm was under way. Their success was immediate and the firm grew to be one of the largest service organizations on the west coast. Sandy and Pop enjoyed such a good relationship that it was a perfect setup for one of Sandy's practical jokes: In front of an unsuspecting client, Sandy would pretend to get angry at Pop and would eventually kick him in the leg. The client, of course, didn't know that Pop had a wooden leg! In one instance Sandy actually broke a broom handle over Pop's leg. On another occasion Pop kicked Sandy back and when a very surprised Sandy later asked why, Pop replied, "Because you kicked the wrong leg!"[5]

In 1924 Sandy assumed the representation of the Kimball company for theatre sales in the northwest and from 1924 to 1929 he sold and installed around 20 Kimball theatre organs. He also installed at least nine Robert-Morton theatre organs during this same period. He developed a friendship with R. P. Elliot, head of Kimball's

Sandy Balcom (1899-　) examines a krumet pipe in the KNX radio studio in Hollywood, California. In this installation Sandy started with a 2/8 Wurlitzer, built a new three-manual console and added three ranks of Gottfried pipes: post horn, krumet and French horn. This was one of his favorite installations.

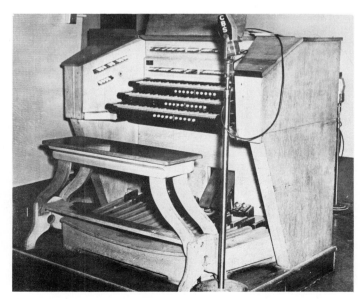

This Balcom & Vaughn console in the KNX studios in Hollywood, California wouldn't win any beauty contests. It typifies the style often used by the firm for their theatre-type installations.

BALCOM & VAUGHAN	FOR	ROLLERLAND RINK		
SEATTLE. WASH.	LOCATION	Renton, Washington.		
Shop Specification	BUILDER	Robert Morton-B &V. #425		

ACCOMPANIMENT SWELL			SOLO GREAT		
STOP	PITCH	DERIVATION	STOP	PITCH	DERIVATION
Existing Stops, plus			Existing Stops, plus		
Trumpet	8'	Trumpet	Trumpet	8'	Unit Tr.
Substitute Kinura	8'	Kinura	Substitute present		
for present Vox Hum.			Clarinet 8' for:		
Substitute present			Tibia	8'	Unit Tib.
Clarinet for:			Tibia	4'	"
*Tibia	16'	Tibia			
Tibia	8'	"	BOMBARDE		
Tibia	5⅓'	"			
Tibia	4'	"	Great to Bombard	16'	straight
			Great to Bombard	8'	"
*Don Ishem furnishes			Great to Bombard	4'	"
Wurlitzer Tibia Pipes					
** Wurlitzer Wood Diaphone from			SOLO		
Rialto Tacoma.					
***Don Ishem will supply			Great to Solo	8'	straight
Diaphone.			Great to Solo	4'	"

PEDAL			ACCESSORIES		
STOP	PITCH	DERIVATION			
Existing Stops, plus			PISTONS:	SW.	
Trumpet	8'	Unit Tr.		GT.	
Substitute present				PED.	
Clarinet 8' for:					
Tibia	8'	Unit Tib.	EXPRESSION PEDALS	Two for foot rest.	
Add:					
**Ophicliede	16'	Unit Tr. ext.	INDICATOR LIGHTS	Current.	
***Diphone (will be	16'	" Op.ext.			
substituted for pre-			DETAILS Original console will be stripped		
sent Bourdon 16' pipes.			and installed in special 4 man. of		
			our design. Regulator and Trem. will be		
			added for Tibia. We will supply Tibia and		
			Trumpet chests. We will not use Bourdon16'		
			Present Harp will have repeat action.		

APPROVED C. M. Balcom.	BEGUN	COMPLETED Jan 76

The Rollerland Rink in Renton, Washington featured a 4/8 Balcom & Vaughn installed in 1946. As in most Balcom & Vaughn rink installations, the pipes were unenclosed. At left, a form like this was made out by Sandy Balcom for each of the theatre organs he converted for other uses.

pipe organ division, and after Elliot went to Aeolian in 1928 Sandy sold and installed half of the Aeolian theatre organs ever built.[6] (See the Aeolian article elsewhere in this volume). Around 1930 a Spokane man, J. Riley Chase, joined the firm briefly and for about five weeks the firm was known as Balcom, Vaughn & Chase, after which it again became Balcom & Vaughn, the name it retains in 1983 despite Pop Vaughn's death in 1947 and Sandy Balcom's retirement in 1966.[7]

During the 1920s Balcom & Vaughn's primary business was selling, installing and servicing organs made by other firms. When the Depression severely cut new organ sales, Balcom & Vaughn continued in the service business and also did a number of transplants of theatre organs to new locations. These transplants frequently included additional ranks of pipes ordered from Gottfried and new or enlarged consoles. Until 1944 the business was conducted

This rather attractive Balcom & Vaughn console started its life as a two-manual Smith. Installed in the Redondo Rink in Redondo Beach, Washington, it controlled ten ranks of pipes.

The Northwest Recording Studio in Seattle contained a 3/9 Balcom & Vaughn installed in 1946. The Kimball console was modernized to look like the one in the WGN radio studios in Chicago.

This instrument in the KGW/KEX studios in Portland, Oregon started its life as a 2/6 style D Wurlitzer. Balcom & Vaughn added the third manual and three additional ranks of pipes.

out of the basement of Sandy's home at 114 East 51st Street in Seattle. In 1944 the old Meridian Theatre building at 5413 Meridian Avenue North was purchased and renovated and still serves as the firm's headquarters in 1983. It is interesting to note that, around 1923, Sandy installed a style 20 Fotoplayer in this very building![8]

In 1939 a young organist with exceptional mechanical skills named William J. Bunch (1918-) joined the Balcom & Vaughn firm and stayed with them for 17 years, leaving in 1956 to join Aeolian-Skinner in Boston. In 1966 Sandy Balcom was ready to retire and Bill Bunch seized the opportunity to return to his native Seattle, purchasing the Balcom & Vaughn firm from Sandy Balcom who was absolutely delighted that "little Willy," as Sandy called him, would continue the business. Under Bill Bunch's leadership the firm gained a reputation for tonal similarity to Aeolian-Skinner instruments but Bill Bunch never lost his enthusiasm for theatre organs. In the 1970s the firm received contracts to build two four-manual Wurlitzer replica consoles to replace those destroyed by arsonists in the Grant Union High School in Sacramento, California and Century II in Wichita, Kansas, home of the famous New York Paramount 4/36 Wurlitzer.[9]

Sandy Balcom was much more interested in installing organs than in keeping records and, as a result, information concerning his installations in the 1930s and 1940s is incomplete. In 1944 Bill Bunch began keeping an opus list. He asked Sandy how many organs he had installed and Sandy replied, "Oh, about 400." So Bill began the numbered opus list with #401! As of 1983 opus 856 is being built in the Balcom & Vaughn shop.[10]

The replacement console for the New York Paramount Wur-litzer is pictured before decorative carvings were applied. Strict adherence to Wurlitzer dimensions ensured an authentic appearing replica although on the inside Bill Bunch designed a combination action mechanism similar to Kimball's which allows for much easier maintenance and accessibility.

This Balcom & Vaughn console was built for Grant Union High School, Sacramento, California in 1975. It looks like a Wurlitzer on the outside, but is all electric inside, using Reisner stop action magnets.

BALCOM & VAUGHN OPUS LIST

Following are those theatre-type instruments known to have been installed under this firm's nameplate. All had original theatre organs as their basis and many had Balcom & Vaughn additions as well. Sizes shown are those of the Balcom & Vaughn installations—not necessarily those of the original instruments.

CITY/STATE	LOCATION	SIZE	YR	REMARKS
CALIFORNIA				
Hollywood	KNX Radio, Columbia Sq.	3/11	1937	Wurlitzer opus 1516, plus post horn, krumet and French horn.
Sacramento	Carl Greer Inn	4/16	1964	Moved Robert-Morton from Fox (Music Hall) (7th Avenue) Theatre, Seattle, Washington; cost $ 3,500.
	Grant Union High School	4/	1975	Build console only, Wurlitzer replica;. cost $ 33,000.
IDAHO				
Moscow	Dr. Frank B. Robinson	2/5	1931	Geneva from Madrona Gardens Theatre, Seattle, Wash.
KANSAS				
Wichita	Century II Th.	4/	1971	Build console only for N.Y. Paramount Wurlitzer; cost $ 39,400.
OREGON				
Medford	Ice Arena Rink	2/6	1941	Robert-Morton from Grants Pass Theatre, Grants Pass, Oregon.
Portland	Ice Arena Rink	2/8	1944	Kimball from T&D Theatre, Aberdeen, Wash.; B&V opus 401.
	Imperial Rink	3/8	1935	Additions to Wood organ.
			1941	Additions.
		3/18	1955	Add Wurlitzer opus 1327.
	KGW/KEX Radio	3/9	1936	Wurlitzer opus 957 plus 3 ranks; destroyed by fire in 1946.
	KOIN Radio	3/6	1935	Robert-Morton.

CITY/STATE	LOCATION	SIZE	YR	REMARKS
Salem	Russell Morelle residence	2/5	1950	Wurlitzer opus 2017.

WASHINGTON

CITY/STATE	LOCATION	SIZE	YR	REMARKS
Anacortes	Empire Theatre	2/4	1937	Wurlitzer opus 1022.
Centralia	Fox Theatre	2/10	193?	Additions.
Ellensburg	Jim Bundy residence	3/6	1952	Wurlitzer from As You Like It Tavern, Seattle, Wash.
Everett	Balboa Theatre	2/4	1930	Wurlitzer opus 1339.
	William Morrison residence	3/13	1962	Marr & Colton; B&V opus 698.
	Rollerfair Rink	3/5	1956	Wurlitzer opus 451.
Federal Way	Roller Gardens Rink	3/10	1954	Robert-Morton from Pantages (Orpheum) Theatre, Portland, Oregon; B&V opus 616; cost $ 8,067.
Mount Vernon	unidentified residence	2/4	1955	Wurlitzer.
Olympia	Olympia Skating Rink	2/8	1944	Wurlitzer; later destroyed by fire.
Redondo Beach	Redondo Rink	4/10	1948	Wurlitzer; B&V opus 469; later destroyed by fire.
Renton	Maple Leaf Tavern	3/5	1946	Kimball from Olympic (Woodland) Theatre, Seattle, Wash.
	Rollerland Rink	4/8	1946	Robert-Morton from Pantages Theatre, Seattle, Wash.; B&V opus 425.
Seattle	As You Like It Tavern	3/6	1945	Wurlitzer; B&V opus 410.
	C. M. Balcom residence	2/10	1941	
			1946	B&V opus 430
	D. Deane Bottker residence	2/9	1951	Some used parts.
	William Bunch residence	3/15	1949	
	Diamond Horseshoe Night Club	2/4	1946	Wurlitzer; later destroyed by fire.
	Donald Drew residence	2/5	1941	Wurlitzer opus 607.
	Louis DuMoulin residence	3/12	1960	Smith from Liberty Theatre, Enumclaw, Wash.
	Robert Dyer residence	2/5	1941	Wurlitzer opus 607.
	Bennett Fisher residence	3/10	1961	Wurlitzer/B&V from KOMO Radio, Seattle; B&V opus 683.
	Garden of Allah Night Club	2/5	1939	Wurlitzer opus 379.
	Kenneth Graves, old residence	2/4	1942	Wurlitzer.
	Kenneth Graves, Magnolia residence	3/14	1946	Wurlitzer opus 178; B&V opus 442.
			1950	Additions; B&V opus 507.
	William Hubley residence	2/3	1947	Estey Minuette enlarged to 2/12.
	Ice Arena Rink	3/8	1941	Wurlitzer opus 1427.
			1964	Disconnected.
			1966	Reinstalled.
	KOL Radio	3/12	1931	Kimball, 5 ranks, from Grand Theatre, Seattle; Wurlitzer console.
	KOMO Radio	3/10	1939	Wurlitzer opus 1194, plus 3 ranks.
	Elliott Lawrence residence	3/8	1965	Many parts.
	Elmer Lindgaard residence	3/15	1949	Used parts; B&V opus 498.
	Lyon's Music Hall	2/6	1936	Robert-Morton from Lark Theatre, McMinnvile, Oregon.
	Edwin L. Neuman residence	2/7	1946	Robert Morton; B&V opus 443.
	Northwest Recording Studio	3/9	1946	Wurlitzer opus 341 plus 2 ranks; Kimball console; destroyed by fire in 1951.
	Pacific Recording Studios	2/4	1945	Wurlitzer; B&V opus 414.
			1946	Additions; B&V opus 438.
	Playland Rink	3/5	1945	Wurlitzer opus 451.
	Ridge Rink	2/9	1946	Wurlitzer; B&V opus 447; replaced a burned 2/9 Wurlitzer.
	Rolladium Rink	3/10	1953	Wurlitzer opus 977; B&V opus 547 and 565.
	Rollerbowl Rink	3/10	1946	Wurlitzer opus 50 with Robert-Morton console from KSTP, Minneapolis; destroyed by fire in 1951.
	Show Box Club	3/8	1943	Wurlitzer opus 776.
	S. W. Smith residence	2/5	1961	Wurlitzer opus 1022; B&V opus 684; cost $ 3,796.
	Hollister T. Sprague residence	3/28	1933	Kilgen, Estey and Wurlitzer.
	Edwin Stern residence	3/4	1964	Wurlitzer; B&V opus 716; cost $ 4,600.
Spokane	Fox Theatre	3/13	1931	Wurlitzer opus 263.
	KFPY Radio	3/	1943	Wurlitzer opus 977.
		3/	1945	Additions; B&V opus 412.
	KHQ Radio	3/	1939	Wurlitzer opus 792.
Sumner	Dan Epperson residence	3/8	1946	Wurlitzer; B&V opus 448.
			1949	Additions; B&V opus 479; cost $ 4,000.
			1953	Additions; B&V opus 506.
Tacoma	King's Skating Rink	2/8	1940	Wurlitzer opus 389.
	KMO Radio	2/	1931	Robert-Morton, 8-ranks, from Park Theatre, Tacoma.
	Rollerbowl Rink	3/8	1941	Wurlitzer opus 389.
Tieton	C. R. Strand residence	2/5	1947	Wurlitzer; B&V opus 457.
Yakima	KIT Radio	2/5	1939	Wurlitzer opus 835; destroyed by fire in 1961.
	Larry Langevin residence	2/7	195?	Wurlitzer opus 69.
	Mrs. George O. Meeker residence	2/4	1939	Kilgen.

BARCKHOFF ORGAN COMPANY

Carl Barckhoff was a colorful figure in American organ building history. He was divorced twice because of romantic interests with other women, while horse racing and gambling were his other favorite pastimes. He was not noted for telling the truth either to church committees or in his advertising and was a businessman of questionable ethics who more than once declared bankruptcy and then moved to another community to repeat the process. His organs had a reputation for being the lowest priced in the country[1] with quality to match.[2]

Barckhoff was the son of German organ builder Felix Barckhoff who moved his family to Philadelphia in 1865 and established a business known as Felix Barckhoff & Sons. Following his father's death in 1878 Carl Barckhoff moved the firm to Allegheny County which is now the north side of Pittsburgh, Pennsylvania. In 1882 the firm moved to Salem, Ohio where it remained until 1895 when a move was made to Mendelssohn, a community now incorporated in Clairton, Pennsylvania. Following a fire of suspicious origin in 1897, the firm moved to Latrobe, Pennsylvania, lasting there until 1900 when another move was made to Pomeroy, Ohio. Here the Barckhoff Church Organ Company had its greatest success and at one time was building three organs per week.[3]

Following a disastrous flood of the Ohio river in 1913 which wiped out the factory, Barckhoff moved for the last time to Basic, Virginia, a community now incorporated in Waynesboro, Virginia. By October of 1916 the firm was again bankrupt and in 1917 control was assumed by E. C. Malarkey who changed the name of the firm to his own. Carl Barckhoff died two years later in 1919.[4]

The vast majority of Barckhoff organs featured tracker action although experimentation with tubular pneumatic action was begun in the 1890s and some electric action organs were made. Most records of the Barckhoff firm were lost to fire or flood.[5]

*Carl Barckhoff
(1849-1919)*[6]

Barckhoff ad in the October 1910 Diapason. Perhaps some of these "self-playing organs" or "orchestrions" were sold to theatres.

BARCKHOFF OPUS LIST

Records of the Kinetic Engineering Company reveal that four blowers were sold to Barckhoff with theatre destinations.

CITY/STATE	LOCATION	SIZE	YR	BLWR	HP	WP	REMARKS
NEW YORK							
Buffalo	Eastern Vaudeville Co.		1911	8270K	½	3"	
OHIO							
Toledo	Brailey Th.		1911	7739K	1	3½"	
PENNSYLVANIA							
Pittsburgh	Cameraphone Th.		1914	C343	¾	3½"	
VIRGINIA							
Petersburg	Palace Th.		1914	C148	½	3½"	

S. H. Barrington operated an organ business in the Philadelphia area and installed at least two theatre organs bearing his nameplate. The 5/21 in the Ardmore Theatre, Ardmore, Pennsylvania was apparently Mr. Barrington's magnum opus and is the console featured on his letterhead.[1] It was actually an enlargement of an earlier 3/13 United States Pipe Organ Company instrument which had been installed in 1922.[2] Mr. Barrington added eight ranks and a five-manual console in 1925, all of which were purchased from Gottfried.[3] The blower for these added ranks was a 7½ horsepower Kinetic, #N328B, rated at 15" wind pressure.[4]

The other Barrington theatre organ was a 4/19 in the Marketplace (Markley) Theatre in Norristown, Pennsylvania for which Barrington himself built the console, patterning it after Wurlitzer stylings. He used a Klann combination action, however, and other components for the organ were ordered from Gottfried, Dennison and Durst-Boegle. The theatre was destroyed by a freak accident in 1930 when a gasoline tank truck exploded and set ablaze nearly the entire block in which the theatre stood.

Barrington built a third theatre organ, a 3/9 for the Norris Theatre in Norristown, but the contract was cancelled and he installed the organ in a church instead, minus its traps.[5]

S. H. Barrington at the console of one of his installations.

F. A. Bartholomay (?-1942) started in the organ industry in 1879. In 1922 his firm moved to an old school building at the corner of American and Bainbridge Streets in Philadelphia[1] and remained in business there until 1954.[2] A major part of their business was rebuilding, but they also built some new organs. Because quality was good, some of their organs and tracker electrifications of sixty years ago are still playing today.

Two Bartholomay organs are known to have been installed in theatres: A two-manual in the Lansdale Theatre, Lansdale, Pennsylvania in 1922 and a 2/8 in the Avenue Theatre, Wilmington, Delaware. At least one of these organs may have sported a horseshoe console: New York historian Biff Buttler recalls having seen a beautiful two-manual Bartholomay horseshoe console in the early 1960s.

Bartholomay nameplate c. 1930.

Bartholomay ad in the April 1923 Diapason.

BARTOLA MUSICAL INSTRUMENT COMPANY

MAKERS OF

Oshkosh, Wis.

The story of the Barton organ company is a classic tale of a high school dropout[4] (Dan Barton) who made good. He proved that a man can be inventive and intelligent despite the lack of a formal education. Little did Barton know as he pursued a career as a percussionist in his mid-twenties that one day a firm bearing his name would become the fifth largest builder of theatre organs in the country. Although being in the organ business was the farthest thing from his mind at the time, Dan was always quick to seize an opportunity—and one opportunity seemed to lead to another until his career reached its zenith with the production of the Chicago Stadium organ. This six-manual behemoth was perhaps the most thrilling theatre organ of them all . . . but that's getting ahead of the story! Let's allow Dan Barton to tell this tale in his own words:

"When I was a boy in grade school my father bought me a drum. When about ten years old I was playing in the Grand Army Drum Corps. By dint of a lot of practice and some experience with the town band and local dance orchestra I became good enough [that] I left home to be a professional drummer. I held jobs with Salisbury's Concert Orchestra playing lyceums and chautauquas, Fischer's Orchestra at Statler's Inside Inn at the St. Louis World's Fair, Kiltie's Concert Band of Canada, Al Sweet's famous fifty-piece concert band with Ringling Bros. Circus and Orpheum circuit vaudeville theatres in Kansas City, Indianapolis . . . Memphis . . . and some other engagements that did not rate quite as high from a prestige standpoint. This included a couple of carnivals, a dog and pony show,

Uncle Tom's Cabin, dance bands and several combination vaudeville and motion picture houses.[5]

"In 1909 I was with the Ringling Brothers circus band and shortly before the end of the season received word of the death of my mother. I returned to my home in Oshkosh, Wisconsin to be with my father who was an invalid. The only job in town was at the Bijou Theatre [which had] 450 seats, three acts of vaudeville and a motion picture, three shows a day. The orchestra [consisted of] a pianist and a drummer. They needed a drummer so I took the job.[6]

"The piano used in the orchestra was a Shoninger. There were some bells inside the piano; the pianist pulled a lever and the bells would play from the treble end of the keyboard. The orchestra pianist never used them so I took them out and mounted them on electric door bell mechanisms and strung them all over the theatre, both side walls, in the rear, under the balcony, all over. I attached them to a keyboard which I played from the orchestra pit. They made a big hit and I got an idea—make up such sets of bells with a keyboard and sell them to drummers in the nearby towns. I rented a closed up machine shop, had patterns made and bells cast in a brass foundry. I tuned and mounted the bells [and] made up the keyboards. This gave me 16 sets of bells and I had a sideline. Then I found out something: the drummers I contacted had no money or if they had money they had no intention of spending it for an attraction that they thought the theatre manager should buy. The theatre owners had no idea of buying equipment for the drummer and only about one in ten of the surrounding theatres even had a drummer. So there I was with 16 sets of bells, about $600 invested, paying rent on a mchine shop and I could not sell even one set of bells. I still had the job in the theatre and I quit trying to sell the bells.

"One stormy night with few people in the theatre during the last show the piano player started to kid a dancing act. He reached up to the highest octave on the piano and played the act's music for their soft shoe dance. It got a laugh from the dancing act and I got an idea. Why

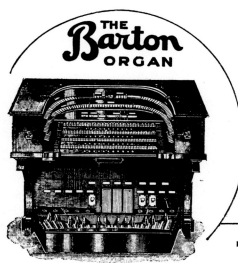

THE **Barton** ORGAN

SALES AND
DEMONSTRATION ROOMS
314 MALLERS BUILDING
CHICAGO, ILLINOIS

W. G. MAXCY
PRES. AND TREAS.

I. T. MAXCY
SECRETARY

D. W. BARTON
GENERAL MANAGER

GENERAL OFFICES
AND FACTORY
OSHKOSH, WIS.

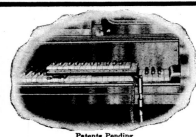

The June 29, 1912 issue of Motion Picture World *carried one of Dan Barton's first ads. His bells were the precursor of the Bartola.*

The Barton factory in Oshkosh, Wisconsin, above and below, as it appeared in 1963. The site is now a parking lot.

couldn't the piano player play the bells from the bell keyboard at the same time he played the piano, bass and [accompaniment] with his left hand and the melody on the bells with his right hand. We tried it and it worked. I had a standard made that set on the floor with the bell keyboard mounted so it would swing over the piano keys or away as desired. To shorten this part of the story I . . . sold all 16 sets in less than six weeks to . . . theatre [owners] for the [pianists] to play. I . . . applied for a patent on the swinging keyboard, quit the theatre and . . . was in the bell business.

"Now more ideas . . . if the pianist could play bells from the keyboard why couldn't he play other instruments from the same keyboard. I hired a couple of fellows to help me, one being Walter Gollnick who was just out of an electrical engineering school. He helped with the electric actions and later became the head installer for the Barton organs . . . I went to see the [Wangerin-Weickhardt] Company in Milwaukee. They agreed to make an organ chest having pipes to sound like a violin, flute, clarinet and vox humana or human voice. In the machine shop we added a xylophone, orchestra bells and chimes. We made a foot board to fit around the piano pedals for bass drum, snare drum, tom tom, castanets, cymbal crash and bird whistle.

"We made two wood cases to be installed in the orchestra pit, one on each side of the piano, mahogany fininsh, with an open grille in the front. We arranged the keyboard with switches so the instruments could be played singly or in any combination, the organ pipes in one case and the xylopone, orchestra bells, drums and effects in the other. The chimes were mounted on a rack outside the cases. It took time and a lot of experimenting but finally we had it complete.[7] I never considered my contraption as an organ but as an arrangement able to produce an orchestral result and as such thought it should have a name. That was back in the days of the Victrola so I used the 'ola' and created the name Bartola.[8]

"The local automobile dealers held an auto show in the local armory and we put the Bartola on display at the auto show. There were two experienced vaudeville piano players in town, Harry Awe and Bernard Cowham. They were both talented and spent many hours playing this first experiment and helped greatly from the musical standpoint . . . They both were with me many years and became great Barton organists. Back to the auto show— there were big crowds and the new music box was the talk of the town—even a write-up and a picture in the local paper.

"Now the Bartola got a break. Mr. Walter Keefe was a vaudeville booking agent in Chicago, booking acts and feature pictures in theatres all over the middle west. Mr. Keefe's parents lived in Oshkosh and he was here on a visit and attended the auto show. To him the Bartola was more than a musical device. He saw the possibilities of marketing it and with his acquaintance with the owners of many theatres he was confident of the result. He made an arrangement with Mr. Tink Humphreys, also a vaudeville booking agent in Chicago, to become his partner to take on the sale of the Bartola.

". . . At that time there was a national association of

A selling point of the Bartola was the presence of the human element; it was not a mechanically played instrument.

The Bartola was the precursor of the Barton theatre organ. Note how the divided keyboards can be swung into place over the piano keys. The chimes on the left used direct electric action, as did all Bartola percussions. The low wind pressure used on Bartola pipework, 3½-5", made pneumatic percussion actions impractical.

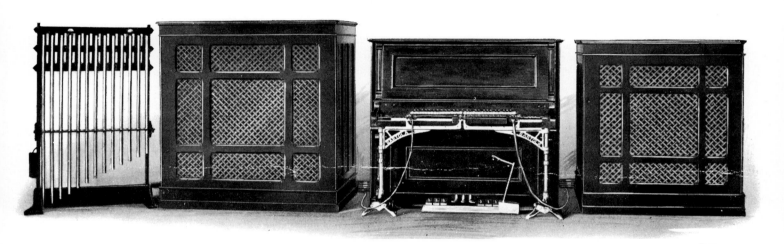

motion picture exhibitors who held a convention every year. There were exhibits of all kinds: motion picture projectors, screens, theatre seats, popcorn machines, electric signs and many more items used in theatres. This convention was opening in two weeks in New York City. Keefe and Humphreys [lost no time and] were going to show the Bartola at this big show. We packed up the experimental Bartola and to the convention we went taking Walter Gollnick to set it up and Bernard Cowham to play it.

". . . There were other musical instruments being shown [with] pneumatic action played from a roll with some pipes, drums and traps. They could also be played manually. Their musical qualities were loud and boistrous. They sounded like a modified merry-go-round organ. The Bartola had an electric action and real organ pipes voiced to have the tonal quality of orchestral instruments and the advantage of the human element. The automatic organs played what was on the music roll . . . but Cowham demonstrated how the Bartola could follow every change of action in the picture and with beautiful tonal quality.

"The convention lasted a week and Keefe sold 18 Bartolas and would have sold more if I had not stopped him.

All I had was an experimental Bartola and a small machine shop with three people to help me. What was I going to do with 18 orders? It would take a factory, woodworking machinery, assembly space . . . trained help and money. Keefe and Humphreys knew nothing of manufacturing and I knew even less. I was desperate with success! And then the Bartola got another break.

"When I arrived back in Oshkosh with orders for 18 Bartolas and no way to build them, the boys in the shop told me that Mr. W. G. Maxcy had stopped in to see how I was doing. Mr. Maxcy was the man I had rented the machine shop from. He was a wealthy man and [was] interested in many projects. He owned several public utilities, had an interest in an auto truck plant, had once operated a carriage factory, manufactured automatic bridge gates and [was involved in several] other ventures. I went to see Mr. Maxcy . . . told him the story, showed him the orders for the 18 Bartolas and told him I was stuck. He had a conference with Keefe and Humphreys and took over the manufacturing of the Bartola—Mr. Maxcy to handle the manufacturing, Keefe and Humphreys the sales and Barton to operate the factory. The very first thing was to advise the exhibitors who had signed the 18 contracts that we could not fill the orders without a

The Greatest Improvement in Organs since the Electric Action

Solves the Problem—Unlimited musical possibilities with standard playing methods.

THE DIVIDED MANUAL

offers thousands of new and original tonal combinations of exquisite beauty—new musical creations never before possible.

No unifying, duplexing, synthetics, or double touch.
No previous organ of any size or price adequately compares with the musical attainment and ease of playing the Barton Organ introduces.

*Write today for booklet "Organ Improvement"
fully describing the Barton Organ*

The Bartola Musical Instrument Co.
312-314 Mallers Bldg.   5 S. Wabash Ave.   Chicago, Ill.

Early ad for the Barton organ in the December 1920 Diapason. The divided manual organ was designed to assist Bartola players, who were accustomed to two divided keyboards, in getting used to larger Barton organs. Organists weren't as enthusiastic about the divided manual consoles as the Barton company was, with the result that few were sold.

long delay and explained the reason to them. They were to advise if they did not care to wait. Not one order was cancelled.

"We rented space in a factory building, installed machinery and hired more men. In six months we had a small but complete factory in operation and the Bartola was on the way. We developed four . . . models . . . a second keyboard was added on the left side of the pianist with an 8' stopped bourdon so if the occasion demanded the Bartola became a pipe organ.[9] Also at this time a pipe stop was added that had a new tone quality. The pipes were developed by Jerome Meyer . . . of Milwaukee [and] were of large scale, metal, with a high pure tin content and were capped; a very fine nicking was used. The voicing produced a tone that especially in the upper registers resembled a soprano voice. This stop at the 2' pitch was used in the Bartola . . . providing a tone one octave higher than the other pipes. This stop was new and had no name so I coined one—Bartolina. The Bartolina was a valuable addition to the tonal makeup of the Bartola and

was used several years later as the upper register of the Barton organ tibia.[10]

"Keefe and Humphreys rented space in the Schiller Building on Randolph Street in Chicago. We installed a demonstrator and Keefe brought in Kenneth Kurtz from Benton Harbor, Michigan to play it. Kurtz was a trained vaudeville and picture pianist. He became a great Bartola player [and] developed into a star salesman and manager of our Chicago office and was with the company for many years. C. C. Pyle was made sales manager. He was a fine salesman and promoter. He was acquainted with a great many theatre owners through his promotion of feature pictures. Later [he] became famous as the owner of a New York City professional football team and promoter of a foot race across the entire United States.

"In my early experience as a drummer I had played in two theatres which were combination vaudeville and picture houses and had installed church organs to accompany the pictures. These organs were in trouble a great deal of the time. The church organ mechanism would not stand up under the grueling use in a picture show. These organs received more hours of use in one day than they received in [a] church in a month or more. When out of order there was always a delay in getting a repair man from the factory. Sometimes for days the theatre would have to revert to a piano for music. In one instance the organ was finally abandoned. In developing the Bartola I remembered this experience. I determined to build the Bartola so it would stand up under severe usage. We used tungsten contact points, weatherproof cable [and] California sugar pine with an exact moisture content to avoid shrinking and swelling. All moving parts and magnets were oversize. The Holtzer-Cabot Company developed a special motor-generator set that furnished plenty of low voltage electricity and caused little trouble. No expense was spared to produce a mechanism that would stand up in a theatre.

"We decided to work only a limited territory so we could give prompt service to all our installations. [This territory included] Wisconsin, Illinois, Michigan, Iowa, Minnesota, North and South Dakota, Nebraska, Kansas, Indiana and Ohio. No installation was more than an overnight sleeper ride from Chicago. We had standby roadmen ready at all times to answer a call for service from any point in our territory. I installed a system of inspection. Every time we installed a Bartola the road installer stopped in all the nearby cities where we had Bartolas and gave them a check, always making sure the owner knew he was there and making sure the owner realized he was receiving service he had not even asked for'. This manner of building the Bartola to quality and giving inspections paid off later on in a manner I never dreamed of at the time we were doing it.

"From the very start I realized that it would take a talented pianist to successfully play the Bartola. To follow the picture action they would have to improvise and to know dozens of tunes to play without music. We used pianists like Harry Awe, Bernard Cowham, Eddie Hanson, Jay Hurlbutt and others. They played the Bartola the opening week and during the week taught the local pianist how to play the instrument. These boys were wizards

Daniel W. Barton (1884-1974) photographed in 1972 at his Oshkosh, Wisconsin home.

Ad in the July 1923 Diapason.

Bernard Cowham plays a Barton divided-manual organ. Employed by the Barton company, he gave opening week recitals on the firm's newly installed organs in the early 1920s.[3]

This ad in the October 1926 Diapason *appeared as the demand for theatre organists reached its zenith. Only one year later the axe fell when movies started to talk.*

and I sometimes wondered at the musical results they attained. This scheme did not work. The local piano [players] many times lacked talent, would not practice . . . had no experience playing the picture action and little ability in many cases.

"After our demonstrator left the musical results were disappointing and sometimes pretty sad. The management hopped on the local organist. What was the trouble? Why didn't the Bartola sound the same as the first week with the factory demonstrator? The local pianist was on the spot and was not going to admit he lacked ability so he told the boss our demonstrator had failed to show him anything or else said the Bartola had gone on the bum and he could do no better owing to the poor shape the instrument was in. Whatever he said, it was trouble for us. It was soon apparent that besides building the Bartola we also had to produce the fellow [who] played it.

"We moved our Chicago office to larger space in the Mallers Building at Madison and Wabash Avenue and started a school for Bartola players. We continued to send a demonstrator for the opening week but told the purchaser at the time he signed the contract it would take a properly talented and trained operator to give him results.

If he wanted to use his local pianist it would be necessary for him to send the pianist to our school. If the pianist turned out okay that was fine, otherwise we would furnish him a competent operator. Ralph Emerson ran the school and also demonstrated for prospects [who] came to the office. The students paid for the instructions. They received big dividends on their investment. If they lacked ability or talent they were quickly told they were wasting their time. We wanted only the pianists [who] would develop into A-1 Bartola players. Many were sent on positions at salaries they never would have received as motion picture piano players.

"Soon after we started placing Bartola players the word went out and we soon had more applicants than we could handle. From the bigger cities and small towns they came and some from great distances. Many later became famous Barton organists. Our business was steadily growing. We increased our factory space [and] trained more people for both factory and road work. We were selling to some growing theatre circuits. The personal acquaintance that Keefe, Humphreys and Pyle had with theatre owners helped a great deal, but the biggest factor in our success was the fact that the Bartola made good. Working a territory never more than a sleeper jump out of Chicago, our service was always ready. We furnished competent and well-trained musicians and built friendship with our customers. We had the most valuable advertising in the world—theatre owners boosting the Bartola to their friends who owned theatres.

"Among our friends and good boosters were W. S. Butterfield and Ed Beatty of the Butterfield circuit in Michigan, Nate Ascher of the Ascher circuit in Chicago, Schaefer Brothers who operated a chain of neighborhood theatres in Chicago, Tom Saxe of the Saxe circuit of Milwaukee, Wisconsin, Jules Rubens of Great States Theatres with theatres throughout Illinois outside of Chicago, S. J. Gregory of the Gregory Theatres in northern Indiana and Chicago suburbs, Abe Blank of the Blank circuit throughout Iowa [and] Barney Balaban and Sam Katz of Balaban & Katz.[11] We were kept busy manufacturing Bartolas for the next ten years. Then came the start of the big theatres with organ lofts. The first such theatre in the middle west was Balaban & Katz' Central Park in Chicago. We installed a Bartola in the organ lofts and it just did not work. The days of the pit organs were over and I got busy designing a console unit organ.[12]

"We were in good shape to make the addition. More space was available in our building. We had developed an organ action for the Bartola that stood up in theatres. We had a successful school and many skilled Bartola players easily converted to console organists. The electrical application to console keyboards, organ relays and switches

Opposite page: A Barton ad in Motion Picture News *for April 5, 1924 promoted dual-console installations. Despite this advertising campaign, illustrating the Lincoln Square Theatre, Decatur, Illinois, only one other twin-console job is known: the 3&3/17 in the Wisconsin Theatre, Milwaukee, Wisconsin.*

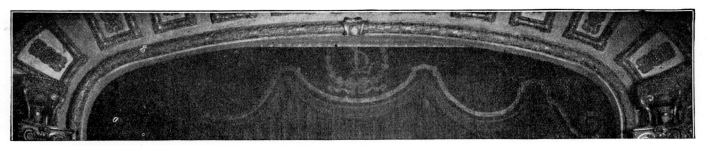

The New Barton Twin Console Double Organ
A Musical Sensation!

Lincoln Square Theatre, Decatur, Ill.

The Barton Pitless Console Lifts occupy only 12 inches of vertical space. They rest on top of the orchestra pit floor and raise five feet. Now every theater can be equipped at a cost tremendously lower than for the pit type. This is exclusively a Barton feature.

A Box Office sensation, too! This is a new way of featuring music that has tremendous audience pulling power. This new Barton Two Console Double Orchestral Organ has gained instant favor. The theater shown above is only one of many we are similarly equipping.

This new Barton can be played by two players simultaneously, or by one player from either console. Each console is mounted on the new Barton Pitless Console Lift that raises it five feet to the audience's amazement and lowers it below the sight lines of first row seats quickly and easily.

Remember that Barton Orchestral Organ has the richest tonal quality and is the most flexible, reliable, and practical theater music equipment ever built. Now that this innovation is provided, this organ is more profitable than ever for any theater to own.

Will you be the first in your city to exploit the New Barton Two Console Double Organ? There is money in it. Write or wire for particulars.

IT'S A *Barton* ORCHESTRAL ORGAN

BARTOLA MUSICAL INSTRUMENT CO.
59 East Madison Street   **CHICAGO, ILL.**

The Console illustrated here is the beautiful Barton Organ installed in the Fair Park Auditorium, Dallas, Texas.

The Golden Voice Barton Brings Silver to Your Box Office

What brings the crowd back next night? What fills those last remaining seats — *your profit seats?* The Picture? Yes — and NO! Somewhere — hidden in the orchestra pit, or in full view — there is a man or woman who makes your shows infinitely better. He or she — the organist — sways your audience to the moods of the presentation.

Has your organist the equipment to move your audience? Consider if he or she sends them away forever — or to come back again? To handi-cap your organist is a mighty big risk. To give your organist full co-operation is to install a "Barton."

The Barton Orchestral Organ is bringing capacity crowds to many leading theaters of the country. It can do likewise for yours.

The Barton has an exceptionally wide and varied range. Its interpretations are conceded to be "next to human." Its completeness, its flexibility make the Barton truly an organ with an appeal — a box office appeal.

Of course, the New Wisconsin—being an advanced theater chose the Barton as well as did the Joliet theater, Joliet, Ill., and Retlaw theater, Fond du Lac, Wis.—All these are C. W. and Geo. L. Rapp designed theaters.

Let us send you full particulars about the Barton without obligation. Merely give us the size of your theater.

IT'S A *Barton* ORCHESTRAL ORGAN

BARTOLA MUSICAL INSTRUMENT CO.,
313-316 Mallers Bldg.   Chicago.

Al Melgard prepares to broadcast on the Barton in the WBBM studios, Chicago.

Barton four-poster lifts were very popular because they could be installed without excavating a pit. They were sold for use under many non-Barton consoles, too. The four screws are stationary and bolted to a bottom frame. A three-horsepower motor under the lift platform powers a chain which traverses the perimeter of the platform and rotates four nuts, causing the platform to move up or down depending on the direction of rotation. Barton lifts are of exceptionally heavy construction, as anyone who has attempted to move one will attest.

One popular Barton console design featured carvings in the shape of candelabra. This example was a 3/10 in the Colonial Theatre, Milwaukee, Wisconsin.

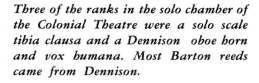

Three of the ranks in the solo chamber of the Colonial Theatre were a solo scale tibia clausa and a Dennison oboe horn and vox humana. Most Barton reeds came from Dennison.

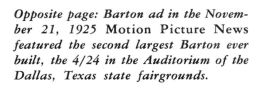

Opposite page: Barton ad in the November 21, 1925 Motion Picture News featured the second largest Barton ever built, the 4/24 in the Auditorium of the Dallas, Texas state fairgrounds.

Joe Gibbs Spring opened the 3/11 Barton in the Orpheum Theatre, Springfield, Illinois in 1927.

[was] little different from the electrical application we used in the Bartola. The Bartola was known for beautiful tone quality. Our big competition in the deluxe theatres was an eastern concern which featured a big solid tone. I decided to stay with the softer voicing that had become a feature of the Bartola. I did not know if it would be better or worse, but it would be different, and we could not be accused of making a copy of our competitor's instruments.[11] (Author's note: This tonal philosophy was indeed true of Barton instruments in the early 1920s but the philosophy certainly changed, as we shall see later!) "And that was the start of the Barton organ. The building boom was on. All the big circuits began building larger theatres. Now you must realize why the history of the Barton organ cannot be told without first relating the history of the Bartola.

"Wurlitzer, Page, Robert-Morton, Kimball, Marr & Colton all were after this new rush of theatre building. We were right there with the Barton organ—Butterfield in Michigan, Saxe in Wisconsin, Blank in Iowa, Gregory in Indiana and Chicago suburbs and many others. The squeeze was on the exhibitor with the small theatre. To protect himself from the circuits, many of them started building larger theatres. Our past reputation now paid off. The big organ companies were driving for the business, but the Barton . . . company had for years been building friendship and a reputation for fair dealing, a good product, service and a player service during the days of the Bartola.

"We had more business than we could handle. Our old friends stuck with us and we made good—the same close territory, prompt service and an organ that became known for beautiful tone quality. Our Chicago office was enlarged, a three-manual organ installed and we turned

experienced Bartola players into A-1 Barton organists. Many of them became famous! In some instances we had two crews of installation men in the same town at the same time. We were still building the Bartola. The exhibitor with the small theatre bought a Bartola to get better musical results and protect himself against the big new theatre being built down the street. We had one crew installing the Bartola in the small theatre and another crew installing the Barton organ in the new theatre.

". . . The deluxe theatres were started in the east. The Wurlitzer organ factory was in the east and they had a large New York City retail store and with Hope-Jones as the designer, [their] organ had a new sound and greatly multiplied the possiblities of the organist to produce new tonal combinations and effects . . . The Mighty Wurlitzer became the organ installed in a great many of the super deluxe theatres throughout the country . . . Having built a reputation with the Bartola for a reliable instrument, good service and an organist school, we were in line for a lot of installations in theatres a notch down from the super deluxers. Balaban & Katz, the big Chicago operators, had two super deluxers: the Chicago in the Loop and the Tivoli on the south side, but the organs in Balaban & Katz' . . . Central Park and Regal were three-manual Barton organs with several two-manual organs in their smaller theatres.

"The Wisconsin Theatre in Milwaukee and the Indiana Theatre in Indianapolis were super deluxers, not as super as theatres in Chicago or New York City, but super just the same. Ascher Brothers' Highland Theatre on Chicago's south side was a 2,500-seater with a large Barton installation. Michigan had several prestige Bartons: the Hollywood . . . the largest neighborhood theatre in Detroit; the Majestic in Grand Rapids; the [Michigan in]

One of the most ornate consoles Barton built was this beautiful 3/17 in the Indiana Theatre, Indianapolis, Indiana.

Dan Barton (right) poses at the console of the 4/21 Barton in the Rialto Theatre, Joliet, Illinois, following a concert by premiere Barton enthusiast Kay McAbee (left) in 1965. The Rialto had a unique lobby organ consisting of one rank of pipes (an 8' tibia clausa on 10" wind) and a chrysoglott. The lobby organ didn't have a console, but by activating a stop on the far right side of the main console's backrail, the lobby organ would play from whatever flute and chrysoglott stops were registered on the main console. The idea was that patrons waiting in the cavernous lobby would be entertained without the expense of an additional musician. Counting the lobby organ, the Rialto actually had 22 ranks, making it the third largest Barton theatre organ.

The 3/14 Barton in the Regal Theatre in Chicago featured a deluxe red and gold console, above, in a smaller than usual shell. This was the only thing about the Regal that was small! When Dan Barton was "discovered" by enthusiasts in the 1950s, the Regal was one of four organs he recalled vividly. At 47th Street and Southparkway, it was in the heart of Chicago's south side. He recalled that area Negroes were "getting tired of their ecclesiastical Kimballs so we decided to give them a real jazz organ!"[1] Pipework scaling was incredible—the clarinet was the size of a small diapason and tibia trebles were nearly the size of teacups. And the Dennison post horn—whew! Below, master xylophone in the Regal. Featuring hard rubber mallets and tertiary action, Barton xylophones were among the snappiest built by any firm.

Ann Arbor; the Capitol in Kalamazoo—all three-manual Bartons. Other prestige installations were the Capitol in Madison, Wisconsin, [the] Rialto in Joliet and [the Coronado] in Rockford, Illinois. The auditorium in Hibbing, Minnesota and the auditorium in the State Fair Park in Dallas, Texas were big Bartons we were very proud of—a pretty fair list of prestige installations for an organ company that had the smallest factory, worked the smallest territory and had the smallest capitalization of all organ companies that manufactured orchestral type unit theatre organs.

"Now the BIG ONE—the Chicago Stadium . . . One of the features was to be a giant pipe organ, to be spectacular in both console appearance and musical sound, designed to fill this giant auditorium when filled with 25,000 people, and an instrumentation that could follow all the

3/8 Barton in the Boehm Theatre, Albion, Michigan.

This two-manual double bolster Barton of nine ranks was originally installed in the Egyptian Theatre, Milwaukee, Wisconsin in 1927. It is actually a three-manual shell with only two manuals present. The organ later saw many years of service in a Roman Catholic church in Eagle River, Wisconsin with all its traps intact and playable. Even its Barton lift was called into service: its four posts decorated the front steps of the church!

Barton deluxe red and gold console in the residence of Roland Treul, Garden Grove, California. This 2/7 was originally installed in the Brin Theatre, Menasha, Wisconsin in 1929.

Above, 4/11 Barton in the Fischer Theatre, Fond du Lac, Wisconsin. This Wangerin-built console certainly wouldn't win any beauty contests. Contrasted at left is the beautiful 4/21 in the Hollywood Theatre, said to be one of the two best theatre organs in Detroit. Barton red and gold consoles such as this, while known officially as the deluxe style, are sometimes referred to today as "circus wagon" styles. The resemblance is probably not accidental considering Dan Barton's youthful employment in circus bands. The Hollywood was one of the only Bartons to contain a brass trumpet which in this case was made by Gottfried.

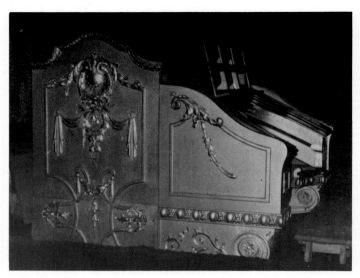

The last Barton theatre organ ever built, installed in the Newport News, Virginia Paramount in 1931, featured a console influenced by Wurlitzer styles. The organ itself was stop-for-stop identical to a 3/10 Wurlitzer and also contained Wurlitzer-style three-valve reservoirs.

4/21 Barton console from the Highland Theatre in Chicago as it appeared in the residence of Dr. Dan Andriesian, Cottage Grove, Oregon in 1965, with what appears to be a non-original music rack. The Rialto Theatre in Joliet, Illinois has an identical console with a glass music rack.

action of the sports events to be presented—an organ in size and sound the like of which had never before been built. Every big organ company in the United States was bidding for the installation: organ companies famous for concert organs and organ builders famous for organs in super deluxe motion picture theatres. The final selections were among twelve companies. And who got the contract? BARTON! But why? It was the talk of the organ industry—how did Barton, the smallest company among the bidders, walk away with this great prestige deal? Here is the story:

"A short time after we installed the Barton organ in [a] theatre on the south side of Chicago a man came into our Chicago office to see me. He was Charles Elgar who told me he was the leader of Elgar's Dance Band playing at the Dreamland Ballroom on Chicago's west side. The Dreamland had a problem. The Chicago west side elevated railroad tracks ran right across the top of the Dreamland building. Every time an elevated train ran by, which was every few minutes, the sound of the train drowned out the music of the orchestra. They had enlarged the dance band but with no success. The orchestra was located on a platform in the center of the dance floor and except for the dancers close to the platform all others just stopped dancing until the elevated train had passed. Elgar had heard the new Barton installation in the . . . theatre and wondered if we could help his orchestra in such a situation. Elgar and I had an interview with Paddy Harmon, the owner of the Dreamland. I arranged a demonstration having Ralph Emerson, our Chicago office demonstrator, show Mr. Harmon the possiblities of our heavy tones in various Chicago theatres and I then went to the Dreamland that night to learn how much noise the elevated trains created. I told Paddy Harmon I thought we could do the job but would not guarantee the results. Paddy said it was worth a gamble and to go

ahead.

"I designed a two-manual organ to be installed alongside the orchestra platform . . . We had Emerson instruct one of Elgar's pianists how to use this organ with the orchestra. The organ was never used except when the elevated train crossed the building. When the organist heard the train coming he cut in the organ and as the noise increased he moved down the crescendo pedal to full organ. The music was then more organ than orchestra but it did the trick. No one stopped dancing and Paddy Harmon's music troubles at the Dreamland were over. Paddy Harmon was the most pleased customer I had ever seen.

"The very next evening Mr. Harmon took me to the Arcadia Ballroom on the north side of Chicago. Harmon ran the Arcadia, which was a very large place with very poor acoustics. The orchestra was on a platform in the center of the floor. When the crowd was large the music could not be heard in either end of the ballroom. The result was [that] the dancers all crowded around the bandstand and both ends of the dance floor were empty. The result of the crowd around the band was a poor dancing situation and many dissatisfied customers. Mr. Harmon told me to see if we could correct this situation. I designed two organs, both exactly alike, with heavy bass and solo stops. One organ was installed in one end of the ballroom and one organ in the opposite end. Heavy drapes were hung behind the organs to improve the acoustics. A two-manual console was installed on the orchestra platform. The same stops from each organ were connected to one stop tablet on the console, making both organs sound exactly alike. The double organs were played continually with the orchestra. The problem was solved. There was no more crowding around the center of the dance floor. Paddy Harmon was very

Oriental-styled 3/14 Barton in the Oriental Theatre, Milwaukee, Wisconsin. At least two other Barton consoles sported the dragon motif: the Redford in Detroit and the Coronado in Rockford, Illinois. At the right is shown a portion of the solo chamber of the Oriental Theatre. From back to front are the glockenspiel, solo string, post horn, oboe horn, orchestral oboe, kinura, and vox humana. The post horn and vox were built by Gottfried; Dennison supplied the other four ranks pictured here.

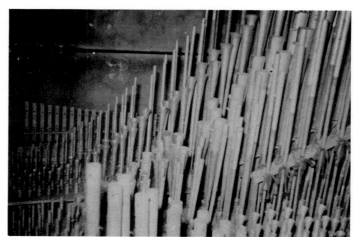

The 3/14 Barton in the Iowa Theatre, Cedar Rapids, Iowa was installed in 1927 and was the largest of the Wangerin-built organs sold under the Barton nameplate. This console's decoration is unique and fabulous: it is covered in black velvet studded with rhinestones in swirling patterns and is trimmed with larger jewels around the perimeters of the lid and keydesk. When Dan Barton was first contacted by organ enthusiasts in the 1950s, this was one of the four instruments he recalled vividly because of its unique console.

This photograph of the solo chamber of the Iowa Theatre shows, from right to left, the vox humana, saxophone, oboe horn, kinura, post horn and solo string. Wangerin theatre organ strings are the loudest and keenest the author has ever experienced. For example, if one registers full organ on this particular instrument, including the post horn, the solo string can be heard above the ensemble even at the 16' pitch level!

Very plain "economy model" console of the 3/10 Barton in the Glen Theatre, Glen Ellyn, Illinois. This organ sported a saxophone instead of the usual oboe horn.

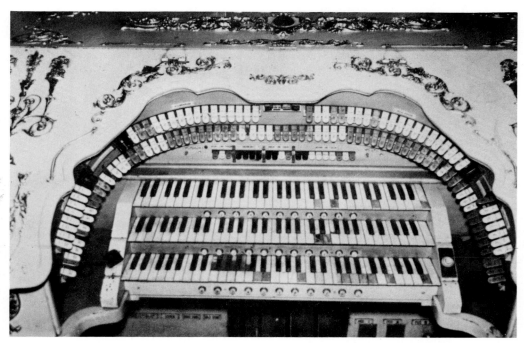

The 3/17 Barton in the Wisconsin Theatre, Milwaukee sported two Wangerin-built consoles in the orchestra pit. These consoles were so petite that all of the combination action valve boxes wouldn't fit inside them and as a result, one of the boxes was mounted underneath the lift platform and tubed up through the floor.

Solo chamber pipework in the Wisconsin Theatre. From left to right: 8' tibia, trumpet, orchestral oboe, oboe horn, and saxophone. All these reeds were built by Dennison. The swell shades and action are Wangerin-built. Barton commonly ordered parts from Wangerin when their factory capacity was exceeded by a heavy influx of orders.

pleased. The Dreamland and Arcadia special installations made money for Paddy Harmon and the Barton Organ Company made a friend.

"Now we move forward . . . Paddy Harmon was promoting the Chicago Stadium. Twelve organ companies [were] bidding for the organ contract [and] the decision was to be made by the 16 big wheels of the Chicago business world who composed the board of directors. As is usual a meeting was held with the board of directors and representatives of all the organ companies. Each representative was allotted a specific time to state the merits of his organ to

the board of directors. The representatives were assembled in a room adjacent to the board of directors' room. One of the keenest memories of my organ career was the laugh a bunch of these representatives gave me when I walked in. 'Hi Barton—what are you doing here? The organ lofts will be larger than your factory! This contract belongs to a big company' and many more such remarks showing their contempt for a little outfit like Barton even showing up to bid against the big outfits.

"I was the very last to be called in; I later learned that this had been arranged by Mr. Harmon. I had no more than started my talk when Paddy Harmon interrupted and to the best of my recollection here is what he said to the directors: 'Gentlemen, we are going to have the finest sports arena in the country and we want the organ to be one of its great features. We do not want a church type organ or a concert organ or a theatre organ. We do not have a church nor a concert hall nor a theatre. This must be a special organ, the like of which has never been built before. It must have volume ample to fill this arena with 25,000 people comprising the audience. It must be designed to play the action of a circus performance, ice hockey, boxing, bicycle races or any other sports event. It must be designed by a man with a showman's background. I am convinced Barton is the man. Early in his life he played in circus bands, carnivals and other shows and he has proven to me he can design organs for special purposes. Let me explain,' and Mr. Harmon told the directors about the special organs we had installed in his Dreamland and Arcadia dance halls.

"I have received many compliments for selling the giant Stadium organ but while I may have laid the ground work at the Dreamland and Arcadia, I did not sell the Chicago

The Chicago Stadium installation was celebrated in a two page ad in the February 1929 issue of The Diapason, *reproduced on the following two pages.*

The World's Greatest Organ

Barton Organ
CHURCH · AUDITORIUM · THEATRE

in The World's Greatest Stadium

MANY organs have been given the compliment of being named "greatest." This new Barton Organ installed in the immense Chicago Stadium that Paddy Harmon built, *is* great. It is *the* greatest because it has both tremendous volume and flexibility. It has the roar of Niagara and the modulation of whispering angel voices. It has tone and range and power. It has, in short, everything.

We leave it to you to judge. It is the only six-manual unit constructed organ in the world! There are 828 stop tablets on the console, all within easy playing reach. Straight unit construction. Wind pressure 15", 25", 35" and 50", with a 100-horsepower blower, the largest blower ever known to have been built. Chimes are Deagan Tower Bells, struck with 9-pound hammers on 50" wind pressure. Over four tons of wire were used on relays and cables. The console is 8' 2" wide, 7' deep and 6' 8" high.

Mr. Harmon conceived the idea of this tremendous organ and Barton built it, putting into it all the famous golden-voiced tones that have made Barton Organs the most popular radio organs, the finest of church organs and the most paying of theatre organs. Music is all pervading, it sways as it charms and Barton knows how to build, either large or small, the "greatest" organs in the world. We are proud that Mr. Harmon paid us the fine compliment of this selection. *Send for complete details and estimates.*

The Bartola Musical Instrument Co.
314 Mallers Building, CHICAGO

Barton Organ
CHURCH · AUDITORIUM · THEATRE

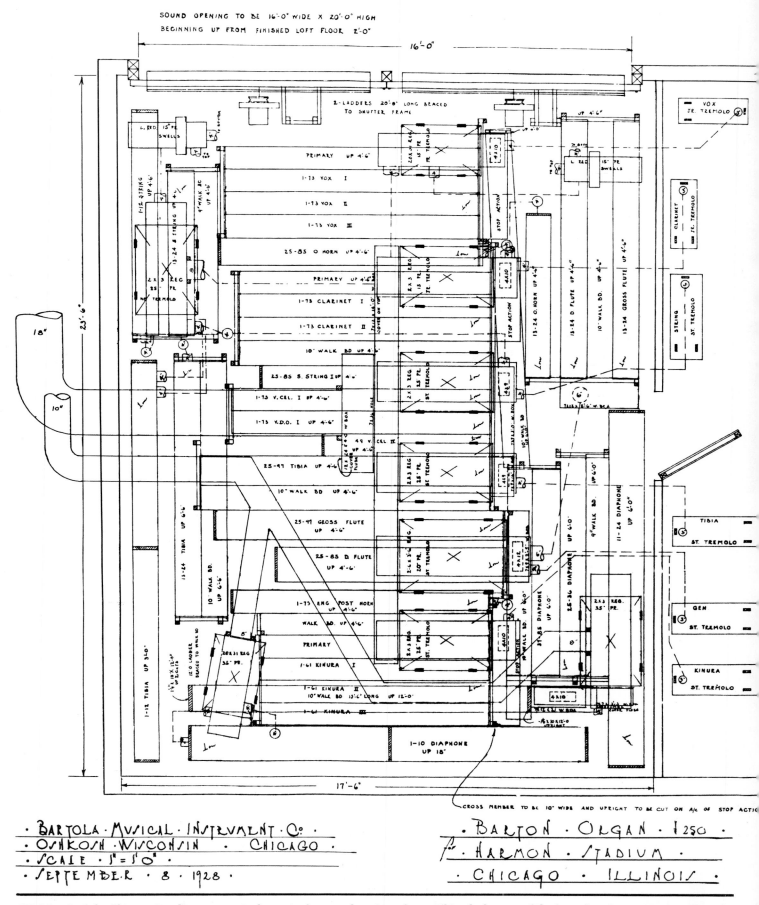

Division I of the Chicago Stadium organ is shown in factory drawing above. This, the largest of the four chambers, contains 18 ranks of pipes. Note the special room on the right for silencing the noise of the tremolos. There are 25 tremolos in the organ contained in four such rooms, one for each chamber.

Division I as photographed from the walkboard in front of the 16' diaphone. All ranks are visible except for the three kinuras which are below the photographer's feet. Note the wall-to-wall and floor-to-ceiling swell shades which restrict virtually none of the intense sounds generated by these large scale, high pressure pipes.

Stadium organ. My good friend Mr. Paddy Harmon did that for me. I will let you imagine what I said to the eleven representatives of the big organ companies when the announcement was made in the anteroom!

"There were four parts to the success of this big organ: first, to be awarded the contract; second, to build the organ; third, to have the organ properly installed; [and] fourth, an organist who could play such an organ. At the time we sold the S. J. Gregory circuit a three-manual . . . organ for a new theatre he was building in Cicero, Illinois, Mr. Gregory said he had an organist playing for him in Hammond, Indiana who he wanted to play the Cicero organ. We suggested he send the organist to our Chicago office organ school for instructions and so we met Al Melgard. Instructions? Al could play more organ than the instructor! Melgard had everything—a wizard organist if ever there was one. After one season on the Cicero organ we put Melgard into our Chicago office as demonstrator and to handle our organ school.

"Who would play the Stadium organ with its six manuals and over 800 stops? There was not even a second thought—Al Melgard. The Stadium opened on March 30, 1929 with a circus performance with Al Melgard at the console. He has been one of the features of the Stadium ever since. Al holds all records for long time jobs on a unit organ—over thirty years and still playing the giant Barton for all attractions at the Stadium. Al has made many record-

Al Melgard (1890-1977) was master of the Stadium Barton for over four decades.

Above is pictured some of the enormous scale pipework in division III of the Stadium Barton. In the left foreground note the stentorphone which is so large that even its 4' octave is on an offset chest. In the center foreground is the 8' octave of the trumpet which is actually another post horn on 25" wind. In the right foreground is the 8' octave of the tibia plena, one of six tibias in the organ. Below, division I is viewed from the walkboard in front of the 8' solo string. All of these pipes can be identified by referring to the drawing on page 76.

6/51 BARTON THEATRE ORGAN
Chicago Stadium, Chicago, Illinois

CHAMBER ANALYSIS

DIVISION I (blue dots on stop keys)

		Pipes	WP
16′	Diaphone I	85	35″
16′	Tibia Clausa I	97	25″
16′	Solo String I	85	25″
8′	Viole d'Orchestre I	73	25″
8′	Viole Celeste I	73	25″
4′	Viole Celeste IV	49	25″
8′	English Post Horn I	73	25″
8′	Kinuras (3 ranks)	183	25″
8′	Gross Flute	85	20″
8′	Double Flute	73	20″
8′	Vox Humana (3 ranks)	219	15″
8′	Clarinet (2 ranks)	146	15″
8′	Oboe Horn I	73	15″
		1,314	

DIVISION III (green dots on stop keys)

		Pipes	WP
16′	Stentorphone I	73	25″
16′	Tuba Profunda	85	15″
8′	Tibia Clausa III	73	25″
8′	Trumpet	73	25″
8′	Gamba	73	25″
8′	Gamba Celeste I	73	25″
4′	Gamba Celeste II	49	25″
8′	Tibia Plena	73	20″
8′	Solo Diapason I	73	15″
8′	French Horn	73	15″
		718	

DIVISION II (pink dots on stop keys)

		Pipes	WP
16′	Diaphone II	85	35″
16′	Solo String II	85	25″
16′	Major Flute	97	20″
8′	Tibia Clausa II	85	25″
8′	Tuba Celeste (3 ranks)	159	25″
8′	English Post Horn II	73	25″
8′	Viole d'Orchestre II	73	25″
8′	Viole Celeste II	73	25″
4′	Viole Celeste V	49	25″
8′	Oboe Horn II	73	15″
		852	

DIVISION IV (violet dots on stop keys)

		Pipes	WP
16′	Tuba Mirabilis	85	25″
16′	English Horn	85	25″
16′	Stentorphone II	73	25″
8′	Tibia Clausa IV	73	25″
8′	Viole d'Orchestre III	73	25″
8′	Viole Celeste III	73	25″
4′	Viole Celeste VI	49	25″
8′	Tibia Molis	73	20″
8′	Solo Diapason II	73	15″
8′	Solo Tuba	73	15″
8′	Saxophone	61	15″
		791	

STOPLIST

PEDAL ORGAN

32′	Acoustic Bass	8′	Major Flute	8′	Gamba
32′	Contra Bass	8′	Gross Flute	8′	Gamba Celeste I
16′	Diaphone I	8′	Double Flute	8′	Viole d'Orchest I
16′	Diaphone II	8′	Tibia Plena	8′	Viole d'Orchest II
16′	Stentorphone I	8′	Tibia Molis	8′	Viole d'Orchest III
16′	Stentorphone II	8′	Tibia Clausa I	8′	Viole Celeste I
16′	Major Flute	8′	Tibia Clausa II	8′	Viole Celeste II
16′	Tibia Clausa I	8′	Tibia Clausa III	8′	Viole Celeste III
16′	Tuba Mirabilis	8′	Tibia Clausa IV	4′	Octave I
16′	Tuba Profunda	8′	Oboe Horn I	4′	Octave II
16′	English Horn	8′	Oboe Horn II	4′	Tuba Mirabilis
16′	Solo String I	8′	Solo Tuba	4′	Tuba Profunda
16′	Solo String II	8′	Tuba Profunda		Bass Drums
8′	Diaphone I	8′	Tuba Mirabilis		Cymbals
8′	Diaphone II	8′	English Horn		Crash Cymbals
8′	Stentorphone I	8′	English Posthorn I	8′	Gt. to Ped.
8′	Stentorphone II	8′	English Posthorn II	8′	Bom. to Ped.
8′	Solo Diapason I	8′	Solo String I	4′	Ped. to Ped.
8′	Solo Diapason II	8′	Solo String II		Six red blank stops

ENSEMBLE PEDAL ORGAN

16′	Diaphones
16′	Stentorphones
16′	Tibias-Flutes
16′	Reeds
16′	Strings
8′	Diaphones
8′	Stentorphones
8′	Tibias-Flutes
8′	Reeds
8′	Strings
4′	Fours
	Bass Drums
	Cymbals
8′	Gt. to Ped.
8′	Bom. to Ped.
4′	Ped. to Ped.

ACCOMPANIMENT ORGAN

16'	Major Flute		Three yellow blank stops
16'	Gross Flute TC	8'	Viole d'Orchest I
16'	Double Flute TC	8'	Viole d'Orchest II
16'	Tibia Plena TC	8'	Viole d'Orchest III
16'	Tibia Molis TC	8'	Viole Celeste I
16'	Solo String I	8'	Viole Celeste II
16'	Solo String II	8'	Viole Celeste III
16'	Gamba Celeste I TC	8'	Viole Celeste IV
16'	Viole d'Orchest I TC	8'	Viole Celeste V
16'	Viole d'Orchest II TC	8'	Viole Celeste VI
16'	Viole d'Orchest III TC	4'	Octave I
16'	Viole Celeste I TC	4'	Octave II
16'	Viole Celeste II TC	4'	Major Flute
16'	Viole Celeste III TC	4'	Gross Flute
8'	Diaphone I	4'	Double Flute
8'	Diaphone II	4'	Tibia Plena
8'	Stentorphone I	4'	Tibia Molis
8'	Stentorphone II	4'	Tibia Clausa I
8'	Major Flute	4'	Tibia Clausa II
8'	Gross Flute	4'	Tibia Clausa III
8'	Double Flute	4'	Tibia Clausa IV
8'	Tibia Plena	4'	Tuba Profunda
8'	Tibia Molis	4'	Tuba Mirabilis
8'	Tibia Clausa I	4'	English Horn
8'	Tibia Clausa II	4'	Solo String I
8'	Tibia Clausa III	4'	Solo String II
8'	Tibia Clausa IV	4'	Gamba
8'	Oboe Horn I	4'	Gamba Celeste I
8'	Oboe Horn II	4'	Viole d'Orchest I
8'	Vox Humana 3-rk Chorus	4'	Viole d'Orchest II
8'	Clarinet 2 Ranks	4'	Viole d'Orchest III
8'	Solo Tuba	4'	Viole Celeste I
8'	Tuba Profunda	4'	Viole Celeste II
8'	Tuba Mirabilis	4'	Viole Celeste III
8'	English Horn	2 2/3'	Major Nazard
8'	English Posthorn I	2'	Major Piccolo
8'	English Posthorn II	1 3/5'	Major Tierce
8'	Tuba Celeste (3 ranks)	2 2/3'	Tibia Twelfth I
8'	Solo String I	2'	Tibia Piccolo I
8'	Solo String II	1 3/5'	Tibia Tierce I
8'	Gamba	4'	Harp
8'	Gamba Celeste I		Snare Drums I
8'	Gamba Celeste II		Snare Drums II
	Tambourines, Castinets	4'	Acc. to Acc.

ENSEMBLE ACCOMPANIMENT ORGAN

16'	Flutes	4'	Flutes
16'	Strings	4'	Tibia Clausas
8'	Diapasons	4'	Reeds
8'	Flutes	4'	Strings
8'	Tibia Clausas		Snare Drums
8'	Heavy Reeds	4'	Acc. to Acc.
8'	Light Reeds		2nd Touch Stops Light
8'	Heavy Strings		2nd Touch Stops Heavy
8'	Light Strings	8'	Solo to Acc.

ENSEMBLE GREAT ORGAN

16'	Diapasons	8'	Kinuras
16'	Flutes	8'	Heavy Strings
16'	Tibia Clausas	8'	Light Strings
16'	Reeds	4'	Flutes
16'	Strings	4'	Tibia Clausas
8'	Heavy Diapasons	4'	Reeds
8'	Light Diapasons	4'	Strings
8'	Flutes	M	Mutations
8'	Tibia Clausas	16'	Gt. to Gt.
8'	Heavy Reeds	4'	Gt. to Gt.
8'	Light Reeds		2nd Touch Stops Light
8'	Clarinets		2nd Touch Stops Heavy

ENSEMBLE JAZZ ORGAN

8'	Heavy Diapasons	8'	Strings
8'	Light Diapasons	M	Tibia Mutations
8'	Flutes	8'	Xylophones
8'	Tibia Clausas	4'	Glockenspiels
8'	Heavy Tubas	16'	Jazz to Jazz
8'	Light Tubas	4'	Jazz to Jazz
8'	English Horns		

GREAT ORGAN

16'	Diaphone I	8'	Kinura 3 Ranks
16'	Diaphone II	8'	Tuba Celeste 3 Ranks
16'	Stentorphone I	8'	Solo String I
16'	Stentorphone II	8'	Solo String II
16'	Major Flute	8'	Gamba
16'	Gross Flute TC	8'	Gamba Celeste I
16'	Double Flute TC	8'	Gamba Celeste II
16'	Tibia Plena TC	8'	Viole d'Orchest I
16'	Tibia Molis TC	8'	Viole d'Orchest II
16'	Tibia Clausa I	8'	Viole d'Orchest III
16'	Tibia Clausa II TC	8'	Viole Celeste I
16'	Tibia Clausa III TC	8'	Viole Celeste II
16'	Tibia Clausa IV TC	8'	Viole Celeste III
16'	Oboe Horn I TC	8'	Viole Celeste IV
16'	Oboe Horn II TC	8'	Viole Celeste V
16'	Vox Humana 3-rk Chorus TC	8'	Viole Celeste VI
16'	Clarinet 2 Ranks TC	4'	Octave I
16'	Solo Tuba TC	4'	Octave II
16'	Tuba Profunda	4'	Major Flute
16'	Tuba Mirabilis	4'	Gross Flute
16'	English Horn	4'	Double Flute
16'	Trumpet TC	4'	Tibia Plena
16'	Solo String I	4'	Tibia Molis
16'	Solo String. II	4'	Tibia Clausa I
16'	Gamba Celeste I TC	4'	Tibia Clausa II
16'	Viole d'Orchest I TC	4'	Tibia Clausa III
16'	Viole d'Orchest II TC	4'	Tibia Clausa IV
16'	Viole d'Orchest III TC	4'	Vox Humana 3-rk Chorus
16'	Viole Celeste I TC	4'	Tuba Profunda
16'	Viole Celeste II TC	4'	Tuba Mirabilis
16'	Viole Celeste III TC		yellow blank stop
8'	Diaphone I	4'	Solo String I
8'	Diaphone II	4'	Solo String II
8'	Stentorphone I	4'	Gamba
8'	Stentorphone II	4'	Gamba Celeste I
8'	Solo Diapason I	4'	Viole d'Orchest I
8'	Solo Diapason II	4'	Viole d'Orchest II
8'	Major Flute	4'	Viole d'Orchest III
8'	Gross Flute	4'	Viole Celeste I
8'	Double Flute	4'	Viole Celeste II
8'	Tibia Plena	4'	Viole Celeste III
8'	Tibia Molis	2 2/3'	Major Nazard
8'	Tibia Clausa I	2'	Major Piccolo
8'	Tibia Clausa II	1 3/5'	Major Tierce
8'	Tibia Clausa III	2 2/3'	Tibia Twelth I
8'	Tibia Clausa IV	2 2/3'	Tibia Twelth II
8'	Oboe Horn I	2'	Tibia Piccolo I
8'	Oboe Horn II	2'	Tibia Piccolo II
8'	French Horn	1 3/5'	Tibia Tierce I
8'	Saxophone	1 3/5'	Tibia Tierce II
8'	Vox Humana 3-rk Chorus	8'	Xylophones I
8'	Clarinet 2 Ranks	8'	Xylophones II
8'	Solo Tuba	4'	Orchest Bells I
8'	Tuba Profunda	4'	Orchest Bells II
8'	Tuba Mirabilis	4'	Harp
8'	English Horn	8'	Cathedral Chimes
8'	English Posthorn I	16'	Gt. to Gt.
8'	English Posthorn II	4'	Gt. to Gt.
8'	Trumpet		

ENSEMBLE BOMBARDE ORGAN

16'	Diapasons	8'	Light Reeds
16'	Flutes	8'	Heavy Strings
16'	Tibia Clausas	8'	Light Strings
16'	Reeds	4'	Flutes
16'	Strings	4'	Tibia Clausas
8'	Heavy Diapasons	4'	Strings
8'	Light Diapasons	16'	Bom. to Bom.
8'	Flutes	4'	Bom. to Bom.
8'	Tibia Clausas		2nd Touch Stops Light
8'	Heavy Reeds		2nd Touch Stops Heavy

BOMBARDE ORGAN

16'	Diaphone I	16'	Gross Flute TC
16'	Diaphone II	16'	Double Flute TC
16'	Stentorphone I	16'	Tibia Plena TC
16'	Stentorphone II	16'	Tibia Molis TC
16'	Major Flute	16'	Tibia Clausa I

BOMBARDE ORGAN, continued

16′	Tibia Clausa II TC		8′	Solo String II
16′	Tibia Clausa III TC		8′	Gamba
16′	Tibia Clausa IV TC		8′	Gamba Celeste I
16′	Oboe Horn I TC		8′	Gamba Celeste II
16′	Oboe Horn II TC		8′	Viole d'Orchest I
16′	Solo Tuba TC		8′	Viole d'Orchest II
16′	Tuba Profunda		8′	Viole d'Orchest III
16′	Tuba Mirabilis		8′	Viole Celeste I
16′	English Horn		8′	Viole Celeste II
16′	English Posthorn I TC		8′	Viole Celeste III
16′	English Posthorn II TC		8′	Viole Celeste IV
16′	Trumpet TC		8′	Viole Celeste V
16′	Solo String I		8′	Viole Celeste VI
16′	Solo String II		4′	Octave I
16′	Gamba Celeste I TC		4′	Octave II
16′	Viole d'Orchest I TC		4′	Major Flute
16′	Viole d'Orchest II TC		4′	Gross Flute
16′	Viole d'Orchest III TC		4′	Double Flute
16′	Viole Celeste I TC		4′	Tibia Plena
16′	Viole Celeste II TC		4′	Tibia Molis
16′	Viole Celeste III TC		4′	Tibia Clausa I
8′	Diaphone I		4′	Tibia Clausa II
8′	Diaphone II		4′	Tibia Clausa III
8′	Stentorphone I		4′	Tibia Clausa IV
8′	Stentorphone II		4′	Tuba Profunda
8′	Solo Diapason I		4′	Tuba Mirabilis
8′	Solo Diapason II		4′	Solo String I
8′	Major Flute		4′	Solo String II
8′	Gross Flute		4′	Gamba
8′	Double Flute		4′	Gamba Celeste I
8′	Tibia Plena		4′	Viole d'Orchest I
8′	Tibia Molis		4′	Viole d'Orchest II
8′	Tibia Clausa I		4′	Viole d'Orchest III
8′	Tibia Clausa II		4′	Viole Celeste I
8′	Tibia Clausa III		4′	Viole Celeste II
8′	Tibia Clausa IV		4′	Viole Celeste III
8′	Oboe Horn I		2 2/3′	Major Nazard
8′	Oboe Horn II		2′	Major Piccolo
8′	French Horn		1 3/5′	Major Tierce
8′	Saxophone		2 2/3′	Tibia Twelfth I
8′	Solo Tuba		2 2/3′	Tibia Twelfth II
8′	Tuba Profunda		2′	Tibia Piccolo I
8′	Tuba Mirabilis		2′	Tibia Piccolo II
8′	English Horn		1 3/5′	Tibia Tierce I
8′	English Posthorn I		1 3/5′	Tibia Tierce II
8′	English Posthorn II			Snare Drums I
8′	Trumpet			Snare Drums II
8′	Tuba Celeste 3 Ranks		16′	Bom. to Bom.
8′	Solo String I		4′	Bom. to Bom.

JAZZ ORGAN

16′	Solo String I		8′	Viole Celeste III
16′	Solo String II		4′	Octave I
16′	Viole d'Orchest I TC		4′	Octave II
16′	Viole d'Orchest II TC		4′	Tibia Clausa I
8′	Diaphone I		4′	Tibia Clausa II
8′	Diaphone II		4′	Tibia Clausa III
8′	Stentorphone I		4′	Tibia Clausa IV
8′	Stentorphone II		4′	Oboe Horn I
8′	Solo Diapason I		4′	Oboe Horn II
8′	Solo Diapason II		4′	Tuba Profunda
8′	Major Flute		4′	Tuba Mirabilis
8′	Gross Flute		4′	English Horn
8′	Double Flute		4′	English Posthorn I
8′	Tibia Plena		4′	English Posthorn II
8′	Tibia Molis		4′	Solo String I
8′	Tibia Clausa I		4′	Solo String II
8′	Tibia Clausa II		4′	Gamba
8′	Tibia Clausa III		4′	Gamba Celeste I
8′	Tibia Clausa IV		4′	Viole d'Orchest I
8′	Oboe Horn I		4′	Viole d'Orchest II
8′	Oboe Horn II		4′	Viole d'Orchest III
8′	Solo Tuba		4′	Viole Celeste I
8′	Tuba Profunda		4′	Viole Celeste II
8′	Tuba Mirabilis		4′	Viole Celeste III
8′	English Horn		M	Tibia Mutation I
8′	English Posthorn I		M	Tibia Mutation II
8′	English Posthorn II		8′	Xylophones I
8′	Trumpet		8′	Xylophones II
8′	Kinura 3 Ranks		4′	Glockenspiels I
8′	Solo String I		4′	Glockenspiels II
8′	Solo String II		4′	Orchest Bells I
8′	Gamba		4′	Orchest Bells II
8′	Gamba Celeste I		16′	Jazz to Jazz
8′	Viole d'Orchest I		4′	Jazz to Jazz
8′	Viole d'Orchest II			Jazz Third
8′	Viole d'Orchest III			Jazz Fifth
8′	Viole Celeste I			Jazz Seventh
8′	Viole Celeste II			Jazz Twelth

ENSEMBLE ORCHESTRAL ORGAN

16′	English Horns		8′	English Horns
16′	Vox Humanas		8′	Strings
16′	Strings		4′	Tibia Clausas
8′	Diapasons		4′	Strings
8′	Flutes		M	Mutations
8′	Tibia Clausas		16′	Orch. to Orch.
8′	Reeds		4′	Orch. to Orch.

ORCHESTRAL ORGAN

16′	Tibia Clausa I		8′	Tibia Clausa III		4′	Major Flute	8′	Xylophones I
16′	Tibia Clausa II TC		8′	Tibia Clausa IV		4′	Gross Flute	8′	Xylophones II
16′	Tibia Clausa III TC		8′	Oboe Horn I		4′	Double Flute	4′	Orchest Bells I
16′	Tibia Clausa IV TC		8′	Oboe Horn II		4′	Tibia Plena	4′	Orchest Bells II
16′	Oboe Horn I TC		8′	French Horn		4′	Tibia Molis	4′	Harp
16′	Oboe Horn II TC		8′	Saxophone		4′	Tibia Clausa I	8′	Cathedral Chimes
16′	Vox Humana 3-rk Chorus TC		8′	Vox Humana 3-rk Chorus		4′	Tibia Clausa II		Snare Drums I
16′	Clarinet 2 Ranks TC		8′	Clarinet 2 Ranks		4′	Tibia Clausa III		Snare Drums II
16′	English Horn		8′	Solo Tuba		4′	Tibia Clausa IV	16′	Orch. to Orch.
16′	English Posthorn I TC		8′	Tuba Profunda		4′	Vox Humana 3-rk Chorus	4′	Orch. to Orch.
16′	English Posthorn II TC		8′	Tuba Mirabilis		4′	English Horn		
16′	Solo String I		8′	English Horn		4′	Solo String I		
16′	Solo String II		8′	English Posthorn I		4′	Solo String II		
16′	Viole d'Orchest I TC		8′	English Posthorn II		4′	Gamba		
16′	Viole d'Orchest II TC		8′	Trumpet		4′	Gamba Celeste I		
8′	Diaphone I		8′	Kinura 3 ranks		4′	Viole d'Orchest I		
8′	Diaphone II		8′	Tuba Celeste 3 ranks		4′	Viole Celeste I		
8′	Stentorphone I		8′	Solo String I		4′	Viole Celeste II		
8′	Stentorphone II		8′	Solo String II		4′	Viole Celeste III		
8′	Solo Diapason I		8′	Gamba		2 2/3′	Major Nazard		
8′	Solo Diapason II		8′	Gamba Celeste I		2′	Major Piccolo		
8′	Major Flute		8′	Viole d'Orchest I		1 3/5′	Major Tierce		
8′	Gross Flute		8′	Viole d'Orchest II		2 2/3′	Tibia Twelfth I		
8′	Double Flute		8′	Viole d'Orchest III		2 2/3′	Tibia Twelfth II		
8′	Tibia Plena		8′	Viole Celeste I		2′	Tibia Piccolo I		
8′	Tibia Molis		8′	Viole Celeste II		2′	Tibia Piccolo II		
8′	Tibia Clausa I		8′	Viole Celeste III		1 3/5′	Tibia Tierce I		
8′	Tibia Clausa II		4′	Octave I		1 3/5′	Tibia Tierce II		

ENSEMBLE SOLO ORGAN

16′	Tibia Clausas
16′	Reeds
16′	Strings
8′	Diapasons
8′	Flutes
8′	Tibia Clausas
8′	Reeds
8′	English Horns
8′	Vox Humanas
8′	Strings
4′	Tibia Clausas
4′	Strings
8′	Chimes
16′	Solo to Solo
4′	Solo to Solo

SOLO ORGAN		ACCOMP. 2nd TOUCH	
16'	Tibia Clausa I	8'	Diaphone I
16'	Tibia Clausa II TC	8'	Diaphone II
16'	Tibia Clausa III TC	8'	Tibia Clausa I
16'	Tibia Clausa IV TC	8'	Tibia Clausa II
16'	Oboe Horn I TC	8'	Tibia Clausa III
16'	Oboe Horn II TC	8'	Tibia Clausa IV
16'	Clarinet 2 Ranks TC	8'	Solo Tuba
16'	English Horn	8'	Tuba M
16'	English Posthorn I TC	8'	Tuba P
16'	English Posthorn II TC	8'	Solo String I
16'	Solo String I	8'	Solo String II
16'	Solo String II	8'	Gamba
16'	Viole d'Orchest I TC	8'	Gamba Celeste I
16'	Viole d'Orchest II TC	8'	Viole d'Orchest I
8'	Diaphone I	8'	Viole d'Orchest II
8'	Diaphone II	8'	Viole d'Orchest III
8'	Solo Diapason I	8'	Viole Celeste I
8'	Solo Diapason II	8'	Viole Celeste II
8'	Major Flute	8'	Viole Celeste III
8'	Gross Flute	8'	Chimes
8'	Double Flute	8'	Solo to Accomp.
8'	Tibia Plena		
8'	Tibia Molis	**GREAT 2nd TOUCH**	
8'	Tibia Clausa I	8'	Diaphone I
8'	Tibia Clausa II	8'	Diaphone II
8'	Tibia Clausa III	8'	Solo Diapason I
8'	Tibia Clausa IV	8'	Solo Diapason II
8'	Oboe Horn I	8'	Tibia Clausa I
8'	Oboe Horn II	8'	Tibia Clausa II
8'	French Horn	8'	Tibia Clausa III
8'	Saxophone	8'	Tibia Clausa IV
8'	Vox Humana 3-rk Chorus	8'	Solo Tuba
8'	Clarinet 2 Ranks	8'	Tuba P
8'	Solo Tuba	8'	Tuba M
8'	Tuba Profunda	8'	Solo String I
8'	Tuba Mirabilis	8'	Solo String II
8'	English Horn	8'	Gamba
8'	English Posthorn I	8'	Gamba Celeste I
8'	English Posthorn II	8'	Viole d'Orchest I
8'	Trumpet	8'	Viole d'Orchest II
8'	Kinura 3 Ranks	8'	Viole d'Orchest III
8'	Tuba Celeste 3 Ranks	8'	Viole Celeste I
8'	Solo String I	8'	Viole Celeste II
8'	Solo String II	8'	Viole Celeste III
8'	Gamba		
8'	Gamba Celeste I	**BOMBARDE 2nd TOUCH**	
8'	Viole d'Orchest I	16'	Tuba P
8'	Viole Celeste I	16'	Tuba M
8'	Viole d'Orchest II	8'	Diaphone I
8'	Viole Celeste II	8'	Diaphone II
8'	Viole d'Orchest III	8'	Stentorphone I
8'	Viole Celeste III	8'	Stentorphone II
4'	Tibia Clausa I	8'	Solo Diapason I
4'	Tibia Clausa II	8'	Solo Diapason II
4'	Tibia Clausa III	8'	Tibia Clausa I
4'	Tibia Clausa IV	8'	Tibia Clausa II
4'	Solo String I	8'	Tibia Clausa III
4'	Solo String II	8'	Tibia Clausa IV
4'	Gamba	8'	Tuba P
4'	Gamba Celeste I	8'	Solo Tuba
4'	Viole d'Orchest I	8'	Tuba M
4'	Viole d'Orchest II		Two white blank stops
4'	Viole Celeste I		
4'	Viole Celeste II	**TREMULANTS**	
4'	Viole Celeste III	General Division I	
M	Tibia Mutation I	General Division II	
M	Tibia Mutation II	General Division III	
8'	Xylophones I	General Division IV	
8'	Xylophones II	Solo Diapasons	
4'	Glockenspiels I	Tibias	
4'	Glockenspiels II	Voxes	
4'	Orchest Bells I	Reeds	
4'	Orchest Bells II	Brass	
8'	Cathedral Chimes	Tubas	
16'	Solo to Solo	Strings	
4'	Solo to Solo	(These stops control 24 separate tremolos.)	

PEDAL 2nd TOUCH

Six white blank stops

ings with the big Barton and also operates a highly successful school for organists. Al Melgard, the dean of all the fine unit organists."[13] (Author's note: This was written, of course, when the late Mr. Melgard was still alive.)

"The talking pictures killed the theatre organ business . . . The Barton organ factory was closed, the machinery and equipment sold and the remaining organ parts disposed of. The records were stored in a vault in the office of Mr. W. G. Maxcy, who was the president of the company. Mr. Maxcy died soon thereafter and the executors of his estate, seeing no reason to save records of a concern that was then out of business, destroyed all of the Barton company records.

"To me the theatre organ business became just a pleasant memory. I went to Chicago to work for Wurlitzer. For twelve years I had been battling Wurlitzer for theatre organ business in the midwest, and Mr. Tom Clancy, the sales manager of the Wurlitzer company, must have taken some note of the battle for he offered me a position in the Chicago retail store to take charge of a new department selling a newly developed electric refrigerator. After several months it was decided that kitchen refrigerators and musical instruments did not synchronize in the public mind and Wurlitzer gave up the refrigerator business.

"I then started a poster advertising business in Chicago and soon learned I knew more about the theatre organ business than advertising and, not wanting to spend the time to learn a new business, I quit and returned to my home in Oshkosh, Wisconsin. I purchased four large houses and remodeled them into apartments. I became the busiest handyman in the community. I was a carpenter, house painter, interior decorator, electrician, plumber, upholsterer and even did cement work. I did everything but cook and babysit for the tenants. During those years I gave little thought to the theatre organ business."[14]

In the above recollections Dan Barton credits many of the people responsible for the success of his organization but fails to tell about his own extraordinary salesmanship. He had a quality product to offer, to be sure, but his incredible ability as a salesman was the underlying reason for the fact that his small firm achieved the rank of fifth largest theatre organ builder. Only the large firms— Wurlitzer, Robert-Morton, Kimball and Moller—sold more theatre organs than did Barton. Dan had quite a reputation for popularity with the ladies and rumor has it that he was especially successful at selling to female clients. In a soap opera-like romance Dan divorced his first wife and married his Chicago office secretary, with whom he spent fifty happy years.

The author's favorite examples of Barton salesmanship are the last three new organs the company built in 1931 for Paramount theatres in Hamilton and Middletown, Ohio and in Newport News, Virginia. These organs were sold at a time when theatre organs were all but dead, due to the combined effects of talking pictures and the Depression, and they were stop-for-stop identical to Wurlitzer models and even had consoles influenced by Wurlitzer stylings rather than the usual Barton "circus wagon" approach. Even the reservoirs on these late organs copied the Wurlitzer three-valve system. This wasn't the first time that Barton allowed Wurlitzer influence to help make a sale, however: the 3/17 in the Wisconsin Theatre in Milwaukee was sold on the assurance that it would be a duplicate of the Wurlitzer in the Tivoli Theatre which at the time (1924) was acclaimed the best theatre organ in Chicago. As a result, the Wisconsin Theatre had the only Barton known to contain tuned sleigh bells and a 32' diaphone. Other examples of Wurlitzer-influenced sales were the three 4/21 Bartons in the Highland Theatre, Chicago, the Rialto in Joliet, Illinois and the Hollywood in Detroit. These organs are obvious copies of 4/20 Wurlitzer models, even having 4' tibia stops engraved 'piccolo' as per Wurlitzer practice. These 4/21 Bartons contained one extra rank each, however—post horns (made by Gottfried)—thus alleviating a major deficiency in the Wurlitzer design and making these Bartons really jazzy organs.

Dan Barton's claim that his organs were built to stand up under heavy use is absolutely true. Their burly construction makes some other organs look like toys by comparison. The author knows of some Bartons which are sixty years old and still playing well; even the leather used in chests was of exceptional quality. Tonal quality was quite variable, however. To paraphrase an old fairy tale, when they were good they were very, very good, but when they were bad they were horrid! Examples of the latter are the style B-3 economy models favored by the Butterfield chain in Michigan. These 3/11 abortions had six *straight* ranks of pipes, were poorly specified, were voiced on low wind pressures (except for 10" tibias) and had only a 16' bourdon in the pedal. The consoles were loaded with dozens of blank stops to give the audience something to look at inasmuch as there was little to hear. The B-3 model made by the Hammond Clock Company made much more music!

Fortunately, many Bartons were excellent tonally and some were quite thrilling in the impact they made in their theatres. One outstanding example, ironically enough, was also in the state of Michigan, the home of so many of

those puny style B-3s. The 4/21 Barton in Detroit's Hollywood Theatre was fondly remembered by several old timers as the second best organ in town—and that's up against competition from some fine large Wurlitzers such as the Fox 4/36, Fisher 4/34, Michigan 5/28 and the State and Capitol 4/20s. In the author's opinion it is fair to state that, percentage-wise, Barton probably produced the same relative quantities of inferior, so-so and outstanding instruments as did the Wurlitzer company—and that's not a poor batting average!

The Barton factory was relatively small considering its output. Much of its efficiency was due to factory superintendent Al Stoll. In the words of Dan Barton, "We needed [a boy] to run errands, unpack stock and help wherever he was needed. Al Stoll was this boy. He was a bright kid and asked plenty of questions. One day he showed me a wiring diagram of a Bartola keyboard and wanted to know if he had figured the wiring correctly. Here was a fellow who wanted to learn something. We were adding more men. Al was put on assembling and a new boy was hired. I moved Al to other departments and always he wanted to know *why*! At the end of two years he was in charge of the testing. All Bartolas were assembled in the factory and given a final test before shipment was made. More of my time was needed away from the factory and Al, with his keen brain and ability to grasp knowledge, became more valuable. In less than five years Al Stoll went from errand boy to factory superintendent. One of the factors in the success of the Barton organ was the manner in which Al handled the production."[15]

According to some Barton employees, Stoll ruled the factory with an iron hand. He never asked or told anyone what to do. Instead he would write out an order or instruction on a piece of paper and hand it to the individual who would be expected to keep it on file for future reference! Despite Stoll's efficiency the factory often couldn't keep up with Dan Barton's selling pace. The

Barton organ being erected in the Madison studios of University of Wisconsin radio station WHA c. 1934. Original location of the organ is unknown. The installation was made by Anthony J. Endres, left, supervised by organist Frederick Fuller, right.[2] After the end of World War II Mr. Fuller operated an organ business using the Maxcy-Barton name. The Barton name was also used by James Huber of Chippewa Falls, Wisconsin in the 1950s. Neither of these men had any connection with the original Barton company which went out of business about 1935.

2/6 Barton in the Fox Theatre, Marinette, Wisconsin as it appeared in 1966. The theatre manager had six children and to keep them out of his hair, allowed them to play in the organ chamber!

organs were contracted for specific delivery dates and in order to meet schedules, parts were sometimes ordered from the Wangerin Organ Company in Milwaukee. Barton had an excellent business relationship with Wangerin from the earliest days of the Bartola, and Wangerin products featured the same excellent quality as Barton's. Sometimes the factory schedule was so tight that the entire organ was built by Wangerin. Around forty completely Wangerin-built organs were thus sold under the Barton nameplate.

With the exception of these occasional Wangerin parts, most parts of Barton organs were made in the Oshkosh factory except metal pipes. Jerome B. Meyer & Sons of Milwaukee made the metal trebles for Barton flutes and tibias and also supplied most of the diapasons. Meyer also built about half of Barton's strings, especially those voiced on 5" and 7" wind, while Dennison received orders for the rest of the strings and for most of the reeds. Some reeds and an occasional solo string were ordered from Gottfried, and National Organ Supply was called upon for an occasional clarinet or tuba. The author's impression from talking to Dan Barton was that delivery was the most important factor in deciding which firm got the pipework order, with tonal quality and price only secondary considerations.

If the Barton firm were remembered for no other reason, it will go down in organ history as the builder of one of the most spectacular organs ever built, the 6/51 behemoth in the Chicago Stadium. The word "loud" doesn't do it justice: "thrilling" comes a little closer. Some commercially available recordings of the Stadium organ were made by an organist past his prime when the organ was dreadfully out of tune, with the unfortunate result that many people have a totally erroneous conception of the

Stadium Barton's potential. Those of us who have heard it in person played by a good musician will never forget the overpowering emotional experience.

Because the Stadium Barton is so unique a number of rumors have persisted which the author would like to lay to rest. One story is that the expense of the project caused the failure of the Barton firm. According to Dan Barton, the Stadium organ made money for the company. Furthermore, the Barton firm was still in business six years after the opening of the Stadium organ in 1929. Other specious rumors about the organ's size and wind pressures were started by Barton himself. He shouldn't have had to make anything up; the actual statistics are impressive enough! With six manuals and 51 ranks of pipes it was the largest fully unified organ ever built. It had the largest organ blower ever built (100 horsepower) and was certainly one of the loudest musical instruments of all time.

Early in 1929 the Barton firm changed its name to the Maxcy-Barton Organ Company.[16] After the theatre organ business started its sharp decline, the firm tried to enter the church organ market and found that their Bartola name tended to alienate churches. A mere name change proved insufficient to capture the church market which seemed to elude most theatre organ builders, however, and the last new Barton organ was sold in 1931. A number of theatre customers who had bought Bartons on credit stopped making payments after the advent of talking pictures. Barton repossessed a number of these defaulted organs and tried to resell them to churches. Eventually, recalled Dan Barton, the company stopped repossessing organs they were entitled to, simply because they ran out of space to store them all. The firm finally went out of business around 1935.

BARTON OPUS LIST

Following are this firm's known theatre-type installations. Barton didn't use "opus" numbers, saying, for example, "107 organ" instead of the conventional "opus 107." These numbers, where known, are shown in Barton fashion under the "remarks" column.

CITY/STATE	LOCATION	SIZE	YR	BLWR	HP	WP	REMARKS
ARKANSAS							
Bentonville	Meteor Th.	2/3	1927	20410	1	12"	
Eldorado	Mission Th.	2/3	1927	19833	1	12"	
Fayetteville	Victory (Palace) Th.	2/4	1926	19061	2	12"	107 organ.
FLORIDA							
Miami	unidentified theatre	2/7					
	Victory Th.	3/	1920	11346	2	7"	Divided manual.
ILLINOIS							
Arlington Heights	Arlington Th.	2/3	1925	16922	1	12"	
Aurora	Rialto Th.	3/	1926	19034	5	13"	
Bensonville	Center Th.	2/3	1925	17807	1	12"	
Berwyn	Parthenon (Berwyn) Th.	4/16	1924	16003	10	15"	112 organ.
Bloomington	Majestic Th.	3/11	1926	19232	5	13"	
Canton	Garden Th.	2/	1922	13736	2	12"	
Champaign	Rialto Th.	2/7	1926	19059	1	12"	
Chicago	Arcadia Ballroom	3/	1923	14647	5	10"	
	Barton Organ School	2/	1923	14532	2	8"	
	Barton Organ School	3/11	1926	19078	5	18"	197 organ; moved in 1930 to WLS Radio, Chicago, Illinois as 197A organ.
	Belpark Th.	3/17	1927	20293	10	15"	
	Capital Th.	2/	1924	15715	2	12"	
	Central Park Th.	3/9	1919	10428	3	7"	
		3/10	1923	14034	5	5"&10"	Replaced earlier Barton organ.
	Chicago Stadium	6/51	1929	22655	100	25"&35"	250 organ.
	Colony Th.	3/10	1926	18428	5	18"	
	Crystal Th.	3/	1920	11220	3	7"	Divided manual.
	Dreamland Ballroom	2/6	1919	9723	2	7"	
			1922	13662	3	12"	Additions to earlier organ.
	Embassy Th.	3/10	1925	17921	5	18"	
	Highland Th.	4/21	1925	18196	15	18½"	157 organ.
	James Coston Th.	2/7	1925	17839	2	12"	
	Jeffery Th.	2/6	1924	16397	3	14"	
	Loomis Bldg. Corp./new th.		1925	17839	2	12"	
	Maplewood Th.	2/	1927	20754	2	12"	
	Midwest Th.	3/10					
	Milo Th.	3/8					
	Montclare Th.	3/10	1928	22642	7½	19"	
	New Pershing Th.	2/	1927	19834	1	12"	
	Ogden Th.	2/3	1927	20583	1	12"	
	Park Th.	2/	1924	15699	2	12"	
	Patio Th.	3/17	1926	19685	10	19"	
	Regal Th.	3/14	1927	21334	10	19"	222 organ.
	Rivera Th.	2/9	1918	9073	3	7"	First Barton organ; built by Wangerin—opus 270.
	Savoy Th.	2/	1927	19791	2	12"	
	Schindler's Th.		1926	19295	3	13"	
	Spaulding Th.	2/	1925	17990	2	12"	
	WBBM Radio	2/	1926	18653	2	12"	
	WBBM Radio	3/10	1929	22890	7½	13"	Moved in 1935 to Olympia Stadium, Detroit, Michigan and enlarged to 3/14, with blower #16737, rated at 5 hp, 18" wp.
	WCFL Radio	3/10	1923	14240	5	5"&10"	
	Windsor Park Th.	2/	1925	16852	2	12"	
	Woodlawn Th.	3/	1928	21593	7½	19"	
Cicero	Palace Th.	3/10	1926	19623	5	18"	
Danville	Fischer Th.	2/6	1924	16096	2	12"	Two ranks added to a 2/4 Robert-Morton.
Decatur	Empress Th.	3/9	1928	22084	3	13"	
	Lincoln Th.	3/	1924	15417	5	10"	Twin consoles.
Dixon	Dixon Th.	3/9	1922	13070	3	7"	Divided manual.
Elgin	Grover Th.	2/3	1921	12482	1	7"	
Elmhurst	York Th.	3/10					
Evanston	Park (Coronet) Th.	2/	1924	16078	1	12"	
Forest Park	Forest Th.	2/6	1928	21801	3	13"	
Galesburg	Orpheum Th.	3/11	1926	18932	5	13"	
	West Th.	2/	1926	19205	1	12"	
Glen Ellyn	Glen Th.	3/10	1926	19648	5	18"	
Granite City	Washington Th.		1923	15173	3	5"&10"	
Highland Park	Alcyon Th.	3/13	1925	17419	5	12½"	
Highwood	Bartlett Th.	2/3	1927	19850	1	12"	Style 20, Wangerin opus 507; cost $ 2,750.
Joliet	Rialto Th.	4/21	1926	18365	15	18½"	
				18552	1	12"	For one-rank lobby organ controlled from auditorium console.

CITY/STATE	LOCATION	SIZE	YR	BLWR	HP	WP	REMARKS
ILLINOIS							
Kankakee	unidentified theatre						
La Grange	La Grange Th.	4/10	1925	16676	7½	18″	126 organ.
La Salle	La Salle Th.	2/6	1928	21544	3	13″	267 organ.
	Majestic Th.	2/	1926	19651	2	12″	
Lombard	Parkside Th.	2/8					
Peoria	WMBD Radio	3/					
Quincy	Washington Th.	3/7	1924	15563	3	5″&10″	
Rockford	Coronado Th.	4/17	1927	20750	15	19″	207 organ.
	Orpheum Th.	3/	1925				Divided manual.
	Rialto Th.	2/7	1928	21621	2	12″	
Springfield	Orpheum theatre	3/11	1927	20063	7½	19″	
Sterling	unidentified theatre		1923				Built by Wangerin—opus 384.
Streator	Lyric (Plum) Th.	2/5	1926	18504	1	12″	
	Majestic Th.	2/	1927	20558	2	12″	
Waukegan	Academy Th.	2/7	1926	19761	2	12″	
	Genesee Th.	3/10	1927	20899	7½	19″	
Woodstock	Miller Th.	2/6	1927	20647	3	13″	Style 23.
INDIANA							
Bloomington	Indiana Th.		1923	14777	3	5″&10″	
Crown Point	Crown Th.	2/	1924	16671	1	9″	
Gary	Grand Th.	2/	1922	13964	2	9″	Built by Wangerin—opus 368.
	Grand Th.	2/	1928	21631	3	13″	Replaced earlier Barton.
	Tivoli Th.	3/12	1928	22332	10	19″	Later moved to Paramount Th., Hammond, Indiana.
Greencastle	Greencastle Th.	2/7	1925	17693	2	12″	
Indianapolis	Indiana Th.	3/17	1927	20187	15	19″	228 organ.
	Walker Th.	2/6	1927	21155	3	13″	
Terre Haute	Hippodrome Th.	2/	1926	18852	2	12″	
Washington	Liberty Th.	2/7	1925	17606	2	12″	
IOWA							
Boone	Princess Th.	2/	1927	19835	1	12″	
Cedar Rapids	Iowa Th.	3/14	1927	21294	7½	19″	Built by Wangerin—opus 510; cost $ 13,000.
Clinton	unidentified theatre						
Des Moines	A. H. Blank circuit	3/8					Divided manual.
Fort Dodge	Strand Th.	2/4	1927	20665	2	12″	Style 21; built by Wangerin—opus 508; cost $ 3,395; moved in 1937 to KOY Radio, Phoenix, AZ.
Iowa City	unidentified theatre	2/					
	Englert	2/	1926	19524	3	13″	
Keokuk	Regent Th.	2/	1927	20299	1	12″	
Shenandoah	Majestic Th.	2/	1921	12140	1	7″	
Sioux City	Capitol Th.	3/10	1928	21349	7½	19″	
Waterloo	unidentified theatre	2/8					
	Paramount Th.	3/10	1927	20890	7½	18″	
KENTUCKY							
Ashland	Capitol Th.	3/	1923	14352	3	10″	Divided manual.
	Grand Th.	2/	1928	21793	2	13″	
Paducah	Arcade Th.	2/	1926	18304	2	12″	
	Columbia Th.	2/7					
	Orpheum	2/	1925	18181	2	12″	
LOUISIANA							
Shreveport	Capitol Th.	2/4	1925	17530	2	12″	
MICHIGAN							
Albion	Boehm Th.	3/8	1928	21726	3	13″	
Ann Arbor	Michigan Th.	3/13	1927	21127	7½	19″	
Battle Creek	Bijou Th.	2/	1921	12053	1	7″	
Bay City	Orpheum Th.	2/	1921	12068	1	7″	
Coldwater	Tibbetts Th.	2/3	1926	19674	1	12″	
Detroit	Avalon Th.	3/10	1927	21172	7½	19″	Built by Wangerin—opus 519.
	Birmingham Th.	3/10	1927	20920	7½	18″	259 organ.
	Hollywood Th.	4/21	1927	20548	15	19″	234 organ.
	Linwood-La Salle Th.	2/8	1928	22025	3	13″	
	Oakman	2/	1921	12106	1	7″	
	Redford Th.	3/10	1927	20999	7½	18″	258 organ.
	West End Th.	3/10	1926	18745	5	13½″	
Flint	Capitol Th.	3/11	1927	19801	5	13″	
	Ritz (Globe) Th.	2/6	1925	17762	2	12″	
Gladstone	Rialto Th.	2/9	1927	20991	2	12″	Built by Wangerin—opus 517; cost $ 3,395.
Grand Haven	Grand Th.	2/6	1927	21136	3	13″	
Grand Rapids	Majestic Th.	3/11	1926	19493	5	13″	
Iron Mountain	Colonial Th.	2/	1927	20110	2	12″	
Ironwood	Ironwood Th.	2/7	1928	21737	3	13″	
	Rex Th.	2/3	1926	18726	1	12″	
	Rialto Th.	2/7	1925	16979	1	12″	
Jackson	unidentified theatre	2/					

CITY/STATE	LOCATION	SIZE	YR	BLWR	HP	WP	REMARKS
MICHIGAN							
Kalamazoo	Bijou (Majestic) Th.		1924	15938	5	10"	
	Capitol Th.	3/11	1924				108 organ.
	State Th.	3/11	1927	20247	5	15"	
Lansing	Strand (Michigan) Th.	3/11	1925	18053	5	13"	206 organ.
			1928	21911	5	13"	Replacement blower.
Marshall	Garden Th.	2/6	1927	20333	2	12"	
Menominee	Lloyd Th.	2/7	1926	19237	2	12"	212 organ.
Monroe	Family Th.	2/	1923	13872	2	5"	Built by Wangerin—opus 364.
Muskegon	Majestic Th.	2/6	1927	20903	3	13"	Style 23; built by Wangerin—opus 512; cost $ 5,350.
	Michigan	3/8					
	Regent	2/6	1927	20905	3	13"	Style 23; built by Wangerin—opus 513; cost $ 5,630.
Negaunee	Vista Th.	2/	1926	18985	2	12"	
Niles	Ready Th.	2/8	1927	20689	3	13"	247 organ.
Owosso	Capitol Th.	2/7	1926	18301	3	13"	
Pontiac	Oakland Th.	3/12	1925	16683	5	14"	
	Orpheum Th.	2/6	1925	18134	2	12"	
	State	2/7	1926	18384	2	12"	
	Strand Th.	3/	1920	11201	3	7"	Divided manual.
River Rouge	Fleur dy Lys Th.	2/7	1927	19820	2	12"	
Royal Oak	Baldwin (Washington) Th.	2/	1922	13006	3	7"	
	Royal Oak Th.	3/10	1927	21232	7½	19"	257 organ.
Saginaw	Franklin Th.	3/11					
	Mecca Th.	2/7	1927	20100	3	13"	
	Temple Th.	3/11	1927	19838	5	13"	
Sault Ste. Marie	Temple Th.	2/6	1927	19802	2	12"	
Wyandotte	Majestic Th.	2/					
Ypsilanti	unidentified theatre	2/					
MINNNESOTA							
Albert Lea	Rivoli		1922	13418	3	7"	
Faribault	unidentified theatre						
Hibbing	High School	3/12	1923	14452	10	15"	
Mankato	unidentified theatre						
Minneapolis	American Th.	2/	1922	13414	2	12"	
Owatonna	unidentified theatre	2/					
Rochester	Empress Th.	2/					
	Lawler Th.	2/					
St. Paul	Oxford Th.	3/8	1921	12535	3	7"	Divided manual.
	Tower Th.	3/8	1921	12540	3	7"	
Spring Grove	unidentified theatre	2/7					
Winona	Apollo Th.	2/6	1925	18150	3	12"	
	unidentified theatre						
NEBRASKA							
Fremont	Empress Th.	2/4	1922				
Grand Island	Majestic Th.	2/	1921	12131	1	7"	
Hastings	Strand Th.	2/	1921	12077	1	7"	
North Platte	Paramount	3/10	1930	24426	5	19"	
Omaha	Mueller Th.	2/7	1926	19072	2	12"	
	Roseland Th.	2/8	1922	13779	3	10"	
	Uptown Th.	2/4					
NORTH CAROLINA							
Winston-Salem	unidentified theatre	3/					
NORTH DAKOTA							
Fargo	WDAY Radio	2/3	1925	17488	1	12"	
	unidentified theatre						
OHIO							
Ashtabula	Majestic Th.		1923	14691	3	9"	
Canton	Alhambra Th.	2/	1922	13706	2	12"	
	Mozart Th.	2/	1922				
Cleveland	Five Points Th.	3/	1920	11498	3	7"	Divided manual.
	Jewel Th.	3/	1920	10939	2	7"	Divided manual.
	University Th.		1928	22155	3	13"	
East Palestine	Liberty Th.	2/3	1920	10967	1	6"	
Hamilton	Paramount Th.	3/14	1931	24455	10	18"	343 organ.
Middletown	Paramount Th.	3/14	1931	24454	10	18"	345 organ.
Toledo	East Auditorium	2/	1928	22153	2	13"	
	Eastwood Th.	2/3	1921	11890	1	7"	
		2/7	1928	22146	2	12"	Replaced earlier Barton.
	Westwood Th.		1927	21181	3	13"	
	World Th.	3/8	1920	11326	2	7"	Divided manual.
SOUTH DAKOTA							
Mitchell	unidentified theatre	2/3					

CITY/STATE	LOCATION	SIZE	YR	BLWR	HP	WP	REMARKS
TEXAS							
Coleman	Howell Th.	2/6	1928	21944	3	13"	
Dallas	Capitol Th.	3/10					
	Fair Park Auditorium	4/24	1925	17333	7½	15"	
			1925	17355	15	15"	One blower for each chamber.
	Ideal Th.	2/					
	Midway Th.	2/6					Moved in 1932 to Texas Theatre, Dallas, Texas.
	Phil Pierce Agency	2/3	1920	11820	1	7"	Demonstration organ.
Denison	Denison Th.	3/10	1926				
Fort Worth	Ritz Th.	2/7	1924	16077	2	9"	
Galveston	Dixie Th.	2/7	1925	17244	2	12"	
	Martini Th.	3/10	1924	16085	5	10"	
Houston	Wier Th.	2/3	1927	20914	1	12"	
Lubbock	Majestic Th.	3/10					
Lufkin	Pines Th.	2/6	1925	17370	2	12"	
Waco	Strand Th.	2/7	1925	16823	2	12"	
VIRGINIA							
Lynchburg	Paramount Th.	3/10	1930	24337	7½	18"	255 organ.
Newport News	Paramount Th.	3/10	1931	24761	7½	18"	350 organ; last Barton built.
Norfolk	unidentified theatre	3/					
WISCONSIN							
Antigo	Opera House (Palace) Th.	2/6	1928	21658	3	13"	Later moved to Fox Th., Marinette, Wisc.
Appleton	Appleton Th.	2/9					
	Elite Th.	2/	1923	13748	1	12"	
	Majestic Th.	2/	1922	13620	2	10"	
Baraboo	Ringling Th.	3/9	1928	21966	3	13"	
Beaver Dam	Davidson Th.	2/	1924	16208	1	12"	
Beloit	Majestic Th.	2/					
Burlington	Orpheum	2/5	1927	20470	2	12"	Style 22; built by Wangerin—opus 503; cost $ 4,637.
	Plaza Th.	2/4	1927	21122	1	12"	
Cudahy	Majestic Th.	2/4	1927	20511	2	12"	Style 21, with duplex roll player; built by Wangerin—opus 496; cost: $ 4,000.
Delavan	Pastime Th.	2/	1921	12132	1	7"	
Elkhorn	Sprague Th.	2/4	1928	21773	2	12"	
Fond du Lac	Fischer (Fond du Lac) Th.	4/11	1925	17908	5	13½"	
	Garrick Th.	2/					
	Retlaw Th.	3/11	1925	17910	5	13½"	129 organ.
Green Bay	Colonial Th.	2/	1925	17454	2	12"	
	Orpheum Th.	3/10	1930	24191	5	13"	
Janesville	Beverly Th.	2/	1927	20297	2	12"	
	Jeffery Th.	2/	1924	16146	3	12"	
	unidentified theatre		1922				Built by Wangerin—opus 363.
Kenosha	Burke Th.	2/3	1925	18241	1	12"	184 organ.
	Cameo Th.	2/					
	Gateway (Lake) Th.	3/10	1927	21154	7½	19"	
	Lincoln Th.	2/					
	Orpheum	3/	1921	12874	3	7"	
Kiel	Pastime Th.	2/4					99 organ.
La Crosse	Casino Th.	2/					
	Strand Th.	2/					
Lake Geneva	Gump Th.	2/5	1928	21852	2	12"	
Madison	Capitol Th.	3/14	1927	20952	7½	19"	249 organ.
	Eastwood Th.		1923	14055	3	5"&10"	
	Majestic Th.	2/3	1921	11885	1	7"	
		2/	1923	15158	3	5"&10"	Replaced earlier Barton.
	Parkway	3/	1926	19388	5	13"	
	WHA Radio	2/					Transplanted from unknown location.
Manitowoc	Capitol Th.	2/	1921	12114	1	7"	
	Strand Th.						
Marinette	Rialto Th.	2/	1923	14100	1	12"	
Marshfield	Adler Th.	2/6	1922	13744	2	12"	Built by Wangerin—opus 362.
Menasha	Brin Th.	2/7	1928	22631	3	13"	
	Rialto (Fox Valley) Th.	3/	1920	11041	2	7"	Divided manual.
Milwaukee	Burleigh Th.	2/6	1924	15902	2	12"	
	Climax Th.	2/					
	Colonial Th.	3/10	1926	19698	5	19"	215 organ.
	Egyptain Th.	2/9	1927	21008	5	12"	254 organ; double bolster.
	Garfield Th.	3/11	1927	20492	7½	19"	
	Grace Th.	2/	1925	17896	2	12"	
	Granada Th.	2/	1927	20129	2	12"	
	Hollywood Th.	2/	1927	20567	2	12"	
	Idle Hour Th.	2/	1922	13555	2	12"	
		3/9	1926	19082	3	12"	
	Layton Park Th.	2/5	1924	16092	2	12"	
	Liberty Th.	2/5					
	Lincoln Th.	2/3	1927	20086	1	12"	167 organ.
	Majestic Th.	2/8	1925	17131	3	13"	

CITY/STATE	LOCATION	SIZE	YR	BLWR	HP	WP	REMARKS
WISCONSIN							
Milwaukee	Miller Th.	2/	1921	12552	2	7″	
	Mirth Th.	2/3	1922	13548	1	7″	
		2/7	1924	16135	2	12″	Replaced earlier Barton.
	Modjeska Th.	3/10	1924	15791	7½	20″	
	Murray Th.	2/	1925				
	National	3/10	1927	21192	7½	19″	Built by Wangerin—opus 516.
	Oriental Th.	3/14	1927	20066	7½	19″	236 organ.
	Pearl Th.	2/5	1924	16093	2	12″	111 organ.
	Princess Th.						100 organ; not built.
	Regent Th.	2/7	1922	13550	2	12″	
	Savoy Th.	2/	1926	18808	1	12″	
		2/8	1926	19126	3	12″	
	Strand Th.	2/6	1925	17571	3	14″	
	Studio Th.	2/4	1925	18130	1	12″	
	Teutonia (Milwaukee) Th.	2/9					Additions: tibia, kinura, oboe horn, chrysoglott and new console for existing Wurlitzer—opus 559.
	Tower Th.	3/10	1926	18435	5	18″	176 organ.
	Uptown Th.	3/10	1926	19710	7½	19″	198 organ.
	Wisconsin Th.	3/17	1924	15310	15	15″	Twin consoles.
	Wisc. College of Music		1927	20457	3	13″	
	WTMJ Radio	3/	1929	23331	3	12″	
Mineral Point	World Th.	2/	1923	15064	1	12″	
Neenah	Neenah Opera House (Embassy) (Neenah) Th.	2/8	1922	13111	3	7″	
New London	Grand Th.	2/					
Oshkosh	Maxcy residence						
	Opera House						
	Orpheum Th.	3/	1922	13058	3	7″	
	Oshkosh Th.	3/	1926	19669	5	19″	
	Strand Th.	3/11	1927	19662	5	13″	274 organ.
Portage	Portage Th.	2/9	1927	19847	2	12″	223 organ.
Port Washington	Ozaukee Th.	2/5	1927	20577	2	12″	Style 22; Built by Wangerin—opus 504; cost $4,637.
Racine	Crown Th.	2/4	1926	19671	1	12″	
	Douglas Th.	2/6					
	Rex Th.	3/10					
	State Th.	2/6	1926	19403	2	12″	
Rhinelander	State Th.	2/6	1926	18422	2	12″	
Sheboygan	Majestic Th.	2/	1923	15020	3	12″	
	Majestic Th.	2/11	1923	15178	3	5″&10″	May also have been known as Wisconsin Theatre.
	Opera House (Vander Vaart) (Wisconsin) Th.	2/6	1925	17597	2	12″	
Shorewood	Shorewood Th.	2/7	1927	19831	2	12″	185 organ.
South Milwaukee	Grand Th.	2/3	1927	20352	1	12″	
Stevens Point	Fox Th.	2/					
	Lyric Th.	2/					
Two Rivers	Opera House	2/					
	Rivoli Th.	2/6	1922	13750	2	12″	Built by Wangerin—opus 359.
			1922	13813			Replacement blower.
Watertown	Classic Th.	2/	1922	13771	2	12″	Built by Wangerin—opus 358.
Waukesha	Park Th.	2/8	1926	18775	2	12″	
Waupaca	Palace (Rosa) Th.	3/	1920	11311	3	7″	Divided manual.
Wausau	Stuart Th.	2/	1926	18923	2	12″	
West Allis	Allis Th.	2/	1925	17611	2	12″	
West Bend	West Bend Th.	2/5	1929	23514	3	13″	
Whitewater	unidentified theatre	2/4	1927				Style 21; Built by Wangerin—opus 494; cost $3,470.
Wisconsin Rapids	Palace Th.	2/	1927	20937	2	12″	Built by Wangerin—opus 518; cost $3,500.

BEMAN ORGAN COMPANY, BINGHAMTON, N. Y.

*Builders of Electric and Electro-Pneumatic Pipe Organs,
and the "Celestafon," a Fine Standard Pipe
Organ Designed for Small Churches*

Established in 1884, this firm's original name was Frank Beman & Son. Through the teens the firm was also known as the Beman Symphonie Organ Company, Inc. and Beman Symphonie Orchestra Company,[1] "Symphonie" being a trademark for automatic organs produced by the firm.[2] By late 1919 the firm name had become simply the Beman Organ Company.[3]

In the early 1970s the author had an opportunity to examine an original Beman installation in the Highland Theatre, Fort Thomas, Kentucky. Among its distinguishing features were a wooden string on the manuals and a particularly ugly console! The metal pipes had apparently been given to the World War II metal scrap drives, a not uncommon fate of neglected theatre organs, and the console was stored backstage. It is unfortunate that no photographs were taken then; the theatre was gutted and the organ thrown out in 1975.[4]

Beman advertisement in the April 1919 Diapason.

BEMAN OPUS LIST

CITY/STATE	THEATRE	SIZE	YR	BLWR	HP	WP	REMARKS
KENTUCKY							
Fort Thomas	Highland Th.	2/	1923				
			1927	P70B	3	8"	
NEW JERSEY							
Union City	Summit Th.	2/	1915	6265			
NEW YORK							
Binghamton	Star Th.	2/	1917	8669			
	Symphony Th.		1913	5070			
Buffalo	Allendale Th.		1915	C515	5	16"	
				C514	¾		
Johnson City	Goodwill Th.	2/15	1920	10459			With 2-rank echo.
New York City	Washington Th.		1915	C622	3½	12"	
				C772	½	21" vacuum.	
OHIO							
Youngstown	Hippodrome Th.	2/	1914				
PENNSYLVANIA							
Wellsboro	Arcadia Th.		1921	12650			

Trade publications often published specifications of new organs. The above announcement is reproduced from the October 1919 issue of The Diapason.

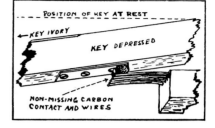
Beman ad in the June 1923 Diapason.

Beman ad in the April 1924 Diapason.

JAMES BENNETT

"Jim" Bennett operated an extensive service and rebuilding business in Columbus, Ohio during the 1920s and '30s. At least one theatre organ was installed bearing his nameplate: a two-manual instrument in the Clinton Theatre, Clintonville, Ohio. Installed in 1926, this organ had Spencer blower #19535 and consisted primarily of components purchasd from Organ Supply.[1]

Bennett advertisement in the July 1935 issue of The Diapason.

THE BENNETT ORGAN COMPANY
PIPE ORGAN BUILDERS
ROCKFORD, ILLINOIS

ELECTRO PNEUMATIC
ACTIONS
ELECTRIC MOTORS, ETC.

The history of the Bennett Organ Company is a convoluted story involving nine different nameplates. The story begins with four brothers in Ripon, Wisconsin in 1864. George, Thomas, Edward and Octavius Marshall had purchased an organ from Willis in their native England and donated it to their church. John L. Lancashire was sent from the Willis factory to erect the organ. The Marshall brothers had some money to invest and easily persuaded Lancashire to join them in organizing an organ factory in Ripon which became known as the Marshall Brothers Organ Company. Lancashire persuaded three Willis men to join the enterprise: Charles S. Barlow, William H. Turner and Edward "Ted" Harris, an excellent pipemaker.[1]

In 1867 the firm was joined by Phillip Odenbrett who had been building organs in Waupun, Wisconsin and the company name was changed to Marshall & Odenbrett. Following a disastrous fire in 1870 the firm relocated to Milwaukee, Wisconsin. At this time George and Octavius appeared to be the only Marshall brothers still associated with the business. Shortly after the move Odenbrett left to form the firm of Odenbrett & Abler. Trouble was also brewing between the Willis men and George Marshall and in 1872 John Lancashire and William Turner filed a lawsuit against Marshall from which they collected over $1,300.[2] The allegations of this suit are unknown.

The Lancashire and Turner nameplate made its debut about 1873 after these gentlemen left Milwaukee to form their own company in Moline, Illinois. They maintained a cordial relationship with Octavius Marshall who represented the firm in Milwaukee. In 1879 Lancashire and Turner sought additional capital and incorporated the Moline Pipe Organ Company. The organs they built at this time, all trackers, were among the finest in America both tonally and mechanically.[3]

In 1891 Octavius Marshall decided to invest $25,000 in the company, doubling its capitalization. He moved to Moline and changed the name to the Lancashire-Marshall Company. After Lancashire died of pneumonia in the late 1890s Marshall went looking for a shop superintendent. In 1902 he hired Robert J. Bennett and (you guessed it!) changed the name of the firm to the Marshall-Bennett Organ Company.

Bennett had apprenticed with George S. Hutchings in Boston and over a ten-year period had learned many organ building skills. Around 1894 Bennett had joined the Lyon & Healy Company of Chicago and by 1895 had become superintendent of their pipe organ division. Bennett apparently maintained cordial relations with Lyon & Healy, who stopped manufacturing organs around 1910. Some of the later Bennett theatre organs were sold under the Lyon & Healy nameplate.[4]

Bennett, or "R. J." as he was known among his employees, introduced a number of changes. Prior to his arrival only tracker organs had been built, but Bennett invented a new tubular pneumatic action which company nameplates thereafter referred to as the "Bennett System." Bennett chests were similar to Kilgen's but were consid-

Robert J. Bennett
(1864-1938)

Bennett advertisement
in the May 1914
Diapason.

erably more complex with two pouches per note. In 1916 the firm switched to electropneumatic action, retaining the same complicated chest design. Although expensive to build, these chests worked well. The same couldn't be said for Bennett consoles, however. "R. J." was forever experimenting with new designs for key and combination actions, most of which were unreliable.[5] Bennett was not averse to horsehoe consoles, however, and used them on many church organs as well as on theatre instruments.

The instruments crafted under John Lancashire's supervision followed the English tradition of Willis, but Bennett introduced tonal changes. He had developed his ideas in the Hutchings factory where the tonal "reform" (many people prefer "decadence") of the early twentieth century was underway. It is interesting to note that not a single mixture stop was offered in any of the numerous church organ specifications in a 1910 Bennett catalog.[6] The pipework continued to be of excellent quality, however. Bennett's Hoyt metal is especially noteworthy, much of it still retaining its sheen even after sixty years.

In the 1960s, organ builder, scholar and historian Robert E. Coleberd, Jr. extensively researched the colorful history of the Bennett Organ Company. Its continuing saga unfolds in his own words:

"In 1908 Octavius Marshall left the firm and Bennett assumed full control. He rewrote the corporate charter as the Bennett Organ Company which was now located in Rock Island because of a change in municipal boundaries with adjacent Moline.

". . . The future of the firm now rested upon the business acumen of Bennett who personally solicited most of the contracts. Friendly and humorous, this slender dark-haired man was beyond question a capable and clever salesman. He had all the answers when talking to a church committee about an organ and they in turn appeared to swallow everything he said. On one occasion, for exam-

ple, a Lutheran church in Swedeborg, Iowa complained that the primary action on the newly installed Bennett organ was too noisy and called Bennett. He drove over to the church, listened to the action and then explained that the fault was not in the instrument but was caused by the church being acoustically too alive. If the church were not so alive, he told the committee, the problem wouldn't exist. They bought the story!

"As was true of other midwestern builders up through the early 1920s, the Bennett company did not employ full time sales representatives in territories across the nation. The majority of the installations were in the immediate neighborhood—within driving distance of the home office.

". . . The task of directing the enterprise proved difficult for Robert J. Bennett. He purposely or inadvertently alienated stockholders and employees. It was generally known among the employees that he forced Octavius Marshall out of the business in 1908 . . . and they accused him of having a personal financial interest in contracts for theatre organs the company was building for Lyon & Healy. He was forever trying to persuade the employees to trade a portion of their wages for stock in the company. This drove several valuable men away . . . Needless to say, those who bought stock in the Bennett company never received a nickel on their investment.

"Bennett found an escape from his personality clashes and his lack of business ability in his fascination for console mechanisms. He experimented endlessly with various forms of combination and key action, but he changed his ideas so often that he never succeeded in producing a satisfactory mechanism. He eagerly pursued the work of other builders seeking to learn their methods, but then he changed the designs so much they wouldn't work. His mistakes were costly, tied up shop labor, and incurred the bitterness of churches. On one occasion the combination action didn't last long enough for the dedicatory recital. The company survived largely because of the dedication of a handful of able craftsmen, men like Ed and Charles Wright, the Canadian-born pipemakers, Albert Stannke,

This is how the Bennett factory, above left, appeared after a 10,000 square foot addition was made in 1921, bringing total factory area to 26,000 square feet.[8] Other rare photos on this page show interior of the factory.

the voicer who came from Aeolian in 1924, Carl Nyquist, the console maker, and Theodore Sandberg, the shop superintendent.

". . . By 1923 the financial condition of the company had deteriorated so drastically that it was technically insolvent. Hovering on the brink of bankruptcy, Bennett was forced to resort to issuing promissory notes to suppliers and installation crews. Wages were the only cash disbursements. The critical cash flow problems of organ building vexed most builders; they simply overwhelmed Bennett!

". . . In 1927 Bennett changed the corporate charter to the Rock Island Organ Company, a legal subterfuge employed surreptitiously to avoid the lawsuits threatening the company brought by irate chuches disillusioned with the malfunctioning Bennett organs. By then he could no longer ignore the precarious financial condition of his

enterprise and so he went looking for a buyer . . . A business promoter from Rockford (near Rock Island) named Robert Stack learned that the company needed funds and could be bought. He approached the wealthy Sunstrand brothers in Rockford who had recently sold their adding machine business . . . for a reported $3,000,000 . . . Stack somehow convinced them that the pipe organ business was promising and they agreed to buy the Bennett company. They were reportedly prepared to sink a half million dollars into it. Bennett was elated. He talked all the creditors into cancelling their claims agains the company, a condition necessary under Illinois law before the firm could be sold; all but one, a former road man, who demanded his money. When Bennett heard about this hold out he flew into a rage, but the employee collected the full amount of his claim.

"The Sunstrand brothers . . . purchased a tract of land in Rockford where the factory was to be moved and hired an architect to draw up the plans for the buildings. But they knew virtually nothing about the organ business, least of all the problems of the Bennett company. They began by making the incredibly unfortunate mistake of hiring Bennett as the general manger at the munificent salary of $10,000 per year . . . When they became aware very shortly that matters were not going well they began to ask questions. Bennett, who had buried himself in his experiments, seemingly oblivious to the critical stage of things or subconsciously bent upon destroying the firm, found a scapegoat in Theodore Sandberg, the shop superintendent. One day Bennett left unannounced and journeyed to North Tonawanda, New York where he called at the Rudolph Wurlitzer Company and persuaded a young draftsman named Hollingsworth to come back to Rock Island as shop superintendent.

"When they returned Bennett fired Sandberg and announced triumphantly to the stockholders that the problems were solved [and that] everything would be in order. In 47 years experience beginning with the Moline era, Sandberg, who was popular with the employees, had acquired an encyclopedic knowledge of organ building. The survival of the firm in the 1920s rested in large measure upon his abilities and his loyalty. As events soon proved, his dismissal, the most irrational act conceivable, sealed the fate of the Bennett Organ Company. But for a short time it appeared that Bennett was right. Hollingsworth restored discipline in the factory, which had broken down completely because Bennett overruled Sandberg when the latter tried to fire poor help, and work began moving through the shop again. Then it came time to lay out new organs and Hollingsworth, who was supposedly a draftsman, was found wanting.

By this time the Sundstrands . . . were thoroughly disillusioned . . . They concluded the situation was hopeless and . . . liquidation proceedings began. At a sale in the spring of 1930, employees bought the tools, console shells and other miscellaneous materials . . . The unfinished contacts were completed by the Hinners company in Pekin under Bennett's supervision.

". . . Approximately 1,100 pipe organs [were] built during [the company's] 66 years of operation . . . Only a handful of instruments were built . . . for residences, funeral homes, and lodge halls, [the majority being for churches] . . . As was true of numerous other builders in the midwestern industry, the Bennett company built fewer than half a dozen four-manual organs.

". . . The history of the Bennett company reveals most dramatically in the career of Robert J. Bennett that the nameplate is but the lengthened shadow of the key figure in the enterprise. A man tortured inside, Bennett's life was a series of contradictions. He dreamed of his own nameplate and when he got it he had great difficulty man-

aging it. He recognized the importance of non-mechanical action in windchest design, yet he couldn't or wouldn't build a workable console. He knew he needed money, but when he got it he couldn't make it work for him. But for all his weaknesses, R. J. Bennett was a likeable man, one of those figures in the rich history of American organ building who wanted to build pipe organs more than anything else."[7]

3-MANUAL BENNETT THEATRE ORGAN, OPUS 867
Liberty Theatre, Davenport, Iowa

Following is an interesting specification of a unified Bennett organ installed in 1919. Since Davenport is just across the Mississippi River from Bennett's Rock Island factory, this instrument may have been one of the company's "show" organs. The author would certainly like to know what the "solo ukeleke" was!

GREAT

8'	Diapason	8'	Tuba
8'	Major Flute	4'	Tuba Clarion
8'	Violoncello	16'	Tuba Profunda
8'	Flauto Dolce		Harp, 61 notes
4'	Flute Harmonic		Chimes, 20 notes

SWELL

8'	Diapason	8'	Flauto
8'	Clarabella	4'	Flute
8'	Viola	4'	Violina
8'	Viola Celeste	8'	Oboe Orchestral

ECHO

8'	Concert Flute		Chimes, 20 notes
8'	Flute Celeste		Xylophone, 49 notes
8'	Vox Humana		

ORCHESTRAL

8'	French Horn	2'	Piccolo
8'	Viole d'Orchestre	8'	Clarinet
8'	Viole Celeste	8'	Saxophone
8'	Quintadena		Chimes, 20 notes
4'	Musette		Solo Ukelele, 37 notes
4'	Whistling Flute		

PEDAL

16'	Double Bass
16'	Trombone
8'	Tuba
16'	Violone
8'	Cello
8'	Flute
	Bass Drum
	Bass Drum & Cymbals

COMBINATION PISTONS

(adjustable)
5 for great and pedal
5 for swell and pedal
5 for orchestral and pedal

The specification also included couplers, but their disposition is unknown.

TRAPS

(played from pedal studs)	Second Kettle Drum Roll
First Kettle Drum Single Stroke	Snare Drum Single Stroke
First Kettle Drum Roll	Snare Drum Roll
Second Kettle Drum Single Stroke	Bass Drum Single Stroke
	Bass Drum & Cymbals

This 2/5 Bennett in the Luther Memorial Church, Tacoma, Washington was originally installed in the State Theatre in Seattle.

BENNETT OPUS LIST

CITY/STATE	LOCATION	SIZE	OPUS	YR	BLWR	HP	WP	REMARKS
FLORIDA								
Jacksonville	WJAX Radio	2/		1928	21473			
ILLINOIS								
Chicago	Barbee's Loop Th.	2/12	873	1919				
	Lyric Th.	3/	883	1920	11865			
	Morrison Th.			1919	10392			
	State & Congress Th.	3/	880	1920				
East St. Louis	Erber (Lyric) Th.	2/7	894	1921	11521	1	5"	
Freeport	Lincoln Th.	3/8	902	1922				
Moline	Lyric Th.	1/7		1912				
	Savoy Th.	2/	947	1925				
Monmouth	Monmouth Th.			1917	8405			
Peoria	Apollo Th.	2/9	803	1914				Tubular pneumatic action.
				1921	12092			
Rock Island	Colonial Th.	2/		1918	9132			
	Fort Armstrong Th.	2/		1921	11671			
	Spencer Square Th.	2/16		1915				
INDIANA								
Fort Wayne	Lyric Th.	2/14	811	1914	5684			Tubular pneumatic action.
	Strand Th.	2/	234X	1919				Rebuilt.
IOWA								
Davenport	Liberty Th.	3/	867	1919	9387	5		With echo.
Sioux City	Strand Th.	2/19	829	1916				
KENTUCKY								
Henderson	Princess Th.	2/	872	1919	9973			
MICHIGAN								
Flint	Bijou Th.	2/7		1920				
MINNESOTA								
Pipestone	Orpheum Th.	2/5	967	1925				
Montevideo	Eagle Th.	2/	1002	1928				
St. Paul	Tower Th.	3/		1928				
MISSOURI								
St. Joseph	Orpheum Th.	2/	823	1915				With echo.
NEBRASKA								
Omaha	Magic Th.	2/4	959	1925				
OHIO								
Portsmouth	La Roy Th.	3/	952	1925				
SOUTH DAKOTA								
Brookings	Grand Th.	2/	1008	1928	21931			
TENNESSEE								
Chattanooga	Rialto Th.	2/8	879	1920	10474	1	5"	
					11515	¾	5"	
TEXAS								
Dallas	KLRD Radio	2/7		1928	21985			In Adolphus Hotel.
VIRGINIA								
Quantico	U. S. Theatre Barracks	3/	893	1920				
WASHINGTON								
Seattle	State Th.	2/5						
WISCONSIN								
Kenosha	Burke	2/9	881	1921	10636			
Menomonie	Opera House	2/						
Racine	Bijou Th.	2/	909	1922	13599			Model C-4.

BUHL & BLASHFIELD ORGAN COMPANY

P. C. Buhl and Frank E. Blashfield were in partnership by at least the mid teens doing business under the firm name of Barnes & Buhl Company.[1] At least two theatre instruments were installed under this nameplate, both in the firm's home town of Utica, New York. By 1920 the firm name had become the Buhl & Blashfield Organ Company. In late 1926 Messrs. Buhl and Blashfield amicably dissolved their partnership; Frank Blashfield moved to Cleveland, Ohio where he operated a business specializing in the modernizing of old organs[2] and Mr. Buhl continued doing business in Utica under the Buhl Organ Company, Inc. name.[3]

Ad in the January 1915 Diapason.

Ad in the September 1927 Diapason.

Ad in the August 1924 Diapason.

John DeMello plays the 3/14 Buhl & Blashfield organ in the Kaimuki Theatre, Honolulu, Hawaii, c. 1930.

BUHL & BLASHFIELD OPUS LIST

CITY/STATE	LOCATION	SIZE	YR	BLWR	HP	WP	NAMEPLATE & REMARKS
HAWAII							
Honolulu	Kaimuki Th.	3/14	1921	11686	3	10″	Buhl & Blashfield.
NEW YORK							
Endicott	Elvin Th.		1928	12514TUR			Buhl Organ Company; may have been a rebuild of a Link organ.
Little Falls	Gateway Th.		1923	14884			Buhl & Blashfield.
			1923	14944			
Utica	Deluxe Th.		1924	16393			Buhl & Blashfield.
			1924	16519			
	Schubert Th.	3/	1915	6683			Barnes & Buhl.
	State Th.	3/	1915				Barnes & Buhl.
PENNSYLVANIA							
Pittsburgh	Cameraphone Th.		1920	11281			Buhl & Blashfield; may have been a rebuild of a Moller organ.

BURLINGTON PIPE ORGAN COMPANY

Little is known to the author about this firm which was located in Burlington, Iowa at Fourth and Division Streets. In March 1910 their superintendent was R. C. Verney, who had earlier operated his own organ business in Mason City, Iowa[1] and had represented the Barckhoff Organ Company at one time.[2] One Burlington organ is known to have been installed at the Crystal Theatre, Waterloo, Iowa in 1912. It used Kinetic blower #A265 which had a ¾ horsepower motor and a 3½" wind capacity.

John E. Byington started his business in a Dixon, Illinois barn in 1913. Essentially a one-man shop, he specialized in rebuilding. He was also a representative for Bennett and ordered some parts from them for organs sold under his nameplate. He moved to Rockford, Illinois around 1929[1], remaining there until 1948 when he sold the business and moved to Whittier, California as a representative of M. P. Moller, Inc.[2]

During 1913 he installed an organ in the Eagle (State) Theatre, Princeton, Illinois and in 1917 Spencer sold him blower #8644, shipping it to the Palm Theatre at Rockford, Illinois. As valuable as the Spencer records are, they also have limitations as illustrated by this entry: rarely is the *purpose* of the blower disclosed. In this case the Palm Theatre's blower *may* have been for a new Byington organ, but it could also have been a replacement for an exisiting organ by another manufactuer which Byington was merely servicing.

Byington advertisement in the February 1932 Diapason.

CASAVANT BROS.

The Casavant story begins in 1837 when Joseph Casavant rebuilt an organ for a college near Montreal. In 1840 he built his first new organ and followed that with sixteen more before his retirement in 1866. Joseph Casavant died in 1874, whereupon his sons Claver and Samuel traveled to Europe to study organ building. They returned to their home town of St. Hyacinthe, Quebec in 1879 and established the firm of Casavant Freres. Claver was twenty-four and Samuel was only twenty years of age.[1]

By 1899 opus 100 had been produced. Opus 200 came in 1904 and opus 500 in 1912.[2] An American branch factory was opened in 1912 at South Haven, Michigan with complete facilities for organ building. This factory was superintended by J. E. Pepin who had been in charge of Casavant's Montreal office.[3] In 1918 the American plant stopped organ building to go into war production work.[4] The parent company in St. Hyacinthe was not affected and remains in business today. Over 3,400 organs have been built there as of 1983.

Though the firm unfortunately has no records of the instruments built at South Haven[5] at least three are known to have been installed in theatres: The Strand (Park) (Capitol) Theatre in Indianapolis, Indiana had a 2/13; the Montrose Theatre in Chicago, installed in 1913, had Spencer blower #5140; and the Rex Theatre in Duluth, Minnesota had a three-manual console and a 7½ horsepower Spencer Orgoblo.

The Canadian factory built two organs for Canadian theatres: Opus 641, a 2/20, was installed in the Regent Theatre in Ottawa, Ontario in 1915, and opus 1207, a

Casavant ad in the June 1917 Diapason.

2/14 Casavant in the Kerrisdale Theatre, Vancouver, British Columbia, Canada. Note the peculiarly shaped swell shoes, a Casavant trademark.

3/30, was installed in the Capitol Theatre in Quebec in 1927.

Other Casavants have also been reported in the Alma, Kerrisdale and Windsor Theatres in Vancouver, British Columbia.[6] These do not appear in Casavant records.[7] It is a possibility that they were built at the South Haven plant or perhaps were transplanted from other locations unbeknownst to the factory.

This photo appeared in a 1917 ad which touted the Bartola for adding orchestral voices to existing organs. The Casavant console may have been the one in the Rex Theatre, Duluth, Minnesota.

CLARK & FENTON

When the Losh brothers assumed control of the Midmer company in 1920, Arthur L. Fenton had already been superintendent there for five years. He decided to leave the company[1] and joined the firm of M. A. Clark & Sons in Nyack, New York which specialized in maintenance and rebuilding. In 1923 the firm purchased a building formerly used as a pail factory and changed its name to Clark & Fenton.[2] The manufacture of new organs became an increasing part of their business and in 1926 they sold what was apparently their only theatre organ to the Pearl River Theatre in Pearl River, New York. This organ used Spencer blower #18352 and was a two-manual instrument with chimes, xylophone and traps.[3]

Clark & Fenton advertising in *The Diapason* ceased in 1932, replaced by ads for the Fenton Organ Co. which note that its proprietor, A. L. Fenton, was "formerly with Clark & Fenton."

Clark & Fenton ad in the May 1928 Diapason.

Walter S. Coburn started in the organ business during the 1880s.[1] In 1896 he moved to Chicago and established the firm of Walter S. Coburn & Company. In 1900 he formed the partnership of Coburn & Taylor with a tuner, George Taylor. After Taylor left in 1909 the firm became the Coburn Organ Company. Coburn remained in business until 1935 after which their building was taken over by Arthur R. Temple, doing business as the Temple Organ Company.[2] In the 1920s Art Temple had been the Chicago area sales representative for Marr & Colton.

The Coburn firm built some new organs but specialized in rebuilding older instruments. Some new organs bearing the Coburn nameplate were actually the work of other firms such as Felgemaker[3] and Wicks.[4] Three Coburn theatre installations are known: a two-manual in the Iris Theatre in Houston, Texas, installed in 1911; a 2/9 installed in the Strand Thetare in Lexington, Kentucky in 1915; and a 2/7 installed in the Castle Theatre in Chicago in 1915. The latter two organs were purchased from Felgemaker and were Felgemaker opus numbers 1215 and 1218, respectively.

A typical Coburn nameplate.

Coburn ad in the March 1911 Diapason.

Perry Cozatt received his training from the Hinners Organ Company and went on to operate a small organ firm and printing shop at his home in Danville, Illinois. Two Cozatt theatre organs have been discovered: a 4/8 in the Cozatt residence in Danville and a three-manual in the Fine Arts Theatre, Monmouth, Illinois. The Fine Arts organ was installed in 1928 and was in service only a year before the theatre burned to the ground.[1] Cozatt's son, as of the late 1970s, was still carrying on a segment of his father's business: the manufacture of calliopes.

Perry Cozatt's residence and organ shop included a console in the log cabin at the left and organ chambers in the building behind it. Note the extraordinary width of the stop keys on the 4/8 console.

Cozatt ad in the February 1932 Diapason.

The Pulling Power Of Good Music Has Been Proven By The Most Successful Tteater Managers Everywhere.

We Take Pleasure In Presenting The

Cozatt Pipe Organ

The Cozatt organ is a genuine Theater Organ, Built on years of experience in Motion Picture Theater Music. Built to overcome the monotony of the Pipe Organ. Designed to have beautiful tone-quality, Unlimited playing Possibilities, and stadnard construction familiar to all Organist.

The Cozatt Organ will be a musical feature in your theater that will mean more business and the Elimination of your music worry to you Pipe Organs from $500.00 up.

Cozatt ad in a Western Motion Picture Company catalog; the entire catalog was printed by Cozatt as well. One can only hope that the quality of his organs was better than his proofreading skills! The console in the ad is a Barton, c. 1920. Perhaps Cozatt hadn't yet made a console of his own to photograph.

Security State Bank
Of Marine
Capital and Surplus
$15,000.00
Marine on St. Croix, Minn.

March 29, 1924
Cozatt Organ Co.,
Danville, Ill.
Dear Sir:
I am herewith enclosing our St. Paul draft in the sum of $75.00 as payment in full for Electric Blower ordered by Arthur Ecklund of this place for the Swedish Lutheran Church.
As I understand it, this gives entire satisfaction and wish to thank you for your courtesy in this transaction.
Yours very truly,
JOHN ROSELL,
Treas.

Another Cozatt specialty was the production of blowers of his own design. This ad copy appearing in the May 1924 Diapason was unusual to say the least.

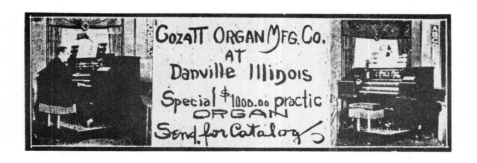

Cozatt ad in the July 1928 Diapason featured the three-manual instrument installed in the Fine Arts Theatre, Monmouth, Illinois. As a prospective client, would you consider purchasing an organ from a firm whose ad was not typeset and contained a misspelled word to boot?

Nicholas Doerr hung out his shingle in 1919, having served with the Kimball company for eleven years.[1] Under his own nameplate he rebuilt and enlarged several early Kimballs in local theatres: a 2/7 in the Douglas Theatre, Chicago;[2] the Melrose Park (Rose) Theatre, Melrose Park, Illinois in 1929 (with Spencer blower #22830); and the Marshall Square Theatre, Chicago in 1927 (with Spencer blower #20673). The Marshall Square instrument, a highly unified 3/12, was his pride and joy

and was featured prominently on his letterhead. He also installed a new 2/6 unit organ with orchestra bells in the residence of Frank A. Bryce, Grand Ledge, Michigan in 1931.[3]

"Nick" Doerr was still in business in the early 1970s and delighted several Chicago area enthusiasts by selling them choice parts left over from theatre days, such as a 16' string and a saxophone.

Estey was one of the giants of American organ building. Although they produced around 3,000 pipe organs, the firm is best known for their reed organs which were manufactured by the hundreds of thousands. Reed organ production began in 1846 and continued through the 1970s. Pipe organs weren't built by the firm until about half a century after its founding but they grew to represent a major portion of the firm's business in the first few decades of the twentieth century. The last new Estey pipe organ was opus 3261 built in 1960.[2] The tonal quality of Estey organs was unremarkable but the Estey name will be long remembered for several innovations including Haskell pipes, the "luminous" console and the Minuette ser-

ies of small organs.

The name of William E. Haskell is nearly as well known as that of Estey itself. Haskell began his organ career by working for his father who was superintendent of the Roosevelt organ factory in Philadelphia.[3] Father and son went into business on their own when the Roosevelt factory closed in 1891.[4] (See the Haskell section in this volume for further details about this firm.) William Haskell left his father's company in 1901 to join Estey as factory superintendent, a position held until he was overtaken by a serious illness in 1924.[5]

During Haskell's tenure at Estey he invented several varieties of flue pipes which sounded like reeds, includ-

AN INDUSTRIAL GENEALOGY
Five Generations of Esteys—Fourth now in Control
And Fifth is Preparing

Julius J. Estey, President
1890 ~ 1902

J. Gray Estey, President
1902 ~ 1930

J. Harry Estey, Treasurer
1902 ~ 1920

Jacob Estey,
son of Jacob P.

Jacob Estey, Founder
President, 1846 ~ 1890

Wilson Gray Estey,
son of Joseph G.

Jacob P. Estey ~ President
1930 ~~

THE ESTEY ORGAN COMPANY
Organ makers for 84 years
and for many years to come

Joseph G. Estey, Treasurer
1930 ~~

Estey's most renowned employee, William E. Haskell (1865-1927)[1], voices one of his reedless oboe ranks.

ing the reedless oboe, reedless saxophone, reedless clarinet and gamba tuba. He also developed a method of reducing the length of open pipes without changing their tonality. Such pipes are commonly referred to today as Haskell basses. Mr. Haskell was an exceptionally talented voicer and his string stops are perhaps the most distinguished feature of Estey organs.

The Estey company had a lifelong fascination with console stop controls. Mr. Haskell brought to Estey a design wherein the stops took the form of a miniature keyboard. Depressing the "naturals" turned the stops on, and they were cancelled by pushing the adjacent "sharps." A photograph of such a console is reproduced on page 158.

The "luminous" console, an innovation introduced in 1922, was available on the company's church and residence organs as well as on instruments destined for theatres. Estey felt that the luminous console was a major development in the art of organ building but few organists shared the factory's enthusiasm. Changing large numbers of stops rapidly was difficult; light bulbs would burn out and create confusion as to which stops were activated and occasionally the metallic buttons would deliver a nasty shock to unwary organists!

An apocryphal but nonetheless fabulous story is told about legendary organ builder G. Donald Harrison who was sent to service the Estey in New York's Capitol Theatre shortly after his arrival in the United States from his native England. The day after Harrison's visit, patrons in the balcony started laughing even before the organist started his solo. It seems that Harrison had reset the general combination pistons so that the luminous buttons would spell out dirty words![6]

The luminous console's failure in the marketplace was a source of embarrassment to the Estey organization. In a rather clever attempt to save face, the firm announced in February of 1929 the development of a new "master keydesk." According to the Estey advertising department, the "master keydesk" represented the latest in technology and was really something new.[7] All that was new, however, was a catchy name for something which had been a standard design with other firms for years.

Another Estey innovation was the Minuette series of organs wherein three ranks of pipes were squeezed into cabinets requiring no more floor space than an upright or grand piano.

Estey's most famous organ was installed in the Capitol Theatre in New York. Major Edward Bowes was building the largest theatre ever constructed (in 1919) and wanted

Although no Minuettes were sold directly to theatres, they were relatively portable and frequently saw service in several locations. At left is an upright model whose case design was not nearly as appealing as the more popular grand model. Photo below shows a grand Minuette in the Art Deco splendor of the lobby of the Fox Wilshire Theatre in Beverly Hills, California.

Through the use of Haskell basses an entire 16′ open string rank was squeezed into a Minuette. This particular example even included a set of chimes mounted horizontally along the angled edge of the case. Some of the 16′ string pipes have been removed in this photo to show the placement of other pipes beneath them.

Estey "Minuette" Pipe Organ
(Patented and additional patents pending)

Two Manuals: Compass CCC to C. 61 Notes each.
Dimensions: Height 3'-3". Length 8'-4". Width 5'-5", not including Bench.
Organ Bench: Piano type, finished to match Organ.
Console Face: Circular type with tablets above keys.
Pedal Board: Concave and radiating, CCC to G. 32 Notes.
Pitch: A-440.
Action: Especial simplified electric. Patent No. 1,286,059 Unit Action Patent. Other Patents pending.
Pipes: Estey patented construction.
Finish: Standard finishes are Mahogany, Walnut, Oak, Ebonized. Special finishes may be obtained.

SWELL ORGAN

Bass Viol	16 feet
Diapason	8 feet
Oboe (*Syn.*)	8 feet
Clarinet (*Syn.*)	8 feet
Tibia Clausa	8 feet
Violin	8 feet
Saxophone (*Syn.*)	8 feet
Diapason	4 feet
Flute D'Amour	4 feet
Violina	4 feet
Twelfth	2 2/3 feet
Piccolo	2 feet
Tierce	1 3/5 feet

GREAT ORGAN

Violone	16 feet
Diapason	8 feet
Viola	8 feet
Gedackt	8 feet
Diapason	4 feet
String	4 feet
Flute	4 feet

PEDAL ORGAN

Contra Viol	16 feet
Viola	8 feet
Flute	8 feet

GENERAL

General Tremolo   Expression Pedal

ACCESSORIES

25 feet Flexible Coupling

Music Rack   Organ Bench (*Piano Style*)   Motor

Blower and Generator   Current and Wind Light

Four Spare contacts in Console (*Swell Manual*) for additions.
Seven Spare contacts in Console (*Great Manual*) for additions.
Four Spare contacts on Pedal Board for additions.

Note: Spare Contacts are not generally provided in organs. These allow for additions to be made at small cost. Interior Action plated with cadmium, which is about 2,000 times as rust-resistant as nickel plate.

Accessories and Additions

Any or all of the following may be added to the foregoing basic specification.

Dual Expression—To make any organ twice as effective (available only on Estey Magnetic instruments). By the means of two-way tablets, one may set each stop of pipes individually as to volume. For instance, by setting the Violin loud and Flute and Clarinet soft, a gradation can be established so that the effect would be that of a Violin soloist accompanied very faintly by a Clarinet and Flute. Likewise, any stop or group of stops can be made to predominate.

All of the Dual Expression is behind the master expression, so that the possibilities of gradation of volume are unlimited.

Electrically controlled Master Shutters for expression should be added, although this can be added without the Dual Expression.

Automatic Bass Accompaniment—For use when a pedal board is not required.

Chimes—Five Notes on separate keyboard.

Stop Tablets may be added within the range of the specification.

Toe Pistons—Round, heavy cast and plated.

Indicator Lights, such as "Wind" and "Current," placed over stop tablets.

Console Interior Lights—Two placed in Console. Arranged to work on 6, 12 or 18 volts through step-down transformer.

Note: If additional lights of any number are to be added to Console, and are wired to the organ generator current, there will be an extra charge; this also applies to the addition of stop tablets provided a larger generator is required.

Flexible Wind Conduit (extra over 25 feet).

Pedal Cable (extra over 20 feet which comes with Pedal as standard equipment).

Cable (extra beyond that which is standard equipment up to 32 Notes).

TRAP UNIT

Accompaniment Organ—Snare Drum, Tambourine, Castanets.

Pedal Organ—Bass Drum, Tympani, Cymbal.

GLOCKENSPIEL, ORCHESTRAL BELLS UNIT

Accompaniment Organ—Glockenspiel.
Solo Melody Organ—Orchestral Bells, Glockenspiel.

XYLOPHONE UNIT

Accompaniment Organ—Xylophone.
Solo Melody Organ—Xylophone.

Raised and ornate finishes prices quoted on request. Silver, Gold, Polychrome, mottled Bronze, two weeks special notice required.

Other additions subject to individual quotation from factory. All extras should be installed at factory. They may be added after the original installation, and purchaser must then pay an extra charge for installation.

Solo, Accompaniment and Pedal Players can be added to operate any of these organs, but they are not recommended unless the Dual Expression is a part of the organ. The equivalent of a six-stop organ will result from the player when the automatic player is added to the specifications.

Estey players may be added to the Minuette. These players take the Estey library of over 1500 rolls.

Estey produced a 20-page illustrated brochure for prospective Minutte purchasers. The text from several of its interesting pages is reproduced above.

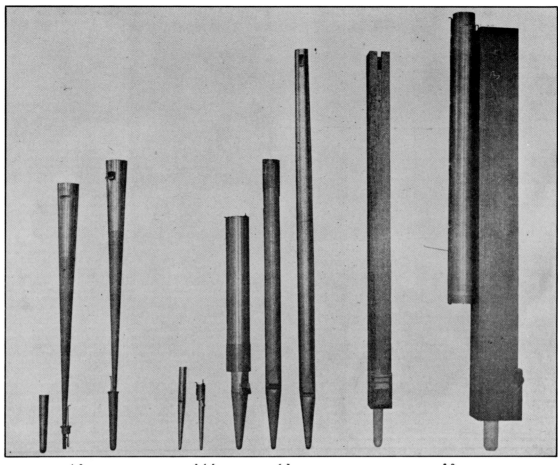

1, 2	3, 4, 5	6, 7	8, 9
A TYPICAL REED	REEDLESS CLARINET	REEDLESS OBOE	REEDLESS SAXOPHONE Normal position of cylinder on No. 9 is inside pipe

THE VALUE OF ESTEY REEDLESS REEDS

The first value of the Estey Reedless Reed Stops is their imitative qualities.
"—the wonderful imitative labial Saxophone—yields a compound tone so closely imitative of that of the true saxophone as to be positively deceptive to the ear. We were naturally very doubtful regarding the possibility of producing so complex a tonality from wood labial pipes; but all doubts were put to rest, on our being afforded the means of judging by direct comparison of the tones of the stop with those of the true saxophone, performed upon within the organ immediately alongside the stop. The imitation was practically perfect while in certain parts of the compass the Saxophone of the Organ was more even and pleasing than the reed instrument." This quotation is from—"Organ Stops and their Artistic Registration" by Dr. George Ashdown Audsley.

The second value of these Stops is that they stay in tune.
Every organist knows that pipes with a vibrating reed can be tuned practically every day. The Estey Reedless Reeds produce a reed tone from a labial pipe and consequently need no more attention from the tuner than any other stop. The dependability of these special stops has been the subject of favorable comment from many organists.

The Estey Reedless Oboe, Saxophone, Clarinet and Tuba Mirabilis are installed in organs like the National Cash Register Concert Organ, The Capitol Theatre, and the Third Church of Christ Scientist, New York,—especially for their distinctive tone. In other installations the elimination of constant tuning is the attractive feature.

ESTEY ORGAN COMPANY
BRATTLEBORO, VERMONT

This ad in the February 1924 Diapason *illustrates several of the Haskell reedless reeds. Among those not featured is the gamba tuba, a wooden rank of enormous power which flares larger at its open end than at its mouth. The fanfare division of the Atlantic City Convention Hall organ contains three of these ranks on 20″ pressure. See the photograph on page 337 of this volume.*

2/5 ESTEY PIPE ORGAN, OPUS 2680
Palace Theatre, Rockville, Connecticut
This contract, dating from 1927, illustrates a typical Estey theatre instrument.

CONTRACT

It is this day agreed by and between the ESTEY ORGAN CO., of Brattleboro, Vermont, party of the first part, and _____ **PUTNAM THEATER COMPANY** _____ **PUTNAM, CONNECTICUT** _____ party of the second part, as follows:—

The party of the first part agrees to build an organ in accordance with the annexed specifications, which are made a part hereof, and erect the same in _____ **Palace Theater** _____ **Rockville, Connecticut** _____ complete and ready for use on or before the _____ **First** _____ day of _____ **September** _____ A. D. 192_ or as soon thereafter as possible.

Should said organ, upon completion, not comply with the terms and specifications of this agreement the party of first part agrees at its own cost to remedy such defects or remove the organ.

The said party of the first part further agrees that it will, at its own cost and expense, at any time after the completion of said organ, remedy all structural defects therein, if any, natural wear, damage done by fire, water, or other cause not connected with the construction of said organ, excepted.

The said party of the second part agrees to test and examine said organ immediately upon completion of same, in presence of the representative of said party of the first part, and, if found in accordance with specifications hereto attached, will then accept and settle for same as follows:—

The said party of the second part hereby agrees to pay to the said ESTEY ORGAN CO., the party of the first part, the sum of **Five Thousand Five Hundred ($5500.)** _ _ _ dollars: **One Thousand Three Hundred Seventy-five ($1375.) Dollars at time of signing contracts, One Thousand Three Hundred Seventy-five ($1375.) Dollars on installation of organ in theater, and the balance to be evidenced by three (3) notes maturing in thirty (30), sixty (60), and ninety (90) days for Nine Hundred Sixteen ($916.) Dollars, Nine Hundred Sixteen ($916.) Dollars, and Nine Hundred Eighteen ($918.) Dollars respectively.**

The said party of the second part also agrees to pay all freight and drayage charges on the organ and parts thereof, together with hoisting charges, if any, and also to transfer organ to the premises promptly on notification of its arrival.

And it is agreed by both the parties hereto that the said organ shall be and remain the property of the said ESTEY ORGAN CO. until all the purchase price thereof, whether evidenced by note, account, or otherwise, xxxxxxxxxxxx, shall have been paid in full.

The said party of the second part also agrees that the building will be in proper condition for the installation of the organ **Ten (10)** days previous to the date of completion; and that they will allow, free from interruption, suitable convenience and opportunity for the installation in the building and provide such a condition of quiet as is necessary for proper tone regulation and tuning, together with the necessary heat, light and power.

If water or electric motor is included in these specifications the party of the second part agrees to provide foundation and enclosures when necessary; to furnish and install wind conductor between blower and organ; to do all wiring or plumbing connected therewith; to install such lights as may be needed for the erection and future care of the organ, and to do any necessary cutting of floors, partitions, or alterations to any other parts of the building. In the event that local regulations require the use of an automatic or remote control switch or motor starter, electric conduits or other special equipment, they are to be furnished by the party of the second part.

It is further agreed that if the party of the first part is subjected to any expense by reason of delay in the aforementioned preparation for organ or motor, said expense shall be paid by the party of the second part.

For the mutual protection of the manufacturer and purchaser, it is understood that no verbal agreement, not covered by this contract, will be recognized, or in any way modify this agreement; and it is further understood and agreed that this contract is submitted to the purchaser subject to the acceptance and approval of the said ESTEY ORGAN CO., at its home office in Brattleboro, Vermont, and that only when so accepted and approved shall it become a binding contract between said parties.

Witness our signatures at _____ this _____ day of _____ A. D. 192_

It is further understood and agreed by the party of the first part with the party of the second part, that they will not record this agreement and sale of this organ except on failure to pay any of the notes as specified in this agreement.

ESTEY ORGAN COMPANY | Party of the First Part

| Party of the Second Part

Brattleboro, Vermont, _____ 192_.

The above contract is this day accepted and approved.

ESTEY ORGAN COMPANY

By _____
President.

DETAILS OF CONSTRUCTION

~~The Case is to be constructed of native hard wood of appropriate design; the large Metal Pipes in the front to be decorated in plain dull gold bronze.~~

The Ground Sill is to be extra heavy and with the upright frame is to be rigidly constructed of well-seasoned material, every portion firmly put together.

The Swell Box is to be constructed of heavy material framed together. The Shades to be vertical, to swing on metal pins, bushed with felt, and so constructed as to insure tight closing and noiseless operation.

The Bellows and Regulators are to be of ample size to supply sufficient wind for the greatest possible demand and to furnish wind at a uniform pressure, no matter what the demand. They are to be framed with panels screwed on, to be double-leathered, with the best alum-tanned sheepskin, to be provided with automatic safety valve and regulating valve.

Wind Chests. The Wind Chests are to be of the individual valve type so that each pipe will have its own individual supply of wind, preventing robbing or unsteadiness of speech. The use of compressed air through tubes and channels to operate each individual valve avoids complicated levers and kindred devices, thus insuring instantaneous operation and repetition.

Couplers. The Coupler action is to be operated pneumatically, eliminating entirely any variation in the weight of the touch whether or not the couplers are in use.

Pipes. No stopped or mitred basses shall be used in any normally open stop. The Wood Pipes shall be made of the best selected stock, glue-sized on the inside and coated with two coats of shellac varnish on the outside, all to be supplied with wooden feet, metal toes being used for the smaller pipes and gates for the larger. The small Metal Pipes shall be made of the best quality and appropriate weight of annealed zinc. All other Metal Pipes to be made of a composition of tin and lead in the proper proportions to give the best results for the quality of tone required.

The scale of all pipes shall be in accordance with the best standards, and the voicing shall be of the highest order of excellence, with the proper volume throughout.

Stop Action. The Stop Action shall be of the ~~stop~~ tablet type, with the tablets placed over the swell manual and plainly marked with the name of the stop or coupler, stops to be indicated in black, couplers in red.

The Crescendo Pedal shall be so arranged as to bring on the stops in accordance with the strength of tone and cancel them in the reverse order. It, however, shall be made adjustable, so that any stop not desired on the Crescendo Pedal can be disconnected from it.

Combination Pistons. The Combination Pistons, whenever provided for, are to be adjustable at the Console, double acting, so that they can be adjusted to bring on or cancel any stops which are so set. They shall also be so arranged that the couplers can be set to act with the Combination Pistons if desired.

With a view to securing the greatest possible durability and utility none but the best and most improved materials and methods of construction shall be used in any part of the instrument, so that the complete instrument shall be of the highest order of excellence.

the largest possible pipe organ for it. The contract was awarded to Estey, so the story goes, because their proposal called for the largest organ of all the firms who submitted bids! In 1923 the original stop key console was replaced with a new luminous model. The luminous console did not meet expectations of playability or reliability and was replaced with a horseshoe console in 1927 at which time the organ was also enlarged.[8] The Capitol Estey was a powerful organ but it was strictly a concert instrument and lacked the sobbing tibias and heavy tremulants necessary for the successful performance of popular music.

Another famous Estey which wasn't successful at performing popular music was installed in 1921 in the old Trinity Baptist Church in Camden, New Jersey, which was being used as a recording studio by the Victor Talking Machine Company. Contrary to some reports, the 2/12 Estey was purchased by Victor for recording purposes and was not the instrument previously used for church services in the building. The organ was enlarged to a 3/13 in 1925 and was again enlarged in 1926 to upwards of twenty ranks, several of which were on 15" wind pressure although most were on 5".[9] Some wag changed the wording on the general cancel piston to read "no sale," reflecting the fact that luminous consoles were often referred to as "cash register" consoles because of the style of buttons and because one of the first luminous console installations was in the auditorium of the National Cash Register Company in Dayton, Ohio.[10]

ESTEY ORGAN COMPANY

Brattleboro, Vt., U. S. A.

SPECIFICATION FOR A TWO MANUAL PIPE ORGAN WITH PEDALS
COMPASS OF MANUALS CC TO C' 61 NOTES
COMPASS OF PEDALS CCC TO G 32 NOTES
TO BE BUILT FOR

PALACE THEATER
ROCKVILLE, CONNECTICUT

Name of Stop	ACCOMPANIMENT ORGAN	Pitch	Material	Notes
1. Open Diapason		8 ft.	Metal	61
2. Orch. Bells (Second Touch)				
3. Stopped Flute		8 ft.	Wood	61
4. Viol d'Orchestre		8 ft.	Metal	61
5. Octave		4 ft.	Metal	61
6. Flute d'Amour		4 ft.	Wood	61
7. Violina		4 ft.	Metal	61
8. Vox Humana		8 ft.	Reeds	61
9. Vox Humana		4 ft.	Reeds	61
10. Orchestral Bells (repeating action)				
11. Snare Drum				
12. Tambourine				
13. Castanets				
14. Tom-Tom				
15. Wood Block				
16. Door Bell (push button)				

SOLO ORGAN

17. Bourdon, Tenor C	16 ft.	Wood	61	
18. Open Diapason	8 ft.	Metal	73	
19. Stopped Flute	8 ft.	Wood	73	
20. Viol d'Orchestre	8 ft.	Metal	73	
21. Tibia	8 ft.	Wood	73	
22. Principal	4 ft.	Metal	73	
23. Flute	4 ft.	Wood	73	
24. Flute d'Amour	4 ft.	Wood	73	
25. Piccolo	2 ft.	Wood & Metal	61	
26. Nazard	2-2/3 ft.	Wood & Metal	61	
27. Tierce	1-3/5 ft.	Wood & Metal	61	
28. Vox Humana, Tenor C	16 ft.	Reeds	61	
29. Vox Humana	8 ft.	Reeds	73	
30. Vox Humana	4 ft.	Reeds	61	
31. Xylophone			37 bars	
32. Glockenspiel (single stroke)			37 bars	
33. Cathedral Chimes				

PEDAL ORGAN

34. Bourdon	16 ft.	Wood	32	
35. Open Diapason	8 ft.	Metal	32	
36. Gedeckt	8 ft.	Wood	32	
37. Violin Cello	8 ft.	Metal	32	
38. Tibia	8 ft.	Wood	32	
39. Octave	4 ft.	Metal	32	
40. Bass Drum				
41. Cymbal				

TOE STUDS

42. Crash Cymbal
43. Triangle
44. Boat Whistle
45. Bird Whistle
46. Fire Gong
47. Siren

ANALYSIS

Bourdon	16 ft.	Wood	97 pipes	
Open Diapason	8 ft.	Metal	73 pipes	
Viol d'Orchestre	8 ft.	Metal	73 pipes	
Vox Humana	8 ft.	Reeds	73 pipes	
Tibia	8 ft.	Wood	73 pipes	
Xylophone				
Glockenspiel				
Chimes				

PEDAL MOVEMENTS
AND
MECHANICAL ACCESSORIES

Balanced Crescendo Pedal

Expression Pedal

Tremulant

Crescendo Indicator

Wind Indicator

Stop-Tablet Console

Electric Motor and Organ Blower

Action Current Generator

COUPLERS

Solo to Pedal 8'
Solo to Pedal 4'
Solo to Solo 16'
Solo to Solo 4'
Solo to Accompaniment 16'
Solo to Accompaniment 8'
Solo to Accompaniment 4'
Solo Unison

Nos. 25-26-27, Traps and Percussions not affected
by Couplers.

Victor recording director Ray Sooey conducts tenor George Hopkins accompanied by E. J. Quinby on the Estey in the Victor Talking Machine Company studios in 1930.[11] At least one famous musician recorded some organ solos on this instrument: "Fats" Waller.

Console of the Estey Theatre Pipe Organ recently
installed in the Capitol Theatre, New York City

An *ESTEY ORGAN* equal to an
orchestra of 200 musicians

The largest theatre in the world required the largest organ in the world.   They chose an Estey.

The Capitol Theatre represents the last word in theatre construction and equipment. The Estey organ was built into the Capitol Theatre while it was in course of construction.   Its pipes produce a volume of sound equivalent to 200 musicians.   Our experts can fit a small organ to your theatre, whatever its size.

The Estey has been a big factor in the success of every theatre that has installed one.   No instrument can produce such thrilling tones as an organ. Churches realize this.   So should every wide-awake manager.

Hear an Estey Pipe Organ at any of the studios listed below, or write for a list of theatres near you.   We will send an expert to talk with you wherever you are, whenever you say.

An Estey residence organ adds a valued touch of refinement to
the homes of many of our most celebrated artists and producers

THE ESTEY ORGAN COMPANY, Brattleboro, Vermont

OTHER STUDIOS AT

NEW YORK, 11 West 49th Street   BOSTON, 120 Boylston Street
LOS ANGELES, 633 South Hill Street   PHILADELPHIA, 1701 Walnut Street

Original stop key console in the Capitol Theatre is shown on the opposite page in an ad from the March 13, 1920 Motion Picture News. At right, C. A. J. Parmentier plays the second console in June 1923. One can just imagine the words that could be spelled out on those luminous buttons! The third console, below, featured both stop keys and luminous buttons. It's too bad the organ didn't sound as theatrical as it looked after this 1927 facelift.

Some of the theatres that have installed Estey Organs

THE ALLSTEN THEATRE, BOSTON, MASS.

THE SHAWMUT THEATRE, BOSTON, MASS

THE DUDLEY THEATRE, BOSTON, MASS.

CLEMMER THEATRE, SEATTLE, WASH.

YAKIMA THEATRE, YAKIMA, WASH.

Big profits come to the men who do big things. Good pictures attract people to your theatre— Good music brings them back—regularly.

You can always have good music if you have an Estey Organ. You will be independent of labor troubles, for in many theatres the Estey Organ does the work of an entire orchestra. It has no union hours, it is always there. You will save the cost of the organ, times over, in what you save on musician's salaries; and your organ is growing better all the time.

Your organ will be built to fit your theatre, just as the organ in the Capitol Theatre was built to fit that theatre. Its cost depends upon the size, and the way it is built in,—and it doesn't cost as much as you think it will.

We will send an expert to talk with you, wherever you are, whenever you say.

Ask the home office—

THE ESTEY ORGAN COMPANY

Brattleboro, Vermont

You can hear the Estey Pipe Organ at any one of these branches:

Studios in

New York, 11 West 49th Street   Philadelphia. 1701 Walnut Street
Boston, 120 Boylston Street   Los Angeles, 633 South Hill Street

Shortly after the opening of New York's Capitol Theatre, Estey ran a four-page advertising insert in theatrical trade magazines describing its installation in the Manhattan showplace. The last page is reproduced above. This particular ad campaign appeared in the November 1, 1919 issue of Motion Picture News.

THE EXETER STREET THEATER, SITUATED IN THE EXCLUSIVE BACK BAY RESIDENTIAL DISTRICT OF BOSTON. THEY INSTALLED AN ESTEY THEATRE ORGAN TO BETTER INTERPRET THE PICTURES, INCREASED THE SEATING CAPACITY BY 1000, AND ARE SATISFYING CAPACITY CROWDS WITH THE NEW MUSIC.

See Its Success for Yourself

Many of the first-class large theatres of the country depend on the Estey Pipe Organ for all their music —the music that goes with the pictures and the additional music program.

There must be a reason for this new and successful development in the motion picture world.

The Estey Theatre Organ

is unquestionably the best music for picture theatres.

On request we will tell you some theatre near you that has an Estey Organ, so you can see it, hear it and talk with the owner.

One by one, we are telling you of high-class theatres in whose success the Estey Pipe Organ has played a prominent part, but there are hundreds of others.

Without cost to you we will send an expert to look at your theatre, tell you what kind of an organ you could use best, and give you an estimate of the cost.

THE ESTEY ORGAN COMPANY, BRATTLEBORO, VERMONT.

You can hear the Estey Pipe Organ at any of these branches:

Studios in New York, 11 West 49th Street; Philadelphia, 1701 Walnut Street; Boston, 120 Boylston Street; Los Angeles, 633 South Hill Street.

Estey ran a series of full page ads similar to that above in the late teens. This particular one ran in the April 12, 1919 issue of Motion Picture News. The Exeter Street Theatre was formerly a church containing a Hutchings organ.

Lloyd Del Castillo poses at the 3/7 Estey in his theatre organ school. This instrument was moved to WEEI Radio in Boston after the Castillo enterprise closed. In 1983 Mr. Castillo celebrated his 90th birthday.

One of two two-manual Esteys in the Castillo Theatre Organ School, Boston, Massachusetts.

Sept. 20. '14.

Shipped *Sept. 2 '14.*		Motor	*Orgoblo.*	
Cost Card			*Chimes.*	
Pipe Organ No. **1290**	Style	*4-4-1*		
Sold to *G.G. Merrill & C.A. Howe.*	*for.*	*Owl Theatre*		
3050.		*Riverside Cal*	*incl. annual*	

Case, Des. No. *no Case* Finish *wood Birch*	24 sq. ft. @ 4.31	305	102 12
Ext. to lay. Used *Extra for Birch Draps Projector*		4677	3 10
Console *1911* *Detached*		4639	200 48
Pedal *1911*			13 96
Bench			6 37
Front { 50 Pipes *Dull* } 230 sq. ft. @ .66		155	134 50
Finish *Bronze.*		4883	17 47
Action for Chimes. 1/2 of 4389)		4389	5 14
Inside Pipes *Chimes*			439 10
Frame and Sills *Special.*		4667	12 49
Bellows { Reservoir *3-3-1*			19 64
Feeders			—
Bellows Action			—
Crank Shaft and Connections			—
Chests { Pedal *Special*		4668	18 75
Great *4 st. 6'3"*			33 35
Swell *4 st. 6'3" sp.*		4673	36 72
Pneumatic Work and Setting Pipes		4635	25 21
Pneumatics			24 53
Wind Trunks *4-4-1*			4 44
Swell Box *none*			—
Shade Frames *2 Shade Frames, A & C.*			20 20
Swell Action		4637	10 08
Crescendo		4638	14 29
Tubing { Stock		4635	85 59
Labor		4635	39 36
Setting Up		4635	50 86
Extra Stock		4635	21 78
Voicing and Regulating		4958	154 60
Automatic			—
Boxing and Packing		4636	44 71
Packing Expense			23 49

		1617 53
Selling Expense		539 85
Factory Cost		2157 38
Motor and Attachments		116
Freight		269
Installation { Labor		55 75
Expense		66 18
Special Expenses		
Total Cost		2464 31

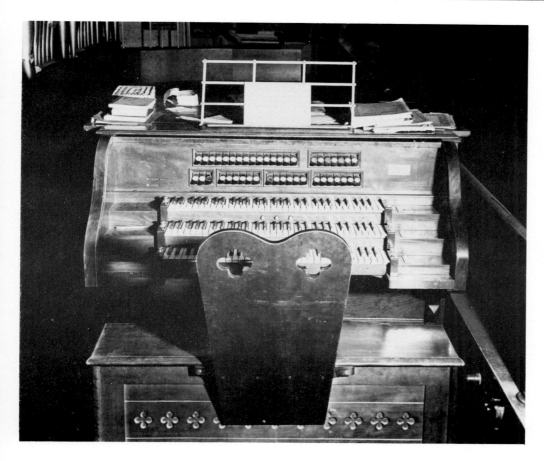

This three-manual tubular pneumatic Estey was originally installed in Seattle's Dream Theatre in 1908. It is shown here at its new home in St. Joseph's Church in Yakima, Washington.

Sectional view of an Estey ventil chest. Note channels C exhaust individual note pneumatics V, one for each pipe. Stop action pneumatic A controls ventil valve B allowing air pressure to enter the chest when the rank is on. Valve E allows chest pressure to escape when the rank is turned off.

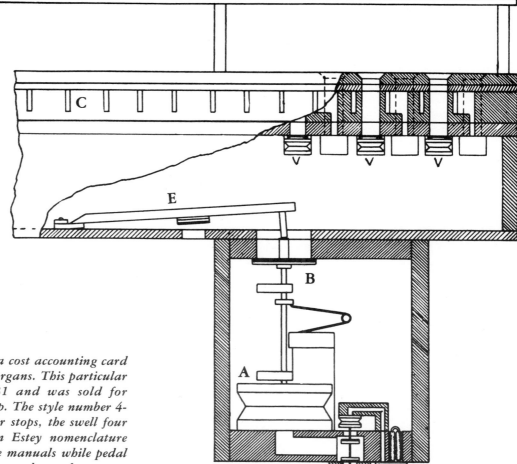

(opposite page) Estey maintained a cost accounting card such as this for each of their pipe organs. This particular organ cost the factory $2,464.31 and was sold for $3,050, certainly a modest markup. The style number 4-4-1 means that the great had four stops, the swell four stops and the pedal one stop. In Estey nomenclature "stop" translates to "rank" on the manuals while pedal stops might be either independent ranks or borrows.

Estey opus 2812 was installed on one of the sound stages at the United Artists Studios in Los Angeles. Note the protective house around the console to shelter it from careless stage hands when not in use. It's too bad that Estey waited so long (1930) to build such an attractive console.

Closeup view of the luminous stop control buttons on a 2/5 Estey theatre organ console.

Above, 2/6 Estey in the Princess Theatre, Bloomington, Indiana. The large clock at the right of the organ grille is an unsual feature for 1927. The 3/32 Estey on the right was installed in Boston's Beacon Theatre in 1916. The organ was quite large for such a small house. Considering the size of the organ, this must have been a deluxe theatre in its day, although one might never guess that by looking at the "plain Jane" architecture.

The Estey factory at Brattleboro, Vermont, looking southwest.

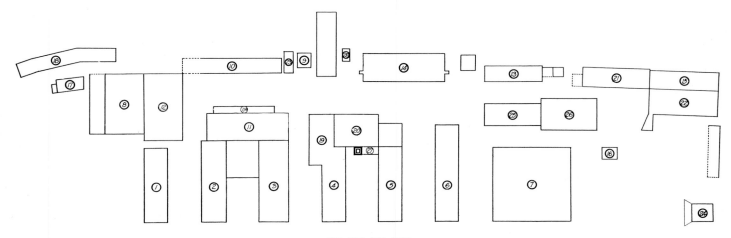

PLAT PLAN

1. Key making, cabinet and case work
2. Cabinet and box shop
3. Mill, planers, molders, gluing and veneering
4. Reed organ parts and assembly
5. Reed organ bellows making and assembly
6. Offices, drafting and production rooms
7. Chest, wood pipe, console, pneumatic and electric action making
8. Veneer and dried lumber storage
9. Electric transformers
10. Lumber storage sheds
11. Sanding, saw filing and belt room
12. Dry kilns
13. Pipe voicing
14. Machine shop, metal pipe making and bronzing
15. Packing and shipping supplies
16. Varnish and oil storage
17. Fire protection
18. Special lumber storage
19. Engine room
20. Boiler room
21. Packing and shipping
22. Packing and shipping
23. Metal casting
24. Garage
25. Erecting room
26. Erecting room
27. Fire pump
28. Water supply pump

The Estey factory looking north. The building on the left (#8 on map) was used for veneer and dried lumber storage, while the structure on its right (#1 on map) was used for key making, cabinet and case work. In the foreground is the lumber yard. This photo was taken prior to 1915.

The Estey factory buildings seen above are numbers 5, 20 and 19. In upper right is a general view of the lumber yard looking from the third floor of building #1. Photo at right shows the machine shop (#14 on map).

Boards on the four walls of the production department allowed the progress of each part of an organ's construction to be monitored.

This photo shows about half of Estey's general offices.

Wood was seasoned in dry kilns. A track extended to the lumber yard where the kiln cars were loaded and the lumber handled only once.

This section of the mill room contained a large self-feeding sanding machine.

Every organ was first "built" on paper in the drafting room.

This special machine cut the mouths and caps of wood pipes, replacing the hand labor of six men working with chisels and drills.

Estey's keyboard department manufactured manuals by the hundreds of thousands.

Reed preparation and voicing room. The voicer even made his own shallots.

Pipe metal casting department.

These four views show various sections of the metal pipe department.

Case work department is seen above and at right.

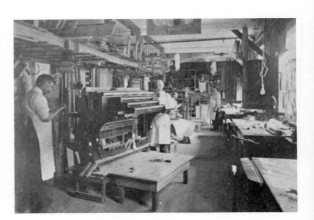

Console department.

Machine shop.

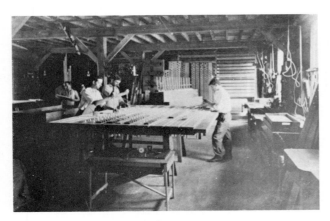

Some Estey horseshoe consoles featured roll tops.

Chest department.

A two-manual Estey with luminous console and player mechanism is set up for testing in a corner of an erecting room. A number of bass pipes have been "Haskelled," thereby shortening them for a low ceiling clearance. The fact that these pipes aren't mitred allows the organ to consume a much smaller floor area.

There were two erecting rooms at the Estey factory. Pictured here are views of each.

ESTEY OPUS LIST

Following is a list of this firm's known theatre-type installations. An alphabetical index appears first, enabling one to locate instruments on a city/state/installation site basis, with a corresponding opus number shown adjoining. This number can be used to find an organ in the accompanying chronological list. Statistics on each organ are shown only in the latter list. Installations in the alphabetical index with opus numbers shown as "unknown" will be found at the end of the chronological list.

CITY/STATE	LOCATION	OPUS
ARIZONA (AZ)		
Phoenix	KTAR Radio	2831
CALIFORNIA (CA)		
Bell	Alcazar Th.	2214
	Maybell Th.	1983
Burbank	KELW Radio	2831
	Walt Disney Studio	2812
Glendale	Glendale Th.	1864
Hollywood	Iris Th.	1925
	United Artists Studio	2812
Inglewood	Seville (Palms) Th.	2195
Long Beach	Hoyt's Th.	1468
	Queen Th.	1925
Los Angeles	KHJ Radio	1699
	Liberty Th.	427
	Mike Gore Th.	unknown
	West Coast Th.	2214
Monterey Park	Monterey Th.	2256
Ontario	J. V. Spaugh	1777
Riverside	Loring Opera House	1665
	Owl (Regent) Th.	1290
San Diego	Dream Th.	1027
	Rudder's Cafe	1125
Whittier	Scenic Th.	1766
	Strand (Roxy) Th.	2181
COLORADO (CO)		
Denver	Isis Th.	776
CONNECTICUT (CT)		
Plainville	Strand Th.	2609
Putnam	Bradley Th.	2681
Rockville	Palace Th.	2680
FLORIDA (FL)		
Miami	Alcazar Hotel	2830
St. Petersburg	WSUN Radio	2830
IDAHO (ID)		
Wallace	Isis (Liberty) Th.	1139
ILLINOIS (IL)		
Chicago	Ashland Th.	2196
	Masonic Temple	2504—2516
Springfield	Gaiety Th.	unknown
INDIANA (IN)		
Bloomington	Princess Th.	2072
Logansport	Colonial Th.	2026
Rochester	Char-Bell Th.	2192
Wabash	Eagles Th.	2060
LOUISIANA (LA)		
Bastrop	F. J. Goodwin	2602
MARYLAND (MD)		
Cumberland	Capitol Th.	2012
MASSACHUSETTS (MA)		
Allston	Allston Th.	1721
Athol	Colonial Th.	2578
Boston	Beacon Th.	1463
	Castillo Studio	2617, 2618, 2712
	Dudley Th.	1525
	Exeter Street Th.	1495
	Modern Th.	2528
	Shawmut Th.	1600
	Star Th.	1789
	WEEI Radio	2618
Fitchburg	Universal Th.	2138
Framingham	Gorman Th.	2318

CITY/STATE	LOCATION	OPUS
MASSACHUSETTS (MA)		
Gardner	Gardner Th.	2317
	Orpheum Th.	2333
Greenfield	Lawler Th.	2686
Haverhill	Strand (Haverhill) Th.	1884
Holyoke	Strand Th.	2578
Jamaica Plain	Hyde Square Th.	1966
Lawrence	Capitol Th.	2729
Malden	Mystic Th.	1936
Methuen	Century Th.	2000
Northampton	Calvin Th.	2222
Roxbury	Criterion Th.	1954
Springfield	Capitol Th.	unknown
Stoughton	Stoughton Th.	2682
Westfield	Strand Th.	2579
MICHIGAN (MI)		
Battle Creek	Post Th.	1788
	Regent Th.	1688
Detroit	WWJ Radio	2909
MINNESOTA (MN)		
Alexandria	State Th.	2360
MISSOURI (MO)		
Cape Girardeau	Columbia Broadcasting Co.	2895
Trenton	Opal Webb Th.	unknown
MONTANA (MT)		
Missoula	Empress	1139
NEBRASKA (NE)		
Omaha	Muse Th.	unknown
NEW HAMPSHIRE (NH)		
Keene	Latchis Th.	2147
NEW JERSEY (NJ)		
Camden	Victor Talking Machine Co.	1850, 2370, 2529
Newark	Bergen Th.	1832
Parsipanny	WCDA Radio	2829
Paterson	Garden Th.	1485
Weehawken	Schuyler Th.	313
NEW YORK (NY)		
Astoria	Paramount Studios	2852
Bronx	Luxor Th.	2219
Brooklyn	Borough Park Th.	1902
	Coliseum Th.	1293
	Shore Road Th.	2138
New York City	American Recording Studio	3037
	Byers Recording Studio	3037
	Capitol Th.	1710, 2651
	Connie's Inn	2800
	Irving Th.	2562
	Mr. MacDougall	2042
	Metropolitan Th.	unknown
	NBC Studios	2853
	Paramount Studios	2833
OREGON (OR)		
Eugene	Rex (Progressive) Th.	1078
Portland	Arcade Th.	844
	Irvington Th.	2277
	Star Th.	unknown
PENNSYLVANIA (PA)		
Allentown	Colonial Th.	1843
	Strand Th.	1594
Bethlehem	Colonial (Kurtz) Th.	1824
	Lorenz Th.	1407

CITY/STATE	LOCATION	OPUS
PENNSYLVANIA (PA)		
Monaca	Olympic Th.	241
New Brighton	Grand Th.	241
TEXAS (TX)		
Austin	Majestic (Paramount) Th.	1378
Mineral Wells	Crazy (Grand) Th.	1863
Texarkana	Majestic Th.	unknown
VERMONT (VT)		
Brattleboro	Latchis Th.	1849
WASHINGTON (WA)		
Bremerton	Dream Th.	1531
North Yakima	Majestic Th.	1154
Seattle	Clemmer Th.	981
	Dream Th.	579

CITY/STATE	LOCATOIN	OPUS
WASHINGTON (WA)		
Seattle	Jewell Th.	578
	KJR Radio	2945
	Savoy Th.	1106
Spokane	Clemmer (Casino) Th.	81
Tacoma	Colonial Th.	unknown
Vancouver	Court Th.	443
AUSTRALIA		
Sydney	Crystal Palace Th.	591
ENGLAND		
London	Cafe Royal	2610
SOUTH AFRICA		
Durban	Prince of Wales Th.	2493

OPUS	LOCATION/CITY/STATE	SIZE	YR	PRICE	BLWR	HP	WP	REMARKS
81	Clemmer (Casino) Th., Spokane, WA	2/8	1903					
241	Estey Store, St. Louis, MO	1/7	1906					58-note roll player; no pedals.
241	Olympic Th., Monaca, PA	1/7	1915					Moved from Estey Store, St. Louis, Missouri.
241	Grand Th., New Brighton, PA	1/7						Moved from Olympic Theatre, Monaca, Pennsylvania.
313	Schuyler Th., Weehawken, NJ	2/8	1906					
427	Liberty Th., Los Angeles, CA	1/7	1907					58-note roll player; no pedals.
443	Court Th., Vancouver, WA	1/7	1907					58-note roll player; no pedals.
578	Jewell Th., Seattle, WA	1/7	1908					58-note roll player; no pedals.
579	Dream Th., Seattle, WA	3/	1908					Tubular pneumatic.
591	Crystal Palace, Sydney, Australia	2/11	1908					
776	Isis Th., Denver, CO	2/15	1910					
844	Arcade Th., Portland, OR	2/8	1910					
981	Clemmer Th., Seattle, WA	3/28	1912					
		4/32	1916					Additions: 4-rank echo and 4-manual console.
1027	Dream Th., San Diego, CA	2/7	1912					
1078	Rex (Progressive) Th., Eugene, OR	2/10	1912					
1106	Savoy Th., Seattle, WA	2/8	1913	$ 2,760.00				Tubular pneumatic.
1125	Rudder's Cafe, San Diego, CA	2/14	1913	$ 3,095.00	A736	2		With roll player.
1139	Empress Th., Missoula, MT	2/13	1913		4663			
1139	Isis (Liberty) Th., Wallace, ID	2/13						Moved from Empress Th., Missoula, Montana.
1154	Majestic Th., North Yakima, WA	2/14	1913		4835			Tubular pneumatic.
		3/	1917		7676			Enlarged and electrified.
1241	Modern Th., Boston, MA	3/38	1914		5320	7½		See opus 2528.
1290	Owl (Regent) Th., Riverside, CA	2/9	1914	$ 3,050.00	5766			
			1923					Enlarged.
1293	Coliseum Th., Brooklyn, NY	2/9	1914	$ 2,700.00				
1378	Majestic (Paramount) Th., Austin, TX	2/10	1915		6455			
1384	Haverhill (Strand) Th., Haverhill, MA	2/13	1915		6451			See opus 1884.
1407	Lorenz Th., Bethlehem, PA	2/12	1915	$ 3,000.00	6619			
1463	Beacon Th., Boston, MA	3/32	1916		7445	7½		
1468	Southern Calif. Music Co., Los Angeles, CA	2/18	1916					With roll player.
1468	Hoyt's Th., Long Beach, CA	2/18	1916					Sold by Southern Calif. Music Co.
1485	Garden Th., Paterson, NJ	2/18	1916		7350			
1495	Exeter Street Th., Boston, MA	3/28	1917		7745	5		Former church building converted to theatre use; case of existing Hutchings organ, opus 139, to be retained.
1525	Dudley Th., Boston, MA	2/17	1917		7877			
1531	Dream Th., Bremerton, WA	2/11	1917		7913			
1594	Strand Th., Allentown, PA	2/13	1917		9608			
1600	Shawmut Th., Boston, MA	3/32	1917		8460	7½		
1634	Estey Studio, Boston, MA	2/	1918					See opus 1954.
1665	Loring Opera House, Riverside, CA	2/16	1918		9120	7½		
1688	Regent Th., Battle Creek, MI	2/15	1918		9230			
			1918		9344			
1699	Estey Studio, Los Angeles, CA	2/16	1920		9408			With roll player.
1699	KHJ Radio, Los Angeles, CA	2/16						Moved from previous location; later enlarged.

OPUS	LOCATION/CITY/STATE	SIZE	YR	PRICE	BLWR	HP	WP	REMARKS
1710	Capitol Th., New York City, NY	4/45	1919	$ 16,000.00	9952 10196	15 15		
		4/46	1923	$ 2,500.00				Additions: vox humana and luminous console; see opus 2651.
1721	Allston Th., Allston, MA	3/18	1919		9787			
			1924		16272			
1766	Scenic Th., Whittier, CA	2/16	1920	$ 9,450.00	10149			
1777	J. V. Spaugh	2/10	1920		10310			
1788	Post Th., Battle Creek, MI	2/14	1920	$ 4,200.00	10689			
1789	Star Th., Boston, MA	2/15	1920	$ 5,000.00	10432			
			1920		10596			
1824	Colonial (Kurtz) Th., Bethlehem, PA	3/25	1921	$ 10,000.00	11373	5	6"	
1832	Bergen Th., Newark, NJ	2/20	1920	$ 8,500.00	10957	2	6"	
			1920		10971	2	6"	
1843	Colonial Th., Allentown, PA	3/25	1920	$ 12,000.00	11305	5	6"	
1849	Latchis Th., Brattleboro, VT	2/12	1920	$ 3,800.00				
			1926		18573			
1850	Victor Talking Machine Co., Camden, NJ	2/12	1921					With roll player; see opus 2370.
1863	Crazy (Grand) Th., Mineral Wells, TX	2/13	1921		11283			
1864	W. C. & Louis Goodno, Pasadena, CA	3/27	1920		11454	5	6"	
1864	Glendale Th., Glendale, CA	3/27						Moved from previous location.
1872	Lyon & Healy Store, Chicago, IL	2/7	1921					"Theatre organ stoplist" according to Estey records.
1884	Strand (Haverhill) Th., Haverhill, MA	3/31	1922					Enlargement of opus 1384.
1902	Borough Park Th., Brooklyn, NY	3/22	1921		12090			
1924	Renaissance Th., New York City, NY	2/14	1921					Order cancelled.
1925	Queen Th., Long Beach, CA	2/10	1921					
1925	Iris Th., Hollywood, CA	2/10						Moved from Queen Th., Long Beach, California.
1936	Mystic Th., Malden, MA	2/13	1921		12494			
			1921		12615			
1954	Criterion Th., Roxbury, MA	3/19	1921		12300			Incorported opus 1634.
1966	Hyde Square Th., Jamaica Plain, MA	2/17	1921		12586			
1983	Maybell Th., Bell, CA	2/10	1922		12753			
2000	Century Th., Methuen, MA	2/14	1922		12863			
2012	Capitol Th., Cumberland, MD	2/11	1922		13052			
2026	Colonial Th., Logansport, IN	2/5	1922		8292			Luminous console.
2042	Mr. MacDougall, New York, NY	2/6	1922		13769			Luminous console.
2060	Eagles Th., Wabash, IN	2/6	1922		13624			Luminous console.
2072	Princess Th., Bloomington, IN	2/5	1923		14037			Luminous console.
		2/6	1927					Additions: one rank.
2138	Shore Road Th., Brooklyn, NY	2/17	1924		15348			Luminous console.
2138	Universal Th., Fitchburg, MA	2/17						Moved from Shore Road Th., Brooklyn, New York.
2147	Latchis Th., Keene, NH	2/23	1923	$ 11,500.00	14893			Luminous console.
2181	Strand (Roxy) Th., Whittier, CA	2/5	1924	$ 7,175.00	15278			Luminous console.
2192	Char-Bell Th., Rochester, IN	2/	1924		15321			Luminous console.
2195	Seville (Palms) Th., Inglewood, CA	2/5	1924	$ 7,500.00	15324			Luminous console.
2196	Ashland Th., Chicago, IL	2/4	1924	$ 4,968.00				Luminous console.
2214	Alcazar Th., Bell, CA	2/10	1925	$ 15.375.00	15876			
2214	West Coast Th., Los Angeles, CA							Located at Vermont & Washington Streets; moved from previous location.
2219	Luxor Th., Bronx, NY	2/	1924	$ 9,000.00				Luminous console.
2222	Calvin Th., Northampton, MA	2/19	1924	$ 8,500.00	15743			Luminous console.
2256	Monterey Th., Monterey Park, CA	2/5	1924	$ 7,450.00	16896			Luminous console.
2277	Irvington Th., Portland, OR	2/10	1924	$ 10,036.00	16344			Luminous console.
2317	Gardner Th., Gardner, MA	2/17	1925	$ 6,650.00	16757			
			1925		17007			
2318	Gorman Th., Framingham, MA	2/17	1925		16756			
2333	Orpheum Th., Gardner, MA	2/17	1925					
2360	State Th., Alexandria, MN	2/4	1926		17142			Luminous console.
2370	Victor Talking Machine Co., Camden, NJ	3/13	1925					Rebuild opus 1850; additions: VDO and luminous console; see opus 2529.
2493	Prince of Wales Th., Durban, South Africa	2/7	1926		18649			Luminous console.
2504	Masonic Temple, Chicago, IL	2/5	1926					Practice organ.
2505	Masonic Temple, Chicago, IL	2/5	1926					Practice organ.
2506	Masonic Temple, Chicago, IL	2/5	1926					Practice organ.
2507	Masonic Temple, Chicago, IL	2/5	1926					Practice organ.
2508	Masonic Temple, Chicago, IL	2/5	1926					Practice organ.
2509	Masonic Temple, Chicago, IL	2/5	1926					Practice organ.
2510	Masonic Temple, Chicago, IL	2/5	1926					Practice organ.
2511	Masonic Temple, Chicago, IL	2/5	1926					Practice organ.
2512	Masonic Temple, Chicago, IL	2/5	1926					Practice organ.
2513	Masonic Temple, Chicago, IL	2/5	1926					Practice organ.
2514	Masonic Temple, Chicago, IL	2/6	1926					Practice organ.
2515	Masonic Temple, Chicago, IL	2/6	1926					Practice organ.
2516	Masonic Temple Auditorium, Chicago, IL	2/8	1926					
2528	Modern Th., Boston, MA	3/38	1926					Rebuild of opus 1241.
2529	Victor Talking Machine Co., Camden, NJ	3/	1926		18937			Rebuild and enlarge opus 2370.

OPUS	LOCATION/CITY/STATE	SIZE	YR	PRICE	BLWR	HP	WP	REMARKS
2562	Irving Th., New York City, NY	2/22	1927					Two luminous consoles.
2578	Strand Th., Holyoke, MA	2/20	1927	$ 8,100.00	19501			
2578	Colonial Th., Athol, MA	2/20						Moved from Strand Th., Holyoke, Mass.
2579	Strand Th., Westfield, MA	2/20	1927	$ 8,100.00				
2602	F. J. Goodwin, Bastrop, LA	2/6	1927		19922			
2609	Strand Th., Plainville, CT	2/7	1927		19911			
2610	Cafe Royal, London, England	2/14	1927		20194	3		With roll player.
2617	Castillo Studio, Boston, MA	2/5	1927					
2618	Castillo Studio, Boston, MA	3/7	1927					
2618	WEEI Radio, Boston, MA	3/7						Moved from Castillo Studio, Boston, Massachusetts.
2651	Capitol Th., New York City, NY	4/	1927		20527			Opus 1710 enlarged plus a new console.
2680	Palace Th., Rockville, CT	2/5	1927	$ 5,500.00				Order cancelled.
2681	Bradley Th., Putnam, CT	2/5	1927	$ 5,500.00	20774			
2682	Stoughton Th., Stoughton, MA	2/5	1927	$ 5,615.00	20783			
2686	Lawler Th., Greenfield, MA	2/6	1928		20761			
2712	Castillo Studio, Boston, MA	2/4	1928					
2729	Capitol Th., Lawrence, MA	2/6	1928		21720			
2800	Connie's Inn, New York City, NY	2/3	1929					First grand Minuette; with 5-note chimes, voiced on 8" wp.
2812	United Artists Studio, Hollywood, CA	3/10	1930		23749	10	10"&12"	
2812	Walt Disney Studio, Burbank, CA	3/10						Moved from United Artists Studio, Hollywood, California.
2829	WCDA Radio, Parsipanny, NJ	2/3	1929					Grand Minuette.
2830	Alcazar Hotel, Miami, FL	2/3	1929					Grand Minutte, with 20-note chimes and 49-note harp.
2830	WSUN Radio, St. Petersburg, FL	2/3						Moved from Alcazar Hotel, Miami, Florida.
2831	KTAR Radio, Phoenix, AZ	2/3	1929					Grand Minuette.
2831	KELW Radio, Burbank, CA	2/3						Moved from KTAR Radio, Phoenix, Arizona.
2832	National Th. Supply Co., St. Louis, MO	2/3	1929					Grand Minuette.
2833	Paramount Studios, New York City, NY	2/3	1929					Grand Minuette.
2852	Paramount Studios, Astoria, NY	2/3	1929	$ 3,032.50	23355			Grand Minuette, with 37-note harp.
2853	NBC Studios, New York City, NY	2/3	1929	$ 2,670.00	23487			Grand Minuette, with tap and repeat action on harp.
2895	Grinnell Bros. Store, Detroit, MI	2/3	1930					Upright Minuette with Clark player.
2895	Columbia Broadcasting Co., Cape Girardeau, MO	2/3		$ 1,750.00				Moved from Grinnell Bros. Store, Detroit, Michigan.
2909	WWJ Radio, Detroit, MI	2/3	1930	$ 1,750.00				Grand Minuette.
2945	KJR Radio, Seattle, WA	2/3	1930		24263			Grand Minuette.
3037	Byers Recording Studio, New York City, NY	2/8	1932		24974			Located at 1780 Broadway.
3037	American Recording Studio, New York City, NY	2/8	1932		24974			Located at 1776 Broadway; probably moved from 1780 Broadway.

CITY/STATE	LOCATION	SIZE	YR	BLWR
CALIFORNIA				
Los Angeles	Mike Gore Th.		1906	
ILLINOIS				
Springfield	Gaiety Th.		1912	
MASSACHUSETTS				
Springfield	Capitol Th.	2/		
MISSOURI				
Trenton	Opal Webb Th.		1915	6511
NEBRASKA				
Omaha	Muse Th.	2/6	1919	
NEW YORK				
New York City	Metropolitan Th.		1908	1472
OREGON				
Portland	Star Th.		1910	
TEXAS				
Texarkana	Majestic Th.		1913	4585
WASHINGTON				
Tacoma	Colonial Th.		1914	5791

FARRAND & VOTEY

The family of William R. Farrand (1854-1930) purchased the Whitney Organ Company during the 1880s while Edwin Scott Votey (1856-1931) was working for the Estey Organ Company.[1] Locating in Detroit, Farrand & Votey's first products were reed organs. Desiring to branch into the pipe organ business, they purchased the firm of Granville Wood and his son William D. Wood in 1890[2] and in 1893 they made the major purchase of the Roosevelt company.[3] Several of the best Roosevelt men also joined the Farrand & Votey firm and they proceeded to build Roosevelt-style organs. One of these was the fourth organ ever installed in an American theatre, an electric action 4/43 in the Pabst Theatre, Milwaukee, Wisconsin in 1895. According to William D. Wood, this organ was only the second in American history to be outfitted with an electric blower.[4]

Farrand & Votey were in business until 1897 when the firm divided into two companies: The Farrand Organ Company made reed organs and the Votey Organ Company made pipe organs. In 1899 the Votey Organ Company merged with the Aeolian Company. Farrand & Votey had been making residence organs for Aeolian since 1893 and Edwin Votey had become a member of the Aeolian Company's board of directors as a result of his inventions and improvements in player piano and player organ technology. In 1901 George Hutchings purchased the Votey Organ Company from Aeolian, forming the Hutchings-Votey Organ Company.[5] This firm lasted until 1908 when the Votey name was dropped and the firm name was shortened to the Hutchings Organ Company.[6] The Votey name surfaced for the last time in the late 1920s when Aeolian tried to branch out of the residence organ market, the name Aeolian-Votey being used for their church and theatre organs.

Edwin S. Votey

William R. Farrand

A. B. FELGEMAKER ORGAN COMPANY

Abraham B. Felgemaker (1836-1905)[1] and Silas L. Derrick established an organ business in Buffalo, New York[2] in 1865.[3] During 1872 the Derrick & Felgemaker firm moved to Erie, Pennsylvania at the instigation of a group of investors there.[4] Sometime after the move the firm name changed to A. B. Felgemaker Organ Company.[5] 1,289 organs were built[6] before the firm went out business voluntarily in 1918,[7] at which time the company assets were acquired by the Tellers Organ Company.[8]

Most of their organs were trackers, although a few electropneumatics were built shortly before the end of production.[9] The company was highly respected in the industry and was the employer of a number of individuals who went on to become owners of their own firms, such as A. E. Kent (Felgemaker factory superintendent 1894-1918),[10] Henry and Ignatius Tellers, W. A. Sommerhof,[11] and M. P. Moller.[12]

This ad was a familiar sight to readers of The Diapason *during the 'teens.*

Several views of the large Felgemaker factory in Erie, Pennsylvania, still standing in 1982.

Workers making electropneumatic chests in the Felgemaker factory. Shortly before the end of production the firm advertised that it was making electropneumatic organs exclusively.

FELGEMAKER OPUS LIST

CITY/STATE	LOCATION	SIZE	OPUS	YR	BLWR	HP	WP	REMARKS
ILLINOIS								
Chicago	Castle Th.	2/7	1218	1915				Electropneumatic; built for Coburn Organ Company.
KENTUCKY								
Lexington	Strand Th.	2/9	1215	1915				Built for Coburn Organ Company.
OHIO								
Steubenville	Rex Th.	2/7	1141	1913	B122	½	3½"	Tracker action.

𝔉𝔯𝔞𝔷𝔢𝔢 𝔒𝔯𝔤𝔞𝔫 ℭ𝔬𝔪𝔭𝔞𝔫𝔶
𝔈𝔳𝔢𝔯𝔢𝔱𝔱, 𝔐𝔞𝔰𝔰.

Leslie H. Frazee (1870-1934)[1] was born in St. John, New Brunswick, and at age 14 went to work for the organ builder in his home town, the F. A. Peters Organ Company. In 1894 Mr. Frazee moved to join Jesse Woodberry in Boston where his first assignment was being in charge of erecting Woodberry organs. By 1901 he was chief voicer and he also developed a successful electro-pneumatic action in collaboration with Edward E. Smallman, plant superintendent.[2]

In 1910 Jesse Woodberry retired and Frazee and Smallman joined Henry D. Kimball to organize the firm of Kimball, Smallman & Frazee.[3] Mr. Kimball had begun his organ career with Hook & Hastings and later was associated with George Hutchings for around thirty years.[4] Mr. Smallman retired in 1915 whereupon the firm name became the Kimball-Frazee Organ Company.[5] Henry Kimball retired due to serious illness in February of 1920 and died later that year at the age of 68.[6] Shortly after

Kimball's death Leslie Frazee's son, H. Norman Frazee, joined his father in the business and the firm name was changed, for the last time, to the Frazee Organ Company.[7]

The firm did not pursue unit theatre organ business until 1927, by which time their entry into the market was too late to result in many sales. It is interesting to note that Norman Frazee's brother Roy was a theatre organist who played at the Keith Memorial Theatre in Boston (on a 3/20 Wurlitzer) and at the Granada in Malden, Massachusetts (on a four-manual Hook & Hastings) and at other Boston area theatres as well.[8]

The quality of workmanship took a decided decline following Leslie Frazee's death in 1934. Also at this time the firm's advertising adopted what has become one of the author's favorite examples of hokey slogans: "Favorably Known for Frazee Tone." Honestly, now, would *you* buy an organ from a firm who advertised that way?

The State Theatre in Milford, Massachusetts featured a 2/5 Frazee unit organ. Equipped with a tibia, diapason, viola, vox humana and tuba, it also had chimes, xylophone, harp and a full complement of traps and effects: snare drum, tambourine, castanets, Chinese block, tom tom, sleigh bells, triangle, horse hooves, surf, birds, train whistle, auto horn, fire gong, steam boat whistle, siren and door bell.[9]

Isn't this little Frazee console cute? The case styling resembles a Wurlitzer although it is even more petite. Installed in the State Theatre, Milford, Massachusetts.

Ads in The Diapason *reflect the firm's changes of name and address. The ad at left appeared in December 1915 and the one on the right was in the September 1920 issue.*

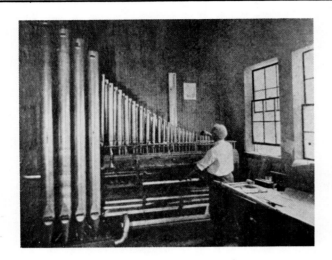
Leslie Frazee is shown at his voicing machine in this ad from the May 1930 Diapason.

FRAZEE OPUS LIST

CITY/STATE	LOCATION	SIZE	YR	BLWR	HP	WP	REMARKS
MARYLAND							
Cumberland	Capitol Th.		1921	525JR			
MASSACHUSETTS							
Boston	Fenway Th.						
	Houghton & Dutton Studio	3/					
	Loew's Orpheum	3/25	1916	D423	7½	6"&15"	Opus 30.
	St. James	3/19	1915	D424	2	6"	Opus 32.
	South End (Loew's New Columbia) Th.	3/	1916				Opus 40.
Lowell	Lowell Th.	4/					
Milford	State Th.	2/5	1927	20652			
Roslindale	Rialto Th.	2/20	19??				
			1928	22329			
			1928	22369			
RHODE ISLAND							
Providence	Forest Theatre Organ School		1927	20316			

GENEVA ORGAN COMPANY

MANUFACTURERS OF HIGH-GRADE
ELECTRO-PNEUMATIC PIPE ORGANS
FOR CHURCH, THEATRE AND HOME

FACTORY AND GENERAL OFFICES
HAMILTON AND RICHARDS STS.

GENEVA, ILL.

The history of the Geneva Organ Company begins in late 1921 with the incorporation of the Smith Unit Organ Company in Chicago. Frederick W. Smith, previously associated with Seeburg in the manufacture of Seeburg-Smith organs, wanted to operate his own firm. He obtained financial backing from Henry Hogans, a building contractor from Oak Park, Illinois and the Smith Unit Organ Company was born.[1][2] The company moved to Geneva, Illinois in early 1924 and continued to advertise in *The Diapason* under the Smith Unit Organ Company name through June 1924. From July through December 1924 the firm's *Diapason* ad copy listed the firm name as Geneva Organ Company, manufacturing both Geneva organs and Smith unit organs. Starting in January 1925 the ads drop the name of Smith altogether, reflecting Smith's departure for California where he again founded his own firm.

During this transition period three nameplates were used for the company's products. At least one of their theatre organs bears the A. F. Johnson nameplate. Some nameplates say Smith-Geneva while others read Geneva Organ Company. After 1926 all the nameplates say Geneva Organ Company. In addition to nameplate changes there were other modifications as well: the troublesome Smith magnets were discarded in favor of the exceptionally reliable Reisner C17s and chest designs were altered dramatically. A pipe shop was set up under the direction of John Wright, who had been in charge of Bennett's pipe shop for the previous thirteen years and who had held a similar position at Estey for a number of years before that. As a result, Geneva made most of their own wooden pipes and many metal pipes, including reeds, and only occasionally purchased pipework from Gottfried or from National Organ Supply.

Another difference between the Geneva and Smith companies was marketing strategy. Smith ads stressed the fact that their products were unit organs. This was fine for theatre business but left most churches cold. Geneva owner Henry Hogans wanted a share of the church market, too, and he got it, selling nearly as many Geneva organs to churches as to theatres.[3] The biggest difference in company philosophy, however, was in giving customers what they wanted, especially in regard to consoles. Smith had one console style. It was aesthetically pleasing and in fact closely resembled a Wurlitzer. However, if one bought a Smith Unit Organ there was no choice: that was the console you got. Geneva, on the other hand, was completely open-minded. Did you need an Art Deco style? No problem! How about English Tudor? Easy! What about a Spanish house with a picket fence? A . . . *what?* See for yourself in the photo on the next page. Geneva certainly carved a niche in the theatre organ hall of fame by producing some of the most unusual consoles ever built.

Attractive three-manual Geneva console in the Fargo Theatre, Geneva, Illinois. This organ was originally installed in the Fargo Theatre, Sycamore, Illinois in 1924.

It's a bird! It's a Spanish house! It's a . . . Geneva console?! Truly one of a kind, this 3/26 in the Varsity Theatre, Evanston, Illinois was the largest Geneva theatre organ ever built, replete with picket fence, even! The organ chambers featured some goodies too, such as a Gottfried post horn, brass trumpet, a floating string division and a set of five Chinese temple blocks. Identity of the organist is not known.

This 2/8 in the Lincoln Theatre, Lincoln, Illinois was apparently built during the transition from Smith-Geneva to Geneva Organ Company. Its nameplate reads "A. F. Johnson, Geneva, Illinois."

One-of-a-kind Art Deco console in the Arcada Theatre, St. Charles, Illinois. Designed by the theatre's owner, Lester J. Norris, the original decorations were executed in silver, black and two shades of red, with a silver heron on each side. The glass diamonds on the front, scrollwork on the lid and builder's nameplate on the backrail were all illuminated from within. This rare photo was provided through the courtesy of John Hill, who for a number of years operated the Century Pipe Organ Company using the old Geneva factory.

Geneva's combination setter mechanism was extremely clever and less expensive to build than the setterboard type systems used by other manufacturers. This example in the Deerpath Theatre is located in the organ relay room and at first glance appears to be an ordinary switchstack. Closer examination reveals that each switch corresponds to a piston on the console and that the switch fingers are movable. By inserting the movable fingers in right or left slots of the switch the respective stops are set to go on or off when the piston is pressed. Leaving a movable finger out altogether sets the stop at neutral so it isn't activated either way on that particular piston.

Geneva console in Spanish Renaissance design, one of two such consoles at the Baker Hotel, St. Charles, Illinois. The music rack is actually a sliding panel concealing a player roll mechanism.

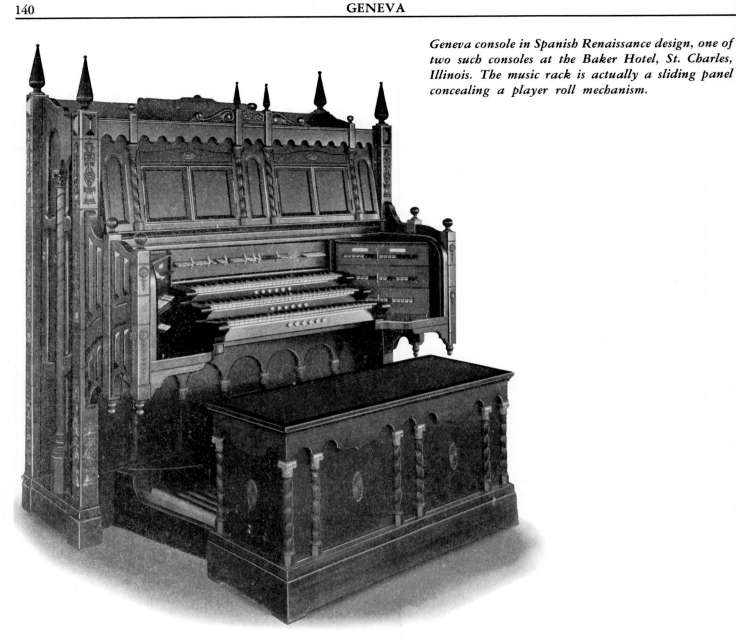

 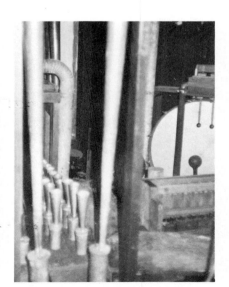 

The 3/10 Geneva console on the left perfectly matches the English Tudor interior of its home, the Deerpath Theatre in Lake Forest, Illinois. To its right are two views of the Deerpath's solo chamber featuring, on the right, an English post horn.

Geneva ad in the January 1925 Diapason. The organ featured was probably in the Tivoli Theatre in Aurora, Illinois, just a few miles from Mooseheart.

This building was occupied by Geneva only a short time before they moved to larger quarters. Half a century later it was occupied by another organ firm, the Century Pipe Organ Company.

Second home of the Geneva Organ Company.

Wood pipe voicing department.

Console at right, perhaps the only four-manual the company ever built, was for the Ambassador (Rockne) Theatre, Chicago and is still in daily service at the Elm Skating Club, Elmhurst, Illinois as of 1983.

Making wood pipes at the Geneva factory.

Making pouchboard style chests at the Geneva factory. Geneva's chests were quite different from the Roosevelt style chests made by their predecessor, the Smith Unit Organ Company.

3/26 GENEVA THEATRE ORGAN
Varsity Theatre, Evanston, Illinois
Installed during 1926, this was the largest theatre organ ever built by Geneva.

PEDAL

32'	Resultant
16'	Diaphone
16'	Tibia Clausa
16'	Bourdon
16'	Contra Violone
16'	Ophicleide
8'	Octave
8'	Tibia Clausa
8'	Concert Flute
8'	Violon Cello
8'	String
8'	Tuba Horn
8'	Saxophone
8'	Clarinet
8'	French Horn
4'	Tibia Clausa
16'	Piano
	Bass Drum
8'	Great to Pedal
8'	Solo to Pedal
8'	String to Pedal
8'	Brass to Pedal

PEDAL 2nd TOUCHES

16'	Diaphone
	Bass Drum
	Cymbal
	Kettle Drum
	Snare Drum
	Crash Cymbal
	Cymbal Tympani
8'	Chimes

BRASS (FLOATING)

16'	Bombarde
8'	Tuba Horn
4'	Tuba Horn
8'	Post Horn
8'	Stentorphone

STRING (FLOATING)

16'	String I
16'	String II
8'	String I
8'	String II
8'	String III
5 1/3'	String II
4'	String I
4'	String II
4'	String IV
2 2/3'	String II
2'	String I
2'	String III

PIZZICATO

16'	Ophicleide
16'	Contra Violone
8'	Solo to Accomp
8'	Brass to Accomp
8'	Solo to Great
8'	Brass to Great

SOSTENUTO

Accomp Sostenuto
Great Sostenuto
Solo Sostenuto

ACCOMPANIMENT

16'	Bourdon
16'	Contra Violone
8'	Diaphonic Diapason
8'	Tibia Clausa
8'	String
8'	Viole De Orchestra
8'	Celeste
8'	Dulciana
8'	Concert Flute
8'	Quintadena
8'	Tuba Sonora
8'	Saxophone
8'	Oboe Horn
8'	Clarinet
8'	French Horn
8'	Vox Humana
4'	Vox Humana
4'	Octave
4'	Tibia Clausa
4'	Flute
4'	Viol
4'	Octave Celeste
2 2/3'	Twelfth
2'	Piccolo
8'	Piano
4'	Piano
8'	Marimba Harp
4'	Marimba Harp
8'	Chrysoglott
16'	Solo to Accomp
8'	Solo to Accomp
4'	Solo to Accomp
8'	String to Accomp
	Snare Drum Soft
	Snare Drum Loud
	Tambourine
	Castanets
	Chinese Block
	Shuffle
	Horse Trot
	Chinese Temple Blocks

ACCOMP 2nd TOUCHES

16'	Ophicleide
8'	Tibia Clausa
8'	Tuba Horn
8'	Trumpet
8'	Saxophone
8'	Clarinet
	Triangle
8'	Solo to Accomp
8'	Brass to Accomp

TREMOLOS

Main
Solo
String
Tibia Clausa
Vox Humana

BALANCE CONTROLS

Main
Solo
Brass
Crescendo

SOLO

16'	Tibia Clausa
16'	Violon Cello
16'	Ophicleide
16'	TC Clarinet
16'	TC Vox Humana
8'	Diaphonic Diapason
8'	Tibia Clausa
8'	Silver Flute
8'	Violon Cello
8'	String I
8'	Viole De Orchestra
8'	Quintadena
8'	Tuba Sonora
8'	Trumpet
8'	Saxophone
8'	Oboe Horn
8'	Clarinet
8'	Orchestral Oboe
8'	Kinura
8'	French Horn
8'	Vox Humana
4'	Vox Humana
4'	Principal
4'	Tibia Clausa
4'	Silver Flute
4'	Violin
4'	Fugaro
4'	Tuba Clarion
2'	Piccolo
8'	Piano
8'	Xylophone
8'	Glockenspiel
8'	Bells
8'	Chimes
4'	Solo to Solo
5 1/3'	Amplex

SOLO 2nd TOUCHES

8'	Diaphonic Diapason
8'	Tuba Sonora
8'	Trumpet
8'	Chimes
8'	Brass to Solo

TOE STUDS

Boat Whistle
Siren
Comedy Whistle
Surf
Klaxon
Fire Gong
Storm
Door Bell
Bird Song
Sforzando
Piano Sustaining
Thunder Crash

PISTONS

Pedal 1-3
Accomp 1-10
Great 1-10
Solo 1-10
General 1-5

GREAT

16'	Diaphone
16'	Tibia Clausa
16'	Bourdon
16'	Contra Violone
16'	Ophicleide
16'	TC Saxophone
16'	TC Clarinet
16'	TC Vox Humana
8'	Diaphonic Diapason
8'	Tibia Clausa
8'	Violon Cello
8'	Viole De Orchestra
8'	Celeste
8'	Concert Flute
8'	Dulciana
8'	Tuba Sonora
8'	Trumpet
8'	Saxophone
8'	Orchestral Oboe
8'	Clarinet
8'	Kinura
8'	French Horn
8'	Vox Humana
4'	Vox Humana
4'	Principal
4'	Tibia Clausa
4'	Concert Flute
4'	Violin
4'	Octave Celeste
4'	Clarion
2 2/3'	Twelfth
2'	Fifteenth
2'	Piccolo
1 3/5'	Tierce
16'	Piano
8'	Piano
4'	Piano
	Mandolin
8'	Marimba Harp
8'	Sleigh Bells
8'	Chrysoglott
8'	Xylophone
8'	Glockenspiel
8'	Bells
8'	Chimes
16'	Great to Great
4'	Great to Great
16'	Solo to Great
8'	Solo to Great
8'	Brass to Great
8'	String to Great
5 1/3'	Amplex

GREAT 2nd TOUCHES

16'	Ophicleide
8'	Tibia Clausa
8'	Clarinet
8'	Glockenspiel
8'	Solo to Great
8'	Brass to Great

GENEVA OPUS LIST

CITY/STATE	LOCATION	SIZE	YR	BLWR	HP	WP	REMARKS
CALIFORNIA							
Los Angeles	Owl Th.	2/5					
Roseville	Roseville	2/8	1926				
San Francisco	Sunset Th.	1925		17946	5		
CONNECTICUT							
Hartford	State Th.	1926		19551			
ILLINOIS							
Aurora	Tivoli Th.	3/12					
Chicago	Ambassador (Rockne) Th.	4/14	1925	17083			
DeKalb	Fargo Th.	2/10					
Des Plaines	Des Plaines Th.	3/	1925	17765	7½		
Evanston	Varsity Th.	3/26	1926	0721B	15	15"	
Hoopeston	Lorraine Th.	3/8	1925	16928	5		
Lake Forest	Deerpath Th.	3/10	1927	21297			
Lincoln	Lincoln Th.	2/8	1924	16304			A. F. Johnson nameplate.
Mooseheart	Mooseheart Auditorium	2/10	1925	17319	5		With player.
Plano	Plano (Gem) Th.	2/3	1925	18211			
Rochelle	Hut Th.						
St. Charles	Arcada Th.	3/16	1927	20401			Enlargement of a 2/10 Marr & Colton, with 3-rank echo.
	Baker Hotel	3/10	1927	20539			Two consoles; with roll player.
Sycamore	Fargo Th.	3/	1924				Later moved to Fargo Theatre, Geneva, Illinois.
INDIANA							
Gary	Roosevelt Th.	1926		19523			
Indianapolis	Irvington School of Music	1926		19447			
	Ritz Th.	2/5	1925	19543	3		
IOWA							
Bloomfield	Iowa Th.	1925		18248	½		
Fairfield	Orpheum Th.	1925		17904	3		
Fort Dodge	Weiss Th.	2/	1924				
Webster City	Isis Th.	2/	1924				
	New Isis Th.	1927		20287			
MICHIGAN							
Hobart	Strand Th.	1928		21696			
MINNEAPOLIS							
Duluth	Orpheum Th.	2/8	1925	18513	3		Smith-Geneva nameplate.
Luverne	Palace Th.	2/5	1925	17942	3		Smith-Geneva nameplate.
Minneapolis	El Lago Th.	2/6					
MISSISSIPPI							
Aberdeen	Temple Th.						
MISSOURI							
Kansas City	Mrs. Madalyn Akkers residence	2/	1927	19863			Moved in 1930 to Beverly Hills Hotel, Beverly Hills, Calif.
NORTH CAROLINA							
Henderson	Stevenson Th.	1927		19863			
High Point	Broadhurst Th.	2/8	1925	17654			
OREGON							
Cottage Grove	Arcade Th.	1927		20298			
PENNSYLVANIA							
Somerset	Park Th.	1926		19310			
Vandergrift	Indiana Th.	1928		21704			
SOUTH CAROLINA							
Rock Hill	Carolina Th.	2/					
TEXAS							
Dallas	Herber Bros. & Wolf	1926		18645			A theatrical supply firm.
Houston	Cameo Th.	1925		17909	3		
Terrell	Lyric Th.	1926		19024			
WASHINGTON							
Renton	Renton-Hall Th.	2/4	1925	16847			Smith-Geneva nameplate.
WISCONSIN							
Eau Claire	New Wisconsin Th.	2/8	1926				

In the early twentieth century Gottfried was America's largest organ supply house, building pipes, chests, consoles and other supplies for dozens of builders who were too busy or too small to make their own. See the section on trade suppliers in *Encyclopedia of the American Theatre Organ*, Volume II, for pictures and advertising concerning this branch of the Gottfried business. Gottfried was the only major firm in American organ building history which was both a parts supplier and a builder of complete organs under its own nameplate. This duality created some animosity in some builders who felt a sense of unfair competition. Sensing the problem, Gottfried stressed only their role as parts suppliers in advertising during the 1920s and mentioned complete organs only after the onset of the Depression.

Anton Gottfried was born in Neulussheim, Germany in 1862.[4] As a younster he received schooling and practical training from his uncle, a tinsmith.[5] As a boy of 16 he built an organ from scratch, including the pipes, and went on to apprenticeship in the shop of organ builder August Laukhuff in Weikersheim.[6] In 1885 he joined the staff of organ builder E. F. Walcker & Co. of Ludwigsburg and in 1888 emigrated to New York where he joined the Hilborne Roosevelt company,[7] first at their New York factory and later at their Philadelphia branch. Yearning to operate his own business, he rented space over a blacksmith shop in Philadelphia in 1890 and began making organ pipes. He hired two young apprentices: Fred Schillinger of Erie, Pennsylvania and Harry Auch of Philadelphia, who were to remain with him for over fifty years.[8]

In 1892 Gottfried entered into a partnership with Henry Kugel[9] and in 1894 received an invitation from A. B. Felgemaker to move to his factory in Erie, Pennsylvania. Gottfried's growing business soon crowded him out of space on the third floor of the Felgemaker factory and he expanded into an old match factory building. Eventually in 1904 he built a three-story building at 19th and Myrtle Streets in Erie[10] which the company would occupy for the next 46 years. At first the firm built only metal pipes but wooden pipes were eventually added to the line.

Reed pipe production began in 1907 and it is for these that the name Gottfried is principally remembered today. Anton Gottfried pioneered the use of the goosebill shallot in reed construction for high pressure theatre organ use and invented or improved a number of stops including the English post horn, French trumpet and krumet horn. In the flue pipe department he invented a variety of reedless oboes and saxophones whose pipes were not circular in cross section but which had flat fronts similar to the letter D.[11]

The quality of Gottfried's pipework was excellent and his firm continued to prosper, much to the consternation of other commercial pipe makers such as Hedges, White, Pierce, Meyer, Gutfleisch and Schopp. These other pipe makers, concerned that Gottfried was getting most of the trade's business, held a meeting with him to discuss what could be done. In an early example of price fixing, Gottfried agreed to charge more for his pipes than did the other suppliers to help them get a better share of the market![12]

After adding wooden and reed pipes to the line, Gottfried branched into the manufacture of other organ parts as well, soon becoming America's largest organ supply house. The firm even had a European representative: International Organ Supply Company of Rotterdam, Holland.[13] Continued success brought the need for more factory space and in 1921 a building was purchased at 25th and Ash streets. At the peak year of production, 1928, 55 people were employed in this building making metal pipes while another 45 employees worked at the old Myrtle Street building.[14] Key personnel at that time were Fred Schillinger, foreman of the metal pipe department; Charles Berlis, head flue voicer; and C. P. Gerrard, head reed voicer. Chester A. Raymond was in charge of the relay and switchboard department and D. D. Symmes was factory superintendent and also in charge of construction of complete organs.[15]

The first complete Gottfried organ was sold around 1916. The total number sold is unknown but the last was built for the Twelfth Street Evangelical United Brethren

Church in Detroit in 1946. The author's estimate is that around 170 were built of which 28 are known to have had theatre destinations. The original factory specification of one theatre instrument is reproduced below:

THE A. GOTTFRIED COMPANY

PIPE ORGANS

ERIE, PA.

Specification   Page ___1.___

No. ___137___   ___October 29,___ ___192 7.___

BROWN & SONS   —   PHILADELPHIA, PA.

___Three___ manuals, compass CC to C ___61___ notes

Pedals, compass CCC to G ___32___ notes

Electro-pneumatic action throughout, with direct current generator.

Console ___to be of the Circular Type___ manual keyboards movable and hinged for convenient access to contacts. Pedals A. G. O. pattern, concave and radiating. Speaking stops and couplers operated by stop keys.

Combinations adjustable at console, visibly affecting the registers, operated by pistons underneath their manuals, pedal combinations by toe pistons.

Pitch ___A -440___

A suitable electric blower of ample capacity to be furnished with the organ.

Adequate foundation or enclosure for organ, electric connections (including remote control starter, if required) and wind ducts from blower to organ, to be supplied and installed by the purchaser.

The purchaser to prepare the space or spaces for the reception of the organ in accordance with plans to be submitted by the organ builder, including the "sound proof" enclosures forming the expression chambers, cutting necessary holes through floors, ceilings and partitions, and provision and installation of conduit for organ cables if required by the local authorities, and necessary electric lights in organ and blower room.

No case or screen is embraced in this contract, except the console case.

This specification being witnessed by initials of parties interested in the same.

Specification

No. ___137.___

PEDAL ORGAN

1. Bourdon	16'	
2. Contra Violin	16'	
3. Ophicleide	16'	
4. Tuba	8'	
5. Open Diapason	8'	
6. Cello	8'	2 ranks
7. Tibia Clausa	8'	
8. French Trumpet	8'	
9. Octave	4'	
10. Flute	4'	
11. Bass Drum		
12. Cymbal		

13. Accomp. to Pedal
14. Orchestra to Pedal
15. Solo to Pedal

SECOND TOUCH

16. Bass Drum	
17. Tympani	
18. Cymbal	
19. Crash Cymbal	
20. Triangle	
21. Chimes	
22. Tuba	8'
23. Open Diapason	8'
24. Tuba	16'

ACCOMPANIMENT ORGAN

25. Contra Violin	16'	
26. Vox Humana T.C.	16'	
27. Diaphonic Diapason	8'	
28. Tibia Clausa	8'	
29. Concert Flute	8'	
30. Viola	8'	
31. Violin	8'	
32. Violin Celeste	8'	
33. Tuba Harmonic	8'	
34. French Trumpet	8'	
35. Vox Humana	8'	
36. Tibia Clausa	4'	
37. Flute	4'	
38. Violin	4'	
39. Violin Celeste	4'	
40. Piccolo	2'	
41. Harp		49 notes
42. Xylophone		37 notes

43. Glockenspiel		37 notes
44. Snare Drum Roll		
45. Snare Drum Tap		
46. Castinets		
47. Tambourine		
48. Chinese Block		
49. Tom Tom		

SECOND TOUCH

50. Trumpet	8'
51. Open Diapason	8'
52. Tibia Clausa	8'
53. Violin	8'
54. Solo Piccolo	4'
55. Snare Drum Tap	
56. Birds (2)	

ORCHESTRAL ORGAN

57. Contra Violin	16'	
58. Bourdon	16'	
59. Diaphonic Diapason	8'	
60. Tibia Clausa	8'	
61. Concert Flute	8'	
62. Viola	8'	
63. Violin	8'	
64. Violin Celeste	8'	
65. French Trumpet	8'	
66. Tuba	8'	
67. Kinura	8'	
68. Clarinet	8'	
69. Vox Humana	8'	
70. Orchestral Oboe	8'	synthetic
71. Nazard	5-1/3'	
72. Violin	4'	
73. Violin Celeste	4'	
74. Viola	4'	
75. Principal	4'	
76. Tibia	4'	
77. Flute	4'	
78. Clarion	4'	
79. French Trumpet	4'	
80. Nazard	2-2/3'	
81. Piccolo	2'	
82. Violin	2'	
83. Tierce	1-3/5'	
84. Orchestral Bells		37 notes
85. Glockenspiel		37 notes
86. Xylophone		37 notes
87. Marimba Harp		49 notes
88. Snare Drum Roll		

89. Solo to Orchestral 8'
90. Solo to Orchestral 4'

SECOND TOUCH

91. Tuba	8'
92. French Trumpet	8'
93. Tibia Clausa	8'
94. Trombone	16'

SOLO ORGAN

95. Tuba	16'	
96. Bourdon	16'	
97. Double Bass Violine	16'	
98. Tibia Clausa T.C.	16'	
99. Tibia Clausa	8'	
100. Open Phonon	8'	
101. Concert Flute	8'	
102. Viola	8'	
103. Violin	8'	
104. Violin Celeste	8'	
105. Tuba	8'	
106. French Trumpet	8'	
107. Clarinet	8'	
108. Kinura	8'	
109. Vox Humana	8'	
110. Oboe	8'	synthetic
111. Saxaphone	8'	"
112. Bassoon	8'	"
113. Nazard	5-1/3'	
114. Clarion	4'	
115. Trumpet	4'	
116. Tibia Clausa	4'	
117. Flute	4'	
118. Vox Humana	4'	
119. Viola	4'	
120. Violin	4'	
121. Celeste	4'	
122. Nazard	2-2/3'	
123. String Nazard	2-2/3'	
124. Piccolo	2'	
125. Viola	2'	
126. Violin	2'	
127. Tierce	1-3/5'	
128. Marimba Harp		49 notes
129. Glockenspiel		37 notes
130. Xylophone		37 notes
131. Orchestral Bells		37 notes
132. Chimes		20 notes

TREMOLOS

Left Main Tremulant
Right Main Tremulant
Vox Tremulant

ADJUSTABLE COMBINATIONS

Six (6) pistons operating Accompaniment and Pedal Stops
Six (6) pistons operating Orchestral and Pedal Stops
Six (6) pistons operating Solo and Pedal Stops
Three (3) Cancel pistons effecting respective manuals
Universal Cancel Pistons effecting entire organ.

PISTONS

Trap Toe Pistons
Triangle, Two Birds, Sleigh Bells, Tympani, Crash Cymbal and
Bass Drum.

ACCESSORIES

Two Balanced Swell Pedals
One Balanced Crescendo Pedal
Crescendo Signal Light
Lights over Stop Registers

BLOWER APPARATUS

An electric Blower of sufficient power and capacity to furnish
ample and perfectly steady wind.

An electric Generator to furnish current suitable for the
action.

GENERAL

The console for the organ to be of the Special Gottfried
style, having a circular front. Wood work for the case to
be of mahogany highly finished.

ANALYSIS

16'	Bass Flute #1 2¾x9¾	97 pipes	Vertical Grain Spruce
16'	Contra Violin 4c 46 6½c	97 pipes	Zinc and 85% Tin
16'	Tuba 4c. 8¼	85 pipes	Brass, Zinc, Plain or Hoyt Metal
8'	Phonon (Open) 4c. 40	73 pipes	Zinc, Plain or Hoyt Metal
8'	Tibia Clausa #1 6x7	73 pipes	Vertical Grain Spruce
8'	Violin	85 pipes	Zinc and 85% Tin
8'	French Trumpet	73 pipes	Zinc and Hoyt Metal
8'	Violin Celeste 4c.71	73 pipes	Zinc and Hoyt Metal
8'	Vox Humana	73 pipes	Brass, Block and Hoyt Metal
8'	Kinura	61 pipes	Brass, Block and Hoyt Metal
8'	Clarinet	61 pipes	Brass, Block and Hoyt Metal

Chimes Class b Deagan	20 Bells
Harp	49 Bars single and repeating
Xylophone Deagan # 2237	37 Bars
Glockenspiel	37 Bells single and repeating
Bass Drum	
Castinets	
Cymbal	
Crash Cymbal	
Triangle	
Snare Drum	
Tambourine	
Chinese Block	
Tom Tom	
Bird Whistle (2)	
Tympani	
Sleigh Bells	

During the 1920s the firm didn't advertise their complete organs but relied instead on representatives. At one time there were ten such local salespersons and one of these was Arthur H. Bewell[17] who nearly sold a 5/179 to the city of Santa Barbara, California. This horseshoe console behemoth was to have been installed outdoors and would have required 16 organ chambers![18] Anton Gottfried himself sold some church instruments. On one trip he made to sell a church organ the pastor was absent on Sunday so Mr. Gottfried, who had once studied to become a minister, preached the morning sermon![19]

Gottfried organs were not inexpensive. In 1935 several firms including Gottfried were bidding for a small practice organ for Ball State University in Muncie, Indiana. The prices quoted by each firm for the same instrument are most interesting:

Pilcher	$2550.00
Gottfried	2280.00
Kimball	2180.00
Wurlitzer	1850.00
Kilgen	1800.00
Moller	1677.50
Wicks	1350.00

Several firms were begun in Erie by former Gottfried employees, just as Gottfried himself had founded his own firm after working for someone else. Henry Kugel, who had joined Gottfried in partnership in 1892, left in 1911 to pursue non-organ related businesses but later decided to enter organ building again and founded National Organ Supply Company in 1920 and Organ Supply Corporation in 1924.[21] Ed Wambsgans, Willie Krebs and Steve Roth left around 1921 to form the Erie Reed Pipe Company and in 1926 Val Durst and Ignace Boegle left to form Durst, Boegle & Co.[22]

Gottfried continued in business until 1950 when, at the age of 88, he sold his firm to the Standaart Organ Company of Suffolk, Virginia. Mr. Standaart's business ethics were not of the highest calibre and this firm was very short lived. Henry Gottfried (1903-   ), son of Anton Gottfried and treasurer of the firm for many years, moved to Florida where he still operates an organ maintenance business in Jacksonville in 1983.[23]

Console of the 4/15 Gottfried in the Carman Theatre, Philadelphia. The organ had two three-manual relays, one for each chamber; the fourth manual, playing percussion stops only, needed no relay.

Two-manual double bolster Gottfried installed in Cleveland's WHK radio studios.

The 3/11 Gottfried in the Brownson Theatre, Philadelphia, had an unorthodox stop arrangement: pedal stops were in the upper left row, followed by the solo stops, and orchestral stops were in the lower left row, followed by the accompaniment stops.

The 3/11 Gottfried console in the Villard Theatre, Villa Park, Illinois was installed in the unusual location of a box below one of the organ grilles. This 1927 theatre is a particularly interesting example of early Art Deco influences.

This page from a 1921 Gottfried catalog illustrates an early model piano console.

Gottfried Organs

A REMARKABLE HISTORY

About fifty-eight years ago a master organ builder of Germany was asked to inspect and pass upon a pipe organ consisting of four stops. Every part of the organ was made by its builder. The pipes were worked out from the raw materials, likewise the chests, and all other actions. After thorough inspection, the master builder pronounced the organ a perfect instrument, superior to many organs he had inspected.

The surprise of the master builder was indescribable, when, after having made the inspection, he learned that the builder of this organ was a sixteen-year-old boy. This boy was Anton Gottfried. From that date Mr. Gottfried's genius in the world of organ tone has been undisputed.

Very early in his career as organ builder, Mr. Gottfried recognized that the future of pipe organ development lay mainly in the development of the tone of the organ pipes. Equipped with a rare genius and an infinite capacity for hard work, Mr. Gottfried set about exploring the field of organ tone. For almost three-score years he applied himself to the task of producing better quality of organ tone. The most marvelous results rewarded his efforts; so that the name of "GOTTFRIED" today stands a synonym for beauty and grandeur of organ tone.

While systematically improving the quality of every known organ stop, and inventing many others with new and wonderful tone qualities, Mr. Gottfried helped to improve the action of the organ. He surrounded himself with experts in every field of organ construction and thus developed the modern Gottfried Organ.

The same painstaking methods which were employed to develop the fine beauties of tone color, were also applied to the action of the organ. No detail was too minute to receive thorough consideration. And so the remarkable thoroughness and beauty of tone has a worthy and fitting counterpart in the action of the Gottfried Organ. IT IS THE LAST WORD IN RELIABILITY AND EXCELLENCY OF MECHANICAL CONSTRUCTION; AND ITS *"Gottfried Tone*—THE SOUL OF THE ORGAN"—IS TRUE ART.

THE A. GOTTFRIED COMPANY
ESTABLISHED 1890

MID-WEST FACTORY BRANCH
2033 BAYER AVENUE
FT. WAYNE, IND.

FACTORIES AND OFFICE
ERIE — PENNA.

Out of deference to their organ building clients, Gottfried didn't advertise the fact that they built complete organs until after the onset of the Depression. This ad appeared in the October 1936 Diapason.

The legend "A. Gottfried Company Organ Supplies" is still faintly visible on the side of the original Gottfried factory at 19th and Myrtle Streets in 1982. The first floor housed Anton Gottfried's voicing room (across the hall from the office) and the shipping department. The second floor was the assembly area and the third floor was the mill room. Pipe metal casting was done in the basement before the pipe shop was moved to the 25th and Ash Street building in 1921. The building had no elevator; large consoles and chests made on the second floor were lowered to the ground via block and tackle.[2]

Anton Gottfried (1862-1954)[3] at work in the first floor voicing room of his Erie, Pennsylvania factory.

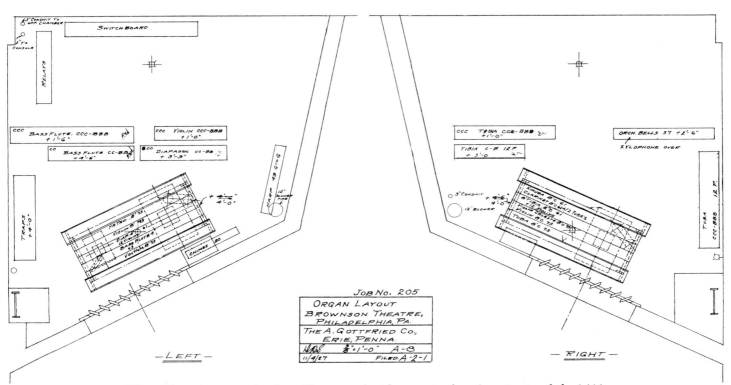

These blueprint reproductions illustrate the placement of various parts of the 3/11 Gottfried whose console is shown on page 148. Some of the larger parts probably came through swell shade openings during the organ's installation since they wouldn't readily fit through the trap doors seen on the extreme left and right.

GOTTFRIED OPUS LIST

CITY/STATE	LOCATION	SIZE	YR	BLWR	HP	WP	REMARKS
ILLINOIS							
Chicago	Alvin Th.		1923	14620			
	Avon Th.						
	Famous Th.		1926	18744			
	Hub Th.		1924	15742			
	Karlov Th.	3/	1928	21483			
				21540			
	Oakley Th.		1927	20222			
	Vision Th.	2/	1925	18099			
Lombard	Lombard (DuPage) Th.	3/10	1928	21536			
Park Ridge	Park Ridge Th.		1924	16436			
Villa Park	Villard Th.	3/11	1927	21318			Opus 203.
MARYLAND							
Baltimore	Hampden Th.		1926	19276			
NEW JERSEY							
Newark	Broadway Th.	4/					Opus 209.
Oaklyn	Oaklyn (Ritz) Th.	2/	1927	P443B	5		
NEW YORK							
New York City	East Side Beauty Th.		1921	12490			Located at 235 Avenue A.
OHIO							
Cleveland	WHK Radio	2/					
Conneaut	State Th.	2/	1925	N813B	3	10″	
PENNSYLVANIA							
Allentown	New Pergola Th.	3/	1926	19693			
				19719			
Ambler	Ambler Th.	3/9	1928	22577			
Brookline	Brookline (Boulevard) Th.	2/6	1928	21902			
Coropolis	Coropolis Th.	2/					
Erie	Aris Th.	2/	1921	11987			
McKeesport	Capitol Th.						
Philadelphia	Apex (Joy) Th.		1928	22418			Located at 51st & Haverford.
	Brownson (Bird) Th.	3/11	1928				Opus 205; cost $ 15,000.
	Carman Th.	4/15	1927	P722B	15	15″	
	Clearfield Th.	2/					
	Hamilton Th.		1923	L618	2	10″	
	Ontario Th.	2/	1927	P652B	5	10″	
	Walton Th.		1923	L554	3	10″	
Pittsburgh	New Kenyon Th.	4/	1927	20877			

Joseph Gratian arrived in Quincy, Illinois from his native England at age 27 in 1857 and moved to Alton, Illinois soon thereafter. He built a modest number of high quality tracker organs until his death in 1897 when his son John W. Gratian took over the business. "Will" Gratian had little or no business ability and also had trouble developing a satisfactory electropneumatic action.[1] The firm bought some components and even complete organs from Wicks.[2]

Gratian's son, Warren, joined him in business for a time[3] and he and his father had severe disagreements at the beginning of the Depression of the 1930s. The company went bankrupt and Warren, in apparent rage, destroyed most of the firm's records. He then worked with several firms including Austin, Estey and Midmer-Losh before returning to Bunker Hill, Illinois around 1938 to re-establish a service business. He later moved to Kenney, Illinois and finally retired from the organ business in 1979.[3][4]

JOHN W. GRATIAN is an experienced organ craftsman, an accomplished musician, and an organist of merit. He has spent several years in Europe, which were devoted to the study of the organs of the most notable builders.

The rare tone quality of the Gratian Organ is due to his skill and ability in voicing.

WARREN BURKE GRATIAN, grandson of the founder, has taken up the family calling and contributes to the business fresh energy, enthusiasm, and impetus.

Much of the mechanical perfection of the modern Gratian Organ is due to his genius for invention and is the result of his untiring interest in the study of electricity, in its direct relation to organ building.

It is unfortunate that the quality of Gratian organs didn't measure up to the promises of their elaborate catalog, a page of which is reproduced here. Knowing that they frequently used Wicks direct electric chests since their own were troublesome, the catalog's statement about electricity's "direct relation to organ building" is particularly amusing.

The Gratian Organ Builders

BUILDERS OF HIGH GRADE INSTRUMENTS
AT MODERATE PRICES

Sales Offices:
Illinois Merchants Bank Bldg.
Chicago, Illinois

Main Office & Factory:
Bunker Hill, Illinois

This ad appeared in an unidentified publication during the 1920s.

The Gratian Organ Company

ALTON, ILL., U. S. A.

Dear Mr. Gratian:

I am writing these lines to express to you my great delight and appreciation of playing one of your master organs at the Alton Hippodrome.

Your work as organ builder is of the highest type and the voicing of the pipes is most excellent.

I sincerely hope that others will appreciate your exquisite work as I do.

Yours for success and prosperity,

RENÉ L. BECKER.

Gratian ad in the July 1916 Diapason.

GRATIAN OPUS LIST

CITY/STATE	LOCATION	SIZE	YR	REMARKS
ILLINOIS				
Alton	Hippodrome Th.	2/28	1916	Spencer blower #6813.
	Princess Th.	2/4	1927	Wicks opus 781.
Gillespie	Colonial Th.	2/14	1922	

GRIFFITH-BEACH COMPANY

Earl Beach had worked with Hope-Jones at his factory in Elmira, New York.[1] In the early 1920s Beach formed a partnership with the Griffith Piano Company of Newark, New Jersey and sold a modest number of organs to churches, theatres and schools under the Griffith-Beach nameplate. The theatre organs were high pressure unified instruments and were undoubtedly competitive with Wurlitzers of the day. After all, they shared the same lineage! Dr. Alfred Ehrhardt told the author that Griffith-Beach instruments had a sweet sound and that they compared favorably with other good theatre organs of the 1920s.[2] Beach apparently used many supply house parts but in at least one example, the Newark Mosque, the console was of his own construction and of high quality.[3]

One Griffith-Beach instrument, the three-manual in the Montauk Theatre in Passaic, New Jersey, had an interesting feature which foreshadowed the computer age. Today it is not uncommon for combination actions to have multiple memories which allow several organists to play the same organ and have instant access to their own piston settings. The Montauk organ had a similar feature in 1923! There were two complete and separate setterboards in a room behind the console; the regular organist used one and the relief organist used the other. A switch at the console controlled which of the "memories"—that is, which setterboard—would be controlled by the pistons.[4]

In the 1930s or '40s Beach developed an electric chime action which was moderately successful. The author had the opportunity to meet Mr. Beach around 1970 and now wishes that the clock could be turned back so an in-depth interview could be conducted!

Griffith-Beach console formerly in the Newark Mosque.

GRIFFITH-BEACH OPUS LIST

CITY/STATE	LOCATION	SIZE	YR	BLWR	HP	WP	REMARKS
NEW JERSEY							
Elizabeth	Branford Th.		1922	K303	5	8"&15"	
	Masonic Temple	3/					
	Regent Th.	3/17	1923				With echo and Steinway grand whose volume was controlled by a separate swell shoe.
Newark	Shrine Auditorium (Mosque Th.)	4/16	1925				
Newton	Newton Th.		1924	M136B	3	12"	
Passaic	Montauk Th.	3/	1923	L551	7½	15"	
			1923	L552	7½	15"	
Paterson	Regent Th.	3/	1923				With echo.
	Rivoli Th.		1925	M1125B	3	12"	
Ridgewood	Ridgewood Opera House	2/	1923				
West Hoboken	Roosevelt Th.	3/	1921	J172	7½	15"	With echo.

THE HALL ORGAN COMPANY

BUILDERS OF   PIPE ORGANS
WEST HAVEN, CONNECTICUT

Harry Hall, a native of England, emigrated to the United States in the 1890s and was first employed by the Hook & Hastings Company.[1] In 1897 he established the business of H. Hall & Company at New Haven, Connecticut.[2] In 1889 George A. North joined the firm as general manager. North was born in England in 1869 and received his early training there, coming to the United States in 1892 to join Hook & Hastings. In 1912 the Hall Organ Company was incorporated and North was elected president and treasurer. This same year the company moved into a new factory building designed by North in West Haven, Connecticut. Two of North's friends from the Hook & Hastings days eventually joined the Hall firm: Frederick Campkin as vice president and manager of the console department and C. B. Floyd as vice president and sales manager. George North's elder son Clifford also worked for the company.[3]

In June 1925 Hall and Welte entered into an agreement wherein some of their corporate stock was exchanged,[4] the apparent objective being that Hall would obtain rights to Welte's player device and that Welte would have access to Hall's manufacturing capabilities. Hall was a

Erecting room at the Hall factory.

Below, plant as it appeared in 1931.

major factor in the church organ business at that time and wanted to enter the residence market aggressively but needed a player mechanism to do so.[5] The Hall-Welte association was short lived, being dissolved by mutal consent in June 1927.[6] Perhaps one reason the association didn't last was that Hall's quality standards were considerably below what Welte's came to be after R. P. Elliot joined Welte in 1925. Despite Hall's standing as one of the major builders, the company had a reputation for some of the poorest quality in the industry. For example, nails would be found in Hall's construction where most builders would use screws, such as the front caps on wood pipes.

Hall never really went after the theatre business. The two dozen or so organs they installed in theatres represented only a fraction of their total production and there is no reason to believe that these instruments differed significantly from their church organs. A glance at their opus list reveals that most of the theatre instruments were sold to locations near the factory, no doubt to non-discriminating clients for whom low price was the basic selling point.

Harry Hall left his firm in 1930 to form the Harry Hall Organ Company in Hamden, Connecticut. He died in 1945 at the age of 75.[7] The Hall Organ Company also went out of business in 1945 and sold its remaining inventory of parts to Moller.[8]

Hall ad in the February 1920 Diapason.

HALL OPUS LIST

CITY/STATE	LOCATION	SIZE	YR	BLWR	HP	WP	REMARKS
CONNECTICUT							
Ansonia	Capitol Th.	3/	1920	11463	3	5"	
Bridgeport	Majestic Th.	3/					
	Poli's Palace Th.	3/48	1921				
	Poli's Th.	3/	1922	13347			
				13815			
Bristol	Princess Th.	3/	1925	17861			
Hartford	Palace Th.	3/	1924	16540			
Middletown	Middlesex Th.	2/4	1927	21312			
	S & S (Capitol) Th.	2/	1926	18667			
	Strand (Palace) Th.	3/					
New Haven	Bijou Th.	3/33					
	Globe Th.	2/	1914	5954			
	Pequot Th.	3/	1924	15409			
Waterbury	Music Hall	2/					Tracker action.
	Poli's Palace (Fox Palace) Th. ...3/		1921	12787	7½		
	Strand Th.	3/	1925	17866			
West Haven	Rivoli Th.	2/4	1929				
	State Th.		1926	19435			
Westport	Fine Arts Th.	2/	1927	20326			
MASSACHUSETTS							
Fall River	Rialto Th.	3/	1920	10776			
Worcester	Loew's Poli Palace Th.	3/	1926	19207			
			1927	20667			
	Poli's Elm Street Th.	3/					
MONTANA							
Anaconda	Bluebeard Th.	2/10	1916	7173			
NEW JERSEY							
Butler	New Fabian Th.		1927	20770			
NEW YORK							
New York City	Kramer show room		1917	7812	½		
	Rio Th.	3/16	1920	10677	3	5"	Moved in 1926 to Strand Th., Lakewood, N J. by M. P. Moller.
	Seamen's Institute Th.	2/8	1928	22479			
NORTH CAROLINA							
Raleigh	Superba Th.	2/	1918	9292			
OHIO							
Cleveland	Liberty Th.	3/	1919	H260	3	5"	

Charles S. Haskell worked in the Philadelphia plant of the Roosevelt company where he and Hilborne Roosevelt patented pneumatic ventil windchest designs in 1885 and 1886. Haskell went into business for himself when the Philadelphia plant was closed in 1891. After Haskell's death in 1904 the business was taken over by his son, C. E. Haskell,[1] who directed the firm until bankruptcy closed it in 1921. Another son, William E. Haskell, joined Estey in 1901 where his revolutionary contributions to organ building ensured the immortality of the name Haskell. Refer to the Estey section of this volume for a discussion of Haskell's remarkable inventions.

A curious form of stop control used on some Haskell organs.

Haskell ad above is from the Decmeber 1914 Diapason. *At right is a document from the archive of* The Console. *Apprentice Benjamin Lenoir later installed several theatre organs under his own nameplate.*

```
                            Sept. 7, 1901.
Names on the pay-roll of C. S. Haskell, Organ Builder
1520-2 Kater St., Philadelphia, at the end of August
1901. Name, occupation and wages. 10 hour day.
Henry Auch      Pipe-maker, metal,p.w.,average-$15.00
A. J. Bowers    Outside voicing                   12.00
W. A. Busby     Action                            18.00
P. J. Cleary    Bellows making                    15.00
W. H. Courter   Mill work                         15.00
Robert Faix     Chest and cabinet work            15.00
J. H. Hallas    Voicer                            24.00
C. T. Harris    Voicer, foreman of voicers.       31.50
G. R. Haskell   Outside setting up etc.           16.50
C. S. Haskell   Proprietor                        50.00
J. G. Hutchinson    Apprentice boy                 5.00
A. Korbinsky    Action                            15.00
F. Krimmelbein  Cabinet and wood-pipe making      15.00
Benj. Lenoir    Apprentice boy                     3.00
Alex. Levinson  Finishing and polishing           10.00
Geo. Maucher    Foreman of cabinet, wood-pipe &
                   and mill work depts.           19.50
Henry Maucher   Apprentice boy                     6.00
G. H. Niles     Clerk in the office               6.00
Robert Pearse   Action and repairing              15.00
F. W. Putzier   Pipe setting                      16.50
W. Russman      Action and repairing              18.00
Geo. F. Renwick   Outside setting up & action     16.50
John Reiser     Porter                            10.50
Peter Schmidt   Foreman of chest dept.            18.00
W. J. Timlin    Metal pipe-maker, p.w., average,  15.00
Edw. Wright     Metal pipe-maker, p.w., average,  17.00
Chas. Zitler    Chest and cabinet work            15.00
```

HASKELL OPUS LIST

CITY/STATE	LOCATION	SIZE	YR	BLWR HP	WP	REMARKS
DELAWARE						
Wilmington	Avenue Th.	2/	1915			
PENNSYLVANIA						
Philadelphia	Arcade Th.	3/	1915			
	Bellevue Th.	2/6	1914	C602	1	6"
				C601	½	25" vacuum.
	Blue Bird Th.	3/	1915	C500	2	6"
	Garrick Th.		1918	G123	1½	4"

HILLGREEN, LANE & CO.

Shortly before the turn of the twentieth century Alfred Hillgreen and Charles Lane were both working for Phillip Wirsching at the Salem Church Organ Company in Salem, Ohio. They struck up a friendship and in 1898 formed their own company in Alliance, Ohio with a third man, Senator Silas S. Williams. After his death Williams' interest in the company was purchased by Hillgreen and Lane who decided to leave the phrase '& Co.' in their firm's name despite the fact that they were the sole owners and the firm was not incorporated.[1]

Alfred Hillgreen and Charles Lane formed an excellent alliance partly because of their widely differing personality traits. Hillgreen was an excellent craftsman and inventor whose greatest desire in life was to build organs with his own hands. Born in Sweden in 1859 and never having received a formal education, he came to America in 1881. He worked first for the Hillstrom Reed Organ Company and then for the Lancashire-Marshall company in Moline, Illinois before joining the Salem Church Organ Company. Charles Lane, on the other hand, was born into a well-to-do family, received a college education and became interested in philosophy, metaphysics and the fine arts. Wielding a hammer or saw was about the farthest thing from Lane's mind; his forte lay in office and managerial skills. Hillgreen was a devout Christian, but when Lane was asked his religion he would reply, with a twinkle in his eye, "Buddhist," leaving considerable doubt as to whether he was being humorous or candid![2]

Alfred Hillgreen was quite an inventor and was fascinated with mechanical devices. A Hillgreen-Lane horseshoe console of the 1920s vies for the title of the most complex organ assembly ever designed. The mechanical combination action required complicated linkages since the stops were arranged in a circle, and key and coupler actions were in the *bottom* of the console, connected to

the manuals by pull wires. Rube Goldberg would have been envious! Another Hillgreen invention was the (in)famous pull-wire ventil chest used until 1951 when the company changed to a standard pitman style chest.[3]

Hillgreen evidently had a fascination with pull wires since they were also featured in the firm's percussion actions. The power pneumatics were mounted inside a windchest and transferred their motion to the outside via a pull wire running through a bushed hole. Not being content to leave well enough alone, Hillgreen further complicated this design by including a second power pneumatic for each note to reverse the motion. Other builders accomplished the same result with a simple spring!

Hillgreen-Lane made their own wooden pipes but turned to another Alliance firm, Gutfleisch & Schopp, for most of their metal pipes, with an occasional order to Organ Supply.[4] Chest magnets were purchased from another local firm, August Klann. Alfred Hillgreen, who was born in Sweden, liked to employ fellow countrymen. In 1927, for example, John Chelberg was draftsman, Gustav Adolphson was console foreman, Oscar Peterson was chest foreman and Hjalmar Peterson was general foreman![5]

Alfred Hillgreen died in 1923 leaving his son Robert to take his place.[6] With the passing of Charles Lane in 1933[7] Robert Hillgreen became sole owner of the company. His son Robert L. Hillgreen, Jr. also took an interest in the organ business and assumed control of the firm during the 1960s. Following the death of his father in 1971, Bob Hillgreen, Jr. began to tire of the many responsibilities of running an organ business and after considerable soul searching decided to cease operations in 1973, the 75th anniversary of the firm. The last organ to leave the factory was opus 1302, a 2/5 destined for St. Matthew's Lutheran

Charles Alva Lane (1854-1933)

Alfred Hillgreen (1859-1923)

Robert Hillgreen (1893-1971)

Front page of an elaborate Hillgreen-Lane catalog.

Church, Medina, Ohio.[8]

Concerned about the welfare of his company's employees, Mr. Hillgreen chose a time when many of them were at retirement age anyway and arranged in an ingenious way for the rest of them to remain employed: he persuaded Bob Schopp, the firm's principal pipe supplier, to take over the Hillgreen-Lane woodworking department. Since Schopp already supplied pipes to the trade it seemed reasonable to offer chests and reservoirs as well.[9]

Bob Hillgreen, Jr. represented Moller for a few years after closing his factory and currently represents VSM Abrasives Corporation. He keeps in touch with the organ industry because, as he says, "it never gets out of your blood," and now calls on his friends at Organ Supply Industries in Erie, Pennsylvania in the role of sandpaper salesman![10]

The name Hillgreen-Lane will be remembered in theatre organ history if for no other reason than for the fact that this firm built the last new organ ever installed in a theatre, the 3/19 in the Odeon Carleton in Toronto in 1948. The Odeon Carleton organ featured a horseshoe console, as did most of this firm's theatre instruments, modest wind pressure (5") and a specification which included many straight stops as well as duplexed and unified ranks.

Hillgreen-Lane console in the Madison Theatre, Detroit, Michigan. This was the firm's largest theatre installation.

Hillgreen-Lane ad in the November 1924 Dia-pason. Horseshoe consoles were a common fea-ture of the firm's church organs.

One of several types of consoles made by
Hillgreen, Lane & Co.

Hillgreen, Lane & Company
ALLIANCE, OHIO

are builders of many important
Church, Theatre and Residence
Organs throughout the United
States and Canada

Factories: Alliance, Ohio
Correspondence Solicited

Cadet Bob MacNeur plays Hillgreen-Lane opus 755 after it was transplanted to the New Mexico Military Institute in Roswell, New Mexico.

This 3/19 Hillgreen-Lane in the Odeon Carleton, Toron-to, Canada, was the last new organ ever installed in a theatre.

HILLGREEN, LANE & COMPANY

Detroit, Michigan, October, 9, 1915.

Hillgreen, Lane & Company,
    Alliance, Ohio.

Gentlemen:—You know of the brutal and unrespecting manner in which I have treated the Organ you placed some time ago in the Majestic Theatre here. I feel I owe some expression of appreciation regarding it.

My attitude results from the fact that is has always withstood these brutal onslaughts, and that I could call upon the instrument for results—double its normal capacity—and find it able to answer every impulse laid against its tonal and mechanical capacity. Further, it seems to improve with each smash I give it, and persists in retaining a concrete semblance of Organ tone and mechanism.

It is being used from 2 o'clock in the afternoon until 11 o'clock in the evening, besides a practice time by the relief shift. It therefore is getting a severe continuous test. And months after its installation it is in good shape.

Cordially and sincerely yours,

Organist Majestic Theatre.   FRANK FRUTTCHEY.

ALLIANCE, OHIO

Interesting testimonial advertisement in the January 1916 Diapason.

3/10 HILLGREEN-LANE THEATRE ORGAN, OPUS 909
Morrison Theatre, Alliance, Ohio

The following specification is typical of this firm's instruments. The Morrison Theatre was in the company's home town and this may have been a "show" organ. In 1927, at a time when even the most conservative builders had jumped on the unit bandwagon for their theatre instruments, only three of these ten ranks were unified.

No...............   **Specifications**   *Page 1*
                              of an Organ for

Morrison Theatre .... of .... Alliance, Ohio.

Prepared and Respectfully Submitted by

HILLGREEN, LANE & CO.
ALLIANCE, OHIO

No. of Manuals .... 3 .... Compass of Manuals CC to C-4 .... 61 Keys.

Compass of Pedals CCC to g .... , 32 Keys.

Action: *Electro Pneumatic Throughout* ....

Console .... Detached ....

Manual Key-board inclined. Convenient access to Key-contacts. Pedal Key-board concave and radiating. (American Guild of Organist's Pattern) unless otherwise specified.

Speaking Stops and Couplers operated by ....

Combinations adjustable at Key-desk, visibly affecting the stops, and operated by pistons located beneath the respective manuals. Pedals combinations operated either by toe-pistons or foot-levers.

Pitch, Philharmonic-440-A. 532. 3-C. (unless otherwise specified.)

A suitable Electric Blower and Motor of ample capacity to be furnished by the Organ Builders. Wiring of Motor (including switches and fixtures) conduits for Organ cables, and also galvanized iron wind-conduits between Blower and Organ to be supplied by the purchaser under the supervision of representatives of said Organ Builders. Suitable chambers or other provision for the housing of the Organ to be prepared by purchaser. A Low-Volt Generator will also be supplied by the Organ Builder to provide current for the Action.

MEMORANDUM OF AGREEMENT, made this 3d. day of June 19 27, by and between HILLGREEN, LANE & COMPANY, of ALLIANCE, OHIO, party of the first part, and Morrison Amusement Co. party of the second part.

WITNESSETH: The party of the first part, in consideration of the agreements hereinafter named, to be made by the party of the second part, hereby agrees to build, install and sell to the party of the second part a 3-Manual Pipe Organ, according to the specifications annexed, said Organ to be erected complete and ready for use in Morrison Theatre on or about the 1st. day of Aug. 1927 subject, however, to delays from causes properly recognized as beyond the control of the party of the first part.

Should said Organ, after completion, and upon examination by a competent and disinterested expert employed by the party of the second part, be found not to accord with specifications and terms of these agreements, said party of the first part agrees, at its own cost and expense, to at once make good any deficiency, or failing in this, to remove said Organ from the building, and refund the payments advanced by the party of the second part, who shall no longer be held by the terms of these agreements.

The party of the first part further agrees, at its own cost and expense, for the term of one year after the completion of said Organ, to remedy any and all defects that may develop therein, this undertaking, however, not including tuning nor such care of the instrument as is necessary to insure its normal preservation.

And the party of the second part, in consideration of the agreements herein of the party of the first part, hereby requests the party of the first part to install said Organ, and agrees to purchase the same, paying therefor the sum of Sixty Eight Hundred Dollars ($6800.00)

as follows:

(1.) Upon the signing of this agreement, the sum of $ 500.00

(2.) When the chief component parts of said Organ are constructed and assembled in the Factory of the party of the first part, the sum of $

(3.) Upon completion of the instrument in accordance with the agreements herein, the balance of said contract price, namely, the sum of $ 1000.00 and the balance of $5300.00 covered by 29 notes of $175.00 and one for $225.00, maturing monthly and bearing 6% interest.

It is further agreed by the party of the second part that said building and Organ Chambers shall be in readiness for the erection, tuning and regulating of said Organ, including the conveniences of light, heat and power and subject to the possession of representatives of the party of the first part for the period of 10 days next, previous to the specified time for completion of the Organ, and that the party of the second part will have the Organ examined immediately upon its completion and in the presence of a representative of the party of the first part.

And the party of the second part further agrees, at its own expense to provide the necessary plumbing and electric wiring, (including switches and fixtures) furnish the required wind Conduits from Blower to Organ, and assume the expense of the cutting of such parts of the building, as may be necessary for the proper installation of the Organ.

And the party of the second part further agrees to assume all risks of damage to said Organ, or parts thereof, when placed inside the building it is to occupy; to receive the Organ upon its arrival, cart it to the building, and pay the freights thereon, said freights and cartage to be deducted from the price of the Organ, and such reception and care not to be construed as an acceptance of said Organ. It is also agreed that the party of the second part shall place upon the instrument, in some reliable Company, adequate insurance for the benefit of the parties hereto, as their respective interests may appear.

It is mutually agreed that in the event of a note or notes being given for any balance of said contract price, the title to and ownership of said Organ shall be and remain in the party of the first part until such note or notes, with accrued interest, shall be paid in full, and in default of payment of any such note or notes, with interest, then all the sum represented by said note or notes, and interests, shall become due and payable, and the party of the first part is hereby authorized at their option to take possession of said instrument without legal process, and all payment heretofore made shall apply as rental for use of said Organ.

It is further agreed that the terms of this agreement shall apply to and bind the heirs, executors, administrators, successors, and assigns of the respective parties.

WITNESS our hands and seals the day and year first above written.

WITNESS   HILLGREEN, LANE & COMPANY

                                By C. A. Lane, Treas. (SEAL) } Party of First Part

                                Morrison Amusement Co
                                By J. A. Morris, Pres (SEAL) } Party of Second Part

                                                    (SEAL)

HILLGREEN, LANE & CO., ALLIANCE, OHIO
PIPE ORGANS

Specification
No._____   Page___2___

-: GREAT ORGAN :-

1.	8 ft.	Stentorphone	Metal	61 pipes
2.	8 ft.	Gamba	Metal	61 pipes
3.	8 ft.	Hohl Flute	Wood	97 pipes
4.	4 ft.	Flute Traverso	Wood	61 notes
5.	2 2/3 ft.	Quint	Wood & Metal	61 notes
6.	2 ft.	Piccolo	Wood & Metal	61 notes
7.	1 3/5 ft.	Tierce	Metal	61 notes
8.	3 rnk.	Mixture	Metal	183 notes
9.	16 ft.	Ophicleide	Reeds	61 notes
10.	8 ft.	Tuba	Reeds	85 pipes
11.	4 ft.	Clarion	Reeds	61 notes
12.		Xylophone	Bars	37 tones

-: SWELL ORGAN :-

13.	16 ft.	Bourdon	Wood	97 pipes
14.	8 ft.	Viol d'Orchestre	Metal	73 pipes
15.	8 ft.	Gedeckt	Wood	73 notes
16.	4 ft.	Flute d'Amour	Wood & Metal	73 notes
17.	2 2/3 ft.	Nazard	Wood & Metal	61 notes
18.	2 ft.	Flautina	Wood & Metal	61 notes
19.	8 ft.	Oboe	Reeds	73 pipes
20.	8 ft.	Vox Humana (Mechanicals only)		
21.		Xylophone	Bars	37 tones
22.		Harp	Bars	37 tones

-: ECHO ORGAN :-

23.	8 ft.	Salicional	Metal	73 pipes
24.	8 ft.	Wald Flute	Wood	73 pipes
25.	8 ft.	Vox Humana	Reeds	73 pipes
26.		Cathedral Chimes	Tubes	20 tones

-: PEDAL ORGAN :-

27.	16 ft.	Bourdon	Wood	32 notes
28.	16 ft.	Lieblich Gedeckt	Wood	32 notes
29.	8 ft.	Flute	Wood	32 notes
30.	8 ft.	Dolce	Wood	32 notes
31.	16 ft.	Trombone	Reeds	32 notes
32.	8 ft.	Tuba	Reeds	32 notes

-: ORCHESTRAL AUXILIARIES :-

33. Bass Drum
34. Snare Drum
35. Tympanium
36. Bird Whistle
37. Cymbal
38. Triangle
39. Castanets
40. Tambourine
41. Tom Tom
42. Chinese Block

-: COUPLERS :-

43. Swell 8' to Pedal
44. Swell 8' to Great
45. Swell 4' to Great
46. Swell 16' to Great
47. Swell 4' to Swell
48. Swell 16' to Swell
49. Great 8' to Pedal

-: COUPLERS :- Continued

50. Great 4' to Great
51. Swell Quint to Pedal
52. Swell Unison Separation
53. Swell 8' to Echo
54. Swell 4' to Echo
55. Swell 16' to Echo
56. Echo 4' to Echo
57. Echo 16' to Echo
58. Echo Unison Separation
59. Echo 8' to Great
60. Echo 4' to Great
61. Echo 16' to Great
62. Echo 8' to Pedal

-: PISTON COMBINATIONS :-
Adjustable at Key Desk and visibly effecting the Stops.

63, 64, 65. Three effecting Great and Pedal Organs.
66, 67, 68, Three effecting Swell and Pedal Organs.
69, 70, 71. Three effecting Echo and Pedal Organs.
72, 73, 74. Three General Pistons effecting all Stops and Couplers.

-: MECHANICALS :-

75. Swell Tremulant
76. Great Tremulant
77. Echo Tremulant
78. Coupler Cancel (Piston)
79. Crescendo Indicator, (Light)
80. Wind Indicator, (Light)

-: PEDAL MOVEMENTS :-

81. Great to Pedal, Reversible
82. Balanced Swell Pedal
83. Balanced Great Pedal
84. Balanced Echo Pedal
85. Sforzando Pedal
86. Balanced Crescendo and Diminuendo Pedal.

-: NOTES :-

It is understood that in the construction of this instrument some used Pipes will be employed after being re-voiced to modern standards. Such Pipes, if used, will be in every respect of value equal to new work.

As of 1982 the Hillgreen-Lane factory is occupied by an electronics firm, but the name of the original occupant is still faintly visible above the front door. The company moved to this building in 1902.[11]

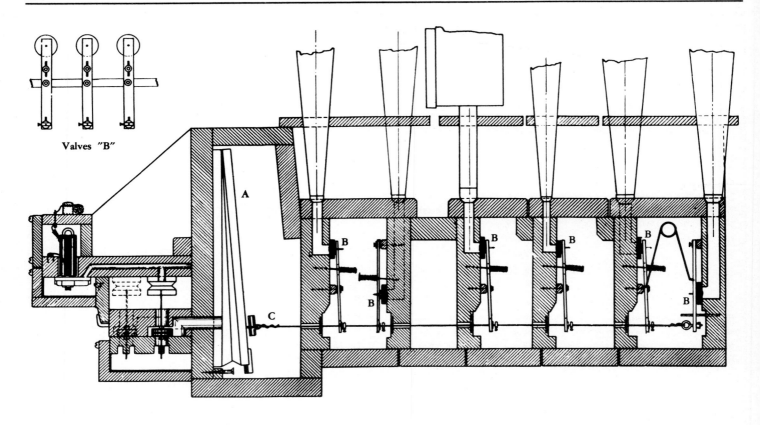

Valves "B"

Sectional view of a Hillgreen-Lane pull-wire ventil chest. Power pneumatic A pulls wire C which opens pipe valves B causing the pipes to speak. Note the Klann chest magnet at the extreme left. Klann magnets were manufactured in Hillgreen-Lane's home town of Alliance, Ohio.

Hillgreen-Lane console in the Capitol Theatre, Detroit, Michigan. This organ was in service only four years before being replaced with a 4/20 Wurlitzer.

HILLGREEN-LANE OPUS LIST

Following is a complete list of this firm's theatre-type installations. An alphabetical index appears first, enabling one to locate instruments on a city/state/installation site basis, with a corresponding opus number shown adjoining. This number can be used to find an organ in the accompanying chronological list. Statistics on each organ are shown only in the latter list.

CITY/STATE	LOCATION	OPUS
ARKANSAS (AK)		
Fort Smith	Joie Th.	573
IOWA (IA)		
Clarinda	Armory Th.	892
Ottumwa	Capitol Th.	874
LOUISIANA (LA)		
Alexandria	Saenger Th.	423
New Orleans	Arcade Th.	582, 612
	Crown Th.	841
	Fern Th.	611
	Granada Th.	840
	Hipp Th.	669
	Iris Th.	638
	Napoleon Th.	787
	New Carrollton (Fine Arts) Th.	469
	Palmer Th.	842
	Poplar Th.	607, 895
	Prytania Th.	567, 891
	Rivoli Th.	566
	Sobel-Richards-Shears (Poplar Th.?)	467
	Variety Th.	651
Shreveport	Saenger Th.	342, 551
MASSACHUSETTS (MA)		
Natick	Natick Th.	720
MICHIGAN (MI)		
Detroit	Adams Th.	518
	Alhambra Th.	371
	Capitol (Paramount) (Broadway-Capitol) (Grand Circus) Th.	630
	Colonial Th.	480
	Columbia Th. (50 Monroe St.)	278
	Empire Th.	332
	Garden Th.	387
	Globe Th.	418
	Kramer Th.	589
	LaSalle Garden (Century) Th.	590
	Liberty Th.	344
	Lincoln Park Th.	825
	Madison Th.	459
	Majestic Th.	389
	Maxine Th.	395
	Miles Th.	601
	Miles-Majestic Th.	558
	Orpheum Th.	495
	Palace Th.	606
	Rialto Th.	446
	Strand Th.	416
	Washington Th.	385
Flint	Regent Th.	571
Grand Rapids	Idlehour Th.	333
	Majestic Th.	411
	Strand Th.	412
Jackson	Majestic Th.	431
Mt. Clemens	Macomb Th.	609
Owosso	Strand Th.	411
Port Huron	Desmond Th.	644
	Harris Th.	409
Saginaw	Palace Th.	429
MISSOURI (MO)		
Maryville	Main Street Th.	861
St. Joseph	Tootle Th.	837
NEBRASKA (NE)		
Beatrice	Ritz Th.	925
Columbus	Swan Th.	465
Crete	Burrus Th.	844

CITY/STATE	LOCATION	OPUS
Grand Island	Cook Th.	890
Hastings	Strand Th.	838
Lincoln	Capitol Th.	876
	Colonial Th.	488
	Rialto (Princess) Th.	485, 522
Lyons	Plaza Th.	849
Nebraska City	Paramount Th.	489, 775
Omaha	Ames (North Star) Th.	583
	Beacon (Suburban) Th.	804
	Dundee Th.	835
	Hower (Circle) Th.	847
	Moon Th.	537
	Rialto Th.	504
	Ritz Th.	430
	Strand Th.	430
Osceola	Auditorim Th.	613
York	Sun Th.	882
NEW MEXICO (NM)		
Albuquerque	Sunshine Th.	755
NEW YORK (NY)		
Newburgh	Park Th.	639
New York City	Magna-Chordia Studio	556
Yonkers	Yonkers Country Club	599
OHIO (OH)		
Alliance	Morrison Th.	909
	Strand Th.	894
Canton	Alhambra Th.	320
Cleveland	Allen's Palace Th.	604
	Amphion Th.	499
	Carlyon Th.	476
	Ezella Th.	886
	Fulton-Lorain Th.	635
	Gordon Square Th.	530
	Grand Th.	500
	Homestead Th.	524
	Jennings Th.	471
	Lakewood Th.	631
	Madison Th.	623
	Miles Th.	496
	Pearl Th.	473
	Rialto Th.	547
	Savoy Th.	523
	Strand Th.	447
	Sun Th.	472, 526
Cuyahoga Falls	Falls Th.	752
Dover	Bexler Th.	918
Elyria	Rialto Th.	943
Fairport	Lyric Th.	917
Lima	Regent Th.	548
Martins Ferry	Fenray Th.	517
Norwalk	Moose Th.	923
Painesville	Park Th.	898
	Utopia Th.	484
Sandusky	Plaza Th.	684
Steubenville	Steuben Amusement Co. (Strand Th.?)	402
	Strand Th.	546
Toronto	Rex Th.	744, 883
Warren	Hippodrome Th.	491
Youngstown	Liberty Th.	478
Zanesville	Imperial Th.	608
	Liberty Th.	572
OKLAHOMA (OK)		
Enid	Aztec Th.	922
Shawnee	Cozy Th.	783
PENNSYLVANIA (PA)		
Braddock	Colonial Th.	508
McKeesport	Avenue Th.	450

CITY/STATE	LOCATION	OPUS
PENNSYLVANIA (PA)		
McKeesport	Liberty Th.	745
	Lyric Th.	442, 454
	Victor Th.	633
Pittsburgh	Alhambra Th.	492
	American Th.	531
	Apollo Th.	441
	Blackstone Th.	348
	Center Square Th.	507
	Elda Th.	464
	Elmore Th.	690
	Garden Th.	578
	Kenyon Th.	579
	Knoxville Strand Th.	468
	Minerva Th.	449
	Superior Th.	552
	Triangle Th.	559
TEXAS (TX)		
Beeville	Rialto Th.	667
Brownwood	Lyric Th.	911
Corsicana	Levine (Ideal) Th.	445
Dallas	Ed Foy (Columbia) Th.	636
	Hulsey (Washington) Th.	315
	W.D. Neville's Th.	309

CITY/STATE	LOCATION	OPUS
Eastland	Carragin Th.	545
Ennis	Grand Picture House	393, 648
Galveston	Dixie Th.	408
Kerrville	Arcadia Th.	864
Mexia	National Th.	658
Nacogdoches	Austin Th.	887
San Antonio	Palace (Alamo) Th.	685
	Rialto Th.	640
	Royal Th.	628
Texarkana	Saenger Th.	424
ALBERTA, CANADA		
Calgary	Allen's Palace Th.	605
Edmonton	Monarch Th.	519
MANITOBA, CANADA		
Winnipeg	Allen Th.	542
ONTARIO, CANADA		
London	Allen Th.	541
Toronto	Allen Th.	479
	Odeon Carleton Th.	1105
SASKATCHEWAN, CANADA		
Regina	Allen Th.	539

OPUS	LOCATION/CITY/STATE	SIZE	YR	PRICE	BLWR	HP	WP	REMARKS
278	Columbia Th., Detroit, MI	2/18	1911	$ 2,700				Located at 50 Monroe Street.
309	W. D. Neville's Th., Dallas, TX	2/11	1912	$ 3,350				Rebuild of an existing organ; make unknown.
315	Hulsey (Washington) Th., Dallas, TX	2/12	1912	$ 4,800				With roll player.
320	Alhambra Th., Canton, OH	2/8	1912	$ 1,500				
332	Empire Th., Detroit, MI	2/8	1913	$ 2,000				
333	Idlehour Th., Grand Rapids, MI	2/8	1913	$ 1,725				
342	Saenger Th., Shreveport, LA	2/8	1913	$ 3,890	4965			See opus 551.
344	Liberty Th., Detroit, MI	2/10	1913	$ 2,700	4938			
			1916		7211			
348	Blackstone Th., Pittsburgh, PA	3/33	1913	$ 6,300	5107			
371	Alhambra Th., Detroit, MI	2/11	1914	$ 2,900	C265	1	5"	
385	Washington Th., Detroit, MI	2/11	1914	$ 2,900				
387	Garden Th., Detroit, MI	2/11	1914	$ 3,200				
389	Majestic Th., Detroit, MI	2/16	1915	$ 4,500	C787	2	9"	
393	Grand Picture House, Ennis, TX	2/9	1915	$ 2,750		¾	3½"	See opus 648.
395	Maxine Th., Detroit, MI	2/9	1915	$ 3,200	6224			
402	Steuben Amusement Co., Steubenville, OH	2/11	1915	$ 2,500				May have been for Strand Theatre; see opus 546.
408	Dixie Th., Galveston, TX	2/11	1915	$ 4,250	6434			
409	Harris Th., Port Huron, MI	2/9	1915	$ 1,400	D211	¾	5"	
411	Majestic Th., Grand Rapids, MI	2/14	1915	$ 3,635	6429			
					D269	2	6"	
					D270	½		Provided vacuum—possibly for roll player.
			19??					Moved to Strand Th., Owosso, Michigan.
412	Strand Th., Grand Rapids, MI	2/10	1916	$ 3,300				
416	Strand Th., Detroit, MI	3/13	1915	$ 3,875	D461	3½	8"	
418	Globe Th., Detroit, MI	2/13	1915	$ 3,500				
423	Saenger Th., Alexandria, LA	2/8	1916	$ 2,475	6849			
424	Saenger Th., Texarkana, TX	2/8	1916	$ 2,475	6827			
429	Palace Th., Saginaw, MI	2/10	1915	$ 3,100	D824	2	6"	
430	Strand Th., Omaha, NE	3/20	1916	$ 4,750	6860	5		Later moved to Ritz Th., Omaha, NE.
431	Majestic Th., Jackson, MI	2/11	1916	$ 3,075	6946			
441	Apollo Th., Pittsburgh, PA	2/9	1916	$ 3,250	7114			
442	Lyric Th., McKeesport, PA	2/17	1916	$ 4,040	7230	5		See opus 454.
445	Levine (Ideal) Th., Corsicana, TX	2/9	1916	$ 4,150				
446	Rialto Th., Detroit, MI	2/22	1916	$ 1,400	7705	5		
447	Strand Th., Cleveland, OH	2/14	1916	$ 4,800	7428			
449	Minerva Th., Pittsburgh, PA	2/11	1916	$ 4,150	7473	5		
450	Avenue Th., McKeesport, PA	3/19	1916	$ 4,500				
454	Lyric Th., McKeesport, PA	2/20	1916	$ 650				Enlargement of opus 442, with a 3-rank echo.
459	Madison Th., Detroit, MI	3/48	1916	$ 10,725	7830			
					7898			

OPUS	LOCATION/CITY/STATE	SIZE	YR	PRICE	BLWR	HP	WP	REMARKS
464	Elda Th., Pittsburgh, PA		1916	$ 1,100				Rebuild of existing organ; make unknown.
465	Swan Th., Columbus, OH	2/6	1917	$ 2,650	7873			
467	Sobel-Richards-Shears, New Orleans, LA	2/7	1917	$ 3,000	7902			May have been Poplar Th.; see opus 607.
468	Knoxville Strand Th., Pittsburgh, PA	2/8	1917	$ 1,800	8031			
469	New Carrollton (Fine Arts) Th., New Orleans, LA	2/9	1917	$ 3,000	7912			
471	Jennings Th., Cleveland, OH	2/16	1917	$ 5,500	8024			
472	Sun Th., Cleveland, OH							Order cancelled; see opus 526.
473	Pearl Th., Cleveland, OH	2/14	1917	$ 3,500	8056			
476	Carlyon Th., Cleveland, OH	2/8	1917	$ 2,200	8076			
478	Liberty Th., Youngstown, OH	2/20	1917	$ 5,275	8627			
479	Allen Th., Toronto, Ontario, Canada	2/21	1917	$ 3,225	8256	3		
480	Colonial Th., Detroit, MI	2/22	1917	$ 4,500	8335			
484	Utopia Th., Painesville, OH	2/14	1917	$ 3,500	8300			
485	Rialto (Princess) Th., Lincoln, NE	2/20	1917	$ 5,250				See opus 522.
488	Colonial Th., Lincoln, NE	2/19	1917	$ 4,850	8413			
489	Paramount Th., Nebraska City, NE	2/9	1917	$ 2,100				See opus 775.
491	Hippodrome Th., Warren, OH	2/19	1917	$ 3,400				
492	Alhambra Th., Pittsburgh, PA	2/17	1917	$ 3,600	8439			
495	Orpheum Th., Detroit, MI	2/23	1917	$ 5,650	8555	5		
496	Miles Th., Cleveland, OH	2/23	1917	$ 5,650	8626	5		
499	Amphion Th., Cleveland, OH	2/14	1917	$ 2,500				
500	Grand Th., Cleveland, OH	2/10	1917	$ 3,800	8513			
504	Rialto Th., Omaha, NE	3/27	1918	$ 8,750	8764	5		
507	Center Square Th., Pittsburgh, PA	2/17	1918	$ 4,235	8763			
508	Colonial Th., Braddock, PA	2/11	1918	$ 3,000	F598	2	6"	
517	Fenray Th., Martins Ferry, OH	2/8	1919	$ 3,000	9481			
518	Adams Th., Detroit, MI	3/28	1918	$ 5,400	9354	5		
519	Monarch Th., Edmonton, Alberta, Canada	2/17	1918	$ 2,500				
522	Rialto (Princess) Th., Lincoln, NE	2/25	1918	$ 1,150				Additions: 5 stops to opus 485.
523	Savoy Th., Cleveland, OH	2/15	1918	$ 4,000	8994			
524	Homestead Th., Cleveland, OH	2/12	1918	$ 3,900	9209			
526	Sun Th., Cleveland, OH	2/12	1918	$ 4,150				
530	Gordon Square Th., Cleveland, OH	2/17	1919	$ 4,875				
531	American Th., Pittsburgh, PA	2/10	1919	$ 3,000	9409			
537	Moon Th., Omaha, NE	3/27	1919	$ 6,825	9686			
539	Allen Th., Regina, Saskatchewan, Canada	2/32	1919	$ 4,542	9774	5		
541	Allen Th., London, Ontario, Canada	2/24	1920	$ 3,800	10464	3	6"	
542	Allen Th., Winnipeg, Manitoba, Canada		1919		10389	5		
545	Carragin Th., Eastland, TX	2/8	1919	$ 4,000	9732			
546	Strand Th., Steubenville, OH		1919	$ 775				Additions to existing organ; see opus 402.
547	Rialto Th., Cleveland, OH	2/17	1919	$ 5,415	10155			
548	Regent Th., Lima, OH	2/16	1919	$ 5,385	9899			
551	Saenger Th., Shreveport, LA	2/8	1919	$ 375				Electrify opus 342.
552	Superior Th., Pittsburgh, PA	2/10	1919	$ 3,200	10108			
556	Magna-Chordia Studio, New York City, NY	2/19	1919	$ 7,520	10161			
558	Miles-Majestic Th., Detroit, MI	2/11	1919	$ 6,200	10174			
559	Triangle Th., Pittsburgh, PA	3/25	1919	$ 6,000	10357			
566	Rivoli Th., New Orleans, LA	2/8	1920	$ 3,775	10687	2	6"	
567	Prytania Th., New Orleans, LA	2/9	1920	$ 3,775	10690	2	6"	See opus 891.
571	Regent Th., Flint, MI	3/27	1920	$ 5,000	10466			
572	Liberty Th., Zanesville, OH	2/14	1920	$ 3,525	11202	3	6"	
573	Joie Th., Fort Smith, AR	2/20	1919	$ 4,635				
578	Garden Th., Pittsburgh, PA	3/23	1920	$ 5,000	10740			
579	Kenyon Th., Pittsburgh, PA	3/27	1920	$ 2,200	10816			
582	Arcade Th., New Orleans, LA	2/9	1920	$ 3,900	10932	2	6"	See opus 612.
583	Ames (North Star) Th., Omaha, NE	2/23	1920	$ 7,250				
589	Kramer Th., Detroit, MI	2/18	1920	$ 7,600	11402	5	8"	
590	LaSalle Garden (Century) Th., Detroit, MI	2/26	1920	$ 7,450	11234	5	8"	
599	Yonkers Country Club, Yonkers, NY	2/13	1920	$ 1,917				
601	Miles Th., Detroit, MI	2/29	1921	$ 9,600	11694			
604	Allen's Palace Th., Cleveland, OH							
605	Allen's Palace Th., Calgary, Alberta, Canada	2/10	1921	$ 2,950				
606	Palace Th., Detroit, MI	2/19	1920	$ 7,875	11596	3	15"	
607	Poplar Th., New Orleans, LA		1921	$ 910	11554	1	5"	Additions: 5 stops; see opus 467.
608	Imperial Th., Zanesville, OH	2/10	1920	$ 4,200				
609	Macomb Th., Mt. Clemens, MI	2/26	1921	$ 8,275	12108			
611	Fern Th., New Orleans, LA	2/9	1921	$ 4,150	11718			
612	Arcade Th., New Orleans, LA	2/9	1921	$ 4,150	11717			See opus 582.
613	Auditorium Th., Osceola, NE	2/10	1921	$ 3,050				
623	Madison Th., Cleveland, OH	2/10	1921	$ 3,750				
628	Royal Th., San Antonio, TX	2/19	1921	$ 8,000	12489			
630	Capitol (Paramount) (Broadway-Capitol) (Grand Circus) Th., Detroit, MI	3/38	1921	$ 20,300	12850	15		
631	Lakewood Th., Cleveland, OH	2/13	1921	$ 4,000	12010			
633	Victor Th., McKeesport, PA	3/19	1921	$ 5,300		5		
635	Fulton-Lorain Th., Cleveland, OH		1921		12739			
636	Ed Foy (Columbia) Th., Dallas, TX	2/13	1921	$ 7,300				
638	Iris Th., New Orleans, LA	2/9	1921	$ 3,950				
639	Park Th., Newburgh, NY	2/14	1921	$ 5,550	12641			

OPUS	LOCATION/CITY/STATE	SIZE	YR	PRICE	BLWR	HP	WP	REMARKS
640	Rialto Th., San Antonio, TX	2/12	1921	$ 6,200	12708			
644	Desmond Th., Port Huron, MI	2/16	1922	$ 8,750	13192 13193			
648	Grand Th., Ennis, TX		1922	$ 695				Enlargement of opus 393.
651	Variety Th., New Orleans, LA	2/9	1922	$ 4,250	13172			
658	National Th., Mexia, TX	2/11	1922	$ 5,950	12785			
667	Rialto Th., Beeville, TX	2/8	1922	$ 4,050	13430			
669	Hipp Th., New Orleans, LA	2/5	1922	$ 2,650				
676	Maus Piano Co., Lima, OH		1922	$ 2,200	13778			Additions to an existing organ; make unknown.
684	Plaza Th., Sandusky, OH	2/10	1922	$ 3,000				
685	Palace (Alamo) Th., San Antonio, TX	2/13	1922	$ 1,600	13972			
690	Elmore Th., Pittsburgh, PA	2/10	1923	$ 5,500	14372			
692	Maus Piano Co., Lima, OH		1922	$ 2,200				Pipes only.
720	Natick Th., Natick, MA	2/11	1923	$ 6,400	14890			
744	Rex Th., Toronto, OH	2/10	1924	$ 4,000	15350			See opus 883.
745	Liberty Th., McKeesport, PA	2/16	1924	$ 10,000				
752	Falls Th., Cuyahoga Falls, OH	2/10	1924	$ 6,000	15645			
755	Sunshine Th., Albuquerque, NM	3/14	1923	$ 11,900	15677			Later moved to New Mexico Military Institute, Roswell, NM.
775	Paramount Th., Nebraska City, NE	2/14	1924	$ 7,000	16230			Replaced opus 489.
783	Cozy Th., Shawnee, OK	2/10	1924	$ 5,765	16248			
787	Napoleon Th., New Orleans, LA	2/5	1924	$ 4,275	16551			
			1925		16945			
804	Beacon (Suburban) Th., Omaha, NE	2/11	1925	$ 6,000				
825	Lincoln Park Th., Detroit, MI	2/7	1925	$ 3,200	17543			
835	Dundee Th., Omaha, NE	2/11	1925	$ 5,500	17858			
837	Tootle Th., St. Joseph, MO	2/11	1925	$ 5,350				
838	Strand Th., Hastings, NE	2/11	1925	$ 5,350	17977			
840	Granada Th., New Orleans, LA		1925		17972			
841	Crown Th., New Orleans, LA	2/6	1925	$ 3,750	17982			
842	Palmer Th., New Orleans, LA	2/6	1925	$ 3,750	17985			
844	Burrus Th., Crete, NE	2/6	1926	$ 3,500	18313			
847	Hower (Circle) Th., Omaha, NE	2/10	1926	$ 5,800	18546			
849	Plaza Th., Lyons, NE	2/4	1926	$ 3,500				
861	Main Street Th., Maryville, MO	2/4	1926	$ 3,300				
864	Arcadia Th., Kerrville, TX	2/4	1926	$ 3,850	18755			
874	Capitol Th., Ottumwa, IA	2/6	1926	$ 6,800				
876	Capitol Th., Lincoln, NE	2/7	1926	$ 6,000	19296			
882	Sun Th., York, NE		1926		19609			
883	Rex Th., Toronto, OH	2/11	1927	$ 8,500	21270			Replaced opus 744.
886	Ezella Th., Cleveland, OH	2/6	1926	$ 8,400				
887	Austin Th., Nacogdoches, TX	2/5	1927	$ 6,000	19841			
890	Cook Th., Grand Island, NE	2/7	1927	$ 6,000				
891	Prytania Th., New Orleans, LA	2/5	1927	$ 4,000	19844			Replaced opus 567.
892	Armory Th., Clarinda, IA	2/6	1927	$ 4,000	20040			
894	Strand Th., Alliance, OH	2/8	1927	$ 5,500	20088			
895	Poplar Th., New Orleans, LA	2/5	1927	$ 3,800	20127			Replaced opus 607.
898	Park Th., Painesville, OH		1927					
909	Morrison Th., Alliance, OH	3/10	1927	$ 6,800	20535 20579			
911	Lyric Th., Brownwood, TX	2/4	1927	$ 6,000	20526			
917	Lyric Th., Fairport, OH	2/7	1927	$ 4,500	20804			
918	Bexler Th., Dover, OH	2/8	1927	$ 6,000				
922	Aztec Th., Enid, OK	2/6	1927	$ 7,500	21167			
923	Moose Th., Norwalk, OH	2/8	1927	$ 5,000				
925	Ritz Th., Beatrice, NE		1928		21581			
943	Rialto Th., Elyria, OH	2/7	1928	$ 4,000				
1105	Odeon Carleton Th., Toronto, Ontario, Canada	3/19	1948	$ 19,200	26834	7½		

ESTABLISHED 1879

HINNERS ORGAN COMPANY

BUILDERS OF HIGH GRADE
PIPE ORGANS AND REED ORGANS

PEKIN, ILLINOIS

John L. Hinners began making reed organs in Pekin, Illinois in 1879 and several years later formed the Hinners & Albertsen partnership with U. J. Albertsen. Tracker pipe organ construction began around 1890. Metal pipes were purchased from Gottfried until the early 1920s when Alfred Gautschi of the Gottfried firm called on Hinners and was persuaded to remain in Pekin to set up a pipe shop in the factory. Wooden pipes and most other parts had always been manufactured right at the plant in Pekin.[1]

The Hinners Organ Company was incorporated in 1902, Albertsen having left to go into the wagon business. Initial capitalization was $35,000 which eventually grew to $237,500 by 1928. The company's peak year was reached in 1921 when 97 persons were employed and three organs were shipped each week. By the time the last organ was produced in 1936 some 3,097 instruments had left the factory. These sales figures are particularly remarkable in light of the fact that the company had no salesmen; most sales were conducted *by mail* with the aid of an elaborately prepared catalog! As a result most of the instruments sold were stock models and only a few large organs were ever built.[2][3]

Hinners products represented perhaps the best value in the entire organ industry. They were of excellent quality but sold for low prices because of mass production techniques and the absence of markup due to salesmen's commissions. And if you were lucky enough to live near Pekin and could pick up the organ at the factory yourself it would cost you—talk about value—only about $75 per rank! And talk about quality—the author knows of several Hinners tracker organs which are still giving excellent service in their original country church locations after over half a century of use with little or no maintenance. The author also knows of two 2/2 Hinners electro-pneumatic practice organs at the University of Illinois in Urbana which were still going strong after enduring thirty years of nearly daily beating.

The Hinners story is full of surprises. They were one of the very few builders to sell tracker organs to theatres and sold nearly two dozen in all—two of them as late as 1916! They never solicited theatre business and in fact one of the stockholders, Hielo J. Rust, pulled out of the company because of a disagreement with Arthur Hinners over whether or not they should even *accept* unit theatre organ orders.[5] Their last two (and largest) theatre contracts were obtained more or less by default. The Pekin Theatre in Pekin was being built virtually around the corner from the Hinners factory and one of the owners of the Madison Theatre in Peoria was a Hinners shareholder.[6]

The ultimate irony is that these two organs, which the company didn't solicit and didn't even want to build, turned out to be excellent theatre organs. They were well specified and contained four 16' ranks each. The author had the good fortune to purchase both of them in the 1970s and still remembers the joy (and shock) of opening the chamber doors to find not the mediocrity he expected but instead absolute treasures! Neither organ was playable due to water damage, so some parts were used in the author's own projects and others were offered for sale. Some quotes from Junchen Pipe Organ Service and Junchen-Collins Organ Corporation sales flyers are not

Hinners factory as it appeared in 1919.

Hinners ad in the May 1914 Diapason. At a time when many builders had switched to electropneumatic action Hinners was doing a land office business selling trackers to country churches throughout the midwest.

Advertisement ten years later in the May 1924 Diapason. By this time Hinners was offering electropneumatic organs although they still produced trackers as late as 1930. Of the 3,097 Hinners organs built only 503 were not trackers; 280 were electric and 223 were tubular.[11]

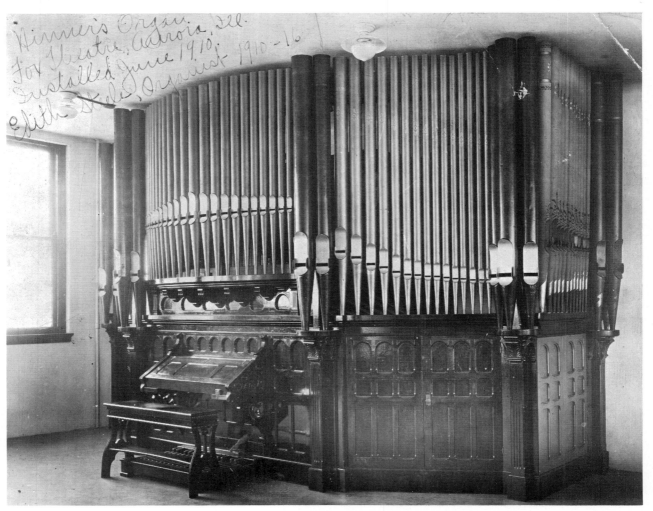

Hinners tracker organ used in the Fox Theater, Aurora, Illinois c. 1910.

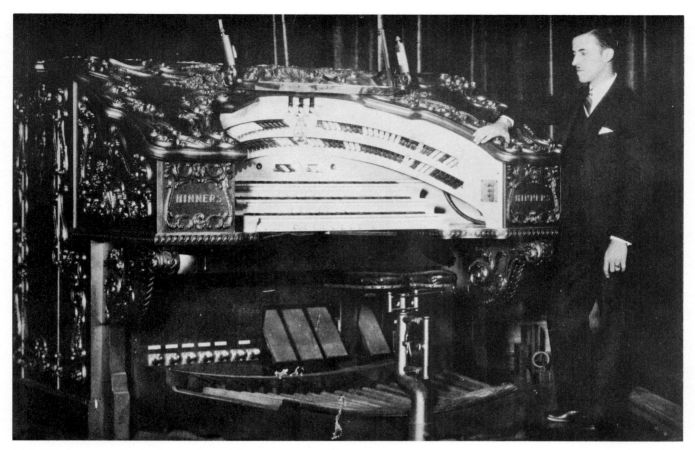

3/11 Hinners console in the Madison Theatre, Peoria, Illinois, Leonard Leigh, organist. Note the three push buttons on the right controlling the console lift turntable: revolve right, revolve left and stop. Three comparable buttons on the left controlled the lift: up, down and stop.

only nostalgic but also reveal some of the Hinners quality as well:

> . . . Deagan master xylophone, 49 notes, with reiterating action. Beautiful. How many 49-note xylophones have you seen? They're rare! . . .[7]
>
> . . . 20-note chimes, Deagan class B, with electropneumatic action. The Hinners action is exceptionally well built and sturdy . . . Each chime has an individual mechanically operated damper which is particularly well designed. One of the best chime actions ever built . . .[8]
>
> . . . Carillon harp, 49 notes G-G, Deagan's largest scale metal harp. The Hinners action is constructed with the power pneumatics *inside* the windchest, which makes for a quieter action as well as leather longevity . . .
>
> . . . 8' kinura . . . similar to a Dennison with nice little duckbill shallots, narrow tongues, and a good bitey kinura snarl! . . .
>
> . . . 8' oboe horn . . . one of the many pleasant surprises in the Hinners—it sounds remarkably like a Wurlitzer style D trumpet . . .
>
> . . . 8' diapason . . . One of the most pleasant surprises we've experienced in a long time, this set has the harmonic development so sadly lacking in a typical Wurlitzer diapason . . .
>
> . . . 8' stopped flute . . . another pleasant surprise . . . shakes on tremulant like a tibia! . . .
>
> . . . 8' tibia clausa . . . If this set were in good condition we'd never sell it—it's one of the finest tibias we've ever

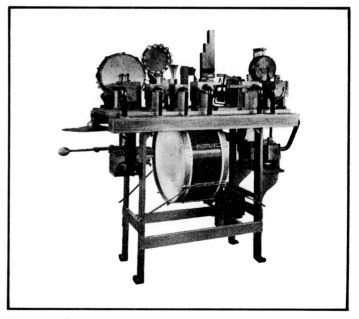

Hinners theatre organs contained top quality trap assemblies furnished by Organ Supply Corporation which were among the few components not actually manufactured in the Hinners factory.

A console with a horseshoe shape and roll top nears completion in the Hinners factory.

heard . . .[9]

Other details of construction of these Hinners theatre organs are also noteworthy. Someone on the Hinners staff must have examined a Barton since the reservoirs, swell shades, relays, tibias and console shapes were remarkably similar to Barton designs although obviously built in the Hinners plant. Like Bartons, they were also built like battleships. The consoles featured Reisner electric stop actions so no air was required. The chests were of standard pouchboard design using first quality leather and some of them are still functioning perfectly in the 1980s, some 55 years after they were built. The theatre organ world would have been much better off had more Hinners instruments been sold.

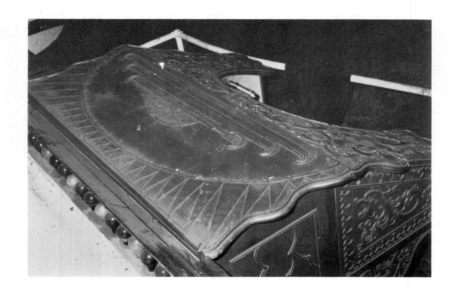

John L. Hinners (1846-1906) died of cancer, after which his son Arthur became president of the company.[10]

Above and at right are views of the 3/11 Hinners in its original home, the Pekin Theatre. Its large size was for appearance only; the console was relatively empty since the stops were activated by Reisner electric actions. The elaborate plaster decorations were pleasant although not quite in keeping with the Chinese atmospheric design of the theatre.

HINNERS OPUS LIST

CITY/STATE	LOCATION	SIZE	YR	ACTION	BLWR	HP	WP	REMARKS
ILLINOIS								
Aurora	Fox Th.	2/						Moved to theatre from local hall.
Beardstown	Gem Th.	2/		Electric				
	Princess Th.	2/		Electric				
Bloomington	Castle Th.	?/5	1910	Tracker				
		2/10	1915	Tubular	6518			
Champaign	Cooper Th.	2/8	1924	Unit				
	Park Th.	2/	1921	Unit	12210			
			1923		14350			
			1923		14985			
Chicago	Alcazar Th.	?/5	1908	Tracker				
	Dunlap Th.	?/5	1909	Tracker				
	Franklin Th.	?/5	1912	Tracker				
	Goodman Marx Th.	?/7	1912	Tracker				
	Howard Th.		1917		8528			
	Niemann Th.	2/	1916	Tubular				
	Orpheum Th.	2/6	1909	Tracker				
	Parkway Th.	?/5	1912	Tracker				
	Temple Th.	?/7	1912	Tracker				
	Vendome Th.	2/9	1918	Tubular	9311			
	World Th.	?/7	1915	Tracker				
Decatur	Avon Th.	2/	1916	Tubular				With echo.
Joliet	Colonial Th.	?/5	1915	Tracker				
	Princess Th.	2/10	1913	Tubular	4878			
La Salle	Majestic Th.	?/5	1915	Tracker				
Ottawa	Robinson Th.	?/5	1912	Tracker				
Pekin	Pekin Th.	3/11	1928	Unit	22526	7½	12"	
Peoria	Columbia Th.	2/7	1913	Tracker				
	Dutchess Th.	?/6	1913	Tracker				
	Garden Th.	?/6	1916	Tracker				
	Hippodrome Th.	?/5	1913	Tracker				
	Madison Th.		1920		10754	3	8"	
		3/11	1927	Unit	20625	7½	18"	
Rushville	Princess Th.	2/5	1923	Unit	15258			
Springfield	Vaudette Th.	?/5	1912	Tracker				
Streator	Majestic Th.	2/	1921	Unit	12445			
Urbana	Princess Th.	?/7	1923	Tubular				
INDIANA								
Indianapolis	Mystic (Orpheum) Th.	1/6	1910	Tracker				
Terre Haute	American Th.	3/	1914	Tubular				
IOWA								
Des Moines	Unique Th.	?/5	1915	Tracker				
Fort Madison	Strand Th.	2/10	1919	Electric	9534			
Mt. Pleasant	Wm. Ferguson Th.		1923	Unit				
Muscatine	Amuse-U Th.	?/8	1916	Tracker				
LOUISIANA								
New Orleans	Washington Th.	?/8	1917	Tubular				
MARYLAND								
Baltimore	West End Th.		1921		12093			
MICHIGAN								
Bridgman	Bridgman Th.	?/8	1921	Tubular	12821			
Port Huron	Regent Th.		1922		13300			
MINNESOTA								
Duluth	Brunswick Th.	2/10	1913	Tubular				
MISSOURI								
Hannibal	Star Th.	?/5	1910	Tracker				
OKLAHOMA								
Tulsa	Ralph Talbot Th.		1921		12850			
TEXAS								
McKinney	McKinney (Pope) Th.	2/						
WISCONSIN								
Milwaukee	Princess Th.	?/5	1909	Tracker				

The following article appeared in the June 1936 *Diapason* and is reprinted in its entirety. In addition to telling the Hook & Hastings story, it also illustrates the tremendous wealth of historical information contained in the pages of *The Diapason* every month from 1909 to the present.

FINIS WRITTEN AFTER CAREER OF 109 YEARS

HOOK & HASTINGS LIQUIDATE

Historic Firm Announces Retirement from Field After Long Activity— Founded by E. & G. G. Hook— Large Organs Among Works.

Memories of the earliest days of American organ building are conjured up by the official announcement within the last month that the old firm of Hook & Hastings has definitely decided to go out of business. The assets of the company are being liquidated and the doors of the factory at Kendal Green, Mass., a suburb of Boston, are to be closed. Several months ago advertisements appeared in THE DIAPASON offering the business for sale as a going concern.

The Hook & Hastings Company looks back on a history of 109 years. Until a few years ago the company was one of the most prominent in the field and among its most famous works of the present generation are the large organ in the Riverside Church, New York, and the older but famous instrument in the Mother Church of Christian Science in Boston. Hook & Hastings organs may be found in all the larger cities of the United States and the reputation of the firm built up by E. & G. G. Hook, its founders, was an enviable one.

In 1827 Elias Hook, who had studied organ building with William M. Goodrich, one of the earliest builders of New England, began the construction of organs in Salem, Mass., with his brother George, under the name of E. & G. G. Hook. Five years later, in 1832, they moved to Boston and located at Leverett and Brighton streets, with a salesroom on Friend street. They continued to build organs at the Leverett street factory until 1853, when they moved to 1131 Tremont street, in that part of Boston known as Roxbury.

In 1885 Francis H. Hastings entered their employment and ten years later was admitted as a partner, the firm name being changed to E. & G. G. Hook & Hastings. The Hook brothers both lived beyond the allotted age of man, and died within nine months of each other, one in 1880 and the other in 1881.

In 1885 the present factory was built at Kendal Green and the business was transferred from Boston to the new factory during that year and the year following. In 1895 the business was incorporated under the name of the Hook & Hastings Company. The present officials of the company are: Alfred R. Pratt, president; Norman Jacobsen, vice-president, and Anna C. Hastings, treasurer.

A number of years before Mr. Hasting's death in 1916 he relinquished the active management to his associates.

The first organ built by the company is still intact, and may be found in the Essex Institute.

HOOK & HASTINGS OPUS LIST

OPUS	LOCATION	CITY/STATE	SIZE	YR	BLWR	HP	WP
2338	Globe Th.	Philadelphia, PA	3/	1914	B829	3½	5"
2339	Arcadia Th.	Philadelphia, PA	3/	1914	C110	3½	4"
2374	Circle Th.	Indianapolis, IN	2/16	1916	E116	2	5"
2414	Rialto Th.	Providence, RI	2/20	1917			
2460	Gordon's Olympia (Brockton) Th.	Brockton, MA	2/24	1921			
2464	unidentified theatre	Newton, MA		1921			
no #	Hyannis Th.	Hyannis, MA		1923	14469		
no #	Rialto (Fields Corner) Th.	Dorchester, MA	2/10	1924	15299		
no #	Granada (Malden) Th.	Malden, MA	4/	1927	19009		

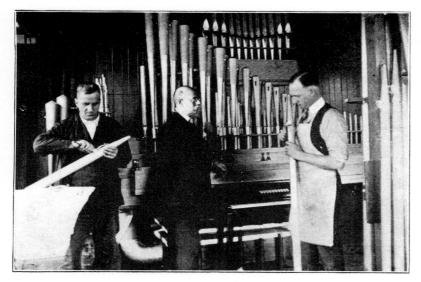

THE voicing of an organ is especially fascinating and important. Our voicers not only preserve faithfully the distinctive characteristics of each individual stop, but they devote equal attention to the proper blending and to complete co-ordination in the finished whole.

A French Horn is here shown on the voicing machine. Many eminent musicians have pronounced the voicing of our French Horn as unexcelled.

On the bench at the left are shown pipes of ou patented Orchestral Flute. This, too, is creating special attention, and those who have heard it concede that it is an absolute reproduction of the orchestral instrument, and not the usual imitation.

Voicing Department
(Hook & Hastings)

HOOK & HASTINGS COMPANY
Main Office and Works, Kendal Green, Mass.

These ads in The Diapason *appeared, above, in June 1925 and below, in October 1925.*

HOOK & HASTINGS
ORGAN FACTORY

THE illustration is of our main plant. The spacious yards in the rear afford fine opportunity for lumber in process of seasoning.

As can be seen, the plant is surrounded with beauty which nature has provided. The atmosphere of the interior is equally attractive, with an abundance of sunshine and pure air throughout.

The conditions are appropriate for creating artistic instruments. We have always discouraged the "commercial" treatment of our organs.

HOOK & HASTINGS COMPANY
Main Office and Works, Kendal Green, Mass.

Above, a view in the Hook & Hastings action department. At left, a rare acknowledgement of the firm's theatre products in an ad from the February 1923 Diapason. Nearly all of their several thousand organs were church instruments.

H. A. "Pete" Howell was a prodigy who built his first organ in his parents' home in Dixon, Illinois while still a teenager.[1] He became interested in organs after making the acquaintance of John Byington, an organ builder in Dixon, and "because my sister dropped me on the head when I was a baby!" He often journeyed to Chicago to hear his favorite organists: Harry Zimmerman at the Belmont and Preston Sellers at the Oriental (both having 4/20 Wurlitzers) and Al Carney at the WHT 4/15 Page on the seventh floor of the Wrigley Building. Carney took a shine to the precocious youth and allowed him to sit next to him on the bench while he played the Page for broadcasts. Carney introduced Howell to another young organ man, Ken Simpson, who was then in his early twenties and who had a reputation as a real "whiz" with Wurlitzers.[2]

Al Carney dreamed of owning his own instrument on which to do recordings and broadcasts. In 1929 twenty-one-year-old Pete Howell agreed to build this organ with help from Ken Simpson. Carney was to pay for all materials, deferring payments for labor until profits from use of the organ came rolling in. The first item purchased was a four-manual Wurlitzer console which had been damaged by a malfunctioning lift in the Chicago Theatre. Fifteen choice ranks of pipes were purchased from Gottfried including two tibias, a brass saxophone, an English post horn and a krumet horn. Not surprisingly, the rank list paralleled that of the 4/15 Page on which Carney had been broadcasting. Percussions (including a 49-note xylophone) were purchased from Deagan and a ten-horsepower Orgoblo (#23435) was ordered. All other parts of the organ were made by Pete Howell himself with the exception of the relay switches which were purchased from the nearby Geneva Organ Company.[3]

Shortly after construction of the organ was under way Pete got into an argument with Ken Simpson's brother over what size to bore some channel holes, after which Simpson and his brother left, leaving Pete to complete the organ on his own.[4] To say that he succeeded admirably is an understatement! For his chests Pete copied Kilgen designs which have never been surpassed for speed. The organ is still playing well in 1983 with no major rebuilding (except for the Wurlitzer console!) over fifty years after its construction. Not bad for a 21 year old!

Al Carney made a few recordings on the organ but died in 1930, with the result that Pete Howell was never paid for his labor.[5] The instrument was eventually acquired by St. Mary of the Lake Seminary in Mundelein, Illinois and was moved to its new auditorium by the Kilgen company in 1934.

Pete Howell dabbled in the organ business in the 1930s and 1940s but made most of his living selling oil burners. After World War II he sold the heating business and went into full time organ building under the name H. A. Howell Pipe Organs, Inc.[6] In the late 1960s a young organist named Curt Schmitt joined the company as tonal director and eventually purchased controlling interest in the firm. Although semi-retired, Pete still visits the shop daily and contributes his inventive genius while keeping a watchful eye on quality control. His most recent invention is an improved quiet-operating organ blower which is now manufactured in the Howell shop for their own instruments as well as being offered to the trade.

Pete Howell (1908-   ) is still building quality pipe organs in 1983.

The 4/15 relay for the Carney organ is being wired in the Howell shop. Pete Howell enlisted the aid of several high school buddies to help in this seemingly endless chore.

Interior of the Al Carney studio at 160 East Illinois Street in Chicago. Note the many drapes to muffle the roar of 15 ranks of Gottfried pipes on 10″ and 15″ wind pressure. Pipework was in two chambers behind the left wall in a space no larger than the studio itself. The grand piano played from the organ and there was a second piano, an upright, in the chamber,[7] making this perhaps the first organ installation ever to include two pianos. The Wurlitzer console originally saw service in the Chicago Theatre where it controlled 27 ranks of pipes. Since the Carney organ had only 15 ranks there were enough stops for extensive unification. For example, each tibia appeared on the accompaniment second touch at 8′, 4′, 2 2/3′, 2′ and 1 3/5′ pitches.

A man who formerly built reservoirs for the Geneva Organ Company plies his trade in the Howell shop for the Carney organ.

HUTCHINGS ORGAN COMPANY

George Sherburne Hutchings was one of America's foremost organ builders and had a reputation for being satisfied with nothing less than the best instrument he could make. His career began in 1857 when he joined the famous Boston builders E. & G. G. Hook as a cabinet maker. He worked his way up through every department in the factory and eventually became plant superintendent, a position he held for ten years.[2] In 1869 he formed a partnership with Dr. J. H. Willcox, M. H. Plaisted and G. V. Nordstrom under the name of J. H. Willcox & Company. In 1872 Dr. Willcox retired due to failing health and Nordstrom's interest was purchased by Hutchings and Plaisted. The new firm of Hutchings, Plaisted & Company operated until Plaisted's departure in 1884, after which the firm name became simply George S. Hutchings.[3]

Early in 1901 a merger was effected with the Votey Organ Company and the new firm established operations in Boston as the Hutchings-Votey Organ Company. After a disastrous fire in 1904 the firm moved to Cambridge, Massachusetts. In 1908 they moved to Waltham, Massachusetts, absorbing the Waltham Church Organ Factory, operated by E. W. Lane, and again changed names, becoming the Hutchings Organ Company. After Mr. Hutchings' death in 1913 Charles A. Flaherty assumed control of the company. A. Perry Martin, who had been superintendent, left at this time to join forces with Ernest M. Skinner,[4] also an ex-Hutchings man.[5] The Hutchings Organ Company voluntarily went out of business in 1917 after completing the work on hand.[6]

Part of Hutchings' prestige came from having installed organs at a number of colleges. After building an organ for Yale in 1903 Hutchings was awarded the honorary degree of master of arts by that college.[7] The handful of Hutchings organs installed in theatres all seem to have been built after Mr. Hutchings' death. At least two were unified orchestral instruments although they sported drawknob consoles! Their interesting specifications are reproduced here from the July 1915 *Diapason:*

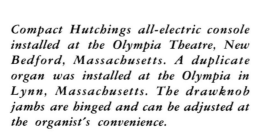

Hutchings ad in the July 1916 Diapason.

*George S. Hutchings
(1835-1913)[1]*

Compact Hutchings all-electric console installed at the Olympia Theatre, New Bedford, Massachusetts. A duplicate organ was installed at the Olympia in Lynn, Massachusetts. The drawknob jambs are hinged and can be adjusted at the organist's convenience.

ORCHESTRAL ORGANS BUILT BY HUTCHINGS

TWO LARGE FOUR-MANUALS

Duplex and Unit Systems Combined in Interesting and Unusual Specifications for Large Theater Syndicate.

The Hutchings Organ Company has completed one orchestral organ and is finishing another. These are for one of the largest syndicates of theater owners in the country and are being built by this company because the buyers desired only the best possible quality of work. They are four-manual companion organs built to combine the best features of both the duplex and the unit systems. They are successes both from a tonal and from a mechanical standpoint. One is to be installed at Lynn, Mass., and the other at New Bedford, Mass. The specifications are given below:

SWELL SECTION 1.
A. Wood Diapason, 16 ft., 97 pipes.
B. Diapason, 8 ft., 73 pipes.
C. Viola da Gamba, 8 ft., 73 pipes.
D. Vibrant Strings, 8 ft., 73 pipes.
E. Double Flute, 8 ft., 73 pipes.
F. Clarinet, 8 ft., 61 pipes.
G. Trumpet, 8 ft., 73 pipes.

SWELL SECTION 2.
H. Bourdon, 16 ft., 97 pipes.
J. Horn Diapason, 8 ft., 73 pipes.
K. Viole d'Orchestre, 8 ft., 73 pipes.
L. Viole Celeste, 8 ft., 73 pipes.
M. Oboe, 8 ft., 61 pipes.
N. Vox Humana, 8 ft., 61 pipes.
O. Tuba, 16 ft., 97 pipes.

TRAPS.
AA. Chimes.
BB. Harp.
CC. Sleigh Bells.
DD. Swiss Bells.
EE. Triangle.
GG. Snare Drum.
HH. Bass Drum.
JJ. Cymbals.

PEDAL ORGAN.
1. Diapason (from A), 16 ft.
2. Bourdon (from H), 16 ft.
3. Great Flute (from A), 8 ft.
4. Stopped Flute (from H), 8 ft.
5. Octave Flute (from A), 4 ft.
6. Trombone (from O), 16 ft.
7. Tromba (from O), 8 ft.
8. Clarion (from O), 4 ft.
9. Chimes (from AA).
10. Bass Drum (single stroke) (from HH), lowest octave.
11. Bass Drum (roll) (from HH), lowest octave.
12. Snare Drum (roll) (from GG), second octave.
13. Cymbals (from JJ), lowest octave.

FIRST MANUAL (Choir).
14. Viola da Gamba (from C), 8 ft.
15. Vibrant Strings (from D), 8 ft.
16. Double Flute (from E), 8 ft.
17. Flute (from A), 4 ft.
18. Harmonic Piccolo (from A), 2 ft.
19. Clarinet (from F), 8 ft.
20. Celesta (harp) (from BB).
21. Sleigh Bells (from CC), 25 bells.
22. Chimes (from AA), 20 notes.
23. Triangle (from EE), second octave
24. Snare Drum (from GG), lowest octave.
25. Swiss Bells (from DD), 20 bells.
26. Tremolo (first and second manuals).

SECOND MANUAL (Great).
27. Diapason (from B), 8 ft.
28. Great Flute (from A), 8 ft.
29. Double Flute (from E), 8 ft.
30. Viola da Gamba (from C), 8 ft.
31. Vibrant Strings (from D), 8 ft.
32. Flute (from A), 4 ft.
33. Harmonic Piccolo (from A), 2 ft.
34. Trumpet (from G), 8 ft.
35. Clarinet (from F), 8 ft.
36. Triangle (from EE), lowest octave.
37. Snare Drum (from GG), second octave.

THIRD MANUAL (Swell).
38. Bourdon (from H), 16 ft.
39. Horn Diapason (from J), 8 ft.
40. Gedeckt (from H), 8 ft.
41. Viole d'Orchestre (from K), 8 ft.
42. Viole Celeste (from L), 8 ft.
43. Flute (from H), 4 ft.
44. Trombone (from O), 16 ft.
45. Tuba (from O), 8 ft.
46. Oboe (from M), 8 ft.
47. Vox Humana (from N), 8 ft.
48. Clarion (from O), 4 ft.
49. Tremolo (third and fourth manuals).

FOURTH MANUAL (Solo).
50. Horn Diapason (from J), 8 ft.
51. Gedeckt (from H), 8 ft.
52. Viole Celeste (from K and L), 8 ft.
53. Flute (from H), 4 ft.
54. Trombone (from O), 16 ft.
55. Tuba (from O), 8 ft.
56. Oboe (from M), 8 ft.
57. Vox Humana (from N), 8 ft.
58. Clarion (from O), 4 ft.
59. Celesta (harp) (from BB).
60. Sleigh Bells (from CC), 25 bells.
61. Swiss Bells (from DD), 20 bells.
62. Chimes (from AA), 20 notes.

ADJUSTABLE COMBINATIONS (operated by pistons)—Six affecting pedal registers and couplers. Six affecting choir registers, all pedal registers and all couplers. Six affecting great registers, all pedal registers and all couplers. Six affecting swell registers, all pedal registers and all couplers. Six affecting solo registers, all pedal registers and all couplers. Five affecting entire organ—all manual registers, all pedal registers and all couplers.

PEDAL STUDS—1. Bass drum—single stroke. 2. Bass drum—roll. 3. Cymbals—crash. 4. Snare drum—single stroke. 5. Snare drum—roll. 6. Triangle—single stroke. 7. Triangle—roll.

The company has also in process of construction organs for Helena, Mont.; Oyster Bay, L. I.; Shreveport, La., and other cities.

Specifications are reproduced as they appeared in the July 1915 Diapason.

HUTCHINGS OPUS LIST

CITY/STATE	LOCATION	SIZE	YR	BLWR HP	WP	REMARKS
MASSACHUSETTS						
Boston	Eagle Th.		1917	8399		
	Exeter Street Th.	3/44				Former church converted into a theatre; opus 139.
Lynn	Gordon's Olympia Th.	4/14	1915	6282	7½	6"&15"
New Bedford	Olympia Th.	4/14	1915	7½		6"&15"
Waltham	Waltham Th.		1916	7551		
Worcester	New Park Th.		1915	6709		
NEW JERSEY						
Newark	Webbe Th.		1913	5161		
	Paramount Th.	3/	1915			
RHODE ISLAND						
Pawtucket	Pawtucket Th.	2/	1916			

KARN-MORRIS PIANO & ORGAN COMPANY

D. W. Karn of Woodstock, Ontario was a builder of tracker organs in the late nineteenth century. During the mid teens (if not before) the Karn-Morris alliance was formed, also operating in Woodstock. Many of their organs of this period were, as Stuart Kennedy is fond of saying, "tubercular rheumatic." Somewhat later the Karn-Morris alliance was dissolved and Karn formed a partnership with Samuel Russell Warren who had been a partner in Clough & Warren of Detroit, Michigan. The Karn-Warren alliance eventually gave way to Warren & Sons which in turn became Woodstock Pipe Organ Buiders. During Warren's association the firm built several Canadian theatre organs, some of which were unit organs.[1] The only shipments to United States theatres were under the Karn-Morris nameplate.

KARN-MORRIS OPUS LIST

CITY/STATE	LOCATION	SIZE	YR	BLWR	HP	WP
BRISTH COLUMBIA, CANADA						
Vancouver	Dewess Th.		1913	B193	3	4"
	Kinemacolor Th.		1913	A724	2	4"
Victoria	Dominion Th.		1913	A723	2	4"
	Kinemacolor Th.		1913	B218	2	4"
ONTARIO, CANADA						
Toronto	Strand Th.		1914	C38	3½	5"&8"
MICHIGAN						
Detroit	Crystal Th.		1916	D758	2	10"
	Grand Boulevard Th.		1915	D556	7½	8"&15"

THOS. KELLY

Kelly ad in the March 1927 Diapason. He reportedly installed an organ in the Oriole Terrace Dance Hall in Detroit c. 1922.

According to the Kilgen public relations department, monks in a monastery near Durlach, Germany taught Sebastian Kilgen organ building skills in 1640. It *is* known that John George Kilgen emigrated to the United States in the mid-nineteenth century and was employed by George Jardine in New York before going into business for himself in 1851. He moved to St. Louis in 1873 and took his son Charles into partnership in 1866 at which time the name of the firm became Geo. Kilgen & Son. Charles Kilgen continued the business after his father's death in 1902 and in 1909 absorbed the Pfeffer Organ Company of St. Louis. In 1924 the four sons of Charles Kilgen joined their father in partnership and the firm became Geo. Kilgen & Son, Inc.[6]

In 1939 Eugene R. Kilgen filed suit against his three brothers, alleging mismanagement. The result was that a court ordered dissolution of the firm, the assets to be sold at public auction.[7] Eugene Kilgen and Max Hess, chief engineer of Geo. Kilgen & Son, Inc., formed a new company called the Kilgen Organ Company, Inc.[8] while the other brothers formed Kilgen Associates, Inc.[9] The two competing firms were in business until the outbreak of World War II, after which only Eugene Kilgen's company survived. Plagued by inadequate financing, this firm teetered on the edge of bankruptcy for a number of years, finally going out of business in 1960. Its direct descendant is the St. Louis Pipe Organ Company operated by

Max Nagel. Mr. Nagel apprenticed with Welte in Germany, coming to St. Louis in 1930 as Kilgen plant superintendent, a position he held until the close of the firm. Having absolutely nothing to do with the demise of the Kilgen firm but amusing nonetheless are the names of several individuals associated with the company in its latter days: Charles Crook was the bookkeeper[10] and Jerry Outlaw and a Mr. Poolshark were janitors![11]

Kilgen products were not the lowest quality organs made (that distinction undoubtedly belonging to Marr & Colton) but they certainly weren't in the same class with Kimball, Aeolian, Wangerin, Skinner and other high quality builders. The author's favorite example of Kilgen cost cutting is their method of attaching metal windlines to chests. A hole was drilled in the chest slightly larger in diameter than the windline. Then cotton string was wrapped around the end of the windline after which it was doused in red sealing wax and shoved into the hole. After a few years the sealing wax started to crack, causing leaks, and woe be unto the poor serviceman who might have to remove one of these windlines!

Despite their inexpensive construction, Kilgen theatre organs sounded good. Their tibias and voxes were sweet and the Dennison Hoyt metal saxophones used were the next best things to late Wurlitzer model brass saxophones. Kilgen organs were also better unified than most although the pedal divisions were usually fairly gutless

Charles C. Kilgen (1859-1932), father of the four Kilgen brothers.[4]

George J. Kilgen

Kilgen was in the entertainment organ business very early, as evidenced by this 4/11 traveling circus organ made for the Ringling Brothers in 1902. Only one manual was operative; the other three were for show only. The action was tubular pneumatic.

with but one lone 16′ bourdon. Kilgen relays were of the matrix type and consumed a remarkably small space. A 3/11 Kilgen relay, for example, is about the same size as a 2/6 Wurlitzer relay.

One factor which kept the company afloat in the 1930s was the success of the Petit Ensemble, Kilgen's name for their self-contained cabinet organ. Several of these were sold for radio use and one found its way into a theatre in 1936. These instruments were not voiced theatrically, unlike several other Kilgen unit organs in radio stations which were quite successful for performing popular music.

The number of Kilgen organs built is difficult to estimate. Opus numbers reached the 7000s by the end of production but many numbers were never assigned and others were given to rebuilds and parts orders. As an example, the Capitol Theatre in Wheeling, West Virginia (which had a 4/17 Marr & Colton) ordered a new blower

bag from the Kilgen factory in 1937. This order was shipped C.O.D. at a cost of $5.00 and was assinged opus number 5910! The following opus numbers were never assigned at all: 3165-3199, 3253-3299, 3764-3799, 4058-4099, 3388-3399, 4294-4299, 4665-4699, 5020-5099[12] and perhaps more. The author's estimate is that around 4,000 new Kilgens were built, certainly placing Kilgen in the top echelon of all companies from a production standpoint.

The existing Kilgen records were placed at the disposal of the author by Max Nagel, plant superintendent from 1930 to 1960. The following pages from one of the old ledger books are reproduced here through his courtesy. This particular organ is one of the few Kilgen theatre organs remaining in its original habitat (as of 1983) and it illustrates the extent to which Kilgen unified their theatre instruments.

Eugene R. Kilgen

Charles C. Kilgen, Jr.

Alfred G. Kilgen

THE VOICE OF THE SILENT DRAMA

MIRABILE AVDITV

3/6 KILGEN THEATRE ORGAN
Grand Theatre, Wausau, Wisconsin

Documents reproduced here are from original factory ledger books and illustrate the extent to which Kilgen unified their theatre instruments. This particular organ is one of the few Kilgen theatre organs remaining in its original habitat as of 1983.

SPECIFICATION U-0-14 X SPECIAL

of   a

KILGEN UNIT ORCHESTRA.

designed   for

GRAND THEATRE   WAUSAU, WIS.

****

DIMENSIONS:	As per plans of Organ Builder. Organ divided.
THREE MANUALS:	Compass CC to C---------------61 notes each.
PEDAL BOARD	A.G.O. Model Concave and Radiating. Compass CCC to G -------------32 notes.
CONSOLE	Circular type including 50 ft. of cable length. Additional cable $4.00 per ft extra.
PITCH:	A-440
PRESSURE:	High Orchestral Pressure

****

PEDAL ORGAN

Resultant	32	Feet
Bourdon	16	"
Tuba	8	"
Tibia	8	"
Cello	8	"
Flute	8	""
Clarion	4	"
Tibia	4	"
Flute	4	"
Bass Drum		
Cymbal		
Tympani		
Great to Pedal		
Accompaniment to Pedal.		

ACCOMPANIMENT ORGAN

Bourdon	16	Feet
Tuba	8	"
Tibia	8	"
Viol D' Orchestre	8	"
Flute	8	"
Vox Humana	8	"
Kimura	8	"
Clarion	4	"
Tibia	4	"
Salicet	4	"
Flute	4	"
Vox Humana	4	"
Twelfth	2 2-3	"
Piccolo	2	"
Marimba		
Harp		
Xylophone		
Snare Drum		
Tambourine		
Castanets		
Chinese Block		
Blank Tablet (Silent)		

1350

3711

ACCOMPANIMENT ORGAN CONTINUED.

Tuba	8 ft.-----------------------	Second Touch		
Tibia	8 "-----------------------	"	"
Tuba	4 "-----------------------	"	"
Tibia	4 "-----------------------	"	"

4 Combination Pistons Controlling Accompaniment and Pedal Stops.

GREAT ORGAN

Tuba	Tenor C	16	Feet
Tibia	Tenor C	16	"
Contra Viol	Tenor C	16	"
Bourdon		16	"
Vox Humana	Tenor C	16	"
Tuba		8	"
Tibia		8	"
Viol D' Orchestre		8	"
Flute		8	"
Vox Humana		8	"
Kimura		8	"
Clarion		4	"
Tibia		4	"
Salicet		4	"
Flute		4	"
Vox Humana		4	"
Twelfth		2 2-3	"
Fifteenth (On String)		2	"
Piccolo		2	"
Tierce		1 3-5	"
Marimba			
Harp			
Xylophone			
Blank Tablet (Silent)			

4 Combination Pistons Controlling Great and Pedal Stops.

SOLO ORGAN.

Tuba	Tenor C	16	Feet
Tibia	Tenor C	16	Feet
Contra Viol	Tenor C	16	"
Bourdon		16	"
Vox Humana	Tenor C	16	"
Tuba		8	"
Tibia		8	"
Orchestral Oboe (Syn.)		8	"
Viol d' Orchestre		8	"
Quintadena (Syn)		8	"
Flute		8	"
Vox Humana		8	"
Tibia		4	"

4 Combination Pistons Controlling Solo and Pedal Stops.

5 Chimes
On Separate Key Board.

3711

Eddie Dunstedter (left) and Leonard Leigh pose at the 4/31 Kilgen in the Capitol Theatre, St. Paul, Minnesota. A twin to this Kilgen was installed in the State Theatre in Minneapolis, St. Paul's twin city. Both organs were erected in 1920 and each was subsequently replaced with a Wurlitzer style 260 special: the Capitol in 1926 and the State in 1924. Several years before this photo was taken Dunstedter had been an apprentice in the Kilgen factory.

EXPRESS GENERAL SOLO
Expression Pedal MAIN
Crescendo Pedal Controlling Great and Pedal Stops.
General Tremolo.
Vox Humana Tremolo.

TOE PISTONS.

Tambourine
Castanets
Tom Tom
Siren
Bird Whistle
Sleigh Bells.

REMARKS.

An electric motor, blower and generator will be furnished and installed with the organ. The purchaser to do all the wiring for same, furnish and install switches, remote control, fuses etc., also furnish and install conduits for wiring and organ cable where local regulations or conditions require it. The purchaser is also to furnish and install the galvanized iron pipe from blower to organ reservoir and to furnish a suitable place with foundation if necessary, for the motor blower and generator, and to enclose same if necessary. The purchaser to make all changes to the building necessary for the proper installation of the organ, motor, blower and generator for the wiring and the galvanized iron pipe, and to cut any openings in walls or floors etc. so that the organ men will not be called on to do any carpenter's mason's or electrician's work.

Purchaser to furnish any exterior decoration for the organ and also to build the organ chambers according to specification ov the organ builders.

GEO. KILGEN & SON INC.
ST. LOUIS MO.
U.S.A.

MM
August 27th, 1926

3711

NAME OF BLDG-------- Grand Theatre
CITY---------------- Wausau Wis.
SOLD BY------------- R R Ounson Dec-31-1921
DELIVERY DATE------- 5 months after Drawings O.K.
PRICE--------------- $8000

TRADE IN------------ Robert Morton Organ

EXTRAS-------------- Console to be shipped 30 days in advance of del. date.
DESCRIBE WOOD------- Birch Mah.
CASE---------------- none
FRONT PIPE---------- none
MOTOR H.P.&PRESSURE- 3 H.P. Simp 110-220 V. 60B S.P. 1750 R.P.M. 10"P. 3" Fl. no val Reg F. outlet
CURRENT-------------
GENERATOR VOLTS &AMP
STOP KEYS----------- Thom - 5667
PIPES--------------- make here
REEDS--------------- Jell. O - 5608 Denn. 5964
PERCUSSIONS-------- Hy. 8 - 5582
CHIMES------------- BLM 5582
VOICED BY----------- Mayhew
SHIPPED VIA WEIGHT-- Frt. 11-17-26 - 1314
    " " " -- Xpress 12-16-26
    " " " -- Frt. 12-10-
    " " " -- CEg, C n.W- 6250 - 12-10-26
        Xpress 12-21-26
        " 12-22-26
    3711

In the Finest Theatres
—the Voice of the Silent Drama

K ILGEN WONDER ORGANS have, during the past few years, won universal preference in those theatres where music selection is a matter of discrimination.

Organists have been unfailing in their approval of the Kilgen; because it is responsive in the expression of all human emotions—joy, sorrow, happiness, tragedy. And throughout the land, an announcement of Kilgen Music wins immediate public approval; because in hundreds of theatres, auditoriums, universities and homes, Kilgen Wonder Organs have told the story of music beauty.

Geo. Kilgen & Son, Inc.
Builders Pipe Organs
ST. LOUIS

Studio—252 Wrigley Bldg.—Chicago

Installations

Below are listed a few of the leading theatres in which Kilgen Wonder Organs are furnishing the Voice of Melody to the Silent Drama

ST. LOUIS	BIRMINGHAM
Grand Central	Lyric
Capitol	
Tivoli	HOUSTON
West End Lyric	Majestic
Del Monte	
Ritz	LITTLE ROCK
	Majestic
CHICAGO	
White Palace	GARY, IND.
Vogue	Broadway
ST. PAUL	KEOKUK, IA.
Capitol Theatre	Grand

CAPE GIRARDEAU, MO.
Broadway

One of the newest commissions for Kilgen craftsmen is the Miracle Play to be staged in the St. Louis Coliseum in December under the direction of Morris Gest. The beauty of flowing, stately melody is of the greatest importance to this spectacle; so it is natural that a Kilgen was chosen.

The organ music at Radio Station WHT, Wrigley Bldg., Chicago, has won comments of praise from delighted auditors throughout the land. It is Kilgen Organ Music.

An Invitation
Let Kilgen Organ architects confer with your builders on the question of an organ installation. The benefit of their long study and knowledge is available without obligation on your part.

Kilgen ad in the November 21, 1925 Motion Picture News.

Kilgen Organs

NET PRICE LIST

AUGUST 1, 1926

———o———

Prices subject to change without notice

———o———

Established U. S. A. 1851

Geo. Kilgen & Son Inc.

Builders

Pipe Organs

Main Office and Plant
4016 Union Blvd.
St. Louis, Mo.

———o———

Studio and Branch
252 Wrigley Bldg.
Chicago, Ill.

CHURCHES AND RESIDENCE ORGANS

Style	Price
Two Manual Unit Organs	
U-1	$ 3,795.00
U-2	4,485.00
U-3	4,945.00
Two Manual Organs	
100	3,680.00
200	4,370.00
300	4,945.00
400	5,520.00
500	6,095.00
600	6,785.00
700	7,590.00
800	7,820.00
900	8,625.00
1000	9,775.00
1100	10,695.00
1200	11,385.00
1300	12,363.00
1400	12,938.00
Three Manual Organs	
1500	10,264.00
1600	11,098.00
1700	11,817.00
1800	12,823.00
1900	13,915.00
2000	14,605.00
2100	15,985.00
2200	17,940.00
2300	20,873.00
2400	23,000.00
2500	26,105.00
Straight 88 Note Player	
Straight Roll	1,000.00
Kilgen Unda Maris Reproducing Player	
Residence Reproducing	3,500.00
Kilgen Rural Direct Action Organ	
6 One Manual	2,500.00
50 Two Manual	3,500.00

KILGEN WONDER ORGANS FOR THEATRES

Style	Price	Divided Add.
Two Manual		
U-O-1	$ 4,950.00	10%
U-O-2	5,600.00	"
U-O-3	6,800.00	"
U-O-4	7,675.00	"
U-O-5	5,600.00	"
U-O-6	6,500.00	"
U-O-7	7,550.00	"
U-O-8	8,600.00	"
U-O-9	8,350.00	"
U-O-10	8,975.00	"
U-O-11	11,200.00	5%
U-O-12	12,350.00	"
U-O-13	15,600.00	"
U-O-14	16,900.00	"
U-O-15	17,550.00	"
U-O-16	22,100.00	"
U-O-17	23,400.00	"
U-O-18	25,625.00	"
U-O-19	27,300.00	"
Three Manual		
U-O-14X	17,825.00	2%
U-O-16X	23,400.00	"
U-O-20	27,250.00	"
U-O-21	31,000.00	"
U-O-22	33,000.00	"
U-O-23	36,000.00	"
U-O-24	37,875.00	"
U-O-25	42,000.00	"
U-O-26	42,125.00	"
U-O-27	45,000.00	"
Roll Player—Single	$1,000.00	
" Double	2,000.00	

"The Voice of the Silent Drama"

Form 32x

NOTE

To the enclosed prices always add cost of division extended Console & Cable, Extra Case Work, and all extras added to printed office copies of Standard Specifications.

Sales books have explanation of how to figure extras and additions.

———o———

All prices F. O. B. Factory, St. Louis, Mo.

———o———

Customer pays freight and drayage, but organ factory installs organs by sending expert mechanics to erect the organs properly in the purchaser's building.

This 1926 Kilgen price schedule offers a large number of stock church and theatre models. The Kilgen company tended to specialize in stock model theatre organs more so than most companies whose instruments were more customized. It is fascinating to note that at the relatively late date of 1926 Kilgen was still offering two models of tracker organs, called "rural direct action organs" in this price schedule. By consulting the opus list one will see that a number of these theatre models were never sold. It is also interesting to compare the inflated prices in this brochure with the prices actually charged by the factory. The difference represents the markup charged by National Theatre Supply, the agency which handled many Kilgen theatre organ sales.

The Palace Theatre in Little Rock, Arkansas featured an early Kilgen installed in 1914.

Horseshoe consoles were out of vogue at Kilgen by the early 1930s. This 2/5 in the WHDH radio studios in Boston was installed in 1935 with an ordinary church-type console belying its theatrical specification.

4/14 Kilgen in the WKY radio studios in Oklahoma City, Oklahoma. Nearly identical consoles were featured on Kilgen organs in WLAC, Nashville; WHAS, Louisville; and KMOX, St. Louis.

Chicago radio station WHT featured a 2/8 Kilgen with two consoles, one at each end of the studio, installed in 1925. Just two years later the Kilgen was replaced by a 4/15 Page.

Auxiliary console at the other end of the WHT studios in Chicago.

The original Kilgen in KMOX Radio, St. Louis was a 2/5 installed in 1926. It was later enlarged several times, finally reaching 4/16 in size.

Herbie Koch poses in the chamber of the 4/14 Kilgen he designed for WHAS Radio in Louisville, Kentucky. The gesture of cupping his hand to his ear is quite amusing when one realizes that this organ featured a battery of reeds on 15" wind pressure which, as Kirk Collins used to say, would "blow you off the console!"

The author tunes a concert flute in the main chamber of the 3/6 Kilgen in the Grand Theatre, Wausau, Wisconsin in 1963.

The 3/6 Kilgen console in the Grand Theatre, Wausau, Wisconsin rises on a Barton four-poster lift. Console is slightly too large for the lift platform and the right rear lift screw actually goes inside the console. Most Kilgen three-manual horseshoe consoles are of this same case design.

This 2/6 Kilgen console (opus 3742) was much more aesthetically pleasing than the company's three-manual models.

Dr. Alfred G. Robyn plays the 3/20 Kilgen in the New Grand Central Theatre, St. Louis. This was the largest unified theatre organ that Kilgen ever built, having one more rank than the famous Piccadilly Theatre in Chicago. Two Kilgen theatre installations were larger: the State in Minneapolis and the Capitol in St. Paul, each of which was a 4/31. These were straight specifications, however. Dr. Robyn, a noted musician in St. Louis and New York, was the brother of Charles C. Kilgen's first wife, Louise.[5]

Kilgen's most prestigious theatre installation was the Piccadilly in Chicago. The Baldwin grand piano in the box below the right organ screen actually played from the organ and had its expression controlled by one of the swell shoes on the console. In the 1960s this piano was removed and has become a feature at the Atlanta Fox Theatre where it is connected to the famous 4/42 Moller. The instrumental harp in the above photo was decorative only and did not play from the organ. At left, solo chamber in the Piccadilly. The brass trumpet did not have spun bells as do most sets, but instead was made of rolled sheet brass with a soldered seam. Cost cutting such as this was not uncommon in Kilgen products.

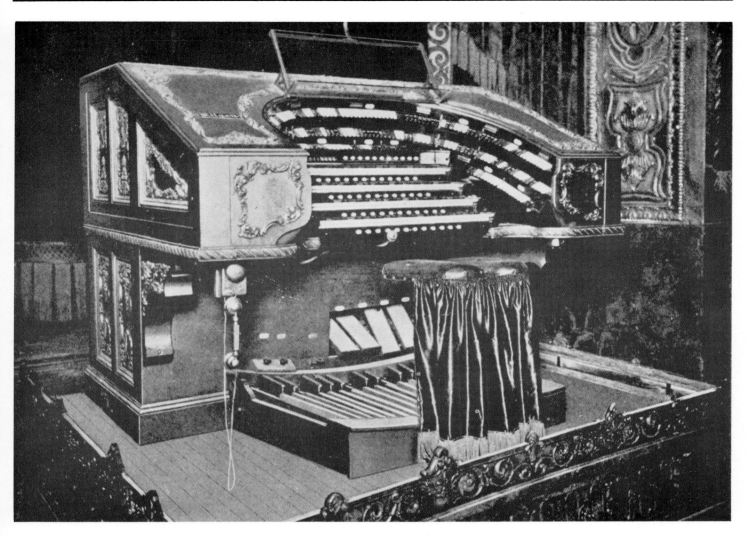

Above: Kilgen's most prestigious theatre installation in the Piccadilly Theatre, Chicago. Factory photo below shows the serviceability of the 4/19 console and also reveals its plain appearance before it received a cosmetic treatment by the Decorators Supply Company of Chicago.

Cover of an elaborate 1927 Kilgen theatre organ catalog.

Soldering the final seam on a salicional pipe in the flue pipe department.

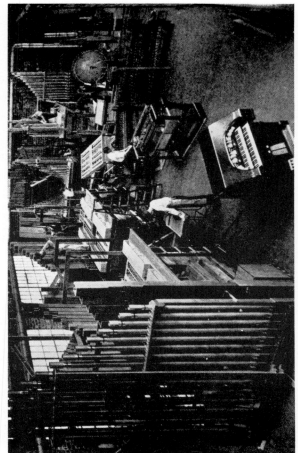

Several organs are being set up at one time in the Kilgen erecting room. Note the enormous bass drum at the right center of the photo. Many Kilgen theatre organs featured a drum of this size.

Soldering a tuba resonator to its block in the reed department.

Assembling a set of chimes in the Kilgen percussion department.

Voicing a tuba in the reed department. Kilgen made some of their own reeds but purchased others from such trade suppliers as Dennison, Badger, Illinois Organ Supply, Erie Reed Pipe Co. and National Organ Supply.[1]

A technician adjusts contacts in a Kilgen matrix style relay tray. This particular tray contains 18 unit switches in an incredibly compact space.

At the right a worker stirs a cauldron of molten pipe metal which will be cast into sheets on the table at left.

Chest department.

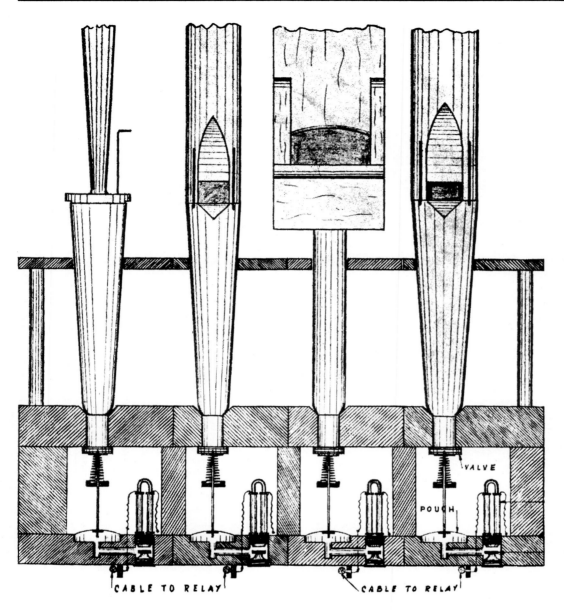

Sectional view of a Kilgen unit chest. The author has long suspected that this style of chest has the fastest response and this was confirmed in 1982 by organ builder David Harris who constructed an experimental chest with several types of action. Measured with an oscilloscope, the response of the Kilgen style action was faster than Wurlitzer, Roosevelt, Moller, or Wicks style actions. In all honesty it must be reported that the responses of these various chest designs are actually very similar to each other, the slight differences probably not being significant from a player's standpoint.

A young woman winds the coils for Kilgen's unique design of chest magnets.

KILGEN STYLE CHART

Following is a guide to the various styles of stock theatre organs found in the Kilgen opus list. The letters UO stand for unit organ.

Style	Size	Features
UO1	2/3	16' flute: 1-24 #2 pedal bourdon scale, 25-97 #1 stopped diapason scale; 8' string 1-73, 65 scale; 8' vox humana 13-61, regular scale; circular console.
UO2	2/3	UO1 plus bass drum, tympani and cymbal on pedals; snare drum, tambourine and castanets on accompaniment.
UO3	2/3	UO2 plus glockenspiel/orchestra bells.
UO4	2/3	UO3 plus 37-note xylophone.
UO5	2/3	UO1 plus 8' vox humana 1-12; 5 chimes; tom tom, siren, birds and sleigh bells on toe studs.
UO6	2/3	UO5 plus additional unification.
UO7	2/3	UO6 plus glockenspiel/orchestra bells, 37 notes.
UO8	2/3	UO7 plus 37-note xylophone.
UO9	2/4	UO1 plus 8' vox humana 1-12; 8' tuba 1-73, 5½" scale; 37-note xylophone; 5 chimes; tom tom, siren, birds and sleigh bells on toe studs.
UO10	2/4	UO2 plus 8' vox humana 1-12; 8' tuba 1-73, 5½" scale; 5 chimes.

Style	Size	Features
UO11	2/4	UO10 plus 37-note orchestra bells.
UO12	2/4	UO11 plus 37-note xylophone.
UO13	2/5	16' flute: 1-24 #1 pedal bourdon scale, 25-97 #1 melodia scale; 8' string 1-85, 65 scale; 8' tuba 1-73; 8' vox humana 1-73, regular scale; 8' tibia clausa 1-73, #2 scale; 37-note marimba; 37-note xylophone; 5 chimes; tambourine, castanets, tom tom, siren, birds and sleigh bells on toe studs only; second touch on accompaniment.
UO14X	3/5	UO13 plus 37-note glockenspiel/orchestra bells; pedal and accompaniment traps.
UO15	2/7	UO13 plus 8' kinura 1-61; 8' open diapason 1-73, 43 scale, with #1 open wood bass 1-12; pedal and accompaniment traps.
UO16X	3/6	UO13 plus 16' tuba 1-12, 10" scale; 8' kinura 1-61; 37-note glockenspiel/orchestra bells; pedal and accompaniment traps.
UO20	3/9	UO16X plus 8' saxophone 1-61; 8' celeste 13-73, 65 scale; 8' open diapason 1-73, 43 scale, with #1 open wood bass 1-12; 37-note chrysoglott.

UO22   3/11 (Only one example built—opus 3648):

Rank	Notes	Chamber	WP	Remarks
16' bourdon	97	main	8"	1-24 #1 pedal bourdon, 25-97 #1 melodia.
16' tibia clausa	97	solo	12"	#1 scale.
16' tuba	85	solo	12"	Made by Dennison.
8' string	73	main	8"	65 scale.
8' celeste	61	main	8"	65 scale.
8' open diapason	73	main	8"	43 scale with #1 open wood bass 1-12.
8' saxophone	61	solo	12"	Made by Dennison.
8' clarinet	61	main	8"	
8' vox humana	73	main	6"	
8' oboe horn	61	main	8"	Made by Dennison.
8' kinura	61	solo	12"	Made by National Organ Supply.
marimba harp	49	solo		
master xylophone	49	main		
chrysoglott	37	main		
orchestra bells	37	main		
chimes	20	solo		

bass drum, cymbal, snare drum, tambourine, castanets, Chinese block, sand block, tom tom, siren, birds, sleigh bells and effects in main chamber.

KILGEN OPUS LIST

Following is a list of this firm's known theatre-type installations. An alphabetical index appears first, enabling one to locate instruments on a city/state/installation site basis, with a corresponding opus number shown adjoining. This number can be used to find an organ in the accompanying chronological list. Statistics on each organ are shown only in the latter list. Installations in the alphabetical index with opus numbers shown as "unknown" will be found at the end of the chronological list.

Kilgen was the only builder to use Simplex blowers in substantial quantities; they were, in fact, Simplex's largest customer. As with other lists in this book, Simplex blowers are identified by an "S" suffix on the serial number, or in a few instances by a lone "S" where the serial number is unknown. Kinetic blowers have one or two letters other than S in their numbers and Spencer Orgoblo numbers have no letters at all.

Kilgen had perhaps the most capricious pricing policy in the industry. Note the wide variations in prices charged for the same style organs in the following list. The policy seems to have been to charge whatever the traffic would bear. Prices were also inflated in instances where a trade-in was involved, often resulting in the company getting a used instrument for virtually nothing, which would then be resold (and assigned an opus number) at an enormous profit. Keep in mind that these are the prices charged by the factory, but not necessarily those paid by theatres; many Kilgen organs were sold by National Theatre Supply Company, whose commission added an average of 60% to the theatre's purchase price. What a racket!

CITY/STATE	LOCATION	OPUS
ALABAMA (AL)		
Birmingham	Alcazar (Empire) Th.	unknown
	Avon Th.	4006
	Bijou Th.	unknown
	Lyric Th.	3459
	Pantages (Bijou) Th.	3934
	Ritz Th.	3629
ARKANSAS (AR)		
Fort Smith	KFPW Radio	5616
Little Rock	Majestic	3458
	Palace Th.	1514
	Park Th.	unknown
CALIFORNIA (CA)		
Crescent City	Enderts Th.	4114
Culver City	Hal Roach Studio (KFVD Radio)	4444
Encintas	La Paloma Th.	4029
Los Angeles	KNX Radio	4931
San Francisco	National Theatre Supply (Radio Station?)	3828
Santa Cruz	Unique Th.	4036
Woodside	Whittall Th.	4230
COLORADO (CO)		
Denver	KLZ Radio	3871
CONNECTICUT (CT)		
Danielson	Orpheum Th.	4152
New Haven	Dreamland Th.	3972
Rockville	Palace Th.	4200B
Stamford	Palace Th.	4113
	Strand Th.	4108
GEORGIA (GA)		
Athens	Stand Th.	3017
Rome	Rivoli Th.	4184
IDAHO (ID)		
Idaho Falls	Paramount Th.	4550
	T. R. Earl	4584
ILLINOIS (IL)		
Aurora	Rialto (Aurora?) Th.	1787
Berwyn	Oakwyn (Ritz) Th.	3473
Chicago	Alamo Th.	3475
	Atlantic Th.	unknown
	Atlantic Th.	3648
	Ben Hur Th.	3761
	Clearing Th.	3670, 4292
	Criterion Th.	3660
	Frolic Th.	3644
	Iris Th.	1717
	Kenwood Th.	3515
	Metropole Th.	3622
	Milford Th.	3728
	Monogram Th.	4003

CITY/STATE	LOCATION	OPUS
Chicago	Oak Th.	3693
	Orchid Th.	3682
	Piccadilly Th.	3647
	Steuben Club	4043
	Twentieth Century Th.	3673
	White Palace Th.	3358
	WHT Radio	3363, 3685
	WIBO Radio	4145
Fairfield	unidentified theatre	3003
Gillespie	Peart Th.	3808
LaGrange	Illinois Th.	3734
Maywood	Lido Th.	3474
Rockford	Capitol Th.	4008
Staunton	Labor Temple	3413
INDIANA (IN)		
Brazil	Citizens (Lark) Th.	4155
Crawfordsville	Strand Th.	3911
Evansville	American Th.	unknown
Gary	Broadway Th.	3432
	Orpheum Th.	3605
	Palace Th.	3431, 4731
	Ritz Th.	3902
Madison	Grand Th.	4163, 4226
IOWA (IA)		
Centerville	Orpheum Th.	1531
Council Bluffs	KOIL Radio	4010
Des Moines	WHO Radio	5621
Keokuk	New Grand Th.	3344
LeMars	Royal Th.	3820
KANSAS (KS)		
Eldorado	Eldorado Th.	3897
Great Bend	Zarah Th.	3900
Hutchinson	Royal Th.	3650
Manhattan	Miller Th.	3690
Pittsburgh	Mystic (Majestic) Th.	1628
Topeka	Jayhawk Th.	3614
Wichita	Orpheum Th.	3126
KENTUCKY (KY)		
Louisville	WHAS Radio	5009, 5124, 5198
		5212, 5769, 7179
LOUISIANA (LA)		
New Orleans	Grand Th.	4198
MARYLAND (MD)		
Baltimore	Community (Arcade) Th.	4126
Bel Air	Argonne	4150B
Cantonsville	Alpha (Canton) Th.	4109
Towson	Towson	4017
MASSACHUSETTS (MA)		
Boston	WHDH Radio	5465

CITY/STATE	LOCATION	OPUS
MASSACHUSETTS (MA)		
Lowell	Crown Th.	4148
Medford	Riverside Th.	3966
Waltham	Embassy (Moody) Th.	4007
MICHIGAN (MI)		
Grand Rapids	Alcazar (Birds State) Th.	3895
Harbor Springs	Lyric Th.	3892
MINNESOTA (MN)		
Minneapolis	Dyckman Hotel	unknown
	Leola Th.	4054
	Loring Th.	3048
	Lyric Th.	unknown
	New Garrick (Century) Th.	1627
	Ritz Th.	3704
	Roof Garden (Blue Mouse) Th.	3020
	State Th.	3038
	Unique Th.	unknown
	WAMD Radio	3671, 3814
Red Wing	Sheldon Memorial Th.	3608
St. Paul	Astor Th.	3019
	Capitol Th.	3037
	Garrick Th.	unknown
	Majestic Th.	unknown
	Princess Th.	unknown
	Strand Th.	unknown
MISSISSIPPI (MS)		
Laurel	Strand (Arabian) Th.	3742
MISSOURI (MO)		
Columbia	Uptown Th.	unknown
Cape Girardeau	Broadway Th.	3460
Hannibal	Star Th.	3421
Kansas City	Alladin Th.	3947
	Empress Th.	unknown
	Garden Th.	unknown
	Ocasso Th.	3806
Malden	Liberty Th.	5004
Moberly	unidentified theatre	1505
St. Joseph	Colonial Th.	3959
	Royal Th.	1472
St. Louis	Alamo Th.	5323
	Arsenal Th.	3149
	Capitol Th.	3069, 3325
	Cinderella Th.	unknown, 3336
	Columbia Th.	3013
	Delmonte	3058, 3800
	Empress Th.	3092
	Gem Th.	unknown
	Grand Opera House	3014
	Kingsland	3337
	KMOX Radio	3502, 4443, 4577, 4816, 5225, 5302, 5471, 5612, 5869
	KXOK Radio	6106
	La Paloma Th.	unknown
	New Grand Central Th.	unknown, 3066, 3204
	New Rex Th.	unknown
	Old Grand Central Th.	unknown
	Pershing Th.	unknown
	Ritz Th.	3471
	Sixth & Chestnut Th.	unknown
	Strand Th.	1654
	Tivoli Th.	3232
	West End Lyric Th.	3067
Springfield	Landers Th.	3652
Webster Groves	Ozark Th.	3345
NEBRASKA (NE)		
Albion	Rex Th.	3891
Beatrice	Rivoli Th.	3676
Fairbury	Bonham Th.	3675
Fremont	Fremont (Goldberg) Th.	3617
Hastings	Rivoli Th.	3677
Holdrege	Sun Th.	3827, 4827
Kearney	Empress Th.	3689
Norfolk	Granada Th.	3733
Omaha	Benson Th.	3707
	Corby Th.	3616

CITY/STATE	LOCATION	OPUS
Omaha	Lathrop Th.	3658
	Leavenworth Avenue Th.	3706
	Minne-Lusa Th.	3516
NEW JERSEY (NJ)		
Asbury Park	Convention Hall	unknown, 4610, 4613, 4619, 4646, 4717
Hackettstown	Strand Th.	4138
Irvington	Liberty Th.	3957, 4045
Mt. Ephraim	Mt. Ephraim Th.	4271
Paterson	Majestic Th.	4005
Westwood	Westwood Th.	4161B
NEW MEXICO (NM)		
Roswell	Princess (Civic) Th.	1619, 3423, 3801
NEW YORK (NY)		
Albany	Paramount Th.	3692
Bronx	Bandbox Th.	4112
	Metro Th.	3894
Brooklyn	Fortway Th.	3893
	Gold Th.	4039
	Graham (Gerrittsen) Th.	4037
	Momart Th.	3898
	Parthenon Th.	unknown
Kingston	Orpheum Th.	3970
New York	Earl Carroll Th.	4258
	Edith Toten Th.	3991
	Cortlandt Th.	4038
	Kilgen Wonder Organ School	unknown
Rochester	Dixie Th.	4206
	Little Th.	5661
Schenectady	Rivoli Th.	3995
NORTH CAROLINA (NC)		
Morehead	Wade Th.	4149B
Mt. Airy	Paramount Grand (Benbow) Th.	4004
OHIO (OH)		
Canton	Lyceum (Young's) Th.	3835
	Palace Th.	3604
Celina	Lakona Th.	3921
Cincinnati	Monte Vista Th.	3861
Cleveland	Mt. Pleasant Th.	3851
Columbus	Hippodrome Th.	3741
Marion	Oakland Th.	4167B
Norwood	Norwood Th.	4172
Sidney	Broad & Larkin	3869
Youngstown	Cameo (Ohio) Th.	3903
OKLAHOMA (OK)		
Ardmore	Ritz Th.	3933
Miami	Glory B Th.	3478
Oklahoma City	WKY Radio	5281
OREGON (OR)		
Portland	Capitol Th.	4157
	Lucien Becker Studio	unknown
PENNSYLVANIA (PA)		
Easton	Seville (Boyd) Th.	4301, 4301A
Kane	Albertson Th.	4049, 4049A
Palmyra	Seltzer Th.	3896
Philadelphia	Forum Th.	4106
	WFIL Radio	5931
Pittsburgh	American Th.	4018
St. Mary's	St. Mary's Th.	4231
Scotdale	Strand Th.	4137
RHODE ISLAND (RI)		
Providence	Hope Th.	3931
Woonsocket	Park Th.	3840
TENNESSEE (TN)		
Memphis	Poplar Street Th.	3926
Nashville	WLAC Radio	6013
TEXAS (TX)		
Brownsville	Capitol Th.	4013
Dallas	Majestic Th.	3054
	Wells Th.	unknown
Fort Worth	Majestic Th.	3127
Houston	Majestic Th.	3129

CITY/STATE	LOCATION	OPUS
TEXAS (TX)		
San Antonio	Majestic (State) Th.	3128, 3481
San Benito	Rivoli Th.	4025
UTAH (UT)		
Cedar City	Woodbury Th.	3822
Salt Lake City	Suburban Th.	3952
VIRGINIA (VA)		
Roanoke	WDBJ Radio	5685
WISCONSIN (WI)		
Baraboo	Ringling Bros. Circus	unknown
Madison	Eastwood Th.	4420
Merrill	Cameo Th.	1796
	Cosmo Th.	3834
Milwaukee	N. W. Conservatory of Music	3857
	Ritz Th.	3615
	WKAF Radio	3740
	Zenith Th.	3915
Racine	Granada Th.	3935
Watertown	Classic Th.	4034
Wausau	Grand Th.	3711
West Bend	Mermac Th.	3514

CITY/STATE	LOCATION	OPUS
AUSTRIA		
Vienna	LaScala (Kiba-Apollo) Th.	4779
CUBA		
Havana	Encanto Th.	4019

OPUS	LOCATION/CITY/STATE	SIZE	YR	PRICE	BLWR	HP	WP	REMARKS
1472	Royal Th., St. Joseph, MO	2/	1912					
1505	unidentified theatre, Moberly, MO	1/6	1912					Tracker action.
1514	Palace Th., Little Rock, AR	2/	1914					
1531	Orpheum Th., Centerville, IA	1/6	1913					Tracker action.
1619	Princess (Civic) Th., Roswell, NM	2/10	1915		6508			
1627	New Garrick (Century) Th., Minneapolis, MN	2/	1915		D195	3	8"	Removed in 1925.
1628	Mystic (Majestic) Th., Pittsburgh, KS	2/8	1915					
1654	Strand Th., St. Louis, MO	2/5	1917		7380			
			1917		8670			
1717	Iris Th., Chicago, IL	2/8	1917		8707			
1787	Wells Th., Norfolk, VA	2/8	1919					Order cancelled.
1787	Rialto (Aurora?) Th., Aurora, IL	2/8	1919					Voiced on 5" wp.
1796	Cameo Th., Merrill, WI		1919					
3003	Theatre, Fairfield, IL	1/	1919					Tracker action.
3013	Columbia Th., St. Louis, MO	2/11	1919		10114			
3014	Grand Opera House, St. Louis, MO	2/10	1919					
3017	Strand Th., Athens, GA	2/7	1919		10176			
3019	Astor Th., St. Paul, MN	2/12	1920		10758			
3020	Roof Garden (Blue Mouse) Th., Minneapolis, MN	2/12	1920					
3037	Capitol Th., St. Paul, MN	4/31	1920		10994	7½	8"	With echo.
			1922		K413	15	10"	
3038	State Th., Minneapolis, MN	4/31	1920		11809	10	8"	With echo.
3048	Loring Th., Minneapolis, MN	2/5	1920		10995	3	7"	
			1920		11441	3	7"	
3054	Majestic Th., Dallas, TX	2/8	1921					
3058	Delmonte Th., St. Louis, MO	2/9	1920		11238	3	6"	
3066	New Grand Central Th., St. Louis, MO		1920					Rebuild of existing Kilgen organ; additions: solo stops and traps.
3067	West End Lyric Th., St. Louis, MO	2/4	1920					
3068	East End Lyric Th., St. Louis, MO	2/5	1919					Order cancelled—never built.
3069	Capitol Th., St. Louis, MO	2/3	1920					See opus 3325.
3077	Pageant Th., St. Louis, MO	2/8	1920					Austin organ moved from Warrensburg, Missouri.
3092	Empress Th., St. Louis, MO	2/10	1921					Kilgen organ moved from Empress Theatre, Kansas City, Missouri.
3126	Orpheum Th., Wichita, KS	2/12	1922					Moved opus 3092; additions: clarinet and oboe.
3127	Majestic Th., Fort Worth, TX	2/10	1923		13712			
3128	Majestic (State) Th., San Antonio, TX	2/10	1923					
3129	Majestic Th., Houston, TX	2/16	1922		13899			
3149	Arsenal Th., St. Louis, MO	3/	1921					3/13 Kilgen from Pershing Theatre, St. Louis, moved and rebuilt.
3204	New Grand Central Th., St. Louis, MO	3/20	1923		15035			Additions to opus 3066.
3232	Tivoli Th., St. Louis, MO	2/6	1923		15292	5	10"	With horseshoe console and 2nd touch.
3325	Capitol Th., St. Louis, MO	2/7	1924		14501 16040			Opus 3069 enlarged.

OPUS	LOCATION/CITY/STATE	SIZE	YR	PRICE	BLWR	HP	WP	REMARKS
3336	Cinderella Th., St. Louis, MO	2/11	1924					Kilgen organ moved from Old Grand Central Th., St. Louis, Missouri.
3337	Kingsland Th., St. Louis, MO	2/10	1924					Kilgen tracker organ moved from Cinderella Th., St. Louis, Missouri.
3344	New Grand Th., Keokuk, IA	2/5	1924		16220	3	8"	
3345	Ozark Th., Webster Groves, MO	2/6	1924		16399	3	8"	
3358	White Palace Th., Chicago, IL	2/5	1924		16467			Style "Hess".
3363	WHT Radio, Chicago, IL	2/8	1925		16927	3	10"	With two consoles; see opus 3685.
3413	Labor Temple, Staunton, IL	2/5	1925					Rebuild and enlargement of existing Seeburg photoplayer; with horseshoe console.
3421	Star Th., Hannibal, MO	2/5	1925		17221	3	10"	
3423	Princess (Civic) Th., Roswell, NM	2/10	1925					New relay for opus 1619.
3431	Palace Th., Gary, IN	3/9	1925		17798	7½	15"	Special.
3432	Broadway Th., Gary, IN	2/4	1925		17306	2	10"	
3458	Majestic Th., Little Rock, AR	2/4	1925		17651	2		
3459	Lyric Th., Birmingham, AL	2/4	1925		17491	2		
3460	Broadway Th., Cape Giradeau, MO	3/8	1925		17559			Style U016X Special.
3471	Ritz Th., St. Louis, MO	2/4	1925			2	10"	
3473	Oakwyn (Ritz) Th., Berwyn, IL	3/9	1926		17702	5	15"	Style U020.
3474	Lido Th., Maywood, IL	3/9	1926					Style U020.
3475	Alamo Th., Chicago, IL	3/9	1926					Style U020.
3478	Glory B Th., Miami, OK	2/4	1925		18302			
3481	Majestic (State) Th., San Antonio, TX	2/10	1925		17700	3		New blower and tune opus 3128.
3502	KMOX Radio, St. Louis, MO	2/5	1926					
3514	Mermac Th., West Bend, WI	2/3	1926					Style U05.
3515	Kenwood Th., Chicago, IL	2/5	1926					Style U012 Special; used Kimball taken in on trade.
3516	Minne-Lusa Th., Omaha, NE	2/3	1926		S	1	10"	Style U05.
3604	Palace Th., Canton, OH	3/9	1926		S	5	10"	Style U020.
3605	Orpheum Th., Gary, IN	2/4	1926		18694			Special.
3608	Sheldon Memorial Th., Red Wing, MN	2/8	1926		S	5	10"	Style U015 Special.
3614	Jay Hawk Th., Topeka, KS	3/9	1926		18734			Style U020 Special.
3615	Ritz Th., Milwaukee, WI	2/5	1926		S	2	10"	Special design by Al Carney.
3616	Corby Th., Omaha, NE	2/4	1926		S	2	10"	Style U011 Special.
3617	Fremont (Goldberg) Th., Fremont, NE	2/4	1926		S	2	10"	Style U011.
3622	Metropole Th., Chicago, IL	2/3	1926		S	1	6"	Style U05.
3629	Ritz Th., Birmingham, AL	2/4	1926		S	1½	8"	Style U09.
3644	Frolic Th., Chicago, IL	2/5	1926		18910			Style U013.
3647	Piccadilly Th., Chicago, IL	4/19	1926		19249	20	15"	Special.
3648	Atlantic Th., Chicago, IL	3/11	1926		19142			Style U022.
3650	Royal Th., Hutchinson, KS	2/3	1926					Style U03.
3652	Landers Th., Springfield, MO	2/3	1926					Style U06.
3658	Lathrop Th., Omaha, NE	2/3	1926		S	1½	8"	Style U01.
3660	Criterion Th., Chicago, IL	2/5	1926					Style U013.
3670	Clearing Th., Chicago, IL	2/3	1926		S	1	6"	Style U05; see opus 4292.
3671	WAMD Radio, Minneapolis, MN	2/4	1926		S	1½	6"	Style U09.
3673	Twentieth Century Th., Chicago, IL	3/5	1926					Style U014X.
3675	Bonham Th., Fairbury, NE	2/4	1926					Style U09.
3676	Rivoli Th., Beatrice, NE	2/4	1926					Style U09.
3677	Rivoli Th., Hastings, NE	2/4	1926		S	2	10"	Style U011.
3681	Janet Th., Chicago, IL		1926					Used Seeburg Celesta DeLuxe or Reproduco.
3682	Orchid Th., Chicago, IL	2/3	1926		S	1		Style U01.
3685	WHT Radio, Chicago, IL	2/8	1926	n/c				Muted viol & glock exchanged for kinura on opus 3363.
3689	Empress Th., Kearney, NE	2/4	1926		S	1½	8"	Style U09 Special.
3690	Miller Th., Manhattan, KS	2/3	1926		S	1	8"	Style U06.
3692	Paramount Th., Albany, NY	3/5	1927	$ 8,130.00	21024			Style U014X, with double roll player.
					21198			
					9276S	3		
3693	Oak Th., Chicago, IL	2/3	1926		S	1½	10"	Style U05.
3697	Pawnee Th., Columbus, NE							No files extant.
3704	Ritz Th., Minneapolis, MN	2/3	1926	$ 3,465.00	5248S	1	6"	Style U01.
3706	Leavenworth Avenue Th., Omaha, NE	2/4	1926	$ 4,000.00	5350S	1½	10"	Style U011.
3707	Benson Th., Omaha, NE	2/4	1926	$ 4,000.00	5351S	1½	10"	Style U010.
3710	Leo Terry (organist), Chicago, IL	1/0	1926					One keyboard only for remote stunts at Piccadilly Th., Chicago, Illinois—opus 3647.
3711	Grand Th., Wausau, WI	3/6	1926	$ 8,000.00	5706S	3	10"	Style U014X Special.
3715	Grand Th., Galena, Il		1926	$ 2,250.00				Use Seeburg.
3718	Dickie Th., Downers Grove, IL		1926					Used photo player.
3719	Springfield Th., Chicago, IL		1926					No files extant.
3727	Clybourn Th., Chicago, IL		1926	$ 2,000.00				Used Seeburg Celesta DeLuxe; old piano traded in.

OPUS	LOCATION/CITY/STATE	SIZE	YR	PRICE	BLWR	HP	WP	REMARKS
3728	Milford Th., Chicago, IL	2/7	1927	$ 14,605.00	6563S	3	10"	Style U015; $8,105 credit allowed for Kimball traded in. Kilgen later moved to State Roller Rink, Hammond, Indiana.
3730	New Era Th., Chicago, IL		1926	$ 940.00				Used Reproduco.
3733	Granada Th., Norfolk, NE	2/4	1927	$ 6,653.00	6242S	1	10"	Style U011 Special; originally sold to but not shipped to Capitol (Grand Island) Theatre, Grand Island, Nebraska.
3734	Illinois Th., LaGrange, IL	2/3	1927	$ 4,900.00	6277S	1	8"	Style U02.
3735	Groveland Th., Chicago, IL	1/	1925	$ 950.00				Used Wurlitzer from Janet Th., Chicago, Illinois.
3738	Marlowe Th., Chicago, IL		1926					Used Kimball from Kenwood Th., Chicago, Illinois.
3740	WKAF Radio, Milwaukee, WI	2/4	1926	$ 11,200.00	6610S	2	8"	Was shipped, but not accepted.
3741	Hippodrome Th., Columbus, OH	2/3	1927	$ 3,150.00	6470S	1½	8"	Style U05; old Symphony organ taken in on trade.
3742	Strand (Arabian) Th., Laurel, MS	2/6	1926	$ 6,950.00	6452S	3	10"	Style U015.
3743	Grayland Th., Chicago, IL		1926	$ 2,250.00				Used Seeburg Celeste.
3745	Olympic Th., Chicago, IL		1926	$ 3,250.00				Special demonstration Reproduco.
3761	Ben Hur Th., Chicago, IL		1926	$ 2,500.00				Used Bartola taken in on trade from
3800	Delmonte Th., St. Louis, MO	2/9	1927	$ 147.00				Additions: extra cable and union board for opus 3058.
3801	Princess (Civic) Th., Roswell, NM	2/10	1927	$ 85.00				Revoiced oboe pipes on opus 1619.
3806	Ocasso Th., Kansas City, MO	2/3	1927	$ 3,250.00	7153S	1½	8"	Style U06.
3808	Peart Th., Gillespie, IL	2/3	1927	$ 2,100.00	7228S	1½	8"	Style U05; photo player taken in on trade.
3814	WAMD Radio, Minneapolis, MN	2/5	1927		7256S	2	10"	Style U013.
3820	Royal Th., LeMars, IA	2/3	1927		7301S	1½	8"	Style U05.
3822	Woodbury Th., Cedar City, UT	2/3	1927	$ 3,190.00				Style U01.
3828	National Theatre Supply, San Francisco, CA	2/5	1927		7186S	2	10"	Style U012; may have been purchased for a radio station.
3834	Cosmo Th., Merrill, WI	2/3	1927	$ 3,500.00	7401S	1½	10"	Style U06 Special; Fotoplayer traded in.
3835	Lyceum (Young's) Th., Canton, OH	2/4	1927	$ 5,000.00				Special.
3835	Lyceum Th., Gary, IN		1927		7542S	2	10"	Repair work; may not be correct opus number.
3836	Sun Th., Holdrege, NE	2/3	1927	$ 2,475.00	7344S	1	8"	Style U01.
3840	Park Th., Woonsocket, RI	2/3	1927	$ 3,870.00	7473S	1½	10"	Style U05.
3851	Mt. Pleasant Th., Cleveland, OH	2/4	1927	$ 5687.50	7543S	1½	8"	Style U010 with Mills Violano which cost $ 1,200.
3854	Lawndale Th., Chicago, IL		1927					Used photo player from Peart Th., Gillespie, Illinois.
3857	N. W. Conservatory of Music, Milwaukee, WI	3/5	1927		7680S	3	8"	Special.
3861	Monte Vista Th., Cincinnati, OH	2/4	1927		7803S	1½	8"	Style U09 Special.
3869	Broad & Larkin Th., Sidney, OH	2/3	1927	$ 2,800.00	7845S	1½	8"	Style U05.
3870	Bugg Th., Chicago, IL		1927					Recover 366 chest pneumatics in Kimball.
3871	KLZ Radio, Denver, CO	2/5	1927		7847S	2	8"	Style U013; vox on 6"wp; organ destroyed by fire in 1933.
3891	Rex Th., Albion, NE	2/3	1927	$ 2,464.00	8225S	1½	8"	Style U05.
3892	Lyric Th., Harbor Springs, MI	2/3	1927	$ 2,868.50	7963S	1½		Style U05 plus xylophone.
3893	Fortway Th., Brooklyn, NY	3/9	1927	$ 11,396.00	20490			Style U020.
3894	Metro Th., Bronx, NY	2/5	1927	$ 6,966.00				Style U013 plus marimba; theatre at Webster & Ford Streets.
3895	Alcazar (Birds State) Th., Grand Rapids, MI	2/4	1927	$ 4,001.00	7962S	1½	8"	Style U09.
3896	Seltzer Th., Palmyra, PA	2/4	1927	$ 4,095.20	9207S	1½	8"	Style U07 Special.
3897	Eldorado Th., Eldorado, KS	2/4	1927	$ 3,423.00	8256S	1½	8"	Style U09.
3898	Momart Th., Brooklyn, NY	2/4	1927	$ 5,675.00	8031S	1½	8"	Style U012.
3900	Zarah Th., Great Bend, KS	2/3	1927	$ 2,029.50	8206S	1	8"	Style U01.
3902	Ritz Th., Gary, IN	2/3	1927	$ 2,796.00	8127S	1½	8"	Style U05 with 88-note player, which cost $ 500.
3902A	Ritz Th., Gary, Indiana	2/3	1927	$ 656.50				Additions: xylophone, bass drum and cymbal.
3903	Cameo (Ohio) Th., Youngstown, OH	2/4	1927	$ 4,267.00	9595S	1½	8"	Style U09.
3911	Strand Th., Crawfordsville, IN	3/5	1927	$ 9599.86	8149S	3	10"	Style U014X with Mills violin which cost $ 1,600.
3915	Zenith Th., Milwaukee, WI	2/7	1927	$ 11,150.00	8297S	3		Special.
3916	Colonial Th., Cedar Rapids, IA		1927	$ 1,500.00				Used Seeburg Celesta from Grand Theatre, Galena, Illinois.
3921	Lakona Th., Celina, OH	2/3	1927		8001S	1½	8"	Style U05.
3926	Poplar Street Th., Memphis, TN	2/3	1927	$ 2,614.00	8314S	1	8"	Style U02 Special, with 5 chimes.
3931	Hope Th., Providence, RI	2/4	1927	$ 5,434.00	20832			Style U012.
3933	Ritz Th., Ardmore, OK	2/4	1927	$ 5,791.50	8420S	1½	8"	Style U09 Special.
3934	Pantages (Bijou) Th., Birmingham, AL	2/5	1927	$ 7,207.20	8366S	2	8"	Style U013; old organ taken in on trade.
3935	Granada Th., Racine, WI	2/3	1928	$ 4,044.00	9332S	1½	8"	Style U07 Special with six swinging bells in organ grille.
3947	Alladin Th., Kansas City, MO	2/5	1927	$ 2,464.00	8467S	1½	8"	Style U05.
3952	Suburban Th., Salt Lake City, UT	2/3	1927	$ 3,377.00	8582S	1	8"	Style U04.

OPUS	LOCATION/CITY/STATE	SIZE	YR	PRICE	BLWR	HP	WP	
3957	Liberty Th., Irvington, NJ	2/4	1927	$ 3,949.00	21025	1½	8"	Style U010.
3959	Colonial Th., St. Joseph, MO	2/3	1927	$ 3,784.00	8569S	1½	8"	Style U08.
3966	Riverside Th., Medford, MA	3/5	1928	$ 7,500.00	21168			Style U014X.
3970	Orpheum Th., Kingston, NY	3/5	1927	$ 7,500.00	21085	3	10"	Style U014X.
3972	Dreamland Th., New Haven, CT	2/3	1928	$ 2,860.00	21295	1½	8"	Style U06.
3991	Edith Toten Th., New York City, NY	3/5	1927		20844			Style U014X.
3995	Rivoli Th., Schenectady, NY	2/3	1927		21016	1½	8"	Style U07.
4003	Monogram Th., Chicago, IL	2/3	1928	$ 2,650.00	9334S	1	8"	Style U02 with roll player.
4004	Paramount Grand (Benbow) Th., Mt. Airy, NC	2/3	1928	$ 3,405.00	9527S	1½	8"	Style U06 with double roll player.
4005	Majestic Th., Paterson, NJ	2/3	1928	$ 3,010.00	21661			Style U08.
4006	Avon Th., Birmingham, AL	2/3	1928	$ 3,772.50	9517S	1½	8"	Style U07 with double roll player.
4007	Embassy (Moody) Th., Waltham, MA	3/9	1928	$ 9,728.25	21367			Style U020.
4008	Capitol Th., Rockford, IL	3/9	1928	$ 8,979.35	9510S	5	12"	Style U020 without chrysoglott.
4010	KOIL Radio, Council Bluffs, IA	2/3	1927	$ 1,732.50	9532S	1	8"	Style U01.
4013	Capitol Th., Brownsville, TX	2/3	1928	$ 2,642.50	9330S	1½	8"	Style U07.
4017	Towson Th., Towson, MD	2/4	1927	$ 3,949.00	21245			Style U010.
4018	American Th., Pittsburgh, PA	2/3	1928	$ 1,960.00				Style U05; moved organ from Ocaso Th., Kansas City, Missouri —opus 3806.
4019	Encanto Th., Havana, Cuba	3/5	1928	$ 6,609.43	21286			Style U014X plus sand block.
4025	Rivoli Th., San Benito, TX	2/3	1928	$ 2,906.75	9539S	1½	8"	Style U07.
4029	La Paloma Th., Encinitas, CA	2/5	1928	$ 5,488.34				Style U012.
4034	Classic Th., Watertown, WI	2/3	1928	$ 3,293.80	9651S	1½	8"	Style U08; harp substituted for xylophone; also listed in original records as Classic Th., Sparta Wisc., with same opus number.
4036	Unique Th., Santa Cruz, CA	2/3	1927	$ 2,686.25	21333			Style U04.
			1928		21504			
4037	Graham (Gerrittsen) Th., Brooklyn, NY	3/5	1928	$ 6,238.75	21394			Style U014X.
4038	Cortlandt Th., New York City, NY	2/3	1928	$ 2,642,50	21352			Style U07.
4039	Gold Th., Brooklyn, NY	2/3	1928	$ 2,642.50				Style U07.
4043	Steuben Club, Chicago, IL	3/6	1929		23716			Style U016X.
4045	Liberty Th., Irvington, NJ	2/4	1928	$ 125.00				Used Kimball xylophone added to opus 3957.
4049	Albertson Th., Kane, PA	2/4	1928	$ 4,481.40	21402			Style U010 with harp/marimba.
4049A	Albertson Th., Kane, PA	2/4		$ 880.00				Addition: double roll player.
4054	Leola Th., Minneapolis, MN	2/3	1928	$ 2,864.00	9966S	1½	8"	Style U08.
4106	Forum Th., Philadelphia, PA	3/9	1928	$ 9,537.50	21552	5	12"	Style U020.
4108	Strand Th., Stamford, CT	3/9	1928	$ 9,728.25	21568			Style U020.
4109	Alpha (Canton) Th., Cantonsville, MD	2/4	1928	$ 3,141.25	21529	1½	8"	Style U010.
4112	Bandbox Th., Bronx, NY	2/3	1928	$ 3,076.00	21557			Style U08 plus effects.
4113	Palace Th., Stamford, CT	3/9	1928	$ 9,728.25	21532			Style U020.
4114	Enderts Th., Crescent City, CA	2/3	1929	$ 2,686.25	21539			Style U04.
4125	West Chicago Th., West Chicago, IL		1928	$ 350.00				Used Bartola from Ben Hur Th., Chicago, Illinois.
4126	Community (Arcade) Th., Baltimore, MD	2/	1928	$ 3,933.25	21614			Style U010 with tibia.
4137	Strand Th., Scotdale, PA	2/4	1928	$ 4,373.40	21729	1½	8"	Style U012.
4138	Strand Th., Hackettstown, NJ	2/3	1928	$ 2,642.50	21771	1½	8"	Style U07.
4144	Shelton Th., Shelton, CT	2/3	1928					Style U08; order cancelled; parts put back in stock.
4145	WIBO Radio, Chicago, IL	2/8	1928		16927	3	10"	Move Kilgen opus 3363.
4148	Crown Th., Lowell, MA	2/3	1928	$ 2,583.00				Style U08.
4149B	Wade Th., Morehead, NC	2/3	1928	$ 3,155.00	21837	1½	8"	Style U06 with double roll player.
4150B	Argonne Th., Bel Air, MD	2/3	1928	$ 2,642.50	21949			Style U08.
4152	Orpheum Th., Danielson, CT	2/3	1928	$ 2,642.50	22122			Style U07.
4155	Citizens (Lark) Th., Brazil, IN	2/5	1928	$ 3,789.50	21851			Style U012 without some traps and second touch.
4157	Capitol Th., Portland, OR	2/4	1928	$ 4,322.50	21853			Style U012.
4161B	Westwood Th., Westwood, NJ	3/9	1928	$ 10,010.00	21826	5	12"	Style U020.
4163	Grand Th., Madison, IN	2/4	1928	$ 3,089.50	21898			Style U09 with player.
4167B	Oakland Th., Marion, OH	2/3	1928	$ 1,960.00	11065S	1½	5"	Style U05.
4172	Norwood Th., Norwood, OH	2/4	1928		21956			Style U011 without traps and 2nd touch.
4184	Rivoli Th., Rome, GA	2/5	1928	$ 5,202.50	22030			Style U012 with double roll player.
4198	Grand Th., New Orleans, LA	2/3	1928	$ 1,960.00	11439S	1	8"	Style U02.
4200B	Palace Th., Rockville, CT	2/3	1928		22170			Style U07.
4206	Dixie Th., Rochester, NY	2/5	1929		22512			Style U011.
4226	Grand Th., Madison, IN	2/4	1929					Roll player for opus 4163.
4230	Whittall Th., Woodside, CA	3/6	1929		22434			Style U014X.
4231	St. Mary's Th., St. Mary's, PA	2/5	1928		22325			Style U012 Special.
4258	Earl Carroll Th., New York, NY	3/6	1929					Style U016X.
4271	Mt. Ephraim Th., Mt. Ephraim, NJ	2/3	1929		22772	1½	8"	Style U08.
4292	Clearing Th., Chicago, IL	2/3	1928	$ 500.00				Additions: traps, orchestra bells and xylophone to opus 3670.
4301	Seville (Boyd) Th., Easton, PA	3/9	1929		22785			Style U020.
4301A	Seville (Boyd) Th., Easton, PA							Extra parts.
4411	East Side Th., Chicago, IL		1929					Additions: 37-note xylophone and 8' kinura, 61-pipes.
4420	Eastwood Th., Madison, WI	2/8	1930		14507S	2	8"	Special.
4443	KMOX Radio, St. Louis, MO	3/10	1930					Enlargement of opus 3502.

OPUS	LOCATION/CITY/STATE	SIZE	YR	PRICE	BLWR	HP	WP	REMARKS
4444	Hal Roach Studio (KFVD Radio), Culver City, CA	3/5	1930					Special.
4515	KEPY Radio, Spokane, WA	2/3	1930					Style U04; order cancelled.
4550	Paramount Th., Idaho Falls, ID	2/3	1930		760S	1½	8"	Style U06.
4577	KMOX Radio, St. Louis, MO	3/10	1930	n/c				New 37-note harp for opus 4443.
4584	T. R. Earl, Idaho Falls, ID	2/3	1930		773S		8"	Style U06.
4610	Convention Hall, Asbury Park, NJ	3/7	1931					Parts.
4613	Convention Hall, Asbury Park, NJ	3/7	1931					Generator.
4619	Convention Hall, Asbury Park, NJ	3/7	1931					Swell shades.
4646	Convention Hall, Asbury Park, NJ	3/7	1931					Parts.
4717	Convention Hall, Asbury Park, NJ	3/7	1931					Rebuild relay.
4731	Palace Th., Gary, IN	3/9	1931					Pipes for opus 3431.
4779	LaScala (Kiba-Apollo) Th., Vienna, Austria	3/10	1931		24731	5		Style U020, plus post horn.
4816	KMOX Radio, St. Louis, MO	3/16	1931					Enlarged opus 4443.
4827	Sun Th., Holdrege, NE	2/3	1931					Parts for opus 3836.
4920	Lincoln Th., Springfield, IL	3/	1932					New console and pedal relay only.
4931	KNX Radio, Los Angeles, CA	2/5	1932					Style U012.
5004	Liberty Th., Malden, MO	2/5	1933					Mostly used parts.
5009	WHAS Radio, Louisville, KY	3/7	1933					
5124	WHAS Radio, Louisville, KY	3/7		$ 212.00				Replace sax with clarinet on opus 5009.
5198	WHAS Radio, Louisville, KY	3/7		n/c				Replace post horn with trumpet on opus 5009.
5212	WHAS Radio, Louisville, KY	3/7		$ 300.00				Electrify player piano owned by WHAS, add mandolin and make playable from organ, opus 5009.
5225	KMOX Radio, St. Louis, MO	4/16	1934					New console for opus 4816.
5232	St. Mary of the Lake Seminary, Mundelein, IL	4/15	1934					Swell shutters for Howell Organ formerly in Al Carney Studio, Chicago, Illinois.
5281	WKY Radio, Oklahoma City, OK	4/10	1935					
5281A	WKY Radio, Oklahoma City, OK	4/14						Additions: four ranks.
5281B	WKY Radio, Oklahoma City, OK	4/14						Added vibrahap.
5281C	WKY Radio, Oklahoma City, OK	4/14						Service.
5281D	WKY Radio, Oklahoma City, OK	4/14						Parts.
5281E	WKY Radio, Oklahoma City, OK	4/14						Parts.
5302	KMOX Radio, St. Louis, MO	4/16	1934					Parts for opus 5225.
5323	Alamo Th., St. Louis, MO		1934					Rebuilt Kilgen—no records on file.
5420	St. Mary of the Lake Seminary, Mundelein, IL	4/15						Additions to Howell organ formerly in Al Carney Studio, Chicago, Illinois.
5465	WHDH Radio, Boston, MA	2/5	1935					
5471	KMOX Radio, St. Louis, MO	4/16	1935					Releather 49 harp pneumatics for opus 5225.
5612	KMOX Radio, St. Louis, MO	4/16	1936					Attach damper action to shuffle for opus 5225.
5616	KFPW Radio, Fort Smith, AR	2/6	1936					
5621	WHO Radio, Des Moines, IA	2/3	1936					Style 7 Petit Ensemble; voiced on 4½" wp.
5661	Little Th., Rochester, NY	2/3	1936					Style 12 Petit Ensemble.
5661A	Little Th., Rochester, NY	2/3	1936					Revoice viola into dulciana!
5685	WDBJ Radio, Roanoke, VA	2/4	1936					Petit Ensemble, style 9 special.
5769	WHAS Radio, Louisville, KY	4/14	1937					Enlarge existing organ, opus 5009; see also opus 7179.
5793	WKRC Radio, Cincinnati, OH		1937					Additions: 8' open diapason, T.C., 49 pipes, chest and switches.
5869	KMOX Radio, St. Louis, MO	4/16	1937	$ 594.25		7½	15"	New blower for opus 5225.
5910	Capitol Th., Wheeling, WV		1937	$ 5.00				Wind bag.
5931	WFIL Radio, Philadelphia, PA	4/14	1937					
5998	Strand Th., Meridian, MS		1937	$ 10.00				Two skins of pneumatic leather.
5999	Saenger Th., New Orleans, LA		1937	$ 20.00				Four skins of pneumatic leather.
6013	WLAC Radio, Nashville, TN	4/12	1938			7½		Enlargement of 9-rank Wurlitzer.
6013A	WLAC Radio, Nashville, TN	4/12						Cable.
6013B	WLAC Radio, Nashville, TN	4/12						Grilles.
6106	KXOK Radio, St. Louis, MO	2/4	1938					Style 50 Petit Ensemble.
7179	WHAS Radio, Louisville, KY	4/14	1949					New console for opus 5769.

Opus numbers for the following Kilgen theatre installations are unknown:

CITY/STATE	LOCATION	SIZE	YR	BLWR	HP	WP	REMARKS
ALABAMA							
Birmingham	Alcazar (Empire) Th.	2/7	1919				
	Bijou Th.	2/10	1919	9635			
ARKANSAS							
Little Rock	Park Th.	2/	1913	B442	2	4½"	
			1914	C113	2	5"	
ILLINOIS							
Chicago	Atlantic Th.		1917	8628			Later moved to Los Angeles Kilgen studios.
INDIANA							
Evansville	American Th.	2/	1912				
MINNESOTA							
Minneapolis	Dyckman Hotel		1914	B596	¾	4"	
	Lyric Th.	2/8	1917	8419			Removed in 1925.
	Unique Th.	2/8	1917				
St. Paul	Garrick Th.	3/	1917	8418			
	Majestic Th.	2/9	1916				
	Princess Th.	2/11	1917				
	Strand Th.	2/8	1917				
MISSOURI							
Columbia	Uptown Th.	2/4					
Kansas City	Empress Th.	2/10	1919				
	Garden Th.	2/14	1919	10321			
St. Louis	Cinderella Th.	2/10	1917	8334			Tracker action; moved from Old Grand Central Th., St. Louis, Missouri.
	Gem Th.	2/	1914				Tubular pneumatic action.
	La Paloma Th.		1927	21241			
	New Grand Central Th.						
	New Rex Th.	2/16	1913	A532	2	4½"	Tubular pneumatic action.
	Old Grand Central Th.	2/10	1911				Tracker action; cost $3,500; moved in 1917 to Cinderella Theatre, St. Louis, Missouri.
	Old Grand Central Th.	2/11	1917				
	Pershing Th.	3/13	1919	9451			
			1919	9730			
	Sixth & Chestnut Th.	2/5	1920				
NEW JERSEY							
Asbury Park	Convention Hall	3/7	1928	22594			
NEW YORK							
Brooklyn	Parthenon Th.		1928				
New York	Kilgen Wonder Organ School		1927				Located at 1560 Broadway, Suite 409; same address as National Theatre Supply Co.
OREGON							
Portland	Lucien Becker Studio	2/7	1920				
TEXAS							
Dallas	Wells Th.	2/9	1919				
WISCONSIN							
Baraboo	Ringling Bros. Circus	4/11	1902				Tubular action; only one manual used, remaining three manuals being dummies; entire organ portable! Cost $4,000.

The history of the W. W. Kimball Company is another classic American success story. William Wallace Kimball moved from his native Maine to Decorah, Iowa in 1853 at the age of 25 and was in the insurance and real estate business there for four years. In 1857 he decided to travel to Chicago to seek his fortune. In many people's eyes he couldn't have picked a worse time: the Panic of 1857 was bankrupting businesses right and left. Over breakfast one morning at the Sherman House, Kimball happened to make the acquaintance of a young piano merchant who, along with many other people at the time, was down on his luck. One thing led to another and eventually the men agreed to trade four Grovensteen & Truslow square grand pianos for some property in Decorah, Iowa. With that simple transaction the Kimball music business was born. Little did Kimball know at the time that his company would one day become the world's largest manufacturer of pianos.[4]

The Kimball business began by retailing instruments of other manufacturers. Though W. W. Kimball knew nothing of the music business and couldn't play a note, he was, however, a shrewd businessman who believed in making money by smaller profits from a larger number of customers rather than by large profits from individual sales. In Kimball's own words, "There are few people who understand that the expenses of running and increasing business do not increase as the business increases; consequently, the point to arrive at is a large volume of trade."[5]

Mr. Kimball tells an interesting story about his first purchase of pianos directly from a manufacturer: "I had a little money and I went on to New York. I didn't know anything about pianos then and supposed you bought them like anything else—like wheat or pork—by the quantity. I called on a house, well known in those days . . . one of the oldest in the trade. After some dickering I had made my bargain and had my roll out to pay for the goods when I said, 'Are you sure you are giving me your lowest prices? Are there not some cheaper pianos being made?'

" 'Oh, yes,' said the piano maker. 'The Fischers make cheaper pianos but we wouldn't put our name on the trash they turn out! Why, they use green lumber!'

" 'I guess,' said I, as a thought struck me and I put my roll back into my pocket, 'that I'll think this thing over and come again in the morning.' I went straight back to my hotel, got a directory and hunted up the address of 'Fisher,' a piano maker. Couldn't find it. Then I looked up 'Fischer' and got it. That day I went to the [J. & C.] Fischer factory and met Mr. Fischer, the light haired one. 'Somebody told me,' said I, 'that you make cheaper pianos than anybody else but that they are no good.'

" 'I think we make nice instruments,' replied Mr. Fischer politely.

" 'Let me see some,' said I. So Mr. Fischer took me through the factory. 'Do you use green lumber?' I asked.

" 'No sir, we could not afford to,' was the quiet reply.

" 'Bye the bye,' said I, 'what kind of pianos do Messrs.--- make?" mentioning the name of the firm I had been to first.

" 'I understand that they make a very nice piano indeed,' said Mr. Fischer.

"That settled it. Fischer got my roll and that purchase was the first of many more. I guess I must have bought over 1,000 Fischer pianos before I made other arrangements. During all that time I never had any trouble with any of their instruments and I found them particularly fine, upright and good people to deal with."[6]

By 1859 Kimball had branched into the reed organ business in an effort to secure an even broader market of customers. Even a cheap piano sold for $200 in those days but a parlor organ could be had for less than half as much. By the mid-1860s American reed organ production reached 15,000 instruments per year and Kimball was selling 25% of them! One major reason for Kimball's success was his inauguration of the installment plan which enabled families of modest means to afford the luxury of owning a piano or an organ. Clever sales gimmicks, in those days before heavy media advertising, also helped. One trick was to load a wagon (horse-drawn, of course) with an instrument and head for a country farmhouse. The wagon was outfitted with a wheel which would fall off on command. The salesman would enlist the aid of the farm family to move the instrument off the "broken" wagon into their house to protect it from the elements until he could return to town to secure repairs to the wagon. Returning a day or so later, the salesman usually found that the farmer's wife had become so enamored of the instrument that she would not allow it to be taken away![7]

In 1879 the Kimball company manufactured its first reed organ in the repair shops above the State Street store in Chicago. In 1881 a four-story factory of 76,800 square feet was leased at 26th and Rockwell Streets and a lumber forest and sawmill were leased in Newport, Arkansas.[9] A 96,000 square foot building was built adjacent to the organ factory in 1887 for piano manufacture and by 1889 production reached 50 organs per day and 50 pianos per week.[10]

Mr. Kimball realized that a market existed for an instrument larger than the largest reed organ yet smaller than a full pipe organ, but as yet no one had invented such a thing. In 1890 a young man of 23 applied for a job to W. W. Lufkin, plant superintendent and nephew of W. W. Kimball. Frederic W. Hedgeland was born in London, the son of an English organ builder, and had already done organ work in St. Paul, Minnesota before coming to Chicago. He was given the go-ahead to produce a portable pipe organ which could be shipped anywhere and installed without the services of an expert.[11]

By late 1891 three styles of portable organs had been developed, all featuring removable keyboards which allowed them to pass through ordinary doors. The smallest style was a one-manual instrument; the second style added a pedalboard and the largest model featured two manuals,[12] six ranks of pipes and two sets of 16' free reeds in the pedal. The pipes were held firmly in place so the organ would be ready to play even if it were shipped upside down! The bellows pump handle could be inserted into either end of the case (remember, this was in the days before electric blowers) and the action was double-pressure tubular pneumatic, the pipes speaking on 3" wind pressure and the action on 6".[13]

Kimball's success in the pipe organ market was immediate. In 1894 the first permanently installed instrument was built and a new five-story building of 96,000 square feet was added to the factory complex. In 1907 a new 60,000 square foot structure was built in order to meet increasing production demands.[14] By 1909, 5,000 pipe organs (mostly portable), 200,000 pianos and 320,000 reed organs had been built in the Kimball factory.[15] Reed organ production ceased in 1922 with 403,390 having been built. The last new Kimball pipe organ, opus 7326, was shipped from the factory on September 26, 1942 to Good Hope Lutheran Church, Bucyrus, Ohio.[16] After the pipe organ division was closed, the company continued manufacturing pianos and in 1948 produced the 500,000th Kimball piano, an industry record.[17] Piano production continues in 1983 along with electronic organs which were added to the line in the 1960s.

Frederic W. Hedgeland was in charge of Kimball's pipe organ division from its inception until 1908. Until his departure the firm had built tubular pneumatic organs exclusively. After he left, a successful electric action was developed and Oscar J. Hagstrom, who had also been with the company since the beginning of pipe organ production in 1890, became superintendent of the organ factory. F. T. Milner joined Kimball around 1901 and in 1905 was appointed manager of the pipe organ department.[19] In this same year George T. Michel joined the

The enormous Kimball factory consumed 17 acres on Chicago's southwest side near 32nd and California Streets. Proclaimed the world's largest piano and organ factory, it contained 850,000 square feet of floor space.

Kimball Hall in Chicago, looking southwest across the corner of Jackson and Wabash Avenues. Few firms in the music industry could boast of owning their own office buildings—especially of this size. This building was built in 1917, replacing a seven-story structure built in 1891 which had served earlier as Kimball headquarters.[3]

George Michel, Kimball head voicer and one of the most talented men who ever exercised his craft, tunes a spotted metal principal in his voicing room at the Kimball factory.

company and within ten years became head voicer.[20]

George Michel, as much as anyone, was responsible for the Kimball sound and he occupied perhaps a unique niche in the industry in being supremely talented at voicing both reeds and flues. His reeds were constructed with a jeweler's precision. They had distinctive tone colors, stood rock solidly in tune and were perhaps more uniform note per note than any ever built. Michel's strings set the standard by which all others were judged. Their richness, timbre and incredible promptness of speech, even in the 32' octave, have never been surpassed. An example of the esteem George Michel's voicing gave the company was the fact that Wanamaker's Department Store in Philadelphia commissioned Kimball to build an 88-rank string organ plus a number of solo reeds for additions to the giant Wanamaker instrument in the late 1920s.

Another Kimball voicer of distinction was Joseph J. Carruthers who had been the right hand man of Robert Hope-Jones from the first organ he built to his last.[21] Mr. Carruthers joined Kimball after Hope-Jones' tragic suicide in 1914 and served the company not only as a voicer but as an engineer thoroughly knowledgeable about Hope-Jones methods in organ building.[22] It was Mr. Carruthers who introduced the Hope-Jones triple-valve reser-

voir to Kimball production in 1930.[23] One of the rare Kimball factory documents still extant reveals that Mr. Carruthers' salary in 1920 was $1.00 per hour. George Michel's salary in the same period was $1.10 per hour.

Several other people prominent in the Kimball organ division should be mentioned. The head of the metal pipe shop until his retirement in 1929 was Frank A. Meyer, a brother of Jerome B. Meyer, owner of the well-known Milwaukee pipe making firm bearing his name.[24] Carl Benson was foreman of the electric action and wiring department until 1925 when he left to join Welte. Previously he had been with E. M. Skinner from 1907 to 1917 and then with Wangerin-Weickhardt until joining Kimball in 1918. Walter D. Hardy, one of the company's best salesmen, was appointed manager of the organ department in 1925[25] and was succeeded in that post by William Wallace Kimball, grand nephew of W. W. Kimball, Sr., in 1930. Wallace Kimball (1901-   ) started in the pipe organ factory in 1925 as a draftsman earning $13 per week and later worked on organ installation crews before assuming the post as department manager.[26] He became president of the company in 1945.[27]

There was one man, however, who, more than any other, was really responsible for the Kimball pipe organ we know today. If George Michel was the voice of the Kimball organ, R. P. Elliot was its soul. Robert Pier Elliot (1871-1941) began his career in the organ industry in 1889 with Granville Wood & Son of Northville, Michigan shortly before that firm was acquired by Farrand & Votey. At the latter firm Mr. Elliot made the acquaintance of John T. Austin and was instrumental in organizing the

Austin Organ Company in 1898, becoming its vice president. When Robert Hope-Jones joined Austin in 1903 as vice president, Elliot became secretary. Angered because the firm accepted Hope-Jones' resignation in his absence, Elliot sold his Austin stock and founded the Kinetic Engineering Company, having obtained the rights to manufacture Kinetic blowers in America during a previous trip to England. After the Kinetic company was well established, Mr. Elliot left the country for a few years, pursuing his other avocation of mining, in Mexico and England. He returned to America in May of 1909 to assume the presidency of the Hope-Jones Organ Company of Elmira, New York but left the country again to pursue his mining interests when the Hope-Jones company failed in 1910.[28][29]

Mr. Elliot returned to America to stay in 1914, becoming eastern United States manager for Kimball.[30] He left this position in October of 1916 to become vice president and general manager of the California Organ Company, which soon became the Robert-Morton Company, and remained there until May of 1918.[31] At that time F. T. Milner resigned as manager of Kimball's organ division due to ill health and Mr. Elliot stepped in to fill his position. One of the first policies instituted by Elliot was the abolition of tubular pneumatic action; after 1918 electropneumatic action was used exclusively.[32]

R. P. Elliot embodied a number of talents which served the Kimball company well: he was well schooled in Hope-Jones principles of electric action organ building; he was a knowledgeable businessman who had experience in the day to day operations of running several organ companies; he knew, socialized with, and was respected by many of the country's leading organists and he was recognized by his peers as one of the leading figures in the entire industry. He was described by Riley Daniels, former president of the Moller company, as "a very polished gentleman" and "a professional letter writer."[33] His letter writing skill kept him in close communication with friends in the industry with the result that he was better informed than most about what was going on in the organ business. He also listened to the needs of organists and did his best to satisfy them; not all firms had such a wise policy!

Elliot's letter writing skills were put to excellent advantage in sales efforts. He was often able to clinch a sale without leaving his Chicago office. Even when a sale seemed lost, Elliot would give one last try as evidenced by the following letter to the owner of the Aldine Theatre in Philadelphia. As it turned out, Elliot lost this sale to Moller's crackerjack salesman, Louis Luberoff: "I have never heard anything more from you . . . about the Aldine Theatre organ so it is a pretty safe guess that it was 'love's labour lost.' I am sorry if that is the case, but as I learn that Luberoff has been visiting our big organs and spending hours studying them, I take it he is getting ready to do his first modern orchestral instrument with proper double touch arrangements, etc., and wants to learn how we do it.

" . . . As a personal friendly tip from a friend . . . and in no sense as a protest or complaint, I want to say that your chance of making good with that theatre against the com-

Robert Pier Elliot (1871-1941)

petition of the New Stanley and the Kugler will be very much stronger with a Kimball organ such as we had agreed upon than with anything those people could build. They are particularly and justly known as builders of organs of nondescript tone. They buy a large proportion of their pipes and they haven't the class of artistic voicers we have for those they make themselves. I am no lover of Wurlitzer's tone but I must say you would have been much more likely to attract the musical people with a Wurlitzer played by a clever player of the Bonawitz type than you will with the other, no matter how it may be played.

"Sounds as though we were proud of ourselves, doesn't it? Well, we are and we have a right to be. I wish you were still on the band wagon."[34]

Kimball's business was so good that the company actually stopped taking orders for 3½ months early in 1920.[35] In Elliot's own words, "Our capacity has been sold out for twelve months ahead all winter and in spite of repeated price increases it has reached a point today about fifteen months ahead, which the company regards as unsafe in consideration of the rapidly rising cost of materials and labor and the fact that contracts for organs taken last year and delivered recently have in some instances shown a loss although there was a good margin of profit at the time the contracts were taken."[36]

Elliot was responsible for Kimball building what they called orchestral instruments. These featured some unification, although not much, and some straight and

THE money invested in Kimball organs in the theatres of Philadelphia alone equals, if indeed it does not surpass that in organs of all other makes (pit and corresponding small automatic instruments, which the Kimball Company has never manufactured, not included in the comparison).

The Stanley Company of America is doubtless the largest owner of fine organs in the United States, their equipment being almost exclusively Kimball and running largely to complete instruments which supplant orchestras altogether in many of the leading houses they operate in Philadelphia, Atlantic City, New York and elsewhere. Frank W. Buhler, General Manager, wrote a fellow exhibitor: "In our experience, which covers a period of fifteen years, there is only one organ that seems to qualify in every department, and that is the Kimball."

The M. E. Comerford Amusement Company, operating the leading theatres in Scranton, Wilkesbarre and over eastern Pennsylvania and southern New York state, is also a heavy Kimball owner and buys Kimballs exclusively.

The Nixon-Nirdlinger group and others of prominence are now joined by H. M. Crandall of Washington, who has ordered a Kimball Unit Orchestra for his new Ambassador Theatre.

C. Howard Crane, architect of many of the finest theatres in existence, wrote in a letter to a client for whom he was building a large house: "In the last three large theatres that I have built Kimball organs have been installed, and to my mind they are the best organs we have ever put into theatres. One particular fact that I wish to speak about is this, that in each and every case, the James Theatre, the Allen, Cleveland, and the Roosevelt, the organs were installed and in fine working order when we opened the theatres, a thing that we never had happen to us before. I am writing you this, in this letter, for the reason that I believe that service of this sort should receive recognition."

In the Empress Theatre, Anchorage, Alaska, where it rains from August until it snows in October, where midsummer humid heat alternates with forty degrees below zero and navigation opens late in May, is a Kimball Orchestral Organ which stood two years without attention and never missed a performance nor had any other tuning or regulation than the organist gave it and was found in good shape when the erecting man visited it after installing the second Kimball in the new Empress Theatre at Cordova, also owned by Capt. Lathrop. Only one visit has been made to these organs in the subsequent four years and both are reported in a recent letter from the management to be in perfect condition.

Its organist writes regarding a Kimball instrument in the hard baked desert country: "I have never in my life come across an organ that stays in such good shape as this organ has, and it really is remarkable considering the climate in this country—the tone quality of this instrument is super-supreme—I have shown them that it is possible to play vaudeville on the organ—I have even played musical comedies with this organ, and if that is not going some, I want to know."

W. C. Quimby of Fort Wayne said, while signing a contract for the new Kimball Unit Orchestra just installed in his Jefferson Theatre: "My old Kimball has played every day for nine years with only one day's shut down, and that was due to motor trouble."

The Organ is the King of Instruments;
The Kimball is the King of Organs

THE FORVM
Singulus Theatrum Unicus
Los Angeles

This Temple of Roman Architecture, dedicated to the fine art of Amusement, will depend for its music upon a Kimball Unit Orchestra, which represents the largest investment ever made in a musical instrument for a theatre.

An extremely rare Kimball theatre organ catalog c. 1923 is reproduced on this (in reduced size) and the following three pages (full size). The company produced a number of elaborate catalogs for its church organs, but promotional literature for its theatre products has proved quite elusive.

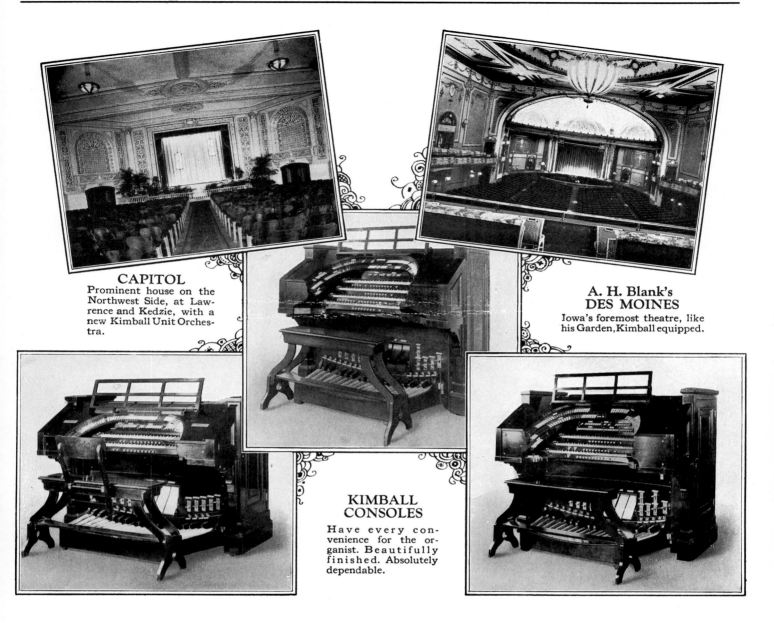

CAPITOL

Prominent house on the Northwest Side, at Lawrence and Kedzie, with a new Kimball Unit Orchestra.

A. H. Blank's DES MOINES

Iowa's foremost theatre, like his Garden, Kimball equipped.

KIMBALL CONSOLES

Have every convenience for the organist. Beautifully finished. Absolutely dependable.

POINTS OF SUPERIORITY

KIMBALLS ARE BUILT TO ORDER, to fit the requirements of each theatre. You would not be satisfied with an architect who built your house inflexibly to a stock, numbered plan.

All Kimball pipes are made and voiced after all conditions are known. There is no "piece work" voicing in Kimball organs. Six sound proof voicing rooms are needed for this work. Pure tin strings, special heavy metal leathered Diapasons, true scale leathered Tibias, genuine Diaphones made under the direction of the man responsible for the first Diaphones, imitative reeds that stand in tune, Deagan Chimes, Deagan Artist's Special Xylophones and other percussions exclusively, with special Kimball piano and reiterating actions having the correct loud and soft and damper controls, Ludwig and Ludwig drums of ample size, their best military band and orchestra equipment.

Adequate wind pressures in ample volume. The Kimball single pressure wind chest with percussion chamber to each pipe.

Perfected Kimball electric action, speedy beyond human testing, with the highest resistance magnet used in organs, made in the Kimball factory, safe and reliable, requiring no regulation. Silver contacts throughout, including relays. Inclined key boards hinged for inspection. All Kimball consoles are rat and vermin proof.

Kimball adjustable double touch combination action with provision for neutral setting. Kimball individual silent electric swells perfectly graduated. Kimball tremolos and vibratos with separate regulation for speed and force. "The organ with the human voice" built that reputation on Kimball scales of Vox Humanas having special vibratos and separate reservoirs with correct wind pressures for the effects desired.

No "ciphers" and no silent notes. Kimball organs require less attention than others. "Ask the man who owns one." Ask especially the man who owns Kimballs and other organs.

The facilities of the Kimball Company are unsurpassed. The Kimball plant is reputed to house the largest musical instrument industry in America and is practically independent of outside assistance. Abundant capital and extensive storage space permit carrying heavy stocks of lumber, metals and other raw materials, which are bought at the most favorable times. Skilled workmen have the assistance of the latest labor saving machinery, much of which is designed and built in the Company's own foundry and machine shops.

Unprejudiced advice can be depended upon from the Kimball technical staff since the Kimball Company builds all types of organs from the true Unit Orchestra through the degrees of unification to absolutely straight organs, as sometimes required in church, school and lodge work. Opportunities to coöperate with owners and architects are welcomed.

Free from financial worry, the inventors and builders of Kimball organs live up to their ideals, and can and do build an instrument which approaches perfection, which is artistic and pleasing tonally, which is instantaneous and reliable in action, and which stands indefinitely without regulation or repairs, *the best investment a theatre man can make.*

NEPTUNE, Seattle

One of the finest theatres in the Northwest, belonging to the *Jensen & Von Herberg* chain. A large three manual Kimball.

CLEMMER, Spokane

Principal house of the city. It has a four manual Kimball with Echo

**ARCADIA
Windber, Pa.**

Illustrating the long type of house, about 800 seats, two manual divided Kimball.

**EMPRESS
Anchorage, Alaska**

The farthest north of theatre organs. This and the Empress, Cordova, have large Kimball Orchestral Units, some of the percussion instruments being visible in the openings under the grilles.

**CAPITOL
Wilkes-Barre, Pa.**

One of *The M. E. Comerford Amusement Co.* houses. They buy Kimballs exclusively.

**Loew's ALLEN
Cleveland**

Ohio's finest theatre. Large three manual Kimball with Echo, the most complete theatre organ in the state.

**KARLTON
Philadelphia**

Typical *Stanley Company* one floor house, its music supplied by a three manual Kimball Unit Orchestra.

**STANLEY
Philadelphia**

Producing house of the *Stanley Company of America*, containing the largest and most costly Unit in the East.

RIVIERA

Keith's Brooklyn theatre with a large divided three manual Kimball.

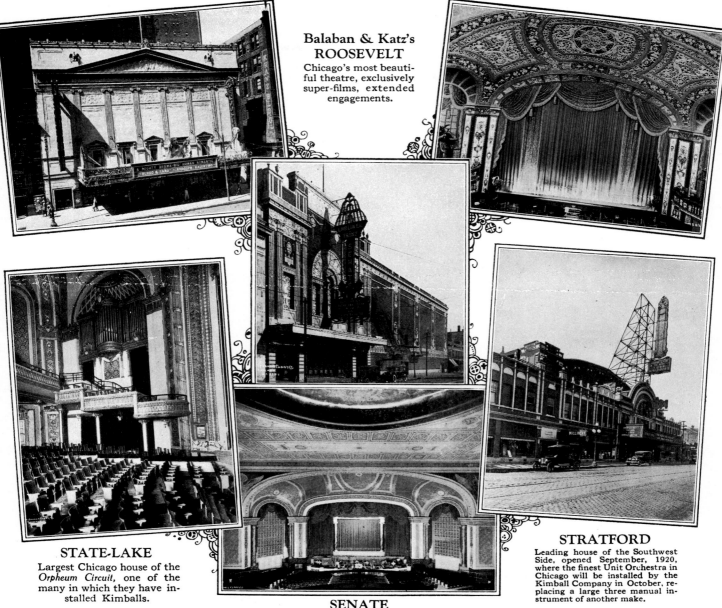

Balaban & Katz's ROOSEVELT
Chicago's most beautiful theatre, exclusively super-films, extended engagements.

STATE-LAKE
Largest Chicago house of the *Orpheum Circuit,* one of the many in which they have installed Kimballs.

SENATE
The leading house of the West Side, picked by a group of eastern theatre owners and architects as the most satisfactory picture house in Chicago.
Lubliner and Trinz.

STRATFORD
Leading house of the Southwest Side, opened September, 1920, where the finest Unit Orchestra in Chicago will be installed by the Kimball Company in October, replacing a large three manual instrument of another make.

WOODLAWN
Prominent South Side first run house. The largest in Chicago on one floor and the first to install a three manual Kimball.

PANTHEON
The palatial house of the North Side, on Sheridan Road at Leland. *Lubliner and Trinz.*

duplexed ranks. A typical example was installed in the Roosevelt Theatre in Chicago where Jesse Crawford's wife-to-be, Helen Anderson, played. Its analysis is reproduced below:

W. W. KIMBALL CO.						
CHICAGO. U.S.A.						
PIPE ORGANS						
Specification					Page 5.	
No. 20131		A N A L Y S I S				
Name.	Pitch	Pipes	Pedal	Orchestral	Great	Swell
Diaphone	16	85	16-8		8-8	
Tibia Clausa	16	85	16	8-8-4-4	8	
Wald Horn	8	85		8	8-4	
Concert Flute	16	97	16-10⅔-8-4	8-4-2	16-8-4-2⅔-1⅓	
Violin I	16	97	16-(8-(4	16-8-4	8-2	
Violin II	8	146	(8-(4	8-4		
Clarabella	16	97	16			16-8-4-2
Horn Diapason	8	73				8
Flute Celeste t.c.	8	61				8
Viola	8	73				8
Muted Violin	8	73				8
Vox Angelica t.c.	8	61				8
Quintadena	4	73				4
Tuba	16	85	16-8-4	16-8	16-8-4-8	
Oboe Horn	16	97	16			16-8-4
Trumpet	8	73				8
Vox Humana	8	61				8
Clarinet	8	73		8		
Kinura	8	61		8		
Saxaphone	8	Syn.		8		
Orchestral Oboe	8	Syn.		8		
Musette	8	Syn.			8	
Violoncello IV	8	Syn.		8		
Harp	8	49		8		8
Marimba					8	8
Chimes	8	20		8	8	
Glockenspiel	4	37		4	4	4
Orchestra Bells				4	4	
Xylophone	4	37		4	4	

In R. P. Elliot's own words, "Upon my resumption of organ building in 1914 at . . . Kimball . . . theatre work was well started but consisted [in other builders] largely of those abominable 'pit instruments' and second hand church organs, usually electified after a fashion and supplied with chimes, drums and traps. We set out to remedy this and for years refused to build [unit orchestras] . . . and we refused to furnish any but the legitimate, musical drums and traps of the concert orchestra."[37] It is fascinating that the man who was president of the Hope-Jones Organ Company should have been so resistant to the idea of fully unified theatre organs. He succumbed, however, to pressure from Kimball's largest theatre customer, the Stanley circuit, to build the first large fully unified Kimball theatre organ in 1921 for the Stanley Theatre in Philadelphia. It was an impressive instrument of 29 ranks, boasting a 32' bombarde. Said Elliot, " . . . came the day when our best customer demanded a 'unit orchestra' and the reason? Wurlitzer-trained players were drifting in, for the most part ex-pianists who had learned a fixed group of 'combinations' and were at sea when confronted with a standard organ."[38]

The Stanley 3/29, designed by Elliot, Hagstrom and Carruthers,[40] set a pattern by which most succeeding Kimball unit theatre organs were built. Although the company built a number of specially designed instruments, sales representatives were encouraged to sell stock styles. Styles U25, U26 and U27 were, respectively, 2/5, 2/6 and 2/7 instruments[41] and it is certain that a number of other unit styles were offered as well although no Kimball catalogs which refer to unit style numbers are known to the author.

The largest Kimball unit orchestra was the 37-rank

instrument installed in the Forum Theatre, Los Angeles in 1924 and later moved to the Western (Wiltern) Theatre in 1931. Its stop arrangement has presented a real challenge to most organists because of its peculiar order. The author used to joke that the factory's method of stop layout was to place all the stops in a bushel basket, coat the stoprails with glue and hurl the stops at the console. Wherever they stuck, that was the order! Closer examination reveals that there really was a method to their madness, however. The stops are arranged by families of tone: foundations, brass, strings, woodwinds and percussisons. Each of these families had a unique stop color scheme as follows:

Family	Stop	Engraving
Foundations	white	black
Brass	red	black
Strings	amber	black
Woodwinds	white	red
Tuned percussions	white	green
Traps	white	black
Couplers	black	white
Vibratos	white	red

Mr. Elliot must have thought that this stop grouping by families made sense for an instrument purporting to be an emulation of an orchestra but few organists thought so. The Forum was one of the last Kimballs built with that stop arrangement; later Kimballs have the stops arranged in order of pitch, as did most other manufacturers. The later stop arrangements, however, continued a peculiar Kimball trait of placing the lowest pitches in the upper row of stops, the opposite of common practice among other builders. Another Kimball aberration was the absence of a great manual. Functionally it was present but it almost always had another name. A four-manual scheme usually had accompaniment, orchestral, solo and percussion manuals. The Roxy had this order with the addition of a bombarde as the fifth manual. Three-manual schemes were usually either accompaniment-solo-percussion or accompaniment-orchestral-solo on later Kimball unit organs.

Kimball enjoyed a reputation for having the highest quality products in the organ industry. Perhaps not everyone would rate Kimball as number one in overall quality (the author is certainly tempted to do so) but a large number of people did. Riley Daniels, former president of M. P. Moller, one of Kimball's chief competitors, told the author about having once examined the 4/56 Kimball installed in 1930 at Ohio Wesleyan University. "It had as fine workmanship as I've ever seen in an organ," reported Mr. Daniels.[42]

Lloyd Davey, once a representative for Welte, tells a wonderful tale about the acquisition of a new four-manual Kimball by the Wilshire Boulevard Temple in Los Angeles. Davey relates his experience of dealing with the chairman of the organ committee, a prominent dentist: "I discussed the merits of my company's product and was treated with consideration by the doctor. After we had finished talking business he invited me to relax and have

The 3/29 console of the Stanley Theatre in Philadelphia is an example of one of the few all-electric consoles built by Kimball c. 1919-1920. Lower left photo illustrates Kimball's method of placing setterboards behind easily accessible swinging doors on either end of the console. Kimball setter switches were rotary and could be positioned on narrow centers, consuming less space than comparable systems of most manufacturers.

Kimball ad in the 1924 Chicago Society of Organists Directory.

Visually clever but probably ineffective ad in the November 8, 1919 Exhibitor's Trade Review.

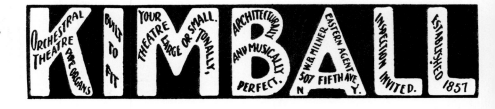

KIMBALL ORCHESTRAL UNIT ORGANS

A TWO MANUAL KIMBALL UNIT - $6000

GENTLEMEN:

When you build a Theatre you employ a competent Architect to design it.

When we build you a *Kimball*, competent Organ Architects design each instrument to fit your theatre Architecturally and *tonely*

BECAUSE

KIMBALL ORGANS are buiit to order whether $6,000. or $60,000. They are *not* stock organs.

W. B. MILNER
Eastern Sales Agent

507 FIFTH AVE.,   N. Y. C.

Murray Hill 0721-0722

The Kimball company always believed in judicious advertising. W. W. Kimball himself used to say, "To have business go where business is and use printer's ink."[8] Source of the above ad is unknown; ad below appeared in the November 21, 1925 issue of Motion Picture News.

Spectacular photo on opposite page provides a panoramic view of the Kimball erecting room where the Forum 4/37 is being assembled. Lower photo show brass chamber of the Forum organ nearing completion. The famous 60" bass drum dwarfs the workman standing beside it.

The Forum Theatre in Los Angeles housed the largest Kimball theatre organ ever built. String, brass and woodwind chambers flanked the stage and a large nine-rank echo division featuring three vox humanas spoke through a grille at the right rear of the house. A unique feature of this division was an additional set of swell shades which allowed it to speak into an outdoor park adjacent to the theatre for the entertainment of waiting patrons. The Kimball's 37 ranks, three of which were on 25″ wind pressure, must have had a stunning impact in this relatively small 1,200-seat house.

Brass division in the Forum Theatre. From left to right: muted conrnet, trumpet, French horn, serpent and tuba. The former three ranks are on 10" wind pressure, the latter two on 25". The incrediby powerful tuba goes harmonic at 8' DD.

4/37 KIMBALL UNIT ORCHESTRA
Forum/Wiltern Theatres, Los Angeles, California
Information in parenthesis is the derivation and is not actually engraved on the stop keys.

PEDAL

32'	Diaphone	4'	Cornet (tuba)		Snare Drum Roll 2
32'	Tibia Bass (16' tibia plus 10 2/3' flute)	16'	Double Bass (cello I)		Drum Rev
		16'	Bass Viols II	8'	Accomp. to Pedal
16'	Diaphone	8'	Cellos III	8'	Orchestral to Pedal
16'	Tibia Clausa	8'	Violins III	32'	Diaphone 2ndT
16'	Diaphonic Horn	4'	Violins III	16'	Serpent 2ndT
16'	Tibia Profunda (clarabella)	16'	Bass Clarinet	8'	Trombone 2ndT
16'	Bourdon	8'	Clarinet	4'	Trumpet 2ndT
8'	Diaphonic Diapason	8'	Bassoon (English horn)	8'	Chimes 2ndT
8'	Tibia Mollis	16'	Piano		Thunder Drum 2ndT
8'	Concert Flute	8'	Piano		Tympani 2ndT
4'	Tibia Dura		Bass Drum Heavy		Bass Drum 2ndT
16'	Tuba		Bass Drum Light		Cymbal 2ndT
16'	Serpent		Cymbal		Persian Cymbal 2ndT
8'	Trumpet		Snare Drum Roll 1		Chinese Gong Stroke 2ndT
8'	Baritone (tuba)				

ACCOMPANIMENT

16'	Bourdon	8'	Viola	8'	Mandolin
8'	Open Diapason (horn diapason)	8'	Muted Violins II	8'	Piano
8'	Tibia Clausa	4'	Violins II	4'	Piano
8'	Wald Horn	4'	Violin I	8'	Harp
8'	Tibia Mollis (clarabella)	4'	Viola	8'	Celesta
8'	Concert Flute	4'	Muted Violins II	4'	Celesta
4'	Gemshorn (wald horn)	8'	Solo Vox Humana II	4'	Xylophone
4'	Tibia Dura (clarabella)	8'	Chorus Vox Humana	2'	Glockenspiel
2'	15th (wald horn)	4'	Chorus Vox Humana		Snare Drum Roll 1
8'	Tuba	8'	Kinura		Snare Drum Roll 2
8'	French Horn	8'	Clarinet		Snare Drum Tap
16'	Bass Viols II	8'	Oboe Horn		Tambourine
16'	Bass Viol I TC	4'	Traverse Flute		Castanets
8'	Violins II	2 2/3'	Nazard Twelfth		Tom Tom
8'	Violin I	2'	Piccolo		Chinese Block Tap

ORCHESTRAL

16′	Contra Clarabella	16′	Bass Viols II	8′	English Horn
16′	Tibia Clausa	16′	Bass Viol I TC	8′	Oboe (synthetic)
8′	Diaphonic Diapason	8′	Cellos II	8′	Kinura
8′	Open Diapason	8′	Cello I	16′	Bass Clarinet
8′	Tibia Clausa	8′	Violins II	8′	Clarinet
8′	Wald Horn	8′	Violin I	8′	Saxophone
8′	Tibia Mollis	8′	Viola	8′	Oboe Horn
8′	Concert Flute	8′	Muted Violins II	4′	Solo Flute (tibia)
4′	Octave (horn diapason)	4′	Violins II	4′	Traverse Flute
4′	Gemshorn (wald horn)	4′	Violin I	2 2/3′	Nazard Twelfth
4′	Tibia Dura (clarabella)	4′	Viola	2′	Piccolo
2 2/3′	String Twelfth (viola)	4′	Muted Violins II	8′	Piano
2′	String 15th (viola)	8′	Solo to Orchestral	4′	Piano
1 3/5′	17th (flute)	4′	Solo to Orchestral	8′	Harp
16′	Tuba	8′	Percussion to Orchestral	8′	Marimba
8′	Flugel Horn (tuba)		Snare Drum Tap	4′	Marimba
4′	Cornet (tuba)	8′	Solo Vox Humana II	4′	Celesta
8′	Trumpet	16′	Chorus Vox Humana TC	2′	Glockenspiel
8′	French Horn	8′	Chorus Vox Humana	4′	Xylophone
4′	Ballad Horn (French horn)	4′	Chorus Vox Humana		

SOLO

16′	Diaphone	16′	Serpent	8′	English Horn
16′	Contra Tibia Clausa	8′	Serpent	8′	Oboe (synthetic)
16′	Tibia Profunda (clarabella)	16′	Ophicleide (French horn)	8′	Kinura
8′	Diaphonic Diapason	8′	French Horn	16′	Bass Clarinet
8′	Tibia Clausa	4′	Ballad Horn (French horn)	8′	Clarinet
8′	Tibia Mollis	8′	Muted Cornet TC	4′	Clarinet
8′	Concert Flute	16′	Double Basses III (violins)	16′	Saxophone TC
4′	Octave (diaphonic diapason)	8′	Cellos III	4′	Solo Flute (tibia)
4′	Tibia Dura	8′	Violins III	4′	Traverse Flute
	Harmonics IV (2′ clarabella, 1 3/5′,	4′	Violins III	2′	Piccolo
	1 1/3′, 1′ viola)	2 2/3′	String Twelfth (viola)	8′	Marimba
16′	Tuba	2′	String 15th (viola)	4′	Celesta
8′	Flugel Horn	16′	Solo Vox Humana II TC	2′	Glockenspiel
16′	Trombone TC	8′	Solo Vox Humana II	2′	Orchestra Bells
8′	Trumpet	16′	Bassoon TC (English horn)	4′	Xylophone
4′	Trumpet				

PERCUSSION

8′	Tibia Clausa
8′	Trumpet
16′	Serpent
8′	Muted Cornet TC
16′	Solo Vox Humana II TC
8′	Solo Vox Humana II
4′	Solo Vox Humana II
8′	English Horn
16′	Kinura TC
8′	Kinura
16′	Bass Clarinet
8′	Clarinet
4′	Solo Flute (tibia)
2′	Whistle (tibia)
16′	Piano
8′	Piano
4′	Piano
8′	Harp
8′	Marimba
4′	Marimba
4′	Celesta
2′	Glockenspiel
2′	Orchestra Bells
4′	Xylophone
2′	Xylophone
2′	Sleigh Bells
8′	Chimes

VIBRATOS

Foundation
Tibia
Brass
String
Wood Wind
Solo Vox Humana
Chorus Vox Humana

ACCOMPANIMENT 2nd TOUCH

8′	Diaphonic Diapason
8′	Tibia Clausa
8′	Tuba
8′	Cellos III
8′	English Horn
8′	Clarinet
8′	Saxophone
4′	Solo Piccolo (tibia)
8′	Chimes
2′	Glockenspiel
	Chinese Block Roll
	Triangle
	Bird Call
	Snare Drum Roll 1
	Snare Drum Roll 2

ORCHESTRAL 2nd TOUCH

8′	Tibia Clausa
16′	Serpent
16′	Tuba
8′	Trumpet
16′	Clarinet
4′	Solo Flute (tibia)
2′	Glockenspiel
2′	Orchestra Bells
2′	Sleigh Bells
4′	Xylophone
	Triangle
	Snare Drum Roll 1
	Snare Drum Roll 2

ECHO PEDAL

	Main Pedal Off
16′	Echo Bass
8′	Flute
8′	Viola

ECHO SOLO

	Solo Organ Off
8′	English Diapason
8′	Gedeckt
8′	Viole Aetheria
4′	Flute d'Amour
4′	Salicet
8′	Vox Humana III
4′	Harp

ECHO PERCUSSION

	Percussion Organ Off
16′	Contra Viole TC
8′	English Diapason
8′	Gedeckt
8′	Flute Celeste
8′	Viole Aetheria
8′	Vox Angelica
4′	Flute d'Amour
4′	Salicet
2′	Echo Piccolo
8′	Echo Horn
8′	Musette (synthetic)
8′	Vox Humana III
4′	Vox Humana III
4′	Harp
	Echo Vibrato

a round of small talk. During our discussion he put me at ease and then said, in an offhand way, 'Just between us, which do you consider to be the second best built organ?' My reply was that Kimball, in my opinion, was second best in the field. You can imagine my surprise, and that of all the others who tried to see their product win acceptance, when we learned that Kimball had been given the contract. It seems that the very smart doctor had asked each of us to relax and have a bit of small talk and had put the same question to each of us in his disarming manner. And each of us had, in our opinion, stated that Kimball was second best!"[43]

A similar story surrounds the acquisition of R. P. Elliot's talents by the Welte company in mid-1925. For years Welte had specialized in residence organs, selling only a modest number in that market which was dominated by Aeolian. Early in 1925 Welte decided that they wanted a share of the church and theatre organ market as well and they inquired of a number of sources as to who would be the ideal man to spearhead such an expansion. "R. P. Elliot" was the universal response, so Welte officials approached him[44] and made an offer he couldn't refuse. Their trust in Mr. Elliot was well founded; virtually overnight he turned Welte into one of the most respected firms in the industry. And well they should have been for under Elliot' leadership the Welte factory was building organs which were virtual duplicates of Kimballs in nearly every detail!

The Welte success story did not go unnoticed in the industry. The Aeolian Company was in an identical situation: nearly all their business was in residence organs and they wanted a share of the church and theatre organ market, too. In October of 1927 Aeolian lured Mr. Elliot away from Welte[45] hoping he could work magic for them, too. Unfortunately, the end of the theatre organ era was just around the corner and Aeolian sold only four of them during the year or so Mr. Elliot was with them. And sure enough, the consoles of those four Aeolian theatre organs were dead ringers for Kimballs!

The next company in line to bid for Mr. Elliot's talents was—would you believe—Wurlitzer! They certainly didn't need Elliot's expertise in the theatre organ realm, but theatre organ sales were slowing down rapidly and Wurlitzer was desperate to get a foothold in the church organ market. They hoped that the magic name of R. P.

Elliot would be their entry, but such was not to be. In May of 1929 Mr. Elliot wrote to his friend Lloyd Davey, "Probably by now you have heard that I gave up the attempt to introduce respectability into the Wurlitzer church organ situation. Not a chance! However, I never was too sure there would be, and they didn't promise definitely as Aeolian did. They held out hopes and inducements but in a showdown *they* governed, and units go.

"They quoted various organists to me as praising organs they had built in churches and I wrote causal letters to some of them asking what they would suggest and how they liked this and that organ and they came back hot and heavy all my way. Kraft, Goldthwaite *et al.* Not content with writing me, they wrote the factory. But nothing will change the leopard's spots.

"They are fine people in some ways. Farny, Rudolph and a few others. But not for me to work with. They were patient and were waiting for me to see things their way. I was the one who became discouraged first and made a showdown necessary. I have a dandy letter from [Meakin] Jones; really sorry I am not going to work things out with them.[46]

"[I] shall in all probability hook up with Kimball again. Should have before, but they wouldn't ante enough. We are getting together now. Walter [Hardy] was here 'till 2:20 AM and I am going [to Chicago] this week. He, of course, realizes the need to help them make money, which they haven't been doing."[47]

Mr. Elliot's last remark was an understatement! In the teens and twenties, theatre organs accounted for around 40% of Kimball's business. Starting in 1928 the theatre organ market took a nosedive and the effect on Kimball's organ division, which operated on a marginal basis anyway, was devastating. To help keep the division afloat, the staff was reduced and heavy salary cuts were instituted from plant superintendent Hagstrom on down the line.[48] Even though times were tough, Kimball quality never suffered; indeed, it may have improved slightly in the 1930s, if that were possible.

By June of 1929 R. P. Elliot was back with Kimball but the circumstances were vastly different from the hectic times of the mid-twenties. Late in 1929 Mr. Elliot wrote, "It is slow everywhere, even Skinner feeling it and cutting very close here on one recent job he made us cut still closer to get. He dropped from $19,000 to $15,000. Some

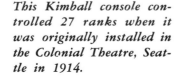

4/27 *Kimball in Detroit's Regent Theatre, installed in 1916.*

This Kimball console controlled 27 ranks when it was originally installed in the Colonial Theatre, Seattle in 1914.

New York, July 30th, 1914.

The W. W. Kimball Company, Chicago, announce the removal of their Eastern headquarters from 150 Fifth Avenue to the Columbia Bank Building, 507 Fifth Avenue, at Forty-second Street.

The personnel and equipment of the new offices provide for every requirement of organ design, sales and maintenance. Technical information regarding weights and dimensions of organ parts and the division and arrangement of organ spaces will be cheerfully supplied to architects and prospective buyers, and expert assistance will be rendered in the solution of acoustical and engineering problems. A trained mechanical staff is attached to this office for the erection of new Kimball organs and the regulation and tuning of organs of all makes under yearly contract.

The W. W. Kimball Company differentiate between the demands of the church service, the theatre and the home, and build organs which are adapted to each distinct purpose. The KIMBALL CHURCH ORGAN is noted for its **devotional character**. The KIMBALL THEATRE ORGAN is a **musical instrument first**, provided with all the accessories that have been found to be desirable, and it is **built to stand constant daily use.** THE KIMBALL RESIDENCE ORGAN combines the musical qualities of both with the **perfect Kimball Solo Player**, giving solo and accompaniment through the compass of manuals and pedals, with or without automatic control of stops and expression. These organs are constructed throughout on principles fully protected by numerous United States patents, owned and used exclusively by the W. W. Kimball Company.

The new offices are most accessible by train, subway, elevated and surface cars and the Fifth Avenue motor 'bus lines. All visitors will be made welcome.

W. W. KIMBALL COMPANY
Robert Elliot, Eastern Manager
James L. Fitzpatrick, Associated
Telephone Murray Hill 2209

Eighty-nine Kimball organs have been contracted for in the twelve months ending September 20, 1919. It has not been possible to produce a Kimball below twenty-five hundred dollars at any time during the year, and the lowest price for a church instrument today is one hundred and fifty dollars higher than that, or for a theatre, five thousand dollars. The majority of these eighty-nine contracts are for organs costing more than ten thousand dollars, and some of them go beyond thirty thousand.

The list includes orders from Alaska to Florida, from New England to China. There are organs going to churches, lodges, residences, auditoriums, colleges, conservatories, restaurants and theatres.

It seems to the W. W. Kimball Company, in view of the recognized high quality of these organs, that this is something of a contribution to the progress of the art of music and the craft of organ building.

Kimball organs are erected, tested and tuned in the factory. The outside men report that they go together without difficulty, "no ciphers or troubles of any kind," and the time sheets prove it.

Let us send a technical representative to discuss your organ problem with you. What he will tell you cannot fail to be helpful, and it will place you under no obligation.

W. W. KIMBALL COMPANY
KIMBALL HALL   Established 1857   **CHICAGO**

These Kimball ads from The Diapason *tell an interesting story. They appeared in the following issues, clockwise from upper left: September 1914, October 1919, February 1920, March 1921, February 1923, August 1924 and January 1927.*

---

40 KIMBALL ORGANS
for
Stanley Theatres

The Stanley Company of America has bought forty Kimball organs for their theatres. Many of these have been used ten to twelve hours a day, six and seven days a week for years and are still giving splendid service. The satisfaction these organs have given is evidenced by their recent order of eight large three-manual instruments for new theatres under construction.

Kimball organ action has stood the theatre test.

Kimball organs for churches and concert halls are equally satisfactory. They are built to specifications and voiced specially to suit their needs. The Kimball organ is the best organ built.

W. W. KIMBALL CO.

220 Kimball Building   *Established 1857*   Chicago, Illinois

The Clemmer Theatre in Spokane, Washington purchased a 4/32 Kimball in 1914 which was presided over by Jesse Crawford in one of his first theatre organ playing engagements. This early instrument certainly has a small complement of pistons for such a large organ.

2/6 Kimball formerly in the 45th Street (Paramount) Theatre in Seattle. This was a very late tubular pneumatic organ installed in 1921. A real economy model, it has no pistons.

Leonard MacClain plays the 2/5 Kimball installed in the 56th Street Theatre, Philadelphia in 1915.

Echo organs were a common feature of early organs in theatres. A typical example is the Arcadia Theatre in Philadelphia which had a 3/20 Kimball installed in 1915. The echo speaks from the grille above arches at the rear center of the house.

The console in the Hollywood Beach Hotel, Hollywood, Florida was extra tall in order to accommodate a player mechanism.

The Kimball at left was installed in the Strand Theatre, Philadelphia in 1917. Note the unusual chamber divisions as etched on two of the swell shoes: orchestral and tuba.

Grand Theatre, Norristown, Pennsylvania, 3/9.

Michigan Theatre, Chicago, Illinois.

The 3/21 console in the North Center Theatre, Chicago featured a stucco finish. This finish was common in midwestern states but was not so prevalent elsewhere in the country. Other unusual features of the North Center Kimball were a 16′ serpent, a shuffle effect which used actual sandpaper and a glass crash effect which consisted of several metal plates about 4″ x 7″ suspended between two reiterating pneumatics.[39]

The Stanley Theatre in Philadelphia ordered the first large Kimball unit orchestra, a 3/29 instrument, in 1921. Its console featured the same style as virtually every other Kimball horseshoe console ever built. This design, with two "ears" on the top, is quite similar to original Hope-Jones concepts. This shouldn't be too surprising given the fact that two of the top people in Kimball's organ department, Joseph J. Carruthers and Robert Pier Elliot, were former Hope-Jones men.

Virginia Theatre, Atlantic City, New Jersey, 3/13.

Palace Theatre, Philadelphia, 4/28. This was the first of only six four-manual horseshoe theatre consoles built by Kimball.

KIMBALL ORGANS

For the Roxy Theatre, New York

Console for Brass Section   MASTER CONSOLE   Woodwind Console

THE LARGEST ORGAN for the LARGEST THEATRE

Soon to be completed

The main auditorium of the Roxy Theatre, with seating capacity of 6200, will have **the largest unit organ ever built**—a Kimball. The three Consoles shown above control this wonderful instrument. The Master Console of five manuals is supplemented by a woodwind section, and a brass section, separate consoles at each side as illustrated. Three organists will play at the same time.

Two Other Kimball Organs for "The Roxy"

The Broadcasting Studio will have a Kimball Organ as well as Kimball concert grand piano. The Console is shown at the left. This will be used during the familiar broadcasts of "Roxy and His Gang."

In the foyer of "The Roxy" a 3-manual Kimball soloist organ will be ready for entertainment of patrons. The Console is shown at right—It may be played manually or with Kimball soloist organ rolls.

Every Kimball Organ is an individual creation

Ask us about your organ problems.

W. W. KIMBALL CO.

220 Kimball Building   Established 1857   Chicago, Illinois

This ad in the December 1926 Diapason *boasts about what was, at the time, the largest theatre organ contract ever awarded. The claim of "largest unit organ ever built" is pure hyperbole; several years earlier the Kimball company itself had built an organ five ranks larger than the Roxy for the Forum Theatre in Los Angeles.*

One chamber of the Atlantic City Convention Hall ballroom organ is being tested in the Kimball erecting room. Designed by organ architect Emerson Richards as a dual-purpose instrument, it contains both classical and theatrical voices in its 55 ranks and includes a full complement of percussions as well as the only Kimball brass trumpet known to the author. It also has the largest four-manual horseshoe console ever built by Kimball.

This beautiful Art Deco console, similar to one in the Pretoria, South Africa Town Hall, was actually built for a theatre in 1936! It has an interesting history: In 1925 E. M. Skinner installed a 4/51 instrument in Boston's Metropolitan Theatre which remained in service only five years before being replaced by a 4/26 Wurlitzer in 1930. The Wurlitzer company, apparently having taken the Skinner in on trade, sold and installed it in the auditorium of the H. J. Heinz Company in Pittsburgh[1] where its console was destroyed in the 1936 flood. Kimball was engaged to build the new console pictured here and to rebuild and enlarge the organ to 67 ranks. The additions included a tibia clausa, tibia plena, post horn and vibraharp.[2]

Studio 3 of WGN Radio in Chicago (left) featured a 2/7 Wurlitzer until 1942 or so when Kimball added three ranks and two three-manual consoles. The organ was moved to studio B in the Tribune Tower (right) in 1947 at which time the console was refinished in ebony. Seated at the console is staff organist Harold Turner who broadcasted on the organ for many years.

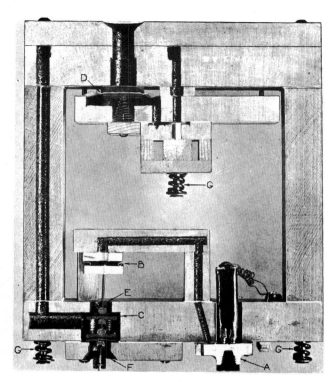

This set of oboe pipes has been voiced by one of the Kimball voicers and is being checked by head voicer George Michel.

Sectional view of a Kimball pitman chest. Their unit chests are identical except for the absence of the pitman rail just under pipe valve D. Kimball magnets (A) were their own unique design with screw-in bakelite caps. Packed joints were held together with screws with compression springs G, an item of quality not used by all manufacturers.

A Kimball artisan solders oboe resonators to their blocks. The upper Hoyt meal portions of the resonators are still covered with whiting which was applied before their zinc stems were soldered. After all soldering operations are completed the whiting will be washed off and the pipes given a coat of clear lacquer.

cut. First was a higher price than he ever expected to get; last was below our schedule. And, as I say, we got it, so draw your own conclusions. And if in doubt, we cut."[49] In September of 1930 Mr. Elliot wrote, "I have not had any salary since a year ago last May and I draw only what I absolutely must have."[50]

In the midst of these hard times (July 1931) Kimball purchased the Welte company[51] which in the past few years had undergone several reorganizations and was foundering. The sale price was $35,000[51] but the only asset of any substantial value was the Welte library of reproducing organ rolls and even its value was questionable considering that the market for reproducing organs was nearly as dead as the theatre organ market. Undoubtedly of greater interest to the Kimball company was the fact that Welte plans and scales were virtual duplicates of Kimball's and would therby be taken off the market.

The theatre organ business being dead, R. P. Elliot concentrated on his first love, the classic organ. He sold and helped design several large four-manual instruments in this period, the last of which was a 4/105 for the Memorial Auditorium in Worcester, Massachusetts. He was increasingly unhappy, however, that Kimball seemed to be putting him on the shelf and he actually considered going to Moller. Writing in late 1932 to his friend Lloyd Davey, Mr. Elliot said, "[Moller's] organ is increasingly better and they mean it to be better still. Whitelegg is good and he is allowed leeway. He is instructed to finish organs properly, whatever it costs. I heard one at Newburgh, a medium three-manual opened by Alex McCurdy,

Front and back views of some Kimball trap assemblies. The observant reader will notice that there are actually four different assemblies pictured.

and it was better than the average Skinner. Action fine, wind absolutely steady, voicing good . . . I like Ted Moller very much and his wife. Always did like old M. P. and he me . . . With them feeling the way they do about progressive organ building, with their plant and money, with Whitelegg and me working together, they would have a good set-up, even if I do say it. Anyhow, I didn't, and if the Kimball company behaves from now on I won't. They're on trial."[52]

In mid-1933 Mr. Elliot made good on this threat and did, in fact, join Moller briefly in their New York sales office.[53] He later worked for the U. S. government[54] and in 1939 joined the staff of WQXR Radio in New York City. In March of 1940 he was persuaded by Ted Moller to rejoin that firm, but, just as before, Moller vice presi-

dent E. O. Shulenberger didn't want him and engineered his departure in August of 1940.[55] Mr. Elliot died just one year later.

The Kimball organ business was halted by order of the War Production Board in 1942. After the ban on production was lifted following World War II, Wallace Kimball decided not to resume organ operations. Much of the remaining inventory such as tin, stopped wood basses, etc. was sold to Aeolian-Skinner.[56] In the mid-1950s other "unsaleable" items, including one of the WGN three-manual horseshoe consoles, were unceremoniously piled into a heap and burned. Most of the factory records were dumped in the alley behind Kimball Hall and were hauled off by the garbage collector.[59]

Views of Kimball percussions: clockwise from upper left are chimes, glockenspiel, xylophone and Chinese gong. Gongs, quite rare on most theatre organs, were common on even smaller Kimball unit orchestras. Kimball's chime action design is similar mechanically to that of an upright piano and is superior to other systems because the mallets are allowed to swing clear of the chime tubes after striking them. Actions of some other builders sometimes strike the chimes twice because their mallets don't have adequate clearance after striking the swinging chime tubes. Kimball xylophones usually featured Deagan's finest quality "artist's special" models. Kimball glockenspiels, struck with hard rubber mallets, were more subdued than those of many other makes which used metal mallets. These others produced a more penetrating tone but Kimball's hard rubber mallets created a result more closely imitative of an actual orchestra. In this case the effect may or may not be desirable, depending on one's taste.

tendency of the noisy type of instrument found in so many of the smaller picture houses.

Succeeding to the tubular pneumatic styles, the modern electric action has made possible the design of an organ, the parts of which may be built in quantity with resultant saving, but which contains every desirable adjunct of the specially built instrument, and which is voiced to suit the requirements of the building in which it is to be installed and the purpose for which it is to be used.

STANDARDIZATION — WHAT IT MEANS

THE Kimball standard style instruments described in the following pages are no cheap "stock" proposition, but are built of the same high grade materials, by the same skilled workmen, as the largest special organ. They have the identical perfected Kimball single pressure windchest, Kimball electric action with contacts of precious metals, the Kimball roll top, stop key console, Kimball adjustable combination action set at the console and moving the registers. The specification of stops is not fixed, but may be changed (when time is given) to any suitable combination within the capacity of the instrument, and the scales are decided, the pipes made and voiced, after all particulars of the auditorium, organ space and proposed use of the organ are known to the head voicer, as in all Kimball organs. The only exceptions are in those instances where an organ is required for immediate delivery and

INTRODUCTION

THERE are Kimball organs for all places and purposes, ranging from great cathedral and auditorium instruments, designed to meet the demands of vast spaces and support the singing of multitudes, to modest two manual organs that satisfy all requirements in smaller buildings. This booklet contains specifications and some description of the latest types of organs built to standardized designs, of real Kimball quality, which may be had at moderate prices.

EVOLUTION OF PRESENT TYPES

THE original product of the Kimball organ factory was a "portable" organ, and for many years these instruments were so built as to permit shipment with the pipes in place and tuned, installation by local dealers being thoroughly practicable. Out of these one and two manual organs grew a great business in larger or stationary organs, still built to standard designs and with few parts, but with the pipes removable for shipment and the services of an organ tuner required for their erection. Hundreds of these instruments, of both types, are giving satisfaction in the churches, lodges and homes of this and other countries, and many have found their way into theatres, where, with the addition of a Vox Humana and perhaps other features, some as new instruments and many as second hand, they stand up to the hard grind of a dozen or more hours' daily work and help to spread a love of good musical tone to counteract the vicious

KIMBALL ORGANS

suitable for

CHURCHES and AUDITORIUMS

of moderate seating capacity

Schools, Lodges and Private Residences

KIMBALL HALL.

W. W. KIMBALL CO.
KIMBALL HALL—CHICAGO
Established 1857

RESEARCH WORK

A WELL appointed experimental division works out all problems, runs "break-down" tests on all new devices, tries out all new materials and makes sure that the Kimball organ shall be the absolutely dependable instrument the buyer has a right to expect. Special problems are taken to the universities and engineering laboratories. Through these means the highest resistance magnet, which is also the safest, quickest operating and best designed for avoidance of trouble from dirt or other causes, was developed and has been in use exclusively in Kimball organs for several years. The best composition of silver contact wire, the proper temper and size for conductivity in each case has been determined. Correct types of pneumatics for their many purposes have been worked out. *No guessing is indulged in.*

FREE MAINTENANCE

A COMPLETE service contract, *including tuning*, prepaid in full for one year following installation of the organ, goes with every Kimball instrument.

THE SOLO PLAYER

IN lodge rooms, private houses and other locations where it may be desired, the Kimball Solo Player, giving solo and accompaniment through the compass of manuals and pedals, with or without automatic control of stops and expression by the music roll at the discretion of the organist, may be applied. This in no way interferes with the normal use of the organ,

---

of voicing skill. Kimball voicers are *not paid "by the piece," but are salaried men, devoting such time as may be necessary or desirable to each stop, and are under no temptation to get rid of it until it is finished to their satisfaction and that of the head voicer and the superintendent.*

TESTS
BEFORE SHIPMENT

THE *instruments are all erected and played upon in the factory, nothing being left to chance.* When the organ is built to go into a chamber the outlines are marked out on the floor and the swell front is erected in the position it will eventually occupy. *Every part is tested before shipment can be permitted.* The organs are then installed, *regulated and tuned by Kimball men*, who again inspect each part before it is assembled, who blow out and brush out each valve hole before the pipes are set in, and *who finish and tune to the Kimball standard.* Kimball organs play from the first note. Kimball magnets never fail. Kimball contacts never break or foul. Every part functions, because it is scientifically designed, accurately manufactured, carefully tested and installed, and there is no skimping in materials or at any stage of the work. Flame-proof manufactured cables are used between console and organ, no bunched and taped wiring being permitted. The National Board of Fire Underwriters has approved the Kimball action and cables and has ruled with respect to their installation that "conduit may be used, but is not required."

---

the buyer has been so fortunate as to find one finished and ready for shipment at the factory.

TONE;
DISTINCTIVE QUALITIES

THE beautiful tone of the Kimball organ is due to many factors. These instruments are entirely expressive, all pipes, including the pedal stops, being enclosed. Adequate wind pressures are used to produce *firm tones of distinctive qualities.* This dictates the use of exceptionally heavy metal and fine, heavy woods in the foundation stops, and special blends even to pure tin for the strings and some solo stops. It makes possible reed tones not obtainable on the old systems, and further, the making of *reeds that stand in tune* so that there is no longer an excuse for imitating reed tones with flue pipes, thus depriving the organ of one of its most important elements.

Kimball tone depends, too, upon other considerations, among them the percussion chamber under each pipe, the method of supplying the wind to the pipe, *an electric action that goes beyond the utmost demands of the most exacting organist*, avoidance of duplication, and the refusal to crowd the pipes, coupled with scientific placing of pipes to avoid sympathy or interference.

VOICING—
THE ARTIST'S TOUCH

WHEN all this has been said of material reasons for tonal excellence, there comes *the ultimate consideration*

The greatest depth at the centre bay is seven feet ten inches.

The swell box is six feet one inch deep by twelve feet at the floor line, the greatest depth of the upper section with swell shades standing open, beginning four feet eight inches from the floor, being six feet eight inches, while the height over all is ten feet. Entrance to the organ is through the front, unless otherwise provided for.

All Kimball organ quotations include a suitable electric motor and blower of ample capacity for the heaviest demand and a direct coupled low voltage generator for the action current, with current indicator at the console.

FACTORS IN FAVORABLE PRICES

The W. W. Kimball Company buys for cash in the most favorable markets and carries immense stocks of lumber, metals, fuel and other necessaries. There is a network of tracks covering the seventeen acres occupied by the Kimball factories and lumber yards at California Boulevard, Twenty-sixth Street and the River, where the company's electric locomotive supplements the work of the railway switching crews. The buildings have a floor area of 850,000 square feet. With its own foundry, machine shops and plating works the Kimball factory is practically independent of outside assistance. It is believed to be the only organ company making all parts of its instruments. The power and heating plant consumes sixty-five tons of coal a day in winter, about thirty-five tons in summer, in addition to

ORGAN CASES

Very handsome cases can be supplied, with and without attached consoles. All speaking pipes being enclosed, the designer has not been hampered by the necessity of taking care of pipes of fixed and awkward dimensions in the decorated front, a matter almost as important to the eye as the absence of the "break" between enclosed and unenclosed pipes to the ear. These cases are made in birch (which takes readily any finish from the natural wood through the shades of mahogany and walnut) and in quartered oak. The displayed pipes are usually done in French gold bronze, but may be decorated in colors to match any interior when so ordered. In these days more organs are sold to go into prepared chambers and behind grilles than with swell boxes and cases, the amount saved in the price of these items usually more than paying for such installations, especially in new buildings where, through co-operation between organ builder and architect, little or nothing is added to the construction cost and much is gained in artistic results. Upon order swell boxes of exceptionally heavy construction are supplied, enclosing not manual pipes only, but all stops of the organ.

DIMENSIONS

These organs as illustrated on the cover page occupy space on the floor seven feet six inches deep by twelve feet six inches wide and the height to the top of the centre pipe is thirteen feet six inches, the lowest point of the front being ten feet six inches.

but combines the merits of the best methods of automatic playing and the straight organ.

PRACTICABLE ADDITIONS—DELIVERY

In chambers of sufficient capacity Chimes, Harp, or certain other features may be added, but any considerable extension of the specifications is not recommended on account of the ease with which a special instrument can be designed for any purpose. This series has been planned with a view to such economy as may result from standardization without sacrifice of character, the saving being mainly in the drafting room, the manufacture of standard parts in quantity, and simplified erection. An additional advantage lies in the ability to deliver these standard organs in a matter of weeks, instead of the months required for the execution of any special order.

ORGANS BUILT TO SPECIAL PLANS

Upon receipt of plans and necessary information, specifications will be drawn up for larger organs or specially built small organs that will go into spaces of unusual shape. Hundreds of successful installations in the large churches, cathedrals, temples, schools and public auditoriums of this and other countries attest the correctness of the Kimball policy, of *planning the disposition of stops, deciding scales and wind pressures and making and voicing all pipes to conform to the conditions encountered in the building and the intended use of the instrument.*

SPECIFICATION NUMBER 41

GREAT

Open Diapason	8' metal
Dulciana	8' metal
Melodia	8' wood
Swell 16'	Great 16'
Swell 8'	Great 8' off
Swell 4'	Great 4'

Three adjustable pistons affecting Great and Pedal stops and couplers. Cancel piston affecting Great stops and couplers.

SWELL

Viola Diapason	8' metal
Stopped Flute	8' wood
Echo Salicional	8' metal
Wald Flute	4' m/w
Tremolo	

Swell 16' Swell 8' off Swell 4'

Three adjustable pistons affecting Swell and Pedal stops and couplers. Cancel piston affecting Swell stops and couplers.

PEDAL

Bourdon	16' wood
Flute	8' wood
Swell 8'	
Great 8'	

ACCESSORIES

Balanced expression pedal, affecting entire organ.

Balanced crescendo pedal, affecting entire organ.

Crescendo indicator.

Action current indicator.

Organ bench.

NOTE.—Aeoline or Salicional, 8', metal, may be substituted for Echo Salicional.

SPECIFICATION NUMBER 40

GREAT

Open Diapason	8' metal
Dulciana	8' metal
Melodia	8' wood
Swell 16'	Great 16'
Swell 8'	Great 8' off
Swell 4'	Great 4'

Three adjustable pistons affecting Great and Pedal stops and couplers. Cancel piston affecting Great stops and couplers.

SWELL

Viola Diapason	8' metal
Stopped Flute	8' wood
Wald Flute	4' m/w
Tremolo	

Swell 16' Swell 8' off Swell 4'

Three adjustable pistons affecting Swell and Pedal stops and couplers. Cancel piston affecting Swell stops and couplers.

PEDAL

Bourdon	16' wood
Flute	8' wood
Swell 8'	
Great 8'	

ACCESSORIES

Balanced expression pedal, affecting entire organ.

Balanced crescendo pedal, affecting entire organ.

Crescendo indicator.

Action current indicator.

Organ bench.

---

some hundreds of electrical horse power furnished by public utilities corporations. There are normally more than eighteen hundred men and women employed in the factory making organs, pianos, phonographs and music rolls, as many as twenty-two hundred having been at work in the busiest seasons.

THE KIMBALL BUILDING

THE general and executive offices and retail stores of the company occupy a considerable part of the first six floors of the New Kimball Building at Jackson Boulevard and Wabash Avenue. Other tenants include some famous conservatories and many nationally known organists and other musicians.

Kimball Hall, with its magnificent four manual concert organ, is the favorite recital hall of Chicago. Here Bonnet, Bauer, Courboin, Casals, Eddy, Ganz, Godowsky, Gabrilowitsch, Lhevinne, Leginska, Novaes, Yon, and others of equal note make their appearances. In addition to the great organ with its two manual and pedal Echo, the building contains six practice organs that are in use from early morning to late at night.

IDEALS BECOME REALITIES

WITH abundant capital and the spirit that exists throughout the organization it would be strange indeed if the technical staff had failed to build a wonderful organ, and this, we represent and can prove, is the standing accomplishment of the Kimball organ factory.

SPECIFICATION NUMBER 42

GREAT

Open Diapason . . . . . 8' metal
Dulciana . . . . 8' wood
Melodia . . . . 8' wood
Swell 16'   Great 8' off
Swell 8'   Great 4'
Swell 4'

Three adjustable pistons affecting Great and Pedal stops and couplers. Cancel piston affecting Great stops and couplers.

SWELL

Viola Diapason . . . . . 8' metal
Stopped Flute . . . . . 8' wood
Wald Flute . . . . . . 4' m/w
Vox Humana, with vibrato . . . . 8' reed
Tremolo
Swell 16'   Swell 8' off   Swell 4'

Three adjustable pistons affecting Swell and Pedal stops and couplers. Cancel piston affecting Swell stops and couplers.

PEDAL

Bourdon . . . . 16' wood
Flute . . . . 8' wood
Swell 8'   Great 8'

ACCESSORIES

Balanced expression pedal, affecting entire organ.
Balanced crescendo pedal, affecting entire organ.
Crescendo indicator.
Action current indicator.
Organ bench.
NOTE.—Oboe Horn, 8', reed, may be substituted for Vox Humana.

SPECIFICATION NUMBER 43

GREAT

Open Diapason . . . . . 8' metal
Dulciana . . . . 8' metal
Melodia . . . . 8' wood
Swell 16'   Great 8' off
Swell 8'   Great 4'
Swell 4'

Three adjustable pistons affecting Great and Pedal stops and couplers. Cancel piston affecting Great stops and couplers.

SWELL

Viola Diapason . . . . . 8' metal
Stopped Flute . . . . . 8' wood
Echo Salicional . . . . 8' metal
Wald Flute . . . . . . 4' m/w
Vox Humana, with vibrato . . . . 8' reed
Tremolo
Swell 16'   Swell 8' off   Swell 4'

Three adjustable pistons affecting Swell and Pedal stops and couplers. Cancel piston affecting Swell stops and couplers.

PEDAL

Bourdon . . . . 16' wood
Flute . . . . 8' wood
Swell 8'   Great 8'

ACCESSORIES

Balanced expression pedal, affecting entire organ.
Balanced crescendo pedal, affecting entire organ.
Crescendo indicator.
Action current indicator.
Organ bench.
NOTE.—Salicional or Aeoline, 8', metal, may be substituted for Echo Salicional. Oboe Horn, 8', reed, may be substituted for Vox Humana.

SPECIFICATION NUMBER 35

GREAT

Open Diapason . . . . . 8' metal
Dulciana . . . . 8' metal
Melodia . . . . 8' wood
Wald Flute . . . . . . 4' m/w
Piccolo . . . . 2' metal
Swell 16'   Great 16'
Swell 8'   Great 8' off
Swell 4'   Great 4'

Three adjustable pistons affecting Great and Pedal stops and couplers. Cancel piston affecting Great stops and couplers.

SWELL

Viola Diapason . . . . . 8' metal
Echo Salicional . . . . 8' metal
Melodia . . . . 8' wood
Wald Flute . . . . . . 4' m/w
Nazard . . . . 2⅔' metal
Piccolo . . . . 2' metal
Orchestral Oboe . . . . 8' synthetic
Tremolo
Swell 16'   Swell 8' off   Swell 4'

Three adjustable pistons affecting Swell and Pedal stops and couplers. Cancel piston affecting Swell stops and couplers.

PEDAL

Bourdon . . . . 16' wood
Flute . . . . 8' wood
Great 8'   Swell 8'

ACCESSORIES

Balanced expression pedal, affecting entire organ.

may be substituted for Echo Salicional. Oboe Horn, 8', reed, may be substituted for Vox Humana.

Balanced crescendo pedal, affecting entire organ.

Crescendo indicator.

Action current indicator.

Organ bench.

ANALYSIS

Name	Pitch	Pipes	Pedal	Great	Swell
Open Diapason	8'	61		8	
Dulciana	8'	61		8	
Melodia	16'	97	16-8	8-4-2	8-4-2⅔-2
Viola Diapason	8'	61			8
Echo Salicional	8'	61			8
Orchestral Oboe	8'	Syn.			8

SPECIFICATION NUMBER 36

GREAT

Open Diapason	8'	metal
Dulciana	8'	metal
Melodia	8'	wood
Wald Flute	4'	w/m
Piccolo	2'	metal

Swell 16'
Swell 8'   Great 8' off
Swell 4'   Great 4'

Three adjustable pistons affecting Great and Pedal stops and couplers. Cancel piston affecting Great stops and couplers.

SWELL

Viola Diapason	8'	metal
Echo Salicional	8'	metal
Melodia	8'	wood
Wald Flute	4'	w/m
Nazard	2⅔'	metal
Piccolo	2'	metal
Orchestral Oboe	8'	synthetic
Vox Humana, with vibrato	8'	reed
Tremolo		

Swell 16' Swell 8' off Swell 4'

Three adjustable pistons affecting Swell and Pedal stops and couplers. Cancel piston affecting Swell stops and couplers.

PEDAL

Bourdon	16'	wood
Flute	8'	wood

Great 8'   Swell 8'

ACCESSORIES

Balanced expression pedal, affecting entire organ.

Balanced crescendo pedal, affecting entire organ.

Crescendo indicator.

Action current indicator.

Organ bench.

ANALYSIS

Name	Pitch	Pipes	Pedal	Great	Swell
Open Diapason	8'	61		8	
Dulciana	8'	61		8	
Melodia	16'	97	16-8	8-4-2	8-4-2⅔-2
Viola Diapason	8'	61			8
Echo Salicional	8'	61			8
Orchestral Oboe	8'	61			8
Vox Humana	8'	Syn.			8

SPECIFICATION NUMBER 48

GREAT

Open Diapason	8'	metal
Dulciana	8'	metal
Clarabella	8'	wood
Stopped Flute	8'	metal
Flute d'Amour	4'	metal
Piccolo	2'	metal

Swell 16'   Great 16'
Swell 8'   Great 8' off
Swell 4'   Great 4'

Four adjustable pistons affecting Great and Pedal stops and couplers. Cancel piston affecting Great stops and couplers.

SWELL

Lieblich Gedeckt	16'	wood
Horn Diapason	8'	metal
Stopped Flute	8'	metal
Salicional	8'	metal
Voix Celeste	8'	metal
Flute d'Amour	4'	metal
Nazard	2⅔'	metal
Piccolo	2'	metal
Oboe Horn	8'	reed
Orchestral Oboe	8'	synthetic
Tremolo		

Swell 16' Swell 8' off Swell 4'

Four adjustable pistons affecting Swell and Pedal stops and couplers. Cancel piston affecting Swell stops and couplers.

PEDAL

Acoustic Bass	32'	resultant
Bourdon	16'	wood
Lieblich Gedeckt	16'	wood
Flute	8'	wood

Great 8'   Swell 8'

ACCESSORIES

Balanced expression pedal, affecting entire organ.

Balanced crescendo pedal, affecting entire organ.

Crescendo indicator.

Action current indicator.

Organ bench.

ANALYSIS

Name	Pitch	Pipes	Pedal	Great	Swell
Open Diapason	8'	61		8	
Clarabella	16'	73	32-16	8	
Dulciana	8'	61		8	
Horn Diapason	8'	61			8
Stopped Flute	16'	97	16-8	8-4-2	16-8-4-2⅔-2
Salicional	8'	61			8
Voix Celeste	8'	61			8
Oboe Horn	8'	61			8
Orchestral Oboe	8'	Syn.			8

NOTE

Vox Humana, with vibrato, 8' reed, may be substituted for Oboe Horn. Aeoline 8' metal may be substituted for Voix Celeste.

QUOTATION SLIP

June 1, 1924.

THE following prices cover the organ with detached roll top console, heavy swell box with electric swell front, electric blower and generator, erected and tuned. Also a Kimball maintenance contract, prepaid in full for one year following installation. In accordance with organ builders' practice the buyer pays delivery charges, motor wiring, wind pipe from blower to organ and any preparatory or structural work, including provision of lights, etc.

Nos. 35 and 40..$4500   No. 41 ....$4850   No. 48 ....$6300
Nos. 36 and 42.. 5000   No. 43 5300

Finished hardwood case with decorated pipes to cover the front of the organ, average installation, extra $500

Deduction when swell box is not required, organ being installed in a chamber prepared in the building, electric swell front only supplied with organ:
Styles 35 to 43, inclusive................$300. Style 48 ....$400

Above and below are addenda attached to the Kimball brochure reproduced on the preceeding six pages. These instruments were designed for smaller churches and lodges but many were sold to theatres which couldn't afford more expensive unit orchestras. But what these little Kimballs lacked in theatricality they more than made up for in reliability and longevity.

The following prices cover the organ erected complete with suitable electric blower and generator, case of birch or (on special order) quartered oak, rubbed finish of any shade, and displayed pipes in french gold bronze or decorated in colors. They do not include freight, local drayage, or any hoisting charges, motor wiring, wind pipe from blower to organ or any other preparatory or structural work. Console detached, within 30' of organ, without extra charge.

Without case, to be covered by grille, or otherwise $400 less
Without swell box, to go in sound proof chamber (sw front sup $300 less

STYLE 40.......... .. $4200   STYLE 42 .... $4700
STYLE 41........... $4550   STYLE 43............. $5000

STYLE 35 .... $5000   STYLE 36 .... $5500

STYLE 44 including chimes (20lg scale Deagan tubular bells)* $5750
  " 44 " glockenspiel and orch bells instead of chimes $5850
  " 44 " chimes and xylophone $6450
  " 44 "   "   "   "   " and unit A drums and traps   7450
  " 44 " chimes, glockenspiel, orch bells, xylophone, and
              Unit A drums and traps, (maximum equipment)..... 8300
  " 45 " chimes (20) large scale Deagan tubular chimes)*   5250
  " 45 " glockenspiel and orch bells, instead of chimes.... 6350
  " 45 " chimes and xylophone 6950
  " 45 " chimes, xylophone, and unit A drums and traps 7950
  " 45 " chimes, glockenspiel, orch bells, xylophone, and
              Unit A drums and traps, (maximum equipment)...... 8800

The above prices cover the organs erected complete with electric blower and generator, electric swell front fitted to chamber opening and detached console located within 30 feet of the organ without extra charge. They do not include freight, local drayage, or any hoisting charges. Motor wiring, wind pipe from blower to organ, or any other preparatory or structural work.
  Swell box for Styles 44 and 45, organ proper, not, including percussions. $400.
  Enlarged swell box or additional swell box to enclose percussions, price according to size and conditions. In some locations, Chimes or glockenspiel are satisfactory unenclosed.

  Case work or decorated pipe fronts, price depends upon area, design, and finish.

  (*Chimes, 5 Deagan tubular bells, Westminster scale, $500, less in all cases)

On the following three pages is reproduced a brochure which sings the praises of Kimball quality. Unlike the hyperbole of some other firms, most claims in this brochure are true. A curious anomaly is the attention given to vox humanas which are generally conceded today to have been the weakest tonal element in Kimball theatre organs. With their "goaty" and sometimes metallic-sounding voicing, Kimball voxes are inferior to those of just about every other theatre organ builder.

KIMBALL

ORCHESTRAL ORGANS AND UNIT ORCHESTRAS

THE Kimball orchestral organ and the Kimball unit orchestra are first of all *musical instruments*. Products of a great and highly organized factory, built by men who were first in legitimate theatre organ work following a long training in the construction and voicing of church, cathedral, concert, lodge and private residence organs in Europe and America, the traditional beauties of "The King of Instruments" have been preserved, and to them have been added the recognized characteristics of the modern orchestra.

WHAT IS AN ORCHESTRAL ORGAN?

KIMBALL theatre organs *are* orchestral, not merely what is too often termed "orchestral." If this seems an invidious distinction, let it be explained that *tones of orchestra instruments are in the main pleasant tones*, and that it has been the fashion of some builders of theatre instruments, who were attracted from other spheres of activity by the sudden development of a seemingly lucrative business, to exaggerate to the point of harshness and to introduce and over-emphasize noisy jazz elements. This applies both to the quality of string and other tones, which in many cases lost all resemblance to their prototypes, and to over-dependence upon the cheaper class of percussion instruments, too many drums and traps and especially too many unmusical "effects," in lieu of the more costly but musical organ pipes and high class percussions, such as full compass chimes, glockenspiel, marimba, harp, celesta, xylophone and piano.

SOME FACTORS IN TONE PRODUCTION

THE beautiful tone of the Kimball organ is due to many factors. These instruments are entirely expressive, all pipes, including the pedal stops, being enclosed. The instant operating, sound-proof, individual electro-pneumatic swell shades are silent—not merely quiet, but *silent*—in operation, and give a perfectly graded crescendo or a full sforzando, accurately timed to the movement of the organist's foot. Adequate wind pressures are used to produce *firm tones of distinctive quality*. This permits, and in fact compels, the use of exceptionally heavy cast special metal and fine, heavy woods in the foundation stops, hard maple for the orchestral flutes, and special blends even to pure tin for the strings and certain wood winds. It makes possible reed tones not obtainable on the old systems, and further, the making of reeds that *stand in tune* so that there is no longer an excuse for imitating reed tones with flue pipes, thus depriving the organ of one of its most important elements.

KIMBALL tone depends, too, upon other considerations; among them the percussion chamber under each pipe, the method of supplying the wind to the pipe, an electric action that goes beyond the utmost demands of the most exacting organist, avoidance of duplication, and the refusal to crowd the pipes, coupled with scientific placing of pipes to avoid sympathy or interference.

VOICING; THE ARTIST'S TOUCH

WHEN all this has been said of material reasons for tonal excellence, there comes the *ultimate consideration of voicing skill. Kimball voicers are not paid "by the piece," but are salaried men, devoting such time as may be necessary or desirable to each stop, and are under no temptation to get rid of it until it is finished to their satisfaction and* that of the head voicer and the superintendent.

REMEMBER

THE scales are decided, the pipes made and voiced, after all particulars of the auditorium, organ space and the proposed use of the organ are known to the head voicer, in Kimball organs.

SOME SPECIALTIES

OUR Vox Humana had a great deal to do with the early popularity of the Kimball organ in theatres. "The Organ with the Human Voice" is still written over the entrance to the Regent in Philadelphia, where Alec Boyd installed the first Kimball orchestral organ in the East, after being brought to Chicago by an observant friend to hear the Kimball in the little old Boston theatre, and particularly, its Vox Humana. For Mr. Boyd, now vice president, and Mr. Buhler, general manager of the Stanley Company of America, the largest buyers of high priced organs in the world, the two rank Vox Humana was developed, along with other specialties. Their leading theatre, the Stanley, has three Vox Humanas, as has the magnificent new Keith-Stanley vaudeville house, the Earle, and Nixon's Grand on North Broad Street, these being the finest and largest unit orchestras in the East. Across the continent, in Los Angeles, the Forum, America's most beautiful theatre, has also its largest and most wonderful unit organ, a Kimball containing three Vox Humanas of one, two and three ranks respectively, unbelievably rich and varied.

Tibias are another Kimball specialty for which requests are made frequently by owners of other organs, but the Company neither buys nor sells its pipes, and the only way to get Kimball Tibias, Flutes, Vox Humanas, Kinuras, Tubas, Trumpets, Saxophones, Oboes, English and French Horns, Diaphones and Diapasons, as to get Kimball magnets,

determined. Correct types of pneumatics for their many purposes have been worked out. *No guessing is indulged in.*

Economy without loss of character, but with marked gain, results from proper standardization of parts, including windchests, reservoirs, tremolos, magnets, switches, relays and console mechanism. There are few people today who do not know what standardized interchangeable parts have done for the automobile industry. Ability to make earlier shipments and great saving in installation time are two valuable considerations. Ease of repair in the event of damage from a leaky roof or steam pipe or otherwise also counts.

Kimball magnets never fail. Kimball organs do not "cypher." Kimball contacts do not break or foul. Every part functions, because it is scientifically designed, accurately manufactured, carefully installed, and there is no skimping in materials or at any stage of the work.

From the Smallest to the Largest

Kimball organs and unit orchestras start with the essentials and build up with such additional features as the size and character of the house may justify or the buyer care to pay for. They are no cheap "stock" proposition. The organ of the smallest Kimball standard specification is built of the same high grade materials and by the same skilled workmen as the largest organ which may be special from start to finish. The identical perfected Kimball single pressure windchest, Kimball electric action with contacts of precious metal, Kimball unit switch boards, Kimball roll top or unit type (curved stop key bolster) console, completely rat and vermin proof, Kimball adjustable combination action set at the console and moving the registers, is employed. The same voicers are responsible

Every part is tested before shipment can be permitted.

The organs are then *installed, regulated and tuned by Kimball men,* who again inspect each part before it is assembled, who blow out and brush out each valve hole before the pipes are set in, and *who finish and tune to the Kimball standard.* The Kimball organ can be finished as the doors are thrown open to the public (as happens not infrequently in theatre building) and it plays from the first note, without a hitch. Flame proof manufactured cables are used between the console and organ, no bunched and taped wiring being permitted. The National Board of Fire Underwriters has approved Kimball action and cables and has ruled with respect to their installation that "conduit may be used, but is not required."

Maintenance

A complete service contract, *including tuning,* prepaid in full for a year following installation, goes with every Kimball organ or unit orchestra. There is nothing left for the buyer to worry about.

We Know What We Are Doing

A well appointed experimental division works out all problems, runs "breakdown" tests on all new devices, tries out all new materials and makes sure that the Kimball organ, when delivered, shall be the absolutely dependable instrument the buyer has a right to expect. Special problems are taken to the universities and engineering laboratories. Through these means the highest resistance magnet, which is also the safest, quickest operating and best designed for avoidance of trouble from dirt or other causes, was developed and has been in use exclusively in Kimball organs for several years. The best composition of silver contact wire, the proper temper (springiness) and size for conductivity in each case has been

actions, chests and consoles, is to buy *Kimball Organs and Kimball Unit Orchestras.*

Percussion Instruments

Deagan high grade Chimes (large scale tubular bells) with Kimball loud and soft quick repeating piano action and individual damper action. Deagan Glockenspiel-Orchestra Bells, Xylophones, Harps, Marimbas, Celestas, Chrysoglots, and other percussion instruments with full scale resonators and Kimball single stroke and repeating actions as their nature may indicate. Kimball percussion actions are *silent* in operation. The tone of the instruments is heard in all its purity and power.

Drums and Traps

Ludwig & Ludwig full military drums with Kimball separate drum sticks for tap or accent and double roll drum sticks, giving the touch of the human drummer. Ludwig & Ludwig authentic cymbals, triangles, and legitimate orchestra traps. Imported tom toms, Chinese blocks, castanets, tambourines, Chinese gongs, genuine Zildjian Turkish cymbals, etc.

Pianos

Kimball large scale grand and upright pianos with mandolin-banjo attachment, soft pedal and a conveniently placed sustaining pedal which operates independent of the position of the organ expression pedal, yet permits the free use of both with one foot.

Why They Stand Up

The instruments are all erected and played *upon in the factory, nothing being left to chance.* When the organ is built to go into a chamber the outlines are marked out on the floor and the swell front is erected in the position it will eventually occupy.

furnished by public utilities corporations. There are normally more than eighteen hundred men and women employed in the factory making organs, pianos, phonographs and music rolls, as many as twenty-two hundred having been at work in the busiest seasons.

The Kimball Building

THE general and executive offices and retail stores of the company occupy a considerable part of the first six floors of the New Kimball Building at Jackson Boulevard and Wabash Avenue. Other tenants include some famous conservatories and many nationally known organists and other musicians.

KIMBALL Hall, with its magnificent four manual (and echo) concert organ, is the favorite recital hall of Chicago. Here Bonnet, Bauer, Courboin, Casals, Eddy, Ganz, Godowsky, Gabrilowitsch, Leginska, Lhevinne, Novaes, Yon, and others of equal note make their appearances. In addition to the great organ with its two manual and pedal Echo, the building contains six teaching and practice organs that are in use from early morning to late at night, training organists for Kimball organs.

Ideals Become Realities

WITH abundant capital and the spirit that exists throughout the organization it would be strange indeed if the technical staff had failed to build a wonderful organ, and this, we represent and can prove, is the standing accomplishment of the Kimball organ factory.

*The Organ is "The King of Instruments."
The Kimball is the King of Organs.*

---

for the tone. No pipes are bought outside, whatever the emergency. A Kimball is a Kimball, from the smallest organ needed for a city apartment, a lodge room or a miniature chapel to the greatest municipal concert organ or theatre unit orchestra.

Wide Scope in Organ Building

CONSIDERATION should be given to the fact that *the Kimball Company is the only one building* ORGANS *of both orchestral and churchly types, and true* UNIT ORCHESTRAS based upon the divisions of the symphony orchestra—string, wood wind, brass and percussion—with the addition of the organ or foundation tones and the muted brass, saxophones and other elements of the modern dance orchestra. *Unprejudiced advice can therefore be depended upon* and all theatre organ requirements can be met properly *with instruments perfectly suited for* motion picture theatres of every size and character, for use with and without orchestras, for vaudeville or "legitimate" houses, for lodge rooms and concert auditoriums.

IT is our belief that *the small house is as deserving of consideration as the largest theatre,* and in many instances it is vastly more important that the small organ be a success, since it is so often called upon to carry the burden of providing all the music, a responsibility which is likely to be shared with an orchestra in the large house. Not only must it be musically satisfactory, but it must be *absolutely dependable*—something the Kimball organ is invariably.

A Service That Serves

THE buyer may send for a Kimball representative with perfect assurance that a *qualified technical man* will respond, a sales engineer whose business it is to know organs, acoustics and all other fac-

tors which enter into the musical equipment of a theatre, and who understands the problems and economics of theatre operation. He will be a man prepared to advise conscientiously, knowing that as much depends upon the judicious selection and correct placing of the organ and its tone outlets as upon the materials and workmanship, all of which, in the Kimball, are of the best.

ALL Kimball theatre organ quotations include a suitable electric motor and blower of ample capacity for the heaviest demand and a direct coupled low voltage generator for the action current, with current indicator at the console. Also a solid bench with adjustable back and height adjustment, signal buttons and lights for "change slide" and other purposes, and exclusive features too numerous to list here. Kimball consoles are portable without extra charge, and can be set on elevators if desired.

Factors in Favorable Prices

THE W. W. Kimball Company buys for cash in the most favorable markets and carries immense stocks of lumber, metals, fuel and other necessaries. There is a network of tracks covering the seventeen acres occupied by the Kimball factories and lumber yards at California Boulevard, Twenty-sixth Street and the River, where the company's electric locomotive supplements the work of the railway switching crews. The buildings have a floor area of 850,000 square feet. With its own foundry, machine shops and plating works the Kimball factory is practically independent of outside assistance. It is believed to be the only organ company making all parts of its instruments. The power and heating plant consumes sixty-five tons of coal a day in winter, about thirty-five tons in summer, in addition to some hundreds of electrical horse power

An information form such as this helped Kimball design an appropriate organ for each theatre's specific circumstances. This particular sheet was prepared by C. M. "Sandy" Balcom, Kimball's northwest representative, for the Colonial Theatre in Portland which indeed purchased a 2/7 Kimball. According to this document the theatre's budget for an organ was $8,000; the actual contract price of the organ they purchased was $8,800.

3/12 KIMBALL THEATRE ORGAN
Bagdad Theatre, Portland, Oregon

The author has long been fascinated by the wording of contracts of various builders. It is a pleasure to reproduce here an example of an extremely rare document: a Kimball theatre organ contract.

Page 1

Designed for:

THE MULTNOMAH THEATRES CORPORATION
PORTLAND, OREGON.

Manuals,____(3)____compass CC to C⁴..61 notes.

Pedals, compass CCC to G..32 notes.

Electro-pneumatic action throughout, with direct current generator.

Console ____Unit circassian Walnut, satin finish.____
Manual keyboards inclined and all keyboards hinged for convenient access to contacts. Pedals A. G. O. pattern, corrected scale, concave and radiating. Speaking stops and couplers operated by stop keys.

Combinations adjustable at console, visibly affecting the registers, operated by pistons underneath their manuals; pedal combinations by toe pistons.

Pitch, Philharmonic, 440-A, 523.3-C.

A suitable electric motor and blower of ample capacity to be furnished with the organ; adequate foundation or enclosure and ventilation for same, electrical connections (including remote control starter, if required) and air tight ducts for distribution of wind from blower to all sections of organ, to be supplied and installed by the purchaser, in accordance with information to be furnished by the organ builder.

The purchaser to prepare the space for the reception of the organ in accordance with information to be furnished by the organ builder, such preparation including the "sound-proof" enclosures forming the expression chambers and means of access thereto, cutting and finishing necessary holes through floors, ceilings and partitions, supplying and installing all conduits for organ cables and mains (if required by local authorities*), electric lights in organ and blower chambers and at console, and adequate ventilation and means of keeping the atmosphere in all parts of the organ and blower room at a proper temperature and free from dampness, dust or other detrimental conditions. The purchaser will also provide necessary light, heat and power during the erection and finishing of the organ.

No case or screen is embraced in this contract, except the console case.

G. M. BALCOM
Tech. Rep.

*Kimball organ installations comply with the Code of the National Board of Fire Underwriters, which specifies: "The outside covering of organ cables not run in conduit must be either flame-proof or covered with a closely wound fire-proof tape. * * * Conduit may be used, but is not required." Kimball cables are flame-proof and damp proof.

Page 2

PEDAL

First Touch	Acoustic Bass	32'	Pipes
	Diaphone	16'	
	Ophicliede	16'	
	Bourdon	16'	
	Diapason Phonon	8'	
	Tibia Clausa	8'	
	Cello	8'	
	Flute	8'	
	Violin	4'	
	Bass Drum (band)		Traps
	Cymbal		
	Bass Drum (orchestra)		
	Snare Drum, roll		
Second Touch	Chinese Gong		Traps
	Bass Drum, band		
	Cymbal T		
	Tympani		

ACCOMPANIMENT

First Touch	Bourdon	16'	Pipes
	English Horn	8'	
	Diapason Phonon	8'	
	Tibia Clausa	8'	
	Violin I	8'	
	Violin II	8'	
	Vox Humana	8'	
	Kinura	8'	
	Flute	8'	
	Tibia Flute	4'	
	Violin I	4'	
	Violin II	4'	
	Vox Humana	4'	
	Forest Flute	4'	
	Piccolo	2'	
	Marimba Harp		Percussion
	Xylophone		
	Glockenspiel		
	Snare Drum, roll		Traps
	Snare Drum, tap		
	Chinese Block, roll		
	Chinese Block, tap		
	Tom Tom		
	Castanet		
	Tambourine		
	Shuffle		
Second Touch	English Horn	8'	Pipes
	Diapason Phonon	8'	
	Tibia Clausa	8'	
	Tibia Flute	4'	
	Glockenspiel		Percussion
	Chimes		
	Snare Drum, roll		Traps
	Chinese Block, roll		
	Triangle		
	Bird		

Page 3

SOLO

First Touch	Trombone	16'	Pipes
	Tibia Clausa	16'	
	Contre Viole	16'	
	Vox Humana	16'	
	English Horn	8'	
	Diapason Phonon	8'	
	Tibia Clausa	8'	
	Violin I	8'	
	Violin II	8'	
	Orchestral Oboe	8'	(synthetic)
	Saxaphone	8'	(synthetic)
	Vox Humana	8'	
	Oboe Horn	8'	
	Muted Cornet	8'	
	Clarinet	8'	
	Solo Cello	8'	
	Kinura	8'	
	Flute	8'	
	Cornet	4'	
	Octave	4'	
	Tibia Flute	4'	
	Violin I	4'	
	Forest Flute	4'	
	Nazard	2 2/3'	
	Fifteenth	2'	
	Piccolo	2'	
	Tierce	1 3/5'	
	Marimba		Percussion
	Xylophone		
	Glockenspiel		
	Orchestra Bells		
	Chimes		
Second Touch	Trombone	16'	Pipes
	Diapason Phonon	8'	

PERCUSSION

First Touch	Tibia Clausa	8'	Pipes
	English Horn	8'	
	Kinura	8'	
	Vox Humana	8'	
	Solo Piccolo	4'	
	Harp	8'	Percussion
	Marimba	8'	
	Marimba	4'	
	Xylophone	4'	
	Xylophone	2'	
	Glockenspiel		
	Orchestra Bells		
	Chimes		
	Bass Drum		Traps
	Cymbal		
	Tympani		
	Chinese Gong		
	Triangle		
	Snare Drum, tap		
	Snare Drum, roll		

Page 4

PERCUSSION cont.

Muffled Drum		Traps
Chinese Block, roll		
Chinese Block, tap		
Tom Tom		
Castanet		
Tambourine		
Shuffle		

VIBRATOS

Right Chamber.
Left Chamber.

ADJUSTABLE COMBINATIONS

Seven toe pistons affecting Pedal.
Seven double touch pistons affecting Acc. and Pedal.
Seven double touch pistons affecting Solo, Acc. and Pedal.
Two cancel pistons affecting respective manual groups.
Drum piston; military drums and cymbal, manual and pedal.
Trap cancel piston.
Vibrato cancel piston.

ADDITIONAL TRAP CONTROLS

Pedals

Chinese Gong, roll, first touch; stroke, second touch.
Grand Crash.

Toe pistons

Triangle
Two Birds

Push Buttons

Two Birds	Telephone Bell
Two Sleigh Bells	Steamboat Whistle
Auto Horn	Locomotive Whistle
Fire Gong, stroke	Siren
Factory gong, reiterating	Aeroplane
Chime	Wood Block

ACCESSORIES

Two balanced expression pedals.
Balanced crescendo pedal.
Sforzando pedal.
Muffled drum pedal.
Signal button. Signal light.
Change-title button, duplicated by toe piston.
Organ bench with adjustable back and adjustable for height.

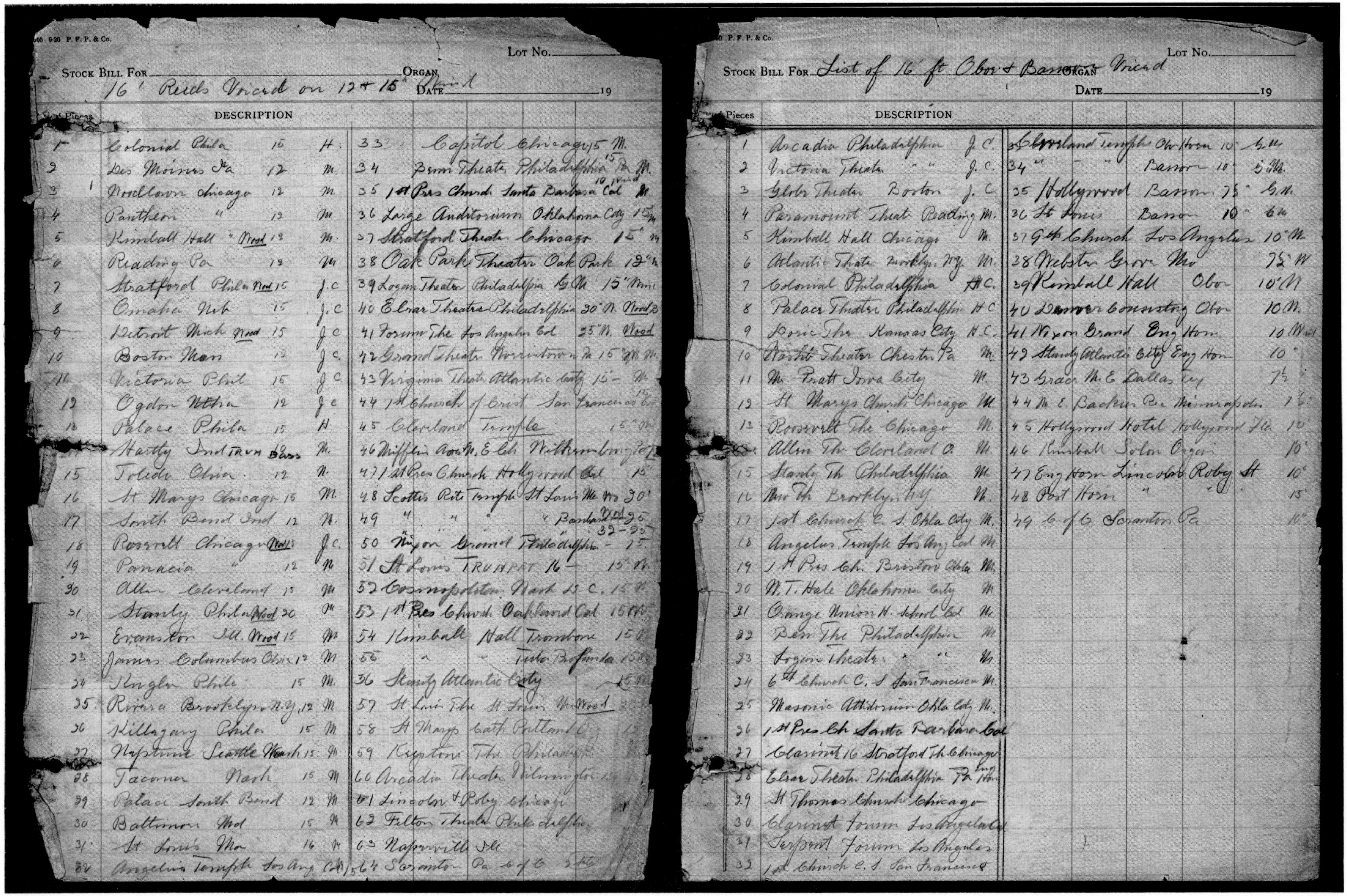

STOCK BILL FOR 16' Reeds Voiced on 12 & 15" Wind ORGAN DATE 19 LOT No.

Pieces	DESCRIPTION						
1	Colonial Phila	15	H.	33	Capitol Chicago	15	M.
2	Des Moines Ia	12	M.	34	Penn Theatr Philadelphia Pa	15	M.
3	Woodlawn Chicago	12	M.	35	1st Pres Church Santa Barbara Cal	10 Wind	M.
4	Pantheon "	12	M	36	Large Auditorium Oklahoma City	15	M
5	Kimball Hall " Wood	12	M.	37	Stratford Theatr Chicago	15"	M
6	Reading Pa	12	M	38	Oak Park Theatr Oak Park	12"	M
7	Stratford Phila Wood	15	J. C	39	Logan Theatr Philadelphia G.M	15"	Mixed
8	Omaha Neb	15	J. C	40	Elrae Theatre Philadelphia	20"	M. Wood B
9	Detroit Mich Wood	15	J C	41	Forum The Los Angeles Cal	25" M.	Wood
10	Boston Mass	15	J C	42	Grand Theatr Norristown Pa	15"	M. M.
11	Victoria Phil	15	J C	43	Virginia Theatr Atlantic City	15"	M
12	Ogden Utha	12	J C	44	1st Church of Crist San Francisco	15	
13	Palace Phila	15	H	45	Cleveland Temple	15"	M
14	Hardy Ind Trum Bass	16	M.	46	Mifflin Ave M.E. Ch. Wilkensburg Pa		
15	Toledo Ohio	12	M.	47	1st Pres Church Hollywood Cal	15"	
16	St Marys Chicago	15	M.	48	Scottish Rite Temple St Louis Mo		30"
17	South Bend Ind	12	M.	49	" " " Bombarde Wood	25	
18	Roosevelt Chicago Wood	15	J C.	50	Nixon Grand Philadelphia	32-20	15"
19	Panacia "	12	M	51	St Louis TRUMPET 16	15"	M.
20	Allen Cleveland	15	M	52	Cosmopolitan Wash D. C.	15	M.
21	Stanly Phila Wood	20	M	53	1st Pres Church Oakland Cal	15	M
22	Evanston Ill. Wood	15	M	54	Kimball Hall Trombone	15	
23	James Columbus Ohio	12	M	55	" Tuba Profunda	15	M
24	Kugler Phila	15	M.	56	Stanly Atlantic City	15	M
25	Rivera Brooklyn N.Y.	12	M	57	St Louis The St Louis Mo Wood		
26	Killagany Phila	15	M	58	St Marys Cath Portland Or		
27	Neptune Seattle Wash	15	M	59	Keystone The Philadelphia		
28	Tacoma Wash	15	M	60	Arcadia Theatr Wilmington		
29	Palace South Bend	12	M	61	Lincoln & Roby Chicago		
30	Baltimore Md	15	M	62	Felton Theatr Philadelphia		
31	St Louis Mo	16	M	63	Naperville Ill		
32	Angelus Temple Los Ang Cal			64	Scranton Pa 6 of 6		

STOCK BILL FOR List of 16 ft Obor & Basson Voiced ORGAN DATE 19 LOT No.

Pieces	DESCRIPTION					
1	Arcadia Philadelphia	J. C.	33	Cleveland Temple Obo Horn	10	G.M.
2	Victoria Theatr " "	J. C.	34	" " Basson	10	G.M.
3	Globe Theatr Boston	J. C	35	Hollywood Basson	7½	G.M.
4	Paramount Theat Reading	M.	36	St Louis Basson	10	G.M.
5	Kimball Hall Chicago	M.	37	9th Church Los Angeles	10"	M.
6	Atlantic Theatr Brooklyn N.Y.	M.	38	Webster Grove Mo	7½	W
7	Colonial Philadelphia	H.C.	39	Kimball Hall Obo	10"	M
8	Palace Theatr Philadelphia	H C	40	Denver Conservatory Obo	10	M.
9	Doric The Kansas City	H. C.	41	Nixon Grand Eng Horn	10	Wind
10	Karlton Theatr Chester Pa	M.	42	Stanly Atlantic City Eng Horn	10"	
11	Mt Pratt Iowa City	M.	43	Grace M. E Dallas Tex	7½	
12	St Marys Church Chicago	M.	44	M. E. Backus Rec Minneapolis	7½	
13	Roosevelt The Chicago	M.	45	Hollywood Hotel Hollywood Fla	10"	
14	Allen The Cleveland O.	M.	46	Kimball Solo Organ	10"	
15	Stanly Th Philadelphia	M.	47	Eng Horn Lincoln & Roby St	10"	
16	Mark Th Brooklyn N.Y.	M.	48	Post Horn "	15"	
17	1st Church C. S. Okla City	M.	49	6 of 6 Scranton Pa	10"	
18	Angelus Temple Los Ang Cal	M.				
19	1st Pres Ch. Bristow Okla	M.				
20	W. T. Hale Oklahoma City	M				
21	Orange Union H. School Cal	M.				
22	Ben The Philadelphia	M				
23	Logan Theatr " "	M				
24	6th Church C. S. San Francisco	M.				
25	Masonic Auditorium Okla City	M.				
26	1st Pres Ch Santa Barbara Cal					
27	Clarinet 16 Stratford Th Chicago					
28	Elrae Theatr Philadelphia Pa Eng Horn					
29	St Thomas Church Chicago					
30	Clarinet Forum Los Angeles Cal					
31	Serpent Forum Los Angeles					
32	1st Church C. S. San Francisco					

Here are some documents especially fascinating to students of Kimball minutiae: records of 16′ reeds produced by the Kimball pipe shop. The list on the left begins in 1918, the right page begins in 1915 and each runs through early 1926. The handwriting belongs to George T. Michel, head voicer, who voiced the majority of these stops. The initials J. C. and H. C. undoubtedly refer to Joseph J. Carruthers and his son Harry. Two Chicago theatres are masquerading under different names: Panacia was the working name for the Senate while it was under construction and Lincoln & Roby was the address of the then unnamed North Center Theatre.

What a disgusting way to picture the interior of an organ chamber! This is the solo side of the Earle Theatre in Philadelphia undergoing demolition during August of 1953.

KIMBALL OPUS LIST

Following are this firm's known theatre-type installations. It was their practice to prefix opus numbers with the letters "KPO" which stood for "Kimball Pipe Organ". Where these numbers are known, they are shown in Kimball fashion under the "remarks" column.

CITY/STATE	LOCATION	SIZE	YR	BLWR	HP	WP	REMARKS
ALABAMA							
Birmingham	WAPI Radio	3/8	1930				
ALASKA							
Anchorage	Empress Th.	2/11	1917	8052	5		
Cordova	Empress Th.	2/	1919				
Fairbanks	Empress Th.	2/7	1927	20242	5		
Juneau	Coliseum Th.	2/8	1928	21387	3		KPO 7019; later moved to 20th Century Th., Juneau, Alaska.
Ketchikan	Coliseum	2/7	1923	15238	2		
ARKANSAS							
Hot Springs	Princess (Palace) Th.	3/13	1920	11621	5	8"	With roll player.
			1921	11962			
Little Rock	Hollenberg Th.	2/					
Pine Bluff	Moon Th.	2/	1910	5126K			Tubular pneumatic action.
CALIFORNIA							
Alameda	Alameda Th.		1916	6964			
Lodi	Lodi Th.	2/					
Los Angeles	Forum Th.	4/37	1924	15111	25	10"&25"	KPO 6644; with 9-rank echo.
	Rimpau (Metro) Th.	2/4	1923	14068			Weighed 8,900 pounds.
Oakland	Photo (Franklin) Th.	2/	1914	5708			
San Francisco	Haight Street Th.	2/					
	Imperial (Premier) (United Artists) (Loew's) (Market St. Cinema) Th.		1914				
	Silver Palace Th.	2/	1910	4042K	1		
San Jose	T & D Th.	2/12					Tubular pneumatic action.
Saratoga	Community Th.		1925	17448			
COLORADO							
Denver	Ogden Th.	3/	1927	20313			
CONNECTICUT							
Greenwich	Greenwich Th.		1919	10088			
DELAWARE							
Wilmington	Arcadia	3/15	1921	12188			
	Strand Th.	3/10					
DISTRICT OF COLUMBIA							
Washington	Ambassador Th.	2/8	1923	14779			
	Cosmopolitan Th.	2/					
	Earle (Warner) Th.	3/10	1924	16604			
FLORIDA							
Coral Gables	Coral Gables Th.	3/	1925	18101			
Hollywood	Hotel Hollywood	3/	1925				
Little River	Tivoli Th.	2/	1925	17975			
Miami Beach	Biscayne Plaza Th.	2/8	1926	18789			
	Miami Beach Pier Th.		1926	18805			
	Plaza Community Th.	3/9	1923	14974			
GEORGIA							
Atlanta	Atlanta Th.	3/					
	Bailey's Eighty-One (Arcade) Th.	2/3	1925	18501			
	Crystal Th.	2/	1925	17980			
	Palace Th.	2/	1924				
Savannah	Arcadia Th.	2/	1919	10371			
	Folly Th.	2/	1919	10451			
	Odeon Th.	2/	1919	10375			
IDAHO							
Coeur d'Alene	Liberty Th.	2/7	1921	11598	3	7½"	Later moved to Hennepin Avenue Th., Minneapolis, Minnesota.
ILLINOIS							
Barrington	Catlow Th.	3/8					KPO 6960.
Bloomington	C. E. Irwin's Th.	?/9	1915	D358	2	5½"	
Blue Island	Grand Th.	2/	1926	19421			
	Lyric Th.	2/	1924	15665			
Cairo	Bijou Th.	2/7	1912	8873K	1	5"	Tubular pneumatic action.
Champaign	Orpheum Th.	2/4	1922	K410	1	7½"	KPO 6667.
Chicago	Academy Th.	2/	1923	14013			

CITY/STATE	LOCATION	SIZE	YR	BLWR	HP	WP	REMARKS
Chicago	Adelphi Th.	2/6	1917	8504			
	A. Karzas Th.		1913	A752	¾	5"	
	American Conservatory of Music	2/8	1923				Fulco Little Model Theatre.
	American Conservatory of Music	3/6					
	American Conservatory of Music	2/5	1925				
	Areon Th.	2/	1914	5808			
	Atlas Th.		1914	5851			
			1915	C559	½		
	Avon Th.		1914	C464	½	5"	
	Banner Th.	2/	1928	22303			
	Beach Th.	2/	1914	5438			
			1914	C114	½	5"	For two-rank echo.
	Boston Th.	2/10					
	Boulevard Th.	2/	1915	D595	1	5½"	
			1915	D596	½	5"	
	Bridgeport Th.		1919	10282			
	Brighton Th.	2/6	1920	11317	2	6½"	
	Broadway Th.		1915	D593	1	5½"	
			1915	D594	½	5"	
	Broadway Hippodrome Th.		1918	9013			
	Broadway Strand Th.	2/8	1917	8327			
	Bryn Mawr Th.	2/7	1913	A785	1	5"	
			1913	B40	1	5"	
	Buckingham Th.	3/	1927	20968			
	Calo Th.		1915	D568	1	5½"	
	Capitol (Alba) Th.	3/	1923			7½	
	Casey's Th.		1917	7884			
	Chateau (Vogue) Th.	3/9	1925	18104			
	Cicero Th.		1916	E154	1	5½"	
	Circle Th.		1914	C210	½	5"	
	Claude P. Ball Organ School	3/	1922				In Kimball Hall.
	Clifton Th.	2/7	1912	A83	1	5"	
	Columbus Th.	2/	1915	D617	1	5½"	
	Commercial Th.	2/10	1919	10122			
			1920	10822	3	8"	
	Coronada Th.	2/	1913	B317	¾	4"	
	Cosmopolitan Th.		1914	B780	1	5"	
			1914	C90	¾	5"	
	Deluxe Th.	2/	1924	16094			
	Douglas Th.	2/7	1914	C385	¾	4"	
			1917	F170	3	7"	
	Drexel Th.		1914	5781			
	Easterly Th.	?/10	1915	D180	2	5½"	
	Edelweiss Th.		1914	C492	¼		Blower for 2 ranks according to Kinetic Co. records.
	Ellentee Th.	2/6					
	Ettleson Th.	2/8	1914	C463	1	5½"	
	Forest Park Th.	2/7	1920	10876	2	7"	
	Frolic Th.	2/9	1915	D501	1	5½"	
			1915	D570	½	5"	
	Garfield Th.	2/9	1916	E136	1	5½"	
	Gold Th.	2/	1914	C145	¾	4"	Tubular pneumatic action.
			1914	C245	½	5"	
			1914	C257	¾	5½"	
	Gold Coast (Globe) (Parkside) (Village) Th.	2/7					
	Grand Th.	2/	1912	A409	¾	5"	
	Gumbiner's Th.		1914	B711	1	5"	
			1914	B712	½	5"	For 2-rank echo.
			1916	E135	1	5½"	
	Halsted Th.		1912	A126	1	5"	
	Hamilton Th.	2/	1916	E428	1	5½"	
	Hamlin (Alex) Th.		1914	C557	1	5½"	KPO 6245; blower for 8-rank main organ.
			1914	C556	½	5"	Blower for stage organ.
			1923	14442			Additions: 6 ranks.
	Harper Th.		1915				
	Highway Th.		1924	16142			
	Howard Th.	3/8	1928	21803			KPO 7042.
	Hoyburn Th.		1915	C669	1	5"	
			1915	C704	1		
	Hub Th.		1914	5418			
	Hyman & Hirsch Th.	2/7	1914	C445	¾	5½"	Tubular pneumatic action.
			1914	C446	½		
	Illington Th.	2/	1916	7105			Tubular pneumatic action.
		2/7	19??				Enlarged and electrified existing organ.
	Imperial Th.	2/6	1918	G4			
	Independence Th.	2/	1914	5511			
			1914	C164	½	5"	
	Iris Th.	3/12	1920				KPO 6789.
	Jefferson Th.		1912	A411	¾	5"	

CITY/STATE	LOCATION	SIZE	YR	BLWR	HP	WP	REMARKS
Chicago	Jewel Th.	2/9	1915	D410	1	5½"	
			1915	D409	½	5"	For 2-rank echo.
	Joy (Orpheus) (Tampico) Th.	2/7					
	Julian Th.	2/	1924	16624			
			1926	19354			
	Keystone Th.	1915		D569	1	5½"	
			1928	21894			
	Kimball Hall	2/	1922				Practice organ.
	Kimbark Th.	3/7	1927	20984		10"	
	Ed Kounovsky's Th.	?/10	1917	F209	3	7¼"	
	Lake Shore Th.	2/					
	Lakeside Th.	2/	1915	D179	2	5½"	
			1915	D356	½	5"	For 2-rank echo.
			1915	D502	1	5½"	
	Lawrence Th.	2/8	1915	D375	1	5½"	
	Lexington Th.	2/12	1925	17677			KPO 6857.
	Little Th., DePaul University	3/	1939				Classic organ.
	Logan Th.	2/	1916	7720			
	Lyric Th.	2/	1912	A197	¾	5"	
		2/8	1919	H409	1	6"	
	Mandarin Inn Restaurant	2/	1912	A339	2	5"	Tubular pneumatic action.
			1919	H562	3	7"	Electrified.
	Manor Th.	3/9					
	Marshall Square Th.	1917		8328			KPO 6431.
	Maywood Th.	1925		17879			
	Metropolitan Th.	2/10					
	Michigan Th.	2/	1922	13873			
	North Center Th.	3/21	1925	17930	15		
	North Shore Th.	2/8	1913	B152	1	5"	Tubular pneumatic action.
	Oakland Th.	2/7	1912	A90	1	5"	Tubular pneumatic action, style 23.
	Oakland Square Th.	2/8	1915	D653	2	5½"	
	Ogden Th.						Located at 1619 W. 63rd Street.
	Olympia Th.	2/9					KPO 6843.
	Orpheum Th.	2/7	1912	A126	1	5"	Tubular pneumatic action; style 23.
			1914	C563	1	5½"	
		2/9	1914	C564	1	4"	Additions: 2 ranks.
	Palace Th.	2/6					
	Panorama Th.	2/	1914	B778	1	5"	
			1914	B779	½	5"	For 2-rank echo.
			1927	20408			
		2/4	1928	21996			KPO 7008; later moved to Regent (400) Theatre, Chicago, Illinois.
	Pantheon Th.	3/	1918	9110	5		KPO 6456.
		3/18	1924	15916			Enlarged.
	Pastime Th.	2/	1919	10268			
	People's Th.	2/9	1924				Located at 47th & Marshfield.
	Prairie Th.	2/9	1915	D654	1	5½"	
			1915	D655	½	5"	For 2-rank echo.
	Randolph Th.	3/	1919				
	Rector's Restaurant	1908		3414K			
	Regent Th.	1915		D591	1	5½"	
			1915	D592	½	5"	
			1926	19631			
	Rex Th.	2/	1923	14184			
	Rialto Th.	1916		7685			
	Roosevelt Th.	3/20	1921	11745	15	10"&15"	KPO 6576.
	Rose Th.	1915		6280			
	Rosedale Th.	1915		D679	3½	8"	
	Schubert Th.	3/					
	Senate Th.	3/	1921				KPO 6643; with drawknob console.
		3/18	1924	15936			
			1925	16916			
	Shakespeare Th.	2/	1914	5292			
	Sheridan Th.	2/8	1915	D376	1	5½"	
	South Shore Th.	1915		D566	1	5½"	
			1915	D567	½	5"	For 2-rank echo.
	S. S. & P. Th.	1913		B95	¾	5"	
	State Lake Th.	3/	1919		5		KPO 6444.
	Strand Th.	2/	1915	D499	1	5½"	
			1915	D500	½	5½"	
	Stratford Th.	3/22	1923	14771			
	Studebaker Th.	3/	1914	5413			
			1915	D122	3	5"	
	Symphony Th.	4/10	1928	21580			KPO 7033.
	Terrace (Avenue) Th.	3/	1921				
	Thos. Gaynor Th.	1913		B153	3½	5½"	
	Vic Th.	3/12	1920	11306	5	8"&12"	KPO 6823; two consoles.
	Vista Th.	2/9	1915	C709	1	5½"	Tubular pneumatic action.
			1915	C710	½	5"	For 2-rank echo.
	Wabash Th.	1924		15793			

CITY/STATE	LOCATION	SIZE	YR	BLWR	HP	WP	REMARKS
Chicago	West End Th.	3/14	1917	8583			
	West Englewood Th.	2/10	1921	11468	3	8"	
	WGN Radio	3/10					Additions to 2/7 Wurlitzer; two consoles.
	Wilson (Four Star) Th.	2/6	1919				
	Wonderland Th.	2/9	1913	B455	1	5"	Tubular pneumatic action; style 26.
	Woodlawn Th.	3/9	1918	8786	7½		
	WTAS Radio	3/					
Chicago Heights	Lincoln Dixie Th.	2/9	1921	11887			KPO 6537.
	Washington Th.	2/	1921	12848			
Cicero	Baltelstein & Gold Th.	1914		C203	½	5"	
Decatur	Bijou Th.		1922	13484			
	Empress Th.	2/	1913	B529	¾	5"	
Des Plaines	Echo Th.	2/	1926	18693			
Evanston	Hoyburn Th.	2/	1915	C704	1	4"	
Harvey	Harvey Th.	2/					
Hawthorne	unidentified new theatre		1921	12643	3	10"	
Joliet	Princess Th.	2/					
	Tavern Th.	2/	1913	B165	¾	5"	Tubular pneumatic action.
Melrose Park	Melrose Park Th.	2/	1919	9380			
Momence	Momence Th.	2/7					
Oak Park	Oak Park (Lamar) Th.	2/10	1913	B535	1	5"	
			1913	159K	¼	5"	For 2-rank echo.
			1915	C691	½	5"	
		2/14	1923	14965			New organ.
Libertyville	Auditorium Th.	2/	1927	20388			
Peoria	unidentified theatre						
Ravinia	Ravinia Park Th.	2/	1910				
Rockford	Palace Th.	2/	1925	18317			KPO 6878.
Roseland	Berkson Th.		1914	C394	½		
			1914	C395	¾		
			1914	C566	1	5"	Replaced blower C395.
	Sam Stoll Th.		1914	C393	½	5"	
Springfield	Roxy (Majestic) Th.	2/4	1927	20128			
Waukegan	W. Q. Spoor's Th.	2/9	1915	D719	2	5½"	With 2-rank echo.
Wheaton	Grand Th.	2/8					
Wilmette	Teatro Del Lago	2/10					KPO 6952.
	Village Th.		1914	5517			
			1914	C163	½	5"	

INDIANA

CITY/STATE	LOCATION	SIZE	YR	BLWR	HP	WP	REMARKS
Anderson	Faulknir & Rosenberg		1913	B593	¾	5"	Tubular pneumatic action.
East Chicago	Hartley Th.	2/9	1920	10895	2	7"	
	Midway Th.	3/					
Elkhart	Bucklin Th.	2/	1915	D651	1	5"	
	Lerner (Elco) Th.	2/8	1924	16167			
Evansville	Grand Th.		1915	17527			
Fort Wayne	Jefferson Th.	2/	1914	C231	¾	5"	
			1914	C326	1	6"	
			1914	C327	½	5"	
			1922	13756			For new unit organ.
Gary	Young Amusement Co.	2/8	1912	8684K	1	5"	
Goshen	Jefferson	2/	1926	19174			
Hammond	Deluxe Th.	2/	1926	18640			
	Gumbiner's Th.	2/	1913	B461	1	5"	
	Orpheum Th.	2/8	1922	13018			KPO 6640.
	Parthenon Th.	2/11	1921	11864			KPO 6569.
	State Th.	3/	1926				
Indianapolis	Garrick (Esquire) Th.	2/7	1914				
	Isis Th.	2/12	1914				
Logansport	Ark Th.	2/	1915				
Richmond	Murette Th.	2/	1919	9951			
South Bend	Auditorium Th.	2/12	1916	7759			KPO 6393.
	Blackstone (State) Th.	2/	1920	11490	7½	8"&12"	
	LaSalle Th.	2/9	1914	C513	1	5½"	With 2-rank echo.
	Strand (Avon) Th.	2/4	1925	17669			KPO 6894.
	Orpheum Th.		1922	13611			
	Palace (Morris Civic) Th.	3/12	1921	12879	7½		
	Studebaker Opera House	2/					
Terre Haute	Brentlinger Th.	2/	1918				
	Terre Haute Th.	3/					
Valparaiso	J. Schelling's Th.	2/8	1914	C465	1	5½"	
Whiting	Capitol Th.	2/	1923	14369			
	Hoosier Th.	3/7	1924	15325			KPO 6749.

IOWA

CITY/STATE	LOCATION	SIZE	YR	BLWR	HP	WP	REMARKS
Burlington	Garrick Th.	2/	1919	9871			
Clinton	Strand Th.	2/	1919	9357			
Davenport	Columbia Th.	2/	1926	18366			
	Esquire Th.	2/					
	Garden Th.	2/	1915	D374	3	6½"	
Des Moines	Des Moines Th.	2/	1919	9497	7½		

CITY/STATE	LOCATION	SIZE	YR	BLWR	HP	WP	REMARKS
Des Moines	Garden Th.		1916	7524	5		
	Orpheum Th.	2/8	1923	14708			
Dubuque	Grand Opera House	2/9	1920	11464	3	8"	
	Strand Th.	2/7	1919	9749			With roll player.
Fort Dodge	Rialto Th.		1920	10498	2	7"	
Oelwein	Orpheum Th.	2/11	1919	9696			
Oskaloosa	Orient Th.	2/	1916	E276	1	5½"	
Ottumwa	Square Th.	2/	1925	17944			
Sioux City	Orpheum Th.	2/	1925	17550			
	Plaza Th.		1916	E142	2	6½"	
			1916	6995			
Waterloo	Plaza Th.	2/	1914	C544	½		
			1914	C545	1	5½"	
			1914	C569	1	5½"	
			1915	D523	½	5½"	
			1921	12945			

KANSAS

CITY/STATE	LOCATION	SIZE	YR	BLWR	HP	WP	REMARKS
Columbus	Christian Th.		1920	11076			
Pittsburgh	Mystic Th.	2/	1915	6630			
Wichita	Orpheum Th.		1922	13529			

LOUISIANA

CITY/STATE	LOCATION	SIZE	YR	BLWR	HP	WP	REMARKS
New Orleans	Palace Th.	2/9	1920	11141	3	8"	

MARYLAND

CITY/STATE	LOCATION	SIZE	YR	BLWR	HP	WP	REMARKS
Baltimore	Astor Th.		1927	21006			
	Avalon Th.	2/	1927	19971			
	Century Th.	2/					
	Linden Th.	2/9	1916	E55	2	6½"	With 2-rank echo.
	Lubin Th.	2/7	1916	E353	2	6½"	
	Mt. Royal Th.	2/9	1916	E54	2	6½"	With 2-rank echo.
	New Belnord Th.	3/8	1921	12209			
	Rivoli Th.	3/	1922	13306	7½		
	Stanley (Stanton) Th.	3/28	1927	20438	15		
Frederick	Opera House	3/	1926				
Sparrows Point	Lyceum Th.		1928	21824			

MASSACHUSETTS

CITY/STATE	LOCATION	SIZE	YR	BLWR	HP	WP	REMARKS
Boston	Columbia Th.	2/	1917	8213			
	Fenway Th.	2/					Replaced by Wurlitzer opus 561.
	Globe (Center) (Pilgrim) Th.	3/14	1916	C686	7½	7½"	With echo.
	St. James Th.	3/	1915	6697			
Salem	New Plaza Th.		1920	11246			

MICHIGAN

CITY/STATE	LOCATION	SIZE	YR	BLWR	HP	WP	REMARKS
Adrian	Crosswell Th.	2/	1925	16944			
Alpena	Maltz Th.	2/	1924	15669			KPO 6839.
			1925	17246			
Battle Creek	Garden Th.		1913	B382	¾	5"	
		2/	1922	13133			
	Strand Th.	2/8	1915	D206	1	5½"	
Cadillac	Lyric Th.	2/	1924	15774			
Detroit	Loop Th.	3/	1928				KPO 7011.
	New Plaza Th.		1922	13560			
	Oriental (Downtown) Th.	3/15	1927	20468			
	Regent (Center) Th.	4/27	1916	6809	10		With echo.
	Rosedale Th.	2/12	1915	D5	1	5"	
Flint	Orpheum Th.	2/8	1915	D366	1	5½"	
Grand Rapids	Empress Th.	3/	1914	5535			
Jackson	Capitol Th.	2/8	1928	21564			KPO 7020.
	Opheum Th.		1916	D739	1	5½"	
Muskegon	N-K Th.	2/6	1928	22144			
Kalamazoo	Elite Th.	2/	1913	B677	¾	5"	
Saginaw	Strand Th.	2/8	1915	D390	1	5½"	
St. Joseph	Caldwell Th.	2/8	1923	14960			Weight: 8,550 pounds.
South Haven	Centre Th.		1925	17245			
Three Rivers	Riviera Th.	2/10					KPO 6861.

MINNESOTA

CITY/STATE	LOCATION	SIZE	YR	BLWR	HP	WP	REMARKS
Crookston	Lyric Th.	2/					
Duluth	Zelda Th.	2/8					Tubular pneumatic action.
Hibbing	State Th.	2/	1921	12725			
Minneapolis	Auditorium (Lyceum) Th.	4/	1904	4617K	35		KPO 577; tubular pneumatic action.
	Blue Mouse Th.		1920	10976	3	8"	
	Curtis Hotel	2/11	1920	10877	5	8"	
	Municipal Auditorium	5/	1928	21848			KPO 7030; two consoles: 5-manual drawknob classic and 4/24 horseshoe theatre.
		4/24	1928				
			1928	13056TUR			For Kimball concert grand piano.
	Orpheum Th.	3/10					Twin consoles.
	Regent Th.	2/8					

CITY/STATE	LOCATION	SIZE	YR	BLWR	HP	WP	REMARKS
St. Paul	Alhambra Th.	2/6					
	Blue Mouse Th.		1913	B219	¾	5"	Style 26.
		2/8	1920	9726			
	Riviera Th.	3/9					
Virginia	Garrick Th.	2/	1917	8100			
MISSOURI							
Kansas City	Doric Th.	3/18	1920	10044	7½		Moved in 1922 to Liberty Th., Council Bluffs, Iowa.
	Gladstone Th.	2/13	1916	D578	½	5"	
			1916	D579	3½	7"	
	Main Street (RKO Missouri) (Empire) Th.	3/10	1924				KPO 6776.
	Orpheum Th.	2/	1925	17691			
	Regent Th.	2/	1916	D801	3	6½	With 2-rank echo.
	Yale Amusement Co.	2/	1910				
St. Louis	Orpheum Th.						
	Rialto Th.		1920	11109			
	St. Louis Th.	4/19	1925	17342			KPO 6852.
Sedalia	Lona Th.		1919	10359			
MONTANA							
Butte	American Th.	2/8	1912	A84	¾	5"	
			1920	I39	¼	3"	
Great Falls	Alcazar Th.	2/7	1913	A135	1	5"	Style 23; tubular pneumatic action.
	Ritz Th.	2/					
Livingston	Livingston Th.	2/10					
	G. M. White's Th.		1916	E237	2	5½"	
	Strand Th.	2/3	1917				
NEBRASKA							
Madison	Brown Th.	2/					
Omaha	Gem (Besse) Th.	2/	1914	5554			Moved in 1925 to Sun (State) Th., Omaha.
			1914	C221	½	5"	
	Sun Th.	2/	1916	7668	7½		
NEW JERSEY							
Atlantic City	Bijou Th.	2/	1915	D221	1	5"	
			1917	E680	3	7"	
	Colonial Th.	2/10	1915	D384	3	7"	
	Convention Hall	4/55	1930	23635	30	10"&15"	KPO 7073; also provided was a second blower for 25"wp, a concert grand piano and a roll player which controlled 13 ranks.
	Earle Th.	3/13	1926	19016			KPO 6913.
	Virginia Th.	3/13	1924	15886			
	Warner (Stanley) (Roxy) Th.	3/26	1925	17268			KPO 6832.
Bardentown	Fox Th.		1923	14445			
Bridgeton	Stanley Th.	3/7	1928	21794			
Burlington	Auditorium Th.	2/	1923	14810			
Camden	Colonial Th.	2/	1917	E758	2	5½"	
	Forest Hill Th.		1919	10372			
			1919	10374			
Iselin	Iselin Th.	2/	1928	21453			
Newark	Court Th.						
	Family Th.	2/	1913	B267	2	5½"	Moved to Regent Th., Philadelphia, Penn., in 1913.
Paterson	U. S. Th.		1926	19446			
Pitman	Broadway Th.	3/8	1926	18696			KPO 6862.
Trenton	State Street Th.		1919	10293			
Woodbury	Rialto Th.	2/7	1920	11089	1	6"	
Woodcliffe	Broadway Th.		1926	19504			
NEW YORK							
Astoria, L.I.	Astoria Strand Th.	2/	1924	16373			
Binghamton	Binghamton	?/11					
	Strand Th.	2/8	1920	10871	3	8"	
Bronx	Forum Th.	3/8	1922	13709			
Brooklyn	Adelphi Th.		1919	10374			
	Atlantic Th.	2/	1919	9485	5		
	Bluebird Th.		1925	17174			
	Boro Hall Th.		1923	15308			
	Commodore Th.	3/8	1922	13508			
	Endicott Th.	3/8	1927	20124			
	Keeney's Bay Ridge Th.		1924	16010			
	Normandy Th.		1919	10260			
	Patio Th.	3/	1928				
	Riviera Th.	3/	1920				
	Roebling Th.		1919	9880			
	St. George Playhouse		1927				
	Savoy Th.	3/8	1925	18152			KPO 6865.
	Sheepshead Th.	3/8	1929	23179			
	Stadium Th.	2/	1920	11229	3	8"	With 4-rank echo.
	Stanley Th.	3/	1928	22310			

CITY/STATE	LOCATION	SIZE	YR	BLWR	HP	WP	REMARKS
Brooklyn	Strand Th.	3/22	1927	20263	15		KPO 6944.
	Utica Th.	3/13	1920	10728	5	8"	
	Werbe Th.		1921	11724			
	Williamsburg Th.		1914	C570	3	6½"	
NEW YORK							
Elmira	Regent Th.	2/	1915	D354	3	7"	
Geneva	unidentified theatre	2/	1919				
Long Island	Park Th.		1922	13206			
Lynbrook, L.I.	Fox Lynbrook Th.	2/9	1923	14139			
Mt. Vernon	Little Play House		1917	F482	3	8½"	
New York	Arena Th.	2/	1918	8936			With double roll player.
			1918	9234			
	Bluebird (Ramona) Th.	2/7	1921	11842	1	6"	
	Broadway Th.		1915	D537	7½	5"&10"	
			1915	D671	½		
			19??				New console and additional ranks.
	City Hall Th.	2/11	1916	E356	3	7"	
	Clinton Th.		1921	12334			
	Empress Th.	2/8	1916	E287	2	5½"	
	First Avenue Th.		1921	12589			
	Forum Th.	2/					
	Gotham Th.	2/	1921	12849			
	Grand Th.	2/	1921	12439			
	Hollywood Th.		1926				
	Ideal Th.		1919	10079			
	Jewel (Grant) Th.	2/	1922	13411			
	Lew White Inst. For Organ	3/8	1927				This or one of the following two organs was later moved to WCBS Radio, New York City and enlarged to a 3/10; one of the three instruments was KPO 7044.
	Lew White Inst. For Organ	2/8	1927				
	Lew White Inst. For Organ	2/5	1927				
	Loew's Commodore Th.	3/12	1926	19047			
	Lyric Th.	2/7	1916	E167	¾	5½"	Tubular pneumatic action.
	M & S Theatre		1919	10323			
	New Law Th.	2/8	1920	10735	1¼	5"	Tubular pneumatic action.
			1921	12528			
	Odeon Th.		1922	12961			
	Orpheum Th.	2/20	1915	C590	7½	7½"&15"	Moved in 1916 to Victoria Th., Philadelphia, PA.
	Roxy Th.	5/34	1927	19767	40		KPO 6889; also had two additional 3-manual consoles.
	Roxy Th.	2/8	1927	19768	5		KPO 6887; located in theatre broadcasting studio.
	Roxy Th.	3/14	1927	19766	7½		KPO 6888; located in grand lobby and equipped with roll player.
	Stanley Th.	2/9	1920	11244	3	8"	
	Tivoli (Adonis) Th.	3/10	1921	12187	7½		
	Velazco Studio	3/8	1928				Later repossessed.
Owego	Tioga Th.	2/	1923	15273			
Richmond Hill	Garden Th.	2/	1921	12899			
Rochester	Fay's Th.	2/	1925	17766			
Waverly	Capitol Th.	2/	1926	19414			
NORTH CAROLINA							
Ahoskie	Richard Th.	3/7	1928	22112			Later moved to WPTF Radio, Raleigh, N.C.
Greensboro	Imperial Th.	2/					
Hendersonville	Rex Th.		1924	16269			
NORTH DAKOTA							
Grand Forks	Grand Th.		1919	10006			
OHIO							
Cleveland	Allen Th.	3/23	1921	11763	7½		KPO 6578; with echo; weight: 28,000 pounds.
	Broadway Th.		1925	16850			
	East Ninth Street Th.	2/	1927				
	Garfield Th.		1927	21130			
	Hilliard Square Th.	2/8	1927	19502			
	Imperial Th.		1926	19505			
	Kinsman Th.	2/	1924	16441			
	Moreland Th.	2/9	1927	21301			
	Palace Th.	3/					
	Variety Th.	3/11	1927	21139			KPO 7001.
Columbus	James (Loew's Broad) Th.	3/15	1921	11354	5	8"&12½"	
Dayton	Auditorium Th.	2/	1917	F292	1	6"	
			1917	F293	½	5½"	
		3/	1919	9846			KPO 6550.
East Liverpool	American Th.		1918	G272	2	6½"	
Kent	Kent Th.		1927	19968			
Lakewood	Lakewood (Detroit) Th.	3/	1923	15153			
Mansfield	Grand Th.	2/	1916	E263	2	7"	With 2-rank echo.
	Majestic Th.	2/	1923				

CITY/STATE	LOCATION	SIZE	YR	BLWR	HP	WP	REMARKS
Mansfield	Ohio Th.	3/9	1928	21281			KPO 7029.
Marion	Marion Th.		1928	21976			
	Marion Photo Player Co.		1914	C391	½	6"	
	Oakland Th.	2/	1922				
Newark	Auditorium Th.						
Springfield	unidentified new theatre	2/10	1920	10695	3	8"	Possibly Sun's Regent Theatre.
	Sun's Fairbanks Th.	2/	1926	18716			
	Sun's Regent Th.						
Toledo	Rivoli Th.	3/12	1920	11320	5	8"&12"	Later moved to Irving Theatre, Carbondale, Penn.
Youngstown	State Th.	3/12	1928	21231			

OKLAHOMA

CITY/STATE	LOCATION	SIZE	YR	BLWR	HP	WP	REMARKS
Oklahoma City	Empress Th.	2/	1912				
	Home Th.	4/	1923				
	Powell Th.	2/7	1911	8346K	1	5"	Tubular pneumatic action.
Tulsa	Alhambra Th.	2/	1923				

OREGON

CITY/STATE	LOCATION	SIZE	YR	BLWR	HP	WP	REMARKS
Medford	Medford Th.	2/8	1924				KPO 6735.
Portland	Bagdad Th.	3/12	1927	19586			Cost $ 16,500.
	Columbia Th.		1913	B268	3½	6½"	
	Heilig Th.	2/5	1925				
	Hudson's Colonial Th.	2/7	1924	16209			Cost: $8,800.
		2/8	1926				Additions: kinura, xylophone and piano, costing $ 1,805.
	Music Box Th.	3/22					Later replaced with a style 4 Wurlitzer.
	National Th.	3/24	1914	5823	5		

PENNSYLVANIA

CITY/STATE	LOCATION	SIZE	YR	BLWR	HP	WP	REMARKS
Allentown	Vermond Knauss School Of Organ Playing	3/	1927	20780			
		2/	1927				
Altoona	Victoria Th.		1922	13384			Moved in 1925 to Midwood Th., Brooklyn, NY.
Bala Cynwood	Egyptian (Bala) Th.	3/8	1927	20591	5	10"	KPO 6925.
Bristol	Forest (Grand) Th.	3/8	1927	21229			KPO 6973.
Bryn Mawr	Seville (Bryn Mawr) Th.		1926	18862			
Chester	Edgemont Th.	2/	1926	18746			
	Washburn's Th.	2/11	1920	11190	5	8"	
	Washington (Stanley) Th.	2/9	1920	11239	3	7½"	
Coatesville	Auditorium Th.	2/15					
Darby	Darby Th.	2/9	1920	10885	3	7½"	
Drexel Hill	Waverly Th.	3/8	1927	20343			KPO 6637; later repossessed.
Easton	Strand Th.	2/9	1920	11597	2	7"	
Edwardsville	Belle Th.	2/	1926	18859			
Ellwood City	Barnes Th.	2/	1927	20763			
Forest City	Freedman Th.	2/	1925	17481			
Glenside	Glenside Th.	2/6	1921	12887			
Hazelton	Capitol Th.	3/8	1926	18785	5		KPO 6883.
Homestead	Stahl (Leona) Th.	3/9	1925	17885			KPO 6860.
Honesdale	Lyric Th.		1919	9579			
Kingston	Kingston Th.	2/	1925	17087			
Lansdowne	Lansdowne Th.	3/8	1927	20201			KPO 6937.
Lewistown	Embassy Th.	3/8	1928	20848			KPO 6992.
Monessen	Olympic Th.		1914	C608	¾	5"	Tubular pneumatic action.
Norristown	Garrick Th.	3/7	1927	20863			
	Grand Th.		1924	15980			
		3/12	192?				KPO 7029.
Norwood	Manor (Norwood) Th.	3/7	1927	20434			
Philadelphia	Alhambra Th.		1915	D86	3	7"	
	Ambassador Th.		1921	12548			
	Apollo Th.		1917	E503	3	7"	
	Arcadia Th.	3/20	1915	C809	4	6½"	With echo.
	Auditorium Th.	2/8	1917	F210	3	7¼"	
	Avon Th.	2/					
	Bell Th.	2/					
	Belmont Th.	2/12	1916	E264	3	7"	
	Benn Th.	2/	1915	D221	1	5"	
		3/13	1923	14375	10		
	Boyd (Sameric) Th.	3/19	1928	22477			KPO 7050.
	Capitol Th.	2/7	1919	9879			Located at 8th and Market.
	Cedar Th.	2/6	1920	H540	1	6"	
	Circle Th.	3/	1929	23276			KPO 6943.
	Colonial Th.	3/20	1919	9967	7½		Located on Germantown Street.
	Colonial Th.						Located on Lancaster Avenue.
	Colonial Th.	3/	1914				Located on Moyamensing Avenue.
	Colonial Th.		1927	21075			Blower for one of Colonial Theatres above.
	Crystal Palace Th.						
	Diamond Th.	3/	1926				
	Drury Th.	2/8	1919	G364	1	6"	
	Earle Th.	3/29	1923	15117			Weight: 44,000 pounds.
	Empress Th.	2/	1918	9075			

CITY/STATE	LOCATION	SIZE	YR	BLWR	HP	WP	REMARKS
Philadelphia	Fairmount Th.	2/8	1921	12259			
	Family Th.	2/10	1917	F38	3	7"	
	Felton Th.	2/	1926	18538			
	56th Street (Photo Play) Th.	2/15	1915	D553	3	7"	
	Globe Th.	2/12	1916	D527	3	7"	
	Grand Th.	3/	1925				
	Imperial Th.	2/9	1916	E469	2	7"	Located at 2nd and Popular Street.
	Imperial Th.	2/11	1917	E583	3	7"	Located at 60th and Walnut Street.
	Imperial Th.	2/8	1925	17615			New organ for one of Imperial Theatres above.
	Jackson Th.	2/					
	Jumbo Th.	2/	1918	G301	1	5"	
		2/4	1924	15352			KPO 6897; replaced earlier instrument.
	Karlton (Midtown) Th.	3/13	1921	12364			
	Kent Th.	3/15	1927	20876			
	Keystone (Lehigh) Th.	1925		17711			
	Killegarry Th.	1921		12402	10		
	Leader Th.	1915		D214	3	7"	
	Lehigh Palace Th.	2/7	1916	E355	2	7"	
	Liberty Th.	2/8	1921	12254			
	Locust Th.	1914		C258	2	6½"	Located on 52nd Street.
	Logan Th.	3/13	1923	15081			
	Market (333) Th.	2/10	1916	E354	3	7"	
	Milgram Th.	1923		15119			
	Nixon Grand Th.	3/19	1924	15997			
	Ogontz Th.	3/15	1926	19676			KPO 6906.
	Olney Th.	1922		12985			
	Orient Th.	2/6	1920	H493	1	6"	
	Orpheum Th.	3/13	1926	19475	10		
	Overbrook Th.	3/10	1926	19627			KPO 6936.
	Oxford Th.	3/	1927	21251			
	Palace Th.	4/28	1919	10123	15		With 5-rank echo.
	Pearl Th.	3/	1927	20570			KPO 6977.
	Princess Th.	2/					
	Regent Th.	2/10	1914	B267	5½		
		2/12	1914	C93	¼	5"	Additions: 2-rank echo.
	Ritz Th.	2/					
	Stanley Th.	3/29	1921	11410	25	10"&25"	KPO 6582.
	State Th.	3/13	1929	23241			KPO 6941.
	Strand Th.	3/	1917	E492	10	11½"&15"	
	Stratford Th.						
	Torresdale Th.	3/8	1923	14041			
	Uptown Th.	3/19	1928	22609			
	Viola Klaiss Studio	1924		16130			
	West Allegheny Th.	1922		13764			
	Windsor Th.	1914		C10	¾	5"	
	Wishart Th.	2/	1924	16391			
	Wynne Th.	2/	1927	20343			
Pittsburgh	Cameraphone Th.	2/8	1913	B647	1	5"	
	Colonial Th.	3/20					
	East Liberty Th.	3/	1928	22522			
	Heinz Auditorium Th.	4/67	1936				Rebuild and new console for existing E. M. Skinner opus 545, plus additions, including unified theatre stops and traps.
	Enright Th.	3/13					
	Olympia Th.	1913		B383	¾	5"	
			1914	C246	¼		
	Olympic Th.	2/	1914	C260	1		Tubular pneumatic action.
			1914	C461	2		
			1914	C537	3	7"	
			1914	C608	¾	5"	
	Stahl Th.	3/					
	Stanley Th.	3/	1926				
Pittston	American Th.	3/9	1924	15730			
	Roman Th.	2/8					
Plymouth	unidentified new theatre		1925	16851			
Pottstown	Strand Th.	1925		18114			
Pottsville	Capitol Th.	3/8	1927	20923			KPO 6990.
Reading	Colonial Th.	2/15	1917	8091	15		
	Paramount Th.	3/					
	Princess Th.	2/	1916	C671	3	5½"	With 2-rank echo.
Sayre	Sayre Th.	2/	1923	13730			
Scranton	Capitol Th.	2/	1924	15680			
	Green Ridge Th.	1925		16853			
	Hyde Park Th.	3/					
	Park Th.	2/	1921	12603			
	Poli's Th.	1925		17655			
	Regent Th.	3/	1917	E763	5	9½"	
			1919	9679			

CITY/STATE	LOCATION	SIZE	YR	BLWR	HP	WP	REMARKS
Scranton	State Th.		1921	12559			
	Strand Th.		1916	E301	3	7"	
		3/12	1924	15761			KPO 6756; replaced existing organ.
	Westside Th.	3/8	1926	19374			
Tarentum	Palace Th.	2/	1920				
Towanda	Keystone Th.		1927	20062			
Upper Darby	69th Street Th.	3/15	1924				
Williamsport	unidentified new theatre		1926	19420			
Windber	Arcadia Th.	2/	1921	12012			
Wilkes-Barre	Capitol Th.	2/					
	Metropolitan Th.	2/8	1920	11189	3	8"	
	Poli's Th.		1925	17675			
	Savoy Th.		1915	D48	3½	6½"	With 2-rank echo.
		3/	1918	8938			

RHODE ISLAND

CITY/STATE	LOCATION	SIZE	YR	BLWR	HP	WP	REMARKS
Providence	Carlton Th.	2/	1927	19912			
	Fay's Th.		1925	17673			
			1925	17787			Moved in 1926 to Columbus Th., New York City.

SOUTH DAKOTA

CITY/STATE	LOCATION	SIZE	YR	BLWR	HP	WP	REMARKS
Aberdeen	Capitol Th.	2/8	1926	19425			
Sioux Falls	Colonial Th.	2/	1926	18950			

TENNESSEE

CITY/STATE	LOCATION	SIZE	YR	BLWR	HP	WP	REMARKS
Memphis	Princess Th.	2/	1916	D762	3½	6½"	With 2-rank echo.
Nashville	Hillsboro (Belcourt) Th.	2/5	1925	16901			
	Knickerbocker Th.	3/12	1916	D732	3½	6½"	With 2-rank echo.

TEXAS

CITY/STATE	LOCATION	SIZE	YR	BLWR	HP	WP	REMARKS
Dallas	Majestic Th.	2/	1920	11617			
Houston	Kirby Th.	2/					
San Antonio	Majestic Th.		1914	5625			

UTAH

CITY/STATE	LOCATION	SIZE	YR	BLWR	HP	WP	REMARKS
Ogden	Alhambra (Paramount) Th.	3/37	1915	6018			With echo.
			1915	6035			
Salt Lake City	American Th.	4/	1913	A794	3	5"	
	Liberty Th.	2/8	1912	A189	2	5"	
	Rex Th.	3/	1912				Moved in 1915 to Diepenbrock (Strand) (State) Theatre, Sacramento, Calif.
Tooele	Tooele Th.	2/8					Tubular pneumatic action.

VIRGINIA

CITY/STATE	LOCATION	SIZE	YR	BLWR	HP	WP	REMARKS
Atlantic City	Virginia Th.	3/					
Norfolk	Wells Th.	2/	1919	9753			

WASHINGTON

CITY/STATE	LOCATION	SIZE	YR	BLWR	HP	WP	REMARKS
Aberdeen	D & R Th.	2/8	1923	15026			KPO 6735.
Bellingham	Egyptian Th.	2/					Tubular pneumatic action.
		2/7	1926	17576	3		KPO 6838; Cost $ 9,000.
	Grand Th.	2/7			5		Tubular pneumatic action.
Centralia	Liberty Th.	2/12	1922				KPO 6651.
Chehalis	St. Helen's Th.	2/6	1924	15357			KPO 6748.
Everett	Apollo Th.	2/10					Tubular pneumatic action.
	Everett Th.	2/	1918	9166			
		2/9	1924	15818			KPO 6760.
	Orpheum Th.	2/8					Tubular pneumatic action.
	Star Th.	2/7	1910				Tubular pneumatic action.
Kent	unidentified theatre	2/9					Tubular pneumatic action.
Kirkland	Gateway Th.	2/7	1919				
Longview	Columbia Th.	3/9	1924	16622			
Port Angeles	Dream Th.	2/7	1916	E273	1	5"	
Seattle	Alhambra Th.	2/7					
	American Th.	2/7					
	Arabian Th.	2/5	1925	16365			Later moved to State (Rivoli) Th., Seattle, Wash.
	Broadway Th.	2/7					Tubular pneumatic action.
	Broadway Society Th.	2/7					Tubular pneumatic action.
	Bruen's Venetian Th.	2/7	1919				Tubular pneumatic action.
	Capitol Th.	3/14	1924	16194			Later moved to Palomar Th., Seattle.
	Cheerio (Stradley) Th.	2/5	1925	16590			KPO 6805.
	Circuit Th.	2/7					
	City Th.	2/7					
	Colonial Th.	3/27	1914	B709	7½	8"	With echo.
	Embassy Th.	2/9	1925	17768			KPO 6859.
	Everett Th.	2/8	1919				
	45th Street (Paramount) Th.	2/6	1921	12294			KPO 6657; tubular pneumatic action; moved in 1924 to Mission Theatre, Seattle.
		2/6	1924	15666			Cost $ 8,250, less $2,000 allowance for old organ traded in.
		2/8					Additions: 2 ranks.
	Gateway Th.	2/4	1925				

CITY/STATE	LOCATION	SIZE	YR	BLWR	HP	WP	REMARKS
Seattle	Grand Th.	2/5					
	Heilig Th.	2/					
	Melbourne Th.	2/8	1913				
	Neptune Th.	3/14	1921	12652	10		
	Olympic (Woodland) Th.	2/7	1925	17361			KPO 6858.
			1925	17791			
	Orpheum Th.						
	Pantages Th.	3/10					
	Queen Anne Th.	2/	1910	5535K	2		
		2/5	1924				
	Ridgemont Th.	2/6	1923	14260			KPO 6842.
Sedro-Wooley	Dream Th.	2/5	1925	17025			
Snohomish	Brown (Smith) Th.	2/4	1924	16137			KPO 6784; Cost $ 6,900.
Spokane	Clem Th.	2/4					
	Clemmer (Audion) (State) Th.	4/32	1914	5789	5		
			1914	C472	½	5″	For 4-rank echo.
	Majestic Th.	2/7	1901				Tubular pneumatic action.
Tacoma	Shrine (Temple) Th.	2/9	1927	20902			
Vancouver	Grand Th.	2/	1914	C12	¾	5″	
WEST VIRGINIA							
Wheeling	Colonial Th.	2/9	1914	C100	1	5½″	With 2-rank echo.
	Virginia Th.	3/	1915	D355	3½	7″	
WISCONSIN							
Fon du Lac	Bijou Th.		1912	A539	¾	5″	
Green Bay	WCLO Radio	2/					
Madison	Fuller Opera House	2/	1921	12647			
	Orpheum Th.	3/9	1927	19808	5		
Milwaukee	Empire Th.		1913	B318	¾	4″	
	State Th.	2/	1915	D603	2	5½″	
		2/6	1924	15805			KPO 6769.
	Warner (Center) Th.	3/28	1931	24559			This organ contains *three consecutive* opus numbers: 6944, 6945 and 6946, all dating from 1927, four years earlier than the blower was shipped and the organ actually installed. Some pipes are marked "KPO 6946 Stanley Theatre, Pittsburgh" although this theatre is known to have installed a 3/27 Wurlitzer late in 1927.
	Warner Bros. Th.		1926	19017			
ALBERTA, CANADA							
Calgary	Strand (Crown) Th.	2/14	1913	B510	2	5″	Tubular pneumatic action.
Edmonton	Dominion Th.	2/9					Tubular pneumatic action.
	Empress Th.	2/	1912	A537	¾	5″	
BRITISH COLUMBIA, CANADA							
Vancouver	CJOR Radio	2/4					
	Princess Th.						
	Strand Th.						
Victoria	Bijou Th.						
MANITOBA, CANADA							
Winnipeg	Orpheum Th.		1921	12678	3		
	Rex Th.		1913	A641	¾	5″	
	Moving Picture Theatre	2/7	1911	7988K	1	5″	Style 23, tubular pneumatic action.
QUEBEC, CANADA							
Montreal	Allen Th.	3/	1920				
CHINA							
Peking	Union Medical College	2/10	1920	10890	3	8″	With solo roll player and traps; used in chapel below and in auditorium above for motion pictures.
ENGLAND							
London	Empire Th., Leicester Square	3/	1920				With echo.

ARTHUR A. KOHL ORGAN COMPANY

Arthur A. Kohl was a Rochester, New York organ man whose business was primarily local.[1] He bought consoles from Durst, Boegle & Company and probably most other parts from supply houses as well. Considering that he installed about fifteen theatre organs in a very short span of years, he would have had his hands full just installing them, with little, if any, time for actual building. His success was apparently due partly to having had a good "in" with the Schine theatre circuit.

This 2/3 Kohl was formerly installed in the Rivoli Theatre, Rochester, New York. The console was built for Kohl by the supply house Durst, Boegle & Company. Note the setterboards which pull out on either side of the lower manual for ease of piston setting by the organist. On many other makes of organs it was necessary to remove a rear or side panel to gain access to the setterboards. Even having a combination action on an organ of only three ranks was a deluxe feature. Photos on the left illustrate, above, pneumatics which move the stop keys and, below, a close-up view of the right setterboard.

This Durst, Boegle & Co. ad in the May 1928 Diapason featured the console Kohl installed in the Monroe Theatre, Rochester, New York.

KOHL OPUS LIST

CITY/STATE	LOCATION	SIZE	YR	BLWR	HP	WP
NEW YORK						
Lyons	Ohman Th.		1927	19944		
Rochester	Arnett Th.	2/	1928	22036		
	Cameo Th.	2/	1926	18322		
	Clinton Th.	2/	1928	21534		
	Empress Th.	2/6				
	Jefferson Th.	2/				
	Lyndhurst Th.	2/				
	Majestic Th.		1926	18335		
	Monroe Th.	3/	1927	21037		
	Palace Th.		1928	22297		
	Plaza Th.	2/	1927	20768		
	Princess Th.	2/	1926	19274		
	Rivoli Th.	2/3	1928	21887	1	6"
	Stanley Th.	2/	1926	19361		
	Sun Th.	2/				
	Thos. W. Finucane Residence		1926	19383		

KRAMER ORGAN COMPANY

The author knows very little about this firm other than its address: 334 W. 44 Street in New York City. They apparently were engaged to install Seeburg-Smith and Smith Unit Organ Company organs in the New York and New Jersey areas, inasmuch as records of the Kinetic blower company reveal that some blowers for these organs were shipped to Kramer's shop. Some blowers were purchased by Kramer while the Seeburg and Smith companies bought others. At least two Smith organs are known to have Kramer nameplates and it is conceivable that other Smith organs installed by Kramer may also bear his nameplate.

KRAMER OPUS LIST

Entries on the following list, with two exceptions, do not appear on the Smith list so it is likely that they are actually Kramer organs. Inasmuch as Smith factory records are incomplete, it is possible that some of these are actually Smith or Seeburg-Smith organs.

CITY/STATE	LOCATION	SIZE	YR	BLWR	HP	WP	REMARKS
NEW JERSEY							
Clifton	Strand Th.	2/4					Piano console; pipes in chambers.
Hoboken	Hespe Th.	3/	1931				
Passaic	Capitol Th.	2/	1921	J120	3		Built by Seeburg-Smith.
NEW YORK							
Amsterdam	Strand Th.		1919	H533	1½	6″	
Bronx	Allerton Th.		1927	P519B	3	10″	
	Daly Th.		1926	0823B	3	10″	
Brooklyn	Gloria Th.		1924	M645B	2	10″	
	Granada Th.	2/8					
	Myrtle Th.		1921	J281	2	8″	
	Singer Th.		1919	9568			
Huntington	Palace Th.		1927	P907B	2	10″	
New York	Avenue A Th.		1918	8771			
	Central Th.		1921	J244	3	10″	
	Cosmo Th.	2/8	1921	J415			Built by Smith.
	Dyckman Th.		1924	M18	2	10″	
	Kramer show rooms		1917	7812	½		Built by Hall.
	Park Lane Th.		1926	G71	2		
	Mr. Rhinelander		1925	N540B	5	8″	
Peekskill	Peekskill Th.		1921	J438	2	10″	

BENJAMIN F. LENOIR

LeNoir was in the organ business in Philadelphia during the 1920s, having apprenticed with C. S. Haskell as early as 1901.[1] It is probably safe to assume that theatre organs bearing his nameplate consist of Organ Supply components, inasmuch as the blowers were sold through this supply house.[2] Judging from the junction board remaining in the Levoy Theatre, LeNoir organs may have been quite nice. This component discloses that the Levoy organ was a 3/10 with the following disposition: tuba horn 16-4, post horn 8-4, diaphonic diapason 16-4, tibia clausa 16TC-4, kinura 8, oboe 8-4, VDO 16TC-4, VDO celeste 8-4, concert flute 16-1 1/3, vox humana 16TC-4, wood harp, glockenspiel, xylophone, chimes, and seventeen traps.[3]

The instrument controlled by this Organ Supply console contained a 16′ tuba, 8′ post horn, 8′ kinura, 8′ clarinet and 8′ vox humana; in all probability it was a Lenoir. Note the vertically oriented combination setter drawers with glass knobs.

LENOIR OPUS LIST

CITY/STATE	LOCATION	SIZE	YR	BLWR	HP	WP
NEW JERSEY						
Clementon	Clementon Th.		1927	P755B	5	12″
Millville	Levoy Th.	3/10	1927	P304B	7½	12″
Runnemede	Runnemede Th.		1928	Q242B	5	10″
Westmont	Westmont Th.		1927	P303B	7½	12″

LINK PIANO COMPANY, INC.

MANUFACTURERS OF *Automatic Musical Instruments* — *Pianos and Organs*

532 REPUBLIC BLDG.
CHICAGO

183-185 WATER ST.

BINGHAMTON, N.Y.

The Link story begins in Huntington, Indiana where George T. Link headed the Schaff Brothers Piano Company. One of Schaff's customers was the Automatic Musical Company of Binghamton, New York.[1] This firm was founded by two brothers named Harris in 1900 or so to manufacture coin-operated musical instruments.[2] By 1910 the Automatic Musical Company was in receivership and a group of creditors appointed George Link's son Edwin to manage the firm. Edwin Link moved to Binghamton with his wife and sons George T. Link and Edwin A. Link, Jr. and managed to get the Automatic Musical Company back on its feet.[3] By February 1913 the plant resumed manufacturing. With the prospect of ever increasing business, Edwin Link purchased the firm from the creditors and incorporated the Link Piano Company in 1916.[4]

The coin-operated piano business was steady until Prohibition was enacted in 1920 when it slumped but picked up again after speakeasies became popular. A factory force of between 60-125 people turned out about six instruments per week right up until the 1929 crash. Around thirty to forty women were employed just to cover pneumatics! George Thayer was plant manager and did much of the design work in the early years; in later years Edwin Link's son, Ed Link, Jr., contributed much of his inventive genius to the firm.[5] Mr. Link's other son, George, became general manager in the mid-1920s when his father retired.[6] Edwin Link, Sr. moved to California because his health couldn't tolerate the New York winters.[7] He was responsible for sales of around two dozen Link organs on the west coast (about 20% of the total production) although most instruments were sold within a few hundred miles of the factory.

The first Link theatre organ consisted of a piano and two side cabinets containing four ranks of pipes and a four-roll player device and was sold around 1918. This instrument was known by the nickname "Peter Flunk." In 1925 Link engaged the services of organist C. Sharpe Minor to design a series of instruments which became known as Link-C. Sharpe Minor Unit Organs. Part of the gimmick to promote sales was that Charley Minor would play the opening concerts, generating publicity for the theatres. Link also built a 3/8 portable organ which Minor took on tour. This organ was housed in six cases and had sequined swell shades, rich velvet curtains surrounding the pipe cases and a jeweled console.

It was quite a vaudeville sensation[8] and when its traveling days were over it was installed permanently in the State Theatre, Ithaca, New York in 1928.[9]

Most of the Link theatre organs were of two-manual size and many were equipped with player mechanisms. Few three-manual organs were built (five are known at the time of this writing) and none of these was equipped with a player. A five-manual instrument was on the drawing boards but was never built.[10] The players were built in at least two varieties: one was built into the console and played ordinary 88-note rolls; another was the famous Link four-roll player which used special Link endless organ rolls. A few of these rolls were hand played but most were mechanically arranged by Bill Sabin who was first clarinetist with John Phillip Sousa's band.[11] A 1925 Link catalog claims that "managers have confided to us that patrons, not knowing the relief was a Link [roll] player, have complimented them on their relief organist and have suggested his promotion to regular organist." At first glance this seems to be typical advertising hyperbole but perhaps it is actually an accurate reflection of the musical abilities of some organists of the day!

Link organs, like their coin-operated piano brethren, were well made. Most of the pipework was puchased from Gottfried although some ranks came from Organ Supply when Gottfried fell behind schedule. A feature of Link design was the use of vacuum to operate almost everything in the organ except the pipes, including the combination actions, relays, swell shades, percussions and roll players.[12] Another feature, especially on the C. Sharpe Minor models, was some of the most extensive unificiation ever employed by any builder. See page 270 for the specification of the organ installed in the Haltnorth Theatre, Cleveland, Ohio containing 154 stops controlling only nine ranks! Note also the use of *seven* different color combinations for the stop keys, one color for the stop itself and another for the lettering.[13]

Ed Link, Jr. started working in the factory during summer school vacations and worked in every department, learning all phases of the business.[14] The first theatre organ he helped install was in the Colonial Theatre, Norwich, New York and he went on to install quite a few more on his own. Link was a prolific inventor and received 35 patents, many of them for theatre organ improvements. Among his patents were unit chests, piz-

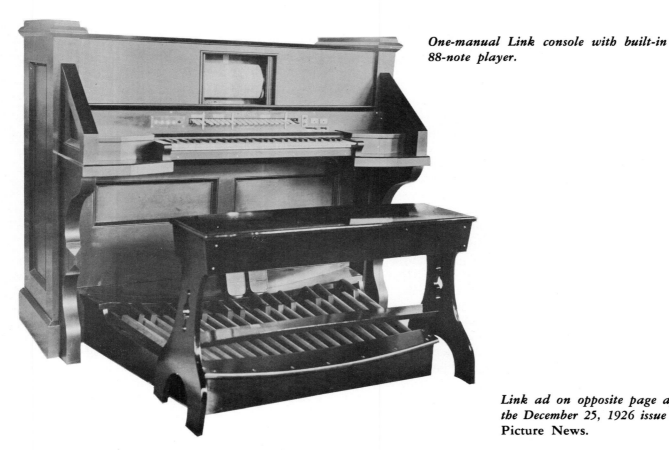

Two-manual Link console with 88-note roll player mechanism.

One-manual Link console with built-in 88-note player.

Link ad on opposite page appeared in the December 25, 1926 issue of Motion Picture News.

An Unprecedented Demand

Leading exhibitors recognize a better organ. That is why Link-C. Sharpe Minor unit organs have created an unprecedented demand—one that keeps the Link factory rushed to capacity.

Link-C. Sharpe Minor Organs Installed by Leading Theatres

Some Noteworthy Installations

Following is a list of some of the recent installations of Link-C. Sharpe Minor Unit Theatre Organs: Haltnorth Theatre, Cleveland, Ohio; New Plaza Theatre, Cleveland, Ohio; Jefferson Theatre, Auburn, New York; Lafayette Theatre, Charlottesville, Va.; Jefferson Theatre, Charlottesville, Va.; Rex Theatre, Bessemer, Mich.; Bush's Egyptian Theatre, San Diego, Calif.; Palace Theatre, San Diego, Calif.; Bradley Theatre, Elko, Nev.; Lincoln Theatre, New Martinsville, W. Va.; New Theatre, Utica, New York; Glen Park Theatre, Gary, Ind.; New Theatre, Clyde, New York; New Theatre, Farrell, Pa.; New Theatre, Lackawanna, New York; Morenci Y. M. C. A., Morenci, Ariz.; Keeney's New Theatre, Binghamton, New York.

NO stronger endorsement of the superiority of Link-C. Sharpe Minor theatre organs can be had than the numerous installations in the country's leading theatres. From coast to coast, exhibitors are building patronage by featuring their Link organs.

Link prestige is growing with leaps and bounds. Today the demand for Link theatre organs surpasses all past records. Even with enlarged manufacturing facilities the Link plant must operate day and night to fill orders.

Link-C. Sharpe Minor Unit Organs incorporate all the latest developments of organ design and many new features that are exclusive with Link-C. Sharpe Minor instruments. Tonal quality, responsiveness and flexibility of expression superimposed upon a basic rugged construction—these are the inherent characteristics that make Link organs definitely superior for theatre use.

Send for Free Booklet

We publish a booklet which contains much interesting and enlightening information of value to you and your organist.
It is our pleasure to send you a free copy—just mail the attached coupon.

MAIL THIS COUPON

Link-C. Sharpe Minor Unit Organs, Binghamton, N. Y.
Please send me .... copies of your new booklet.
Name ....
Theatre ....
Address ....
Number of Seats ....

LINK

C. SHARPE MINOR ⬥⬥⬥ UNIT ORGANS

BINGHAMTON, N. Y.

Link four-roll player in the Mead residence, Los Angeles. The top roll has been removed to show part of the complex mechanism. This 2/5 Link also has an 88-note player built into the console.

3/9 Link console formerly in the Haltnorth Theatre, Cleveland, Ohio. This console was originally finished in mahogany. Its current white and gold garb is similar to the decoration of the 3/11 Link in the Capitol Theatre, Binghamton, New York.

Duane Arey examines the vacuum-operated Link percussions from the Haltnorth Theatre.

3/9 LINK THEATRE ORGAN
Haltnorth Theatre, Cleveland, Ohio

The following specification contains 154 stops controlling only nine ranks! Note the use of *seven* different color combinations for the stop keys, one color for the stop itself and another for the lettering.[13]

PEDAL

32'	Basso Profundo
16'	Tibia Profundo
16'	Violone
16'	Bass Flute
8'	Trombone
8'	Octave
8'	Tibia
8'	Orchestral Oboe
8'	Violon Cello
8'	Flute
PP	Bass Drum
PP	Cymbal
PP	Tympani
FF	Bass Drum
FF	Cymbal
FF	Tympani
	Crash Cymbal
	Martial Drums
	Traps Reverse
16'	Piano
8'	Great to Pedal
8'	Solo to Pedal

ACCOMPANIMENT

16'	Contra Viole
8'	Tuba Trumpet
8'	Open Diapason
8'	Tibia Clausa
8'	Orchestral Oboe
8'	Kinura
8'	Viole d'Orchestre
8'	Viole Celeste
8'	Concert Flute
8'	Vox Humana
4'	Plenette
4'	Oboe
4'	Octave Viole
4'	Octave Celeste
4'	Flute Traverso
4'	Vox Choral
2 2/3'	Tibia
2'	Tibia Piccolo
2'	Harmonic Piccolo
	Harp
	Marimba
8'	Piano
4'	Piano
4'	Accom. to Accom.
8'	Great to Accom.
8'	Solo to Accom.
4'	Solo to Accom.
PP	Snare Drum Tap
PP	Snare Drum Roll
PP	Drums Ensemble
FF	Snare Drum Tap
FF	Snare Drum Roll
FF	Drums Ensemble
	Tambourine
	Castinet (sic)
	Tom Tom
	Sand Block
	Wood Block
	Sleigh Bells
	Traps Reverse

ACCOM. 2nd TOUCH

8'	Tuba
8'	Open Diapason
8'	Tibia
4'	Plenette
4'	Chimes
	Bird Song (Main)
	Triangle
8'	Great
8'	Solo

SOLO

16'	Tibia Major
16'	Vox Basso TC
8'	Tuba Trumpet
8'	Open Diapason
8'	Tibia Clausa
8'	Orchestral Oboe
8'	Kinura
5 1/3'	Tibia Quint
8'	Clarinet Synthetic
8'	Orientale Synthetic
8'	Viole d'Orchestre
8'	Viole Celeste
8'	Concert Flute
8'	Vox Humana
4'	Plenette
4'	Solo Violin
4'	Flute Traverso
4'	Mixture
2'	Tibia Piccolo
	Harp
	Glockenspiel
	Xylophone Stroke
	Marimba
	Orchestra Bells
	Xylophone Roll
	Cathedral Chimes
16'	Solo to Solo
4'	Solo to Solo
10 2/3'	Dominant
6 2/3'	Terz

TOE STUDS

Operator
Pedal 1
Pedal 2
Thunder PP
Wind
Thunder FF
Boat
Train
Siren
Fire
Auto
Horse Trot

GREAT

16'	Ophicleide TC
16'	Diapason TC
16'	Tibia Major
16'	Contra Bassoon TC
16'	Contra Viole
16'	Bass Flute
16'	Vox Basso TC
8'	Tuba Trumpet
8'	Open Diapason
8'	Tibia Clausa
8'	Orchestral Oboe
8'	Kinura
8'	Viole d'Orchestre
8'	Viole Celeste
8'	Concert Flute
8'	Vox Humana
4'	Clarion
4'	Octave
4'	Plenette
4'	Octave Oboe
4'	Kinura
4'	Octave Viole
4'	Octave Celeste
4'	Flute Traverso
4'	Vox Choral
2 2/3'	Twelfth
2'	Tibia Piccolo
2'	Fifteenth
2'	Harmonic Piccolo
1 3/5'	Tierce
	Harp
	Glockenspiel
	Xylophone Stroke
	Marimba
	Orchestra Bells
	Xylophone Roll
16'	Piano
8'	Piano
4'	Piano
2'	Piano
16'	Great to Great
4'	Great to Great
8'	Solo to Great
4'	Solo to Great

TOE LEVERS

Drums and Crash
Thunder with Traps

COMBINATION PISTONS

10 plus suitable bass
  per manual

STOP KEY COLORS

white with red letters:
Flute

*light blue with
  black letters:*
Sforzando

*brown wood grained
  with white letters:*
Marimba
Harp
Xylophone

amber with black letters:
FF Traps
Strings
Pizzicato
Tom Tom
Sand Block
Wood Block

red with white letters:
Tuba
Oboe
Vox
Kinura
Clarinet Synthetic
Orientale Synthetic
Tambourine
Castinet (sic)
Crash Cymbal

black with white letters:
Couplers
Traps Reverse

white with black letters:
All remaining stops

TREMOLOS

Main
Vox
Solo
Tibia

GENERAL

Piano Mandolin
Piano Clog
Pizzicato Great & Accom.
Re-iterating Entire Organ
Sforzando

zicato and sostenuto actions and player mechanism improvements.[15] His very first patent was for the Autovox, a completely mechanical coin-operated phonograph which was developed just before the 1929 stock market crash closed the company.[16]

Ed Link's real passion was aviation and his first invention in that field was the famous Link flight trainer. To quote Mr. Link, "I started the trainers in 1926 so I was working on a trainer before the piano factory folded up. The first trainers were built there; that's why they have so many piano and organ parts in them. When the piano and organ factory folded in 1929 I was working on trainers in my spare time after hours and on Saturdays and Sundays . . . Meanwhile I had learned to fly and I had a commercial license so I had to go out and earn my living by flying. I guess it was a good thing for me that the factory did fold because I did better with trainers than I ever would have with pianos!

". . . Around 1930 [I invented an electrical sign for advertising]. I had a piano roll mechanism in the plane and I would punch out the rolls for different messages. The holes would light the proper lights for "Spaulding Bread," "Enna Jettick Shoes" and others. I put a venturi tube in the slipstream of the airplane and that created the vacuum. It was a player piano in the air! . . . For three or four years I did pretty well with it. I owned the plane and made the sign mechanism. I later put one on a big tri-motor Ford. I had three of them in all. Another thing I did to attract attention was to make a ten-note pipe organ. I had a big wind-driven air compressor under the Ford's wing and the organ was played by rolls! The pipes had to be loud or nobody could hear it."[17]

Using the flight trainers he had invented, Ed Link founded a flying school which became Link Aviation, Inc. Hundreds of Link trainers were sold to the government during World War II. In 1954 Link Aviation, Inc. merged with General Precision Engineering and the manufacture of flight simulators continued.[18] The player piano and organ components used in the original Link "blue boxes" were supplanted by sophisticated electro-mechanical controls in the newer models. In his final years (he died in 1981) Ed Link pursued a new interest, deep sea oceanography, but found time to install a Link theatre organ (from the Haltnorth Theatre) in a special building at his home. He was also instrumental in rescuing the 3/11 Link organ from the Capitol Theatre in Binghamton which he subsequently donated to the Roberson Center for the Arts and Sciences in Binghamton.[19]

Ed Link examines the marimba in the Roberson Center, Binghamton, New York. Note compact design of switchstack on the right.

Ed Link demonstrates the serviceability of the Link vacuum-operated combination action.

Link invoice for a 2/3 organ whose eventual destination was a funeral parlor. Frank A. Leatherman was an Atlanta distributor who also sold instruments made by Seeburg and other manufacturers.

A Link kinura chest with the bottom board removed. The design is similar to Kilgen's. Using Reisner C17 chest magnets, Link chests require no primaries except on the very largest notes.

Interior of the Link factory is revealed in these extremely rare photographs which show the machine shop, console department, relay assembling area and two views of the erecting room. The gentleman in the oval inset is George T. Link, brother of Ed Link, Jr.

On pages 273-277 is reproduced a wonderful Link theatre organ catalog c. 1925. Following it on pages 278-280 is an earlier catalog no doubt written before many Link organ sales had yet materialized. Both these documents represent, in the author's opinion, an ideal balance between persuasive hyperbole and actual facts.

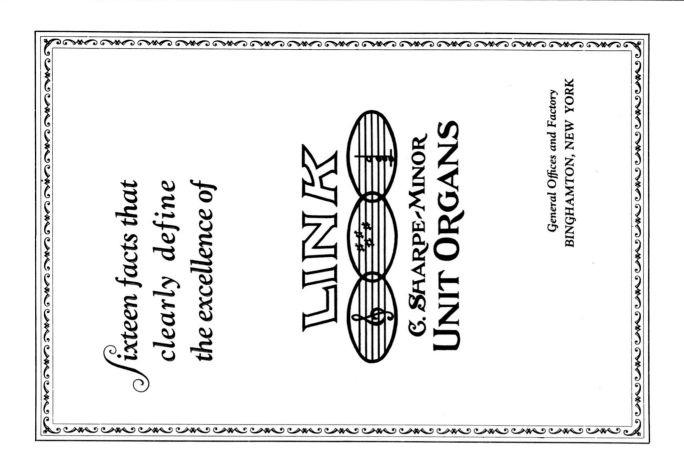

C. SHARPE MINOR — LINK — UNIT ORGANS

READ why Mr. C. Sharpe Minor, the noted theatre organist, chose the LINK as most worthy of his name and recommendation.

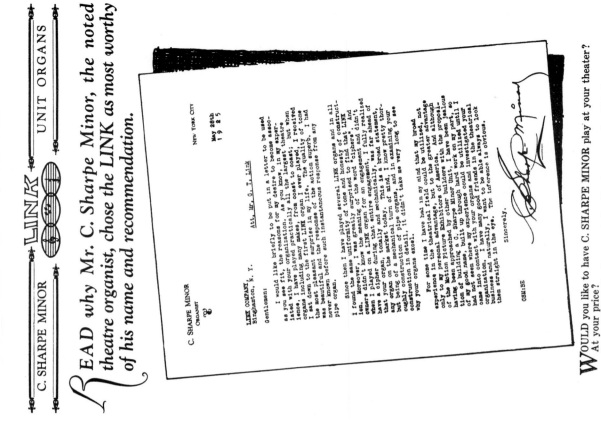

WOULD you like to have C. SHARPE MINOR play at your theater? At your price?

Do you believe he knows what a theatre organ should be?

He chose LINK.

He opens LINK—C. SHARPE MINOR UNIT ORGANS.

C. SHARPE MINOR — LINK — UNIT ORGANS

FOREWORD

TO the live wire EXHIBITOR of TODAY it is not necessary to prove that Good Music is indispensable to the success of his theatre. Nor to the majority of exhibitors is it necessary to prove that in his scheme for good music, a modern Unit Pipe Organ is also indispensable. The well informed Exhibitor would no more think of building his theatre without making provisions for an organ, than he would of leaving out his seats or his screen.

It is extremely unfortunate, however, that there are still too many organs sold that from any point of view cannot be called **theatre** organs. We have invariably found that where an exhibitor still believes that an organ cannot be made an attractive feature in his theatre, the organs which he has heard are either instruments built for church usage, which have no place in the theatre, or these organs are half-way attempts at theatre organs, usually sold at a price without regard to suitability or quality.

Theatres of large capacity maintain their DeLuxe Orchestras at a tremendous cost, and, naturally, they are effective. But it is interesting here to note that these same theatres which maintain such orchestras, without exception, are equipped with an organ, and the larger the orchestra, the larger the organ.

The modern unit organ is a whole orchestra in itself. For following pictures, it is peculiarly adaptable, as it has within itself a range of expression and additional effects of pathos and depth which cannot be reproduced by any other one instrument, or group of musical instruments. The modern organ has truthfully been described many times as the "King of Instruments."

In the pages that follow, we describe to you a "quality instrument" built to a standard, without regard to cost, by men, who, through experience and investigation, know what they are doing. These are not **empty words**. We have made an exhaustive study, not only of our own organs but of all other organs that are worthy of the name. We know their weaknesses and faults and we know that in Link Unit Organs and in LINK-C Sharpe Minor Unit Organs these are eliminated and many additional exclusive features added.

Read the pages that follow. We invite investigation. We know that if you will investigate, your enthusiasm will excel ours, and you will agree that any LINK or LINK-C Sharpe Minor Unit Organ from the smallest style to our Master, which is the largest unit organ ever designed, will make money for you and will, in the end, be the cheapest investment you ever made.

Three Popular Types
of LINK CONSOLES

*Other styles built, up to our Five Manual MASTER
which is the largest unit organ ever designed.*

LINK · C. SHARPE MINOR *Three-Manual Leader Console*

Wᴇ have made refinements in console details that automatically help an organist to secure results. Note the curve of the stop-key layout. This curve has been worked out scientifically by us for the natural sweep of the arm. In addition to the usual indicators, we have incorporated an indicator to show how far open the swell shades are. Also in our larger organs a complete Console Lift and many other features too numerous to mention here.

Eᴀᴄʜ pipe in our organs is carefully voiced and blended to our exact standards. The tone of an organ is important. Therefore, do not overlook the fact that the majority of builders today are producing instruments inadequate tonally for the theatre because they have no one within their organizations who has been able to get away from his immediate job long enough to find out what tone is required from a theatrical instrument.

We voice our pipes not to suit ourselves or to suit you, but to suit the public, as they determine your success or failure. Moreover, the public does not want to hear a church organ in a theatre.

LINK · C. SHARPE MINOR *Two-Manual Baby Grand Console*

A LINK *Two-Manual Console*

Lɪɴᴋ construction and application of principles we know, through actual experience and research, have yet to be equalled or even approached by any other builder. To the best of our knowledge, we are the only organ builders in the world who thoroughly understand and use that extremely powerful f o r c e called vacuum or suction. Through its agency we accomplish results that are really miraculous and cannot be accomplished successfully in any other way.

Moreover, no detail of construction is too small not to merit the most painstaking care and inspection. Our methods mean perfection and true value to the buyer.

C. SHARPE MINOR — LINK — UNIT ORGANS

The Link Selective Roll Reproducing Player

The Theatre's Musical Insurance Policy

Selective control box, operating a player from any distance. Touch of button instantly changes rolls to follow picture.

THE LINK REPRODUCING PLAYER is the most marvelous musical invention of today, because it does that which is beyond the scope of any other player. It not only is self playing, but it plays without mechanical effect, reproducing the "human appeal" characteristic of music when rendered by master musicians.

It plays with exact interpretation anything from the simplest musical composition to the most difficult classic, and it does not require the aid of the human hand in order to bring out the best there is in the music. Our player is the only mechanical player that dominates the whole instrument constantly, obviating the necessity of any hand manipulation during the rendition of any selection.

In Constant Control of Every Note and Expression

The LINK Reproducing Player is distinctly a delight to all accomplished musicians. We challenge any organist to play a pipe organ any better than our mechanical player. One reason why our player will easily win any such contest is because we have through it constant control of every note on the instrument all of the time, and are not obliged to relinquish any part of that control to manipulate stops and swell shades. The organist, at best, has but twelve points of contact with the instrument and must frequently surrender, momentarily at least, some of them in order to manipulate the stops or expression controls. Through our player we have instant control of every function of the instrument, and are, therefore, able to shade expression perfectly and with human deftness, while at the same time we can secure as many additional effects as may be desired, because we are not like the individual, limited to ten fingers and two feet.

C. SHARPE MINOR — LINK — UNIT ORGANS

screen is a most important factor for the successful display of a film, without which the proper effect of the picture is nullified. This is one main reason why even the owners of larger theatres, who, in the past, would not consider a player on their organs, immediately see where the LINK Player can take the place of the relief organist, save them money, and still not lower one iota the high standard of music they want to maintain. In the great majority of cases the LINK Player, through our rolls, made by master musicians, produces even a higher standard of music than before. Managers have confided to us that patrons, not knowing the relief was a LINK Player, have complimented them on their relief organist and have suggested his promotion to regular organist.

Link Players Never Go Out on Strike

We have also had exhibitors tell us that they consider their LINK Player a musical insurance policy. As they say, ,hey insure their building and everything else, why not insure against a performance without music? Their LINK Players never go out on strike.

Perhaps, in print, some of these statements sound exaggerated. We have, however, been very conservative in our claim. Our Player has been proved by the test of time, a thoroughly practical feature in many theatres. Simple and rugged in construction, it is built to withstand hard usage, and to render music which it is impossible to describe through mere words. The LINK REPRODUCING PLAYER actually must be heard to be appreciated fully. Certainly you will agree with us that this Player is an additional feature to our organs which cannot be discounted, and is a gold bond investment for any theatre.

Wide Range - No Rewind Annoyance

The LINK Player is particularly adapted to the needs of the theatre, because it has such a wide range in the character of its music. There are four compartments for endless rolls. Each roll has an equivalent to fifteen selections and runs approximately thirty minutes before repeating, so that with the four rolls you have enough music to play a two hour show and not play the same piece twice.

The rolls are like an endless belt so that you do not have to rewind, thereby eliminating all rewind annoyances. The music on each roll is all of the same character—for instance, one roll may be all dramatic music, another roll love scenes, still another hurry, and another popular songs, dances or marches. If so desired, the same type of music can be put in all four compartments.

Positive Control of Various Types of Music, from a Distance

The control of this wide variety of music is through a master control box. One control box is usually placed in the operator's booth, and as many additional control boxes can be placed throughout the theatre as desired. Instantly by the pressing of a button in one of these control boxes, the the music can be changed from one selection to another, even to the stopping of any selection at any note and the beginning of another of entirely different tempo the next second.

Instantaneous Changes in Music to Co-ordinate with Pictures

The right music at the right time with instantaneous changes from one selection to another, with changing tempo at the instant the scenes are shifted on the

The Link Orchestral Pipe Organ

The Link Orchestral Pipe Organ is the most wonderful musical instrument in the world because it does that which is beyond the scope of any other self-playing instrument. It not only is self-playing, but it plays without mechanical effects, and with the "human touch" characteristic of music when made by skillful musicians.

It plays with expression anything from the simplest musical composition to the most classical production of the greatest composer, and it does not require the aid of the human hand in order to bring out the best there is in the music. Our player is the only mechanical player that dominates the whole instrument constantly, obviating the necessity of any hand manipulation during the rendition of any selection.

The Link Orchestral Pipe Organ is distinctly a musical instrument in the best sense of the word. Heretofore all mechanical musical instruments have been an offense to sensitive ears and a positive torture to musicians. We challenge any organist to play a pipe organ any better than our mechanical player. The reason why our player will easily win any such contest is because we have through it constant contact with every key on the instrument all of the time, and are not obliged to relinquish any part of that control to manipulate stops and swell shades. The organist, at best, has but twelve points of contact with an instrument and must frequently surrender, momentarily at least, some of them in order to manipulate stop or expression controls. Through our player we have instant control of every function of the instrument and are therefore able to shade expression perfectly and with human similarity while at the same time we can play as many of the keys as may be desired because we are not like the individual limited to ten fingers and two feet.

So absolutely perfect is our player that we have assembled such instruments as may be reproduced by pipes and having made up an orchestra, we play it as any good orchestra plays, and without fault or blemish.

The Link Organ in the Theatre

The Link Organ is admirably adapted to the needs of the theatre because it has such a wide range in the character of its music. There are three compartments for endless music rolls. Each roll has an equivalent to fifteen popular pieces and runs approximately forty minutes before repeating, so that with the three rolls you have enough music to play a two-hour show and not play the same piece twice.

The rolls are like an endless belt so that they do not have to rewind, thereby eliminating all rewind annoyances The music on each roll is all

---

The Most Wonderful Musical Instrument in the World

LINK
Orchestral Pipe Organ

LINK PIANO COMPANY, Inc.

FACTORY:
BINGHAMTON, N. Y.

The Link Organ is so versatile (if that term may be applied to a musical instrument) that it will not become tiresome to the listener and it satisfies the most exacting requirements of the critical music-lover. It is possible, with the Link Organ, to play an organ selection or an orchestral number and then to play both the organ and the orchestra in combination. It can be used for dancing as well as an entertainment for your guests.

A space 6ft. deep, 5 ft. high and 14 ft. long will accommodate the Link Organ. A mezzanine floor as a location is usually ideal because music which comes from aloft to the listener sounds better than is the case where it is thrust directly at one.

Even the hotel that maintains a so-called orchestra consisting of a piano, a violin, a bass viol and a flute pays more for its music than it will be obliged to pay if it purchases a Link Organ. The sum paid to five musicians for one year will in that time meet the cost of installing a Link Organ, and once it is paid for the expense for music drops to a trifling sum. There is no up-keep charge on a Link Organ and but a small charge for new music and the electric current necessary to operate the instrument.

What is beyond the financial means of the majority of even first-class hotels in the way of music becomes easily possible with a Link Organ. The hotel which has a Link Organ is always provided with music, and that, too, of the best kind, and at the same time the expense is less than it is where an orchestra of musicians is employed.

In brief, the Link Organ gives a hotel better music than it gets from an orchestra and at less expense—much less. The installation of a Link Organ ends all music troubles and lowers expenses. Therefore, it becomes not only a desirable thing for a good hotel, but really a necessity. Besides, it is exclusive and cannot fail to give the hotel owning it a reputation for its musical entertainments that will increase business. Surely no hotel manager in the country can afford to refuse to consider such a sound business proposition as we present.

Again we desire to emphasize the fact that, while we do not make a strong appeal to the aesthetic and artistic side of the hotel proprietor, our strongest appeal, until he has listened to the Link Organ, is to his pocket book. We come to him with a proposition to make his hotel business more profitable by a radical reduction in his operating expenses. We do not ask him to take into account the prospective increase in his business due to better and more alluring music—although that is not inconsiderable—but we show him beyond dispute that he cannot afford to be without the most wonderful instrument in the world. Every day he is getting along without it, he is paying out money he might keep for his very own. What is more, when he keeps that money through the installation of a Link Organ, he not

---

of the same character,—for instance, one roll may be all classic pipe organ or "sob" music, one roll of light semi-classic, still another of popular songs, dances and marches. If so desired, the same music can be put in all three compartments.

The music is controlled by push buttons placed in the operator's booth, or in any part of the theatre.

Instantaneous Changes

from one selection of music to another with change in tempo at the instant the scenes are shifted on the screen are the most important factors for the successful display of a film. In this the ordinary piano player is deficient, and the effects desired are oftentimes spoiled.

The Right Music at the Right Time

is the most vital for the success of the picture house for without it, the proper effect of the picture is nullified, which means eventual loss of patronage. With the LINK PLAYER the musical program is directly under the control of the one operating the buttons and at his will the music changes instantly by pushing a button even to the stopping of playing one selection at any note and the beginning of another of different tempo the next second. It is thus possible at all times to have melody to correspond and be consistent with each picture shown. If the scene is a sad one and you want "sob" music, all you have to do is to touch a button for the roll containing the "sob" music. When the scene changes and you wish music of a lighter character, push the button controlling the semi-classic music, and the change is made instantly. On the other roll you can have your popular songs, dances or marches for your "News Weeklies" and comedies.

It plays with all the expression and technic of a high-class artist and must be heard to be appreciated. The instrument is not equipped with numerous pedals and hand levers to operate, therefore it does not require a thoroughly competent musician to follow the picture. The flexibility of the LINK ORGAN is so great that it leaves nothing to be desired when it comes to meeting the requirements of the theatre.

The Link Organ for Hotels

The Link Pipe Organ solves the problem of music in a hotel. It not only renders better music than an orchestra—music more pleasing to the guests, and as a rule, of much better grade, but it is vastly cheaper.

The Link Organ is ready at all times, either night or day, and is at hand the year around.

only does not lessen the appeal of his hotel to the public, but actually makes it stronger. He virtually advertises his hotel broadcast by putting in a Link Organ, because his guests are sure to talk about the wonderful music to be heard by those who patronize him. In reason, what more could be desired?

The Link Organ for the Home

The Link Organ is a musical instrument de luxe, designed for the homes of people of culture and means. The price of a Link Organ puts it out of the reach of the great mass of people.

In the home where it is a mere matter of the enjoyment of the best, regardless of expense, the Link Organ will fill a place that has heretofore remained unfilled.

Deep, rich, pipe organ music, which thrills one so exquisitely, has never been equaled by any other instrument. There is a completeness about it which is lacking in the harmony of any other single musical device; heretofore it has not been practicable to install pipe-organs in homes which could afford them because, while there are many piano players, there are comparatively few organists. It is true that there are homes in which the pipe organ has been installed, but they are comparatively few, not because there are not many homes where such instruments are desired, but because of the problem of playing which has always accompanied them.

The Link Organ changes everything in that respect. While there have been self-playing organs in the past, they have never given satisfaction because they were slow in action and liable to get out of order. Then, too, their music was mechanical and expressionless—in fact offensive to the musical ear.

With the Link Organ, however, all this is changed and for the first time the pipe organ becomes the ideal musical instrument for the home. Not only have we made the pipe organ a practical home instrument, but we have attached to it the instruments of an orchestra, with the result that we render such music as has never been made before by any single instrument.

When reference is made to the self-playing of the Link Organ, it will doubtless meet with that disdain which arises from knowledge of such mechanical music as has been the rule. We have stated over and over again that in the Link Organ we have the first musical instrument to produce music by mechanical means, but without mechanical effects. It is true, as we have convinced every person who has ever heard the Link Organ play. Mechanical playing musical instruments other than the Link Organ

are an offense and an abomination to the ears of people of culture and especially so if the one listening has a musical ear and a musical education. However, we have changed all that. Those musicians who have come to scoff at the music of the Link Organ have remained to listen and wonder how it is done. Invariably if they are kept from seeing the tracker-board, they will not believe that the music they are listening to is not made by human hands.

When the inventors of the Link Organ were working on the instrument, they determined to obviate mechanical effects. No other player of a mechanical sort absolutely controls the instrument in its every part while playing, but that is just what the Link Organ player does. Because it does that, it makes music with a human quality about it that is pleasing to the ear and as satisfying as the music of the skilled musicians. It plays the selections that are favorites with the best musicians as easily as it plays the simplest composition.

It is this instrument we introduce into the home of refinement, culture and musical taste. We build it for the room it is to grace and we voice it for the space its harmony is to fill. When the Link Organ is at last installed in the home, its owner has achieved the musical nirvana since it leaves nothing to be desired, musically speaking.

It may be used for such musical entertainments as have heretofore been impossible in the home, except through the engagement of a first-class orchestra. With the Link Organ, impromptu musicals of the very highest order are quite as easily provided as are those at the command of the person satisfied with mere piano music. It can be used for dancing as well as an entertainment for your guests.

Not only may one have the music of an orchestra at will, but the music of a pipe organ whenever desired of the very best kind, all playing together and producing such harmony as no home, before the advent of the Link Organ, has been able to command. All of which sounds improbable and untrue, but the skeptical have but to listen to the Link Organ to be convinced.

LINK OPUS LIST

CITY/STATE	LOCATION	SIZE	YR	BLWR	REMARKS
ARIZONA					
Morenci	YMCA Building		1926	19025	
CALIFORNIA					
Anaheim	Dr. Johnston residence		1928	21900	
			1928	13182TUR	
Culver City	Meralta Th.	2/	1924	15402	
Downey	Meralta Th.	2/	1925		
Laguna Beach	J. L. Beebe		1928	22729	
Los Angeles	Arthur Holliday residence		1926	19442	
	Benjamin Harwoods residence		1923	14373	
	Elks Lodge		1923	15227	
	Epco Model Th.	2/	1923	15228	
	G. D. Chambers		1923	14825	
	Jensen's Melrose Th.		1923	14357	
			1924	15416	
	L. A. Wolf		1928	2455JR	Located at 1958 S. Vermont.
			1929	2639JR	
	Lita Grey Chaplin residence				
	Rampart Th.	2/			
	William Mead residence	2/5	1927	21022	Installation included an 88-note roll player in console and separate 4-roll player for Link Rolls.
Pasadena	Egyptian (Uptown) Th.	2/6	1925	17184	
	Henry L. Warner		1924	16428	
San Diego	Bush's Egyptian (Capri) Th.	2/5	1926	18629	
			1926	10668TUR	
	Palace Th.		1926	19106	
San Francisco	Sherman Clay		1928	22465	Demonstration organ.
DISTRICT OF COLUMBIA					
Washington	Homer L. Kitt		1929	23234	Located at 1330 G Street, NW.
	Truxton Th.		1925	17150	
FLORIDA					
Tampa	Marshall's White Lunch		1925	17071	
	Seminole Th.	2/	1929		
IDAHO					
Kellogg	Liberty Th.		1923	14454	
ILLINOIS					
Chicago	Lyon & Healy Showroom		1926	19109	
	Ralph Waldo Emerson		1926	18837	Portable.
	Ralph Waldo Emerson		1928	12890TUR	Located at 921 Rush Street.
	WLS Radio	2/3	1928	21959	
East St. Louis	Lido Th.		1927	21179	
Spring Valley	Valley Th.		1923	14616	
INDIANA					
Gary	Glen Park Th.	2/	1926	19471	
MAINE					
Calais	St. Croix Opera House		1923	15058	
MASSACHUSETTS					
Palmer	Empire Th.		1922	13540	
MICHIGAN					
Bad Axe	Bad Axe Th.	2/3			
Bessemer	Rex Th.	2/	1926	19291	
MINNESOTA					
Blue Earth	Blue Earth Th.	2/3			
MISSOURI					
St. Louis	Cherokee Th.		1924	15663	
	Melva Th.		1924	15664	

CITY/STATE	LOCATION	SIZE	YR	BLWR	REMARKS
NEVADA					
Elko	Bradley (Hunter) Th.	2/	1926	19339	With 4-roll player.
NEW JERSEY					
Newark	Griffith Piano Co.		1928	21958	
	Griffith Piano Co.		1928	22466	
	Griffith Piano Co.		1928	22690	
NEW YORK					
Albany	Clinton Square Th.		1918	8841	
Angola	unidentified new theatre		1924	16539	
Arcade	Hammond Th.		1926	12534	
Auburn	Jefferson Th.	2/	1926	19624	
Binghamton	Cameo Th.				
	Capitol Th.	3/11	1927	20240	
	Empire Th.	2/			
	Glenwood Th.	2/	1927		
	Keeney's Th.		1927	11592TUR	
	Robinson Th.		1928	21428	
	Suburba Th.	2/	1928	21440	
	Sun Th.	2/			With 4-roll player.
	Symphony Th.	2/	1926	18416	
			1926	10192TUR	
Buffalo	Academy Th.		1926	18907	
	Broadway Lyceum Th.		1921	12124	
	Capitol Th.	2/7	1927	19904	
	Columbia Th.		1924	16623	
	Elmwood School of Music	2/			
	Fleming Sales Co. (store/studio)		1928	21598	Later moved to Fleming store in Syracuse, NY.
	Frontier Th.		1928	21650	
	Lyric Th.		1921	12768	
	Maxine Th.		1928	21649	
	Savoy Th.		1927	21182	
	Sheldon Th.		1928	21640	
	New Try-It (Unity) Th.		1923	15261	
Clyde	Clyde Th.		1927	20012	
Elmhurst, L.I.	Queensboro Th.	3/10	1928	22120	
			1928	13492TUR	
Elmira	Capitol Th.	3/			
	Colonial Th.	2/6	1928	21395	
			1928	12851TUR	
			1928	13953TUR	
Endicott	Endicott Th.		1922	13996	
	Lyric Th.		1922	13897	
	Strand Th.		1927	19989	
Holley	Holleywood Th.		1928	22260	
Ithaca	Cornell Th.		1928	12890TUR	
	Happy Hour Th.		1928	22560	
	State Th.	3/8	1928		Formerly organist C. Sharpe Minor's portable organ.
	Strand Th.		1919	9500	
	Temple Th.	2/3			
Jamestown	Roosevelt Th.		1925	18112	
Lackawanna	Ridge Th.	2/	1927	19823	
Lake Placid	Happy Hour Th.		1922	13946	
Lyons	Regent Th.		1922	12007	
New York	Commodore Hotel		1928	21958	For piano convention.
	Wirth & Hamid				
Norwich	Colonial Th.				
Rochester	Plymouth Th.		1921	12221	
Saranac Lake	Pontiac Th.	2/	1923	13835	
Silver Creek	Geitner Th.		1921	12781	
Solvay	Allen Th.		1927	21252	
Syracuse	Elmwood Th.	2/4	1927	20696	
	Hotel Syracuse		1928	22345	
Union	Dittrich Th.		1922	13513	
Utica	James Th.	2/	1927		
	Slotnick Th.		1926	19635	
Westfield	Zimmerman Th.		1924	16401	
Williamsville	Glen Th.		1927	21071	
OHIO					
Cleveland	Astor Th.	3/	1927	20980	
			1927	12490TUR	
	Haltnorth Th.	3/9	1926	19031	5hp, 15"wp; opus 616.
			1926	10785TUR	1hp, 16 oz. vac.
	Homestead Th.				

CITY/STATE	LOCATION	SIZE	YR	BLWR	REMARKS
Cleveland	New Plaza Th.	2/	1926	19299	
Mansfield	Lido Th.		1927	21132	
Orrville	Grand Th.		1924	16251	

PENNSYLVANIA

Corry	Grand Th.		1923	13199	
Farrell	Capitol Th.	2/	1927		
Northeast	Keller Th.	2/	1923	14122	
Old Forge	Holland Th.	2/	1925	17812	

VIRGINIA

Charlottesville	Jefferson Th.		1926	19070	
	Lafayette Th.	2/4	1926	19069	
Fredericksburg	Pitts Th.		1928	22506	
Norfolk	Manhattan Th.		1921	11971	
Waynesboro	Wayne Th.		1925	17808	

WEST VIRGINIA

New Martinsville	Lincoln Th.		1925	18218	

WISCONSIN

Edgerton	Rialto Th.	2/6	1923	14622	
Elkhorn	Princess Th.		1922	13791	
Madison	Palace Th.		1921	12404	
Mauston	Majestic Th.	2/	1926		
Milwaukee	Edward Gram Inc.		1929	22760	

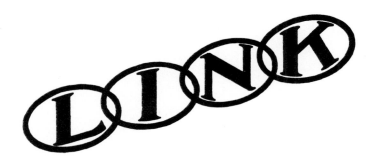

LOUISVILLE PIPE ORGAN COMPANY, INC.

The Louisville Pipe Organ Company was formed in 1925 by W. T. Quilty, August Prante and a third man who may have been either A. H. Tod or Arthur Sperbeck. Quilty was formerly with Votteler-Holtkamp-Sparling and Prante's father had been a well-known organ builder in the late nineteenth and early twentieth centuries.[1] At the time of Louisville's receivership in 1930, Tod was president and Sperbeck, a former Bennett man, was secretary and treasurer.[2]

Business for the company must have been good, for in mid 1928 the city of Terre Haute, Indiana persuaded Louisville to move there, the incentive being the subscription of $20,000 worth of additional stock and the gratis renovation of a factory building at a cost of $4,000.[3] The enthusiasm of the Terre Haute financiers was soon replaced with gloom, however, for the firm sold only about a half dozen new organs in Terre Haute until its failure in 1929.[4]

Fortunately the opus book of this otherwise forgotten firm was saved by Arthur Sperbeck. It was later acquired from Ben Sperbeck, also a Bennett man, by Milwaukee historian Stanton Peters who graciously made it available for inclusion in this volume. It discloses forty opus numbers assigned to new organs and forty-one to "rebuilds and parts" during the short span of the company's life (1925-29). Exactly half of the new organs were theatre instruments.[5] Judging by the several known to the author, these were well unified and were good theatre organs both mechanically and tonally.

Gorgeous photograph of opus 523 on the erecting floor. Main division is on the left, solo on the right. A Louisville church console sits in the background on the right.

Nameplate from opus 523. Note catchy trade name for the company's unified theatre organs.

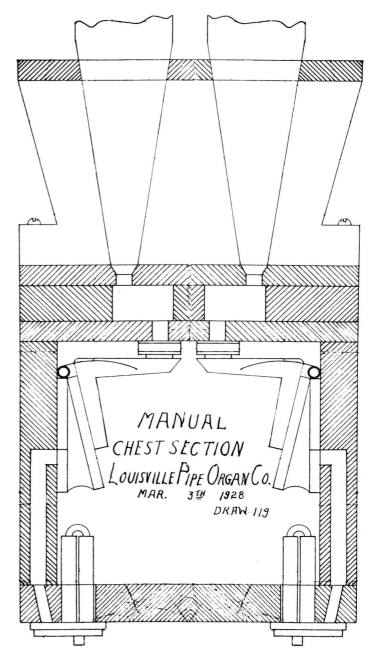

Original drawing of a Louisville chest. Note the absense of primaries, made possible by the use of Reisner C17 chest magnets.

LOUISVILLE OPUS LIST

Following is a complete list of this firm's theatre installations.

OPUS	LOCATION	CITY/STATE	SIZE	YR	BLWR	REMARKS
NEW ORGANS						
508	Cozy Th.	Louisville, KY		1926		
512	Oriental Th.	Indianapolis, IN		1926		
513	Grand Th.	Frankfort, KY		1926		
514	Jacob Markum	Indianapolis, IN	2/	1926		
515	Virginia Th.	Hazard, KY		1926		
516	Towers (Knox) Th.	Louisville, KY	2/12	1926	19253	
517	Crescent Th.	Louisville, KY		1926		
519	Oak Th.	Louisville, KY	2/10	1926	19697	
523	Labor Temple	Louisville, KY	3/10	1927	20330	
524	Hilltop Th.	Louisville, KY		1927		
526	St. Clair Th.	Indianapolis, IN	2/	1927	20488	
528	Kentucky Th.	Louisville, KY	2/6	1927	20916	
530	Grand Th.	New Albany, IN		1927		
531	Uptown Th.	Louisville, KY		1928		Originally planned for Sipe Theatre, Kokomo, Indiana.

OPUS	LOCATION	CITY/STATE	SIZE	YR	BLWR	REMARKS
532	Lerose Th.	Jeffersonville, KY		1927		
533	A & G Th.	Bay St. Louis, MS		1928		
535	Stratford Amusement Co.	Indianapolis, IN	2/	1928		
536	Dream (Grand) Th.	Indianapolis, IN	2/4	1928	22371	
537	Markum Theatre Circuit	Indianapolis, IN	2/	1928		
539	Frederick H. Cesander	Strandburg, SD		1929		

Opus numbers 514, 535 and 537 apply to the following organs, but which is which is unknown:

	Tacoma Th.	Indianapolis, IN	2/			
	Talbott Th.	Indianapolis, IN	2/5			
	Tuxedo Th.	Indianapolis, IN	2/			

REBUILT ORGANS AND PARTS

OPUS	LOCATION	CITY/STATE	SIZE	YR	BLWR	REMARKS
201x	Louis C. Lahaise	Fort Wayne, IN		1925		
203x	Louis C. Lahaise	Fort Wayne, IN		1925		
204x	W. E. Seilkop	Cincinnati, OH		1925		
205x	Frank Muckensturm	Indianapolis, IN		1925		
208x	Alamo (Ohio, 1937-39) Th.	Louisville, KY		1926		Wurlitzer—opus 65.
214x	Rex Th.	Louisville, KY		1927		
216x	Oriental Th.	Indianapolis, IN		1927	20514	Louisville opus 512.
217x	Rialto Th.	Louisville, KY		1927		Pilcher—opus 1076.
219x	Riviera Th.	Anderson, IN		1927		Wurlitzer—opus 1806.
220x	Switow's Th.	Lexington, KY		1927		
221x	Evelann Th.	St. Matthews, KY		1927		Fotoplayer organ.
223x	Switow's Th.	Terre Haute, IN		1927		American Fotoplayer organ.
224x	Switow's Th.	New Albany, IN		1927		American Fotoplayer organ.
225x	Frank Muckensturm	Indianapolis, IN		1927		
226x	Louis Hayes	Henderson, KY		1927		
233x	Stratford Th.	Indianapolis, IN		1928		Photoplayer.
234x	Temple Israel	Terre Haute, IN	3/10	1929	20330	New location for opus 523.

MAAS ORGAN CO.

Louis Mass (pronounced "mass") became interested in organs during 1910 while working as a projectionist in a San Francisco theatre located on Fillmore Street. In 1911 he went to work for Eilers Music Co., the San Francisco agents for Kimball. There he began learning organ building and orchestrion maintenance under the tutelage of Leo Schoenstein. In 1914 he joined Wurlitzer, which had opened a store next door to Eilers, and in 1916 he went to work for Sherman, Clay.[1]

While servicing theatre organs in San Francisco, Maas became acquainted with organist Jesse Crawford who recommended that he apply for a job with the Robert-Morton factory in Van Nuys. Young Maas was so sharp and talented that Robert-Morton president H. J. Werner hired him as assistant plant superintendent at a salary nearly as great as that of superintendent Stanley Williams. The first thing Maas did at Robert-Morton was to design new and snappier-acting trap actions. He also changed the reservoirs from the curtain valve design then in use to the Wurlitzer three-valve system. Another Maas contribution was an improvement of the Robert-

Morton diaphone.[2]

In 1922 Maas left Robert-Morton to go into his own tuning and maintenance business[3] where he was kept busy for the next decade working on southern California theatre organs. When the Robert-Morton factory closed in 1931, Maas purchased the pipe making tools and hired Archie March, a Robert-Morton pipemaker, to continue making pipes. In the early 1930s Maas was hired to install several organs for Fox West Coast Theatres. Maas would take a small existing organ, usually a Wurlitzer or a Robert-Morton, and would soup it up with new pipework made by Archie March and perhaps a restyled console shell. One such Maas installation, which organist Gordon Kibbee remembers as being a real honey, was in the Arlington Theatre in Santa Barbara, California. Originally a 2/6 style D Wurlitzer, this organ sported Maas additons of an oboe horn, clarinet, post horn, tibia unification and couplers, making it a jazzy little 2/9. Maas also built at least two organs for Los Angeles area radio stations wherein all the components were of his own manufacture.[4]

As organ work became sparse in the 1930s, Maas devised a way to keep his business going: he invented a new style of chime. These chimes were quite successful and eventually sold so well that the organ business was discontinued altogether. The Maas factory was in a building at 3105 Casitas Avenue in Los Angeles. Another man renting space in the same building was Paul Rowe (1910-1968) who operated a plastics business. The two men became friends and in 1947 the Maas-Rowe Electromusic Corporation was formed. In the 1950s Louis Maas retired and sold his interest in the business to his partner. Paul Rowe later changed the company name to Maas-Rowe Carillons, Inc. and moved the firm to Escondido, California where it continues in business today under the able direction of his son, Paul Rowe, Jr.[5]

The Fox Wilshire Theatre in Beverly Hills, California, featured a 3/12 Maas which started its life as a two-manual Wurlitzer. The new console shell was a perfect complement to the theatre's Art Deco ambience.

Louis Maas's first ad in The Diapason, *May 1922.*

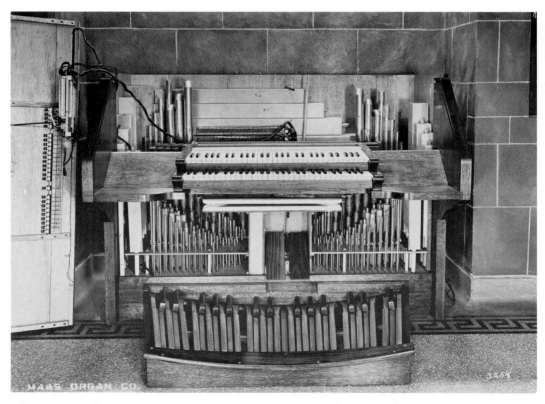

This three-rank Maas organ fits in a compact space little larger than an ordinary console. Not surprisingly, several construction details are nearly identical to Robert-Morton practice including the switches, junction boards and vox humana pipes.

MAAS OPUS LIST

CITY/STATE	LOCATION	SIZE	REMARKS
ARIZONA			
Phoenix	Fox Th.	2/10	Installed in 1932; former Wurlitzer, 2/9, plus post horn and couplers.
CALIFORNIA			
Beverly Hills	Fox Wilshire Th.	3/12	Former Wurlitzer, 2/9, plus second tibia, oboe horn and post horn; 10 hp blower.
Hanford	Fox (Hanford) Th.	2/7	Former Wurlitzer—opus 860, plus 3 ranks.
Los Angeles	KFI Radio	2/4	New Maas organ.
San Luis Obispo	Obispo Th.	2/	Former Wurlitzer, plus 3 ranks.
Long Beach	KFOX Radio	2/4	New Maas organ.
Santa Barbara	Arlington Th.	2/9	Former Wurlitzer style D, plus oboe horn, clarinet and post horn.
Visalia	Fox Th.	2/8	Former Robert-Morton, 2/5, from LaPetite Theatre, Ocean Park, Calif., plus oboe horn, tibia and clarinet.
Westwood	Fox Westwood Village Th.	2/8	Former Wurlitzer, 2/5, plus clarinet, oboe horn and baritone (open diapason).

E. C. MALARKEY

E. C. Malarkey took over the Barckhoff Organ Company of Basic, Virginia in 1917 after that firm declared bankruptcy in October of 1916. Malarkey's firm went out of business in 1926.[1]

This advertisement appeared in the March 1921 Diapason.

MALARKEY OPUS LIST

Records of the Spencer Turbine Company disclose that
at least four blowers were sold to this firm with theatre
destinations.

CITY/STATE	LOCATION	SIZE	YR	BLWR	HP	WP
PENNSYLVANIA						
Hazelwood	Hazelwood Th.		1920	11046	1	5"
Shamokin	Majestic Th.		1920	10394		
Pittsburgh	Fineman (People's?) Th.		1920	11508	1	5"
TENNESSEE						
Johnson City	DeLuxe Th.		1921	11700		

America's Finest Concert Organ

David Marr began his lifelong career in the organ business in Birkenhead, England in 1892 with the Hope-Jones Electric Organ Company. In 1894 he entered the employ of Norman Bros. & Beard of Norwich, England and worked there for eight years, emigrating to the United States in 1904. His first employment in this country was with his old boss at the Hope-Jones & Harrison Company of Watsessing, New Jersey. He later worked for E. M. Skinner and later still for the Hope-Jones Organ Company of Elmira, New York, where he was their pacific coast representative. John J. Colton joined the Hope-Jones firm in 1908, apprenticing in the voicing department. When Wurlitzer acquired the Hope-Jones company in 1910, Marr and Colton went along, remaining there until 1915 when they started a business of their own in a garage in Warsaw, New York.[3][4]

Among the first products of the firm was an instrument called the New Era Organ.[5] It consisted of a small cabinet containing two ranks of pipes played from a keyboard attached to a theatre's pit piano.[6] As business prospered, several larger factory buildings were built to keep pace with the mid-1920s demand for theatre instruments. The firm built about 300 theatre organs, ranking as the country's sixth largest theatre organ builder. A few church organs were also built but the firm never gained a foothold in that market, with the result that when the demand for theatre organs died, so did Marr & Colton.

The firm last advertised in August of 1931 and at about the same time purchased their last blower from the Kinetic Engineering Company.[7] After the firm closed, John Colton joined Kilgen as a salesman and died shortly thereaftrer. David Marr stayed in the organ business in Warsaw and operated a firm called the David Marr Company until 1947 when he incorporated the Marr and Collins Company in Westons Mills, New York with Clyde W. Collins.[8][9] David J. Marr died in 1951 at the age of 69.[10]

*David Jackson Marr
(1882-1951)[2]*

John J. Colton

Marr & Colton organs had some distinctive features. They had one basic console design from which they rarely deviated. This design was closely patterned after the original Hope-Jones style with two "ears" on top. Many models featured a slide whistle among the effects, a feature virtually never encountered on other brands of organs. Some were equipped with another gimmick: a variable thunder operated by a swell shoe. Perhaps the ultimate gimmick was their symphonic registrator which was, in reality, merely a combination action which used stop keys instead of pistons., The stops were labeled with fanciful names such as "anger," "jealousy," "excitement," "happiness," etc. which were supposed to reflect the moods of the silent drama. This novel feature found little acceptance; few were ever sold.

Marr & Coltons had a distinctive sound. Their tibias were usually very pretty and their strings, diapasons and voxes were usually excellent. Their Dennison kinuras and post horns were another story, however. The kinu-

ras were loud, squawky and non-blending and could easily be heard quacking above full organ—a most unpleasant and unmusical effect. So far as the post horns were concerned, it was thoughtful of Marr & Colton to provide them routinely on even eight- and nine-rank organs. Their scale and voicing, unfortunately, caused them to sound like squawking trumpets. Another characteristic of Marr & Colton organs was their avoidance of wind pressures over 10". This resulted in organs which didn't sound as large as they really were. On the instruments in large houses the volume could be inadequate without using the kinura and post horn; but using these ranks turned the ensemble into an ugly buzz. Would you rather die of cancer or tuberculosis?

There is one characteristic in which Marr & Coltons stand alone and that is their quality—or, more precisely, the lack thereof. Marr & Colton is at the absolute bottom of the quality scale. No other commercial instruments were built so cheaply. Wherever a corner could be

This ad in the November 1916 Diapason *sought employees for the fledgling Marr & Colton firm.*

cut, it was, and then some. David Marr was sharp: he knew exactly how thin a piece of lumber to use, how green it could be, and how small a pneumatic it could make and still be barely functional. Throughout the organ the same design concept is apparent: cut every corner possible, eliminate every frill and make every part as cheaply as possible and still have it marginally functional. The company's advertising slogan was "America's finest organ." This was a joke! Even David Marr admitted privately that the organs were deliber-ately built to last only ten years: "After that they should buy a new one!" was his philosophy.[11]

In the opus list it will be seen that over half of the sales were to locations within 300 miles of the factory. The unusual concentration of sales in Detroit is due to the talents of Reginald Webb, a crackerjack salesman. He maintained a showroom in Detroit equipped with two Marr & Coltons: a 3/10 and a 2/4. The larger organ was broadcast over WJR Radio and the smaller was rented out for practice.

Important Points to be considered
when making

Organ Layouts

for the convenience of
Architects

Suggested by

THE MARR & COLTON COMPANY
Organ Builders

General Offices and Factory, WARSAW, N.Y., U.S.A.

2013 PARAMOUNT BUILDING, NEW YORK, N.Y.
708 CONGRESS BANK BUILDING, 506 SO. WABASH AVE., CHICAGO, ILL.
3001 E. GRAND BLVD., DETROIT, MICH.

On this and the following three pages is reproduced a rare document which gives advice to architects concerning the installation of Marr & Colton organs.

We Render Valuable Assistance to Architects

Our staff of organ architects has had long and successful experience in designing, building and installing organs of the highest quality. They will render valuable assistance to architects and are always available for the dissemination of thoroughly reliable organ information.

Correspondence is invited.

Products

Pipe Organs for churches, schools, lodges and residences.

Concert and **Unit Organs** for motion picture, vaudeville and other theaters, with or without roll players.

America's Finest Organ

Tonally and mechanically, Marr & Colton organs have won first place in the esteem of noted organists. Our list of installations shows the prestige which many years of fine work has created for us.

The flexibility of our organs allows the architect to overcome any structural difficulty. Reliability is assured through simplicity. Accurate points of adjustment are of metal. Each stop is carefully considered, and, with our special scales, high grade materials and highly skilled voicers, the very finest quality of tone is obtained.

Every Marr & Colton organ carries with it an absolute guarantee.

Types of Marr & Colton Organs

Church Organs—Arranged for the accompaniment of a large number of voices, with additional stops for recital work, with or without echo organ.

Concert and Unit Organs—These contain harps, marimbas, chimes, xylophones and other percussion instruments.

Consoles

Three principal types of consoles are available, all with the modern stop key, inclined manuals, concave and radiating pedal board and adjustable combinations moving the registers.

Console elevators (see illustration) can be provided so that console can be lifted from the orchestra pit to the stage or platform for special occasions. Further particulars on request.

Important Points to Be Considered When Making Organ Layouts

Organ Chamber—All walls and ceiling in the organ chamber should be plastered smooth and a wood floor should be provided regardless of style and construction of the building. Show all breaks and projections in the organ chamber. Avoid all beam projections below ceiling in organ chamber, as this seriously handicaps the tone and hinders the proper placing of the organ pipes.

Steam and water pipes should not be run above the organ chamber. If impossible to follow these recommendations, all pipes should be heavily insulated to avoid radiation and condensation. Wherever possible, all outside walls should be made dampproof. Dampness in any form should be eliminated from the organ chamber.

Circular Type

Access Doors—Standard fireproof doors in any desirable location, should be provided in the organ chamber for means of access. A light should be provided at the entrance, also a light with basket protection for working on the organ.

Organ Chamber Openings—These should be as central as possible in the chamber and their area should be calculated at approximately 5% to 7% of the cubic capacity of the organ chamber.

Example: Given a chamber 12 ft. long, 7 ft. deep and 10 ft. high. This chamber contains 840 cu. ft. Seven per cent of 840 equals 60. Therefore opening should be 60 sq. ft., or approximately 10 ft. long by 6 ft. high.

The openings should be at the top of the organ chambers.

Organ Blower—The organ blower can be placed in the basement or in any room that is not located too far away from the organ chamber. The room must be dustproof and dampproof, a door should be provided for means of access, and a small grille (12x12 in.) with a fine copper wire mesh screen should be placed in the door.

Provide remote control for the organ motor; the push button can be placed at the key board of the organ. The wiring for the motor should be brought into the blower room.

A foundation should be provided for the organ blower.

Give accurate plan and elevation of organ blower room, showing position of any breaks in the room and of beams, ducts and plumbing pipes.

Roll Top Type

Push Button Controlled Elevator Type

Organ Cable Conduit—Sharp bends in the organ cable conduit should be avoided and pull boxes should be provided to allow the organ cable to be pulled through easily.

Wind Trunk—Consult the organ builder regarding the position of the wind trunk, which should be placed in the building during construction. The wind trunk must be soldered absolutely airtight and sleeves in the floor should have a ½-in. clearance all around the wind trunking.

Dust Filters—Under certain conditions, dust filters are necessary. Information on request.

Grille Work—In theaters, auditoriums, hotels, etc., grille work is used; in churches, front pipes are used.

If sound is transmitted through grille work, architects should be careful to design the grille so that the area of the grille *openings* shall be as large or larger than the area of the organ chamber openings, so as not to retard the tone from passing through the grille.

If draperies are to be used, additional allowances should be made in the organ chamber and grille openings, and draperies shall be as light in weight as possible.

CAUTION—Conduits for cables should not be laid in solid cement, because they sweat

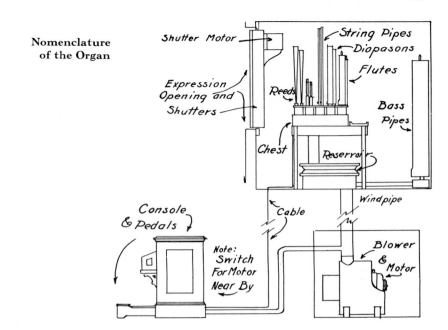

Nomenclature of the Organ

and become moist. The cables should be kept clean and water tight. The wind conductors in the blower room and the chambers should be wind tight. Solder with no sharp angles to obstruct wind passage.

Chamber floors should be painted and the plaster of the chamber should be of a hard enamel finish. An even temperature of 68° Farenheit in the chamber makes perfect organ operation.

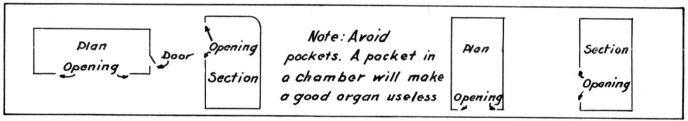

Correct Design   *Incorrect Design*

Correct and Incorrect Designs of Organ Chambers

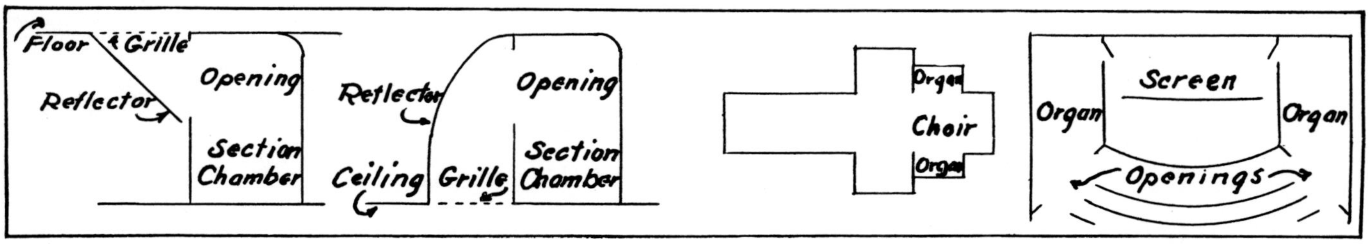

Organ in Basement   *Organ in Attic*   *Church Installation*   *Theater Installation*

Typical Location of Organ Chambers

Marr & Colton Organ Data

Number of organ chambers used	Minimum dimensions of each organ chamber, ft.-in.			Organ chamber openings, ft.-in.		Minimum blower room sizes, ft.-in.			Blower motor hp.	Windpipe diameter, in.	Approximate weight, tons	Console dimensions, ft.-in.		
	Length	Depth	Height	Length	Height	Length	Depth	Height				Length	Depth	Height
1	12-6	6-0	10-6	9-0	6-0	7-0	5-0	7-0	3	6	1¾	5-1	4-2½	4-6½
1	16-0	8-0	10-6	12-0	6-0	7-0	5-0	7-0	5	8	2½	5-1	4-4	4-6½
1	12-0	10-0	12-6	18-0	8-0	9-0	7-0	7-0	7½	10	4	6-9	4-6½	4-9¼
2	14-0	8-0	12-6	12-0	7-0	9-0	7-0	7-0	7½	8	4	6-9	4-6½	4-9¼
1	24-0	14-0	12-6	20-0	8-0	9-0	7-0	7-0	10	12	6	6-9	4-6½	4-9¼
2	16-0	10-0	12-6	12-0	7-0	9-0	7-0	7-0	10	8	6	6-9	4-6½	4-9¼

Cable from organ to console requires 2½ in. conduit.

Preliminary Sketch

The New Automatic Self-Playing

MARR & COLTON
Residence Organ

THIS organ has just been developed by the Marr & Colton Company. Case work is beautifully finished in Walnut, Mahogany or Polychrome. Special designed case work if desired. Plays from rolls. The ideal pipe organ for the home. Write for further information.

The MARR & COLTON COMPANY
Factories and General Offices
WARSAW, NEW YORK

New York Office	*Detroit Office*	*Chicago Office*
Suite 2013, Paramount Bldg.	3001 E. Grand Blvd.	708 Congress Bank Bldg.
Times Square, New York	Detroit, Mich.	506 So. Wabash Ave., Chicago

Marr & Colton
"America's Finest Organ"

For Every Size Theatre

WHETHER your theatre is large or small we build "America's Finest Organ" to suit the acoustic requirements of your particular theatre at a price within your reach.

Every Marr & Colton instrument is a distinctive work of art.

We do not build stock organs. Every organ is designed and constructed under the personal supervision of David Marr and John J. Colton—recognized authorities on organ construction.

WRITE FOR OUR CATALOG
ASK ABOUT OUR EASY PAYMENT PLAN

The Marr & Colton Company
Factories—Warsaw, N. Y.

Eastern Sales Office, 437 Fifth Avenue, New York
Western Sales Office, 906 Merritt Bldg., Los Angeles, Calif.

Branch Offices—Buffalo, N. Y.—Pittsburgh, Pa.—Indianapolis, Ind.—Portland, Oregon—San Francisco, Calif. Detroit, Mich.—Rochester, N. Y.—Philadelphia, Pa. Toledo, Ohio.

Marr & Colton ad in the March 28, 1925 Exhibitors Herald.

Top center—*Hope Ha*

Lower center—*Stra*

Top left—*Rivoli Theater, Philadelph*

Lower Left—*Palace Theatre, Jamest*

Top

Low

Reproduced above is the centerfold from a rare Marr & Colton catalog c. 192

Marr & Colton console
Niagara Falls, N. Y.

...nial Theatre, Brooklyn, N. Y.
...rand Theatre, Schenectady, N. Y.

Marr & Colton ad in the April 1922 Diapason.

Advertisement for Marr & Colton from an exhibitor trade publication c. 1925.

Beautiful brass nameplate found on the rare symphonic registrator models. What a pity that the mechanical construction of the organ didn't match the quality of the nameplate.

Console of the 4/18 Marr & Colton in the Roosevelt Theatre, Buffalo, New York. At right, main chamber. From front to back the ranks are kinura, horn diapason, solo string, French horn, trumpet and vox humana. Below, solo chamber.

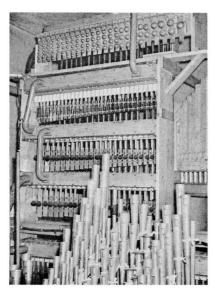

Eddie May plays at the Riviera Theatre, Rochester, New York. This console had a standard case painted in an interesting design instead of the usual varnished finish.

The 3/9 Marr & Colton in the Fountain Square Theatre in Indianapolis featured a one-of-a-kind console (above and at right) of striking design, one of the few the firm built which differed from their standard case style.

This 3/10 Marr & Colton in the Admiral Theatre in Chicago featured the firm's usual standard console case. It sat on a Barton four poster lift shown here in concert position.

Photo below shows console placement at the Apollo Theatre, Indianapolis in the unusually narrow horseshoe balcony.

This double bolstered two-manual Marr & Colton in the home/studio of theatre organist Paul Forster in Syracuse, New York controlled only six ranks of pipes. It replaced an earlier Wangerin instrument which had been moved to the Forster studio following its original installation in the Costello Theatre, New York City in 1916.[1]

The only five-manual organ ever built by Marr & Colton was this 24-ranker in the Rochester Theatre, Rochester, New York. It was the firm's second largest theatre organ, four ranks smaller than that in the Piccadilly Theatre in New York.

Marr & Colton piano formerly installed in the Piccadilly Theatre, New York. The organ keyboard simplified tuning the piano whose keyboard had been replaced with a pneumatic stack.

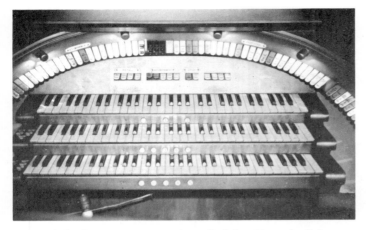

One of the last organs ever installed by Marr & Colton was this 1929 3/8 in the Garden Theatre, Greenfield, Massachusetts. The right chamber (below) contains a 16' tibia (the only 16' rank in the organ), 8' diapason and 8' kinura as well as glockenspiel, chimes and traps. This organ is divided most peculiarly into "right" and "left" chambers rather than the conventional solo and main. Pictured in the left chamber (photo at right) are 8' bass offsets of, front to back, post horn, trumpet and string. Other ranks in this chamber are flute and vox humana as well as xylophone and chrysoglott.

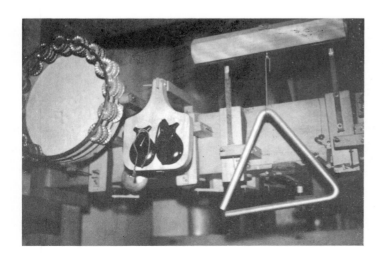

Close-up view of a Marr & Colton toy counter showing tambourine, door bell, castanets, Chinese block and triangle.

Two views of the largest Marr & Colton theatre organ in its second home, the Warner Theatre in Hollywood, California. The original location of this 4/28 was the Piccadilly Theatre, New York, New York. It was moved to Hollywood in 1928.

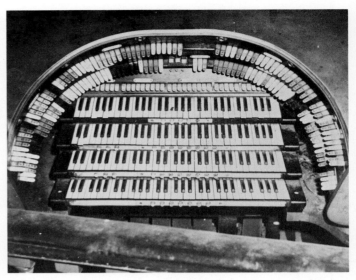

The Marr & Colton in the Rivoli Theatre, Toledo, Ohio was the third largest theatre organ built by the firm. This instrument contained, as did other early Marr & Coltons, several straight ranks of pipes.

This Marr & Colton Symphonic Registator organ was originally installed in the Academy Theatre, Lebanon, Pennsylvania. Upper row of stops is the registrator presets which have such fanciful names as "hatred," "suspense," "gruesome" and "pathetic." These were supposed to refer to moods in the silent film and not to the quality of the organ!

Marr & Colton factory as it appeared in 1962, unoccupied and abandoned for years. Original building on the left was built in the late teens. The center structure was added in 1922 and the building on the right in 1926, used primarily for lumber storage. After the 1922 addition the original building was used for the console department, small parts fabrication and leathering. In the center building the business offices were on the right side of the first floor near the front door and the accounting department was on the left. Behind them was the single-story erecting room. A railroad siding ran behind the building for convenient shipping of the organs. On the front end of the second floor was the drafting room and engraving department. Behind them was the main workroom where most action work was done. At one side was the voicing room and at the rear of the second floor was the mill room and wood pipe department.[12][13]

David Marr, far right, and John Colton, second from right, confer with customers in the Marr & Colton offices. Above them is an artist's view of the factory c. 1925 and, in the oval, their first shop c. 1915.

This group of women leathered pneumatics used in Marr & Colton chests and other actions.

Chest department.

Four scenes show assembling and wiring of Marr & Colton relays.

A heavily retouched photo of the console department.   *A portion of the mill room.*

Console cabinet and finishing departments.

Metal pipe department. Marr & Colton did not make their own metal pipes but instead purchased them, primarily from Dennison and National Organ Supply.

Gluing tibias and 16' strings in the wood department. Despite the inferior quality of Marr & Colton wood pipe construction they sounded amazingly good. Many of their medium sized instruments featured these 16' strings, a feature usually found only in larger organs of other manufacturers.

Making electrical cables.

Assembling contact blocks.

Two views of the erecting room. The ceiling is quite low compared to erecting rooms of most organ factories.

MARR & COLTON OPUS LIST

CITY/STATE	LOCATION	SIZE	YR	BLWR	HP	WP	REMARKS
CALIFORNIA							
Fullerton	Alician Court Th.	3/16	1925				
Long Beach	Brayton Th.	2/8					
Los Angeles	Tempest Th.		1925	N455B	3	9½"	
Stockton	Rialto Th.	2/7					
CONNECTICUT							
Danbury	Empress Th.	2/	1927	20620			
	Palace Th.	3/10	1928	22058			
Hartford	Colonial Th.	2/8	1927	19906			With Symphonic Registrator.
	Embassy Th.	2/	1926				
New Britain	Rialto Th.		1926	O660B	2	8"	
New London	Capitol Th.	2/8	1926	O116B	5	10"	With Symphonic Registrator.
	Crown Th.	3/	1926				
Norwalk	Empress (Princess) Th.	3/9	1928				

CITY/STATE	LOCATION	SIZE	YR	BLWR	HP	WP	REMARKS
FLORIDA							
Miami	Rio Th.		1926	O560B	2......10		
Palm Beach	Flamingo Th.		1927	19972			
ILLINOIS							
Chicago	Admiral Th.	3/10	1926	19961			
	Chelten Th.	3/9	1927	21316			
	Hi-Way Th.	3/9					
	Randolph Th.	2/	1927	20518			
	Shore Th.	3/9	1927	21255			
Danville	unidentified theatre	2/5					
Hinsdale	Hinsdale Th.	3/10	1925	N116B	7½.....12"		
Ottawa	Gayety (Roxy) Th.	2/	1927	20636			
Paris	Dixie Th.		1925	N760B	2.....10"		
St. Charles	Arcada Th.	2/10	1926	O27B	5......9½		
INDIANA							
Auburn	Court Th.	2/7	1927	20897			
Indianapolis	Apollo Th.	2/	1923	L524	3.......7"		
			1926	O22B	5 8"&15"		
	Fountain Square Th.	3/9	1928	21356			
	Lyric Th.	4/15	1927	O616B	10 10"&14"		
	Ohio Th.	3/10	1919	10278			
			1923	14916			
	Zaring Th.	2/	1925	N133B	7½.....12"		
Kendallville	Princess Th.	2/	1926				
	Strand Th.	2/4	1926	O561B	1½.....10"		
Mishawaka	Mishawaka Theatre Corp.		1925	M1011B	5.....7½"		
Richmond	Ritz Th.		1926	O702B	5.....10"		
	Washington Th.		1925	N500B	3......9½		
Shelbyville	Strand Th.		1924	M930B	5......9"		
South Bend	Armo Th.	3/	1928				
Warsaw	Centennial Th.	2/	1926	O805B	1½......8"		
KANSAS							
Garden City	State (Garden) Th.	2/3	1929	228S	1½......8"		
MARYLAND							
Baltimore	Vilma Th.	2/	1928	21628			
Bethesda	Hiser Th.	2/5	1928	Q602B	2......8"		
MASSACHUSETTS							
Charlestown	Hollywood (Charlestown) Th.	2/5	1928	21242			
	Thompson Square Th.	2/5					
Chicopee	Rivoli (Elms) Th.	2/6	1923	14076			
Fall River	Durfee Th.	3/13	1922				
	Nathan Yamins		1929	23121			
Falmouth	Elizabeth Th.	2/	1928	21257			
Greenfield	Garden Th.	3/8	1929	22871			
Roxbury	Egleston Square Th.	2/7	1928	20633			
	Puritan Th.	2/					
Pittsfield	Capitol Th.	3/	1922	13054			
Wakefield	Princess Th.	2/					
MICHIGAN							
Bay City	State Th.	2/4	1924	M717B	1½......8"		
	Washington Th.	2/4	1924	M554B	1½......8"		Later moved to Bay Theatre, Bay City, Michigan.
	West Side Th.		1924	M555B	1......6"		
Charlotte	Rialto Th.		1926	N1018B	2.....10"		
Dearborn	Calvin Th.	2/5					
Detroit	Academy Th.	2/4	1924	M630B	1½......8"		
	Dexter Th.	2/5	1926	O419B	2.....10"		
	East End Th.		1926	O515B	7½.....10"		
	Echo Th.	2/7	1926	P724B	1½.....10"		
	Ferry Field (Beacon) Th.		1926	O119B	7½.....10"		
	Flamingo Th.		1925	N617B	3.....10"		
	Gladwin (Booth) Th.	3/	1925	17743			
	Grande Th.	2/5	1929	22930			
	Great Lakes (Vest Pocket) Th.	3/9	1927	20873			
	Grosse Point Park Th.		1924	M632B	3.....&10"		
	Harmony (Admiral) Th.		1921	J92	3......7"		
	Harper Th.		1922	K537	2......7"		
	Lasky Th.	3/9	1926	N1105B	7½.....10"		
	LaVeeda (DeSoto) (Oakland) Th.	2/4	1926	O324B	1½.....10"		
	Lee Palace (Palace) Th.		1923	K1154	2......9"		
	Martha Washington (Campau) Th.	2/8	1923	L462	5......8"		
		3/14	1924	L1136	.......8"&15"		Enlargement of exisiting instrument.
	New Astor Th.		1923				
	Oakman Th.	3/	1927	20700			
	Orient (Oriole) Th.	3/17	1927	19822	15		

CITY/STATE	LOCATION	SIZE	YR	BLWR	HP	WP	REMARKS
Detroit	Reginald Webb Studio	3/10	1928	Q120B	5	10"	Broadcast over WJR Radio.
		2/4	1928				Second organ.
Fordson	Fordson Th.						
Highland Park	Humber (Woodward) Th.	2/4	1924	M631B	2	8"	
Marine City	unidentified new theatre	2/4	1927	20827			
Marquette	Delft Th.	2/	1924	15687			
Wyandotte	Majestic Th.	2/	1928	M1002B	5	10"	
MINNESOTA							
Fairmont	Opera House (Nicholas) Th.	2/5	1927	20220			
Rochester	Chateau Th.	2/9	1927	20464			
Minneapolis	Calhoun Th.	2/					
	Granada Th.	2/5					
	Lagoon Th.	2/7	1927	19982			
	McPhail School of Music	2/5	1927	20441			
		2/5	1927				Two 2/5 practice organs.
NEBRASKA							
Columbus	Columbus Th.	2/5	1926	O806B	2	8"	
Holdredge	Auditorium Th.	2/					
Kearney	Kearney Th.		1926	P27B	2	8"	
McCook	World (Fox) Th.	2/5	1926	O807B	2	8"	
Omaha	Omaha Academy of Music	2/5	1927	19758			
Scottsbluff	Midwest Amuse. & Realty Co.		1927	20588			
NEW JERSEY							
Asbury Park	Lyric Th.		1926	O701B	2	8"	
Berlin	Palace Th.	2/	1927				
Bogota	Queen Anne Th.	3/8	1928				
Moorestown	Criterion Th.		1920		½	5"	
Perth Amboy	Crescent Th.		1926	P740B	1½	8"	
Salem	Palace Th.	2/					
South Orange	Paramount Th.	3/	1921	11558	2	7"	
Westfield	Rialto (Putnam) Th.		1922	K564	2	7"	
Westville	Westville Th.		1923	L463	1½	8"	
NEW YORK							
Auburn	Strand Th.	3/11	1925	N561B	7½	12"	
	Universal Th.	2/	1921				
Baldwinsville	Variety Th.		1927	20856			
Bayside	Treasureland Th.		1928	21353			
Brockport	Strand Th.		1923	L520	½	5"	
Brooklyn	Colonial (Stanley) Th.	2/	1917	8421			
			1921	11113			
	Dyker Th.	3/12	1926				
	Electra Th.		1923	L437	2	8"	
	Elton Amusement Co.		1927	20161			
	Shore Road Th.	2/	1926	O415B	7½	12"	
			1928	Q23B	3	9½	
	Victoria Th.		1920	10611	1/3	5"	
				10766	½	5"	
Buffalo	Broadway Th.	2/	1922	K903	1½	7½"	
	Central Park Th.		1927	20065			
	Clinton Strand Th.		1923	L631	3	8"	
	Commodore Th.	2/7	1926	O517B	5	10"	
	Genessee Th.	4/18	1927	20719			Later repossessed.
	Kensington Th.		1924	M354B	2	8"	
	Orpheum Th.		1917	8437			
	Roosevelt Th.	4/18	1927	19880	15		
	Varsity Th.		1923	15057			
Dansville	Star Th.	2/4					
East Rochester	Rialto Th.						
Elmira	State (Keeney's) (Elmira) (Clemens Center) Th.	3/20	1926	N117B	10	12"	With 3-rank echo.
Fairport	Rivoli Th.	2/5					
Fredonia	Fredonia Opera House		1926	O535B	3	9½"	
	Winter Garden Th.	2/					
Gloversville	unidentified theatre	3/10					
Ithaca	Crescent Th.	2/	1916	7624			
Jamestown	Palace Th.	2/8	1923	14076			
			1923	14083			
		3/16	1925	N348B	7½	12"	Exiting instrument enlarged.
	Winter Garden Th.		1925	N354B	3	10"	
			1926	O416B	7½	12"	
Johnstown	Smalley Th.	3/	1928	Q207B	5	10"	
Lancaster	New Albert Th.	2/	1919	10170			
LeRoy	LeRoy Th.	2/					
Mt. Morris	Family Th.		1923	L562	1	6"	
Naples	Pictureland Th.		1928	Q703B	1	6"	
New York	Costello Th.		1926	P323B	3	9½"	
	Marr & Colton store						Located in Paramount Theatre building.

CITY/STATE	LOCATION	SIZE	YR	BLWR	HP	WP	REMARKS
New York	Piccadilly Th.	4/28	1924	M462B	15	10"&15"	Second blower for echo chamber; entire organ
				M461B	1	8"	moved in 1928 to Warner (Hollywood Pacific) Th., Hollywood, California.
	Times Th.		1917	8403			Located on 8th Avenue.
	Whitehall Th.		1927	20911			
	WNEW Radio		1928	22362			
Niagara Falls	Cataract Th.	2/	1923	K1026	2	10"	
	New Lumberg Th.	2/	1916	7732			
	Strand Th.	2/	1922	13455			
		3/17	1926	O353B	10	12"	Existing instrument enlarged.
North Tonawanda	Oliver Th.	2/	1921				
Nunda	Acadamy Th.	2/	1928				
Olean	Gem Th.	2/	1921				
Oneida	Madison Th.	3/9	1927	20634			
Oneonta	Palace Th.	2/					
Palmyra	Strand Th.	2/5					
Perry	Auditorium Th.		1925	N744B	1½	8"	
Port Chester	Embassy Th.	2/8	1926	N1004B	3	9½	
				O522B	5	10"	
Queens	Belvedere Th.	3/	1922				
Richmond Hill	Our Civic (Casino) Th.	3/5	1923	14124			Top manual a dummy.
Rochester	Chili Th.		1926	O148B	1½	8"	
	Culver Th.	2/					
	Eastman School of Music	2/5					Practice organ.
	Eastman School of Music	2/					Practice organ.
	Family Th.	2/					
	Hub Th.	2/					
	Hudson Th.	2/					
	Lake Th.	2/	1927	21302			
	Lyric Th.	2/	1917	7908			
	Rialto Th.	1/					
	Riviera Th.	3/11	1926	O523B	7½	12"	
				O839B	10	12"	
	Rochester Th.	5/24	1927			.20	
	Strand (Happy Hour) Th.		1915	6817			
		3/14	1921	J331	3	7"	Existing instrument enlarged.
		4/15	1926	O753B	15	10"&15"	Further enlargement.
	Thurston Th.		1925	N743B	2	8"	
	Victoria Th.	3/	1927				
Rome	Carroll Th.	3/	1921				
Schenectady	New Strand Th.	2/	1921	J365	2	7"	
			1924	M721B	2	10"	
	State Th.	3/	1928				
	Van Cyler Th.		1927	20847			
Syracuse	Avon Th.	3/8	1926	O233B	5	10"	
	Brighton Th.	3/10	1928	22357			
	Civic (Syracuse) Th.	3/10	1927	20120			
	Crescent Th.	1/2	1920	11011	1/3	5"	Attached to piano.
	Eckel Th.	2/	1916	7236			
			1924	M566B	2	10"	
	Empire Th.	3/10	1925	N30B	7½	12"	
	Gedder Street Th.		1926	O710B	3	10"	
	Happy Hour Th.		1920	10613			
	Paul Forster Studio	2/6	1928	Q241B	2	8"	Double bolster console.
	Regent Th.	3/13	1926	N1107B	10	12"	
	Rivoli Th.	2/6	1922	K113	3	7"	
	Savoy Th.	2/8	1920	11374	2	6"	
	Swan Th.		1920	10555	1/3	5"	
	System Th.		1924	L904	3	8"	
	Temple Th.	2/7					
Troy	Strand Th.		1918	8752			
Utica	Majestic Th.						
	Olympic Th.	2/	1926	N115B	5	10"	
	Robbins Amusement Co.	2/	1921				
	South Street Th.		1917				
	Uptown Th.	3/11	1927	20706			
Warsaw	Oatka Th.	2/	1916	6970			First Marr & Colton built.
	Warner Th.		1926				
Watertown	Stand Th.	2/	1916	7584			
Wayland	Legion (Wayland) Th.	2/5	1928				

NORTH DAKOTA

CITY/STATE	LOCATION	SIZE	YR	BLWR	HP	WP	REMARKS
Bismarck	Bismarck (Eltinge) Th.	2/5	1927	20746			
Fargo	State Th.	2/7	1928	21563			

OHIO

CITY/STATE	LOCATION	SIZE	YR	BLWR	HP	WP	REMARKS
Bowling Green	Cla-Zel Th.	2/	1926	O10B	3	9½"	
Bryan	Temple Th.		1926	O832B	2	10"	
Cleveland	Euclid Th.		1925	M1048B	5	10"	
	Manhattan Th.		1926	O28B	1½	8"	
	West Park Th.		1925	M1047B	3	10"	

CITY/STATE	LOCATION	SIZE	YR	BLWR	HP	WP	REMARKS
Columbus	Columbus Th.		1926	O806B	2		
	Midwest Engr. & Const. Co.		1928	Q817B	1	6″	
Conneaut	La Grande Th.	2/					
Ironton	unidentified theatre		1920	10955	1/3	5″	
Springfield	Alhambra Th.	2/					
Toledo	Palace Th.	2/11	1925	N507B	5	10″	
	Rivoli Th.	4/	1926	O461B	15	10″&14″	
	State Th.	3/11	1927	20794	10		

OREGON

Astoria	Viking Th.	3/					
Coquille	Liberty (Coquille) Th.	2/6	1923	14548			
Forest Grove	Forest Grove Th.	2/	1925				
Portland	Walnut Park Th.	2/14	1923	L717	3	8″	

PENNSYLVANIA

Allentown	Cameo Th.		1927	P351B	5	10″	
	Franklin Th.		1926	O659B	2	8″	
	Orpheum Th.	2/	1924	15520			
			1925	16878			Existing instrument enlarged.
Altoona	State Th.		1925	N560B	7½	12″	
Ambridge	Princess Th.	3/	1928	22391			
Beaver Falls	Rialto Th.	3/7	1928	22364			
Bedford	Richelieu Th.		1921				
Bellevue	Bellevue Amusement Co.		1924	M578B	3	10″	
Berwick	Palace Th.		1925	N527B	2	8″	
Carlisle	Orpheum (Strand) Th.		1924	M744B	1	8″	
Carnegie	Liberty Th.	2/	1928				
	Lyric Th.		1923	L334	3	8″	
Catasaqua	Majestic Th.		1924	M109	¾	6″	
				M842B	1½	8″	
Connellsville	Wallace Th.	3/	1928				
Duquesne	Emar Th.	3/	1928	22644			
	Liberty Th.		1922	K732	½	5″	
Easton	Berwick Th.		1924	M258B	1	6″	
	Embassy Th.	3/	1927	O943B	7½	12″	
	Fourth Street Th.		1926	N939B	1½	8″	
	Opera House	2/					
	State Th.	3/	1926	N919B	7½	12″	
East Stroudsburg	Plaza Th.	3/	1927	P503B	7½	10″	
	Sherman Th.	4/	1928				
Exeter	Liberty Th.	2/	1927	P344B	2	10″	
Forty Fort	Pepe's Th.		1925	N543B	1	8″	
Gettysburg	Motion Picture Th.		1926	N902B	2	10″	
Harrisburg	State Th.	3/	1926	O239B	10	12″	
	Victoria Th.	3/	1925	M1002B	5	10″	
			1928	P1022B	7½	12″	
Hazelton	Feeley Th.	3/11	1926	19695			
Indiana	Indiana Th.	2/	1924	M231B	5	10″	Later moved to Ritz (Manos) Theatre, Indiana, PA.
Irwin	Maute Th.	2/8	1924	L837	3	8″	
Johnsonburg	Palace Th.	2/	1927	P902B	1½	8″	
Kulpmont	Imperial Th.	3/10	1929	22527			
Lebanon	Academy Th.	2/10	1926	O1002B	3	10″	
	Strand Th.		1924	M135B	¾	6″	
Lewistown	Pastime Th.		1925	N639B	3	9½″	
			1925	N844B	5	10″	
Mahonoy City	Elk Th.	2/	1925	N619B	2	10″	
McAdoo	Palace Th.		1925	M1026B	2	10″	
Minersville	Minersville Opera House		1924	M301B	1	8″	
Mt. Carmel	Arcade Th.		1926	O609B	3	10″	
Nesquebonig	James Newton		1924	M834B	1½	8″	
New Ambridge	New Ambridge Th.	3/	1928				
Northampton	Lyric Th.		1924	M220B	1½	8″	
Pittsburgh	Brighton Th.	3/	1928	22225			
	Liberty Th.						
Philadelphia	Colonial Th.		1923	K902	1½	7½″	
	Great Northern Th.		1928	K321B	5	15″	
	Lenox Th.	3/9	1926	O738B	7½	10″	
	Littleton Th.		1925	N526B	2	8″	
	Metropolitan Opera House		1926	O534B	3	8″	
	Pastime Th.		1924	M14	2	8″	
	Rivoli Th.	3/	1920				With echo.
			1923	L4	1½	8″	
Reading	Capitol Th.	3/12	1926	O237B	10	12″	
	Royal Th.		1926	O227B	2	10″	
Renovo	Rialto Th.	3/9					
Shenandoah	Oppenheimer & Sweet		1925	N704B	2	10″	
Slatington	Opera House		1924	M460B	1½	8″	
Stroudsburg	New Schuerman Th.		1928	22579			
	Park Th.						

CITY/STATE	LOCATION	SIZE	YR	BLWR	HP	WP	REMARKS
Taylor	Thomas Th.		1926	O1032B	3	10″	
Union City	Palace Th.		1927	20003			
West Pittston	Garden Th.		1924	M15	¾	6″	
Williamsport	Keystone Th.		1928	22601			
	Park Th.	3/10	1928	21374			

RHODE ISLAND

Providence	Olympic Th.	2/	1926	O516B	3	10″	

SOUTH DAKOTA

Huron	Huron Th.	2/					

VIRGINIA

Richmond	Lyric Th.	2/	1926	O303B	3	9½″	
	Bijou (Strand) Th.	2/	1924	M110B	1½	8″	
Norfolk	Granby (Lee) Th.		1926	O504B	7½	10″	
	Wells Th.		1926	O238B	10	12″	

WASHINGTON

Spokane	American Th.	2/	1925				
	Hippodrome Th.	2/8	1919				

WEST VIRGINIA

Ashland	Palace Th.	3/					
Martinsburg	unidentified theatre	2/6					
Wheeling	Capitol Th.	4/17	1928	22126			

WISCONSIN

Jefferson	Allen Th.	2/	1927	20541			
Kenosha	Roosevelt Th.	3/7	1927	20817			
Milwaukee	Arnold Krueger residence	2/7					
	Avelyn Kerr School of Organ	3/8	1927	20113			Broadcast over WSOE and WISN Radio.
	Plaza Th.	2/7					
Racine	Majestic (Uptown) Th.	3/7	1928	1093S	5	7½″	

ALFRED MATHERS CHURCH ORGAN CO.

Quoting from an article in *The Diapason*: "A visit to the well-equipped factory of the Alfred Mathers company inspires respect for a man who, unaided and without capital, has built up a business by integrity and hard work. Coming to this country from England, a thorough organist, Mr. Mathers was familiar with the construction of the instrument. He started business in a small way, doing most of his work himself. His activities grew rapidly, and in 1907 he took over the business of Koehnken & Grim, established in 1847. He also built a factory equipped with all the latest machinery for building modern organs."[1]

As of 1923 the company was being operated by Richard Mathers. On January 2, 1924 the factory caught fire, causing an estimated $25,000 in damage.[2] Apparently the firm continued in business, because in 1926 Spencer sold blower #19670 to them and shipped it to the Park Theatre in Cincinnati. Whether or not this blower was intended for a new organ is not disclosed by the Spencer records. The only Mathers organ known to be installed in a theatre was a 1916 two-manual instrument in the New Lyceum in Dayton, Ohio.

Mathers ad in the September 1916 Diapason.

MEISEL & SULLIVAN

Meisel & Sullivan did business in the Los Angeles area in the 1920s and 1930s. Historical details concerning the firm are lacking but their reputation for shoddy workmanship is keenly remembered by contemporary Los Angeles organ builders.[1] It is reasonable to assume that the firm purchased most of the component parts of their organs and that they did little, if any, actual building themselves.

Four theatre instruments bearing the Meisel & Sullivan nameplate are known to have been installed: a 2/6 in the Huntley Theatre in Hollywood, California; a 2/6 in the Lompoc Theatre in Lompoc, California; a two-manual in the Rialto Theatre in Winslow, Arizona; and a 3/11 in the Paramount, nee Orpheum Theatre in Phoenix, Arizona. A curious fact about the latter organ is that its Spencer Orgoblo (#22334, 7½ horsepower, 12" wind) was sold to Pasadena, California organ builder E. A. Spencer in 1928. This may indicate that Mr. Spencer was involved in the construction of the organ, or he may have purchased the blower for Meisel & Sullivan as a courtesy, perhaps because they didn't have an account with the Spencer Turbine Company.

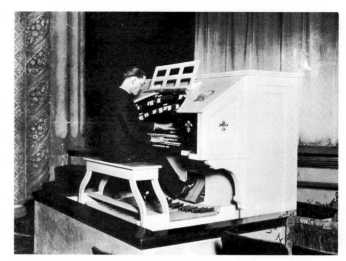

Ray Sawyer plays the 3/11 Meisel & Sullivan in the Phoenix Paramount. The console was built by Gott-fried.[2]

ESTABLISHED 1860

FORMERLY REUBEN MIDMER & SON

MIDMER-LOSH

INCORPORATED

PIPE ORGANS

Factory:
Telephone, Freeport 1862

City Office:
9723 East 127th Street
Richmond Hill, N. Y.
Tel., CLeveland 3-3629

Merrick, Long Island, N. Y.,

Reuben Midmer, an Englishman, came to the United States in 1840 as a boy of 16 and apprenticed with organ builder Thomas Hall of New York City. He later joined the Ferris & Stuart firm, also of New York, as foreman, resigning to go into business for himself in 1860. He built a factory at 18 High Street in Brooklyn and moved to 97 Steuben Street in 1875. His son, Reed Midmer, joined him in business at the age of 14 and the firm name later became Reuben Midmer & Son, Inc. Reuben Midmer retired in 1895 and in 1906 the firm moved to a new and larger building in Merrick, New York. Machinery was operated by a steam engine since elec-tricity wasn't available in Merrick at the time. The firm enjoyed an industry-wide reputation for high quality and sold most of their output by favorable word-of-mouth reports rather than by salesmen or elaborate advertising.[1][2]

In the mid-teens Reed Midmer's health began to fail and he sold his interest in the company to Maximillion Averbeck, treasurer of All Angels Episcopal Church in New York, which had recently installed a large Midmer organ.[3] Mr. Midmer continued to work as his health permitted but he died in 1918 after which his son Reed, a long time employee, became a director of the firm.[4] In

Reed Midmer
(?-1918)

Charles Seibert Losh
(1880-1934)

Reuben Midmer
(1824-?)

George Losh
(1892-1975)

1920 the company was purchased by Seibert Losh.[5]

Seibert Losh grew up in Hagerstown, Maryland where his father managed the M. P. Moller Piano Company, a local music retailer. Seibert worked in this store and later went on the road selling Moller organs. In 1909 he became eastern sales manager, headquartered in New York.[6] He was a terrific salesman and was full of new ideas for improving the musical results obtainable from an organ. He was a pioneer in the sale of organs to theatres and was responsible for the sales of dozens of intruments to the Loew and Fox theatre chains.[7] He was also quite a liar, according to Senator Emerson Richards.[8] Perhaps this was one of the reasons for his success as a salesman! One of his many schemes was a proposal for an organ to be built on the New Jersey Palisades which could be heard across the Hudson River in New York City.[9] This plan never materialized; in fact, it actually paled by comparison with the instrument Losh actually did get to build in Atlantic City. But more on that later!

Seibert Losh quit Moller in 1918 and did freelance organ promoting and selling for a couple of years. When the Midmer company came up for sale in 1920 Losh lost

no time in acquiring it. Their well-equipped factory was just the ticket for carrying out Seibert's schemes. He was joined in the new venture by his younger brother George, who had also worked for Moller, and who soon became plant superintendent. George had a degree in mechanical engineering from the Pratt Institute which would later serve him well in supervising the construction of the world's largest organ. Other key men in the factory were William Voris, a skilled chest maker, console maker Robert Dewar and Gustav Palmgreen, who ran the mill and was also a fine wood pipe maker. For many years George Badger operated an independent pipe shop in the Midmer factory and supplied reed and metal pipes to Midmer as well as to the trade. Mr. Badger died early in 1920 and his son-in-law, Walter V. Elliott, carried on the business. In 1921 the Badger company moved out of the Midmer building and Seibert Losh hired Walter McLaughlin from the Estey company to set up a shop for making metal pipes. James Campbell was head voicer.[10]

The Midmer firm prospered under Seibert Losh's dynamic leadership. Additional factory buildings were acquired in 1921[11] and 1923[12] and in 1925 a new building 3½ stories high and 104 feet long was constructed.[13] The firm name was changed to Midmer-Losh, Inc. in 1924. Before Seibert Losh came on the scene the conservative old Midmer firm had never built an instrument for a theatre. Losh, of course, changed all that and proceeded to sell several dozen such instruments. Losh's conception of the ideal organ for a theatre was an orchestral instrument largely straight or duplexed and with little unification. Many of his theatre installations had no traps (undoubtedly enabling them to be sold less expensively) and only a few had tibia clausas. The contract for one such instrument is reproduced on the next page.

2-MANUAL MIDMER-LOSH THEATRE ORGAN
Essex Theatre, New York City, New York

SPECIFICATION No. 5204

........2......Manuals and Pedals
Compass of Manuals, CC to ..04.—..61.. Notes
Compass of Pedals, CCC to ....G..—..32.. Notes

No.	NAME OF STOP		Tone	Material	Pi

Electro-pneumatic action.
Detached console.
Electric blower and current generator

Rebuilt from Lebanon organ.

GREAT ORGAN

1	Open Diapason	8'		58 Pipes
2	Gamba	8'	Revoice Dulc.	58 "
3	Melodia	8'		58 "
4	Principal	4'		58 "
5	Flute	4'		58 "
6	Fifteenth	2'		58 "

SWELL ORGAN

7	Open Diapason	8'	46 Pipes
8	Salicional	8'	58 "
9	Vox Celeste	8'	46 "
10	Stopped Diapason	8'	58 "
11	Flute Harmonique	4'	58 "
12	Piccolo	2'	58 "
13	Oboe	8'	46 "
14	Vox Humana (New)	8'	58 "
15	Chimes (New)		20 Tubes

PEDAL ORGAN

16	Bourdon	16'	30 Pipes
17	FLUTE	8'	30 Notes

COUPLERS

1 Great to Pedal
2 Swell to Pedal
3 Swell to Great 8'
4 Swell to Great 4'
5 Swell to Great 16'
6 Swell to Swell 4'
7 Swell to Swell 16'
8 Great to Great 4'

PISTON COMBINATIONS

Four pistons operating Great and Pedals
Four pistons operating Swell and Pedals

ACCESSORIES

1 Tremulant
2 Grand Crescendo Pedal
3 Great to Pedal, reversible
4 Crescendo Indicator
5 Balanced Expression Pedal

Tuba tablet in console Great also tablet for Doppel Flute

To Chester Amusement Co., Inc.

103d Street & Broadway

New York City

1.— We propose to build for you and erect in ...Essex Theatre, Broadway........
...& 103d Street, New York City.....................a pipe organ, in accordance with
the annexed specification, complete and ready for use on or about the 1st day of....May........192.6
subject, however, to delays from fire, water, strikes, or causes not within our control.

2.— We warrant that said completed organ shall be free from defects in either material or workmanship, and undertake to replace or repair any such defective parts at our own expense during the term of one year after the completion of said instrument upon written notice thereof. This warranty does not include tuning, regulating, or care of said instrument.

3.— Your acceptance of this will constitute a contract, and we will proceed with the building of said organ and to construct and erect the same, and you agree to accept the completed instrument and pay therefor the sum of Three thousand two hundred fifty Dollars as follows:
Upon the acceptance of this proposal the sum of....Fifteen hundred.....Dollars.
On presentation of bill of lading or other evidence of shipment of the organ or principal parts thereof the sum of...one thousand........Dollars. Balance $750.00 30 days after complete
In the event that the said organ be ready for shipment and the buildings are not ready to receive it, there shall become due and payable (within thirty days after notice has been given to you that the said organ is ready for delivery and installation) an additional sum on account which will bring the total payments to............per cent of the purchase price.
Upon the complete installation of said organ, the balance of said purchase price will be paid by you.

4.— Immediately upon the complete installation of the said organ you will with and in the presence of our representative examine said organ, and if in accord with this contract will then give acceptance of the same.

5.— You agree to provide the proper space and floor therein for the said organ, also to furnish a suitable room or enclosure for the organ blower, and the necessary galvanized metal piping to convey the organ wind from the blower to the organ and console, constructed and installed in accordance with our directions. You further agree to have the motor and generator wired and to provide the required switches, to furnish and install iron conduits for organ cables and wires, if demanded by local conditions, and to supply light, heat, and power during the period of the organ installation, if and when needed. You also agree to pay all freight and drayage on the organ, and parts thereof, as well as hoisting charges if any.

6.— You agree to assume all responsibility for said organ and parts thereof, covering loss or damage, from the time the said organ or parts thereof have been delivered to a common carrier, and will, until the above-mentioned purchase price is fully satisfied, keep the said organ and parts thereof fully insured against any and all loss or damage, such insurance to protect both parties hereto as their interests may appear and be established.

7.— You will execute and deliver such other and further papers herein as may be proper or necessary to give full, legal force and protection to us in said State where such instrument is or is to be installed.

8.— That said instrument is to be and remain personal property, and the title to and ownership thereof shall continue to vest in us until such time as the contract price shall be fully paid in cash or its equivalent.

9.— It is mutually agreed that in the event you shall fail to comply with the terms of this contract, or any of them, that all sums herein paid to us shall at our election be considered and treated as liquidated damages for the breach hereof, and we shall have the right to remove and take to ourselves said organ or portion thereof wheresoever the same may be.

10.— It is agreed that there are no verbal or other agreements or representations except as contained herein, and the same and any changes whatsoever must be in writing and signed by us.

DATE: Mar. 10, 1926   REUBEN MIDMER & SON
                                                           MIDMER-LOSH
                                                              INCORPORATED

ACCEPTED:

_____   WITNESS:

_____   _____

                                          _____

Early Midmer advertising was plain and conservative such as this example in the February 1915 Diapason. The firm built no instruments for theatres until after the Losh brothers assumed control in 1920.

*This ad in the January 1927 Diapason
stressed the merits of seven-octave manuals.
Seibert Losh thought this was a tremendous
advance in the art of organ building but few
organists seemed to think so.*

*3/10 console in the Cove Theatre, Glen Cove, New York.
Typical of many Midmer-Losh theatre instruments, it had a
seven-octave lower manual, slightly curved stoprails and
very limited unification. Above, part of the orchestral division. From left to right are the tuba, gamba, gamba celeste
and flute celeste.*

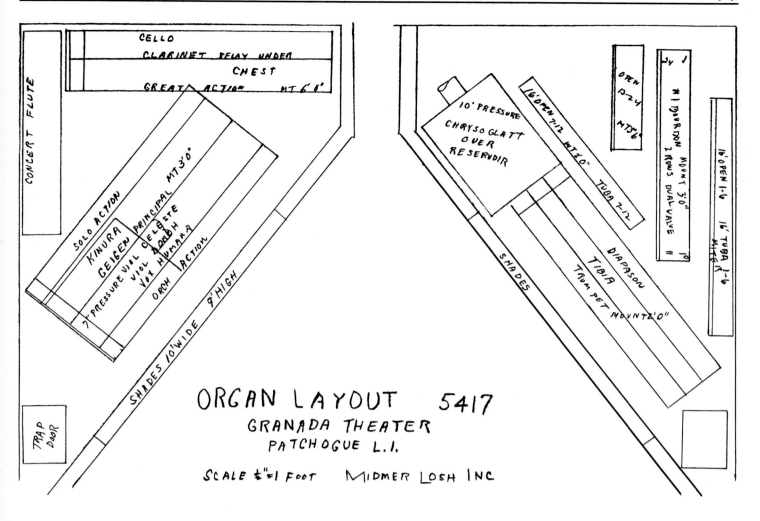

ORGAN LAYOUT 5417
GRANADA THEATER
PATCHOGUE L.I.

SCALE ¼"=1 FOOT   MIDMER LOSH INC

This sketch of one of the last Midmer-Losh theatre installations illustrates the almost haphazard planning by the firm. Layouts of most other builders were considerably more detailed. Perhaps Midmer-Losh organs weren't pre-erected at the factory, in which case an elaborate plan would be unnecessary.

This ad appeared in the March 1929 Diapason shortly before the contract was let for Atlantic City's Convention Hall. Midmer-Losh ads continued to be rather plain even after they received the contract to construct the world's largest organ. The firm stopped advertising nationally in April 1932.

ATLANTIC CITY! The very words bring a chill of excitement to organ enthusiasts eveywhere. To most of the population, Atlantic City conjures images of the Boardwalk, Miss America pageants or possibly the gambling casinos. But to diehard organ buffs Atlantic City will be forever remembered as the location of the largest organ ever built. And were it not for this instrument, the name Midmer-Losh would undoubtedly long since have passed into relative obscurity.

Where does one begin to tell about the world's largest organ? An entire book could easily be devoted to it and someday it should be. Within the scope of the present volume, however, only a few highlights can be touched upon. Let's begin with some rhetoric by one of the all-time great organ promoters, Seibert Losh. These remarks were contained in a booklet entitled *Under the Sassafras Tree* published by Midmer-Losh in 1930 when the Atlantic City organ was about a third completed. Don't forget what Senator Richards said earlier about Mr. Losh! Most of the following statements are factual, however:

The Convention Hall Organ

 MERSON L. RICHARDS, architect of the Convention Hall organ for the city of Atlantic City, widely experienced in the design of a great variety of instruments including some of the most distinguished in America, has acted as consultant in many cases where he was not employed officially. With five organs for his home, including various enlargements and rebuilds, he was able to perform considerable experiment and development of original character, at his own expense. Instruments of his design have been constructed by eight or ten different builders, but three of the most notable ones have been constructed by the Midmer-Losh Company, and it is fair to state at this time that architect Richards has never been interested financially, directly or indirectly, in the Midmer-Losh Company, or any other organ company, and that he has carefully preserved a disinterested and unbiased position.

Many notable improvements have been introduced in the past 20 years under his direction. For instance, in 1910 a small organ was built in the Methodist Church in Pleasantville, N. J., under his supervision, which embodied the very first octave duplex, this being a tubular organ. In the High School organ in Atlantic City, he pioneered the introduction of Schulze type Diapasons and the redevelopment of the Mixture with its allied idea, the derived harmonics.

Senator Richards has personally examined the organs of England and other European countries and has investigated the details of construction, and the factory facilities of the principal American builders and may be considered a leading world authority in organ design and well qualified to design this, the world's greatest musical instrument. This organ will undoubtedly set a mark in size and completeness for the next 100 years.

Engineering Detail

Much uncertainty and confusion still exists about acoustical matters and with all the progress of science, no one has been able to precisely predict the acoustic results in a given auditorium before it is actually completed. A few rules are safe guides. The one immutable law that the intensity of the sound is inversely proportional to the square of the distance, cannot be violated, and this seven-acre space of the auditorium calls for volume and intensity of tone never before required, the furthest portions of the auditorium being 500 feet from the instrument.

The hall is equipped with a public address system with a capacity of 28 times the natural tone, but the organ is intended to have an adequate volume without the amplification system and the necessary distortion of amplified sound.

Elaborate preliminary tests were made and the organ was built sectionally with careful tests as the work progressed, both with the auditorium empty and in service. It has been found necessary to provide a tone approximately six times more powerful than any other existing pipe organ. This is evidenced not only in the horse power employed and the scale of the pipes and wind pressure, but with many other special methods to give a greater rigidity to the pipes and to give a better control of the highly energized wind stream.

Step-down regulators are not employed in the blower rooms to eliminate the noise of the fans and to conceal the noisy valves, but the regulators were located in the arched trusses immediately adjacent to the organ chamber and delivered to the pipes with a single regulation utilizing all of the original energy to blow the pipes.

The Brass Chorus was the first department constructed, a tonal department complete in itself and as designed by architect Richards a highly original and immensely effective division. This includes not only the usual octave and harmonic intervals but the unique interval of the Fifth which architect Richards had discovered and proved to be a practical and natural interval of the Chorus Reeds. The harmonic intervals of this Brass Chorus are undoubtedly more powerful than any similar harmonic intervals previously produced in any instrument and are frankly aimed at a tremendous power and brilliancy.

The String Organ No. 2 includes thirty ranks of pipes, ranging in tone from a Geigen quality to exceedingly slim scale string, reinforced with octave and mixture intervals, also with a Gedeckt 8', and a Flute Twelfth, and fattened with a new Chorus Reed called Reed String, highly suggestive of large Gamba tone but adding a meaty richness to the ensemble.

This String Organ was the first of the departments to be enclosed in the new type of aluminum swell shades originated and designed in and for this Atlantic City organ. The lightness of these shades permits a speed and accent in expression not approached by any other method or material.

When opened these shades do not obstruct the passage of the sound as they consist of two blades of metal built on blocks, permitting the sound to travel between the blades as well as between the shades, and practically no wood is used in the construction, thus there is no absorption of tone by that material.

This division is equipped with Pizzicato and with the regular couplers as well as the Melody Couplers which the Midmer-Losh Company pioneered in America, and these special couplers make this department sing with a balanced and brilliant tone impossible with the ordinary couplers.

The Echo Organ is a department of thirty sets of pipes with some voices extended to provide an ensemble of fifty stops. This department is on 15" wind, except two strings and one reed, which are on 25", and includes a 32' Violone with double languids. It also includes a number of stops never before used in this country, such as Tibia Mollis, Flute Sylvestris, German Bassoon, and a Tuba with wooden barrels throughout.

The Chorus of Flutes is a classification of a dozen Flute stops, mostly harmonic and double languid, on very high pressure to furnish a fundamental quality as required, enclosed in a department by themselves and fully developed with all mutation.

The big stop of this division is a Jubal Flute of very large scale, harmonic and double languid, with an intensity and brilliance of tone never attempted in any other organ flutes.

The Diapason Chorus in the opposite gallery comprises a division of double languid Diapasons of very large scale complete with harmonic corroboration, providing the dominant organ voice of the Gallery Organs. These Diapasons are undoubtedly the most powerful and brilliant ever voiced and at the same time have a ringing sweetness startlingly beautiful to the visitor at the first hearing. This is radically different from the usual loud Diapason which is commonly a rather hideous tone quality, the character being sacrificed to secure the necessary volume.

These Diapasons are all harmoniously beautiful and compare in quality with any low pressure Diapasons of moderate scale. The secret of this brilliant beauty lies in the application of the so-called double languid or rather "truss languid" in the new method developed by Midmer-Losh, which permits a low cut mouth and resulting brilliancy of tone even in pipes of the largest scale.

The masterly work of Henry Vincent Willis, son of the inventor of double languid pipes, in this department, will place his name in the hall of fame with his famous father and grandfather.

In the vault above this department is the FANFARE ORGAN and the STRING ORGAN No. 3.

The Fanfare consists basically of a Chorus of Flutes and a Chorus of mighty reeds, many of them of special design and volume and brilliancy and with pressures far in excess of previous practice.

The favorable position of this department and the extraordinary treatment, pours a volume of tone from its elevated position of grandeur and thrilling brilliancy sufficient to lift an audience to its feet. As a dominating leading note for a hymn tune in a great religious convention nothing so inspiring could be conceived, and the general utility of the department is evident.

One notable feature of this section is the most powerful and brilliant Mixture ever voiced, in reality a complete Diapason Chorus of Seven ranks of pipes, or extraordinary large scale with flared resonators and on 35" wind pressure. A chorus of most powerful and specially designed reeds on 50" pressure provide a clang of brass of overpowering grandeur.

String Organ No. 3 in this same ceiling vault chamber consists of twenty ranks of strings of the more conventional type planned to provide accompanimental material for the Echo department and, as the milder ensemble of Strings, effects of great delicacy and beauty are obtainable from this department. The reinforcing Reed of this section is an English Horn and several of the Solo Strings are of highly special construction and character but relatively mildly voiced.

The Solo Reed Voices in a gallery chamber adjoining the Diapason is a division of solo reed voices,—Saxophones, Clarinets, Euphone, Egyptian Bazu, Musette, and a bold Brass Trumpet, and several other voices which provide a surprisingly effective ensemble of reed tone, blending unexpectedly with the Diapasons in the adjoining chamber and providing characteristic solo voices near the audience where they will be heard with all their bloom and beauty.

Enclosed Choir Organ. The gallery chamber in the corner of the room next the large chambers is devoted to the Enclosed Choir organ, a department of 30 sets, with selected extension to 50 registers, —a part of the main organ ensemble, but by reason of its special location provides some of the special effects belonging to the Gallery divisions.

This department contains the softest stops of the organ,—a Dulciana which is about the proportion tonally of a well developed Violin Diapason as commonly found in Church organs. This is a fair key to the problem of an adequate volume for this tremendous place.

The specifications of the Enclosed Choir follow conventional lines but also include a set of healthy Chorus Reeds of a newly designed Tromba type, highly valuable as a solo voice as well as ensemble.

Mechanical Details

The Gallery Organs are powered by two 40 h.p. Kinetic blowers located in the basement on each side of the auditorium and one 50 h.p. Allen Air Appliance blower, operated at 3500 r.p.m., supplying 100" pressure. This blower is located under the stage and the wind is delivered through a 12" galvanized pipe, 450 feet long. The requirements of the two 100" stops supplied would require only 2½" pipe but the large pipe is used to permit the cooling effect of its area and the expansion, so that the wind is delivered to the pipes very nearly

at normal temperature. This Allen blower is a centrifugal blower with a machined cast iron casing with cast and machined aluminum blades on 32nd inch clearance. This small clearance provides not only a greater efficiency, but delivers the wind in a relatively cool condition as the amount of wind slippage is very small. This is the first employment of this type of blower for organ work.

The Kinetic blowers are of special design with inbuilt screens of steel wool saturated with oil, for the removal of atmospheric dust, after the design of Seibert Losh. This screen also prevents the fan sounds escaping into the blower pipe, and tends to cool and stabilize the wind. These Kinetic blowers are used on all pressures up to and including 50". The gallery organs alone consume the entire potential of 130 h.p., and the main organ chambers are provided with 210 h.p. additional.

The magnets of this instrument are special designed and varied somewhat to suit the purposes of the widely varied pressures. The magnets provided to exhaust the larger valves are a new pattern with inbuilt primary so that the armature is of the smallest dimensions and with the slightest motion. The magnets are all high resistance and the stop action magnets and other continuous duty material as well as most of the low pressure magnets are 400 ohms resistance, so that the amount of current consumed is moderate, considering the size of the organ.

The cables of the organ are made to special specification, of tinned enameled wire. Braided cable is used throughout the job, with beeswax saturation.

All contacts are genuine silver in both members, and the relay contacts are contained in a large wind chest accessible to the tuner while the wind is on the organ. so that they can be examined and regulated while working.

The consoles are all-electric and the specially designed stop keys are operated by a special Riesner magnet mechanism which cuts off the impulse to the registers not to be actuated by the pistons.

The wind regulators in this organ are not of the bellows type, contain no leather, and are not dependent upon glue. They are diaphragmatic, positive and silent in action, and are a development of the standard type employed by the Midmer-Losh company for the past 10 years, being singularly adaptable to the unusual conditions and the extraordinary high pressures employed in this organ. Practically none of them are located in the organ chambers where they would form an obstruction and tend to absorb tone.

Under the high pressures employed, a long wind pipe to the chest, if of sufficient size, is no disadvantage as the power of the wind has a favorable ratio to its inertia when high pressures are employed.

The first set of specifications for the Convention Hall organ was let out for bids in late 1928. Three firms (but not Midmer-Losh) submitted bids, all of which far exceeded the $300,000 appropriation voted by the city council. After modifications to the specifications such as reducing the number of ranks and reducing the number of general pistons from 54 to _only_ 36 (!) bids were again sought. Midmer-Losh was the lowest of three bidders (at $347,200) and this bid was accepted. The original specifications included 297 stops and called for two consoles of five and six manuals, respectively.[14] Subsequent contracts increased the number of manuals in the main console to seven and the number of stops to 320, for a total of 452 ranks of pipes controlled by 1,240 stop keys on the main console.

After working on the Convention Hall project for a

couple of years Seibert Losh began to be more vocal in disagreements with Senator Richards. At one point Losh called on Atlantic City Mayor Anthony Ruffu to complain about Richards' philosophies. This was the last straw for Richards and he issued an order barring Losh from Convention Hall. This order was enforced by Convention Hall guards and Losh became so despondent that he left his firm in 1931 before the completion of his magnum opus[15] and joined the Wicks Organ Company. He died three years later at only 53 years of age.[16] The Midmer-Losh presidency was assumed by Otto Strack in 1931 following Seibert Losh's departure. Strack was a wealthy architect and engineer who lived in a penthouse apartment atop a New York skyscraper he had designed and built. Seibert Losh sold Strack an organ for this apartment in 1921 and in 1925 Strack designed the new Midmer-Losh factory building in Merrick. In his earlier days he had been chief engineer for the American Bridge Company[17] and earlier still had been the architect for the Pabst Theatre in Milwaukee, Wisconsin. This theatre is

interesting in organ history because it contained the fourth organ ever installed in an American theatre, a 4/43 Farrand & Votey.

The Atlantic City organ was completed mechanically in mid-1932. The project had nearly, but not quite, bankrupted the Midmer-Losh company, and Senator Richards tried unsuccessfully to get a further appropriation from the city to complete the tonal finishing.[18] Otto Strack died in 1935 at the age of 78, leaving control of the firm to George Losh. In 1938 Losh officially dissolved the corporation and the bank foreclosed the mortgage on their Merrick factory. Fortunately, Losh was able to rent back about one ninth of it to continue the business along with long time employees William Voris and James Light. In 1958 Mr. Losh went into partnership with James Campagnone who had joined the firm in 1953. George Losh retired in 1973 and died in 1975 at the age of 83.[19] [20] After the death of Mr. Campagnone the Midmer-Losh firm was acquired by W. F. Benzeno, Inc. and remains in the organ business today.[21]

This beautiful and elegant console controlled all 452 ranks of the Convention Hall organ but had only half as many stops as the main seven-manual console. It has been disconnected and now reposes in storage in a corner of the organ shop behind the right main chamber.

Mammoth console of the world's largest organ. The decorative kiosk which forms the console case was designed by Otto Strack. The entire area above the stoprails is acoustically transparent grillework so no sound is impeded in reaching the organist.

CONTRACT FOR 5&7/452 MIDMER-LOSH ORGAN, OPUS 5550 Convention Hall, Atlantic City, New Jersey

On this and the following three pages are reproduced excerpts from the contract for the world's largest organ. Note the many specific and stringent conditions imposed by organ architect Emerson Richards. Few organ contracts contain such specifics but, then, few organs compare to the Atlantic City behemoth! It is obvious that Senator Richards was extremely well versed in the esoterics of organ building. Furthermore, his legal background allowed him to express many otherwise tenuous and indefinite concepts in clear English. He knew exactly what he wanted—and he got it!

The Specifications

These specifications, together with the invitation to bidders and other chapters of the contract, cover all the labor and material and accessories necessary for the complete construction ready to play of a tonally satisfactory concert pipe organ of the highest grade, suitable at all times to command and fill the Convention Hall Auditorium under all conditions.

The drawings of the construction architects, Lockwood, Greene & Company, relative to the details of the building when made to scale are approximate only and are not to be considered as relieving the contractor of the necessity of making his own measurements on the site of the work.

The contractor must bring upon the work a suitable voicing machine and complete the voicing and regulation of each stop or voice in the auditorium under which it will be required to play of speak. The architect shall have the right to reject or condemn any part of the work or any voicing or any stop or voice which, in his opinion, is inadequate or unsatisfactory or does not produce the effect desired, and the contractor shall replace the work or voice in a manner satisfactory to the architect. The voicers and finishers must be artists of experience and ability, and when required the contractor must submit the names and other data that may be required of the ability and experience of the voicers who are to voice the pipe work, and the architect must be assured to his own satisfaction that the men so employed are satisfactory.

If the rate of progress is not such as to insure completion of each stage of the work within the time agreed to by the contractor, the architect shall have the right to order the contractor to employ more men or increase his facilities so as to complete the work in the time specified, time being of the essence of the contract. Upon the completion of the permanent work, the contractor shall remove from the site all materials, debris and temporary construction not forming a part of the permanent construction of the organ.

GENERAL LAY-OUT

Paragraph 1. The contractor shall, within twenty (20) working days after the execution of the contract, submit for the approval of the architect scale drawings of the lay-out of the organ. Great care must be taken to so lay out the organ that every division shall have the freest opportunity to speak. The lay-out when approved shall not be changed, except with the consent of the architect; provided, however, that the architect may, if acoustical or other conditions seem in his judgment to demand it, require the contractor during the course of the work to alter or change the lay-out in order to improve conditions. The detailed drawings must consist of both floor and elevation and sectional plans. No work is to proceed until the lay-out is approved.

Paragraph 8. The contractor will be required to locate and connect his blowing apparatus in the respective blower rooms with the main feed lines and also to connect the same with the blower pipes already in position. He will likewise be required to connect his wind supply in the organ chambers with the conductor pipes entering therein. The contractor will use the cable conduits already installed for the running of all cables between the console and the organ chambers.

Paragraph 9. The contractor must examine the conductor and conduit pipes before submitting his bid, and if he finds them unsuitable in any particular, must so inform the architect at least forty-eight hours before the bids are to be opened; otherwise, if, after submitting his bid, the contractor should discover that either the conduits or conductors are either insufficient or improperly located or inadequate he will be compelled to run any additional conductors or conduits required for the completion of the work at his own cost and expense.

Paragraph 10. The work will be concealed behind open grills in the case of all eight chambers. The grills and general ornamentation will be supplied by the general contractor. No case work or display pipes will be required from the organ contractor.

FRAMING

Paragraph 1. The framing of the main divisions of the organ located in chambers Nos. 1 and 2 shall be made of steel or iron girders, angles and posts so as to support the main chests in a solid and substantial manner according to the detailed drawings to be submitted by the contractor and approved by the architect. Subsidiary framing and the framing in chambers Nos. 5 and 6, 7, 8, 9 and 10 shall be of heavy well seasoned white oak, North Carolina long-left yellow pine, or Douglas fir, free from knots, checks, sap or other imperfections.

WIND SUPPLY

Paragraph 1. Each blower chamber shall be equipped with one or more centrifugal fan blowers of the type manufactures by the Organ Power Company of Hartford, Connecticut, or the Kinetic Engineering Company of Philadelphia, Pennsylvania, to be approved by the architect to generate the wind supply for the organ. Since high and low pressure wind will be required, more than one blower must be provided in each room. The blowers must be equipped with approved air filters and humidifying devices. They must be located on substantial foundations, free from noise or vibration, and equipped with reservoirs to prevent noise reaching the organ chambers. They must be equipped with approved remote control starting switches and such remote controls must be run to the organ console platform. The contractor must provide approved key switches for the operation of the remote controls.*

Paragraph 2. All wind conductors in the organ shall be made of metal, either of copper or heavy gauge galvanized iron, to be fitted in all cases with wooden collars faced with leather and to be screwed to the parts to be supplied. The collars are to be fitted to the pipe in such manner as to make a thoroughly wind-tight connection. Wick and glue joints will not be permitted.

Paragraph 3. The wind supply to all parts of the organ must be perfectly tight and noiseless. Wind leakage will not be permitted. Wherever a wind joint is made, the parts shall be leathered and joined with suitable screws arranged with expansion springs and washers on the screw heads in order to keep the joint under tension at all times. All joints and connections must be made in the manner described above and to the approval of the architect, and so arranged that they may be dismantled without injury to the parts to which they are attached.

Paragraph 4. The main feed wires and switches have been run by the general contractors to the blower rooms. All connections thereto must be made by the contractor. The contractor must inspect the electrical supply provided and if inadequate shall notify the architect forty-eight hours before presenting his bid.

---

*A single blowing plant may be substituted for that specified by the architect, subject to his approval and the procuring of a suitable site in the basement, but the cost of running the additional conductor pipes must be borne by the contractor.

Paragraph 5. In the case of the high pressure blowers, the contractor must be prepared to provide means to cool the compressed air should it be found that the conductor run in insufficient for this purpose.

Paragraph 6. The wind supply for all divisions of the organ must be entirely adequate so that there is no fall from the designed pressure under any conditions. There must be no robbing or dropping of the pitch in any voice or division under any circumstances. A perfectly steady, copious supply of wind will be required. The wind pressures designated will be required at the languid of the pipe and not in the chest. Consequently the chest valves and the pipe toe openings must be of such size as to admit of a full supply of wind at the pressure designated reaching the speaking parts of the pipe, so that there shall be a copious supply of wind at the pressure designated at all times controlling the speaking of the pipe. Attention is called to the fact that double languid pipes require an especially copious supply of wind and that the chests must be made accordingly.

WOOD WORK

Paragraph 7. All of the wood used in this organ shall be of the best quality, free from the slightest imperfection. The chests shall be made of genuine white pine or hardwood or other approved material; the swell boxes of approved material. All wood must be absolutely free from knots, checks, sap or other imperfections. It must be thoroughly planed and sanded to a smooth finish. Wherever worked, all tool marks must be eradicated.

Paragraph 8. All wood work must be protected by waterproof covering of genuine shellac, pyroxilin, lacquer, first-class varnish, or other approved protective coating to the number of coats or degree directed by the architect and applied in a suitable and workmanlike manner. This shall apply to all interior parts as well as exterior parts and particularly to the interiors of the wind chests, reservoirs, swell boxes or other organ parts.

Paragraph 9. All action parts containing borings or grooves adjacent to each other three inches or less of ingrain, shall be thoroughly saturated by dipping in silicate of soda, genuine shellac, or other suitable approved sealing compound. All glueing is to be done with the best animal glue, under suitable compression, and with the materials heated as well as the glue. Fish glue, casein and other substitutes are forbidden. All other exterior parts, whether of wood or metal, are to be suitably painted, including conductor pipes in the organ or blower chambers.

Paragraph 10. The attention of the contractor is called to the fact that this organ will stand within 400 feet of the Atlantic Ocean, under conditions where there may be sudden changes in temperature of very considerable extent and where there may be excessive humidity or at other times excessive dryness. For this reason all parts must be so painted or treated as to be impervious to weather conditions incident to the site of the work, and to afford permanent protection from the actions of the elements.

SWELL BOXES AND REGULATORS

Paragraph 11. The swell boxes in the main chambers shall be of ample size as approved by the architect. Swell boxes Nos. 1, 2, 5, and 7 shall not be less than twenty feet in height. Swell boxes Nos. 3, 4 and 6 shall not be less than twelve feet in height. The boxes shall be suitably framed and the walls thereof shall be constructed either of wood paneling or other approved material of a total thickness of not less than three inches. The swell shades shall be not less than two and one-quarter inches thick to cover the entire front of the swell boxes with such additional shades upon the side or top as the architect may direct.

Paragraph 12. All swell shades shall be actuated by individual motors and shall be graduated in size so that those first opening shall be of comparatively small size, while those last opening shall be of large size presenting the minimum amount of obstruction to the egress of sound. All shades shall close tightly, be equipped with proper felting, be mounted upon suitable bearings, and equipped with a recoil mechanism to prevent slamming when the shades are closed suddenly. The construction of the swell boxes and their operation must be such as to provide a dampening of the total volume of sound enclosed at least 50 per cent. The contractor will be held responsible for the results obtained.

Paragraph 13. The regulators shall be made of approved wood and leather, shall be of a spring type and operated with a positive valve, so that the regulator will function properly under all conditions. The tremolo mechanism shall be approved by the architect.

PIPE WORK

Paragraph 14. All wood pipes under four feet in length are to have at least hardwood fronts and backs and all other wooden pipes, except where made entirely of hardwood, are to have their mouths and the facings of their languids and caps made of straight grained mahogany. All pipe wood must be clear of even the slightest imperfections and must be suitably varnished or shellaced on the outside and coated on the inside with either shellac or animal glue sizing properly applied and free from surplus accumulations.

Paragraph 15. The thickness of the pipe walls must be such as to properly withstand vibration according to the pressures employed. All thicknesses must be approved by the architect, and if brought on the job without his approval, will be subject to instant rejection. The workmanship and finish of all pipe work must be in accordance with the highest standards of the art, subject to the complete satisfaction and approval of the architect. All bass pipes must be voiced upon a voicing machine and means adopted to properly regulate the position of the lips, caps and languids. The smaller pipes are to be constructed with approved metal feet for purposes of regulation. Bass pipes are to be supplied with proper valves in the feet for regulation. All pipes must be provided with sliding tuners. Metal shades will not be permitted.

Paragraph 16. In the case of high pressure pipes of either wood or metal, means must be provided to prevent the smaller pipes from blowing out of the holes, and in all cases the pipe feet must fit in the top boards in such manner that there will be no wind leakage. Rack boards must be bored perfectly true and pipes placed in perpendicular position in all cases in regular rows, according to the best practice in the art. All pipes of either wood or metal over four feet in length must be stayed or otherwise supported.

Metal Pipes

Paragraph 17. Metal pipes shall be of the materials specified. The alloy for the diapasons and other stops where "metal" is specified shall consist of pure tin and lead containing at least 30 per cent of tin. Spotted metal shall consist of an alloy of pure tin and lead, free of other injurious metals, and containing at least 45 per cent tin. Tin pipes shall be at least 90 per cent pure tin. All metal pipes and reed resonators shall be equipped with metal slide tuners sprung tightly around the pipes, free from rattle, and where necessary, insulated with proper deadening material. No coneing will be permitted.

Paragraph 18. All pipes four feet or under shall be made of the material specified. Basses over four feet in length may be made of zinc of proper thickness. The thickness of the metal shall in all cases be subject to the approval of the architect, and where he shall deem the metal walls too thin, heavier pipes must be provided. In the case of the diapasons, all pipes standing on 8-inch wind or less must weigh an average of 180 pounds from tenor C to the top note for a 40-scale diapason; pipe work on wind pressure between 8 inches and 20 inches, at least 230 pounds from tenor C to the top note; between 20 inches and 40 inches, at least 280 pounds from tenor C to the top note. The weight of the basses shall be in proportion. The above weights shall not apply to the string toned pipes, the weights of which will be determined by the architect; or to any pipes of extraordinary or special construction or which stand upon especially heavy wind pressures.

Paragraph 19. The foregoing shall apply in general to both wood and metal resonators of the reeds. All chorus reeds shall be constructed with a mitered hood. All metal reed resonators shall be loaded with true organ metal or extra heavy Moyt metal bells. The bells in the 32' octaves shall be loaded at least one-fifth of the length; in the 16' octaves, one-third of the length, and so in proportion. Organ metal will be required in all resonators above 1' c. Reed blocks shall be accurately machined, and escholots made of heavy brass securely and firmly anchored in the block. The reeds shall be firmly anchored in place by a method satisfactory to the architect. Wooden wedges subject to shrinkage will not be allowed. Leathering of escholots will only be allowed under exceptional circumstances and with the express approval of the architect. Tuning wires must be of exceptionally heavy material and so arranged and supported that there will be no spring left in the wire to cause derangements in the tuning or regulating. Reed boots must be of ample size. Wooden reed boots will be permitted. In the case of 32' and 64' reeds, wooden boots with removable panels will be required. Weights when attached to the reeds must be screwed and locked in place. No sweating or soldering will be allowed.

Paragraph 20. Where harmonic bridges are inserted in either wooden or metal pipes, the bridges must be of straight grained mahogany or similar hardwood or metal, accurately placed by means of projecting ears and screwed in place after being properly set so that they cannot move from the prescribed position. In the case of double languid flue pipes, special directions for the construction, manipulation and voicing will be supplied by the architect.

Paragraph 21. The workmanship on all pipes of either wood or metal must be of the highest quality known to the art and all inferior material will be summarily rejected and must be removed from the job and not returned thereto under any circumstances. The voicing in all cases shall be the responsibility of the contractor. Every pipe must speak with the greatest promptness, free from windiness, chirp, or any defect or deficiency in its speech or attack. All of the reeds must speak very promptly. (This must be specially true of the 32' and 64' voices. It necessary motors to start and stop the reeds must be supplied for the 32' and 64' voices.) The architect will describe the effect to be obtained and the contractor will be obliged to obtain this effect, and hereby warrants that there is nothing in the specification or indicated therein that cannot, in the present state of the art, be produced. The specifications will contain further descriptions of the special tonal qualities required, but shall not be final and conclusive. Additional details in each case and covering each voice will be supplied by the architect from time to time as the work progresses.

THE ACTION

Paragraph 22. The action shall be of the electro-pneumatic type. It must be perfect in operation, giving instantaneous attack and rapid repetition.

Paragraph 23. The chests shall have individual valves operated by individual pneumatics. The primaries are to be built integral with the chests without requiring tubing from the magnets or primaries. The action design must not include sliding wooden parts or other parts which might become bound or loose by expansion or contraction of the wood, due to atmospheric conditions. All screws or other metal fittings for demountable parts shall be of brass. This shall apply to the entire organ as well as the chests. The electric action shall be supplied to all parts of the organ. No basses shall be operated by tubing from the main action, but shall be supplied from their own switches and magnets. No lead, paper or rubber tubing shall be used in any part of the organ. All pneumatic material shall be of the finest grade leather of suitable and adequate strength for the pressures specified. Pneumatic leathers are to be submitted for a chemical test and to be free of acid or other latent harmful ingredients which might become active through the action of light, dampness or other condition. All pneumatic or other glueing in the chests or action parts to be of the best animal glue, with materials heated as well as the glue, and under suitable compression. Fish glue and other substitutes are forbidden.

Paragraph 24. The chests shall be so constructed as to supply an adequate and copious supply of wind to the pipe work. The valve ports and valves leading to the pipe feet must be of ample size and capacity. The valves or ports must not be obstructed by action parts so as to cause eddies in the wind supply or initial vacuums in the attack. The chests under the valve ports shall be not less than nine inches deep, inside measurement, and must be so arranged as to prevent robbing or other undesirable conditions in the wind supply to the pipes. All voices where the scale is No. 50 or larger (or its equivalent in the case of wood pipes or reeds), shall have the bass pipes mounted on separate bass chests. The chests must be so laid out as to give every pipe ample speaking room without interference, shading or sympathy between adjacent ranks.

Paragraph 25. The lay-out of the chests, position of walk boards and other details must be submitted to the architect in the form of drawings by the contractor and approved by him before construction is started. Access to the various chests and divisions shall be by suitable stairs and platforms, and not by ladders or walking over bass pipes.

Paragraph 26. The chests shall be generally constructed of hardwood and all materials must be first approved by the architect. Not more than eight voices may be planted upon any one chest or operated by one primary. Unduly large chests will not be permitted.

Paragraph 27. The magnets used in the entire action must be of high resistance, 150 ohms or more, to be made of enamelled wire with paper or other insulation in between the wrappings, to be thoroughly waterproof and covered with a waterproof covering on each spool; the cores to be of the best soft iron without residual magnetism, and the armatures rendered soundless by approved methods. The

magnet covers to be thoroughly air-tight, and the armatures to be of soft iron plated with a noncorroding material. The base to be made of a noncorroding material. No brass will be permitted. German silver, aluminum alloy or other composition proof against corrosion will be required. The magnet is to be a complete assembled unit attached by screws and must not be driven into prepared holes. The magnet must be arranged to be easily demounted and its operating parts must be externally accessible for inspection, adjustment and repair. The high pressure magnets may deviate from these requirements as may become necessary, with the special approval of the architect. The exceptionally high pressures involved may be treated in a special manner by the contractor, with the approval of the architect; but all action parts, and particularly all magnets and magnet parts, the method of mounting and the assembly, must be of the highest grade and applied in the best manner known to the art.

All buss bars shall be of German silver or other noncorroding conducting metal, and all contacts to be of silver of a percentage of not less than 77 per cent. This includes all relay and coupler contacts, or wherever an electric connection or contact is to be made. All connections must be soldered and the soldering washed off with alcohol and shellaced. No binding screws will be allowed.

Paragraph 28. All wires throughout the organ are to be tinned and enamelled and protected with at least two coats of cotton insulation on each wire, and the cables covered with two coats of asbestos covering; the wires to be paraffined individually and the entire cables to be boiled in paraffin and re-paraffined at all joints where the cable is bent after installation. Built-up cables will not be allowed. Where the main cable is not run through metal conduit, it shall first be enclosed in an armored protective covering either of lead or similar material of a type approved by the architect. The main cables will not be run in conduit.

Paragraph 29. Attention is again called to the fact that this organ is located near the Atlantic Ocean and that great care must be taken because of the corrosive action of salt air to protect all parts of the action against corrosion or other damage or against the action of moisture, incident to the location.

Paragraph 30. The action repetition must be faster than the pipes can be made to speak. The wind supply must be so sufficient that when a full major chord is held in the bass, rapid staccato passages can be played in the treble without affecting the bass chord in either pitch or steadiness; and similarly, with the major chord held in the treble staccato chords may be played in the bass without affecting the treble notes in pitch or steadiness.

A project of the scope of the Atlantic City organ requires an enormous team of talented workmen. In most organ installations the crew at the site is responsible only for erecting an instrument which has already been assembled in the builder's factory. At Atlantic City, however, much of the organ was built right in Convention Hall. Some of the team responsible appear in this photograph taken in January of 1930 in front of one of the organ's diaphones. In the back row, from left to right, are H. Lamb, W. Brook, G. Fabry, C. Gould, W. Varneke, F. Gordon and E. Watson. In the center row are B. Allan, J. Zidlick, J. Hanrahan, J. Cameron, H. Breu, C. Dargis and J. Winter. In the front row are Mrs. Henry V. Willis, Seibert Losh, Senator Emerson Richards, Arthur Scott Brook, Henry V. Willis and R. Douglas. Messrs. Richards and Brook are holding one of the reed pipes voiced on 100″ pressure by Mr. Willis.[14]

Senator Richards demonstrates that, despite its enormous size, the Atlantic City console is quite playable. Its 1,240 stops are arranged in a spherical fashion corresponding to the natural arc of an organist's arm.

Console action of the world's largest organ is all electric with all parts readily accessible for service. Note steel framework supporting the manuals, and the enormous crescendo mechanism at the top center of the console. Stop key actions are of Reisner manufacture, as are the stop keys themselves. The mechanism of the console was designed by George Losh and Harry Van Wart, former superintendent of the Steere Organ Company, and was built by Charles T. Sandberg, former superintendent of the Bennett Organ Company.[24]

Each manual and its associated coupler action is individually removable for ease of maintenance.

Gallery I features two of the loudest reeds ever voiced, trumpet mirabilis and tuba maxima. Their resonators are hooded to focus their high intensity sounds directly toward the audience. Note the springs which keep the 100" wind pressure from blowing the pipes right out of their chests.

Part of gallery IV. From left to right are the brass trumpet, major clarinet, euphone and Egyptian horn, all on 25″ wind pressure. With the exception of the major clarinet, these particular stops were supplied and voiced by Anton Gottfried.

Above: one level of the solo division. The fat metal pipes in the foreground are the tibia rex, having double languids and speaking on 30″ wind pressure.

One section of the swell division. In the foregound is the 8-rank cymbal mixture. This one stop contains 640 pipes.

In the foreground above are trumpets of the great division. The relatively innocent looking pipes behind them are perhaps the most powerful ever built: the ophicleide on 100″ pressure. Springs are used to hold the pipes on their chest so they won't be blown off by the high pressure. The treble pipes are constructed like calliope whistles with mouths the entire circumference of the pipes.

The 16′ octave of the ophicleide, left, has wooden resonators held to their boots with turnbuckles. Tuning wires are screwed solidly to their resonators so the intense vibrations won't cause them to move and throw the pipes out of tune. These pipes were voiced by Roscoe Evans who learned his trade in the Wurlitzer factory. After the entire organ was completed, Mr. Evans was its caretaker for twenty years.[22]

Pipework in the great-solo division. Above, left to right, are the clarinet, French horn, saxophone, tibia clausa, English horn, oboe horn and the 16′ full-length octaves of the saxophone, English horn and French horn. Behind the 16′ French horn is low CCCCC of the 64′ diaphone, whose 59′ resonator passes through several chambers. In the photo below, left to right, are the krummhorn, orchestral oboe, orchestral saxophone, 16′ baryton, vox humana and kinura. On the perch board are pipes of the orchestral saxophone and kinura, showing its goosebill shallot.

Wooden pipes of the 32' contra bombarde and 32' contra diaphone are being made in the left main chamber. Note the exceptional thickness of lumber used; these pipes must withstand the intense vibrations produced by 50" wind pressure.

John Zidlick, the man in charge of pipe construction in Convention Hall, stands in front of the heaviest metal pipe ever made. Constructed of zinc 5/16" thick, this pipe measures 24" in diameter, 38½' long and weighs 2,200 pounds. Its unusual construction required a method not usually employed in a pipe shop: the use of a smokestack rolling machine! The eight pipes pictured are the lowest notes of voice #12, the 32' pedal diapason in the left main chamber. This set is voiced on 20" wind pressure and the low CCCC pipe rumbles at only 16 vibrations per second.

Henry Vincent Willis (above) tunes the seven-rank stentor mixture on 35″ wind in the fanfare division. Considering that this is the most powerful mixture ever built, it is amazing that he isn't wearing ear protection! These pipes are constructed with double languids and are flared to be of wider diamter at the tops than at the mouths. Below, tuning the 32′ contra trombone in the fanfare division, mounted in the ceiling at the left center of the auditorium, about 90′ above the main floor. The diaphragm reservoir suppling 35″ wind is mounted above the pipes on the right side.

Above: The fanfare division features a 4' major clarion with its pipes pointed directly at the ceiling grille. This rank is on 50"
wind pressure, as are the reeds behind it, some of which are triple harmonic. Note that reeds here and throughout the organ
are equipped with tuning collars. Organ architect Emerson Richards specified that no pipes could be cone or scroll tuned.
Echo divison (below) is mounted above the ceiling at the right center of the auditorium directly across from the fanfare
division on the opposite side of the building. The echo contains 27 ranks on 15" and 25" pressure and has the effect in the
building of a full swell in an ordinary church organ. Barely visible behind the chimes on the right are some pipes of the 32'
double languid wooden violone which are laid on their sides due to height restrictions. This rank, voice #298, was the first
addition in a series of contracts which expanded the organ after the original contract for 297 stops was signed.

Tuning the gamba tuba in the fanfare division. This incredibly powerful labial stop was invented by William E. Haskell of the Estey company. The examples here speak on 20″ wind pressure. In the foreground is a mutation-pitched tromba of unusual construction.

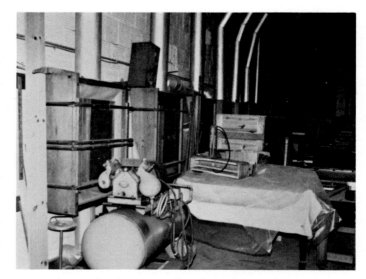

All reservoirs in the organ are of the diaphragm type and are mounted outside the organ chambers. These photos show the reservoirs behind the right main chamber. The one on the wall next to the chamber door is for the 100″ ophicleide. Atop the reservoir is a lever for removing the incredibly heavy springs. The 100″ pressure creates a force of about 3,000 pounds on the reservoir lid! Each spring, therefore, must contribute about 375 pounds of this force. Space behind the reservoirs is used as a workshop and storage area for organ maintenance man William Rosser and was originally the shop where some of the organ was built.

Above: some of the beaters for the 64' diaphone. Covers have been removed from the DDDDD# beater box to show the enormous beater which vibrates at only ten beats per second. This stop is one of only two complete and full-length 64' ranks in the world (the other being in the Sydney, Australia Town Hall). Below: one portion of the remote capture combination action. An entire room full of similar equipment is required to control all 1,240 stops of the main console. Alas, this mechanism no longer operates, having been severely damaged in a 1945 hurricane.

Wiring the relay for the left main chamber. Each of the four main relays in the organ is enclosed in an airtight room and can be regulated in actual operation.

Close-up view of the relay for the right main chamber. Each of these large relay pneumatics controls one note of the great manual. The author, certainly no stranger to large relays, experienced quite a sense of awe standing in the midst of such complexity as the scope of this enormous undertaking became dramatically apparent. The workmanship here is meticulous, as it is throughout the instrument.

5&7/452 MIDMER-LOSH PIPE ORGAN, OPUS 5550
Convention Hall, Atlantic City, New Jersey

Abbreviations for listings under the materials column: ST (stopped); OP (open); W (wood); M (metal); DL (double languid); HARM (harmonic).

RANK LIST OF THE WORLD'S LARGEST ORGAN

VOICE #	PITCH/RANK NAME	MAT'L	SCALE	WP	#
	PEDAL—Right Main Chamber				
1.	32′ Contra Tibia Clausa	StW	24x30	20″	85
2.	16′ Diaphone Phonon	W&M	24x24	50″	39
3.	16′ Tibia Major	OpWDL	17x20	30″	85
4.	16′ Principal	W	10x12	30″	85
5.	16′ Contra Viol	MDL	41	30″	85
6.	12 4/5′ Gross Tierce	M	42	20″	68
7.	9 2/7′ Septieme	M	53	20″	68
8.	32′ Contra Bombardon	M	24″	40″	85
9.	16′ Ophicleide	W&M	15x15	100″	85
10.	16′ Trumpet	M	8½″	20″	85
17.	64′ Diaphone Profundo	W	27x27	35″	85
320.	16′ Major Diapason	W	20x24	20″	32
	PEDAL—Left Main Chamber				
11.	32′ Contra Diaphone	W&M	30x30	50″	85
12.	32′ Diapason	M	24″	20″	85
13.	16′ Diaphonic Diapason	M	14″	35″	85
14.	16′ Bass Viol	OpW&M	7x9	20″	85
15.	16′ Tibia Clausa	StW	13x16	20″	85
16.	Stentor Sesquialtera, 7 ranks: 1-5-8-10-12-14-15	M	42	20″	224
18.	32′ Contra Bombard	W&M	24x24	50″	85
19.	32′ Contra Fagotto	M	8″	20″	85
20.	16′ Major Posuane	M	9″	50″	44
	GREAT—Right Main Chamber				
21.	32′ Sub Principal	W&M	13x17	20″	121
22.	16′ Diapason 1	W&MDL	12x14	20″	97
23.	16′ Diapason 2	M	30	15″	73
24.	16′ Diapason 3	M	32	10″	73
25.	10 2/3′ Sub Quint	M	33	15″	73
26.	8′ Diapason I	MDL	34	30″	73
27.	8′ Diapason II	MDL	38	30″	73
28.	8′ Diapason III	MDL	39	20″	73
29.	8′ Diapason IV	M	38	15″	73
30.	8′ Diapason V	M	41	15″	73
31.	8′ Diapason VI	M	37	15″	73
32.	8′ Diapason VII	M	42	10″	73
33.	8′ Diapason VIII	M	41	10″	73
34.	8′ Diapason IX	M	41	10″	73
35.	8′ Diapason X	M	43	4″	73
36.	5 1/3′ Quint	M	45	20″	73
37.	4′ Octave I	MDL	48	20″	73

VOICE #	PITCH/RANK NAME	MAT'L	SCALE	WP	#
	GREAT-SOLO—Right Main Chamber, continued				
91.	6 2/5′ Gemshorn Terz	M	46	15″	109
92.	5 1/3′ Gemshorn Fifth	M	49	15″	109
93.	4 4/7′ Septieme	M	55	15″	97
64.	2 2/3′ Flute Twelfth	StW	3¾x5	15″	73
94.	Xylophone				49
95.	16′ Oboe Horn	M	4½″	15″	97
96.	16′ Saxophone	M	3″	15″	97
97.	16′ English Horn	M	1¼″	15″	97
98.	16′ French Horn	M	7½″	15″	97
99.	16′ Baryton	M	7″	15″	85
100.	16′ Krummhorn	M	5″	15″	85
101.	8′ Clarinet	M	1¾″	15″	73
102.	8′ Orchestral Saxophone	M	7½″	15″	73
103.	8′ Orchestral Oboe	M	3″	15″	73
104.	8′ French Horn (in Solo)	M	6¼″	20″	61
105.	8′ Vox Humana	M	1½″	15″	85
106.	8′ Kinura	M	1¾″	15″	73
107.	Harp				61
108.	Chimes			25″	37
	BRASS CHORUS—Right Forward Gallery				
109.	16′ Trombone	M	8″	25″	73
110.	8′ Trombone 1	M	6½″	25″	73
111.	8′ Trombone 2	M	5½″	25″	73
112.	5 1/3′ Tromba Quint	M	4¼″	20″	73
113.	4′ Trombone	M	4½″	25″	73
114.	2 2/3′ Tromba Twelfth	M	3¼″	20″	73
115.	2′ Trombone	M	3½″	25″	73
116.	Tierce Mixture, 3 ranks: 10-17-22	M		20″	219
	SWELL—Left Main Chamber				
117.	16′ Diapason	M	32	15″	104
118.	8′ Diapason I	M	41	15″	80
119.	8′ Diapason II	M	45	15″	80
120.	8′ Wald Horn	M	43	15″	80
121.	4′ Octave	M	52	15″	73
122.	2′ Fifteenth	M	65	15″	73
123.	Fourniture, 5 ranks: 12-15-19-22-26	M		15″	400
124.	8′ Tibia Plena	OpW	8x10	15″	80
125.	8′ Hohl Flute	OpW	6x7	15″	80
126.	8′ Gross Gedeckt	StW	6½x9	15″	80
127.	8′ Harmonic Flute	M	44	15″	80

38.	4′ Octave II	MDL	52	20″	73
39.	4′ Octave III	M	50	15″	73
40.	4′ Octave IV	M	54	10″	73
41.	4′ Octave V	M	56	10″	73
42.	3 1/5′ Gross Tierce	M	55	15″	73
43.	2 2/3′ Major Twelfth	M	54	20″	73
44.	2′ Fifteenth I	MDL	60	20″	73
45.	2′ Fifteenth II	M	61	15″	73
46.	2′ Fifteenth III	M	66	10″	73
47.	Rausch Quint, 2 ranks: 5-8	M	52-56	30″	146
48.	Rausch Quint, 2 ranks: 12-15	M	60-64	30″	146
49.	Grand Cornet, 11 ranks: -4, 1-5-8-10-12-14-15-17-19-22	M		20″	803
50.	Sesquialtera, 5 ranks: 10-15-17-19-22	M		20″	365
51.	Mixture (Schulze), 5 ranks: 15-19-22-26-29	M		4″	365
52.	Fourniture, 6 ranks: 17-22-26-29-33-36	M		15″	404
53.	8′ Harmonic Flute	M	40	15″	73
54.	8′ Flute Overte	M	40	4″	73
55.	4′ Harmonic Flute	M	52	15″	73
56.	16′ Trumpet	M	6½″	30″	73
57.	8′ Harmonic Trumpet	M	5½″	30″	73
58.	4′ Harmonic Clarion	M	3¾″	30″	73

SOLO—Right Main Chamber

59.	16′ Major Flute	OpWDL	12x14	30″	85
60.	8′ Tibia Rex	MDL	30	30″	61
61.	8′ Hohl Flute	OpW	6⅜ x7 ⅜	20″	61
62.	8′ Flute Overte	M	36	20″	61
63.	4′ Wald Flute	MDL	48	30″	61
65.	2′ Harmonic Piccolo	M	60	20″	61
66.	8′ Cello Pomposa	M	48	20″	61
67.	8′ Cello Celeste	M	48	20″	61
68.	8′ Violin	M	53-49	20″	61
69.	8′ Viol Celeste	M	53-49	20″	61
70.	4′ Viola Pomposa	M	60	20″	61
71.	8′ Stentor Diapason	MDL	37	30″	61
72.	4′ Stentor Octave	MDL	50	30″	61
73.	16′ Tuba Magna	M&W	12x12	50″	85
74.	16′ Trumpet Profunda	M	9″	30″	85
75.	8′ Tuba Imperial	M	8″	100″	61
76.	8′ Trumpet Royal	M	6″	30″	61
77.	8′ English Post Horn	M	5″	30″	61
78.	8′ Bugle	Brass	5¼″	50″	61
79.	Grand Chorus, 9 ranks: 1-5-8-12-15-19-22-26-29	M		30″	549
80.	Carillon, 4 ranks: 17-19-21-24	M		30″	244

GREAT-SOLO—Right Main Chamber

81.	16′ Wald Flute	OpW	10x10	15″	104
82.	16′ Geigen Principal	M	36	15″	109
83.	16′ Tibia Clausa	StW	11x13	15″	104
84.	8′ Diapason Phonon	MDL	40	15″	85
85.	8′ Horn Diapason	M	42	15″	85
86.	8′ Doppel Gedeckt	StW	4x7	15″	85
87.	8′ Gemshorn	M	48	15″	109
88.	8′ Gemshorn Celeste	M	48	15″	101
89.	8′ Viola d'Gamba	Tin	55	15″	85
90.	8′ Viol Celeste	Tin	55	15″	85

128.	4′ Ocarina	MDL	52-46	15″	73
129.	4′ Traverse Flute	OpWHarm.	3x4	15″	80
130.	2′ Piccolo	WHarm.	3½x3½	15″	80
131.	16′ Contra Gamba	M	50	15″	104
132.	8′ Violin	Tin	68	15″	80
133.	8′ Viol Celeste I, 2 ranks	Tin	68	15″	134
134.	8′ Viol Celeste II, 2 ranks		63	15″	148
135.	8′ Cone Gamba	M	54-58	15″	80
136.	8′ Cone Gamba Celeste	M	54-58	15″	80
137.	4′ Gambette	M	70-66	15″	73
138.	16′ Double Trumpet	M	6″	30″	104
139.	8′ Harmonic Trumpet	M	6″	30″	104
140.	8′ Field Trumpet	M	8″	30″	80
141.	4′ Clarion Harmonic	M	3½″	30″	80
142.	16′ Double Horn	M	7½″	15″	104
143.	8′ Posuane	M	6″	15″	80
144.	8′ Cornopean	M	5½″	15″	80
145.	8′ Flugel Horn	M	3 3/8″	15″	80
146.	Plein Jeu, 7 ranks: 15-19-22-26-29-33-36	M		15″	560
312.	8′ Harmonic Flute Celeste	M	44	15″	80
313.	4′ Silver Flute	M	5″ to 3½″	15″	80
314.	8′ Muted Trumpet	M	1½″	15″	80
315.	8′ Krummhorn	M	2½″	15″	80
316.	8′ Vox Humana	M	1⅝″	15″	80
317.	Cymbal, 8 ranks: 12-15-17-19-21-22-23-26	M		15″	640

CHOIR-SWELL—Left Main Chamber

147.	16′ Doppel Gedeckt	StW	9x14	15″	97
148.	16′ Cone Gamba	M	50	15″	97
149.	8′ Clarabella	OpW	3¼x4	15″	92
150.	8′ Doppel Spitz Flute	OpW	2¾x4	10″	97
151.	4′ Zauber Flute	StWHarm.	2⅝x3⅜	15″	97
152.	8′ Gemshorn	M	53	15″	97
153.	8′ Gemshorn Celeste 1	M	53	15″	97
154.	8′ Gemshorn Celeste 2	M	53	15″	97
155.	6 2/5′ Third	M	58	10″	97
156.	5 1/3′ Fifth	M	56	10″	97
157.	4 4/7′ Seventh	M	65	10″	97
158.	3 5/9′ Ninth	M	68	10″	85
159.	2 10/11′ Eleventh	M	70	10″	85
160.	16′ Contra Oboe	M	4⅛″	15″	97
161.	16′ Bass Clarinet	M	2¾″	15″	97
162.	16′ Vox Humana	M	2⅞″	15″	97
163.	Marimba Harp				49
164.	Glockenspiel				49
311.	16′ Stopped Diapason	StW	6⅝x8⅞	15″	97

UNENCLOSED CHOIR—Left Forward Gallery

165.	16′ Quintaton	StM	48	3½″	73
166.	8′ Diapason	M	44	3½″	73
167.	8′ Holz Flute	OpW	3½x3½	3½″	73
168.	4′ Octave	M	57	3½″	73
169.	2′ Fifteenth	M	70	3½″	73
170.	Rausch, 2 ranks: 12-15	M	72	3½″	146

ENCLOSED CHOIR—Left Forward Gallery

VOICE #/PITCH/RANK NAME	MAT'L	SCALE	WP	#
171. 16′ Dulciana	M	32	10″	85
172. 8′ Diapason I	M	43	10″	73
173. 8′ Diapason II	M	45	10″	73
174. 8′ Dulciana Celeste	M	50	10″	73
175. 4′ Dolce	M	64	10″	85
176. 16′ Melodia	OpW	8x10	10″	109
177. 8′ Philomela	OpW	7x9	10″	73
178. 8′ Concert Flute	OpWHarm.	5x7	10″	73
179. 8′ Unda Maris	OpWHarm.	5x7	10″	73
180. 4′ Spindle Flute	M	48	10″	73
181. 4′ Flute Overte	M	52	10″	73
182. 2′ Flageolet 15th.	M	66	10″	73
183. Flute Mixture, 3 ranks: 15-17-19	M			219
184. 8′ Gemshorn	M	50	10″	73
185. 8′ Gemshorn Celeste	M	50	10″	73
186. 8′ Viola Pomposa	M	62	10″	73
187. 8′ Viola Celeste	M	62	10″	73
308. 8′ Nachthorn	StM	5½″	10″	73
309. 4′ Fugara	M	60	10″	73
310. 8′ Voix Celeste, 2 ranks	M	60	10″	134
188. 16′ Contra Tromba	M	7½″	20″	97
189. 8′ Tromba Real	M	6″	20″	73
190. 8′ Brass Cornet	Brass	6″	20″	73
191. 8′ French Horn	M	7″	10″	73
192. 8′ Clarinet	M	1¾″	10″	73
193. 8′ Bassett Horn	M	3¾″	10″	73
194. 8′ Cor Anglais (free reed)	M	4″	10″	73
195. 8′ Kinura	M	1⅝″	10″	73
196. Acuta, 6 ranks: 19-22-24-26-29-31	M			438

FANFARE—Left Center Ceiling Grille

VOICE #/PITCH/RANK NAME	MAT'L	SCALE	WP	#
197. 16′ Major Flute	OpWDL	16x20	20″	85
198. 8′ Stentor Flute	OpWDL	10x12	35″	61
199. 8′ Stentorphone	MDL	40	20″	61
200. 8′ Pileata Magna	StW	8½x10½	20″	61
201. 4′ Flute Octaviante	M	46	20″	61
202. 2 2/3′ Recorder Twelfth	M	58	20″	61
203. 2′ Fife 15th.	MHarm.	54	20″	61
204. Cymbal, 5 ranks: 19-22-26-29-33	MHarm.		20″	305
205. 16′ Contra Posuane	M	10″	50″	85
206. 16′ Contra Bombardon	M	13″	35″	85
207. 8′ Tuba Harmonic	M	8½″	50″	73
208. 8′ Ophicleide	M	7½″	50″	61
209. 10 2/3′ Tromba Quint	M	10″	20″	73
210. 6 2/5′ Tromba Tierce	M	7″	20″	73
211. 4′ Major Clarion	M	6″	50″	61
212. Stentor Mixture, 7 ranks: 1-5-8-12-15-19-22	MHar.		35″	427
299. 32′ Contra Trombone	W&M	19¼x19¼	35″	12
299. 16′ Contra Trombone	W&M	9½x9½	35″	73
304. 8′ Gamba Tuba	OpW	3½x3½	20″	61
305. 8′ Gamba Tuba Celeste	OpW	3½x3½	20″	61
306. 4′ Gamba Clarion	OpW	2⅝x2⅝	20″	61
307. Harmonic Mixture, 6 ranks: 17-21-22-23-26-29	MHarm.		20″	366

GALLERY ORGAN IV—Left Center Gallery

VOICE #/PITCH/RANK NAME	MAT'L	SCALE	WP	#
249. 16′ Contra Saxophone	Brass&Copper	5½″	25″	85
250. 8′ Major Oboe	M	3⅛″	25″	73
251. 8′ Musette Mirabilis	M	1⅞″	25″	73
252. 8′ Cor d'Orchestre	M	5″	25″	73
253. 8′ Major Clarinet	M	4″	25″	73
300. 8′ Brass Trumpet	Brass	5½″	25″	73
301. 8′ Euphone	M	5″	25″	73
302. 8′ Egyptian Horn	Brass&Copper	4″	25″	73

STRING ORGAN I—Left Main Chamber

VOICE #/PITCH/RANK NAME	MAT'L	SCALE	WP	#
254. 16′ Contra Basso	MDL	44	25″	97
255. 8′ Cello	MDL	50	25″	73
256. 8′ Cello Celeste, 2 ranks	M	53	25″	146
257. 8′ Cello Celeste, 2 ranks	M	55	25″	134
258. 8′ First Violins, 2 ranks	Tin	60	25″	146
259. 8′ First Violins, 2 ranks	Tin	64	25″	134
260. 8′ First Violins, 2 ranks	Tin	62	25″	146
261. 8′ First Violins, 2 ranks	Tin	66	25″	134
262. 8′ Secundo Violins, 2 ranks	M	57	25″	146
263. 8′ Secundo Violins, 2 ranks	M	59	25″	134
264. 4′ Secundo Violins, 2 ranks	Tin	68	25″	146

STRING ORGAN II—Right Forward Gallery

VOICE #/PITCH/RANK NAME	MAT'L	SCALE	WP	#
265. 16′ Double Bass	MDL	40	15″	97
266. 16′ Contra Bass	OpW	5x5	15″	97
267. 16′ Contra Viol	M	50	15″	97
268. 8′ Viola Diapason	M	48	15″	73
269. 8′ Violin Cello	Opw	2¾x4	15″	73
270. 8′ Cello Phonon	MDL	52	15″	73
271. 8′ Cello	MDL	58	15″	73
272. 8′ Cello Celeste, 2 ranks	MDL	58	15″	146
273. 8′ Viola Phonon	MDL	55	15″	73
274. 8′ Viola Celeste, 2 ranks	M	60	15″	134
275. 8′ Violin Phonon	MDL	60	15″	73
276. 8′ Violin	Tin	62	15″	73
277. 8′ Viol Celeste, 2 ranks, I	M	62	15″	146
278. 8′ Viol Celeste, 2 ranks, II	Tin	66	15″	134
279. 8′ Viol Celeste, 2 ranks, III	MDL	72	15″	134
280. 8′ Viol Celeste, 2 ranks, IV	Tin	67	15″	134
281. 8′ Viol Celeste, 2 ranks, V	M	68	15″	134
282. 4′ Violin, 2 ranks	M	68	15″	146
283. 4′ Violas, 2 ranks	M	68	15″	134
284. 4′ Viol Principal	M	58	15″	73
285. String Mixture, 5 ranks: 10-15-17-19-22	M		15″	305
286. 8′ Tromba d'Amour	M	5″	15″	73
287. 5 1/3′ Quint Flute	StW	3¾x3	15″	73
288. 2 2/3′ Flute Twelth	StW	2½x3½	15″	73

ECHO—Right Center Ceiling Grille

No.	Stop	Material	Scale	Pressure	Pipes
213.	16' Contra Gamba	M	52	15"	85
214.	16' Contra Spire Flute	M	40-44	15"	97
215.	8' Diapason	M	44	15"	61
216.	8' Spitz Flute	M	50	15"	61
217.	8' Flute Celeste 1	M	50	15"	61
218.	8' Flute Celeste 2	M	50	15"	61
219.	8' Wald Horn	M	48	15"	61
220.	16' Bourdon	StW	5¼x6½	15"	12
220.	8' Clarabella	OpW	4¾x6	15"	85
221.	8' Tibia Mollis	StM	39	15"	61
222.	8' Flute Sylvestre	M	52	15"	61
223.	8' Flute Celeste	M	52	15"	61
224.	4' Rohr Flute	StM	48	15"	61
225.	Mixture Aetheria, 6 ranks: 15-17-19-22-26-29	M		15"	366
226.	16' Contra Bassoon (free reed)	Papier-mache	3¾"	15"	73
227.	16' Chalumeau	M	2½x3½	15"	85
228.	8' Trumpet Minor	M	3½	15"	61
229.	8' Cor d'Amour	M	5"	15"	61
230.	16' Vox Humana	M	3¾"	15"	85
231.	16' Tuba d'Amour	W	8x8	25"	85
232.	Chimes			15"	25
298.	32' Contra Violone	W&MDL	9¼x9½	25"	97
303.	8' Vox Humana	M	3⅞"	15"	61
319.	8' Viol Celeste	MDL	50	25"	56

GALLERY ORGAN I—Right Center Gallery

No.	Stop	Material	Scale	Pressure	Pipes
233.	16' Contra Diaphone	W&M	14¼x14¼	25"	85
234.	8' Tuba Maxima	M	6"	100"	73
235.	16' Trumpet Mirabilis	M	5½	100"	85
318.	Mixture Mirabilis, 7 ranks: 1-5-8-12-15-19-22	MDL		25"	511

GALLERY ORGAN III—Left Center Gallery

No.	Stop	Material	Scale	Pressure	Pipes
236.	16' Diapason	W&MDL	10x12¼	20"	97
237.	8' Diapason	MDL	37-33	20"	73
238.	8' Diapason II	MDL	40-36	20"	73
239.	4' Octave I	M	47-43	20"	73
240.	2' Fifteenth	M	57-53	20"	73
241.	Mixture, 4 ranks: 12-15-19-22	M	B.54-50	20"	292

GALLERY ORGAN II—Right Center Gallery

No.	Stop	Material	Scale	Pressure	Pipes
242.	16' Flauto Maggiore	StWDL	11x14	25"	97
243.	8' Jubal Flute	OpW	7x9½	25"	73
244.	8' Flute Harmonic	MDL	42	25"	73
245.	4' Flute Harmonic	MDL	54	25"	73
246.	2 2/3' Harmonic Twelfth	M	62	25"	61
247.	2' Harmonic Piccolo	MDL	68	25"	61
248.	Harmonic Cornet, 3 ranks: 17-19-22	M		25"	183

STRING ORGAN III—Left Center Ceiling Grille

No.	Stop	Material	Scale	Pressure	Pipes
289.	8' Cello Celeste, 2 ranks	Tin&M	62	15"	146
290.	8' Cello Celeste, 2 ranks	M	58	15"	146
291.	8' Cello Celeste, 2 ranks	Tin	62	15"	146
292.	8' Violins, 2 ranks	M flat face	56	15"	146
293.	8' Violins, 2 ranks	Tin	80	15"	134
294.	8' Violins, 2 ranks	M	66	15"	146
295.	8' Violins, 2 ranks	W&M	70-1x1TenC	15"	134
296.	8' Violins, 2 ranks	Tin	Slim, Tapered	15"	146
297.	8' Cor Anglais	M	4½"	15"	73

PERCUSSIONS

A. 16' Grand Piano, 85 notes
B. Contra Bass Drum
C. Bass Drum
D. Bass Drum
E. Snare Drum
F. Snare Drum
G. Snare Drum
H. Cymbal
I. Chinese Gong
J. Persian Cymbal
K. Persian Cymbal
L. Tambours
M. Castanets
N. Triangle
O. Wood Block
P. Tom Tom

MIDMER-LOSH OPUS LIST

CITY/STATE	LOCATION	SIZE	YR	BLWR	HP	WP	REMARKS
CONNECTICUT							
New Haven	Bijou Th.	2/	1921	I606	2	6"	
MARYLAND							
Takoma Park	Takoma Th.	2/	1923	L256	1½	6"	
MASSACHUSETTS							
Fall River	Savoy Th.	3/					
NEW JERSEY							
Asbury Park	Asbury Park Th.		1920	I537	¾	5"	
Atlantic City	Convention Hall	5&7/452	1929	R320B	40	15"&30"	Opus 5550.
			1929	R914B	40	20"&50"	
			1930	R1107B	30	15"&30"	
			1930	R1108B	60	25"&50"	
			1930	R1109B	60	25"&50"	
			1931	T105B	50	20"	
			1931	T106B	60	50"	
				Allen	50	100"	
	Steel Pier Casino	2/8	1928	Q24B	5	10"	Opus 5435.
	Steel Pier Music Hall	3/	1930				
West Orange	Edison Recording Labs	3/	1926				
NEW YORK							
Babylon	Babylon Th.	2/	1925				
Baldwin	Baldwin Th.	2/	1925				
Brooklyn	Atlantic Playhouse	2/	1921				
	Congregation Beth Elom Community Building Th.	3/10	1929				
	DeKalb Th.	3/	1921				
	Halsey Th.	3/	1921	J43	2	5"	
East Rockaway	Waldowski (East Rockaway) Th.	2/	1926	0970B	1½	5"	
Freeport	Plaza (Freeport) Th.	2/8	1924				
Glen Cove	Cove Th.	3/10	1927	P326B	5	10"	Opus 5315.
Hempstead	Hempstead Th.	3/	1922				
	Rivoli Th.	3/	1926	N1131B	3	7"	
	State Th.	2/	1927	P518B	1	7"	
Hicksville	Hicksville Th.						
Jamaica	Rialto Th.	3/	1920				
Long Beach	Lido Th.	2/	1928	P1015B	2	7"	
Lynbrook	Arcade Th.		1927	P117B	1	5"	
Mineola	RKO Theatre	2/					
New York	Adelphi Th.	2/	1922				
	Empire Th.		1920				
	Essex Th.	2/15	1926	H516	1½		Opus 5204; records indicate "rebuilt from Lebanon organ."
	Garden Th.	2/	1923	L558	2	5"	
	Gotham Th.	2/	1920				
	Hippodrome Th.	2/					
		3/	1924	L1158	3	8"	Enlarged.
	Rio Th.	2/	1920				
	77th Street Th.	2/	1925				
	Spooner Th.	3/	1920				
	Stoddard Th.	2/	1928	Q702B	3	10"	Opus 5419; opened as Standard Theatre in 1914.
	Symphony Th.	2/	1922				
Patchogue	Granada Th.	3/11	1928	Q729B	3	10"	Opus 5417.
Queens	Queens Community House	3/	1924	M706B	3	6"	
	Rialto Th.	3/	1920				
Roosevelt	Roosevelt Th.	2/	1925				
Valley Stream	Valley Stream Th.	2/8	1927				
Westbury	Westbury Th.	2/6	1927	P723B	1½	7"	

ESTABLISHED 1880

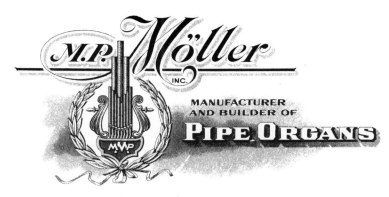

M.P. Möller INC.

MANUFACTURER AND BUILDER OF

PIPE ORGANS

Hagerstown, Maryland, U.S.A.

The Moller story is a wonderful tale of luck, wisdom and perseverance. Mathias Peter Moller was born in 1854 on the Danish island of Bornholm. Denmark went to war with Germany in 1862 and after the war many Danes were in debt. Mathias Moller's family lost their 130-acre farm and the fourteen year-old lad needed to find a trade for himself. In his own words, "It seemed a terrible calamity, but like a good many calamities it turned out the best thing that could have happened to me. The only good I could see in it was that it gave me a chance to be a woodworker. I had always had a sort of secret wish for that.

"I packed up my things and went to the port town of Ronne and apprenticed myself to a carriage maker. He was a master workman; I used to think him a wonderful person. There were four of us apprentice boys. We lived right in the place. I think an eight-hour law would have scared us to death! We had to be up early every morning and clean up the place, then get breakfast. In the winter time, of course, there were fires to build and ashes to care for. We worked all day and then after supper in the evening.

"We got no money—just food and lodging; and after the plenty I had always been used to on the farm the food seemed pretty sad. But I learned, and he taught us thoroughly all the uses of every tool. I got so interested in the woodworking that I don't think I would have cared if the victuals had been a good deal worse even than they were. The second year I was there I built myself a bicycle. It was a proud day when I rode it the sixteen miles out to my old home."[1]

Shortly after Mathias Moller finished his three years of apprenticeship his sister married a neighbor's son who had just returned from America. Enticed by the tales of opportunity in the New World, Mathias joined the newlyweds on a trip to America. He was only seventeen years of age but was full of the ambition and perseverance that would later make him a successful and wealthy man. His traveling companions wanted him to accompany them to Nebraska to take up farming but Moller's hands itched to be working with tools.[2] He chose instead to stay with a half brother, George Moller, in Warren, Pennsylvania[3] and joined him in working at the Greenlund Brothers furniture factory.[4] Cabinet making did not particularly appeal to him and he soon found a woodworking job at

the Derrick & Felgemaker organ factory in Erie, Pennsylvania.[5]

Quoting Mr. Moller again, "All I did was to put in a full day and a little more, but I had the advantage of loving what I was doing. I spent two years in Erie. I learned all I could in the shop but I studied in all my spare time. I was not a musician; I was just a woodworker. It seemed to me the finest thing in the world that could be done with wood was to make it into an organ. A carriage was a utility, but to find and fix, in something you had made out of wood, all the tones and harmonies of music, had something mysterious and reverent about it."[6]

By the end of 1874 at age twenty Moller had designed a new wind chest and had a number of novel ideas about organ construction.[7] He was also developing the ambition to have his own factory and some years later in retrospect admitted that was a pretty audacious wish for just a boy. He had no money other than what he managed to save from his employment with Derrick & Felgemaker. But he just had to find out whether or not he could actually build an organ on his own. His stepbrother in Warren, Pennsylvania agreed to let Moller use his front parlor as a shop. Moller's savings just covered the cost of purchasing the materials[8] and in January 1875 he started building the organ. By September it was finished and Moller had proved that he could build an organ on his own.[9] He also discovered that he could sell it and a local church soon had the two-manual instrument and Mathias Moller had $500.[10]

Spurred by this success, Moller decided to move to Philadelphia where he rented an old piano factory and hired the only two workmen left there.[11] He had wanted to build an organ to display at the 1876 Centennial but did not complete it in time.[12] This must have been a severe disappointment to him, especially after seeing and hearing the great Roosevelt organ at the Centennial; but Moller was even more determined that he would build an even greater organ himself someday. Before leaving his Philadelphia shop he built four organs in less than two years.[13]

In Moller's own words, "Competition was pretty stiff in those days. There were about four times as many organ factories as there are now [1925]. There were six in New Jersey and a dozen in New York. A small shop had hard work getting business. It was pretty discouraging some-times. Three or four times I was tempted to give up. I suppose a lot of men would have quit, but I always hated the idea of getting out of anything I started. I said to myself, 'This is my business. If I can't make a living building organs in a big country like this, what in the world can I make it at?' So I hung on.

"At last I thought the way was clear. A friend of mine came to me and proposed that we set up business in Greencastle. All the plans were made and then he backed out. Once more it was up to me to go on. I did. I started the business in Greencastle myself on next to nothing [in 1877[14]] just as I had before.

"I used to go over to Hagerstown, Maryland occasion-ally. There was a hardware firm here. One day they asked me why I didn't move my business to Hagerstown. I asked what the inducement was. They said I'd get what-ever I needed. I drew them a plan of the plant that I wanted to build. They told me to come on—and I did [in 1881[15]]. The father of Senator L. E. McComas owned a lot of land. He let me have the plot I wanted without any interest for ten years. Then I started out to get the money to build the plant.

"I went to the First National Bank and asked them to lend me $2,000. They asked me who my endorser was. I said I hadn't any endorser. They told me if I couldn't go out and find somebody to endorse my note I couldn't have the money. I told them I was not going to start in Hagerstown by asking somebody to endorse my paper. If I couldn't get the money I could go back to Greencastle.

"I got outside and stood looking up and down the street trying to decide what to do. Across the way I saw a little private bank [Hagerstown Trust Company]. It was a chance. I went over and I got the loan! Do you know, I've been doing business with that bank ever since. It's quite a large institution now [1925]." And modest Mr. Moller at the time of that statement was the bank's vice president,[16] but that's getting ahead of the story!

By April 1881 Moller's first shop in Hagerstown, a modest two-story building, was ready to start building organs. Over the next eleven years the structure was enlarged five times and production reached twenty organs per year. A tragic blow came in 1895, however, when the entire factory was destroyed by fire, including six organs completed and ready for delivery. Only a fraction of the loss was covered by insurance but Mathias Moller had made many friends in Hagerstown and several of them offered to go into partnership with him. He was bound and determined, however, to make a success of the busi-ness on his own.[17] To quote Mr. Moller, "I have never had to let a workman go for lack of work. I have never asked anybody to endorse my paper. I have never taken outside money into my business. What I can't do myself I let alone."[18]

By January 1896 a new factory building on the outskirts of town was completed[19] and the rest, as they say, is his-tory. Growth of the Moller firm exceeded that of any organ builder in the world before or since. Thirty-three years after building his first organ Moller built his one thousandth. The second thousand organs were built in only seven years; the third thousand in five years; the

fourth thousand in four years; and the fifth thousand in just three years.[20] The only builder who ever even approached this record was Wurlitzer, who reached a peak production of one organ per day in 1926.[21] But Moller averaged one organ per day through the *entire decade* of the 1920s. As of 1983 M. P. Moller, Inc. has made over 11,600 pipe organs,[22] nearly double the number of any other builder in history.

In the years following the opening of the new factory in 1896 so many additions were made to the plant that no one today remembers just how many there were. The last addition was completed in 1925, the fiftieth anniversary of Mathias Moller's entry into the organ business. The magnitude of this addition was appropriate to the occa-sion, consisting of a two-story office building and the world's largest erecting room measuring 52' x 113' x 40' high. (The former erecting room was *only* 26'x90'.)[23] At 125,000 square feet the Moller factory still reigns in 1983 as the largest ever built exclusively for the manufacture of pipe organs.

Mathias Moller had a number of interests besides pipe organs. His connection with the Hagerstown Trust Com-pany has already been noted. He was interested in any number of other local businesses as well and was presi-dent of several and a member of the boards of directors of several more.[24] Perhaps the most interesting of these was the automobile business. Around 1902[25] Mr. Moller had become interested in the Crawford bicycle factory in Hagerstown[26] and was later instrumental in founding the Crawford Automobile Company. Later still he bought out all the shareholders and changed the name of the firm to the M. P. Moller Motor Car Company. The best known products of this firm were the Dagmar luxury sedan, named after one of Mr. Moller's daughters, and the Luxor taxicab. The M. P. Moller Motor Car Company continued in business until the founder's death in 1937.[27]

In 1925 Susquehanna University conferred on Mathias Moller the honorary degree of doctor of music. He was also president of the Organ Builders Association of America for a time. But his highest honor was bestowed in 1928 by King Christian X of Denmark who made Mr. Moller a Knight of Dannebrog,[28] the highest honor that could be bestowed on anyone other than Danish nobility.[29]

Following Mathias Moller's death in 1937 control of the organ company passed to his son M. P. Moller, Jr. who was then 35 years of age. "Ted" Moller was even more interested in music than was his father and did post-graduate work at Peabody Conservatory in Baltimore as well as private study with several eminent musicians. In 1954 he received the honorary degree of doctor of laws from Muhlenburg College. Like his father he was active in civic affairs[30] and was also president of the Hagerstown Trust Company.[31] Under his leadership the company pro-duced one instrument which was unique in several ways: it was the company's first five-manual organ, easily the company's most famous organ and also one of the finest theatre organs ever built. And it was built in 1938! It was, of course, the famous Reginald Foort traveling organ of which much more will be said later.

After the untimely death of M. P. Moller, Jr. in 1961 at

This Dagmar Victoria Speedster of 1925 could achieve 87 miles per hour. Other models manufactured by the M. P. Moller Motor Car Company included the Astor, 20th. Century, Moller, Blue Light, Super Paramount, Aristocrat, Five Boro, the Elysee delivery car ("for the deliveries of merchants of importance") and the Luxor taxicab.[50] The Moller radiator medallion was undoubtedly the only one ever to feature a crest of organ pipes!

only 59 years of age[32] the Moller presidency passed to W. Riley Daniels. Mr. Daniels had married Martha Moller, one of Mathias Moller's daughters, and had joined the company in 1930.[33] The Moller labor force was unionized in 1938 and due to the agreement with the AFL-CIO there was a mandatory retirement at age 68, even for company executives who, of course, were not members of the union. Mr. Daniels negotiated this agreement himself and recalls that at the time he never considered how it might affect *him* someday! But on his 68th birthday in 1978 Mr. Daniels retired and was succeeded in the presidency by Kevin Moller, son of M. P. Moller, Jr.[34] Peter Moller Daniels, son of Riley Daniels, assumed the presidency in 1984.

In any larger company a number of men are responsible for its success. This is especially true of M. P. Moller, Inc., the world's largest builder of pipe organs. Only some of the historically important people in the Moller organization will be mentioned here. Limitations of space unfortunately preclude mentioning all of the many people who contributed to Moller's success.

The company was fortunate to have several excellent

E. O. Shulenberger (left) and M. P. Moller, Jr. confer on a large contract in the Moller offices. "Ted" Moller may have been president of the company but "Shuly" ruled the roost politically, his power no doubt resulting from having sold hundreds of Moller organs. For example, Ted Moller wanted to advertise the prestige enjoyed by the firm as a result of having Richard Whitelegg as tonal director. Shuly vetoed the idea. In another instance, over Shuly's objections, Ted engaged the services of noted organ personality R. P. Elliot in 1941. Mr. Elliot lasted only five months before Shuly engineered a political maneuver to oust him.[78]

salesmen on their staff. The company was also in an excellent position financially and was willing to carry long-term paper for "leasing" organs. These propitious circumstances were largely responsible for Moller's standing as the fourth largest builder of theatre instruments, despite the fact that most of them were *not* high pressure unified instruments. Indeed, two-thirds of Moller's theatre instruments were on the modest pressure of 5", the norm for Moller church organs of the day.

C. Seibert Losh, who later gained notoriety with the Midmer-Losh organization, was head of the Moller sales office in New York City through 1918 and was responsible for landing Moller's largest single customer: the Marcus Loew syndicate. Losh believed that there was no essential difference between church and theatre organs, and this philosophy was apparently shared by Ernst Luz, general musical director of the Loew syndicate.[35]

After Losh left Moller in 1918 many of the Loew sales were handled by Elden O. Shulenberger, Moller secretary and sales manager. Mr. Shulenberger deservedly held an industry-wide reputation as one of the finest organ salesmen who ever lived. It was not unusual for "Shuly" to sell several organs at once on one contract. One time he sold *six* 3/17s on one contract to William Fox (#2739-2744); he also sold six 3/17s at once to the Loew syndicate (#2871-2876). On another occasion he sold four 3/32s at the same time to Loew (#4376-4379). In all, Loew bought over *six dozen* Moller organs for their theatres.[36]

One particularly fascinating aspect of Mr. Shulenberger's salesmanship was that he frequently sold organs to established customers without a formal sales contract! He would write a letter to the prospect saying "Here's the specification of the organ I discussed with you on the telephone today. Just sign this letter and return it to me with your down payment and that will constitute our sales agreement."[37] What an operator!

One of the most popular Moller theatre models, accounting for about 20% of all theatre sales, was a three-manual of 16 or 17 ranks, typified by the specification of opus 2953 reproduced below. Note that several ranks are straight, a few are unit and most are duplexed. Eighty-five percent of Moller's theatre instruments were characterized by this same design philosophy, the fully unified theatre organs not making their appearance until the late 1920s.

SPECIFICATIONS OF THREE MANUAL DUPLEX CONCERT ORGAN

MANUALS:- Compass CC to C, 61 Notes.
PEDALS:- Compass CCC to G, 32 Notes.
ACTION:- Moller's Patent Electro Pneumatic throughout.
Stops controlled by Stop Keys over Sw.
No casing or display pipes.

GREAT ORGAN

1	16'	Violin Diapason	Tenor C	73 Pipes
2	8'	Open Diapason		85 "
3	8'	Viol d'Orchestre		73 "
4	8'	Doppel Floete		73 "
5	4'	Octave	from #2	73 Notes
6	4'	Zart Flute	from #14	61 "
7	2'	Piccolo	from #17	61 "
8	3 Rks.	Mixture	From #14-16-17	61 "
9	8'	French Horn	(Reed)	73 Pipes
10	4'	Octave Horn	from #9	61 Notes
11	16'	Bass Clarinet	Tenor C..From #20	61 "
		Cathedral Chimes		20 "

ORCHESTRAL ORGAN

12	8'	Violin Diapason	from #1	73 Notes
13	8'	Horn Diapason	(Synthetic)	73 "
14	8'	Quintadena		73 Pipes
15	8'	Viol d'Orchestre	from #3	73 Notes
16	8'	Viol Celeste	Tenor C	73 Pipes
17	4'	Flute Harmonic	(Ex. Large &Brilliant)	73 "
18	8'	Orchestral Oboe		73 "
19	16'	Fagotto	Tenor C..From #18	61 Notes
20	8'	Clarinet		73 Pipes
		Orchestral Bells		25 Notes
		Concert Harp		37 "
		Glockenspiel		37 "
		Tremulant		

SOLO ORGAN

21	8'	Gross Flute	(Big)	85 Pipes
22	8'	Concert Flute		73 "
23	8'	Gemshorn		85 "
24	8'	Violoncello		73 "
25	4'	Flute Overte..Tenor C, from #21		53 Notes
26	4'	Gemshorn	Tenor C,from #23	53 "
27	8'	Tuba		73 Pipes
28	16'	Bass Tuba	Tenor C, from #17	61 Notes
29	8'	Vox Humana		73 Pipes
		Xylophone		25 Notes
		Tremulant		

PEDAL ORGAN

30	16'	Open Diapason	from #21	32 Notes
31	16'	Sub Bass		32 Pipes
32	16'	Gemshorn	from #23	32 Notes
33	16'	Lieblich Gedeckt	from #31	32 "
34	8'	Violoncello	from #24	32 "
35	8'	Flute	from #22	32 "
36		Thunder Effect	(Operated by PedalStud)	

```
                    COUPLERS
37              Solo to Great
38              Solo to Great 4'
39              Solo to Great 16'
40              Orchestral to Great
41              Orchestral to Great 4'
42              Orchestral to Great 16'
43              Great 4'
44              Solo to Orchestral
45              Orchestral to Solo
46              Solo 4'
47              Solo 16'
48              Orchestral 4'
49              Orchestral 16'
50              Solo to Pedal
51              Orchestral to Pedal
52              Great to Pedal
53              Great to Pedal 4'

                   MECHANICALS
54              Orchestral Tremulant
55              Solo Tremulant
                Crescendo Indicator

            ADJUSTABLE COMBINATIONS
    (Operated by pistons placed under respective manuals)

Pistons No. 1-2-3-4-5-6   Affecting Orchestral & PEDAL

Pistons No. 1-2-3-4-5-6   Affecting Great & Pedal

Pistons No. 1-2-3-4-5-6   Affecting Solo & Pedal

                  PEDAL MOVEMENTS
1               Great to Pedal Reversible
2               Orchestral to Pedal Reversible
3               Balanced Solo Pedal
4               Balanced Orchestral Pedal
5               Grand Crescendo Pedal

                Organ Bench with Music Shelf
                Concave Pedal
                Electric blower and generator
                of ample capacity.

New York City, N. Y.
Oct. 23, 1919. S.
```

Louis Luberoff, another crackerjack Moller salesman, was in charge of the Philadelphia sales office for many years and was responsible for a substantial percentage of Moller's sales of the day. Luberoff was one of the few Moller salesmen who ever paid for his own advertising. He was also the only Moller representative who ever had a theatre organ in his showroom. At one time the factory discovered that Mr. Luberoff was participating in some, shall we say, questionable business practices. This would have been grounds for dismissal in most companies but Mr. Luberoff merely got his wrist slapped;[38] he was too valuable to the company to let go!

Luberoff pioneered a sales technique which won many

Style 100 3/10 theatre organ in the Philadelphia showroom operated by Louis Luberoff.

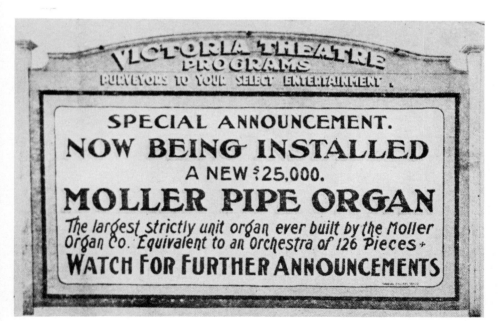

This billboard was paid for by Moller representative Louis Luberoff, a terrific salesman not noted for his honesty or consistency. Actual cost of this 3/13 organ was $14,000,[51] not $25,000 as stated on the billboard. Also, from the tone of this announcement, one would get the idea that Mr. Luberoff thought unit organs were pretty hot stuff. However, in the same year this advertisement was erected, 1923, Mr. Luberoff wrote a five-page article for The American Organist *denouncing the unified organ concept.[52]*

Louis Luberoff

3/10 MOLLER THEATRE ORGAN, OPUS 4980
Victoria Theatre, Shamokin, Pennsylvania
The following represents a typical "lease" agreement.

C O P Y

ORGAN

#4980

This Agreement of Lease. Made this .....20th .day of... October ...
A. D., 192.7..., by and between **M. P. MOLLER, Inc.,** of Hagerstown, Maryland, party of
the first part, as Lessor and hereinafter called the Builder, and........................
...Chamberlain. Amusement. Enterprises. Inc., of. Shamokin, Pa...
party of the second part, hereinafter called the Lessee.

WITNESSETH
FIRST. That the party of the first part hereby agrees to build for and deliver to the Lessee
an organ after and according to the annexed specifications and details of construction hereby approved by the Lessee and made a part of this contract, and to erect it in............
...Victoria. Theatre,. Shamokin,. Pa...........................
ready for use, on or before the....10th........day of...December.......A. D., 1927...,
or as soon thereafter as possible in the event of delays beyond control of builder, according
to the following conditions and covenants;

(a) In consideration of the above, the party of the second part hereby agrees to pay to
M. P. MOLLER, Inc., or his order, a total rental of .... Sixteen. Thousand. Dollars
.........................($16,000.00)...........................
AS FOLLOWS:—$..10%....in cash upon signing this agreement: $........receipt of
which is hereby acknowledged
organ parts are delivered to building $......10%. in cash when said organ is completed
and ready for service, and the residue of the said above reserved rent... payable.in..
.thirty. six. equal. monthly. installments...........................
....
....
with interest upon all deferred payments at the legal rate per annum.

(b) The Lessee hereby agrees that it will provide a suitable place or places in which to
install the organ and sufficient foundations and supports therefore; and that the building
shall be in a proper condition for the installation of the organ... four ...weeks previous to
the above mentioned date of completion, and further agrees that it will furnish, at its own
expense, to the Builder all the necessary light, heat and power, and such a condition of quiet-
ness as may be required for the proper tone regulation and tuning of the organ, and that at
all times it will protect the Builder or his employees engaged in the installation of the organ
from any molestation or interruption, and will allow them free access to the building at all
necessary times with suitable conveniences, conditions and opportunities for the proper installation of the organ.

(c) The Lessee hereby agrees that it will, as the agent of the said M. P. MOLLER, Inc.,
and for the benefit of himself, his successors or assigns, but at its cost, fully insure and keep
the said organ fully insured, and its parts insured from the time that any of the parts are
delivered in the building until the said organ shall be paid in full, in such companies and for
such an amount as shall be satisfactory to the said Builder, and the loss, if any, by fire, water, tornado or otherwise, shall be payable to the Builder as his interest may appear, and
shall be collected and received by him.

(d) If electric motor is included in specifications the Lessee agrees to provide suitable
foundation and enclosures when necessary for motor and blowing apparatus, to do all wiring connected therewith and to install wind conductor between blower and organ, to install
such lights as may be needed for the erection and future care of the organ and do any necessary cutting of floors, partitions, or other parts of the building. In the event that local
regulations require the use of an automatic remote control motor starter, electrical conduits
or other special equipment, they are to be furnished by the Lessee.
d2. This organ is to be the same in every respect and
detail as the style Special 100 located in the Moller De
Luxe Unit Studio, 13th & Vine Sts., Philadelphia.

(e) The Lessee agrees that it will use said organ and all of its parts carefully and will
not suffer any other person, firm or corporation, to have the custody or control of it, and
that it will not sell or underlet or remove it or any of its parts from the above mentioned
building, nor assign this contract without the written consent of the Builder, his legal representative or assigns.

(f) The Lessee further agrees that if any judgment at law shall be obtained against it,
or if bankruptcy proceedings shall be instituted by it, or against it, or if it shall become insolvent, or if the above payments shall not be fully made on or before the day stipulated, or
if default is made in any of the said payments with interest thereon or in respect of any
agreements or condition on its part herein, then this agreement may at the option of the
Builder, his representative or assigns, be forfeited and ended upon five days notice to the
Lessee, and the said Lessee, or its successors in interest agrees forthwith to deliver the said
property to said Builder, or will permit the said Builder, or it agents, to enter into or upon any premises where said organ may be, and, without let or hindrance, take the same together with the fixtures and appurtenances thereto belonging and included in this lease, using such force as may be necessary for the taking thereof, hereby releasing all errors and
right of action that said Lessee may have for such forcible taking and waiving any right of
action for trespass or damage therefore. It is further agreed that all money paid or payable
to said Builder prior to said re-possession shall be retained as rent or hire for the use of said
property without abatement or reduction. It is further agreed by the said Lessee that it
will at the expiration of the term for which said property was leased, return the same to the
said Builder in as good order as when received, reasonable wear and tear excepted.

SECOND: The Builder agrees that the organ when completed shall be first-class in every
respect and agrees to correct defects in material or workmanship that may be brought to his
attention within one year from date of completion, without cost to the Lessee, but this shall
not include tuning or ordinary care and maintenance of the organ.

THIRD: The said Builder agrees that said Lessee shall and may peaceably and quietly
have, hold and enjoy the property above described for the term of this lease, provided it shall
and does faithfully pay the rent above reserved when due and payable hereunder and perform and keep the covenants and agreements herein contained. Said Builder further agrees
that if, at or before the expiration of the term of this lease, the said Lessee, or its legal representatives or assigns, shall wish to purchase said organ, the Builder will make and deliver
to said Lessee, or said representatives or assigns a Bill of Sale thereof upon payment of such
sum as will with previous payments of rent amount to the total sum of the above mentioned
rent reserved with interest.

It is expressly understood and agreed by and between the said parties to this agreement
that no title to said organ either legal or equitable shall vest in the Lessee except as Lessee
under this lease, until the terms of purchase as above provided have been complied with and
the aforesaid Bill of Sale has been fully delivered by the said Builder.

FOURTH: It is mutually agreed that all representations, agreements and understandings,
whether oral or written, are merged in this contract, and the specifications and details of
construction attached hereto.

---

customers for the Moller company. This was a plan
whereby the organ would be "leased" to the client with
little or no money down and payments spread out over
several years. In reality the transaction was merely an
installment sale in which the Moller company carried the
paper at terms favorable to the client. Whatever it was
called, the proposal enabled a number of Moller organs to
be sold to customers who otherwise might not have been
able to afford any brand of organ.

Perhaps the greatest testimony to Mr. Luberoff's sales-
manship was the fabulous 4/39 he sold in 1928 to the
Stanley Company of America for the Metropolitan Opera
House in Philadelphia. For over ten years the Stanley
Company was a steady customer of Kimball and they also
bought a few Wurlitzers for their later prestige houses.
Consequently, persuading the Stanley Company to purchase a Moller was a real feather in Mr. Luberoff's cap.
Ironically, a Moller had once before graced the Met; opus
1993 was installed there in 1915 but lasted less than a year
before being removed.[39] The big 4/39 Moller of 1928
itself displaced a small Marr & Colton which had been
installed in 1926 and which, on only 8" wind pressure,[40]
was woefully inadequate in the cavernous Met.

The Met Moller was *anything* but inadequate! Voiced

Ads on this page were all financed by super salesman Louis Luberoff. 1923 ad at left foretold Moller's leasing program which was actually a sales gimmick whereby Moller carried the paper for theatre customers at very favorable terms. Luberoff never missed a bet. If he couldn't sell a new Moller to a theatre, he tried to interest them in a second-hand instrument as in the lower left ad from the June 1, 1922 Exhibitor. Lower right ad from the December 1, 1923 Exhibitor featured opus 3509, the 3/22 in the Philadelphia Fox Theatre.

Interior Victoria Theater, Shamokin, Pa., 1800 Seats

Interior Victoria Theater, Mt. Carmel, Pa., 1750 Seats

A Leading Exhibitor

CONCLUDED to personally study Pipe Organ
construction and musical design, visiting different factories, and with an organist of his own selection tested a number of large representative organs.

The result was the selection of

M. P. MÖLLER
Concert Theatre Organs

as standard equipment for theaters of

Chamberlain Amusement Enterprises, Shamokin, Pa.

and the placing of orders with us as follows:

Victoria Theater, Shamokin, Pa., four manuals
Victoria Theater, Mt. Carmel, Pa., three manuals
Victoria Theater, Mahanoy City, Pa., three manuals

Any of our customers will be glad to tell why they
selected a Möller Organ, and why they continue to
select them. A study of our list of organs will interest you.

M. P. MÖLLER, Hagerstown, Maryland

1928 N. 7th St.,   1203 Loew Bldg., 1540 Broadway,   6054 Cottage Grove Ave.,
Philadelphia, Pa.   New York City   Chicago

210 Hord Bldg.,   1630 Euclid Ave.,   Strand   Theatre   Bldg.,
Los Angeles   Memphis   (Oakland), Pittsburgh

                        109 Ponce De Leon Place,
                               Atlanta

Exterior Victoria Theater, Mahanoy City, Pa., Now Under Construction,
1850 Seats.

Exterior Victoria Theater, Mt. Carmel, Pa., 1750 Seats

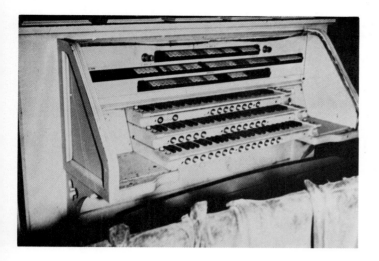

3/25 duplexed Moller in the Victoria Theatre, Mt. Carmel, Pennsylvania. This organ was installed in 1925, replacing a 3/13 unified Moller which had been in service only two years.

(opposite page) Moller ad in the October 1924 Diapason *is an interesting piece of hype, and a really fascinating story lurks beneath the surface. The Shamokin Victoria purchased a 3/16 Moller in 1917, trading it in on a new 3/13 unified Moller in 1923, a particularly early example of a fully unit Moller theatre organ. The Mt. Carmel Victoria bought an identical 3/13 unified Moller at this same time, in mid-1923. These 3/13's cost $14,000 apiece and were relatively expensive compared to other Mollers of the day. Re-reading the testimonial letter in this ad, one can now see that the unit organs spoken about so disparagingly are in fact Moller organs! In early 1925 the Mt. Carmel Victoria 3/13 unit was replaced by a 3/25 costing $18,500. This gives an idea of the great difference in cost between a unit and a duplexed organ. At the same time, early 1925, a 3/29 Moller was purchased for the Mahanoy City Victoria. The four-manual organ in the ad for the Shamokin Victoria was indeed ordered but the contract was later cancelled and the organ was never built.*[47]

At right, Moller ad in the June 1928 Diapason.

A Diapason ad in September 1924 touts the 4/41 Moller installed in Loew's State Theatre, New York City, but fails to mention that it displaced an earlier three-manual Moller installed in 1921.

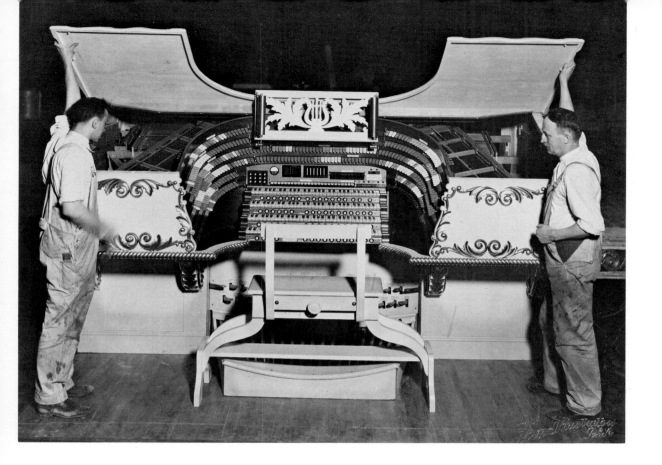

These two views reveal the interior of the largest console ever installed in a theatre, the fabulous 4/39 Moller in the Philadelphia Met. The enormous size wasn't just for show; it was actually necessary to house all the coupler and combination action mechanisms. Note that the combination action is the standard Moller mechanical tripper type. It was quite an engineering accomplishment to fit this straight-line mechanical system to the horseshoe arrangement of those 375 stops.

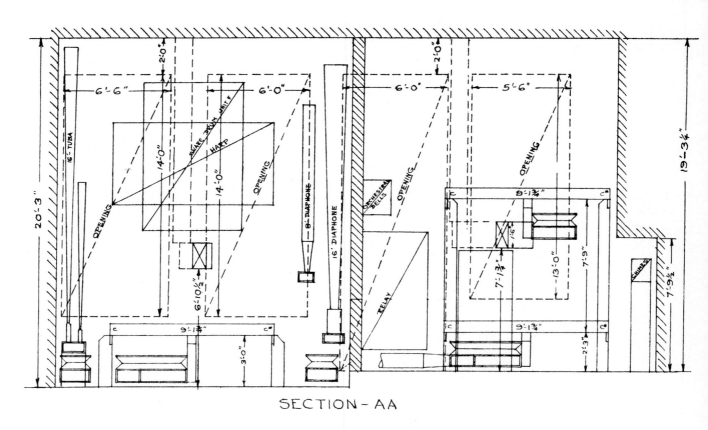

SECTION-AA

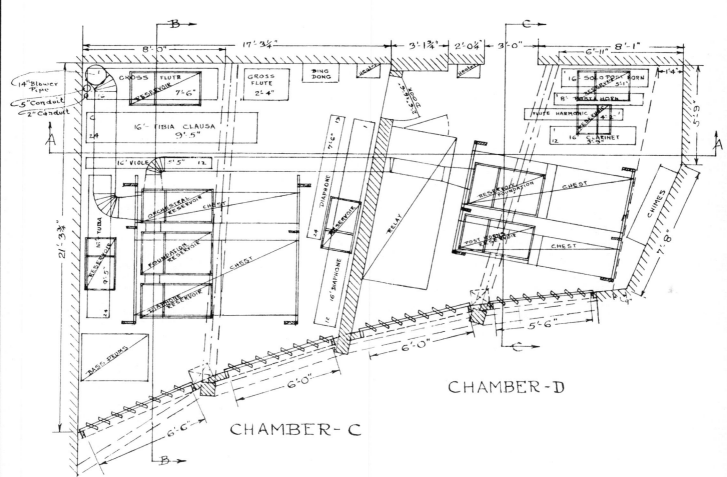

CHAMBER-C

CHAMBER-D

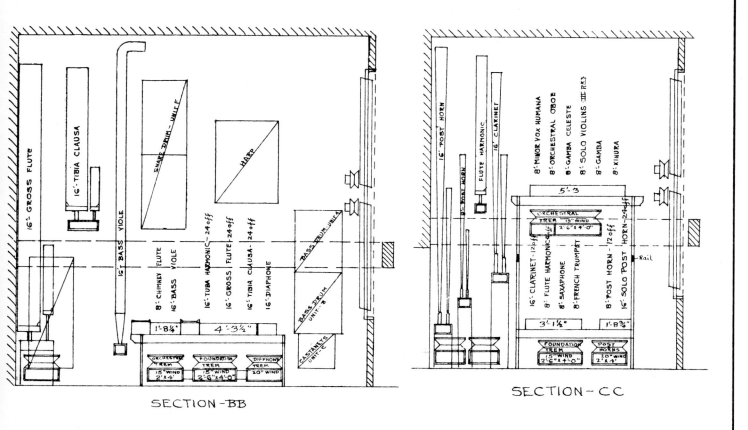

SECTION-BB

SECTION-CC

PLAN of RIGHT HAND
ORGAN CHAMBERS

DRAWN-By L.W.R.
CHECKED-By M.P.M Jr.
TRACED-By W.S.R.

STANLEY'S · METROPOLITAN · OPERA · HOUSE
PHILADELPHIA · PA

5315	SCALE - ¼"=1'-0"	M.P. Möller Pipe Organ M'f'r.
	DATE - 7-5-28	Hagerstown, Md.

4/39 MOLLER THEATRE ORGAN, OPUS 5315
Met Theatre, Philadelphia, Pennsylvania
Specifications for this instrument are reproduced in full below.

M. P. MÖLLER Organ Factory

Pipe Organ No. 5315	Date June 1st, 1928
For Stanley's Metropolitan Opera House, Philadelphia, Pennsylvania.	
Action Unit Electric thruout	Console Detached – DE LUXE CIRCLE"ART
Casing No. White Pine, Mahogany Interior	Finish Special Cream White, Gold Trim
Decorations Carvings	Motor Electric
Width of Key-bed	Stop Controls Colored Stop Keys
No. Manuals Four	Wind Pressure 15" and 20"
To be completed Sept. 1, 1928	Blower pipe furnished by Theatre

SPECIFICATIONS
A-N-A-L-Y-S-I-S

EAST SECTION
CHAMBER "A"

				Pipes Off Tremolo
A	16'	DIAPHONE - Largest scale wood Diaphone bass - zinc 36 scale at 8'C..Bearded..48 scale at 4'C-100 guage metal Hoyt - leathered....20" Wind....85 Pipes		24
B	16'	BASS VIOLE (VIOLA) - Zinc bass 44 scale at 16'C - zinc at 8'C 56 scale - spot metal treble - not too keen - moderate tone.....15" Wind.....97 Pipes		12
C	16'	TIBIA CLAUSA - Regular large heavy theatre scale same as Style 150..Leathered..15" Wind....97 Pipes		24
D	16'	GROSS FLUTE - 16' & 8' Octaves Large Pedal Open Scale Treble - #1 Scale Gross..15" Wind....85 Pipes		24
E	8'	CHIMNEY FLUTE - Orchestral Tone..Metal..15" Wind..85 Pipes		
F	16'	TUBA HARMONIC - Zinc bass..Big Scale..Harmonic at 4' FF.. ......15" Wind....85 Pipes		24
G	4'	HARP - metal resonators....dampers..single stroke only.. 61 Bars		
H		ALL DRUMS AND TRAPS - Unit a. Bass Drum I and Small Cymbal I. Unit b. Bass Drum II an Small Cymbal II. Unit c. Castanets I & II (4), Triangles I & II, Tambourines I & II, and Sleigh Bells. Unit d. Slap Sticks I. Unit e. Slap Sticks II. Unit f. Snare Drums I & II, Chinese Blocks I & II, Tom Tom, Persian Cymbals I & II, Chinese Gongs I & II, Sirens I & II, Song Birds I & II (8), Ford Horn, Auto Horn, Door Bell, Crash Cymbals. Unit g. Wind Effect I. Unit h. Wind effect II. Unit j. Aeroplane Effect. Unit k. Thunder Storm.		

CHAMBER "B"

M	8'	FLUTE HARMONIC - open wood bass...large scale metal treble ......15" Wind....85 Pipes		12
N	8'	SOLO VIOLIN III Ranks - heavy tin..new scale..15" Wind... ......255 Pipes		
P	16'	SOLO POST HORN..big tone..outstanding..20" Wind..85 Pipes		24
Q	8'	POST HORN.........20" Wind..73 Pipes		12
R	8'	GAMBA - Heavy Tin..56 Scale..biggest string..15" Wind.. ......85 Pipes		
S	8'	GAMBA CELESTE - Same as above..heavier..15" Wind..85 Pipes		
O	16'	CLARINET..big solo stop thru to 16'C..15" Wind..85 Pipes		12
T	8'	KINURA - jazzy...big...bright........15" Wind..73 Pipes		

				Pipes Off Tremolo
		CHAMBER "B" (CONT'D)		
U	8'	ORCHESTRAL OBOE..........15 Wind.....73 Pipes		
V	8'	SAXAPHONE......characteristic tone..15" Wind..73 Pipes		
W	8'	MINOR VOX HUMANA.....feminine tone..15" Wind..73 Pipes		
X	8'	FRENCH TRUMPET........15" Wind..73 Pipes		
Y		ORCHESTRAL BELLS..single & repeat strokes..37 Bars		
Z		CHIMES.........1½" bells..G to G..dampers..25 Bells		

WEST SECTION
CHAMBER "C"

AA	16'	BOURDON - 16' Oct..Large Bdn...8' Oct..Stopped tapering to 4' Oct..Open Wood Concert Scale..... Orchestral tone.....15" Wind....97 Pipes		24
BB	16'	STRING BASS ('CELLO) - 16' Oct..Heavy Wood Violine Scale Treble Spot Metal 56 Scale..Broad Tone.... Real Cello Quality..15" Wind....97 Pipes		12
CC	8'	VIOLONCELLO CELESTE - same scale as BB..15" Wind..80 Pipes		
DD	8'	STENTORPHONE - 38 Scale Inverted Languid Dig..15" Wind.. ......73 Pipes		12
EE	8'	SOLO TIBIA CLAUSA - 4 notes larger than 'C'..heavier Hard wood fronts..polished lips..... Sobby tone..Solo..20" Wind....85 Pipes		12
FF	16'	DOMBARDE - Heavy Wood Bass..Band Trombone Tone..very powerful..loudest stop..meaty..20" Wind..85 Pipes		24
GG	16'	DOUBLE TRUMPET - Very Orchestral..Brilliant..15" Wind.. ......85 Pipes		24
HH	8'	ENGLISH HORN - Characteristic......15" Wind..73 Pipes		
JJ	8'	MAJOR VOX HUMANA..big..throaty..full toned..S.S.D. .....20" Wind..73 Pipes		
KK		MARIMBA - single and repeat strokes..metal resonators 49 Bars		

CHAMBER "D"

MM	16'	TIBIA PLENA - X Large Open Bass..biggest scale..... Heavy Wood......15" Wind..85 Pipes		24
NN	8'	ORCHESTRAL VIOLINS III RANKS - tin..64 scale..... ......15" Wind..255 Pipes		
PP	8'	MUTED VIOLINS II Ranks - tin..68 scale..tapered.... ......15" Wind..146 Pipes		
RR	8'	SOLO TRUMPET..like orchestral prototype..15" Wind..73 Pipes		12
SS	8'	JAZZ CORNET..new patent stop..........15" Wind..73 Pipes		
TT	8'	FRENCH HORN..............15" Wind..73 Pipes		12
UU	8'	MEZZO VOX HUMANA..also full toned..S.S.D.15" Wind..73 Pipes		
XX		XYLOPHONE - Repeat Stroke Only..Metal Resonators.. Dig..49 Bars		
ZZ		CHRYSOGLOTT - 49 Bars if can be made..........37 Bars		

BOMBARDE ORGAN Fourth (Top) Manual.
73 Note Station.

1	16'	Diaphone...........From #A...........73 Notes
2	16'	Brass Ensemble VIII Ranks.. From #F, P, Q, X, FF, GG, RR & SS.....73
3	16'	Flute Ensemble II Ranks..From #D & MM.....73
4	16'	Strings II Ranks..Tenor C..from #R & S.....61
5	16'	Vox Humana IV Ranks..T.C...from #W & UU..61
6	8'	Diapasons II Ranks.......73
7	8'	Tibia Ensemble II Rks.......#C, EE & MM..73
8	8'	String Ensemble, XIII Ranks..From #D,N,R,S,DD,CC,NN,PP,..73
9	8'	Brass Ensemble VIII Ranks..from #F,P,Q,X, FF,GG,RR & SS..73
10	8'	Wood Wind Ensemble VI Ranks..from #O,U,T,V,HH & TT..73
11	8'	Vox Humana Chorus IX Ranks (16'& 8'&4')..From #W,JJ & UU..73
12	4'	Tibia Ensemble III Ranks..from C,EE & MM..73
13	4'	Violins Ensemble X Rks..From #N,R,S, NN & PP..73
14	4'	Wood Wind Ensemble VI Ranks..from #O,U,T,V,HH & TT..61
15	2'	Tibias II Ranks..from #C & EE..61
16	1⅗'	Fifes III Ranks..from #C, AA & EE..61
17	(4')	Xylophone..From #XX..Repeat Bottom Octave..61
18		Orchestral Bells..From #Y..Repeat Bottom & Top Octaves..61
19		Glockenspiel...from #Y..Repeat Bottom & Top Octaves Single Stroke...61
20		Marimba...from #KK..Repeat Bottom Octave..Repeat Stroke..61 Notes
21		Marimbaphone..From #KK..Repeat Bottom Octave..Single Stroke..61
22		Chrysoglott..From #ZZ..Repeat Bottom & Top Octaves..61
23		Chimes......wired 20 to 44..From #Z..25

SOLO ORGAN   Third Manual
73 Note Station.

24	16'	Diaphone..........From #A.....73 Notes
25	16'	Tibia Clausa..........C..73
26	16'	String Bass, IV Rks..........N & DD..73
27	16'	Tuba..........F..73
28	16'	Solo Trumpet..T.C...........RR..73
29	16'	Double Trumpet..........GG..73
30	16'	Bass Saxaphone..T.C...........V..61
31	16'	Vox Humana, III Rks..........W,JJ & UU..T.C...61
32	8'	Diaphonic Diapason..........A..73
33	8'	Stentorphone..........DD..73
34	8'	Tibia Plena..........MM..73
35	8'	Solo Tibia Clausa..........EE..73
36	8'	Tibia Clausa..........C..73
37	8'	Gross Flute..........D..73
38	8'	Flute Harmonic..........M..73
39	8'	Concert Flute..........AA..73
40	8'	Chimney Flute..........E..73
41	8'	Gamba..........R..73
42	8'	Gamba Celeste..........S..73
43	8'	Violoncellos..II Rks..........DD & CC..73
44	8'	Solo Violins..III Rks..........N..73
45	8'	Orch...........III..NN..73
46	8'	Muted..II..........PP..73
47	8'	Viola..........R..73
48	8'	Bombarde..........FF..73
49	8'	Tuba Harmonic..........F..73
50	8'	Solo Post Horn..........P..73
51	8'	Post Horn..........Q..73
52	8'	Solo Trumpet..........RR..73
53	8'	French Trumpet..........X..73
54	8'	Trumpet..........GG..73

Octave Orchestral Bells " Y Repeat Two Top Octaves
Repeat Stroke 61 "

SOLO ORGAN   (CONT'D)

55	8'	Jazz Cornet..........From #SS..73 Notes
56	8'	Saxaphone..........V..73 "
57	8'	French Horn..........TT..73 "
58	8'	English Horn..........HH..73 "
59	8'	Orchestral Oboe..........U..73 "
60	8'	Clarinet..........O..73 "
61	8'	Kinura..........T..73 "
62	8'	Major Vox Humana..........JJ..73 "
63	8'	Mezzo Vox Humana..........UU..73 "
64	8'	Minor Vox Humana..........W..73 "
65	4'	Solo Tibia Clausa..........EE..73 "
66	4'	Tibia Clausa..........C..73 "
67	4'	Flute Harmonic..........M..73 "
68	4'	Concert Flute..........AA..73 "
69	4'	Chimney Flute..........E..73 "
70	4'	Gamba..........R..73 "
71	4'	Gamba Celeste..........S..73 "
72	4'	Solo Violins III Rks..........N..73 "
73	4'	Orch.Violins III Rks..........NN..73 "
74	4'	Violoncellos II Rks..........DD & CC..73 "
75	4'	Viola..........R..73 "
76	4'	French Horn..........X..61 "
77	4'	Solo Trumpet..........RR..61 "
78	4'	Trumpet..........GG..61 "
79	4'	Jazz Cornet..........SS..61 "
80	4'	French Horn..........TT..61 "
81	4'	Kinura..........T..61 "
82	4'	Mezzo Vox Humana..........UU..61 "
83	4'	Minor Vox Humana..........W..61 "
84	4'	Clarinet..........O..61 "
85	2-2/3'	Solo Tibia Clausa..........EE..61 "
86	2-2/3'	Flute Harmonic..........M..61 "
87	2-2/3'	Solo Violins III Rks..........N..61 "
88	2-2/3'	Solo Tibia Clausa..........EE..61 "
89	2'	Flute Harmonic..........M..61 "
90	2'	Concert Flute..........AA..61 "
91	2'	Solo Violins III Rks..........N..61 "
92	1-3/5'	Flute Harmonic..........M..61 "
93	1-3/5'	Flute Harmonic..........M..61 "
94	1-1/7'	Solo Tibia Clausa..........EE..61 "
95	1'	Solo Tibia Clausa..........EE..61 "
96	1'	Solo Violins III Rks..........N..61 "
97	(4')	Harp..........G..61 "
98	(8')	Harp.....Tenor C..........G..61 "
99	(4')	Xylophone..........XX..Repeat Bottom Oct..61 "
100	(2')	Octave Xylophone..........XX..Repeat Bottom Oct..61 "
101		Orchestral Bells..........Y..Repeat Top & Bottom Octaves..Repeat Stroke..61

102		Glockenspiel	"	Y...Repeat Top & Bottom
		Octaves..Single Stroke	"	...61
103		Marimba	"	XX...Repeat Botton Octave...
		...Repeat Stroke	"	...61
104		Marimbaphone	"	XX...Repeat Botton Octave
		Single Stroke	"	...61
105		Chrysoglott	"	ZZ...Repeat Top & Bottom
		Octaves	"	...61
106		Chimes....wired 32-56	"	Z....25
107		First Snare Drum (Roll)	113	Chinese Blocks (Tap)
108		First Snare Drum (Tap)	114	Tambourines
109		Second Snare Drum (Roll)	115	Castanets
110		Second Snare Drum (Tap)	116	Song Birds
111		Ton Tom	117	Triangles
112		Chinese Blocks (Roll)		

-5- GREAT ORGAN   Second Manual   73 Note Station

118	16'	Tibia Clausa	From #C....73 Notes
119	16'	Bourdon	AA....73
120	16'	String Bass	BB....73
121	16'	Bass Viole	B....73
122	16'	Gamba	R...Tenor C..61
123	16'	Gamba Celeste (String Bass)	S&G...Tenor C..61
124	16'	Bombarde	FF....73
125	16'	Tuba	F....73
126	16'	Double Trumpet	GG....73
127	16'	English Horn	HH...Tenor C..61
128	16'	Orchestral Oboe	U...Tenor C..61
129	16'	Clarinet	O....73
130	16'	Kinura	T...Tenor C..61
131	16'	Major Vox Humana	JJ...Tenor C..61
132	16'	Mezzo Vox Humana	UU...Tenor C..61
133	8'	Diaphonic Diapason	A....73
134	8'	Stentorphone	DD....73
135	8'	Solo Tibia Clausa	EE....73
136	8'	Tibia Plena	MM....73
137	8'	Tibia Clausa	C....73
138	8'	Gross Flute	D....73
139	8'	Flute Harmonic	M....73
140	8'	Concert Flute	AA....73
141	8'	Chimney Flute	E....73
142	8'	Gamba	R....73
143	8'	Gamba Celeste	S....73
144	8'	Violoncellos II Ranks	DD & CC....73
145	8'	Viola	B....73
146	8'	Solo Violins III Rks	N....73
147	8'	Orch. Violins III Rks	NN....73
148	8'	Muted Violins II Rks	PP....73
149	8'	Bombarde	FF....73
150	8'	Tuba Harmonic	F....73
151	8'	Solo Post Horn	P....73
152	8'	Post Horn	Q....73
153	8'	French Trumpet	L....73
154	8'	Solo Trumpet	RR....73
155	8'	Trumpet	GG....73
156	8'	Jazz Cornet	SS....73
157	8'	Saxophone	V....73
158	8'	French Horn	TT....73
159	8'	English Horn	HH....73
160	8'	Orchestral Oboe	U....73
161	8'	Clarinet	O....73
162	8'	Kinura	T....73
163	8'	Major Vox Humana	JJ....73
164	8'	Mezzo Vox Humana	UU....73
165	8'	Minor Vox Humana	W....73
166	4'	Stentorphone	DD....61
167	4'	Solo Tibia Clausa	EE....73
168	4'	Tibia Clausa	C....73
169	4'	Flute Harmonic	M....73
170	4'	Concert Flute	AA....73
171	4'	Chimney Flute	E....73
172	4'	Gambas II Ranks	R & S....73
173	4'	Solo Violins III Rks	N....73
174	4'	Solo Post Horn	P....61
175	4'	French Trumpet	L....61
176	4'	Solo Trumpet	RR....61
177	4'	Trumpet	GG....61

-6- GREAT ORGAN (CONT'D)

178	4'	Jazz Cornet	From #SS....61 Notes
179	4'	French Horn	TT....61
180	4'	Clarinet	O....61
181	4'	Kinura	T....61
182	4'	Major Vox Humana	JJ....61
183	4'	Mezzo Vox Humana	UU....61
184	4'	Minor Vox Humana	W....61
185	2-2/3'	Solo Tibia Clausa	EE....61
186	2-2/3'	Tibia Clausa	C....61
187	2-2/3'	Gambas II Ranks	R & S....61
188	2-2/3'	Violoncellos II Ranks	DD & CC....61
189	2'	Solo Tibia Clausa	EE....61
190	2'	Tibia Clausa	C....61
191	2'	Flute Harmonic	M....61
192	2'	Concert Flute	AA....61
193	2'	Chimney Flute	E....61
194	2'	Solo Violins III Rks	N....61
195	2'	Orch. Violins III Rks	NN....61
196	(4')	Harp	G....73
197	(8')	Harp..Repeat Bottom Oct	G....73
198	(4')	Xylophone	XX...Repeat Botton Oct.61
199	(2')	Octave Xylophone	XX...Repeat Top Octave.61
200		Orchestral Bells	Y...Repeat Top & Botton Octaves....Repeat Stroke....61
201		Octave Orchestral Bells	YY...Repeat Stroke...Octaves...61
202		Glockenspiel	Y...Repeat Top & Bottom Octaves....Single Stroke...61
203		Marimba	KK...Repeat Botton Octave...Repeat Stroke.61
204		Marimbaphone	KK...Repeat Botton Octave...Single Stroke.61
205		Chrysoglott	ZZ...Repeat Top & Bottom Octaves....61
206		Chimes	Z....Wired 20 to 44....25

GREAT ORGAN SECOND TOUCH   61 Note Station

207	16'	Diaphone	From #A....61 Notes
208	16'	Gamba	R...Tenor C..49
209	16'	Gamba Celeste	S...Tenor C..49
210	16'	Bombarde	FF....61
211	16'	Solo Post Horn	P....61
212	8'	Diaphonic Diapason	A....61
213	8'	Tibia Plena	MM....61
214	8'	Solo Tibia Clausa	EE....61
215	8'	Tibia Clausa	C....61
216	8'	Gross Flute	D....61
217	8'	Gamba	R....61
218	8'	Gamba Celeste	S....61
219	8'	Bombarde	FF....61
220	8'	Tuba Harmonic	F....61
221	8'	Post Horns II Ranks	P & Q....61
222	8'	Solo Trumpet	RR....61
223		Snare Drums (Roll) (Both Drums)	

-7- ACCOMPANIMENT ORGAN   First (Bottom) Manual   73 Note Station

224	16'	Bourdon	From #AA....73 Notes
225	16'	String Bass	BB....73
226	16'	Clarinet	O....73
227	8'	Diaphonic Diapason	A....73
228	8'	Stentorphone	DD....73
229	8'	Solo Tibia Clausa	EE....73
230	8'	Tibia Clausa	C....73
231	8'	Flute Harmonic	M....73
232	8'	Concert Flute	AA....73
233	8'	Chimney Flute	E....73
234	8'	Gamba	R....73
235	8'	Gamba Celeste	S....73
236	8'	Violoncellos II Ranks	DD & CC....73
237	8'	Viola	B....73
238	8'	Solo Violins III Ranks	N....73
239	8'	Orch. Violins III Ranks	NN....73
240	8'	Muted Violins II Ranks	PP....73
241	8'	Solo Post Horn	P....73
242	8'	Post Horn	Q....73
243	8'	French Trumpet	L....73
244	8'	Solo Trumpet	RR....73
245	8'	Jazz Cornet	SS....73
246	8'	Saxophone	V....73
247	8'	French Horn	TT....73
248	8'	English Horn	HH....73
249	8'	Orchestral Oboe	U....73
250	8'	Clarinet	O....73
251	8'	Kinura	T....73
252	8'	Major Vox Humana	JJ....73
253	8'	Mezzo Vox Humana	UU....73
254	8'	Minor Vox Humana	W....73
255	4'	Tibia Clausa	C....73
256	4'	Flute Harmonic	M....73
257	4'	Concert Flute	AA....73
258	4'	Violoncello	DD....73
259	4'	Viola	B....73
260	4'	Solo Violins III Ranks	N....73
261	4'	Muted Violins II Ranks	PP....61
262	4'	Jazz Cornet	SS....61
263	4'	French Horn	TT....61
264	4'	Kinura	T....61
265	4'	Mezzo Vox Humana	UU....61
266	2-2/3'	Flute Harmonic	M....61
267	2-2/3'	Violoncello	DD....61
268	2'	Concert Flute	AA....61
269	2'	Violoncello	DD....61
270	2'	Viola	B....61
271	1-3/5'	Viola	B....61
272	(4')	Harp	G....73
273	(8')	Harp...Repeat Botton Oct	G....73
274	(4')	Xylophone	XX...Repeat Botton Octave....61
275	(2')	Octave Xylophone	XX...Repeat Top & Botton Octaves....61
276		Orchestral Bells	Y...Repeat Top & Botton Octaves....Repeat Stroke....61
277		Marimba	KK...Repeat Botton Octave....61
278		Marimbaphone	KK...Repeat Botton Octave...Single Stroke....61
279		Chrysoglott	ZZ...Repeat Top & Botton Octaves....61
280		Chimes	Z...Wired 8 to 32....25

-8- ACCOMPANIMENT ORGAN (CONT'D.)

281	First Snare Drum (Roll)
282	First Snare Drum (Tap)
283	Second Snare Drum (Roll)
284	Second Snare Drum (Tap)
285	Muffled Drum (Roll)
286	Ton Tom
287	Chinese Blocks (Roll)
288	Chinese Blocks (Tap)
289	Tambourines
290	Castanets

ACCOMPANIMENT ORGAN SECOND TOUCH   61 Note Station

291	16'	Bombarde	From #FF....61 Notes
292	16'	Tuba	F....61
293	16'	Solo Post Horn	P....61
294	8'	Diaphonic Diapason	A....61
295	8'	Tibia Plena	MM....61
296	8'	Solo Tibia Clausa	EE....61
297	8'	Gross Flute	D....61
298	8'	Gamba	R....61
299	8'	Gamba Celeste	S....61
300	8'	Solo Violins III Ranks	N....61
301	8'	Orch. Violins III Ranks	NN....61
302	8'	Post Horns II Ranks	P & Q....61
303	8'	Trumpets III Ranks	L, GG & RR....61
304	8'	French Horn	TT....61
305	8'	Clarinet	O....61
306	(4')	Xylophone	XX...Repeat Stroke....61
307		Glockenspiel	Y...Repeat Top & Botton Octaves...Single Stroke....61
308		Chimes....wired 8 to 32	Z....25
309		Snare Drums (Roll) (Both Drums)	
310		Triangles	
311		Song Birds	

PEDAL ORGAN

32 Note Station

312	32'	Acoustic Bass...........From A & C.............32 Notes
313	32'	Resultant Bombarde....... " FF..............32 "
314	16'	Diaphone............... " A..............32 "
315	16'	Tibia Plena............ " MM.............32 "
316	16'	Tibia Clausa........... " C..............32 "
317	16'	Gross Flute............ " D..............32 "
318	16'	Bourdon................ " AA.............32 "
319	16'	String Bass............ " DD.............32 "
320	16'	Bass Viole............. " S..............32 "
321	16'	Bombarde............... " FF.............32 "
322	16'	Tuba................... " F..............32 "
323	16'	Solo Post Horn......... " P..............32 "
324	16'	Double Trumpet......... " GG.............32 "
325	16'	Clarinet............... " O..............32 "
326	8'	Diaphonic Diapason..... " A..............32 "
327	8'	Stentorphone.......... " DD.............32 "
328	8'	Tibia Plena........... " MM.............32 "
329	8'	Solo Tibia Clausa..... " EE.............32 "
330	8'	Tibia Clausa.......... " C..............32 "
331	8'	Gross Flute........... " D..............32 "
332	8'	Gambas II Ranks....... " R & S.........32 "
333	8'	Violoncellos II Ranks. " BB & CC........32 "
334	8'	Solo Violins III Ranks. " N............32 "
335	8'	Orchestral Violins III Rks. " NN......32 "

-9-
PEDAL ORGAN (CONT'D)

336	8'	Bombarde................From FF.............32 Notes
337	8'	Tuba................... " F..............32 "
338	4'	Tibia Clausa II Ranks.. " C & EE.........32 "
339	4'	Gambas................. " R & S.........32 "
340	4'	Violoncellos II Ranks.. " BB & CC........32 "
341	4'	Solo Violins III Ranks. " N.............32 "
342	4'	Tuba................... " F..............32 "
343	4'	Bombarde............... " FF.............32 "

PEDAL ORGAN SECOND TOUCH

32 Notes Station

344	16'	Diaphone...............From A.............32 Notes
345	16'	Bombarde............... " FF.............32 "
346	16'	Solo Post Horn........ " P..............32 "
347	16'	Double Trumpet........ " GG.............32 "
348	8'	Solo Tibia Clausa..... " EE.............32 "
349	8'	Bombarde.............. " FF.............32 "
350	8'	Tuba.................. " F..............32 "
351		Chimes....wired 8 to 32.. " Z............25 "
352		First Bass Drum
353		Second Bass Drum
354		First Cymbal
355		Second Cymbal
356		Kettle Drums (On both Bass Drums)
357		Snare Drums (Roll) (Both Drums)
358		Persian Cymbals
359		Chinese Gongs

COUPLERS

360		Bombarde 4'
361		Bombarde 2'
362		Solo 4'
363		Great 4'
364		Accomp. 4'
365		Accomp. to Great 8'
366		Solo to Great (8')
367		Bombarde to Great (8')
368		Solo to Pedal (8')
369		Bombarde to Pedal (8')
370		Great to Pedal (8')
371		Accomp. to Pedal (8')
372		Pedal Octave

TRICK COUPLERS

Not affected by Combinations or Crescendo.

373		Great to Solo 4-4/7'
374		Great to Solo 5-1/3'
375		Great to Solo 6-2/5'

EFFECTS

(By Spring Stop Keys Over Solo)

376		Song Birds I (4 Birds)
377		Song Birds II (4 Birds)
378		Siren I (Megaphone)
379		Siren II (Megaphone)
380		Ford Horn (Pneumatic Switch)
381		Door Bell (Telephone)
382		Slap Sticks (2 Sets)
383		Steamboat Whistle (Separate Pipes)
384		Auto Horn

-10-
EFFECTS (CONT'D.)

385		Aeroplane Effect
386		Triangle
387		Persian Cymbals (1st touch, repeat stroke; 2nd touch, single stroke, 3 Hammers)
388		Chinese Gongs (1st touch, repeat stroke; 2nd touch, single stroke, 3 Hammers)
389		Grand Crash (1st touch, Snare Drum Roll; 2nd touch, Crash)
390		Cymbals (Small)
391		Grand Cymbals (Chinese Crash) 2 Cymbals
392		Sleigh Bells (Reversible)
393		Wind Effect (Reversible-Also for Surf Effect (2 outfits)
394		Storm (Thunder Roll Soft Graduated)
395		Thunder Crash (1st touch, Roll; 2nd touch, Crash-Graduated)
396		Chime Peal (Reversible)
397		Ding Dong I
398		Ding Dong II

(By Spring Foot Levers)

399		Triangles-2
400		Persian Cymbals (1st touch, repeat stroke; 2nd touch, single stroke, 3 Hammers)
401		Chinese Gongs (1st touch, repeat stroke; 2nd touch, single stroke, 3 Hammers)
402		Grand Crash (1st touch, Snare Drum Roll; 2nd touch, Crash)
403		Cymbals (Small)
404		Grand Cymbals (Chinese Crash) 2 Cymbals
405		Sleigh Bells (Reversible)
406		Wind Effect (Reversible-Also for Surf Effect) (2 outfits)
407		Storm (Thunder Roll Soft Graduated)
408		Thunder Crash (1st touch, Roll; 2nd touch, Crash-Graduated)
409		Chime Peal (Reversible)
410		Ding Dong I
411		Ding Dong II

TREMOLOS (Engraved Vibrato)

412		Diaphone - Affecting Stop A
413		Post Horns - Affecting Stops P & Q
414		Major Vox Humana - Affecting Stop JJ
415		Mezzo Vox Humana - Affecting Stop UU
416		Violoncellos - Affecting Stops BB & CC
417		East Foundation - Affecting Stops C,D,F,M,O,V & X
418		East Orchestral - Affecting Stops B,E,N,R,T,U & W
419		West 20" Foundation - Affecting Stops EE & FF
420		West Foundation - Affecting Stops AA,DD,GG, & HH,LL,RR & TT.
421		West Orchestral - Affecting Stops NN, PP & SS.

ADJUSTABLE COMBINATIONS

(Adjustable at the Bench by the Pistons)

Six Double Acting Pistons and Cancel affecting on 1st touch the Bombarde Stops; ~~XXXXXXXXXXXXXXXXXXXXXXXXXXXXXX~~ on 2nd touch, the Pedal Stops.

Six Double Acting Pistons and Cancel affecting on 1st touch the Solo Stops; on 2nd touch, the Pedal Stops

Six Double Acting Pistons and Cancel affecting on 1st touch the Great Stops; on 2nd touch, the Pedal Stops.

Six Double Acting Pistons and Cancel affecting on 1st touch the Accompaniment Stops; on 2nd touch the Pedal Stops

Six Pistons and Cancel affecting the Pedal Stops;
Six Pistons and Cancel affecting the Entire Organ.

-11-
ACCESSORIES
Manual

1	Locking Slides Connecting any or all Expression to any Pedal.
	Sforzando Piston (reversible) under Great Manual-Cancels percussions & tremolos-green light when on)
2	Trap Cancel Piston-Moves Stop Keys.
3	Vibrate Cancel Piston-Moves Stop Keys.
4	Coupler Cancel Piston-Moves Stop Keys.
5	2nd Touch Cancel Piston-Moves Stop Keys.
6	Drum Pistons ("On" and "Off")-(Snare Drums Roll on Accompaniment Manual; Bass Drum and Cymbal on Pedal Organ, 2nd touch White light when On)
7	Electric Piston for Operator's Booth.
8	Electric Piston for Attendant.
9	Red Light for Crescendo.
10	Natural Light for Generator Test.
11	Red and White Disk Indicators for Expression and Crescendo Pedals.
12	Yellow Light for Harp Dampers when "On".
13	Purple Light for Chime Dampers when "On".
14	Voltmeter

(Pedal)

15	Lever for Chime Dampers (reversible)
16	Lever for Harp Dampers (reversible)
17	Sforzando Lever (reversible-duplicating action of 1.)
18	Balanced Expression Pedal I)
19	Balanced Expression Pedal II)
20	Balanced Expression Pedal III) Concaved Smooth Raw Wood & Lettered
21	Balanced Expression Pedal IV)
22	Crescendo Pedal (Cancels percussions & tremolos)
23	Balanced Master Expression Pedal affecting all Expressions.

One Blower, Motor and Generator of ample capacity under any test.
Electric lights for Stop Controls and Pedal Board.
Organists bench with Adjustable Spring Back.
Wide music rack with three way nickle plated adjustment.
Circular Lever Board above Pedal Keys.
Concave and Radiating Pedal Clavier, extended Naturals.
New type flat wire relay.
Silver wire for all stop action and other round wire contacts.
Moller Unit System in this organ - separate outside magnets for each pipe; and separate primary for relay and each chest valve over one half inch in diameter.

When organ is not in use, swell shades to be closed.

ALM
6/5/28
Checked by........................date...................,.....

entirely on 15" and 20" wind pressure (even the voxes!) and having 375 stops, it ranks as one of the most tremendous theatre organs ever built.

Louis Luberoff and the Moller company apparently wanted the Met contract pretty badly; the contract price of $20,000 was probably below Moller's actual cost. (As a comparison, note that the Atlanta Fox 4/42 Moller cost $42,000.) The Met contract differed from Moller's standard contracts of the day by including several stringent provisions. One of the provisions was that "The organ shall equal, if not surpass, any make organ now installed in any theatre in [the] United States of American for the purposes of lessee's business requirements." Another clause stated that the organ would be "subject to the entire approval and satisfaction of any disinterested expert that lessee may appoint." Perhaps the most stringent part

ANOTHER DISTINCT TRIUMPH!

THE
M. P. MÖLLER UNIT THEATRE ORGAN

For a number of years we have carefully watched and studied the trend of the screen theatre organ, observed its rigid requirements and realize that the demand is for the unit type of construction. We felt, however, that when Möller makes a Unit Theatre Organ, it must be more mechanically dependable in order to withstand the tremendous usage given it, that it must tonally be vastly improved and that its response should be instantaneous.

It was resolved by us not to build unit organs until these improvements could be had, and that, furthermore, the method of construction must come from an entirely different angle. Such an organ must be radical—new—it must perform in a manner compared with the degree of excellence enjoyed by the Möller Church and Concert Organs and by the Möller "Artiste" Reproducing Organ. In short, it must be THE BEST, and it is with the greatest pride and pleasure that we announce its accomplishment.

To begin with, the Möller Unit Theatre Organ (with the exception of the percussion) is built under our own roof and is positively guaranteed not to be an assembled instrument. Its magnets are of our improved "outside" type with armatures that move within a brass cylindrical container and that are REMOVABLE and REPLACEABLE without interruption of playing. Percussion parts are obtained from the highest specialized manufacturers and cymbals are of imported make. The Möller relay is a distinct achievement in electrical engineering. Fewer contacts are employed to produce greater results than have heretofore been used to obtain lesser ones. Traps, harps, xylophones, etc., operate with marvelous response and purity and naturalness of tone, and the specialized attention given to the voicing of the pipes accounts for their beautiful individual and ensemble musical effect.

All these points of superiority in the Möller Unit Theatre Organ make it responsive to every single mood expression of the organist as called for from the picture and assure durability of the instrument, positive and quick mechanical performance and, in their total, make a unit type of theatre organ that may unfailingly be depended upon in every respect.

The manufacturing cost of such an organ is, of course, relatively high, but due to the very large Möller factory facilities, output and purchasing power, it is possible to absorb it and to provide these instruments at competitive prices.

M. P. MÖLLER,
Factory and Executive Offices
Hagerstown, Maryland

1203 LOEW BLDG., 1540 BROADWAY, NEW YORK CITY	224 LATHROP BLDG., KANSAS CITY	1203 FRANKLIN TRUST BLDG., PHILADELPHIA
6054 COTTAGE GROVE AVE., CHICAGO	2367-73 MARKET ST., SAN FRANCISCO	MEDICAL ARTS BLDG., MEMPHIS
4109 LYNDALE AVE., S., MINNEAPOLIS	333 JACKSON BLDG. BUFFALO	129 NORTH AVE., N. E., ATLANTA
1626 CALIFORNIA ST., DENVER	1514 FORBES ST., PITTSBURGH	1009 FIRST AVE., SEATTLE

This Diapason ad of May 1928 offers a somewhat lame excuse for Moller's late entry into the unit theatre organ market. The truth was that M. P. Moller, Sr. personally despised unit organs and resigned himself to building them only when the demand for his straight/duplex style of theatre organ had nearly ceased.

Opus 5819 for the Philadelphia Convention Hall nears completion in the enormous Moller erecting room. This organ contained the first metal 32' pipes built in the Moller factory.[53]

of the contract, virtually *never* included in any ordinary organ sales agreement, provided that Moller would "change any tonality of the organ at its own cost and expense that it may be directed to change by lessee and to continue making such changes until lessee is thoroughly pleased and satisfied in every detail."[41]

The Met organ was removed in the 1940s and placed in a railroad box car, reportedly for shipment to a college in a western state. The man responsible for the shipment "liberated" one of the 20" post horns. That rank today is the only known remnant of the fabulous Met organ; the rest of it was destroyed by fire before reaching its destination.[42]

A close cousin of the Met organ was the 4/42 Moller installed in the Atlanta Fox just one year after the Met was installed. Although the Fox organ was three ranks larger than the Met it had fewer stops (350 as compared to the Met's 375) and had no pressures higher than 15". In the Atlanta organ ten ranks in the ethereal chamber are on only 6" wind while the other 32 ranks are on 15" pressure. A particularly unusual and interesting feature of the

Fox organ is a set of 25 tuned bird whistles, playable only from the accompaniment second touch.[43] The Atlanta Fox organ reigned for three years as the largest unit organ in a theatre until the 58-rank Wurlitzer was installed in the Radio City Music Hall in 1932.

As stated earlier, 85% of Moller's theatre instruments were essentially similar to Moller's church organ designs of the period. Most had little unification and were on modest pressures such as 5". By the mid-1920s demand for this style of organ had diminished considerably and Moller realized that to secure continued theatre business, fully unified organs would have to be offered. At least six styles of unit organs were developed as follows:

Style	Size	# Sold
40	2/4	2
50	2/5	2
60	2/6	2
70	3/7	5
100	3/10	5
150	3/15	0

A Masterpiece

Webster defines the word masterpiece as "a work show-ing the hands of a master; *an admirable production.*"

Such a work is the huge

Two-Console Four-Manual "Artiste"
M. P. MÖLLER ORGAN

just completed in the

Philadelphia Municipal Auditorium

Built by M. P. Möller—master organ builder of over fifty years' expe-rience—with a staff of extraordinarily skilled workmen and the finest, most up-to-date equipment in the largest organ plant in existence.

M P MÖLLER
The Artist of Organs   The Organ of Artists
Hagerstown   Maryland

Ad in the September 1931 Diapason *features Moller opus 5819. The theatre console plays 20 of the organ's 86 ranks; the drawknob console controls 85 ranks, omitting only the kinura. Note the splendid Art Deco cases on the consoles and roll player.*

STYLE 70 MOLLER THEATRE ORGAN
Specifications of this relatively popular style are reproduced below.

STYLE 70 UNIT THEATRE ORGAN

M. P. MÖLLER Organ Factory

Pipe Organ No. 5214	Date Jan. 27, 1928
For Strand Theatre, Sunbury, Pa.	
Action Unit Electric	Console Detached 50'
Casing No. Console only-quartered oak	Finish
Decorations No case grille or display pipes	Motor Elec
Width of Key-bed	Stop Controls Colored Stop Keys in circle
No. Manuals Three	Wind Pressure Pipes-10". Traps on blower wind reservoir.
To be completed Aug. 15, 1928	Blower pipe furnished by Theatre

SPECIFICATIONS
A-N-A-L-Y-S-I-S
Chamber One

A	16'	TIBIA CLAUSA..1-12 X Heavy Pedal-Rest Largest Theatre Scale-Leathered	97 Pipes 1-24 Off
B	16'	VIOLE D' ORCHESTRE..16' Octave-45 scale-stringy metal bass mitered to 10' 6"-8' Octave & treble-large scale	97 Pipes
C	8'	VIOLE CELESTE..Sharp. Scale.tin. Large feet	85 Pipes
D	8'	KINURA..Jazz type. Duck Bill	73 "
E		CHIMES 1¼"	20 Bells
F		ORCHESTRAL BELLS..Standard metal resonators	37 Bars
G		All drums and traps	
		Unit a.- Bass Drum and Small Cymbal.	
		Unit b.- Castanets (2), Triangle, Tambourine and Sleigh Bells.	
		Unit c.- Slap Sticks.	
		Unit d.- Snare Drum, Chinese Block, Tom Tom, Siren, etc.	

Chamber Two

H	8'	DIAPASON..38 Sc.Zinc bass-Inverted Languid-Zinc bearded bass Leathered X Heavy Metal	73 Pipes 1-12 Off
I	8'	TUBA HARMONIC.....5½ 8' C	73 " 1-12 Off
J	8'	VOX HUMANA.....Alto Vox S.S.B	73 "
K		XYLOPHONE..Standard Metal Resonators-Repeat Stroke Only..49 Bars	

SOLO ORGAN

		Top Manual		73 Station	
1	8'	Diapason Phonon	From #F	73	Notes
2	8'	Tibia Clausa	" A	73	"
3	8'	Violas II Rks.	" B & C	73	"
4	4'	Solo Piccolo	" A	73	"
5	4'	Violins II Rks.	" B & C	73	"
6	2-2/3'	Tibia Twelfth	" A	61	"
7	2'	Whistle	" A	61	"
8	16'	Tuba Profunda	T.C. " I	73	"
9	8'	Tuba Harmonic	" I	61	"
10	8'	Kinura	" D	73	"
11	8'	Vox Humana	" J	73	"
12	4'	Kinura	" D	61	"
13		Chimes (34-53)	" E	20	"
14		Xylophone	" K-Repeat Bot. Oct.	61	"

SOLO ORGAN (Cont'd.)

15		Octave Xylophone	From #K-Repeat Top Octave.	61 Notes
16		Glockenspiel-(Single Stroke)	" F- " & Bot.Oct.	61 "
17		Orchestral Bells (Repeat Stroke)	F- " " " "	61 "
18	8'	*Harp Celeste		
19	8'	*French Trumpet		
20	8'	*Orchestral Flute		
21	4'	*Flute		
22	8'	*Viole d'Amour		
23	8'	*Clarinet		

GREAT ORGAN

		Middle Manual		73 Station	
24	16'	Contra Tibia	Tenor C.From #A	61 Notes
25	16'	Bass Viole	Tenor C. " B	61 "
26	8'	Diapason Phonon	" H	73 "
27	8'	Tibia Clausa	" A	73 "
28	8'	Viole d'Orchestre	" B	73 "
29	8'	Viole Celeste	" C	73 "
30	4'	Solo Piccolo	" A	73 "
31	4'	Violin	" B	73 "
32	4'	Violins II	" B & C	73 "
32a	3-2/3'	Nazard Viole	" B-(switch only-no stop control)	
33	2-2/3'	Tibia Twelfth	" A	61 Notes
34	2'	Whistle	" A	61 "
35	2'	Viole Fifteenth	" B	61 "
36	1-3/5'	Viole Tierce	" C	61 "
37	1'	Fife	" A	61 "
38	16'	Tuba Profunda	Tenor C. " I	61 "
39	8'	Tuba Harmonic	" I	73 "
40	8'	Kinura	" D	73 "
41	8'	Vox Humana	" J	73 "
42	8'	Orchestral Oboe	(Syn.) Draws 28,29 & 23	61 "
43	8'	Saxophone	(Syn.) Draws 27,29,29,32a & 40	61 "
44	4'	Kinura	From #D	61 "
45	4'	Vox Humana	" J	61 "
46		Chimes (22-41)	" E	20 "
47		Xylophone	" K-Repeat Bottom Octave.	61 Notes
48		Orchestral Bells-(Repeat Stroke)	F- " & Top "	61 "
49		Glockenspiel-(Single Stroke)	From F- " " "	61 "
50	8'	*Harp Celeste		
51	4'	*Harp Celeste		
52	8'	*French Trumpet		
53	8'	*Orchestral Flute		
54	4'	*Flute		
55	8'	*Viole d'Amour		
56	16'	*Bourdon		

ACCOMPANIMENT ORGAN

		Bottom Manual		73 Station	
57	16'	Bass Viole	Tenor C. From #B	61 Notes
58	8'	Diapason Phonon	" H	73 "
59	8'	Tibia Clausa	" A	73 "
60	8'	Viole d'Orchestre	" B	73 "
61	8'	Viole Celeste	" C	73 "
62	4'	Solo Piccolo	" A	73 "
63	4'	Violin	" B	73 "
64	4'	Violins II	" B & C	73 "
64a	2-2/3'	Twelfth	" A-(switch only-no stop control)	
65	2-2/3'	Nazard Viole	" B	61 Notes
66	2'	Whistle	" A	61 "
67	2'	Viole Fifteenth	" B	61 "
68	1-3/5'	Viole Tierce	" C	61 "
69	1'	Violette	" B	61 "
70	16'	Vox Human	Tenor C. " J	73 "
71	8'	Tuba Harmonic	" I	73 "
72	8'	Kinura	" D	73 "
73	8'	Vox Humana	" J	73 "
74	8'	Orchestral Oboe	(Syn.) Draws #50,61 & 64a	73 "
75	8'	Saxophone	(Syn.) Draws #59,60,61,65 & 72	73 "
76		Chimes (10-29)	From #E	20 "
77		Orchestral Bells-(Repeat Stroke)	F-(Repeat Bottom & Top Octave	61 Notes
78		Glockenspiel-(Single Stroke)	From F-(Repeat Bottom & Top Octave	61 Notes
79	16'	*Bourdon		
80	8'	*Harp Celeste		
81	4'	*Harp Celeste		
82	8'	*Orchestral Flute		
83	4'	*Flute		
84	8'	*French Trumpet		
85	8'	*Viole d'Amour		
86		Snare Drum Roll-(Two Strikers)		
87		Snare Drum Tap		
88		Muffled Drum Roll		
89		Chinese Block Roll		
90		Chinese Block Tap		
91		Tom Tom (Large)		
92		Castanets (2)		
93		Tambourine		
94		Slap Sticks		

(SECOND TOUCH)

				61 Station	
95	8'	Tibia	From #A	61	Notes
96	8'	Diapason Phonon	" H	61	"
97	8'	Tuba Harmonic	" I	61	"
98	8'	Cellos II Rks.	" B & C	61	"
99		Glockenspiel (Single Stroke)	F-Repeat Bottom & Top Oct	61 Notes
100		Xylophone	" K-Repeat Bottom Octave	61 Notes
101	8'	*French Trumpet		
102	16'	*Tuba Profunda		
103	8'	*Clarinet		

PEDAL ORGAN

				32 Station	
104	32'	Acoustic Bass	From #A & B	32	Notes
105	16'	Viole	" B	32	"
106	16'	Bass	" A	32	"
107	8'	Diaphonic Diapason	" H	32	"
108	8'	Tibia Clausa	" A	32	"
109	8'	Cellos II Rks.	" B & C	32	"
110	8'	Viola	" B	32	"
111	4'	Violins II Rks.	" B & C	32	"
112	4'	Flute	" A	32	"
113	8'	Tuba Harmonic	" I	32	"
114	16'	*Tuba		
115	16'	*Bourdon		

(SECOND TOUCH)

				32 Station	
116	32'	Acoustic Bass	From #A & C	32	Notes
117	8'	Diapason	" H	32	"
118		Bass Drum		
119		Cymbal		
120		Slapsticks		
121		Kettle Drum (Roll or Bass Drum)		
122	16'	*Tuba - Relay & Console only.		

COUPLERS

123		Solo to Solo 4'
124		Great to Great 4'
125		Solo to Great (8')
126		Accompaniment to Accompaniment 4'
127		Great to Pedal (8')
128		Solo to Pedal (8')
129		Accompaniment to Pedal (8')

TRICK COUPLERS
Not affected by Combinations or Crescendo

130		Great to Solo 4-4/7'
131		Great to Solo 5-1/3'
132		Great to Solo 6-2/5'

EFFECTS
(By Spring Stop Keys Over Solo)

133		Song Bird I
134		Song Bird II
135		Siren (Megaphone)
136		Ford Horn (Pneumatic Switch)
137		Door Bell
138		Slap Sticks
139		Steamboat Whistle (Separate Pipes)
140		Blank Stop Control
141		Blank Stop Control
		(By Spring Foot Levers)
142		Triangle
143		Persian Cymbal (1st touch, repeat stroke; 2nd touch, single stroke, 3 Hammers
144		Chinese Gong (1st " , repeat stroke; 2nd touch single stroke, 3 Hammers
145		Grand Crash (1st " , Snare Drum Roll; 2nd touch, Crash)

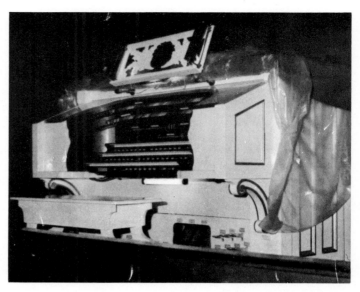

```
                    EFFECTS   (Cont'd.)

146        Cymbal (Small)
147        Grand Cymbal (Chinese Crash)
148        Sleigh Bells (Reversible Levers)
149        Wind Effect (Reversible Lever-Also for Surf Effect)
150        Storm (Thunder Roll Soft Graduated)
151        Thunder Crash (1st touch, Roll; 2nd touch, Crash-Graduated)

                    T R E M O L O S   (Engraved vibrato)

152        Right Foundation (Stops A)
153        Right Orchestral (Stops B, C & D)
154        Left Foundation (Stops H & I)
155        Left Orchestral  (Stops J)

                    ADJUSTABLE COMBINATIONS
               (Adjustable at the Bench by the Pistons)

     Six Double Acting Pistons and Cancel affecting on 1st touch, the Great
                    Stops; on 2nd touch the Pedal Stops.
     Six Double Acting Pistons and Cancel affecting on 1st touch, the Solo
                    Stops; on 2nd touch the Pedal Stops.
     Six Double Acting Pistons and Cancel affecting on 1st touch, the Accompan-
                    iment Stops; on 2nd touch the Pedal Stops.
     Six Pistons and Cancel affecting the Pedal Stops.
     Six Pistons and Cancel affecting the Entire Organ.

                    ACCESSORIES
                    (Manual)

 1     Sforzando Piston (reversible) under Great Manual-Cancels percussions
                    & tremolos-green light when on).
 2     Trap Cancel Piston-Moves Stop Keys.
 3     Vibrato Cancel Piston-Moves Stop Keys.
 4     Coupler Cancel Piston-Moves Stop Keys.
 5     2nd Touch Cancel Piston-Moves Stop Keys.
 6     Drum Pistons ("On and "Off")-(Snare Drum on Accompaniment Manual;
                    Bass Drum and Cymbal on Pedal Organ White light when on)
 7     Electric Piston for Operator's Booth.
 8     Electric Piston for Attendant.
 9     Red Light for Crescendo.
10     Natural Light for Generator Test.
11     Red and White Disk Indicators for Expression and Crescendo Pedal.
12     Yellow Light for Harp Dampers when "On".
13     Lever for Harp Dampers (reversible)
14     Sforzando Lever (reversible-duplicating action of 1.)
15     Balanced Expression Pedal, Right Chamber. Concaved Smooth Raw Wood
                    & lettered.
16     Balanced Expression Pedal, Left Chamber, Concaved Smooth Raw Wood &
                    lettered.
17     Crescendo Pedal (Cancels percussions & tremolos)



     One Blower Motor and Generator of ample capacity under any test.
     Electric lights for Stop Controls and Pedal Board.
     Organists bench with Adjustable Spring Back.
     Wide music rack with three way nickle plated adjustment.
     Circular Lever Board above Pedal Keys.
     Concave and Radiating Pedal Clavier, extended Naturals.
     New type flat wire relay.
     Silver wire for all stop action and other round wire contacts.
     Moller Unit System in this organ - separate outside magnets for each pipe
     and separate primary for relay and each chest valve over one half inch in diameter.
     All stops marked (*) are preparations in console and relay only-no pipes or
     chest included.

ALM

Checked by.........................date.....................
```

3/7 style 70 Moller in the Capitol Theatre, Rome, New York.

These styles featured interesting specifications and offered more than much of the competition did for a similar size of organ. Even so, only 16 organs of all six styles were sold. Most of the Moller unit theatre organs, like most other Moller organs of all types, featured unique specifications custom designed for each instrument.

Well after the end of the theatre organ era in this country, Moller received a contract for their first five-manual organ. This instrument was quite unlike any organ ever built before or since inasmuch as it was designed for portable use in vaudeville performances. The idea of a portable organ was not new but never had it been attempted on such a grand scale, with 27 ranks of large-scale theatre pipework including four full-length 16' stops. The completed organ became the most famous Moller ever built and indeed is one of the most famous organs in history. Now permanently installed in the Pasadena Civic Auditorium in California, it is among the three or four finest theatre organs extant in the 1980s. It is, of course, the famous Reginald Foort 5/27 Moller, opus 6690.

The organ was constructed in 1938 at the giveaway price of $24,615 with the hope that the publicity it would generate would result in the sale of a number of Moller organs in the British Isles. Unfortunately, World War II erupted less than a year after the organ arrived in England, precluding its use for touring. Contrary to some rumors, the organ was paid for, finally, in 1946, but despite the enormous amount of publicity it generated, no other Moller organs were ever sold to the British Isles.[44]

The factory man most directly responsible for the Foort organ was Richard Oliver Whitelegg who took special pride in it since he was an Englishman. Before coming to the United States, Whitelegg had worked for several English organ builders including Willis and Harrison & Harrison. His first American employment was at the Aeolian factory in 1926 as a reed voicer. In 1927 he became head voicer at Welte and joined Moller in late 1931[54] when Welte's demise was imminent. Whitelegg was the first person to assume the post of tonal director at Moller[55] and his work was certainly the equal of another famous Englishman, G. Donald Harrison. Unfortunately, Whitelegg's work isn't as well remembered today inasmuch as he predeceased Harrison by twelve years.

Whitelegg did much of the engineering work on the Foort organ as well as its scaling and some voicing. In his directions to the factory, Reginald Foort specified that the chorus trumpet was to be "of Whitelegg type of voicing . . . a real church organ type of Willis chorus reed" and that the smaller of the two diapasons was to be "a perfect Whitelegg type of church organ diapason."[56]

The man responsible for most of the reed voicing in the Foort organ was Adolf Zajic,[57] one of the finest reed voicers who ever lived. Mr. Zajic began his career by working in the erecting room of the Welte factory and soon realized his ambition to become a voicer. He left Welte to join Moller along with Richard Whitelegg in late 1931.[58] Although he had to retire from Moller at age 68 in accordance with union regulations, Mr. Zajic is still voicing reeds as well as ever in the 1980s in the Hagerstown shop of the Trivo Company, Inc., where he works with Homer

Richard O. Whitelegg
(1890-1944)[71]

M. P. Moller, Sr. (right) is about to enter a New York City theater with famous organ architect George Ashdown Audsley, no doubt to enjoy a performance on a Moller organ.

This 4/11 Moller was installed in the Chicago Musical College in 1926.

Lewis and Joseph Clipp who were once his trainees at the Moller plant.

Before Richard Whitelegg joined the Moller organization there had never been a tonal director as such. In the later 1920s M. P. Moller, Jr. did much of the scaling and Louis Luberoff had a considerable influence on the tonal concepts of the DeLuxe unified theatre organs. Many Moller organs were specified by organ architects such as G. A. Audsley or William H. Barnes who were consultants hired by the purchasers and were not on the Moller payroll. In those days Moller would build *anything!* One of the author's favorite examples is the following theatre organ specification. Have you ever heard of a string celeste *tierce*? Well, you're about to!

3/24 MOLLER THEATRE ORGAN, OPUS 4777
Allegheny Theatre, Philadelphia, Pennsylvania

M. P. MÖLLER Organ Factory

4777

Pipe Organ No.	Date July 8, 1926
For	Allegheny Theatre, Philadelphia, Pa.,
Action	Electric Console Detached
Casing No.	Finish
Decorations None	Motor Elec.
Width of Key-bed Three	Stop Controls
No. Manuals	Wind Pressure 10"
To be completed January 15, 1927	Blower pipe furnished by Theatre

SPECIFICATIONS

A-440
SWELL CHAMBERS; By Purchaser

SOLO ORGAN - top manual
in upper chamber - right side - 61 Chest.

1	8'	STENTORPHONE..unit-38 scale-wood bass....................61	Pipes
2	8'	HARMONIC FLUTE..unit-stopped wood bass-metal treble....85	"
3	4'	Flute........from #2.........................61	Notes
4	2-2/3'	Flute.........from #2.........................61	"
5	8'	POST HORN.....unit..VERY-POWERFUL...............61	Pipes
6	8'	VOX HUMANA.......unit..MAJOR-SCALE............61	"
7	16'	OBOE HORN......unit..capped pipes..............85	"
8	8'	Oboe Horn........from #7.......................61	Notes
9	4'	Oboe Clarion.......from #7....................61	"
10		MARIMBA HARP..single stroke-wood bar..........49	Bars
11		Marimbaphone..repeat stroke-on #10...........49	Notes

in lower chamber - right side - 73 chest

12	16'	String.........Tenor C...from #14............61	Notes
13	16'	String Celeste...Tenor C...from #15...........61	"
14	8'	STRING.....unit..Major scale..pure tin.........85	Pipes
15	8'	STRING CELESTE...Major scale..pure tin..........85	"
16	8'	TIBIA CLAUSA....unit..largest scale.............73	"
17	4'	Strings.........II Ranks..from #54 & 55.........73	Notes
18	4'	String.........from #14.......................73	"
19	4'	String Celeste.......from #15.................73	"
20	4'	Piccolo.........from #16......................61	"
21	2-2/3'	Strings....II Ranks....from #14 & 15...........66	"
22	2'	String Fifteenth.......from #14...............61	"
23	2'	String Fifteenth Celeste...from #15............61	"
24	1-3/5'	String Tierce.......from #14..................61	"
25	1-3/5'	String Tierce Celeste.......from #15..........61	"
26	1'	String Harmonic.......from #14................61	"
27	8'	CLARINET.....................................61	Pipes
28	8'	KINURA.......................................61	"
29	8'	Saxophone.......from #14,15,16 & 28...........73	Notes
30		ORCHESTRAL BELLS..repeat stroke-metal.........37	Bars
31		Glockenspiel...single stroke on 30...........37	Notes
32		XYLOPHONE....repeat stroke - wood............49	Bars

ACCOMPANIMENT ORGAN - Bottom manual
in upper chamber - right side - 61 chest.

33	8'	Stentorphone..................from #1..........61	Notes
34	8'	Flute.........from #2.........................61	"
35	4'	Flute.........from #2.........................61	"
36	2-2/3'	Flute.........from #2.........................61	"
37	2'	Flute.........from #2.........................61	"
38	1-1/3'	Flute.........from #2.........................61	"
39	1'	Flute.........from #2.........................61	"
40	8'	Post Horn.......from #5.......................61	"
41	8'	Vox Humana.......from #6......................61	"
42	8'	Oboe Horn.......from #7.......................61	"
43	4'	Oboe Clarion.......from #7....................61	"
44		Marimba Harp.......single stroke on #10.......49	"
45		Marimbaphone......repeat stroke on #10........49	"
46		Snare Drum #1 - metal shell - roll)	
47		Snare Drum #2 - maple shell - roll)	
48		Snare Drum - tap (both drums)) Off Combinations except	
49		Tom Tom) "Drum Piston" to be per-	
50		Chinese Block - repeat stroke) manently set in factory	
51		Castanets)	
52		Tambourine)	

in lower chamber - right side - 73 chest

53	16'	String....II Ranks..from #54 & 55..Tenor C..........61	Notes
54	8'	STRING....unit-64 scale spotted metal..........85	Pipes
55	8'	STRING CELESTE..unit..64 scale spotted metal...85	"
56	8'	Strings....II Ranks..from #14 & 15...........73	Notes
57	8'	Tibia Clausa.......from #16...................73	"
58	4'	String.........from #54......................73	"
59	4'	String Celeste.......from #55.................73	"
60	4'	Piccolo.........from #16......................61	"
61	2-2/3'	String.........from #54......................66	"
62	2-2/3'	String Celeste.......from #55.................66	"
63	2'	String Fifteenth.......from #54...............61	"
64	2'	String Fifteenth Celeste...from #55...........61	"
65	1-3/5'	String Tierce.......from #54..................61	"
66	1-3/5'	String Tierce Celeste.......from #55..........61	"
67	8'	Kinura.........from #28......................61	"
68	8'	Saxophone.......from #56,57 & 67..............73	"

Orchestral Bells - 37 Notes..repeat stroke from #30
Glockenspiel.......37 Notes..single stroke from #30
Xylophone.........49 Notes..repeat stroke from #32

ACCOMPANIMENT DOUBLE TOUCH

69	8'	Stentorphone................from #1...........61 Notes	
70	8'	Post Horn.......from #5.......................61	"
71		Triangle.........in right upper chamber	
		Great to Accompaniment 8' Coupler	

GREAT ORGAN
in upper chamber - left side - 61 chest

73	16'	Vox Humana.................Tenor C..from #78....49	Notes
74	8'	OPEN DIAPASON.....duplex to 2nd touch..40 scale....61	"
75	8'	TIBIA PLENA.....duplex to Pedal..largest scale..61	"
76	8'	Gemshorn......duplex.........................73	"
77	4'	Gemshorn.......from #76.......................61	Notes
78	8'	VOX HUMANA.....duplex..MEDIUM-SCALE...........61	Pipes
79	8'	TUBA HARMONIC...duplex to 2nd touch 1-32 unit..61	"
80		CHIMES......................................25	Tubes
81	4'	HARP CELESTE...Low C..Single stroke..metal bass...49	Bars
82	8'	Harp Celeste.......from #81..T.C..............49	Notes

in lower chamber - left side - 73 chest

83	16'	BOURDON.......unit..Pedal Lieblich Gedeckt.1-24..large	
		Stop. Diap..25-97............97	Pipes
84	16'	String.........Tenor C....from #88............61	Notes
85	16'	String Celeste..Tenor C....from #89...........61	"
86	16'	Orchestral Oboe.....Synthetic..Tenor C..84,85,94....61	"
87	8'	Concert Flute.......from #83..................73	"
88	8'	STRING....62 scale spotted metal............85	Pipes
89	8'	STRING CELESTE...unit 62 spotted metal........85	"
90	8'	String.........Tenor C....from #98...........61	Notes
91	8'	String Celeste......Tenor C....from #99.......61	"
92	8'	FRENCH TRUMPET....unit.......................61	Pipes
93	8'	Orchestral Oboe.....Synthetic..#88,89,100.....73	Notes
94	5-1/3'	Flute.........switch only..no stopkey..from #83.	
95	4'	Flute.........from #83.......................73	"
96	4'	String.........from #88......................73	"
97	4'	String Celeste.......From #89.................73	"
98	4'	STRING.....duplex..78 scale tin..............73	Pipes
99	4'	STRING.....duplex..73 scale tin..............73	"
100	2-2/3'	Flute Twelfth.......from #83.................66	Notes
101	2-2/3'	String Twelfth.......from #88................66	"
102	2-2/3'	String Twelfth Celeste..from #89.............66	"
103	2'	String.........from #88......................61	"
104	2'	String Celeste.......from #89.................61	"
105	1-3/5'	String.........from #88......................61	"
106	1-3/5'	String Celeste.......from #89................61	"
		One Blank Stop Key	

GREAT DOUBLE TOUCH

107	16'	Tuba...49 from 79-12 pipes...wood..12"..........61	Notes
108	8'	Diapason.......from #74.......................61	"
109	8'	French Trumpet.......from #92.................61	"
110		Solo to Great 8' Coupler	

PEDAL ORGAN

111	32'	Acoustic Bass.........#'s 112 & 113............32	Notes
112	16'	Diaphonic Diapason...20 from #1..12 pipes....32	"
113	16'	STRING BASS..in right upper chamber 44 scale at CCC...44	Pipes
114	16'	Violone..20 from #75..12 pipes...............32	Notes
115	16'	Tibia Clausa..20 from #16..12 pipes..........32	"
116	16'	Bourdon.........from #83.....................32	"
117	15'	Tuba Profunda.......from #79 & 107...........32	"
118	16'	Bass Horn.......from #7......................32	"
119	8'	Octave.........from #113.....................32	"
120	8'	Cello.........from #113......................32	"
121	8'	Tibia.........from #16.......................32	"
122	8'	Dolce Flute.......from #83...................32	"
123	8'	Strings.......II Ranks..from #14 & 15........32	"
124	8'	Strings.......II Ranks..from #14 & 15........32	"
125	8'	Strings.......II Ranks..from #88 & 89........32	"
126	8'	Clarinet.......from #27......................32	"
127	8'	Tuba.........from #107.......................32	"
128	4'	Strings.......II Ranks..from #14 & 15........32	"
129	4'	Strings.......II Ranks..from #88 & 89........32	"
130	2-2/3'	Twelfth.......II Ranks..from #88 & 89........32	"
131	2-2/3'	Twelfth.......IV Ranks..from #14,15,54,55....32	"
132		Chimes.........from #80......................25	"
133		Bass Drum..#1 metal)) Off combinations	
134		Bass Drum..#2 Wood) All in upper right chamber) except "Drum Piston"	
135		Cymbal.....#1)) see accompaniment	
136		Cymbal.....#2)) Drums.	

COUPLERS

137	Solo 4'
138	Solo 16'
139	Great 4'
140	Accompaniment 4'
141	Accompaniment 16'
142	Great to Solo
143	Great to Solo 4'
144	Great to Solo 16'
145	Solo to Great 4'
146	Great to Pedal
147	Great to Pedal 4'
148	Solo to Pedal
149	Solo to Pedal 4'
150	Pedal Octave
151	Pedal Divide
152	Solo to Great
153	Solo to Great (Double Touch) same as #110
154	Great to Accompaniment
155	Great to Accompaniment (Double Touch) same as #72
	Three Unison separations (Dominoes in Key Jamb)

TREMULANTS

156	Solo and Accompaniment, Heavy and Slow)
157	Solo and Accompaniment, Light and Fast) Grouped together
158	Great, Heavy and Slow)
159	Great Light and Fast)

COMBINATION PISTONS

Pistons No. 1-2-3-4-5-6   Affecting Solo Organ
Pistons No. 1-2-3-4-5-6   Affecting Great Organ
Pistons No. 1-2-3-4-5-6   Affecting Accompaniment Organ
Pistons No. 1-2-3-4-5-6   Affecting Pedal-by studs also
Pistons No. 1-2-3-4-5-6   Affecting Generals
Pedal to Manual Piston couplers in left key jambs
Drum piston On & Off pistons operating 2 snare drums on accompaniment and
2 Bass Drums and 2 Cymbals on Pedal
Coupler Cancel Piston

PEDAL MOVEMENTS - roller contacts

Solo and Accompaniment expression Pedal #1) narrow and short shutters, horizontal
Solo and Accompaniment Expression Pedal #2) in top chamber, Vertical in bottom,
Great Expression Pedal #1   ) Brown sheep skin pneumatics.
Great Expression Pedal #2   )
Crescendo Pedal (Tremolo off after 75% of other stops on.
Three Sforzandos...See J.O.Funkhouser.
(Tremolo off)

EXPRESSION PEDAL COUPLERS
(Rocking tablets in right key jamb)

Swell I to Great I.
Solo I to Solo II.
All Pedals to Solo and Accompaniment II

NUT PISTONS (Over top manual)

Song Birds - 2 sets
Siren (Acme-England patent) (high wind)
Grand Crash (Toe Piston also)
Grand Cymbal (Toe Piston also)
Thunder Roll (lowest 5 notes on all 16' pedal stops
           (and Bass Drum repeat and Metal sheets)
           (Toe Piston also)
Tubular Bell (For opening performance) Toe Piston also
Steamboat Whistle, Chinese Gong, Triangle, Auto Horn (Bosch)
Surf Machine
Persian Cymbal
Aeroplane
Surf
Slap Sticks
Electric Bell Telephone
Buzzer
Sand Block
Ford Horn (Electric)

Electric blower & Motor - on outlet 15"
Electric Generator
Bench with adjustable spring back

Electric lamps for stop keys - see Rowe
Colored stop keys - reeds Red. - Flutes and Diapason White & Black
engraving - strings amber and black engraving and Couplers white red
engraved.-traps White and black engraving same for percussions and tremolos.
Disks for Swell Pedal indicators direct connected red on white off.
Silver wire strip on coupler contact wires and rollers operating Swell Shoes.
Swell Shoes finished bare wood concaved no rubber
Round Swell shoe board to follow pedal keys
Spring back for organists bench and apron paneled on back of bench
Very wide music rack
Separate magnet for every pipe - primary for all valves over 1/2".

STOPS:-Controlled by Colored Stop Keys nickle plated separators
CASING:- None
CONSOLE:- Quartered Oak Jacobean finish on outside, Veneered Mahogany Reg.
frame and key slips - Horse Shoe Type
FRONT PIPES:- None
SWELL CHAMBERS:- By Purchaser.

12/13/26
ACZ
Checked by.................................date...........................

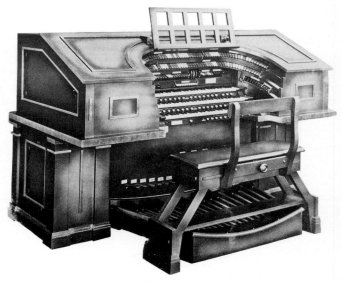

Although relatively plain, this Moller case design featured smoothly flowing lines which helped to disguise its rather elephantine proportions.

Main chamber of the 3/17 Moller installed in the Oakland, California Fox (Orpheum) Theatre in 1922. Resonators on the chrysoglott, in the upper left part of the photo, are wooden and tunable via stoppers. This was a standard feature of Moller harps in the teens and twenties.

The Capitol Theatre in Davenport, Iowa, was an elegant setting for a 4/23 Moller, installed in 1920. The grand piano and harp at the right are decorative only and do not play from the organ. After suffering water damage the Moller was rebuilt into a 3/10 unit organ in 1928 by the Wicks Organ Company.

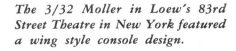

The 3/32 Moller in Loew's 83rd Street Theatre in New York featured a wing style console design.

The beautiful Hillstreet Theatre in Los Angeles (above) featured non-speaking display pipes in front of chambers housing a 3/13 Moller. Decorative pipes such as these were common through the teens, while ornamental grilles were more popular in the twenties.

4/67 Moller concert organ (left) in the Shrine Auditorium, Los Angeles, California. The Shrine is the largest "theatre" in the country, originally seating 6,700 persons.

2/11 Moller at the Edgewater Beach Hotel in Chicago, Illinois. Its sweet tones were featured in many radio broadcasts in the 1930s and '40s.

Ray Sawyer plays the Moller in the Los Angeles Hippodrome. Curiously, this theatre does not appear in Moller factory records. The organ is possibly opus 2743 or 2744; these organs were built for the William Fox syndicate but were put into storage because Fox didn't have a location for them when they were built![45]

Emil Velazco and orchestra pose in his New York City studio. His 2/3 Moller was installed in 1933 and had tibia, violin and saxophone ranks. The organ was sold by R. P. Elliot who was in charge of Moller's New York City sales office for several years after leaving Kimball in 1933. The Velazco organ was later repossessed when its owner couldn't keep up with the relatively modest payments—it cost only $2,640.[48]

Nat Portnoff plays the 3/11 Moller at the Greenbrier Hotel, White Sulphur Springs, West Virginia. This installation also featured an Artiste player in a separate cabinet large enough to include roll storage on each side.

The State Theatre in Roseland, Illinois had a 3/18 largely straight Moller installed in 1921. During 1925 this instrument was traded in on the highly unified 3/12 pictured above. The top manual played only percussions and one rank: the kinura. Also in the organ was an upright piano (left) with vacuum action. A marimba (below) did double duty as a master xylophone via a second set of hard hammers. A similar economizing measure was also used by Moller to obtain both a celesta and a glockenspiel from the same metal-bar instrument.

Pipework in the State Theatre, Roseland, Illinois included both a tibia clausa and tibia plena, the second and third ranks from the left, respectively.

This console originally controlled only nine ranks of pipes in the Gaiety Theatre, Trenton, New Jersey. Shown here in its new home in the Pabst Theatre, Milwaukee, Wisconsin, it now plays 20 ranks of mostly Moller pipework.

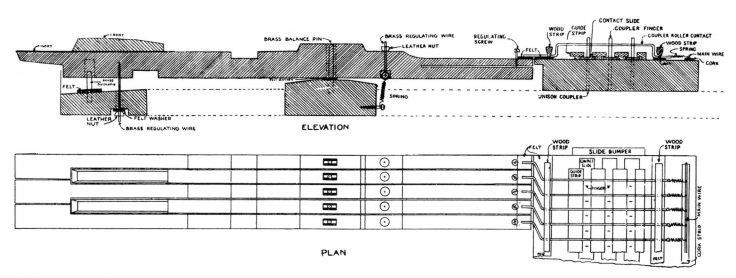

The famous Moller key action. Similar designs were also used by several other builders. Moller relays are constructed using this same matrix principle and are quite compact.

San Francisco's Fox Theatre featured a 3/12 Moller in its lobby,
located on the mezzanine directly
above the grand staircase in the
lower left photo. Lower right photo
shows the console's rarely seen ornamental cover, a much more elegant
means of protection from inquisitive
fingers than a roll top would have
been in the opulent surroundings of
the Fox. Identical Mollers were
installed in the lobbies of the St.
Louis and Detroit Fox Theatres.
Each featured an Artiste player (in
a separate cabinet) so that waiting
theatre patrons could be entertained
without the expense of hiring a musician. What the musician's union had
to say about that is not recorded!

Atlanta Fox console as it looked in 1929 on its ornamental lift platform.

Cut-away model showing construction details of the famous Moller pitman chest.

Close-up view of the enormous Atlanta Fox console.

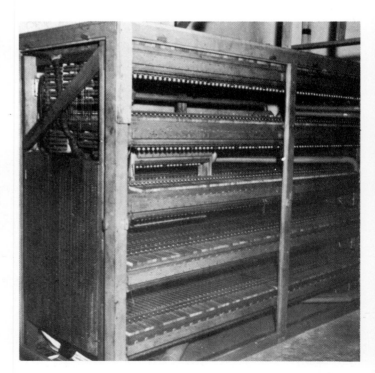

Views inside one chamber at the Atlanta Fox. In the upper left photo the ranks are, left to right, solo violins III ranks, clarinet, orchestral oboe, chimney flute and kinura. At lower right is the relay. Note how compact it is considering the number of functions it controls.

More views of the Atlanta Fox chambers. Clockwise from the upper left the ranks are gamba, French trumpet, solo tibia, diaphonic diapason, post horn, solo post horn, 16′ diaphone, 8′ diaphonic diapason, 8′ French trumpet, orchestral violins III ranks, gemshorn and celeste, mezzo vox humana, English horn, violin cello and celeste, harmonic tuba, concert flute, stentorphone, and saxophone.

Don Gillett has been Moller's tonal director since John Hose's death in 1974, and in 1983 was elected vice president.

After Richard Whitelegg died in 1944, John Hose became tonal director. Mr. Hose had an encyclopedic knowledge of organ building and had served as Moller plant superintendent from 1940 to 1941.[60] Tonally, however, Mr. Whitelegg was a hard act to follow and the instruments scaled by Mr. Hose never received the acclaim of those of Mr. Whitelegg. Of particular interest to theatre organ buffs is the fact that Mr. Hose headed the crew which installed the 4/39 Moller in the Philadelphia Met.[61] Following the death of Mr. Hose in 1974, Don Gillett became tonal director. Mr. Gillett had been president of the Aeolian-Skinner company before its demise in 1972.

In late 1927[63] Moller developed one of the most sophisticated and musically successful inventions ever devised: the Artiste player. Reproducing organ players were certainly nothing new in the 1920s; indeed, Moller's system was the last to be developed of all the major systems. But Moller had something no other firm had: the creative genius of Frederick Albert Hoschke. Technically, the Artiste was the invention of Leonard Peloubet[64] who also invented a twelve-roll changer for it.[65]

Artistically, however, the success of the Artiste belongs to Mr. Hoschke. He originated a technique for recording symphonic compositions wherein the recording artist didn't have to play the actual *notes* but instead recorded only the *rhythm* of the piece. These rhythmic patterns were recorded on a moving piece of paper by a machine called the "nuancer." Later, on a drawing board, notes were drawn in corresponding to the rhythmic patterns. These notes, however, were not limited to what an organist could actually play. The arranger, therefore, could orchestrate a composition with no regard for the technical limitations of a human performer and the finished

result would *sound* hand-played because a live musician had actually recorded the rhythms.[66] In the author's opinion, Mr. Hoschke ranks with other giants such as Gustav Bruder and J. Lawrence Cook as one of the greatest roll arrangers who ever lived. Hearing one of his orchestral transcription masterpieces such as the *Bacchanale* from *Samson and Delilah* is a rare thrill not easily forgotten.

Another feature of the Artiste player was its unique method of stop control. Most other players were designed for a "standard" specification which frequently differed from the actual specifications of the organ to which the players were connected. The Artiste, however, used a system of 47 preset stop combinations which were individually wired for each organ to which the Artiste was attached. Furthermore, a record of these combinations for each instrument was kept at the factory and each roll was custom punched for each particular customer's Artiste! The machine used to perforate these stop combinations in each roll was called the "symphonizer."[67]

Another stop control system unique to the Artiste was the register crescendo mechanism. By an ingenious multiplexing arrangement, 29 of the 133 holes in the tracker bar could be allocated to the register crescendo, whereby the various stops and couplers on the organ would gradually be drawn or retired, just as if an organist were operating an actual crescendo pedal. The 29 crescendo steps were, of course, custom wired on each Artiste for the smoothest possible crescendo on each instrument.

It is truly unfortunate that the Artiste was introduced so late for fewer than 200 were manufactured.[68] By 1934 even roll sales had dwindled to virtually nothing and Mr. Hoschke left Moller to join the Everett Piano Company of South Haven, Michigan where he invented the Everett Orgatron, an electrically amplified reed organ. What an ignominious end to such a glorious career! Mr. Hoschke died in 1936 at the age of 60.[69]

In the 1940s Moller revived the Artiste name for its series of self-contained cabinet organs, none of which was equipped with a player.

*Frederick Albert Hoschke
(1876-1936)[70]*

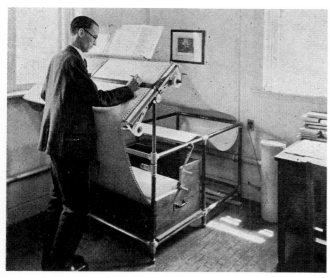

Frederick Albert Hoschke prepares a master roll. The marks he makes will be punched out manually by a technician using several sizes of rectangular punches, after which the master roll will be ready to place in the perforator for the production of multiple copies.

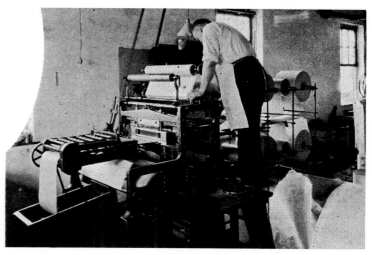

The Moller perforator is completely mechanical, using no pneumatics, and cuts eight rolls at a time. Only the note holes are perforated on this machine; holes controlling registration changes are cut individually for each roll on the "symphonizer."

This early Moller player used ordinary 88-note rolls. Judging from the number of stops and swell shoes, it must have been connected to quite a large organ.

Frederick Albert Hoschke plays the Moller recording organ in the Artiste studio on the second floor of the Moller office building.

Announcing the
M. P. MÖLLER "ARTISTE" REPRODUCING ORGAN
on Our Fifty-Second Anniversary

 THOUGH this House, during past years, had built Reproducing Organs that are giving most satisfactory service, we realized that, in order to substantiate our policy of ever striving to excel, we must create and produce an instrument whose musical and mechanical performances would make its supremacy unquestionable. Announcements of any sort were purposely withheld until an ideal had been attained, and the M. P. Möller "Artiste" Reproducing Organ given the most exacting tests for excellence and dependability. This fondest hope is now realized and with the greatest pride on this, our fifty-second anniversary, we make the present announcement.

This remarkable instrument faithfully preserves and reproduces the master organists' playing.

No registration, mutilation or abridgment of reproduced music. All divisions of organs up to four manuals may play independently any time, anywhere, with unrestricted compass of musical figures or phrases.

Registration of records edited to suit specification requirements of individual organs.

Also equipped to play a special symphonic type of record made by a process distinctively original.

Due to the well-known fact that the extent of the M. P. Möller industry and production makes possible a high quality at a low cost, our "Artiste" Reproducing Organ is to be had at a surprisingly low comparative figure. Further information in this regard will be gladly furnished.

M. P. MÖLLER - Hagerstown, Maryland

BRANCH OFFICES:

1203 Franklin Trust Bldg., Philadelphia

1203 Loew Bldg., 1540 Broadway, New York City

Medical Arts Bldg., Memphis

1514 Forbes St., Pittsburgh, Pa.

1626 California St., Denver

224 Lathrop Bldg., Kansas City, Mo.

6054 Cottage Grove Ave., Chicago

129 North Ave., N. E., Atlanta

1009 First Ave., Seattle

M. P. MÖLLER
Artiste
Reproducing Organ
393
Bacchanale
From "Samson and Delilah"
Saint-Saens-Hoschke
· ·
M. P. MÖLLER
HAGERSTOWN, MD., U.S.A.

Label for one of the finest reproducing organ rolls ever perforated, a masterpiece of arranging by Frederick Albert Hoschke.

This ad in the January 1928 Diapason announced the last of all the major reproducing organ players to be developed. In the author's opinion, this is one instance in which the ad copy wasn't glowing enough; considerably more boasting would have been justified considering how exceptional the Artiste player really is.

All of the 700 or so master rolls for the Artiste still exist at the Moller factory in 1983.

FOORTFOLIO

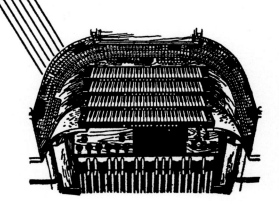

The enclosed collection of authentic stories
is sent with Reginald Foort's compliments
to the News Editor whom he will be glad to
welcome at ....

....

Management :
F. M. W. LTD.,
Carlton House, Regent Street, S.W.1.
ABBEY 2211

Above is the cover of a manila folder for publicity materials supplied by master showman Reginald Foort to promote his various tours and concerts.

Organ No **6690** Blower No. **AA504** Style **8 P 3328**

For **M. P. Moller**
Reginald Foort

City **London** State **England**

H. P. **30** Volts **100/220** Speed **1960/1** Cy. **50**

Generator Amperes **100** Generator Volts **15**

Capacity **6000** @ **15** Outlet **14**

Remarks _____

_____
_____
_____
_____

KINETIC ENGINEERING CO.

Union and Stewart Aves.

LANSDOWNE, PA.

This enormous blower was purchased for the Reginald Foort "portable" Moller but for various reasons was never shipped to England. Before the 1930s Kinetic blowers were constructed with rectangular wooden enclosures painted green. Appropriately, the handwriting on this document is in green ink! In the 1930s the design was changed to a more conventional metal drum although the practice of mounting the machine on steel I-beams was retained. Nearly every Moller was equipped with a Kinetic blower. Mathias Moller purchased stock in the Kinetic Engineering Company and became one of its directors[76] as indeed he should have since Moller purchased half the Kinetic company's output. Moller eventually purchased the company in 1939 and absorbed it into its Hagerstown facility.

Solo chamber of the Foort organ is ready for testing in the Moller erecting room. From the rear forward the ranks are 16' bombarde, 8' tibia III, tuba horn, solo brass trumpet, post horn, tuba mirabilis, vox humana I, tibia III, doppel flute, and tibia I. Ranks on the right chest are, left to right, musette, krumet, saxophone, orchestral oboe and clarinet.

Organ 6690

6690

FACTORY ORDER

MÖLLER ORGAN WORKS

HAGERSTOWN, MARYLAND

To   Fred Carty   Date   September 21, 1938   ROW:T

Please get out the following:

Spidell is not able to put the large Tibia scales on his voicing machine
so please supply him with a new rack board and material so that he may be
able to go ahead with this work.

Shipping Date 9-20-38

Ship via: _____

To _____

Street and No. _____

City _____   Signed by   Daniel

*This factory production order is a rather amusing example of one
of the myriad of problems encountered in the production of the
Reginald Foort organ.*

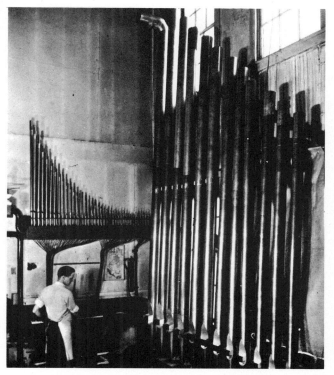

*Foort organ 16' string being voiced. These pipes were
badly battered after several moves and were left in storage for the rest of the Foort tour.*

*Voicing one of the largest scale tibias ever constructed, the #1 tibia in the 5/27
Foort Moller. The halving ratio is such that the treble pipes are wider than
they are tall.*

*Voicing the Foort 16' wood dia-
phone.*

One of the finest reed voicers who ever lived, Adolph Zajic voices the solo brass trumpet in the Foort Moller. This was the first brass rank ever built by Moller. The resonators were purchased from Midmer-Losh (for $75!) who had a set left over from their Atlantic City project.[79]

5/27 relay for the Foort Moller was "portable"—if you had a crane! Note quick-disconnect junctions on the far right. Switch-stacks were built by Reisner but were pneumatically actuated via Moller-built actions. Reisner's factory is just two blocks down Prospect Street from the Moller plant, and at one time Mathias Moller held a large share of Reisner's stock. At left, note that this relay wasn't Moller's usual matrix style. Instead, a design similar to Robert-Morton's was employed in the belief that it would be more reliable after traveling over bumpy English roads.

All traps in the Foort organ were contained in this steel-reinforced framework.

Foort console is about half completed in this photo. Note the Reisner direct electric stop action magnets; Moller felt they would be more reliable in rough traveling service than the standard Moller mechanical combination action.

Main chamber of the Foort organ nears completion on the erecting floor.

The Foort organ console stands completed in the second floor console department of the Moller factory. 1939 photo below shows Reginald Foort (1894-1980) preparing to play one of his orchestral transcription masterpieces on the organ he designed and loved.

The Foort organ is being installed on the stage of one of the many English theatres in which it played. Another section (left) is being wheeled up a ramp while technicians fit a motor to the Discus blower. Several motors were required because of varying electric service encountered in the British Isles.

Assembly of the Foort organ is in progress on the west (left) end of the Moller erecting room. Note steel framework for each section, making them portable. Several other organs are also being erected at the busy factory.

This plaque, a fabulous piece of wit, was presented to Adolf Zajic on the occasion of his retirement from the Moller company. In later years Mr. Zajic voiced a number of post horns of excellent quality for contemporary theatre organ buffs and in this cartoon he is supposedly voicing a 32′ example for Dick Kline, a long-time friend of the Moller company, whose 4/28 residence Wurlitzer already contained a Zajic 8′ post horn. People in the cartoon, from left to right, are Mr. Zajic, Moller executive vice president Pete Daniels (himself a lover of good theatre organ music), factory superintendent Paul "Peck" Kreglo and pipe shop foreman Howard Nalley.

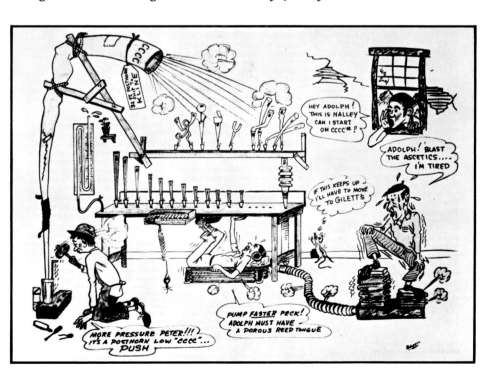

Moller ad copy in the September 1941 Diapason was written by M. P. Moller, Jr. at the suggestion of Reginald Watson, a close friend of Reginald Foort and the liaison between Mr. Foort and the Moller company during construction of the instrument.[49]

Several men prominent in the organ world meet for lunch at Hagerstown in 1940. Left to right are Charles M. Courboin, famous organist of the Wanamaker stores; M. P. Moller, Jr., president of the Moller company; Charles O'Connell of the RCA-Victor Company (Courboin recorded for RCA-Victor in the 1940s); E. O. Shulenberger, Moller vice president and sales manager; and Riley Daniels, secretary of the Moller firm. Mr. Shulenberger died in 1944 at age 67 having been with Moller for 47 years.[46] *Riley Daniels later became executive vice president and succeeded M. P. Moller, Jr. as president following Mr. Moller's untimely death in 1961.*

J. Otterbein Funkhouser (1872-?)[72] *was Moller factory superintendent during most of the period when theatre organs were produced. Successors to the post were Howard Cramers in 1931, Fred Carty in 1937, Jose Hose in 1940, Earl Hoover in 1942 and Paul "Peck" Kreglo in 1967.*[73]

Kevin M. "Chip" Moller was the firm's president from 1978 to 1984.

ENTERTAINMENT PIPE ORGANS
Consoles, Pipes and Parts
by

M.P. MÖLLER, INc.

OF HAGERSTOWN

EUGENE E. POOLE, Western Sales Engineer
165 Lakewood Road - Walnut Creek, California 94598

Although hardly a theatre organ by any stretch of the imagination, the Moller console on the West Point organ (below) is probably the most complex console ever built and is ample evidence that the Moller factory is equal to any challenge. Stops are moved by a specially designed vacuum system and are of a unique angled shape. Among the dozens of special features on this console are sliding bars above the combination pistons which allow the swell shades to be operated by the organist's thumbs. This console was built in 1952 to showcase the talents of West Point organist John A. Davis, Jr.

Ad appearing in the December 1975 Theatre Organ indicated Moller's willingness to supply parts to theatre organ buffs. Post horns voiced by Adolf Zajic were especially popular and were sold by the dozen.

Thirty-five years after building the Foort organ, Moller constructed another theatre instrument. The "Red Devil" was a design similar to a style E Wurlitzer and stayed on the third floor of the factory for about six years before finding a new home in Japan.

John Hose, Moller tonal director until his death in 1974, and Peter Moller Daniels, then executive vice president, pose in the conference room at the Moller offices. A portrait of Mathias Moller hangs on the wall behind them. Pete Daniels became Moller's fifth president in 1984.

A PICTORIAL TOUR OF THE WORLD'S LARGEST PIPE ORGAN FACTORY

Aerial view looking east.

Looking south on Prospect Street in 1937, one saw the newest parts of the factory: the two-story office building erected in 1925 and, immediately behind it, the world's largest erecting room.

One of many factory rooms where action assembly and small parts fabrication took place.

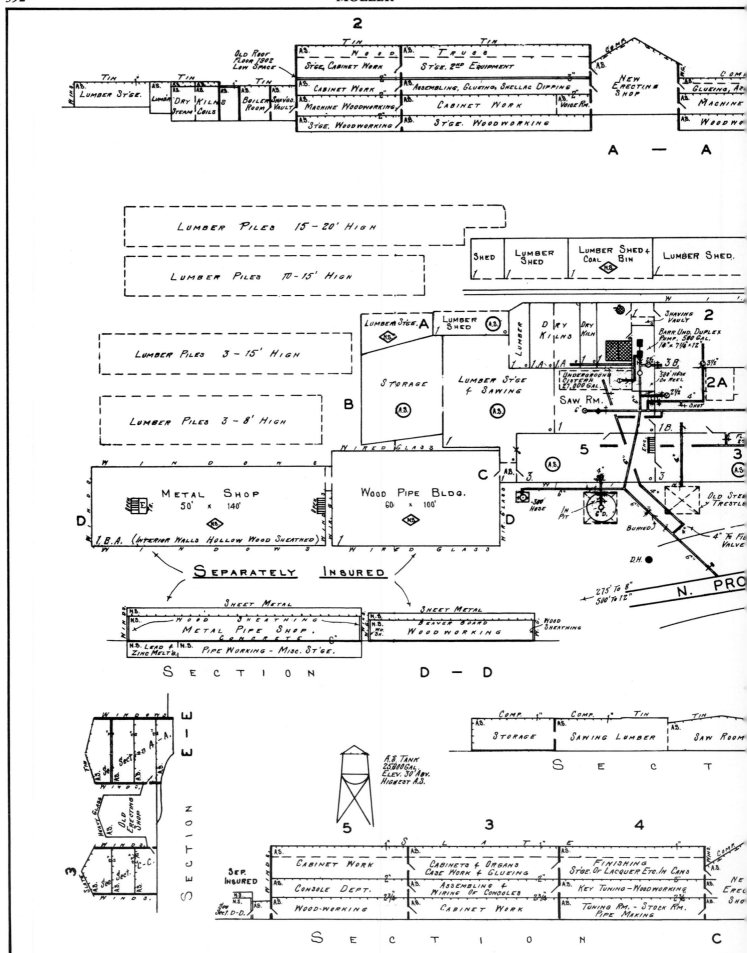

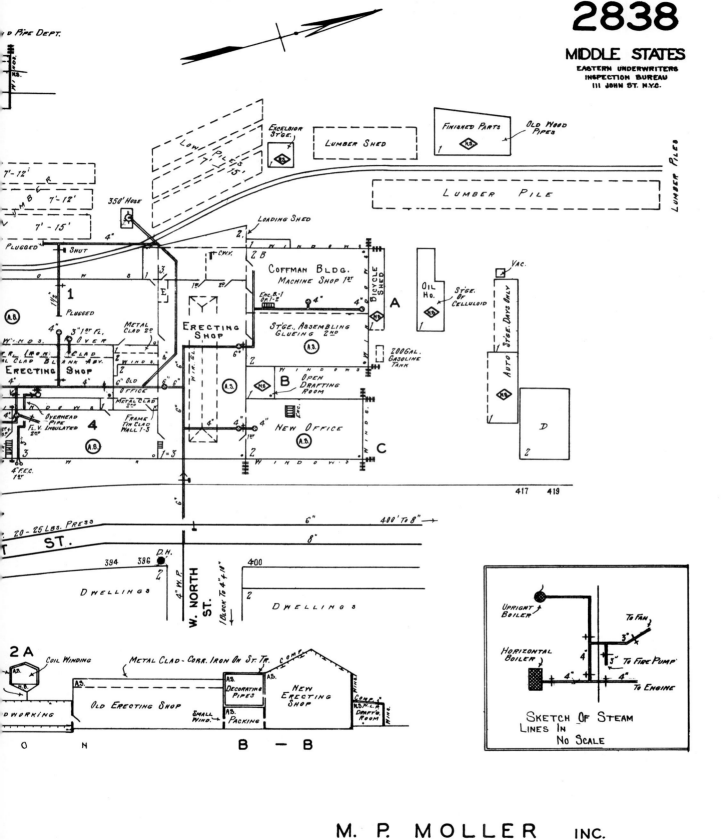

2838

MIDDLE STATES
EASTERN UNDERWRITERS
INSPECTION BUREAU
111 JOHN ST. N.Y.C.

SKETCH OF STEAM
LINES IN
NO SCALE

M. P. MOLLER INC.
HAGERSTOWN WASHINGTON CO. MD.

P. F. RUTH   SCALE 1"=50'   NOV. 7/1934.

One of several action assembly rooms. An organ harp is being assembled near the center of the photo.

In the drafting department c. 1930 are, left to right, Glenn Nichols, Wilbur Remsburg, chief draftsman, Charles Keyser, H. Maynard Iseminger and H. A. Marlotte.

Two million board feet of lumber are stored behind the Moller factory.

Just think how many elephants gave their lives so that Moller keyboards could look and feel good!

Illustrated on this page are a variety of views of the chest department.

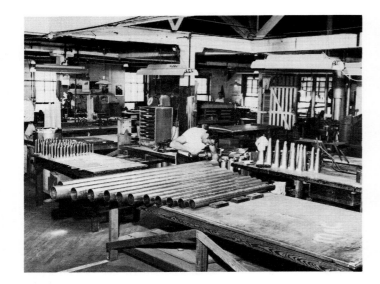

Above, four views in the metal pipe department.

Howard Nalley inspects a brass chamade in the reed pipe shop.

A sheet of spotted metal leaves the casting table after cooling.

Soldering the seam on a 16' pipe.

Above and left, additional scenes in the metal pipe department.

When pipe shop foreman Howard Nalley began working at Moller in 1926 the company had never built a metal 16′ reed.[74] This seems incredible in light of the fact that Moller was the world's largest pipe organ builder. Perhaps the reason lay in Mathias Moller's basic personality as a woodworker. The firm began making zinc pipes in 1894 and by 1896 was making all its own flue pipes.[75] Moller continued to order many reeds, however, from outside suppliers such as Gottfried and Dennison until around 1930.

Voicing a 32′ diapason (above) on the Moller erecting room floor. At left and below, views in the wood pipe department.

Small assembly department in the southeast corner of the third floor. In the foregound Jack Miller tries to solder an all-electric Moller switch-stack . . . with a soldering iron which is not plugged in! Behind Jack a top loading Artiste player is under construction. This very unit in 1984 awaits connecting to the famous Reginald Foort Moller in the Pasadena Civic Auditorium in California.

Making reservoirs on the south end of the third floor.

Adjusting swell shoe contacts in a new Moller console.

Making a piece of grillework in the cabinet department.

Regulating new manual keys is a painstaking task.

The Moller factory (right) was given over entirely to war production from 1942 to 1945. Work progressed around the clock, seven days a week. The airplane wings being assembled on the erecting floor in this photo were used in planes made by Fairchild Aviation, another Hagerstown firm.[62]

Engraving department.

Filling in the engraving on a new set of drawknobs.

Casting pipe metal on a marble-topped casting table.

E. J. Phillips, right, console department foreman, checks a blueprint while Howard Berry poses for the camera.

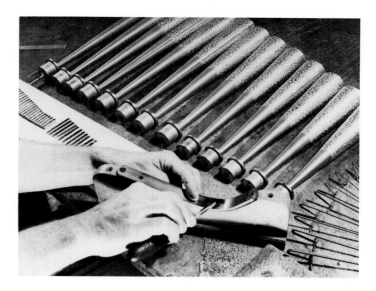

Voicing is a male dominated field in most of the organ industry but Moller employs several talented ladies in the voicing department. In the above photo one of them applies nicking to a new set of spotted metal pipes. Above right, the talented fingers of Adolf Zajic curve a reed tongue. Right, fitting a set of swell shades. At lower right, a Moller employee with half a century of experience fits the manuals into a new console. Below, winding coils for Moller chest magnets.

MOLLER OPUS LIST

Following is a complete list of this firm's theatre installations. An alphabetical index appears first, enabling one to located instruments on a city/state/installation site basis, with a corresponding opus number shown adjoining. This number can be used to find an organ in the accompanying chronological list. Statistics on each organ are shown only in the latter list.

CITY/STATE	LOCATION	OPUS
ALABAMA (AL)		
Anniston	Savoy Th.,	1466
Mobile	Crown Th. #1	1959
Montgomery	Orpheum Th.	1177
ARKANSAS (AR)		
Camden	Rialto Th.	3780
El Dorado	Rialto Th.	4310
CALIFORNIA (CA)		
Long Beach	New Dale Th.	3820
Los Angeles	Astor Th.	4290
	Blake Th.	4130
	Clifton Cafeteria	5366
	Hillstreet Th.	3128
	Loew's State Th.	3140
	Shrine Auditorium	4446
Oakland	Fox (Orpheum) Th.	2741
Riverside	Rubidoux Th.	4343
San Francisco	Fox Th.	5497
	Golden Gate Th.	3131
	Loew's Warfield Th.	3141
COLORADO (CO)		
Denver	Sante Fe Th.	5040
CONNECTICUT (CT)		
Baltic	Jodoin's Th.	2271
Hartford	Poli Th.	2679
New Britain	Fox Th.	1832
New Haven	Poli Th.	2319
Norwich	Palace Th.	3679
DELAWARE (DE)		
Dover	Diamond State Th.	3719
Newark	New Theatre	5337
Wilmington	Aldine Th.	3800
	New Parkway Th.	3184
	Queen Th.	2049
DISTRICT OF COLUMBIA (DC)		
Washington	Avenue Grand Th.	2921
	Central Coliseum Th.	2050
	Crandall Th.	2851
	Knickerbocker Th.	2525
	Lincoln Th.	3259
	Loew's Columbia Th.	3737
	Loew's Palace Th.	4319
	Metropolitan Th.	2561
	Poli Th.	2491
	Republic Th.	4075
	Savoy Th.	2919
	Shoreham Hotel	5849
FLORIDA (FL)		
Miami	Biscayne Fronton Th.	4523
West Palm Beach	Rialto Th.	2491
GEORGIA (GA)		
Athens	Loew's Th.	3068
Atlanta	Fox Th.	5566
ILLINOIS (IL)		
Canton	Garden Th.	4653
Centralia	Illinois Th.	3183
Chicago	Chicago Musical College	4802
	Commodore Th.	3243
	Edgewater Beach Hotel	5530
	Illinois College of Music	5115
	Monroe Th.	2742
	Portage Park Th.	2935
	Sherwood School of Music	4314
	Sherwood School of Music	4315

CITY/STATE	LOCATION	OPUS
Chicago	Sherwood School of Music	4741
	Sherwood School of Music	4742
	Sherwood School of Music	5191
	Stratford Th.	2838
Chicago Heights	Gregory Th.	2988
LaGrange	Illinois Th.	3054
Moline	Bio Th.	2792
Peoria	Palace Th.	2857
	Princess Th.	4275
Rockford	Midway Th.	2509
Roseland	State Th.	4191
INDIANA (IN)		
Clinton	Standard Th.	2905
Evansville	Victory Th.	3109
Fort Wayne	Palace Th.	3389
Indianapolis	Alhambra Th.	1356
	Loew's Th.	2887
	Strand Th.	1821
Kokomo	Victory Th.	2768
Marion	Lyric Th.	2183
Muncie	Columbia Th.	1564
Richmond	Muretti Th.	2791
Valparaiso	Premier Th.	3228
IOWA (IA)		
Davenport	Capitol Th.	2939
Des Moines	Strand Th.	3043
KANSAS (KS)		
Leavenworth	Orpheum Th.	2578
KENTUCKY (KY)		
Louisville	Rex Th.	3159
Newport	Hippodrome Th.	2597
	Temple Th.	4197
Owensboro	Empress Th.	2250
Somerset	Virginia Th.	3483
LOUISIANA (LA)		
Algiers	Folly Th.	2446
Monroe	Saenger Th.	2795
New Orleans	Cosmopolitan Th.	4100
	Crescent Th.	2453
	Crown Th.	4554
	Escorial Th.	2772
	Happyland Th.	4035
	Trianon Th.	1932
	Tudor Th.	1520
Plaquemine	Liberty Th.	2587
MARYLAND (MD)		
Annapolis	Circle Th.	4861
Baltimore	Apollo Th.	3038
	Aurora (Seven East) Th.	2832
	Bridge Th.	2903
	Capitol Th.	2920
	Century Th.	2955
	Columbia Th.	3181
	Eureka Th.	2753
	Forest Park (Forest) Th.	2780
	Garden Th. (at 1100½ S. Charles St.)	2378
	Garden (Keith's-Albee) (Keith's) Th.	2610
	Great Wizard Th.	2699
	Harford Th.	2987
	Hippodrome Th.	1766
	Irvington Th.	3122
	McHenry Th.	2256
	New Theatre	2240
	Palace Th. (at 1351 N. Gay St.)	2664
	Parkway (Five West) Th.	1962
	Peabody Th.	2867

CITY/STATE	LOCATION	OPUS
Baltimore	Picture Garden (Lexway)(Newsreel)(Vogue) (Laffmovie)(World)(Fine Arts) Th.	2082
	Pimlico Th.	3449
	Red Wing Th.	3086
	Schanze Th.	2922
	Strand Th. (at 404 N. Howard St.)	2066
	Victoria Th.	2727
	Walbrook Th.	2726
	Wilson (Rivoli) Th.	1982
	Winter Garden Th.	2205
Cambridge	Grand Opera House (Strand) Th.	3124
Cumberland	Strand Th.	2891
Easton	New Theatre	3258
Hagerstown	Colonial Th.	1797
	Hagerstown Broadcasting Co.	5251
	Maryland Th.	3303
	Nixon Academy Th.	2065
Salisbury	Arcade Th.	2521

MASSACHUSETTS (MA)

Attleboro	Union Th.	5062
Boston	Beacon Th.	4494
	Loew's State Th.	2980
	Olympia (Tremont Row) (Astor) Th.	1601
	Rialto (Rivoli) Th.	4527
Brockton	Colonial Th.	1855
Cambridge	Olympia Th.	2566
Dorchester	Morton Th.	4256
Fall River	New Empire Th.	2559
Revere	Crescent Garden Th.	5310
Springfield	Broadway Th.	4322
	Fox Th.	2028
Westfield	Park Th.	5336

MICHIGAN (MI)

Benton Harbor	Liberty Th.	3177
Detroit	Arcadia Dance Palace	1773
	Fox Th.	5287
	Lakewood Th.	1985
	Washington Th.	2739
Flint	Colonial Th.	3044
	Globe Th.	2893
Lansing	Strand (Michigan) Th.	3001
Munsing	Delft Th.	3916
Petroskey	Hollywood Th.	3054
Saginaw	Wolverine Th.	2894

MINNESOTA (MN)

Fergus Falls	Bijou Th.	2108

MISSISSIPPI (MS)

Clarksdale	McWilliams (Marion) Th.	3345
Hattiesburg	Strand Th.	2528
Meridian	Strand Th.	2022

MISSOURI (MO)

Kansas City	Royal Picture Th.	1716
	12th Street Th.	2233
St. Louis	Fox Th.	5286
	Fox's Liberty Th.	2573

NEW HAMPSHIRE (NH)

Manchester	Star Th.	3207

NEW JERSEY (NJ)

Asbury Park	Main Street Th.	2837
	Mayfair Th.	4809
	St. James (Rosenburg) Th.	2370
Atlantic City	Liberty Th.	3881
	Park Th.	2900
	Royal #1 (Aldine) Th.	2827
	Royal #2 Th.	5204
Audubon	Century Th.	5086
	Highland Th.	3489
Beverly	Riviera Th.	4084
Blackwood	Blackwood Th.	4944
Caldwell	Park Th.	4145
Camden	Liberty Th.	3095
	Lyric Th.	3953
	Princess Th.	2653
	Star Th.	2736
Cape May	Liberty Th.	2817

CITY/STATE	LOCATION	OPUS
Cliffside	Star Th.	4065
Collingswood	Collingswood Th.	3016
Egg Harbor	Colonial Th.	4607
Elizabeth	Fox's Liberty Th.	2572
Gloucester	Apollo Th.	2662
Hackensack	Oritani Th.	4396
Jersey City	Ritz Th.	3322
	State Th.	3323
Long Branch	Broadway Th.	2806
Madison	Madison Th.	4288
Merchantville	Park (State) Th.	2895
Millville	People's Th.	3190
Newark	American Th.	2571
	Hawthorne Th.	4346
	Loew's State Th.	2890
	Lyceum Th.	3411
	Roosevelt Th.	4570
	Terminal Th.	2740
New Brunswick	Reade's State Th.	3090
Ocean City	Moorlyn Th.	3346
	Park Th.	2657
	Strand Th.	2658
Orange	Audubon Th.	4395
Palisade	Palisade Th.	3828
Paterson	American Th.	2605
Perth Amboy	Majestic (Ditman) Th.	4144
Plainfield	Bijou Th.	4143
Princeton	Princeton Th.	2985
Riverside	Fox Th.	4085
Roselle	Rose Park Th.	4313
Roselle Park	Roselle Park Th.	4979
Summit	Summit Th.	4524
Trenton	Gaiety Th.	4451
	Lincoln Th.	5198
	Orpheum Th.	3279
	Palace Th.	3651
	Taylor Opera House	2849
	Trent Th.	2848
Union City	Capitol Th.	4305

NEW YORK (NY)

Astoria	Loew's Astoria Th.	4377
	Steinway Th.	3450
Bayshore	Bayshore Th.	4719
Bronx	Boulevard Th.	2439
	Crotona Th.	2016
	Elsmere Th.	3776
	Empire Th.	1763
	Keith's Fordham Th.	2946
	Loew's Burland Th.	3548
	Loew's Burnside Th.	3773
	Moss's 161st St. (Franklin) Th.	2953
	Victory Th.	3333
Brooklyn	Albermale Th.	2907
	Bedford Th.	2407
	Bijou Th.	2492
	Brevoort Th.	2799
	Comedy Th.	2591
	DeKalb Avenue Th.	2436
	Folly Th.	2027
	Fulton Th.	2099
	Keeney's (Livingston) Th.	2380
	Loew's Alhambra Th.	4376
	Loew's Alpine Th.	2875
	Loew's Broadway Th.	2737
	Loew's Gates Th.	2876
	Loew's Metropolitan Th.	4112
	Loew's Palace Th.	2438
	Meserole Th.	3232
	Metropolitan (Putnam) Th.	2472
	Olympic Th.	4628
	Premier Th.	3370
	Prospector Th.	1361
	Republic (Small's) Th.	3167
	Ridgewood Th.	2408
	Sumner Th.	2606
	Warwick Th.	2437
Buffalo	Cortland-Strand Th.	1464
	Larkin Administration Bldg.	4335
	Loew's Th.	2888

CITY/STATE	LOCATION	OPUS
Buffalo	Loew's State Th.	4318
	Variety Th.	2603
Cedarhurst	Central Th.	3471
Coney Island	Loew's Coney Island Th.	4287
Cornwall	New York Military Academy	4925
East Hampton	East Hampton (Edwards) Th.	4767
Glen Falls	Park Th.	1876
Great Kills	Great Kills Th.	3130
	Strand Th.	5202
Hempstead	Newhouse Theatre Corp.	4312
Herkimer	Liberty Th.	2777
Jamaica	Jamaica Th.	2019
Kingston	Keeney's Th.	2504
Mineola	Mineola Th.	4817
Mt. Vernon	Strand Th.	1598
New Rochelle	Loew's Th.	3088
New York	Academy of Music	3801
	Audubon Th.	3800
	Avenue B Th.	1947
	Chaloner Th.	3426
	Chelsea Th.	3745
	City Th.	2072
	Deluxe Th.	4249
	Dyckman Th.	2344
	86th Street Th.	2129
	Emil Velazco Studio	6189
	14th Street (Mecca) Th.	4629
	Garrick Th.	1965
	Gramercy Park Th.	3822
	Grand Opera House Th.	4117
	Hamilton (at 146th St. & Bdwy)	2238
	Harlem Opera House	1815
	Hippodrome Th.	1580
	Inwood Th.	4357
	Japanese Garden Th.	2008
	Jefferson Th.	2236
	Keith's 81st Street Th.	3037
	Lexington Opera House (Loew's Lexington) Th.	3750
	Loew's American (42nd Street) Th.	2574
	Loew's Circle Th.	2017
	Loew's Delancey Street Th.	2307
	Loew's 83rd Street Th.	4373
	Loew's Greeley Square Th.	2308
	Loew's Lincoln Sqaure Th.	2494
	Loew's 116th Street Th.	2306
	Loew's Rio Th.	4379
	Loew's Spooner Th.	4378
	Loew's State Th.	4111
	Moss's Coliseum (181st Street) Th.	2954
	Moss's Tremont Avenue (Hamilton) Th.	2952
	National Th.	1994
	Nemo Th.	1843
	New York Th.	1910
	New York Theatre Roof Garden	2128
	Orpheum Th.	2096
	Renaissance Th.	3496
	Riviera Th.	2388
	Savoy Th.	3480
	7th Avenue Th.	2493
	Standard (Stoddard) Th.	2643
	Star Th.	2073
	Superior Th.	3746
	Victoria Th.	2322
	Waldorf Astoria Hotel	5766, 5795
	West End Th.	2000
Ogdensburg	Star Th.	1636
Olean	Palace Th.	2198
Patchogue	Patchogue Th.	3550
Peekskill	Colonial Th.	2052
	Ripple Th.	4113
Port Jervis	Strand Th.	5201
Rochester	Gordon's Th.	1493
Rome	Capitol Th.	5371
Saratoga Springs	Congress Th.	2695
Schenectady	Capitol Th.	3349
	Majestic Th.	2411
Springfield Gardens	Garden Th.	3119
Stapleton	Liberty Th.	3129
Suffern	Suffern Th.	3815

CITY/STATE	LOCATION	OPUS
Toms River	Traco Th.	5271
Utica	Park Th.	3123
White Plains	WFAS Radio	6416
Woodhaven	Cross Bay Th.	4149

NORTH CAROLINA (NC)

CITY/STATE	LOCATION	OPUS
Raleigh	WPTF Radio	5792
Spartanburg	WSPA Radio	6184
Winston-Salem	Lincoln Th.	5251

OHIO (OH)

CITY/STATE	LOCATION	OPUS
Akron	Stand Th.	1921
Cambridge	Strand Th.	2682
Cincinnati	Empress Th.	3298
	Lubin Th.	1847
Cleveland	Hippodrome Th.	3434
	Loew's Ohio Th.	2874
	Loew's Park Th.	2871
	Loew's State Th.	2982
	Olympia (Broadway-Wilson) Th.	1299
	Palace Th.	2908
	U. S. Theatre	1351
Columbus	Bill Dalton residence	5356
	Eastern Th.	2942
	Hill Top Th.	3161
	Majestic Th.	2434
	Moby's Inc. Dept. Store	6107
	State Th.	3160
Dayton	Dayton Th.	2471
	Majestic (Loew's) Th.	2089
Elyria	Georgople Th.	3154
Fremont	Strand Th.	1974
Lancaster	Regal Th.	5252
Marietta	Hippodrome Th.	2683
	Putnam Th.	1895
	Strand Th.	4038
Marion	Grand Th.	2312
Middletown	Grand Th.	1772
Newark	Midland Th.	5212
	New Auditorium Th.	5192
Springfield	Alhambra Th.	1681
Toledo	Hippodrome Th.	1998
	Loew's Valentine Th.	2454
Youngstown	Strand Th.	2621

PENNSYLVANIA (PA)

CITY/STATE	LOCATION	OPUS
Allentown	Earle Th.	4946
	Hippodrome Th.	2752
	19th Street Th.	5139
Ashland	New Theatre	5151
	Temple Th.	3980
Bethlehem	College Th.	5211
Bloomsburg	Victoria Th.	2691
Bristol	Forrest Th.	2692
Chambersburg	Capitol (Chambersburg) Th.	4800
Chester	John Keegan Th.	2989
Collingsdale	Villa (Collingsdale) Th.	5311
Columbia	Alto Th.	3696
	Circle Th.	4945
Danville	Opera House	3802
Erie	Strand Th.	1988
Gettysburg	Hotel Gettysburg Co. New Th.	4490
Grove City	Majestic Th.	2231
Harrisburg	Colonial Th.	1952
	Grand Th.	2154
	Regent Th.	1889
Hazelton	Broad Th.	3268
Johnstown	Garden Th.	1861
Lancaster	Grand Th.	5341
	Hippodrome (Aldine) Th.	2839
	Strand Th.	5088
Lawndale	Lawndale Th.	3173
Lebanon	Jackson Th.	2929
Lehighton	Bayer Th.	3532
Lewistown	Rialto Th.	3319
Lock Haven	Garden Th.	4080
Mahanoy City	Victoria Th.	4115
Marcus Hook	Spielmont Th.	3118
Meadville	Park Th.	4030
Mt. Airy	Sedgwick Th.	5230
Mt. Carmel	Victoria Th.	4114

CITY/STATE	LOCATION	OPUS
Nanticoke	Rex Th.	3261
Olyphant	Granada Th.	5331
Palmerton	Colonial Th.	3119
Parsons	Parsons Th.	5203
Philadelphia	Aldine Th.	3179
	Allegheny Th.	4777
	Arcade Palace Th.	2747
	Baltimore Th.	2257
	Belvidere Th.	2416
	Cambria Th.	3125
	Century Th.	5150
	Connie Mack Stadium	2170
	Convention Hall	5819
	Eureka #1 Th.	3138
	Fairhill Th.	2810
	Fox Th. (on 16th Street)	3509
	Franklin Th.	2583
	Grant Th.	3022
	Harrowgate Th.	2949
	Keystone Th.	2765
	Knickerbocker (Fay's) Th.	3112
	Metropolitan Opera House	5315
	Moller Studio	4945
	New Broadway Th.	2693
	New Colonial Th.	2584
	Nixon Th.	2730
	Ridge Avenue Th.	3099
	Ritz (Eureka #2) Th.	3264
	Royal Th.	2766
	Ruby (Arcade) Th.	2244
	Sherwood Th.	2226
	Strand Th.	3083
	Susquehanna Th.	2568
	Tioga Th.	2892
	Tulpehocken Th.	1835
	Wayne Th.	2615
	Wayne Palace Th.	2809
	West Allegheny Th.	2602
Phoenixville	Colonial Th.	3240
Pittsburgh	Alderdice Th.	2652
	Arsenal Th.	2650
	Belmar Th.	2651
	Cameraphone Th.	2109
	Clarence Overend Th.	2060
	Clark Th.	2201
	Columbia Th.	2712
	Foster's Cafeteria	2714
	Grand Th.	3647
	Hill Top Th.	2758
	Lyceum Th.	2675
	Oakland Th.	1997
	Regent Th.	1783
	Roosevelt Th.	5436
	Squirrel Hill Th.	3256
	State Th.	3255
Pottsville	Garden Th.	2536
Pottstown	Hippodrome Th.	3058
Quakertown	Palace Th.	3405
Reading	Arcadia Th.	2880
	Carr & Schad (Loew's) (Strand) Th.	2761
	Lyric Th.	1752
	San Toy Th.	3087
Scranton	Riviera Th.	5351
Shamokin	Majestic Th.	3306
	Victoria Th.	4980
Shenandoah	Strand Th.	5089
Shippensburg	Hollar's Th.	3051
Somerset	Pascal Th.	2759
Souderton	Gillman Th.	3300
Sunbury	Strand Th.	5214
Tamaqua	Higgin's Th.	4067
	Victoria Th.	4355
Uniontown	Penn Th.	2824
Waynesboro	Arcade Th.	3959
Williamsport	Capitol Th.	5352
	Hippodrome Th.	2259
	Keeney's Th.	2505
Wilkinsburgh	Rowland Th.	1941
York	Jackson Th.	3201

CITY/STATE	LOCATION	OPUS
RHODE ISLAND (RI)		
Auburn	Park Th.	4110
East Greenwich	Theatre #1	4416
Pawtucket	Strand Th.	2934
Providence	Broad Street Playhouse	2965
	Modern Th.	2033
	Palace Th.	2938
	Park (Castle) Th.	4388
	Strand Th.	3990
Westerly	United Th.	4449
Woonsocket	Laurier Th.	2882
SOUTH CAROLINA (SC)		
Anderson	unidentified theatre	2962
Charleston	Academy of Music	3689
	Garden Th.	3302
	Gloria Th.	4937
	Victory Th.	3690
Spartanburg	Lester Th.	1723
SOUTH DAKOTA (SD)		
Sioux Falls	Colonial Th.	2537
	Princess Th.	2260
Watertown	unidentified theatre	2945
TENNESSEE (TN)		
Knoxville	Loew's (Lyric) Th.	2811
Memphis	Linden Circle Th.	4551
	Loew's Palace Th.	2872
	Loew's State (Metropolitan) Th.	2873
	Majestic Th.	1873
	Peabody Hotel	5557
Nashville	Loew's Th.	2812
	Parthenon Th.	1942
TEXAS (TX)		
Abilene	Queen Th.	2071
Denison	Rialto Th.	2854
Houston	Zoe (Pearce) Th.	1632
San Antonio	Picture Th.	2353
VIRGINIA (VA)		
Charlottesville	Greek Th. (Univ. of VA)	3060
Lynchburg	Hofheimer's Th.	1778
Norfolk	Granby Th.	2237
Portsmouth	Gates Th.	5272
Richmond	Colonial Th.	1944
	Little (Walker) (Edison) (Regency) Th.	1395
	Odeon Th.	2961
	Regent Th	1777
WASHINGTON (WA)		
Seattle	Coliseum Th.	1964
WEST VIRGINIA (WV)		
Charleston	Rialto Th.	2917
	Virginian Th.	3452
Clarksburg	Grand Th.	1907
	Orpheum Th.	1954
Fairmount	Grand Th.	2194
Martinsburg	Apollo Th.	1919
Moundsville	Strand Th.	4577
Parkersburg	Camden Th.	4456
	Smoot Th.	5098
Shepherdstown	Opera House	2486
White Sulphur Springs	Greenbrier Hotel	5908
WISCONSIN (WI)		
Kenosha	Vogue Th.	3549
LaCrosse	New Theatre	2797
Milwaukee	Parkway Th.	3191
Manitowoc	Mikadow Th.	2785
Portage	Home Th.	4544
QUEBEC, CANADA		
Montreal	Loew's Th.	2585
ENGLAND		
London	Reginald Foort	6690
JAPAN		
Tokyo	Croda Tone Organ Co. Ltd.	11433

OPUS	LOCATION/CITY/STATE	SIZE	YR	PRICE	BLWR	HP	WP	REMARKS
no #	Odeon Th., New York, NY		1910					Not an original installation.
1177	Orpheum Th., Montgomery, AL	2/7	1910	$ 1,350.00				
1188	Majestic Th., Memphis, TN	2/	1910					See opus 1418.
1299	Olympia (Broadway-Wilson) Th., Cleveland, OH	2/14	1911	$ 3,500.00	8164K	3		
1351	U. S. Th., Cleveland, OH	2/	1912		8555K	1	5"	
1356	Alhambra Th., Indianapolis, IN	2/23	1912	$ 5,500.00	A148	3	5"	With 4-rank echo.
1361	14th Street (Mecca) Th., New York, NY	2/13	1912	$ 4,000.00	A85	5	6"	With 65-note roll player; see opus 4629; Moved in 1918 to Prospector Th., Brooklyn, New York.
1395	Little (Walker) (Edison) (Regency) Th., Richmond, VA	2/14	1912	$ 1,500.00	A232	1	4"	With roll player.
1418	Majestic Th., Memphis, TN	2/10	1912	$ 4597.50	A343	1	4½	With 88-note roll player; replaced opus 1188; see opus 1873.
1464	Cortland-Strand Th., Buffalo, NY	2/	1913	$ 3,000.00	A522	1	5"	With roll player.
1466	Savoy Th., Anniston, AL	2/7	1912	$ 2,000.00	A418	½	4"	
1493	Gordon's Th., Rochester, NY	4/17	1913	$ 10,000.00	A599	5	5"&10"	
1520	Tudor Th., New Orleans, LA	2/10	1913	$ 3,000.00	A755	¾		
1564	Columbia Th., Muncie, IN	2/14	1913	$ 3,100.00	B155	1	4"	With roll player.
1580	Hippodrome Th., New York, NY	2/17	1913	$ 4,500.00	B232	7½	10"	
		2/18	1914	$ 1,500.00				Additions: 32' bourdon, 16' tuba and vox humana.
1598	Strand Th., Mt. Vernon, NY	2/9	1913	$ 2,000.00	B360	½	4"	
1601	Olympia (Tremont Row)(Astor) Th., Boston, MA	4/25	1913	$ 15,000.00	B247	7½	5"&10"	With echo.
1632	Zoe (Pearce) Th., Houston, TX	2/	1914		C400	1	5"	
1636	Star Th., Ogdensburg, NY	1/6	1914	$ 2,500.00	C109	1	6"	To be attached to customer's piano.
		2/10	1914	$ 1,000.00				Additions: 2 manual console and 4 ranks; moved 5 original ranks to new echo chamber.
1666	Majestic Th., Columbus, OH	2/	1913	$ 3,600.00	B589	2	5"	See opus 2434.
1681	Alhambra Th., Springfield, OH	2/9	1913	$ 3,100.00	B599	2	5"	With roll player.
1702	Savoy Th., New York, NY	2/7	1914	$ 5,000.00	B695	2	4½"	See opus 2030 and 2592.
					B694	¼	12"	Vacuum for roll player.
1716	Royal Picture Th., Kansas City, MO	2/17	1914	$ 4,200.00	B766	2	4"	
1723	Lester Th., Spartanburg, SC	2/9	1914	$ 2,000.00				Tubular pneumatic action.
1752	Lyric Th., Reading, PA	2/10	1914	$ 3,200.00	C185	1	5"	Tubular pneumatic action; destroyed by fire in 1934.
1763	Empire Th., Bronx, NY	2/9	1914	$ 3,000.00	C99	¾	4"	
1766	Hippodrome Th., Baltimore, MD	2/17	1914	$ 1,000.00	C565	2	5"	Rebuilt used organ; see opus 1856.
1772	Grand Th., Middletown, OH	2/	1914		C392	1	5"	
1773	Arcadia Dance Palace, Detroit, MI	2/8	1914	$ 2,500.00	C216	¾	5"	Tubular pneumatic action.
1777	Regent Th., Richmond, VA	2/10	1914	$ 2,000.00	C170	¾	4"	Tubular pneumatic action.
1778	Hofheimer's Th., Lynchburg, VA	2/	1914		C297	1	5"	
1783	Regent Th., Pittsburgh, PA	2/9	1914	$ 4,730.00	C412	2	6"	With roll player.
		2/14	1915	$ 1,800.00				Additions: 5 ranks.
1786	Cameraphone Th., Pittsburgh, PA	2/7	1914	$ 2,850.00	C334	¾	5"	With 88-note roll player; see opus 2109.
			1914		C343	¾		
1789	Ruby (Arcade) Th., Philadelphia, PA	2/9	1914		C330	1	5"	Tubular pneumatic action; see opus 2257 and 2244.
1790	Broadway Th., Springfield, MA	3/8	1914	$ 3,500.00	C627	2	4½"	See opus 4322.
1792	Academy of Music (#1), New York, NY	3/38	1915	$ 5,700.00	D446	2	4"	Contained many used parts; see opus 3801.
1797	Colonial Th., Hagerstown, MD	2/8	1914	$ 5,000.00	C301	2		Piano console.
			1915					Added electric bells in lobby to be heard on street.
		2/9	1926	$ 1,450.00				Additions: one rank and new horseshoe console.
1815	Harlem Opera House, New York, NY	3/34	1914	$ 10,000.00	C151	7½	6"	
1821	Strand Th., Indianapolis, IN	2/6	1914	$ 1,775.00	C375	½	4"	Tubular pneumatic action.
1832	Fox Th., New Britain, CT	3/24	1915	$ 6,000.00	C511	3½	5"	
1835	Tulpehocken Th., Philadelphia, PA	2/15	1914	$ 2,000.00	C466	1	4"	Used organ rebuilt.
1843	Nemo Th., New York, NY	2/7	1914	$ 4,000.00	C424	2	6"	
1847	Lubin Th., Cincinnati, OH	2/9	1915	$ 2,600.00	D230	2	6"	Piano console.
1855	Colonial Th., Brockton, MA	2/10	1915	$ 3,225.00	C804	1	6"	Player piano console.
1856	Hippodrome Th., Baltimore, MD	2/16	1914	$ 3,100.00				Tubular pneumatic action; replaced opus 1766; see opus 2563.
1861	Garden Th., Johnstown, PA	2/9	1915	$ 3,000.00	C633	2		Player piano console; see opus 2099.
1866	Camden Th., Parkersburg, WV	2/8	1915	$ 2,800.00	C609	2		Player piano console; see opus 4456.
1871	Elsmere Th., Bronx, NY	2/	1914	$ 1,900.00	C585	1	5"	Installed used Misch organ; see opus 3776.
1873	Majestic Th., Memphis, TN	3/20	1915	$ 7,500.00	C634	3½	10"	Replaced opus 1418.
					C635	1	6"	
					D80	½		Vacuum for roll player.
1876	Park Th., Glen Falls, NY	2/11	1915	$ 2,500.00	C657	1	5"	
		3/16	1916	$ 1,150.00				Additions: 5 ranks, harp and 3-manual console.
1889	Regent Th., Harrisburg, PA	2/13	1915	$ 4,100.00	D19	2	5"	Player piano console.
		4/13	1915	$ 350.00				New 4-manual console and staff bells.
1895	Putnam Th., Marietta, OH	2/7	1915	$ 2,000.00	C689	2		
1907	Grand Th., Clarksburg, WV	2/9	1915	$ 3,300.00	C821	2		Player piano console.

OPUS	LOCATION/CITY/STATE	SIZE	YR	PRICE	BLWR	HP	WP	REMARKS
1910	New York Th., New York, NY	3/	1916	$ 5,300.00	E51	2		Used Moller from a New York theatre with a new 3-manual console.
1919	Apollo Th., Martinsburg, WV	2/8	1915	$ 3,250.00	D78	2		Player piano console.
1921	Strand Th., Akron, OH	2/	1915		D238	2	5″	
1930	Great Wizard Th., Baltimore, MD	2/6	1915	$ 2,500.00	D485	1	5″	Player piano console.
			1915		951K	½	32″	Vacuum for player; see opus 2699.
1932	Trianon Th., New Orleans, LA	2/9	1915	$ 3,750.00	D116	2	5″	Player piano console.
1939	Strand Th., Providence, RI	2/15	1915	$ 5,000.00	D132	2	5″	With 3-rank echo; see opus 2267.
1941	Rowland Th., Wilkinsburg, PA	2/16	1915	$ 5,200.00	D232	2	5″	
1942	Parthenon Th., Nashville, TN	2/8	1915	$ 2,500.00	D100	2		Player piano console.
1944	Colonial Th., Richmond, VA	2/9	1915	$ 4,500.00	D209	2	6″	Player piano console.
1947	Avenue B Th., New York, NY	4/31	1916	$ 5,700.00	D757	3	4½″	Contained many used parts.
1952	Colonial Th., Harrisburg, PA	3/12	1915	$ 4,500.00	D282	2	5″	
1954	Orpheum Th., Clarksburg, WV	2/8	1915	$ 3,250.00	D210	2		Player piano console.
1959	Crown Th. #1, Mobile, AL	2/9	1915	$ 3,750.00	D241	2	5″	Player piano console.
1962	Parkway (Five West) Th., Baltimore, MD	2/15	1915	$ 3,500.00	D274	2	5″	
1964	Coliseum Th., Seattle, WA	4/30	1915	$ 12,500.00	D470	7½	6″	
			1915		D483	½	4″	For 4-rank echo; moved in 1918 to Victory Th., Tacoma, WA.
1965	Garrick Th., New York, NY	2/	1915	$ 2,000.00				All used parts.
1974	Strand Th., Fremont, OH	2/8	1915	$ 3,000.00	D392	1	5″	Player piano console.
1982	Wilson (Rivoli) Th., Baltimore, MD	2/	1915		D318	1	5″	See opus 2995.
1985	Lakewood Th., Detroit, MI	2/12	1915	$ 2,850.00	D330	1		
1988	Strand Th., Erie, PA	2/10	1916	$ 3,250.00	D785	2	5″	
1993	Metropolitan Opera House, Philadelphia, PA	2/15	1915	$ 4,000.00	D419	2	5″	See opus 2073 and 5315.
1994	National Th., New York, NY	3/25	1916	$ 5,000.00	D754	3	5″	Contained many used parts.
1997	Oakland Th., Pittsburgh, PA	2/9	1915	$ 2,700.00	D612	1	5″	With roll player.
1998	Hippodrome Th., Toledo, OH	2/	1915		D393	1	5″	
2000	West End Th., New York, NY	3/	1917	$ 4,500.00	E637	3	5″	Contained used parts.
2008	Japanese Garden Th., New York, NY	3/21	1916	$ 5,300.00	D382	3	5″	Tubular pneumatic.
			1925		M1188B	1	10″	
2015	Audubon Th., New York, NY	3/24	1915	$ 7,500.00	D478	2	6″	Blower for great, choir and pedal divisions.
			1915		D507	1	4″	For swell division.
			1916		E379	1	5″	See opus 3800.
2016	Crotona Th., Bronx, NY	3/24	1915	$ 7,500.00	D472	2	6″	Blower for great, choir and pedal.
					D657	1	4″	Blower for swell.
2017	Loew's Circle Th., New York, NY	3/10	1914	$ 4,500.00	B707	1	4″	
2018	Loew's Th., New Rochelle, NY	3/10	1915	$ 3,500.00	D474	1	5″	With used console; see opus 3088.
2019	Jamaica Th., Jamaica, NY	3/21	1915	$ 5,300.00	D471	3	5″	
2022	Strand Th., Meridian, MS	2/11	1915	$ 3,075.00	D493	1	5″	
2027	Folly Th., Brooklyn, NY	3/21	1915	$ 4,300.00	D652	2	5″	With 6-rank echo.
2028	Fox Th., Springfield, MA	3/9	1915	$ 4,000.00	D664	1	5″	
2030	Broadway Th., Long Branch, NJ	2/7	1915	$ 2,100.00	D481	1	4½″	Moved opus 1702; see opus 2806.
2033	Modern Th., Providence, RI	2/13	1916	$ 4,500.00	D747	3	5″	
2047	Colonial Th., Sioux Falls, SD	2/	1916		D759	1	5″	See opus 2537.
2049	Queen Th., Wilmington, DE	3/10	1915	$ 4,500.00	D618	1	5″	
2050	Central Coliseum Th., Washington, DC	2/6	1916	$ 2,750.00	D702	1		With roll player.
2052	Colonial Th., Peekskill, NY	2/16	1918	$ 3,200.00	G321	3	5″	
2060	Clarence Overend Th., Pittsburgh, PA	2/9	1916	$ 2,700.00	D704	1		With roll player.
2065	Nixon Academy Th., Hagerstown, MD	3/19	1916	$ 5,000.00	D733	3	5″	With 4-rank echo.
		3/20	1926	$ 2,650.00				Additions: new 3-manual console and one rank; player piano in orchestra pit also made playable from console.
2066	Strand Th., Baltimore, MD	2/11	1916	$ 2,500.00	D700	1	5″	Located at 404 N. Howard St.
2071	Queen Th., Abilene, TX	2/	1916		D774	1	5″	
2072	City Th., New York, NY	3/21	1916	$ 5,000.00	D736	2	5″	
			1916		D782	1	5″	
2073	Star Th., New York, NY	2/15	1915	$ 3,500.00	D419	2	5″	Moved opus 1993.
2082	Picture Garden (Lexway) (Newsreel) (Vogue) (Laffmovie) (World) (Fine Arts) Th., Baltimore, MD	2/12	1916	$ 2,900.00	E15	1	5″	
2088	Broadway Th., Brooklyn, NY	2/15	1916	$ 3,000.00	D789	5	5″	See opus 2737.
2089	Majestic (Loew's) Th., Dayton, OH	2/	1916		D868	1	5″	
2096	Orpheum Th., New York, NY	3/12	1916	$ 5,000.00	E203	2	5″	
2097	Loew's Columbia Th., Washington, DC	2/7	1916	$ 3,000.00	D870	1	5″	See opus 3737.
2099	Fulton Th., Brooklyn, NY	2/8	1916	$ 3,000.00	E48	1	5″	Player piano console; this organ originally opus 1861.
2108	Bijou Th., Fergus Falls, MN	2/9	1916	$ 2,250.00	E60	1	5″	
2109	Cameraphone Th., Pittsburgh, PA	2/19	1916	$ 2,950.00	E324	¾	5″	Rebuild and enlargement of existing Moller—opus 1786.
2128	New York Th. Roof Garden, New York, NY	3/20	1916	$ 5,500.00	E193	3	5″	
2129	86th Street Th., New York, NY	3/19	1916	$ 5,500.00	E192	3	5″	
2148	Grand Th., Lancaster, PA	3/25	1916	$ 6,300.00	E358	3	5″	See opus 5341.
2154	Grand Th., Harrisburg, PA	3/11	1916	$ 4,000.00	E344	2	5″	
2170	Connie Mack Stadium, Philadelphia, PA	2/8	1916	$ 3,000.00	E367	1	5″	
2171	Strand Th., Youngstown, OH	2/12	1916	$ 3,000.00	E513	2	5″	See opus 2621.
2183	Lyric Th., Marion, IN	2/10	1916	$ 3,500.00	E386	1	5″	With 3-rank echo.
2194	Grand Th., Fairmount, WV	2/7	1916	$ 3,500.00	E392	2	5″	
2198	Palace Th., Olean, NY	3/12	1916	$ 5,000.00	E394	2	5″	

OPUS	LOCATION/CITY/STATE	SIZE	YR	PRICE	BLWR	HP	WP	REMARKS
2201	Clark Th., Pittsburgh, PA	2/11	1916	$ 3,000.00	E429	2	5"	
2205	Winter Garden Th., Baltimore, MD	3/15	1917	$ 4,500.00				
2226	Sherwood Th., Philadelphia, PA	2/9	1916	$ 3,500.00	E433	1	5"	
2231	Majestic Th., Grove City, PA	2/10	1916	$ 2,700.00	E477	2	6"	
2233	12th Street Th., Kansas City, MO	2/9	1916	$ 3,700.00	E474	1	5"	
2236	Jefferson Th., New York, NY	3/14	1917	$ 4,000.00	E636	2	5"	
2237	Granby Th., Norfolk, VA	2/	1916	$ 3,750.00	E491	2	5"	
2238	Hamilton Th., New York, NY	3/15	1917	$ 4,000.00	E637	2	5"	Located at 146th Street and Broadway.
2240	unidentified new theatre, Baltimore, MD	3/14	1916	$ 4,000.00	E484	2	5"	
2244	Ruby (Arcade) Th., Philadelphia, PA	2/11	1916	$ 5,000.00				Replaced opus 1789.
2250	Empress Th., Owensboro, KY	2/11	1917	$ 4,050.00	E551	2	5"	
2251	Terminal Th., Newark, NJ	3/12	1916	$ 4,000.00	E521	2	5"	See opus 2740.
2256	McHenry Th., Baltimore, MD	2/13	1917	$ 3,000.00	F86	2	5"	
2257	Baltimore Th., Philadelphia, PA	2/10	1917	$ 2,100.00	E666	1	5"	Formerly opus 1789, plus additional rank.
2259	Hippodrome Th., Williamsport, PA	2/12	1917	$ 2,975.00	E598	2	5"	
2260	Princess Th., Sioux Falls, SD	2/9	1917	$ 2,750.00	E771	1	5"	Piano console.
2267	Strand Th., Providence, RI	3/28	1917	$ 5,000.00	E767	2	8"	Enlargement of opus 1939; see opus 3990.
			1917		E768	¾	5"	For 4-rank echo.
2271	Jodoin's Th., Baltic, CT	2/6	1917	$ 1,700.00	E642	1	5½"	
2306	Loew's 116th Street Th., New York, NY	3/16	1917	$ 5,000.00	F97	3	5"	
2307	Loew's Delancey Street Th., New York, NY	3/16	1917	$ 5,000.00	F61	3	5"	
2308	Loew's Greeley Square Th., New York, NY	3/16	1917	$ 5,000.00	F62	3	5"	
2312	Grand Th., Marion, OH	3/	1917		F15	3	5"	
2319	Poli Th., New Haven, CT	4/	1917		F330	7½	5"&10"	
2322	Victoria Th., New York, NY	3/17	1917	$ 6,000.00	F156	3	5"	
2344	Dyckman Th., New York, NY	3/16	1920	$ 6,000.00	H692	3	5"	
2353	Picture Th., San Antonio, TX	2/7	1917	$ 2,300.00	F134	¾	5"	Piano console.
2368	McWilliams (Marion) Th., Clarksdale, MS	3/15	1917	$ 5,900.00	F254	3		See opus 3345.
2370	St. James (Rosenburg) Th., Asbury Park, NJ	3/16	1917	$ 6,000.00	F271	3	5"	
2378	Garden Th., Baltimore, MD	2/7	1917	$ 2,100.00	F171	¾	5"	Piano console; located at 1100½ South Charles Street.
2380	Keeney's (Livingston) Th., Brooklyn, NY	3/17	1918	$ 6,000.00	F576	3	5"	
			1926					New console.
2388	Riviera Th., New York, NY	3/16	1917	$ 5,250.00	F274	3	5"	
2407	Bedford Th., Brooklyn, NY	3/16	1917	$ 5,250.00	F527	3	5"	
2408	Ridgewood Th., Brooklyn, NY	3/16	1917	$ 5,250.00	F528	3	5"	
2411	Majestic Th., Schenectady, NY	2/9	1917	$ 3,000.00	F239	1	5"	Tubular pneumatic action.
2415	Knickerbocker (Fay's) Th., Philadelphia, PA	2/16	1917	$ 4,500.00	F268	2	5"	See opus 3112.
2416	Belvidere Th., Philadelphia, PA	2/10	1917	$ 3,150.00	F526	1	5"	Tubular pneumatic action; unknown if theatre name is correct.
2434	Majestic Th., Columbus, OH	4/22	1918	$ 3,100.00	F465	3½	6"	Contained mostly used pipes; with echo; enlargement of opus 1666.
		3/22	1925	$ 1,300.00				New 3-manual console and tremolos.
2436	DeKalb Avenue Th., Brooklyn, NY	3/16	1917		F336	3	5"	
2437	Warwick Th., Brooklyn, NY	3/16	1917	$ 5,500.00	F335	3	5"	
2438	Loew's Palace Th., Brooklyn, NY	3/16	1917		F334	3	5"	
2439	Boulevard Th., Bronx, NY	3/16	1917	$ 6,000.00	F333	3	5"	
2446	Folly Th., Algiers, LA	2/						Unknown if ever built.
2453	Crescent Th., New Orleans, LA	3/16	1917	$ 6,000.00	F365	2	5"	
2454	Loew's Valentine Th., Toledo, OH	3/	1917	$ 4,000.00	F356	2	5"	
2464	Victoria Th., Shamokin, PA	3/16	1917	$ 6,500.00	F550	3	6"	See opus 3614.
2471	Dayton Th., Dayton, OH	3/16	1917	$ 6,000.00	F516	2	6"	
2472	Metropolitan (Putnam) TH., Brooklyn, NY	3/17	1918	$ 6,150.00	F611	3	5"	
2473	Loew's Palace Th., Washington, DC	3/17	1917	$ 6,150.00	F610	3	5"	see opus 4319.
2486	Opera House, Shepherdstown, WV	1/5	1918	$ 875.00	F599	½	5"	Tubular pneumatic action; attached to customer's piano, utilizing used Hook & Hastings parts.
2491	Poli Th., Washington, DC	2/	1917	$ 4,000.00				Order cancelled.
2491	Rialto Th., West Palm Beach, FL	2/10	1918	$ 5,000.00	F616	2	6"	Player piano console with additional roll player for dual roll use.
2492	Bijou Th., Brooklyn, NY	3/16	1918	$ 6,000.00	F637	5	5"	
2493	7th Avenue Th., New York, NY	3/16	1918	$ 6,000.00	F641	5	5"	
2494	Loew's Lincoln Square Th., New York, NY	3/16	1918	$ 6,000.00	F636	3	5"	
2504	Keeney's Th., Kingston, NY	3/13	1918	$ 5,000.00	G243	2	5"	
2505	Keeney's Th., Williamsport, PA	3/13	1918	$ 5,000.00	G244	2	5"	
2509	Midway Th., Rockford, IL	3/13	1918	$ 5,000.00	F661	2	5"	
2521	Arcade Th., Salisbury, MD	2/7	1918	$ 2,500.00	G47	1	5"	
2525	Knickerbocker Th., Washington, DC	2/10	1918	$ 4,000.00	G62	2	5"	
2528	Strand Th., Hattiesburg, MS	2/11	1918	$ 4,000.00	G81	2	5"	
2536	Garden Th., Pottsville, PA	2/11	1918	$ 4,320.00	G209	2	5"	
2537	Colonial Th., Sioux Falls, SD	2/	1918	$ 1,300.00	G89	1	5"	Additions: 4 ranks to existing opus 2047.
2548	Lyceum Th., Pittsburgh, PA	3/16	1918	$ 6,000.00	G389	3	5"	See opus 2548.
2559	New Empire Th, Fall River, MA	2/12	1918	$ 5,500.00	G242	2	5"	
2561	Metropolitan Th., Washington, DC	3/17	1918	$ 6,500.00	G250	3	5"	
2563	Hippodrome Th., Baltimore, MD	3/16	1918	$ 6,000.00				Enlargement of opus 1856.
2566	Olympia Th., Cambridge, MA	4/24	1919	$ 15,000.00	G263			

OPUS	LOCATION/CITY/STATE	SIZE	YR	PRICE	BLWR	HP	WP	REMARKS
2568	Susquehanna Th., Philadelphia, PA	2/11	1918	$ 4,750.00	G237	1	5″	Tubular pneumatic action; with 3-rank echo.
2571	American Th., Newark, NJ	2/7	1918	$ 4,500.00	G175	2	5″	Player piano console.
2572	Fox's Liberty Th., Elizabeth, NJ	3/13	1918	$ 5,500.00	G174	2	5″	
2573	Fox's Liberty Th., St. Louis, MO	3/17	1918	$ 7,500.00	G173	2	5″	
2574	Loew's American (42nd St.) Th., New York, NY	3/16	1918	$ 6,000.00	G239	3	5″	
2578	Orpheum Th., Leavenworth, KS	2/8	1919	$ 4,350.00	G231	1	4″	
2583	Franklin Th., Philadelphia, PA	3/15	1919	$ 6,500.00	G254	3	5″	With 2-rank echo.
no #	Opera House, Dover, DE	2/8	1919	$ 2,500.00				Moved Hope-Jones organ from First Presbyterian Church, Tyrone, Pennsylvania.
2584	New Colonial Th., Philadelphia, PA	3/14	1919	$ 6,500.00	G255	3	5″	With 2-rank echo.
2585	Loew's Th., Montreal, Quebec, Canada	3/24	1919	$ 6,500.00	G252	3		
2587	Liberty Th., Plaquemine, LA	2/11	1919	$ 4,250.00				
2591	Comedy Th., Brooklyn, NY	2/7	1919	$ 4,500.00	G355	2	5″	Player piano console.
2592	Savoy Th., New York, NY	3/12	1919	$ 4,500.00	G397	2	5″	Price included trade-in of existing organ; contained many used parts; see opus 1702 and 3480.
2597	Hippodrome Th., Newport, KY	3/16	1919	$ 6,150.00	G367	2		With 7-rank echo.
2602	West Allegheny Th., Philadelphia, PA	2/7	1919	$ 2,650.00	G300	½	4″	
2603	Variety Th., Buffalo, NY	2/6	1918	$ 2,250.00				
2605	American Th., Paterson, NJ	3/15	1919	$ 5,000.00				With 4-rank echo.
2606	Sumner Th., Brooklyn, NY	3/13	1919	$ 5,500.00	G315	2	5″	
2610	Garden (Keith's-Albee) (Keith's) Th., Baltimore, MD	3/17	1919	$ 6,650.00	G352	3	5″	
2615	Wayne Th., Philadelphia, PA	2/6	1919	$ 3,000.00	G347	½	4″	Tubular pneumatic.
2621	Strand Th., Youngstown, OH	3/15	1919	$ 3,450.00	G398	5	10″	Additions to Moller opus 2171: 3-manual console and 3 ranks.
2643	Standard (Stoddard) Th., New York, NY	3/16	1919	$ 6,750.00	G385	3	4″	
2650	Arsenal Th., Pittsburgh, PA	3/						Probably built for Peloubet.
2651	Belmar Th., Pittsburgh, PA	3/						Probably built for Peloubet.
2652	Alderdice Th., Pittsburgh, PA	3/						Probably built for Peloubet.
2653	Princess Th., Camden, NJ	2/11	1919	$ 5,000.00	H65	2	5″	Purchase price included trade-in of existing organ.
2657	Park Th., Ocean City, NJ	2/11	1919	$ 6,150.00	H64	2	5″	Purchase price discounted $2,000 for trade-in of existing photoplayer.
2658	Strand Th., Ocean City, NJ	2/11	1919	$ 4,150.00	H63	2	5″	
2662	Apollo Th., Gloucester, NJ	2/13	1919	$ 4,850.00	H68	2	5″	
2664	Palace Th., Baltimore, MD	2/10	1919	$ 3,850.00	H92	1	5″	Located at 1351 North Gay Street.
2675	Lyceum Th., Pittsburgh, PA	3/	1919	$ 6,200.00	G329	3		Replaced opus 2548.
2679	Poli Th., Hartford, CT	4/28	1919	$ 11,500.00	H312	5	5″&10″	
					H364	1	5″	For 8-rank lobby organ playable from 2 manuals and pedal of main console.
2682	Strand Th., Cambridge, OH	2/7	1919	$ 3,500.00	H183	¾	5″	Player piano console.
2683	Hippodrome Th., Marietta, OH	2/10	1919	$ 4,500.00	H204	1	5″	Player piano console.
2691	Victoria Th., Bloomsburg, PA	3/16	1919	$ 6,920.00	H185	3	5″	
2692	Forrest Th., Bristol, PA	2/13	1919	$ 5,500.00	H141	2	5″	
2693	New Broadway Th., Philadelphia, PA	2/13	1919	$ 7,000.00	H214		5″	
2695	Congress Th., Saratoga Springs, NY	3/16	1919	$ 6,700.00	H216	3	5″	
2699	Great Wizard Th., Baltimore, MD	2/9	1919	$ 1,150.00				Additions: 3 ranks to Moller opus 1930.
2712	Columbia Th., Pittsburgh, PA	2/						Probably built for Peloubet.
2714	Foster's Cafeteria, Pittsburgh, PA	2/						Probably built for Peloubet.
2715	unidentified theatre, Greenville, SC	2/	1920		I534	¾	5″	Probably built for Peloubet.
2716	Victoria Th., Tamaqua, PA	3/16	1919	$ 6,920.00	H186	3	5″	See opus 4355.
2726	Walbrook Th., Baltimore, MD	2/8	1919	$ 2,600.00	H169	¾	5″	See opus 4861.
2727	Victoria Th., Baltimore, MD	2/9	1919	$ 3,500.00	H257	1	5″	
2730	Nixon Th., Philadelphia, PA	3/9	1919	$ 5,400.00	H284		5″	
2736	Star Th., Camden, NJ	2/11	1919	$ 6,000.00	H213	2	5″	Piano console.
2737	Loew's Broadway Th., Brooklyn, NY	3/16	1918	$ 6,000.00				Replaced opus 2088.
2739	Washington Th., Detroit, MI	3/17	1919	$ 7,000.00	H217	3	5″	
2740	Terminal Th., Newark, NJ	3/17	1921	$ 7,000.00	I629	3	5″	Replaced opus 2251.
2741	Fox (Orpheum) Th., Oakland, CA	3/17	1922	$ 7,000.00	K22	5	6″	
2742	Monroe Th., Chicago, IL	3/17	1924	$ 7,000.00	L913	5	6″	
2743	In storage for William Fox	3/17		$ 7,000.00				
2744	In storage for William Fox	3/17		$ 7,000.00				
2747	Arcade Palace Th., Philadelphia, PA	2/7	1919	$ 3,500.00	H285		5″	
2752	Hippodrome Th., Allentown, PA	2/10	1919	$ 4,000.00	H473	2	5″	
2753	Eureka Th., Baltimore, MD	2/8	1919	$ 2,600.00	H226	¾	5″	
			1921		J396	2	5″	
2757	Schenley Th., Pittsburgh, PA	3/11	1919	$ 4,700.00				Built for Wirsching-Peloubet.
2758	Hill Top Th., Pittsburgh, PA	3/						Probably built for Wirsching-Peloubet.
2759	Pascal Th., Somerset, PA	3/						Probably built for Wirsching-Peloubet.
2760	Grand Th., Atlanta, GA	3/						Built for Wirsching-Peloubet.
2761	Carr & Schad (Loew's) (Strand) Th., Reading, PA	3/16	1919	$ 6,920.00	H597	3	5″	
2765	Keystone Th., Philadelphia, PA	2/9	1919	$ 4,000.00	H286		4″	
2766	Royal Th., Philadelphia, PA	3/22	1919	$ 8,440.00	H287		7″	With 4-rank echo.
2768	Victory Th., Kokomo, IN	2/13	1919	$ 5,000.00	H376	2	5″	

OPUS	LOCATION/CITY/STATE	SIZE	YR	PRICE	BLWR	HP	WP	REMARKS
2772	Escorial Th., New Orleans, LA	2/8	1919	$ 4,000.00	H359	1	5"	
			1920	$ 400.00				Added xylophone.
2777	Liberty Th., Herkimer, NY	3/16	1920	$ 6,000.00	H622	3	5"	
2780	Forest Park (Forest) Th., Baltimore, MD	2/10	1919	$ 3,100.00	H304	1	5"	
2785	Mikadow Th., Manitowoc, WI	3/	1919		H368	2	5"	
2791	Muretti Th., Richmond, IN	2/7	1919	$ 2,700.00	H361	¾	5"	
2792	Bio Th., Moline, IL	2/9	1919	$ 3,000.00	H360	1	5"	
2795	Saenger Th., Monroe, LA	4/18	1921	$ 9,500.00	J80	3	6"	With 4-rank echo.
2797	unidentified new theatre, LaCrosse, WI	2/9	1920	$ 5,000.00	H485	1½	5"	
2799	Brevoort Th., Brooklyn, NY	3/16	1919	$ 6,000.00	H365	5	5"	
2804	Circle Playhouse Th., Annapolis, MD	2/8	1920	$ 2,700.00				See opus 4861.
2806	Broadway Th., Long Branch, NJ	3/16	1920	$ 5,500.00	H482	3	5"	Price included trade-in of existing Moller, opus 1702 and 2030.
2809	Wayne Palace Th., Philadelphia, PA	2/6	1922	$ 3,000.00	H672		5"	
2810	Fairhill Th., Philadelphia, PA	2/6	1920	$ 3,000.00	H673	1	5"	
					I359	2	7"	
2811	Loew's (Lyric) Th., Knoxville, TN	3/16	1919	$ 6,000.00	H219	5	5"	
2812	Loew's Th., Nashville, TN	3/16	1919	$ 6,000.00	H218	5	5"	
2817	Liberty Th., Cape May, NJ	2/6	1920	$ 3,400.00	H489	1	5"	
2824	Penn Th., Uniontown, PA	3/	1920		I26	2	5"	
2827	Royal #1 (Aldine) Th., Atlantic City, NJ	3/	1920		I120	3	5"	
			1923	$ 750.00				Added 5 ranks.
2832	Aurora (Seven East) Th., Baltimore, MD	2/8	1919	$ 2,850.00	H484	¾	5"	
2837	Main Street Th., Asbury Park, NJ	3/16	1920	$ 6,500.00	I334	3	5"	
2838	Stratford Th., Chicago, IL	3/27	1920	$ 10,560.00	I89	5	5"	
2839	Hippodrome (Aldine) Th., Lancaster, PA	4/35	1920	$ 16,000.00	I174	10	6"&10"	
2843	Virginian Th., Charleston, WV	3/10	1920	$ 4,517.50	I28	1½	5"	See opus 3123.
2848	Trent Th., Trenton, NJ	3/17	1919	$ 7,750.00	H521	3	5"	
2849	Taylor Opera House, Trenton, NJ	3/17	1921	$ 7,750.00	I400	3	5"	
2851	Crandall Th., Washington, D.C.	2/8	1920	$ 3,500.00	H572	1½	5"	
2854	Rialto Th., Denison, TX	3/17	1920	$ 7,000.00	H587	3	4½"	
2857	Palace Th., Peoria, IL	3/21	1920	$ 10,000.00	H566	5	5"&10"	
2867	Peabody Th., Baltimore, MD	2/9	1919	$ 3,000.00				
2871	Loew's Park Th., Cleveland, OH	3/17	1920	$ 6,450.00	H645	5	5"	
2872	Loew's Palace Th., Memphis, TN	3/17	1920	$ 6,450.00	H643	5	5"	
2873	Loew's State (Metropolitan) Th., Memphis, TN	3/17	1920	$ 6,450.00	H644		5"	
2874	Loew's Ohio Th., Cleveland, OH	3/17	1921	$ 6,450.00	H648	5	5"	
2875	Loew's Alpine Th., Brooklyn, NY	3/17	1921	$ 6,450.00	H647	5	5"	
2876	Loew's Gates Th., Brooklyn, NY	3/17	1921	$ 6,450.00	H616	5	5"	
2880	Arcadia Th., Reading, PA	4/22	1920		I163	15	8"&20"	
2882	Laurier Th., Woonsocket, RI	2/8	1920	$ 4,350.00	H679	1	5"	
2887	Loew's Th., Indianapolis, IN	3/17	1921	$ 6,450.00	H649	5	5"	
2888	Loew's Th., Buffalo, NY	3/17	1921	$ 6,450.00	H652	5	6"	See opus 4551.
2889	Loew's 83rd Street Th., New York, NY	3/17	1921	$ 6,450.00	H650	5	5"	See opus 4373.
2890	Loew's State Th., Newark, NJ	3/17	1921	$ 6,450.00	H651	5	5"	
2891	Strand Th., Cumberland, MD	2/11	1920	$ 4,750.00	I281	2	5"	
			1924	$ 1,500.00	M137B	3	7"	Rebuilt plus new console.
2892	Tioga Th., Philadelphia, PA	2/12	1920	$ 6,650.00	I61	1½	5"	Piano console.
2893	Globe Th., Flint, MI	2/	1920		I49	2	5"	See opus 3548.
2894	Wolverine Th., Saginaw, MI	2/10	1920	$ 4,000.00	I115	1½	5"	
2895	Park (State) Th., Merchantville, NJ	2/9	1920	$ 4,000.00	I355	2	5"	
2900	Park Th., Atlantic City, NJ	2/11	1920	$ 7,400.00	I87	2	5"	
2901	Liberty Th., Atlantic City, NJ	2/11	1920	$ 7,400.00	I86	2	5"	See opus 3881.
2903	Bridge Th., Baltimore, MD	2/10	1920	$ 4,000.00	H677	1	5"	
2905	Standard Th., Clinton, IN	2/7	1920	$ 3,000.00	I123	¾	5"	
2907	Albermale Th., Brooklyn, NY	3/17	1920	$ 7,500.00	I263	3	5"	
2908	Palace Th., Cleveland, OH	3/	1920		I57	3	5"	
2917	Rialto Th., Charleston, WV	3/10	1920	$ 6,450.00	I165	1½	5"	
2919	Savoy Th., Washington, DC	2/8	1920	$ 4,610.00	I80	1½	5"	
2920	Capitol Th., Baltimore, MD	2/8	1921	$ 5,010.00	I637	2	5"	
2921	Avenue Grand Th., Washington, DC	2/8	1920	$ 4,610.00	I82	1½	5"	
2922	Schanze Th., Baltimore, MD	2/8	1921	$ 5,010.00	I519	1½	5"	
2929	Jackson Th., Lebanon, PA	2/9	1920	$ 6,000.00	I15	1	4"	
2934	Strand Th., Pawtucket, RI	2/15	1920	$ 7,000.00	I56	5	5"&8"	
2935	Portage Park Th., Chicago, IL	3/19	1920	$ 8,650.00	I36	3	5"	
2938	Palace Th., Providence, RI	2/8	1920	$ 4,500.00	I481	1	5"	
2939	Capitol Th., Davenport, IA	4/23	1920	$ 14,405.00	I156	7½	6"&10"	
2942	Eastern Th., Columbus, OH	2/12	1920	$ 6,100.00	C497	2	10"	With 3-rank echo; rebuild of existing Winder organ.
2945	unidentified theatre, Watertown, SD	2/11	1920	$ 5,000.00	I94	2	5"	
2946	Keith's Fordham Th., Bronx, NY	3/17	1921	$ 8,000.00	I67	3	5"	
2949	Harrowgate Th., Philadelphia, PA	2/9	1920	$ 6,000.00	I190	1½	5"	
			1920		I553	2	7"	
2952	Moss's Tremont Avenue (Hamilton) Th., New York, NY	3/17	1921	$ 8,000.00	J449	3	5"	
2953	Moss's 161st. Street (Franklin) Th., Bronx, NY	3/17	1921	$ 8,000.00	I634	3	5"	
2954	Moss's Coliseum (181st. Street) Th., New York, NY	3/15	1920	$ 8,000.00	H560	3	5"	
2955	Century Th., Baltimore, MD	3/	1921		I93	10	7"&10"	
2961	Odeon Th., Richmond, VA	2/						
2962	unidentified theatre, Anderson, SC							

OPUS	LOCATION/CITY/STATE	SIZE	YR	PRICE	BLWR	HP	WP	REMARKS
2965	Broad Street Playhouse, Providence, RI	2/9	1921	$ 4,200.00	I140		5″	
2978	Strand Th., Pittsburgh, PA	3/	1920	$ 3,000.00				Enlarge existing organ for Peloubet.
2980	Loew's State Th., Boston, MA	4/	1922	$ 7,600.00	H617	5	5″	
2981	Loew's State Th., New York, NY	3/	1921	$ 7,600.00	H646	5	6″	See opus 4111.
2982	Loew's State Th., Cleveland, OH	3/	1920	$ 7,600.00	I527	5	5″	
2985	Princeton Th., Princeton, NJ	3/13	1921	$ 7,000.00	I193	2	5″	
2987	Harford Th., Baltimore, MD	2/	1921		I201	1	5″	
2988	Gregory Th., Chicago Heights, IL	3/15	1920	$ 8,400.00	I216	2	5″	With 2-rank echo.
2989	John Keegan Th., Chester, PA	2/5	1921	$ 4,000.00	I217	1	5″	
2995	Rivoli (opened as Wilson) Th., Baltimore, MD	3/15	1920	$ 8,300.00	I391	3	5″	Opus 1982 enlarged.
		3/16	1920	$ 1,300.00				Additions: 1 rank and harp.
3001	Strand (Michigan) Th., Lansing, MI	3/13	1921	$ 7,500.00	I215	2	5″	
3014	Liberty Th., New Kensington, PA	3/10	1921	$ 3,921.25	J27	2	3½	Built for Peloubet.
3015	Strand Th., Sharon, PA	3/10	1921	$ 4,513.84	J12	2	3½	Built for Peloubet.
3016	Collingswood Th., Collingswood, NJ	3/17	1920		I269	3	5″	
3022	Grant Th., Philadelphia, PA	2/6	1920	$ 5,810.00				
		2/10	1922	$ 3,275.00	J625	3	10″	Additions: 4 ranks and traps.
3037	Keith's 81st Street Th., New York, NY	3/17	1921	$ 9,500.00	I324	3	5″	
3038	Apollo Th., Baltimore, MD	2/10	1920	$ 6,000.00	I332	1	5″	
3043	Strand Th., Des Moines, IA	3/17	1921	$ 11,500.00	I372	5	5″&10″	
3044	Colonial Th., Flint, MI	2/7	1921	$ 5,500.00				
3051	Hollar's Th., Shippensburg, PA	2/7	1920	$ 5,400.00	I392	1	5″	Player piano console.
3054	Illinois Th., LaGrange, IL	2/7	1921	$ 6,200.00	J113	1½	5″	Later moved to Hollywood Th., Petroskey, MI.
3058	Hippodrome Th., Pottstown, PA	2/9	1921	$ 5,000.00	J62	3	7″	See opus 3184.
3060	Greek Th. (Univ. of VA), Charlottesville, VA	3/	1921		I628	15	10″&20″	
3068	Loew's Th., Athens, GA	2/10	1920	$ 5,800.00	I444	2	5″	
3083	Strand Th., Philadelphia, PA	2/6	1921	$ 3,820.00	J110	1	5″	
3086	Red Wing Th., Baltimore, MD	2/9	1921	$ 5,000.00	J302	1	5″	
3087	San Toy Th., Reading, PA	2/9	1921	$ 3,000.00				Used pipes; remainder of organ new.
3088	Loew's Th., New Rochelle, NY	3/16	1921	$ 4,500.00				Moller opus 2018 enlarged and new console.
3090	Reade's State Th., New Brunswick, NJ	3/17	1921	$ 9,000.00	J391	3	5″	
3095	Liberty Th., Camden, NJ	2/8	1921	$ 5,000.00	J155	1½	5″	
3099	Ridge Avenue Th., Philadelphia, PA	2/10	1921	$ 10,000.00	J109	3	7″	
3109	Victory Th., Evansville, IN	2/11	1921	$ 7,500.00	J14	2	5″	
3112	Knickerbocker (Fay's) Th., Philadelphia, PA	4/25	1921	$ 16,700.00	J129	15	10″&15″	Replaced opus 2415.
3115	Victory Th., Pittsburgh, PA	3/11	1921					Built for Peloubet.
3116	Crystal Th., Braddock, PA	3/	1922	$ 4,555.63	K714	3	5″	Built for Peloubet; 3-manual console, 8 ranks with chests; total Peloubet organ 3/19.
3118	Spielmont Th., Marcus Hook, PA	2/6	1921	$ 6,000.00	J214	¾	5″	
3119	Colonial Th., Palmerton, PA	2/6	1921	$ 5,700.00	J439	1	5″	
3119	Garden Th., Springfield Gardens, NY	2/6	1925	$ 3,000.00	J439	1	5″	Moved from previous theatre.
3122	Irvington Th., Baltimore, MD	2/10	1924	$ 7,700.00	L404B	1½	6″	
3123	Park Th., Utica, NY	3/10	1923	$ 5,000.00	I28	1½	5″	This organ formerly Moller opus 2843.
3124	Grand Opera House (Strand Th.), Cambridge, MD	2/15	1924	$ 4,500.00	M348B	2	6″	
3125	Cambria Th., Philadelphia, PA	2/12	1922	$ 8,000.00	I617	2	5″	
3128	Hillstreet Th., Los Angeles, CA	3/13	1921	$ 8,500.00	J511	3	5″	
3129	Liberty Th., Stapleton, NY	3/17	1926	$ 7,000.00				
3130	Great Kills Th., Great Kills, NY	3/16	1926	$ 5,850.00	F610	5	5″	
3131	Golden Gate Th., San Francisco, CA	3/13	1922	$ 8,500.00	J512	3	6″	
3138	Eureka Th., Philadelphia, PA	2/7	1922	$ 5,000.00	J509	3	7½″	
			1922		J574	1	5″	
3140	Loew's State Th., Los Angeles, CA	3/18	1921	$ 9,000.00	J270	5	5″	
3141	Loew's Warfield Th., San Francisco, CA	3/18	1922	$ 9,000.00	J501	5	6″	
3154	Georgople Th., Elyria, OH	2/11	1921	$ 7,300.00	J421	2	5″	
3159	Rex Th., Louisville, KY	2/5	1921	$ 3,000.00	J264	1	5″	Price included trade-in of Wurlitzer previously in theatre.
3160	State Th., Columbus, OH	3/16	1921	$ 9,625.00	J250	3	6″	
3161	Hill Top Th., Columbus, OH	3/16	1921	$ 9,625.00				
3167	Republic (Small's) Th., Brooklyn, NY	3/17	1921	$ 10,000.00	J157	3	6″	
3173	Lawndale Th., Lawndale, IL	2/11	1921	$ 8,000.00	J356	2	6″	
3177	Liberty Th., Benton Harbor, MI	2/9	1921	$ 6,000.00	J370	1½	5″	
3179	Aldine Th., Philadelphia, PA	3/27	1921	$ 25,000.00	J128	20	10″&25″	With 2-rank echo.
			1923	$ 937.50				Replace some ranks and revoice others.
3181	Columbia Th., Baltimore, MD	2/10	1921	$ 6,250.00	J396	2	5″	
3183	Illinois Th., Centralia, IL	2/11	1921	$ 6,500.00	J371	2	6″	
3184	New Parkway Th., Wilmington, DE	2/12	1921	$ 4,750.00	J106	3	7″	Moller opus 3058, plus 3 ranks.
3189	State Th., Roseland, IL	3/18	1921	$ 9,000.00	J484	5	6″	See opus 4191.
3190	People's Th., Millville, NJ	2/5	1921	$ 3,000.00	J212	1	6″	
3191	Parkway Th., Milwaukee, WI	2/9	1921	$ 6,200.00	J422	2	5″	
3200	Aldine Th., Wilmington, DE	2/14	1921	$ 10,000.00	J208	10	10″	15″ vacuum; price includes grand piano not connected to organ; see opus 3800.
3201	Jackson Th., York, PA	2/	1921	$ 3,500.00	J220	1	7″	Additions: 5 ranks to existing Robert-Morton organ.
3207	Star Th., Manchester, NH	3/13	1922	$ 10,000.00	K48	2	5″	

OPUS	LOCATION/CITY/STATE	SIZE	YR	PRICE	BLWR	HP	WP	REMARKS
3221	Pennsylvania Amusement Co., Uniontown, PA	3/19	1922	$ 6,000.00	K524	3	6"	With 4-rank echo; built for Wirshing-Peloubet.
3228	Premier Th., Valparaiso, IN	2/10	1921	$ 6,000.00	J330	2	5"	
3232	Meserole Th., Brooklyn, NY	3/17	1921	$ 9,000.00	J256	3	5"	
3240	Colonial Th., Phoenixville, PA	2/6	1921	$ 4,250.00	J257	1	6"	
3243	Commodore Th., Chicago, IL	2/9	1922	$ 6,000.00	J505	2	5"	
3255	State Th., Pittsburgh, PA	3/	1922		J521	3	8"	Probably built for Peloubet.
3256	Squirrel Hill Th., Pittsburgh, PA	3/	1922		J522	3	8"	Probably built for Peloubet.
3258	New Th., Easton, MD	2/7	1922	$ 3,800.00	K3	1	5"	
3259	Lincoln Th., Washington, DC	2/9	1922	$ 5,500.00	J583	3	7½"	
3261	Rex Th., Nanticoke, PA	2/10	1921	$ 5,500.00	J508	3	7½"	
3264	Ritz (Eureka #2) Th., Philadelphia, PA	2/8	1921	$ 3,500.00	J574	1	5"	
3268	Broad Th., Hazelton, PA	2/11	1921	$ 7,500.00	J472	3	7½"	
3279	Orpheum Th., Trenton, NJ	2/9	1921	$ 6,000.00	J481	3	7½"	
3282	Lyric Th., Camden, NJ	2/9	1921	$ 5,850.00				Order cancelled; see opus 3953.
3298	Empress Th., Cincinnati, OH	3/13	1922	$ 7,500.00	J554	3	6"	
3300	Gillman Th., Souderton, PA	2/7	1922	$ 5,500.00	K93	2	5"	
3302	Garden Th., Charleston, SC	3/15	1922		K49	3	6"	
3303	Maryland Th., Hagerstown, MD	3/13	1922	$ 10,000.00	K136	7½	10"	
3306	Majestic Th., Shamokin, PA	4/17	1922	$ 17,500.00	K163	5	7"&10"	With 4-rank echo.
3319	Rialto Th., Lewistown, PA	3/18	1922	$ 15,000.00	K135	10	10"&15"	
3322	Ritz Th., Jersey City, NJ	3/	1922		K38	10	8"&12"	
3323	State Th., Jersey City, NJ	4/25	1922	$ 30,000.00	K63	20	5"&10"&15"	
3333	Victory Th., Bronx, NY	3/17	1922	$ 8,000.00	K118	5	5"	
3345	McWilliams (Marion) Th., Clarksdale, MS	3/15	1922	$ 8,000.00	K76	3	5"	Replaced opus 2368.
3346	Moorlyn Th., Ocean City, NJ	2/8	1922	$ 5,500.00	K112	2	7"	
3349	Capitol Th., Schenectady, NY	3/9	1922	$ 6,000.00	K156	2	5"	
3370	Premier Th., Brooklyn, NY	3/11	1922	$ 12,500.00	K306	10	15"	
3389	Palace Th., Fort Wayne, IN	3/18	1922	$ 10,000.00	K313	7½	8"&12"	
3405	Palace Th., Quakertown, PA	2/7	1922	$ 5,000.00	K346	1½	5"	
3411	Lyceum Th., Newark, NJ	2/9	1922	$ 6,175.00	K404	5	7"&10"	
3426	Chaloner Th., New York, NY	3/16	1922	$ 10,000.00	K417	10	10"&15"	With 3-rank echo.
3434	Hippodrome Th., Cleveland, OH	3/13	1922	$ 8,300.00	K431	3	6"	
3449	Pimlico Th., Baltimore, MD	2/11	1922	$ 6,000.00	K513	2	5"	
3450	Steinway Th., Astoria, NY	2/9	1922	$ 7,900.00	K508	5	10"	
3452	Virginian Th., Charleston, WV	3/	1922		K454	3	6"	Replaced opus 2843.
3471	Central Th., Cedarhurst, NY	3/10	1923	$ 12,100.00	K555	7½	10"&15"	
3472	Capitol Th., Union City, NJ	3/19	1922	$ 22,500.00	K567	10	10"&15"	See opus 4305.
3480	Savoy Th., New York, NY	3/13	1922	$ 8,000.00	K613	5	7"	Replaced opus 2592.
3483	Virginia Th., Somerset, KY	2/7	1922	$ 4,875.00	K625	2	6"	
3489	Highland Th., Audubon, NJ	2/7	1923	$ 4,850.00	K705	3	5"&12"	
3496	Renaissance Th., New York, NY	3/13	1923	$ 9,000.00	K722	5	7"	
3509	Fox Th., Philadelphia, PA	3/22	1923	$ 14,780.00	K756	10	10"&15"	Located on 16th Street.
3515	Victoria Th., Mt. Carmel, PA	3/13	1923	$ 14,000.00	K842	7½	10"&15"	See opus 4114.
3532	Bayer Th., Lehighton, PA	2/	1923	$ 6,375.00	K1019	3	7"&10"	
3548	Loew's Burland Th., Bronx, NY	2/9	1923	$ 4,500.00	I49	2	5"	Former Moller opus 2893.
3549	Vogue Th., Kenosha, WI	2/6	1923	$ 3,850.00	K1008	1	5"	
3550	Patchogue Th., Patchogue, NY	2/8	1923	$ 4,500.00	K1009	1½	5"	
3614	Victoria Th., Shamokin, PA	3/13	1923	$ 14,000.00	L129	7½	10"	15" vacuum; Price was discounted $4,500 for trade-in of existing Moller opus 2464; see opus 4980.
3647	Grand Th., Pittsburgh, PA	3/	1927		O1130B	7½	7"	
3651	Palace Th., Trenton, NJ	3/13	1923	$ 8,500.00	L214	5	7½"&12"	
3679	Palace Th., Norwich, CT	3/13	1923	$ 9,500.00	L259	3	7"	
3689	Academy of Music, Charleston, SC	2/9	1923	$ 2,250.00				
3690	Victory Th., Charleston, SC	2/9	1923	$ 4,750.00	L268	1½	5"	
3696	Alto Th., Columbia, PA	3/21	1923	$ 13,500.00	L285	7½	7½"&12"	
3719	Diamond State Th., Dover, DE	2/9	1923	$ 5,000.00	L332	3	10"	
3737	Loew's Columbia Th., Washington, DC	3/15	1923	$ 6,250.00	L511	5	6"&12"	Replaced opus 2097.
3745	Chelsea Th., New York, NY	2/7	1923	$ 6,000.00	L418	3	7"&10"	
3746	Superior Th., New York, NY	2/7	1923	$ 6,000.00	L419	3	7"&10"	
3750	Lexington Avenue Opera House (Loew's Lexington) Th., New York, NY	3/28	1923	$ 17,500.00	L375	10	7"&12"	
3764	Colonial Th., Wilkinsburg, PA	2/10	1923	$ 2938.25	G32	2		Built for Wirshing-Peloubet.
3773	Loew's Burnside Th., Bronx, NY	3/28	1923	$ 17,500.00	L456	10	7"&12"	
3776	Elsmere Th., Bronx, NY	3/15	1924	$ 10,000.00	L512	7½	7"&10"	Replaced opus 1871.
3780	Rialto Th., Camden, AR	2/7	1923	$ 5,500.00	L510	1½	5"	
3800	Audubon Th., New York, NY	3/15	1923	$ 7,500.00				Price includes trade-in of existing Moller opus 2015.
no #	Aldine Th., Wilmington, DE	2/14	1927	$ 6,600.00				Opus 3800 moved with new console; replaced opus 3200.
3801	Academy of Music, New York, NY	3/15	1924	$ 7,500.00	L612		10"	Replaced opus 1792.
3802	Opera House, Danville, PA	2/12	1923	$ 10,000.00	L632	2	10"	
3815	Suffern Th., Suffern, NY	2/9	1923	$ 6,500.00	L643	2	7"	
3820	New Dale Th., Long Beach, CA	2/8	1924	$ 5,000.00	L704	1½	5"	
3822	Gramercy Park Th., New York, NY	2/6	1924	$ 6,000.00	L706	3	7"&10"	
3828	Palisade Th., Palisade, NJ	2/6	1924	$ 6,500.00	L729	3	7"&10"	
3881	Liberty Th., Atlantic City, NJ	3/16	1924	$ 5,520.00	M102B	2	10"	Additions: 5 ranks and 3-manual console to existing Moller opus 2901.
3916	Delft Th., Munsing, MI	2/9	1924	$ 5,500.00	L1107B	1½	5"	

OPUS	LOCATION/CITY/STATE	SIZE	YR	PRICE	BLWR	HP	WP	REMARKS
3953	Lyric Th., Camden, NJ	3/13	1924	$ 8,850.00	M314B	7½	7"&10"	Bottom manual dummy; see opus 3282.
3959	Arcade Th., Waynesboro, PA	2/8	1924	$ 6,200.00	M56B	2	.6"	
3980	Temple Th, Ashland, PA	3/11	1924	$ 10,000.00	M334B	5	10"	Bottom manual dummy; later repossessed; see opus 5151.
3990	Strand Th., Providence, RI	3/30	1924	$ 4,600.00	M208B	7½	6"&8"	Original Moller opus 2267 rebuilt plus addition of two ranks and percussions. Built for Peloubet.
4030	Park Th., Meadville, PA	3/15	1924	$ 5,500.00	M542B	3	5"	
4035	Happyland Th., New Orleans, LA	2/6	1924	$ 3,250.00	M336B	1½	5"	
4038	Strand Th., Marietta, OH	3/14	1924	$ 5,000.00	M348B	2	6"	
4065	Star Th., Cliffside, NJ	2/6	1924	$ 6,000.00	M441B	3	7"&10"	
4067	Higgin's Th., Tamaqua, PA	3/17	1924	$ 15,000.00	M443B	7½	7"&10"	
4075	Republic Th., Washington, DC	2/	1924	$ 9,200.00	M454B	3	10"	
4080	Garden Th., Lock Haven, PA	2/11	1924	$ 6,000.00	M477B	5	7"&10"	
4084	Riviera Th., Beverly, NJ	2/5	1924	$ 5,000.00	M525B	2	7"	Price was discounted $2,500 for trade-in of style 45 Fotoplayer from Fox Theatre, Riverside, New Jersey.
4085	Fox Th., Riverside, NJ	2/11	1925	$ 6,500.00	M532B	3	10"	
4100	Cosmopolitan Th., New Orleans, LA	2/6	1925	$ 3,700.00	M548B	1½	6"	
4110	Park Th., Auburn, RI	2/9	1925	$ 5,400.00	M616B	2	7"	
4111	Loew's State Th., New York, NY	4/41	1925	$ 15,000.00	M604B	25	7"&15"	Price includes trade-in of existing Moller opus 2981.
4112	Loew's Metropolitan Th., Brooklyn, NY	3/32	1925	$ 12,240.00	M644B	20	7"&12"	Replaced opus 2472.
4113	Victoria Th., Shamokin, PA	4/	1925					Order cancelled; see opus 3614 and 4980.
4113	Ripple Th, Peekskill, NY	3/9	1925	$ 5,000.00				Moved old Moller from a Schenectady, New York theatre.
4114	Victoria Th., Mt. Carmel, PA	3/25	1925	$ 18,500.00	M618B	15	7"&12"	Replaced opus 3515.
4115	Victoria Th., Mahanoy City, PA	3/29	1925	$ 20,000.00	M619B	15	7"&12"	
			1925		N154B	20	7"&12"	
4117	Grand Opera House Th., New York, NY	3/13	1925	$ 10,000.00	M605B	7½	10"	
4130	Blake Th., Los Angeles, CA	2/6	1925	$ 4,150.00	M715B	2	7"	
4143	Bijou Th., Plainfield, NJ	3/15	1925	$ 8,500.00	M748B	5	7"&10"	
4144	Majestic (Ditman) Th., Perth Amboy, NJ	3/15	1925	$ 8,500.00	M749B	5	7"&10"	
4145	Park Th., Caldwell, NJ	3/13	1925	$ 11,000.00	N441B	7½	7"&12"	
4149	Cross Bay Th., Woodhaven, NY	2/13	1925	$ 7,900.00	M763B	7½	7"&12"	
4191	State Th., Roseland, IL	3/12	1925	$ 10,200.00	M960B	15	15"	Price included trade-in of exisiting Moller opus 3189.
4197	Temple Th., Newport, KY	2/6	1925	$ 3,000.00	M1009B	1½	6"	
4249	Deluxe Th., New York, NY	3/15	1925	$ 11,320.00	N44B	5	7"&10"	
4256	Morton Th., Dorchester, MA	3/18	1925	$ 15,000.00	N138B	10	10"	
4275	Princess Th., Peoria, IL	2/5	1925	$ 3,600.00	N152B	3	7"	
4287	Loew's Coney Island Th., Coney Island, NY	3/20	1925	$ 12,500.00	M211B	15	10"&15"	Included some used pipes and parts.
4288	Madison Th., Madison, NJ	2/9	1925	$ 5,500.00				Order cancelled.
4290	Astor Th., Los Angeles, CA	2/8	1925	$ 5,250.00				
4305	Capitol Th., Union City, NJ	3/17	1925	$ 9,500.00				See opus 3472.
4310	Rialto Th., El Dorado, AR	2/13	1925	$ 8,600.00	N162B	5	7"	
4312	Newhouse Theatre Corp., Hempstead, NY	3/12	1925	$ 11,000.00				
4313	Rose Park Th., Roselle, NJ	2/9	1925	$ 5,250.00	N161B	3	7"	
4314	Sherwood School of Music, Chicago, IL	2/6	1925	$ 2,850.00	N262B	¾	5"	
4315	Sherwood School of Music, Chicago, IL	2/6	1925	$ 2,850.00	N261B	¾	5"	
4318	Loew's State Th., Buffalo, NY	3/32	1925	$ 18,390.00	N228B	20	7"&12"	Price was discounted $8,000 for trade-in of old existing organ.
4319	Loew's Palace Th., Washington, DC	3/32	1925	$ 18,390.00	N227B	20	7"&12"	Replaced opus 2473.
no #	unidentified theatre, Whittier, CA	2/	1925	$ 1,800.00				New horseshoe console for existing Estey.
4322	Broadway Th., Springfield, MA	2/9	1925	$ 4,000.00	N254B	2	7"	Price included trade-in of existing Moller opus 1790.
no #	Ramish Th., Los Angeles, CA	3/	1925	$ 1,500.00				New console only.
4335	Larkin Administration Bldg., Buffalo, NY	4/101	1925	$ 63,000.00	N606B	40	7"&20"	With roll player.
4343	Rubidoux Th., Riverside, CA	2/9	1925	$ 6,500.00	N263B	3	7"	
4346	Hawthorne Th., Newark, NJ	2/14	1925	$ 8,000.00	N438B	3	7"	
4347	Summit Th., Summit, NJ	3/14	1925	$ 10,000.00				Order cancelled; see opus 4524.
4355	Victoria Th., Tamaqua, PA	2/10	1925	$ 6,500.00	N302B	5	8"	Price was discounted $2,000 for trade-in of existing Moller opus 2716.
4357	Inwood Th., New York, NY	3/17	1925	$ 9,000.00	N309B	5	7"	
4373	Loew's 83rd Street Th., New York, NY	3/32	1926	$ 18,390.00	N403B	20	7"&12"	Price was discounted $6,450 for trade-in of existing Moller opus 2889.
4376	Loew's Alhambra Th., Brooklyn, NY	3/32	1925	$ 18,390.00	N405B	20	7"&12"	
4377	Loew's Astoria Th., Astoria, NY	3/32	1926	$ 18,390.00	N404B	20	7"&12"	Price was discounted $4,500 for trade-in of exising Austin.
no #	Strand Th., Port Jervis, NY	3/14	1926	$ 6,000.00	O905B	3	7"	Install Austin from Loew's Astoria Theatre, Astoria, NY.
4378	Loew's Spooner Th., New York, NY	3/32	1925	$ 18,390.00	N406B	20	7"&12"	
4379	Loew's Rio Th., New York, NY	3/32	1926	$ 18,390.00	N424B	20	7"&12"	Price was discounted $5,000 for trade-in of existing Hall organ.
no #	Strand Th., Lakewood, NJ	3/16	1926	$ 6,000.00	10677	3	5"	Install Hall from Loew's Rio Theatre, New York, NY.
4388	Park (Castle) Th., Providence, RI	2/9	1926	$ 5,400.00	N434B	3	7"	
4395	Audubon Th., Orange, NJ	3/28	1926	$ 18,000.00	N439B	7½	7"&12"	

OPUS	LOCATION/CITY/STATE	SIZE	YR	PRICE	BLWR	HP	WP	REMARKS
4396	Oritani Th., Hackensack, NJ	3/28	1926	$ 18,000.00	N420B	20	7"&12"	
4416	Theatre #1, East Greenwich, RI	2/9	1926	$ 5,500.00	N472B	5	7"&10"	
4446	Shrine Auditorium, Los Angeles, CA	4/67	1925	$ 35,000.00	N559B	30		
4449	United Th., Westerly, RI	2/9	1926	$ 5,000.00	N538B	2	7"	
4451	Gaiety Th., Trenton, NJ	4/9	1926	$ 6,000.00	N537B	3	7½"	Top two manuals dummies.
4456	Camden Th., Parkersburg, WV	3/18	1925	$ 7,250.00	H646	5	5"	Replaced opus 1866.
4490	Hotel Gettysburg Co. New Th., Gettysburg, PA	2/12	1925	$ 10,000.00	N643B	5	10"	
4494	Beacon Th., Boston, MA	3/31	1926	$ 17,500.00	N718B	20	7"&12"	
4523	Biscayne Fronton Th., Miami, FL	3/32		$ 22,500.00				Possibly not built.
4524	Summit Th., Summit, NJ	2/14	1925	$ 8,000.00	N812B	3	7"	See opus 4347.
4527	Rialto (Rivoli) Th., Boston, MA	3/18	1926	$ 11,000.00	N903B	10	10"	
4544	Home Th., Portage, WI	2/5	1926	$ 3,300.00	N827B	1½	7"	
4551	Linden Circle Th., Memphis, TN	3/16	1926	$ 6,250.00	H652	5	6"	Move Moller opus 2888.
4554	Crown Th., New Orleans, LA	2/5	1926	$ 3,250.00	N921B	2	7"	
4570	Roosevelt Th., Newark, NJ	3/14	1926	$ 10,000.00	N1010B	7½	7"&10"	
4577	Strand Th., Moundsville, WV	3/14	1926	$ 9,300.00	N1052B	3	7"	
4607	Colonial Th., Egg Harbor, NJ	2/10	1926	$ 5,750.00	N1142B	2	7"	
4628	Olympic Th., Brooklyn, NY	3/14	1926	$ 10,000.00	O43B	5	8"	
4629	Mecca Th., New York, NY	3/14	1926	$ 10,000.00	O44B	5	8"	Opened as 14th Street Theatre; see opus 1361.
4653	Garden Th., Canton, IL	2/5	1926	$ 3,800.00	O125B	2	7"	
4719	Bayshore Th., Bayshore, NY	2/8	1926	$ 4,500.00	O339B	3	7"	
4741	Sherwood School of Music, Chicago, IL	4/6	1926	$ 6,500.00	O449B	7½	8"	
4742	Sherwood School of Music, Chicago, IL	4/6	1926	$ 6,500.00	O830B	7½	8"	
4767	East Hampton (Edwards) Th., East Hampton, NY	2/9	1926	$ 5,000.00	O508B	2	7"	
4777	Allegheny Th., Philadelphia, PA	3/24	1927	$ 20,000.00	O319B	3	15"	
4800	Capitol (Chambersburg) Th., Chambersburg, PA	3/14	1926	$ 10,000.00	O630B	5	8"	
4802	Chicago Musical College, Chicago, IL	4/11	1926	$ 9,000.00	O661B	3	5"	
4809	Mayfair Th., Asbury Park, NJ	3/21	1927	$ 15,000.00	O645B	7½	8"	
4817	Mineola Th., Mineola, NY	2/8	1927	$ 4,500.00	O743B	2	7"	
4861	Circle Th., Annapolis, MD	2/13	1927	$ 3,350.00	H169	¾	5"	Move Moller opus 2726, plus new console, 2 ranks and overhauling; replaced opus 2804.
4925	NY Military Academy, Cornwall, NY	4/28	1927	$ 16,750.00	O1153B	10	6"&12"	With 4-rank echo and roll player; "used for motion pictures and other forms of entertainment."
4937	Gloria Th., Charleston, SC	3/14	1927	$ 10,375.00	P29B	7½	10"	
4944	Blackwood Th., Blackwood, NJ	2/5	1927	$ 5,860.00	P205B	5	10"	Style 50.
4945	Moller Studio, Philadelphia, PA	3/10	1927		P201B	7½		Style 100.
4945	Circle Th., Columbia, PA	3/10	1929	$ 9,000.00	P201B	7½		Style 100.
4946	Earle Th., Allentown, PA	3/10	1927	$ 10,000.00	P203B	7½	10"	Style 100 with harp.
4979	Roselle Park Th., Roselle Park, NJ	2/5	1927	$ 9,800.00	P734B	5	10"	Style 50.
4980	Victoria Th., Shamokin, PA	3/10	1927	$ 16,000.00	P204B	7½	10"	Style 100; see opus 4113.
5040	Sante Fe Th., Denver, CO	3/10	1927	$ 7,000.00	P439B	3	7"	
5062	Union Th., Attleboro, MA	2/12	1928	$ 6,000.00	P433B	3	7"	
5086	Century Th., Audubon, NJ	3/10	1928	$ 12,000.00	P937B	7½	10"	Price included trade-in of existing Wurlitzer.
5088	Strand Th., Lancaster, PA	2/5	1927	$ 6,500.00	P841B	2	10"	
5089	Strand Th., Shenandoah, PA	2/5	1928	$ 6,750.00	P1020B	5	10"	
5098	Smoot Th., Parkersburg, WV	3/14	1928	$ 10,000.00	P632B	5	8"	
5115	Illinois College of Music, Chicago, IL	3/6	1927	$ 6,200.00	P710B	2	10"	Later repossessed; may have been moved to Loyola Community Th., Chicago, Illinois.
5139	19th Street Th., Allentown, PA	3/7	1928	$ 10,500.00	P905B	7½	10"	Style 70.
5150	Century Th., Philadelphia, PA	3/10	1928	$ 7,500.00	P1141B	7½	10"	Style 100; repossessed in 1934.
no #	Norris Th., Philadelphia, PA	2/4	1928	$ 1,250.00				Install Robert-Morton from Century Theatre, Philadelphia, PA.
5151	unidentified new theatre, Ashland, PA	3/10	1928	$ 10,500.00	Q620B	7½	10"	Style 100; contract price includes overhauling Moller opus 3980; opus 3980 was later repossessed in settlement of judgment for opus 5151.
5191	Sherwood School of Music, Chicago, IL	3/8	1928	$ 8,000.00	P1017B	7½	10"	
5192	New Auditorium Th., Newark, OH	3/17	1928	$ 7,000.00	P1024B	7½	8"	Price included trade-in of existing Kimball.
5198	Lincoln Th., Trenton, NJ	3/16	1928	$ 16,000.00	P1103B	10	15"	
5201	Strand Th., Port Jervis, NY	2/6	1928	$ 10,000.00	P1035B	5	10"	
5202	Strand Th., Great Kills, NY	2/6	1928	$ 10,000.00	P1106B	5	10"	
5203	Parsons Th., Parsons, PA	2/4	1928	$ 6,000.00	Q133B	5	10"	
5204	Royal Th. #2, Atlantic City, NJ	2/4	1928	$ 5,000.00	P704B	5	10"	
5211	College Th., Bethlehem, PA	3/14	1928	$ 15,000.00	Q345B	10	15"	
5212	Midland Th., Newark, OH	3/11	1928	$ 12,000.00	Q626B	10	15"	
5214	Strand Th., Sunbury, PA	3/7	1928	$ 8,500.00	Q422B	7½	10"	Style 70.
5230	Sedgwick Th., Mt. Airy, PA	3/19	1928	$ 17,000.00	Q116B	15	10"	
5251	Lincoln Th., Winston-Salem, NC	2/4	1928	$ 6,500.00	Q304B	5	10"	Later repossessed.
5251	Hagerstown Broadcasting Co. Hagerstown, MD	2/6	1933	$ 2,000.00				Installation and addition of 2 ranks.
5252	Regal Th., Lancaster, OH	2/6	1928	$ 7,250.00	Q220B	5	10"	
5271	Traco Th., Toms River, NY	2/6	1928	$ 7,000.00	Q219B	5	10"	Style 60.
5272	Gates Th., Portsmouth, VA	2/6	1928	$ 7,500.00	Q222B	5	10"	Style 60.
5286	Fox Th., St. Louis, MO	3/12	1928	$ 10,000.00	Q248B	5	7"	For grand lobby; with Artiste roll player.

OPUS	LOCATION/CITY/STATE	SIZE	YR	PRICE	BLWR	HP	WP	REMARKS
5287	Fox Th., Detroit, MI	3/12	1928	$ 10,000.00	Q249B	5	7″	For grand lobby; with Artiste roll player.
5304	unidentified theatre	3/	1928					Order Cancelled.
5305	unidentified theatre	3/	1928					Order Cancelled.
5310	Crescent Garden Th., Revere, MA	2/6	1928	$ 6,500.00	Q344B	5	10″	
5311	Villa (Collingsdale) Th., Collingsdale, PA	2/4	1928	$ 6,000.00	Q423B	5	10″	Style 40.
5315	Metropolitan Opera House; Philadelphia, PA	4/39	1928	$ 20,000.00	Q328B	50	20″	With Artiste roll player.
		2/	1928	$ 1,200.00				Stage console for Philadelphia Orchestra; see opus 1993.
5331	Granada Th., Olyphant, PA	2/5	1929	$ 6,350.00	R121B	5	10″	
5332	unidentified theatre	2/	1928					Order cancelled.
5336	Park Th., Westfield, MA	2/4	1928	$ 6,000.00	Q517B	5	10″	Style 40.
5337	New Theatre, Newark, DE	2/5	1929	$ 6,000.00	Q1037B	5	10″	Unknown if theatre name correct.
5341	Grand Th., Lancaster, PA	3/11	1928	$ 9,000.00	P703B	7½	10″	Replaced opus 2148.
5342	unidentified theatre	3/	1928					Order cancelled.
5351	Riviera Th., Scranton, PA	3/7	1928	$ 8,500.00	Q434B	7½	10″	Style 70.
5352	Capitol Th., Williamsport, PA	3/7	1928	$ 8,500.00	Q435B	7½	10″	Style 70.
5356	unidentified theatre	2/	1928					Order cancelled.
5356	Bill Dalton residence, Columbus, OH	2/5	1931	$ 1,800.00				Console, trumpet and chests only.
5357	unidentified theatre	2/	1928					Order cancelled.
5361	unidentified theatre	3/	1928					Order cancelled.
5362	unidentified theatre	3/	1928					Order cancelled.
5366	Clifton Cafeteria, Los Angeles, CA	2/7	1933	$ 3,500.00				
5371	Capitol Th., Rome, NY	3/7	1928	$ 8,500.00	Q448B	7½	10″	Style 70.
5372	unidentified theatre	3/	1929					Order cancelled.
5373	unidentified theatre	3/	1929					Order cancelled.
5374	unidentified theatre	3/	1929					Order cancelled.
5436	Roosevelt Th., Pittsburgh, PA	3/9	1929	$ 12,000.00	Q907B	7½	10″	Repossed in 1938.
5497	Fox Th., San Francisco, CA	3/12	1929	$ 10,000.00	Q1019	5	7″	For grand lobby; with Artiste roll player.
5530	Edgewater Beach Hotel, Chicago, IL	2/11	1929	$ 8,000.00	Q1132B	3	7″	With Artiste roll player.
5557	Peabody Hotel, Memphis, TN	2/7	1929	$ 4,200.00	R106B	2	6″	
5566	Fox Th., Atlanta, GA	4/42	1929	$ 42,000.00	R205B	30	15″	
5766	Waldorf Astoria Hotel, New York, NY	3/22	1931	$ 25,000.00	T514B	7½	7″	With Artiste roll player; price included opus 5795.
5792	WPTF Radio, Raleigh, NC	2/6	1930	$ 2,350.00	S115B	1	5″	
5795	Waldorf Astoria Hotel, New York, NY	4/73	1931		S723B	25	15″	With Artiste roll player.
5819	Convention Hall, Philadelphia, PA	4/20	1931	$ 45,000.00	S722B	50	12″&25″	With Artiste roll player.
		4/85			S706B	1½	10″	Blower for consoles only; installation contains 86 ranks total; kinura doesn't play from classic console.
5849	Shoreham Hotel, Washington, DC	2/10	1930	$ 5,000.00	S410B	3	7″	Two consoles—one each for lobby and ballroom.
5908	Greenbrier Hotel, White Sulphur Springs, WV	3/11	1931	$ 6,750.00				With Artiste roll player.
6107	Moby's Inc. Dept. Store, Columbus, OH	3/11	1932	$ 5,500.00				Fully unit, with percussions & traps.
no #	Grand Th., Columbus, OH		1932	$ 969.70				Additions: 16′ string, 12 pipes; 8′ sax, 73 pipes; plus extra unification to existing organ.
6184	WSPA Radio, Spartanburg, NC	2/6	1933	$ 3,400.00	V503B	1½	7″	Price was discounted $500 for trade-in of existing old organ.
6189	Emil Velazco Studio, New York, NY	2/3	1933	$ 2,640.00				Contained tibia, violin and sax; later repossed.
6416	WFAS Radio, White Plains, NY	2/3						
6690	Reginald Foort, London, England	5/27	1938	$ 24,615.00	AA504	30	15″	
R902	Organ Power Pizza, San Diego, CA	5/29	1973		Discus	30	55″	Rebuild and enlarge opus 6690.
11433	Croda Tone Organ Co., Ltd., Tokyo, Japan	2/7	1979	$ 36,000.00				FOB Baltimore, Maryland.

FOOTNOTES

AUTHOR'S PREFACE

1. Conversation with David Hunt, July 1982.
2. Letter from David Hunt, Windsor, Connecticut, July 7, 1982.
3. Conversation with Lester C. Smith, July 1982.
4. Spencer Turbine Company factory records.

INTRODUCTION TO THE
AMERICAN THEATRE ORGAN

1. Conversation with John Schantz, July 1982.
2. B. F. Blower Company records.
3. Conversation with Alfred J. Buttler, February 1983.

AEOLIAN COMPANY

1. Q. David Bowers, *Encyclopedia of Automatic Musical Instruments* (Vestal, New York: Vestal Press, 1972), p. 309.
2. Ibid. p. 788.
3. Aeolian factory records.
4. Bowers, op. cit.
5. Orpha Ochse, *The History of the Organ in the United States* (Bloomington: Indiana University Press, 1975), p. 296.
6. Bowers, op. cit.
7. *The American Organist*, October 1927, p. 263.
8. *The Diapason*, June 1925, p. 3.
9. *The Diapason*, January 1950, p. 6.
10. *The Diapason*, October 1927, p. 1.
11. *The Diapason*, January 1928, p. 3.
12. Aeolian factory records.

AMERICAN MASTER ORGAN COMPANY

1. *The Diapason*, December 1914, p. 8.
2. *Moving Picture World*, July 17, 1915, p. 503.
3. *The Diapason*, January 1916, p. 2.
4. *The Diapason*, November 1917, p. 1.
5. Kinetic factory records.
6. *The Diapason*, August 1916, p. 3.
7. Letter from Ronald Bishop to Alden Miller, c. 1950s.
8. Conversation with C. M. "Sandy" Balcom, April 19, 1983.

ARTCRAFT ORGAN COMPANY

1. *The American Organist*, March 1926, p. 66.
2. Stock purchase agreement between Clarence E. Haldeman, Katherine O. Haldeman, Asa R. Taylor and Margaret Ellis Taylor, November 2, 1925.
3. Conversation with Larry Abbott, 1982.
4. *The Diapason*, August 1923, p. 4.
5. Stock purchase agreement between Clarence E. Haldeman, Katherine O. Haldeman, Asa R. Taylor and Margaret Ellis Taylor, November 2, 1925.
6. Interview with Asa Taylor by Tom B'hend, January 18, 1964.
7. Agreement between Artcraft Organ Company and E. G. Beitel, February 1, 1926.
8. Letter from E. G. Beitel to A. D. Longmore, November 27, 1928.
9. Interview with Asa Taylor by Tom B'hend, January 18, 1964.
10. *The Diapason*, March 1927, p. 3.
11. Interview with Asa Taylor by Tom B'hend, January 18, 1964.
12. Stock purchase agreement between Clarence E. Haldeman, Katherine O. Haldeman, Asa R. Taylor and Margaret Ellis Taylor, July 8, 1927.
13. Letter from E. G. Beitel to A. D. Longmore, November 27, 1928.

AUSTIN ORGAN COMPANY

1. *The Console*, November 1967, p. 7.
2. *Organ Handbook 1984* (Richmond, Virginia: Organ Historical Society, 1984), p. 13.
3. *The Diapason*, October 1948, p. 1.
4. Ibid.
5. *The Diapason*, December 1924, p. 6.
6. Ibid.
7. Austin factory records.
8. *The Diapason*, July 1935, pp. 1-2.
9. *The Diapason*, February 1937, p. 1.
10. *The Diapason*, October 1948, p. 1.
11. Conversation with Allen Miller, July 1982.
12. Ibid.

13. Austin factory records.
14. Lloyd E. Klos, "The Largest Ever Built!", *Theatre Organ*, Volume 21, #5, p. 6.

BALCOM & VAUGHN

1. *The Console*, July 1966, pp. 21-22.
2. Ibid., p. 22.
3. Conversation with Sandy Balcom, April 19, 1983.
4. Ibid.
5. Ibid.
6. *The Console*, July 1966, pp. 22-23.
7. Conversation with Sandy Balcom.
8. *The Console*, July 1966, p. 23.
9. Conversation with Bill Bunch, April 19, 1983.
10. Ibid.

BARCKHOFF ORGAN COMPANY

1. Vernon Brown, "Carl Barckhoff and the Barckhoff Church Organ Company," *The Tracker*, Volume 22 #4, pp. 1-7.
2. Conversation with Randall Wagner, October 1982.
3. Brown, op. cit.
4. Ibid.
5. Ibid.

S. H. BARRINGTON

1. Letter from Samuel H. Barrington, June 24, 1982.
2. Letter from Robert Lent, February 6, 1983.
3. Letter from Samuel H. Barrington.
4. Kinetic Engineering Company factory records.
5. Letter from Samuel H. Barrington.

F. A. BARTHOLOMAY & SONS

1. *The Diapason*, November 1922, p. 22.
2. Conversation with Robert Lent, October 1982.
3. Letter from Alfred J. Buttler, New York, New York, September 28, 1982.

BARTOLA MUSICAL INSTRUMENT COMPANY

1. Conversation with Dan Barton, June 1963.
2. *The Console*, September 1966, p. 2.
3. *The Diapason*, May 1921, p. 20.
4. *Bombarde*, December 1964, p. 8.
5. Dan Barton, "History of the Barton Organ," monograph in the collection of the Oshkosh, Wisconsin Public Museum.
6. *Bombarde*, December 1964, p. 8.
7. Barton, op. cit.
8. *Bombarde*, December 1964, p. 8.
9. Barton, op. cit.
10. *Bombarde*, December 1964, p. 8.
11. Barton, op. cit.
12. *Bombarde*, December 1964, p. 8.
13. Barton, op. cit.
14. *Theatre Organ*, February 1968, p. 18.
15. Barton, op. cit.
16. *The Diapason*, March 1929, p. 2.

BEMAN ORGAN COMPANY

1. *The Diapason*, February 1916, p. 15.
2. *The Diapason*, February 1919, p. 14.
3. *The Diapason*, October 1919, p. 13.
4. Letter from Herb Merritt, Cincinnati, Ohio, August 2, 1982.

JAMES BENNETT

1. Letter from Homer Blanchard, Delaware, Ohio, November 24, 1982.

BENNETT ORGAN COMPANY

1. Robert E. Coleberd, Jr., "Built on the Bennett System: A History of the Bennett Organ Company," *The American Organist*, January 1968, p. 20.
2. Ibid., pp. 20-21.
3. Ibid., pp. 21-22.

4. Ibid., pp. 22-23.
5. Ibid.
6. Ibid.
7. Ibid., pp. 23-25.
8. *The Diapason*, June 1921, p. 17.

BUHL & BLASHFIELD ORGAN COMPANY

1. *The Diapason*, Janury 1915, p. 14.
2. *The Diapason*, December 1926, p. 12.
3. *The Diapason*, September 1927, p. 34.

BURLINGTON PIPE ORGAN COMPANY

1. *The Diapason*, March 1910, p. 2.
2. Philip M. Smith, "A History of the Reuter Organ Company, 1917-1975, An Evolution of Taste," University of Kansas master's thesis, April 1976, p. 12.

JOHN E. BYINGTON

1. Conversation with Pete Howell, December 29, 1982.
2. Letter from John E. Byington to Jerome B. Meyer, December 17, 1948.

CASAVANT BROS.

1. Casavant promotional brochure, c. 1980s.
2. Ibid.
3. *The Diapason*, February 1912, p. 1.
4. *The Diapason*, August 1918, p. 1.
5. Letter from Eugene Laplante, St. Hyacinthe, Quebec, September 2, 1982.
6. Letter from D. Stuart Kennedy, Calgary, Alberta, July 8, 1982, quoting the records of Eugene M. Nye.
7. Laplante letter.

CLARK & FENTON

1. *The Diapason*, February 1920, p. 5.
2. *The Diapason*, April 1923, p. 22.
3. *The Diapason*, October 1927, p. 37.

COBURN ORGAN COMPANY

1. *The Diapason*, March 1911, p. 7.
2. *Organ Handbook 1984* (Richmond, Virginia: Organ Historical Society, 1984), p. 14.
3. Felgemaker factory records.
4. Wicks factory records.

COZATT ORGAN COMPANY

1. Lloyd E. Klos, "Vic Hyde Discovers a Cozatt Theatre Organ," *Theatre Organ*, Volume 19, #1, pp. 12-15.

N. DOERR

1. *The Diapason*, November 1919, p. 2.
2. Conversation with Terry Kleven, 1982.
3. *The Diapason*, June 1931, p. 16.

ESTEY ORGAN COMPANY

1. *The Diapason*, June 1927, p. 1.
2. Estey factory records.
3. *The Diapason*, June 1927, p. 1.
4. *The Diapason*, March 1916, p. 6.
5. *The Diapason*, June 1927, p. 1.
6. *The Console*, January 1972, p. 35.
7. *The Diapason*, February 1929, p. 1.
8. Estey factory records.
9. Ibid.
10. *The Console*, January 1972, p. 37.
11. John W. Landon, *Jesse Crawford, Poet of the Organ; Wizard of the Mighty Wurlitzer* (Vestal, New York: Vestal Press, 1974), p. 184.

FARRAND & VOTEY

1. Orpha Ochse, *The History of the Organ in the United States* (Bloomington: Indiana University Press, 1975), p. 295.
2. *The Diapason*, September 1942, p. 14.
3. Ochse, op. cit.
4. *The Diapason*, September 1942, p. 14.

5. Ochse, p. 296.
6. *The Diapason*, November 1914, p. 10.

A. B. FELGEMAKER COMPANY

1. *The Tracker*, Volume 9, #2, p. 10.
2. Ochse, p. 287.
3. *The Diapason*, June 1918, p. 2.
4. Organ Supply Industries catalog, July 1982, p. 2.
5. Ochse, p. 287.
6. Felgemaker factory records.
7. *The Diapason*, June 1918, p. 2.
8. Ochse, p. 287.
9. Felgemaker factory records.
10. *The Diapason*, June 1918, p. 2.
11. Organ Supply Industries catalog, July 1982, p. 2.
12. Ochse, p. 288.

FRAZEE ORGAN COMPANY

1. *The Diapason*, February 1935, p. 3.
2. Frazee catalog, c. 1926, p. 3.
3. Ibid.
4. *The Diapason*, October 1920, p. 1.
5. Frazee catalog, p. 3.
6. *The Diapason*, October 1920, p. 1.
7. Frazee catalog, p. 3.
8. *Cipher*, September 1964, p. 4.
9. Ibid.

GENEVA ORGAN COMPANY

1. *The Diapason*, December 1921, p. 17.
2. *The Diapason*, January 1929, p. 1.
3. Spencer Turbine Company records.

THE A. GOTTFRIED CO.

1. Conversation with Sam LaRosa, February 1983.
2. Conversation with Henry Gottfried, March 31, 1983.
3. *The Diapason*, November 1954, p. 4.
4. Ibid.
5. *The Diapason*, March 1942, p. 27.
6. *The Diapason*, November 1954, p. 4.
7. *The Diapason*, March 1942, p. 27.
8. *The Diapason*, November 1954, p. 4.
9. *The Diapason*, March 1936, p. 26.
10. *The Diapason*, November 1954, p. 4.
11. Ibid.
12. Conversation with Henry Gottfried.
13. Gottfried factory records.
14. Conversation with Henry Gottfried.
15. *The National Exhibitor*, May 20, 1928, p. 24.
16. *The Diapason*, November 1954, p. 4.
17. Conversation with Henry Gottfried.
18. Gottfried factory records.
19. *The Diapason*, November 1954, p. 4.
20. Gottfried factory records.
21. *The Diapason*, March 1936, p. 26.
22. Conversation with Henry Gottfried.
23. Ibid.

GRATIAN

1. Robert E. Coleberd, Jr., "Joseph Gratian, a Pioneer Builder in the West," *The American Organist*, August 1965, pp. 20-22.
2. Wicks factory records.
3. Coleberd, op. cit.
4. Letter from Richard Schneider, Niantic, Illinois, July 5, 1982.

GRIFFITH-BEACH

1. Hope-Jones factory records, reprinted in *The Console*, November 1969, p. 23.
2. Conversation with Dr. Alfred Ehrhardt, August 26, 1983.
3. Conversation with Bob Lent, October 1982.
4. Conversation with Dr. Alfred Ehrhardt.

HALL ORGAN COMPANY

1. *The Diapason*, October 1945, p. 6.
2. *The Tracker*, Volume 9, #2, p. 11.
3. *The Diapason*, December 1928, p. 3.
4. *The Diapason*, June 1925, p. 28.
5. *The Diapason*, July 1925, p. 3.

6. *The Diapason*, June 1927, p. 12.
7. *The Diapason*, October 1945, p. 6.
8. Conversation with M. P. Moller III, October 1982.

C. S. HASKELL, INC.

1. *The Diapason*, March 1916, p. 6.

HILLGREEN, LANE & CO.

1. *The American Organist*, April 1927, pp. 84-90.
2. Ibid.
3. Conversation with Robert L. Hillgreen, Jr., July 1982.
4. Ibid.
5. *The American Organist*, April 1927, p. 92.
6. Ibid, p. 86.
7. *The Diapason*, September 1933, p. 10.
8. Conversation with Robert L. Hillgreen, Jr.
9. Ibid.
10. Ibid.
11. *The Diapason*, September 1933, p. 10.

HINNERS ORGAN COMPANY

1. Robert E. Coleberd, Jr., "Yesterday's Tracker: The Hinners Organ Story," *The American Organist*, September 1960, pp. 11-12.
2. Ibid, pp. 12-14.
3. John R. Hinners, "Chronicle of the Hinners Organ Company," *The Tracker*, Volume 7, #2, p. 3.
4. Coleberd, p. 12.
5. Ibid.
6. *Theatre Organ*, Volume 1, #2, p. 6.
7. Junchen Pipe Organ Service list of organ parts for sale, October 1970.
8. Junchen-Collins Organ Corp. list of parts for sale, August 1976.
9. Junchen-Collins Organ Corp. list of parts for sale, December 1975.
10. Coleberd, p. 12.
11. Hinners, op. cit.

H. A. HOWELL

1. *The Diapason*, February 1928, p. 41.
2. Conversation with Pete Howell, April 4, 1983.
3. Ibid.
4. Ibid.
5. Ibid.
6. Ibid.
7. Ibid.

HUTCHINGS ORGAN COMPANY

1. *The Diapason*, July 1913, p. 1.
2. Ibid.
3. Ochse, p. 233.
4. *The Diapason*, November 1914, p. 10.
5. Ochse, p. 234.
6. *The Diapason*, November 1917, p. 1.
7. *The Diapason*, July 1913, p. 1.

KARN-MORRIS PIANO AND ORGAN CO.

1. Letter from D. Stuart Kennedy, Calgary, Alberta, November 23, 1982.

GEO. KILGEN & SON, INC.

1. Kilgen factory records.
2. Conversation with David Harris, 1982.
3. H. A. Sommer, "The Kilgen Wonder Organ," *Theatre Organ*, Volume 12, #4, p. 6.
4. *The Diapason*, June 1932, p. 1.
5. Ibid.
6. Ibid.
7. *The Diapason*, July 1939, p. 6.
8. *The Diapason*, December 1939, p. 24.
9. Ibid, p. 27.
10. Conversation with Max Nagel, December 1982.
11. Conversation with William T. Singleton, January 1, 1983.
12. Kilgen factory records.

W. W. KIMBALL COMPANY

1. E. M. Skinner factory records.
2. *The Diapason*, December 1936, pp. 1-2.
3. Van Allen Bradley, *Music for the Millions, the Kimball*

Piano and Organ Story (Chicago: Henry Regnery Co., 1957), pp. 131, 259.
4. Ibid., pp. 1-16.
5. Ibid., pp. 16-26.
6. Ibid., pp. 27-28.
7. Ibid., pp. 35-45.
8. Ibid., p. 65.
9. Ibid., pp. 71-72.
10. Ibid., pp. 108-116.
11. Ibid., pp. 133-134.
12. Ibid., p. 135.
13. Ochse, pp. 302-303.
14. Bradley, p. 185.
15. Ibid., p. 238.
16. Ibid., p. 181.
17. Ibid., p. 290.
19. *The Diapason*, February 1925, p. 6.
20. *The Diapason*, June 1935, p. 11.
21. *The American Organist*, November 1921, p. 366.
22. *The Diapason*, October 1914, p. 9.
23. Letter from R. P. Elliot to Lloyd Davey, December 5, 1930.
24. *The Diapason*, July 1938, p. 29.
25. *The Diapason*, June 1925, p. 4.
26. Bradley, p. 267.
27. Ibid., p. 283.
28. *The Diapason*, November 1941, p. 3.
29. *The Diapason*, January 1910, p. 3.
30. *The Diapason*, July 1941, p. 28.
31. *The American Organist*, March 1926, p. 65.
32. *The Diapason*, February 1925, p. 6.
33. Conversation with Riley Daniels, October 1982.
34. Letter from R. P. Elliot to Fred D. Felt, Philadelphia, Pennsylvania, May 9, 1921.
35. Letter from R. P. Elliot to E. A. Spencer, November 12, 1921.
36. *The Diapason*, March 1920, p. 14.
37. *Rotunda*, Volume 4, #4, March-April 1933, pp. 28-29.
38. Ibid.
39. Conversation with John Shanahan, December 1982.
40. *The Diapason*, April 1921, p. 1.
41. Balcom & Vaughn factory records.
42. Conversation with Riley Daniels, October 1982.
43. *The Console*, February 1971, p. 22.
44. *The American Organist*, July 1925, pp. 7-8.
45. *The American Organist*, October 1927, p. 10.
46. Letter from R. P. Elliot to Lloyd Davey, May 27, 1929.
47. Letter from R. P. Elliot to Lloyd Davey, May 30, 1929.
48. Letter from R. P. Elliot to Lloyd Davey, March 8, 1929.
49. Letter from R. P. Elliot to Lloyd Davey, December 14, 1929.
50. Letter from R. P. Elliot to Lloyd Davey, September 22, 1930.
51. *The Console*, April 1972, p. 11.
52. Letter from R. P. Elliot to Lloyd Davey, November 10, 1932.
53. M. P. Moller factory records.
54. *The Diapason*, November 1941, p. 3.
55. Letter from R. P. Elliot to Lloyd Davey, May 24, 1941.
56. Conversation with Don Gillett, October 1982.
57. Conversation with Kay McAbee, December 1982.

KOHL

1. Letter from Lloyd Klos, Rochester, New York, June 3, 1982.

LOUISVILLE PIPE ORGAN COMPANY, INC.

1. Letter from Sylvester Kohler, Louisville, Kentucky, June 21, 1982.
2. *The Diapason*, February 1930, p. 2.
3. *The Diapason*, May 1928, p. 39.
4. Louisville factory records.
5. Ibid.

BENJAMIN F. LENOIR

1. Haskell factory records.
2. Kinetic factory records.
3. Letter from Martin Wiegand, Millville, New Jersey, September 23, 1982.

LINK PIANO COMPANY, INC.

1. Lloyd Klos, "Edwin A. Link and the Roberson Center Organ," *Theatre Organ*, Volume 11, #6, p. 8.
2. Q. David Bowers, *Encyclopedia of Automatic Musical Instruments* (Vestal, New York: Vestal Press, 1972), p. 481.
3. Klos, op. cit.
4. Bowers, op. cit.
5. Bowers, pp. 481-487.

6. Klos, op. cit.
7. **Bowers,** p. 487.
8. **Klos,** op. cit.
9. Conversation with Harvey Roehl, June 1982.
10. Duane Arey, "Pipe Organs and Pilot Trainers," *Theatre Organ,*
    Volume 4, #4, p. 10.
11. **Bowers,** p. 486.
12. Arey, op. cit.
13. *Theatre Organ,* Volume 4, #4, pp. 12-13.
14. **Bowers,** p. 487.
15. **Klos,** pp. 8-9.
16. **Bowers,** p. 486.
17. Ibid.
18. **Klos,** p. 9.
19. Ibid., pp. 8-9.

MAAS ORGAN CO.

1. Conversation between Louis Maas and Tom B'hend, August 27,
   1963.
2. Ibid.
3. Ibid.
4. Conversation with Gordon Kibbee, 1983.
5. Conversation with Paul Rowe, Jr., May 2, 1983.

E. C. MALARKEY

1. *The Tracker,* Volume 22, #4, p. 5.

MARR & COLTON CO.

1. Spencer Turbine Company factory records.
2. Lloyd Klos, "David J. Marr and the Marr & Colton Co.," *Theatre
   Organ,* Volume 5, #1, pp. 18-22.
3. Marr & Colton Co., *Building America's Finest Organ,* 1925 catalog,
   p. 5.
4. *The Diapason,* January 1925, p. 6.
5. *The Diapason,* November 1917, p. 6.
6. Letter from Stu Green, April 9, 1983.
7. Kinetic Engineering Company factory records.
8. Klos, op. cit.
9. Jerome B. Meyer & Sons, Inc. factory records.
10. Klos, op. cit.
11. Conversation with Roger Mumbrue and Harry Radloff, July 1982.
12. Klos, pp. 18-21.
13. *The Diapason,* February 1922, p. 7.

ALFRED MATHERS CHURCH ORGAN CO.

1. *The Diapason,* September 1915, p. 3.
2. *The Diapason,* February 1924, p. 3.

MEISEL & SULLIVAN

1. Conversation with Larry Abbott, 1982.
2. Conversation with William P. Brown, January 1983.

MIDMER-LOSH, INC.

1. *The Diapason,* December 1917, p. 3.
2. George Losh, *The History of Midmer Losh Organ Company,* typed
   memoirs c. 1974, p. 1.
3. Ibid.
4. *The Diapason,* July 1918, p. 9.
5. Losh, p. 1.
6. Ibid., p. 8.
7. *The Diapason,* February 1934, p. 8.
8. Letter from Emerson Richards to E. O. Shulenberger, July 18, 1938.
9. *The Diapason,* April 1918, p. 9.
10. Losh, pp. 1-11.
11. *The Diapason,* April 1921, p. 20.
12. *The Diapason,* August 1923, p. 9.
13. *The Diapason,* November 1925, p. 13.
14. *The American Organist,* May 1929, pp. 278-285.
15. Losh, pp. 5-6.
16. *The Diapason,* February 1934, p. 8.
17. Losh, p. 3.
18. *The American Organist,* September 1932, p. 558.
19. *The Diapason,* August 1975, p. 18.
20. Losh, p. 14.
21. Letter from William F. Benzeno, June 16, 1982.
22. Losh, pp. 5-7.
23. *The Diapason,* March 1930, p. 43.
24. *The American Organist,* August 1932, p. 489.

M. P. MOLLER, INC.

1. *Success, The Human Magazine,* Volume 9, #2, February 1925,
   pp. 62-63, 118.
2. Ibid., p. 118.
3. Ochse, p. 288.
4. *The Diapason,* May 1929, p. 40.
5. Ochse, p. 289.
6. *Success,* p. 118.
7. Ochse, p. 289.
8. *Success,* p. 118.
9. Ochse, p. 289.
10. *Success,* p. 118.
11. Ibid.
12. Ochse, p. 289.
13. *Success,* p. 118.
14. Ochse, p. 289.
15. Ibid.
16. *Success,* p. 119.
17. Ochse, p. 289.
18. *Success,* p. 120.
19. Ochse, p. 289.
20. Moller factory records.
21. Wurlitzer factory records.
22. Moller factory records.
23. *The American Organist,* January 1926, pp. 17-19.
24. *The Diapason,* May 1937, p. 2.
25. *Theatre Organ,* Volume 8, #1, p. 14.
26. *Success,* p. 120.
27. *Theatre Organ,* Volume 8, #1, p. 14.
28. *The Diapason,* May 1937, p. 2.
29. *Theatre Organ,* Volume 8, #1, p. 14.
30. *The Diapason,* December 1961, p. 1.
31. Ochse, p. 368.
32. *The Diapason,* December 1961, p. 1.
33. Conversation with Riley Daniels, October 1982.
34. Conversation with Riley Daniels, February 11, 1983.
35. *The Diapason,* February 1917, p. 17.
36. Moller factory records.
37. Ibid.
38. Ibid.
39. Ibid.
40. Kinetic Engineering Company records.
41. Moller factory records.
42. Conversation with Sam LaRosa, February 1983.
43. Moller factory records.
44. Ibid.
45. Ibid.
46. *The Diapason,* March 1944, p. 1.
47. Moller factory records.
48. Ibid.
49. Ibid.
50. *Theatre Organ,* Volume 8, #1, p. 14.
51. Moller factory records.
52. *The American Organist,* July 1923, pp. 424-428.
53. Conversation with Howard Nalley, October 1982.
54. *The Tracker,* Volume 16, #1, p. 9.
55. Letter from Harold Ocker, February 22, 1983.
56. Moller factory records.
57. Conversation with Howard Nalley.
58. *Theatre Organ,* February 1974, pp. 24-25.
59. Letter from Harold Ocker.
60. Ibid.
61. Moller factory records.
62. Ibid.
63. *The Diapason,* January 1928, p. 49.
64. *The American Organist,* September 1930, p. 542.
65. Conversation with Riley Daniels, October 1982.
66. *The Diapason,* April 1928, p. 10.
67. Conversation with Pete Daniels, October 1982.
68. Moller factory records.
69. *The Diapason,* October 1936, p. 3.
70. Ibid.
71. *The Diapason,* January 1945, p. 1.
72. *The Diapason,* February 1936, p. 23.
73. Letter from Harold Ocker.
74. Conversation with Howard Nalley.
75. Ochse, p. 290.
76. Conversation with M. P. Moller III, October 1982.
77. *The Diapason,* September 1939, p. 1.
78. Letter from R. P. Elliot to Lloyd Davey, May 24, 1941.
79. Moller factory records.

ILLUSTRATION ACKNOWLEDGMENTS

The author is especially grateful to the following individuals who enhanced the beauty of this book by contributing photographs and documents. Special credit is due Mr. Tom B'hend, editor of the *The Console*, who allowed the author complete access to his enormous archive and in many instances donated halftones to this labor of love. All contributions are acknowledged by page number and, where appropriate, abbreviations of positions on the page as follows: B, bottom; C, center; L, left; R, right; T, top.

FRONTISPIECE: 2, Bill Lamb.

TABLE OF CONTENTS: 6, 7, Mr. & Mrs. Gordon Meyer.

ABOUT THE AUTHOR: 10, author's collection.

AUTHOR'S PREFACE: 13, author's collection. 14, David Hunt.

INTRODUCTION: 17, David Hunt. 18, Pete Daniels.

AEOLIAN: 23, 26B, *The Diapason*. 22T, 24, 25, 26T, author's collection.

AMERICAN MASTER: 28-30, Console collection.

ARTCRAFT: 31T, 32, Console collection.

AUSTIN: 33C, 34BR, 35, 48, author's collection. 34T, 37T, 39BL, 40R, *The Diapason*. 34CL, 38, 40TL, Allen Miller. 36, 37B, 41T, *Theatre Organ*. 39T, 40B, 41B, Console collection. 42T, Harvey Roehl.

BALCOM & VAUGHN: 49L, Console collection. 50, 51TR&B, Bill Bunch. 52, Helena Simonton. 49R, 51TL, Bill Lamb.

BARCKHOFF: 54T, Organ Historical Society.

BARRINGTON: 55T, author's collection. 55R, Console collection.

BARTHOLOMAY: 56T, Robert Whiting. 56C, Organ Historical Society.

BARTON: 57, Mr. & Mrs. Gordon Meyer. 58, 68T, 70L, 72BL, 84, author's collection. 59T, American Theatre Organ Society. 59C, Harvey Roehl. 65 all but TR, 66, 69CL&BL, *Theatre Organ*. 61TL, *Theatre Organ*, John Hill photo. 61B, *The Diapason*. 64, 65TR, 67B, 68B, 69TL, 70R, 77B, 83, Console collection. 67T, Joseph Duci Bella. 69BR, 73T, Bill Lamb. 69TR, Tim Wheat. 71, 73L, John Shanahan. 72T, Bob Arndt and Jim Crawford. 72BR, 76, Theatre Historical Society. 77T, 78, Ron Bogda.

BEMAN: 90T, Mr. & Mrs. Gordon Meyer.

BENNETT: 92C, Mr. & Mrs. Gordon Meyer. 93, Organ Historical Society. 94TL, *The Diapason*. 94 all but TL, Larry Broadmoore. 95, Bill Lamb.

BUHL & BLASHFIELD: 98, *Theatre Organ*.

BYINGTON: 99C, Mr. & Mrs. Gordon Meyer.

CASAVANT: 100R, Bill Bunch. 101, Console collection.

COBURN: 102T, Pete Howell. 102C, Organ Historical Society.

COZATT: 103T, Mr. & Mrs. Gordon Meyer. 103CL&CR, 104TL, *Theatre Organ*.

DOERR: 105T, author's collection.

ESTEY: 105C, 119B, author's collection. 106, 108T, 109, 120B, 122T&C, 123TR&B, 124, 125 all but RC&BC, 126 TR&LC, 127BL, *The Diapason*. 107, 112, 113T, 118R, 127T, Jim Lewis. 108B, 114-117, 119T, 120T, 121, 122B, 123TL&CR, 125RC&BC, 126 all but TR&LC, 127BR, Console collection. 110, Bill Lamb. 113B, Harvey Roehl. 118TL, Del Castillo collection. 118BL, *The American Organist*.

FARRAND & VOTEY: 132, Organ Historical Society.

FELGEMAKER: 133 all but B, author's collection. 133B, Stanton Peters.

FRAZEE: 134, 135T, Console collection.

GENEVA: 137T, Pete Howell. 137B, 138T, 140T, 142, Console collection. 138B, Kay McAbee. 139B, 140RB&CB, Tim Needler. 140LB, *Theatre Organ*. 141BL, author's collection. 141BR, Larry Broadmoore.

GOTTFRIED: 145, Pete Daniels. 146, 147, 148T, 149B, 151, Henry Gottfried. 149T, Theatre Historical Society. 148B, Console collection. 150B, author's collection.

GRATIAN: 153T&R, Mr. & Mrs. Gordon Meyer. 153CL, Console collection.

GRIFFITH-BEACH: 154, Alfred Buttler.

HALL: 155C&B, *The Diapason*. 155T, Jack Bethards.

HASKELL: 157, Robert Whiting. 158T, Organ Historical Society.

HILLGREEN-LANE: 159, 160B, 164B, *The Diapason*. 160T, Franklin Mitchell. 161B, *Theatre Organ*. 162B, 163 all but BR, Robert Hillgreen, Jr. 163BR, 164T, author's collection.

HINNERS: 169T, Mr. & Mrs. Gordon Meyer. 169B, 172TL&CR, Organ Historical Society. 170B, Console collection. 171T, *Theatre Organ*. 171B, 172CL&B, author's collection.

HOOK & HASTINGS: 174T, Jack Bethards. 176, *The Diapason*.

HOWELL: 176C, 177 all but TR, 178B, Pete Howell. 177TR, Curt Schmitt. 178T, Theatre Historical Society.

HUTCHINGS: 179CR, Organ Historical Society. 179BR, Console collection.

KILGEN: 182T, Jack Bethards. 182B, 183B, 188B, *The Diapason*. 183T, 185T, 190TL, *Theatre Organ*. 184T, 190 all but TL, 191T, 193BR, 194-196, author's collection. 184B, 185B, Max Nagel. 186, 192T, Console collection. 187, Clay Holbrook. 188T, Mr. & Mrs. Gordon Meyer. 189B, *The American Organist*. 189T, 191B, 192B, 193TL&BL, Theatre Historical Society. 188C, Bill Lamb.

KIMBALL: 206, 216, 217B, 220B, 221, 223, 226T, 227T, 228B, 234-242, Console collection. 207, 208L, 231B, 233, author's collection. 208R, 218, 248, Dave Krall. 209, 227BL, 232T, *The Diapason*. 210-213, Dave Broskowski. 214, Jerry Critser. 215, 219, 220T, 228T&C, 229, Clay Holbrook. 217T, Al Lightcap. 226BR, 232B, *Theatre Organ*. 226BL, 227BR, 243-245, Bill Lamb. 231T, Pete Daniels. 246, 247, Bill Bunch. 249, Irv Glazer.

KOHL: 261, Bruce Davis.

LE NOIR: 264, Stanton Peters.

LINK: 265, Harvey Roehl. 266, 271C, Clay Holbrook. 267, 268T, 270, 271B, 272, Console Collection. 268C&B, 271T, *Theatre Organ*. 273-280, 283, author's collection.

LOUISVILLE: 285L, Console collection. 284, author's collection. 285R, Stanton Peters.

MAAS: 287, Console collection.

MARR & COLTON: 289C, 290T, *The Diapason*. 291-294, 296, 297, 299B, 300B, 304TR, Bill Lamb. 295, 298TR, 301BR, 302, 303, Console collection. 298B, 299T&C, 301T&BL, 304TL&B, *Theatre Organ*. 300T, author's collection. 305-308, Warren Lubich.

MEISEL & SULLIVAN: 315T, *Bombarde*.

MIDMER-LOSH: 315C, Mr. & Mrs. Gordon Meyer. 316, 327, *The Diapason*. 317T, 319T, W. F. Benzeno. 318B, Console collection. 320, 321, 331B, 332-335, 336T, 339, author's collection. 322, 323, 328-330, 331T, 338, Sid Schrier. 324-326, Nelson Barden. 336B, Pete Daniels.

MOLLER: 345, 348R, 349TL, 350, 355-360, 362, 364, 365L, 366TR, 367, 368L, 371TL&BR, 372T, 375TL, 381, 382, 383TL, 384, 385B, 387T, 388B, 389, 390B, 391-393, 394T, 395T&B, 396 all but CR, 397, 398B, 399T&CL, 400TL, Pete Daniels. 347, 349CR, 351, 369T, 370, 371TR&BL, 386T, 394B, 395C, 398T&CR, 399CR&B, 400CR&BL, 401, Console collection. 348T, 379T&B, 394CR, 398CL, 400BR, Art Pearson. 349BL, 366TL, 378B, 388TR&CR, 400TR, *The Diapason*. 349BR, 353T, 366B, 368R, Bill Lamb. 365R, 369B, 373C, 376, 377, 379C, 383 all but TL, 385T&C, 386B, 387B, 390T, *Theatre Organ*. 372B, 373T, John Shanahan. 373B, 378T, 380, 369CR, author's collection. 374T&BL, Preston Kaufmann. 374BR, Theatre Historical Society. 375TR&B, John McCall.

GLOSSARY: 422, 423B, 424, 425, 426, author's collection. 423T, Harvey Roehl.

BIBLIOGRAPHY

PERIODICALS

The American Organist, journal of the American Guild of Organists.
Theatre Organ, journal of the American Theatre Organ Society.
The Console, an independent magazine of theatre organ news and history.
The Diapason, journal of the American Institute of Organbuilders.
The Tracker, journal of the Organ Historical Society.

BOOKS

William H. Barnes, *The Contemporary American Organ* (Glen Rock, New Jersey: J. Fischer & Bro., 1964)

Q. David Bowers, *Encyclopedia of Automatic Musical Instruments* (Vestal, New York: Vestal Press, 1972)

Reginald Foort, *The Cinema Organ* (Vestal, New York: Vestal Press, 1970)

Ben M. Hall, *The Best Remaining Seats* (New York: Bramhall House, 1961)

John W. Landon, *Jesse Crawford, Poet of the Organ; Wizard of the Mighty Wurlitzer* (Vestal, New York: Vestal Press, 1974)

———*Behold the Mighty Wurlitzer* (Westport, Connecticut: Greenwood Press, 1983)

Orpha Ochse, *The History of the Organ in the United States* (Bloomington: Indiana University Press, 1975)

Reginald Whitworth, *The Cinema and Theatre Organ* (London: Musical Opinion, 1932)

GLOSSARY

ABSOLUTE PITCH. A special memory of musical pitch possessed by some musicians enabling them to identify notes without a comparative reference. For example, if a person with absolute pitch were asked to hum a C#, he could do so solely by relying on his memory of what a C# sounds like. Synonym: perfect pitch.

AMPLEX. 1) A term invented by organist John Seng to denote a stop which adds a rank to the stop keys controlling another rank in a unit organ. For example, an amplex stop engraved 'Vox Humana II On' causes all the vox humana stops in the organ to play the second vox humana rank as well as the first. 2) In Geneva, Smith and Smith-Geneva organs, a stop of 5 1/3' pitch.

ANALYSIS. A detailed accounting in matrix form revealing which stops are derived from which ranks of pipes in a non-straight organ.

AUGMENTED PEDAL. A catchy phrase used by E. M. Skinner to euphemize the fact that some pedal ranks were unified. R. P. Elliot quipped that a more accurate phrase would be "diminished pedal!"

BEARD. A rod placed between the ears of a flue pipe which helps stabilize the pipe's speech. Synonyms: roller, roller beard.

BEATER. The vibrating element in a diaphone consisting of a flat spring to which is attached a round valve.

BLIND COMBINATION ACTION. A combination action which activates the stops electrically but doesn't move the stops physically. Sometimes lights are employed to indicate which stops are activated. Early in the twentieth century a bitter controversy raged as to whether or not a combination action should move the stops. By the 1920s this controversy had largely subsided and today blind combination actions are fortunately quite rare in pipe organs although some electronic organs still use them to reduce costs.

BLOCK. 1) The part of a reed pipe which joins the shallot to the resonator. 2) In a wooden pipe, the part corresponding to the languid of a metal pipe.

BOLSTER. 1) A decorative bracket supporting the keydesk. 2) A row of stop keys in a horseshoe console. A console with two rows of stop keys is called a double bolster console, for example.

BOOT. 1) The foot of a reed pipe. 2) The lower assembly of a reed pipe consisting of the foot, block, shallot and tuning spring.

BORROWED STOP. Any stop which does not have its own unique pipes. For example, consider a 16' fagotto of 61 pipes which plays on a swell manual. If this same rank also plays on the pedal, it is known as a pedal borrow.

BRIDGE. A flat piece of metal soldered between the bottoms of the ears of a quintadena pipe which helps stabilize its speech.

CALLIOPE. An instrument comprising several octaves of stopped metal pipes whose mouths are the entire circumference of the pipes. The pipes may be blown by air or steam pressure. Usually a one-manual instrument frequently seen at circuses and carnivals.

CAP. 1) The part of a wooden pipe forming the lower lip. 2) The cannister top of a stopped metal pipe.

CAPTURE COMBINATION ACTION. A combination action wherein the organist sets selected stops into the system's memory by pushing a special "capture" or "set" piston.

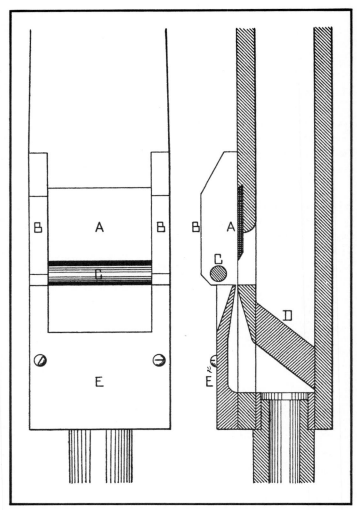

Senator Emerson Richards compares two diaphone beaters in the Atlantic City Convention Hall organ. The beater on the left vibrates at a 16′ pitch, the one on the right at 32′.

Parts of a wood pipe: A, upper lip; B, ears; C, beard; D, block; E, cap.

Parts of a reed pipe: A, block; G and H, two different types of sockets into which resonators fit; H and 10, tuning spring; F, wedge; 2 and 11, shallot; 1, boot; E and 7, reed tongue; 8, reed tongue with a Willis weight attached.

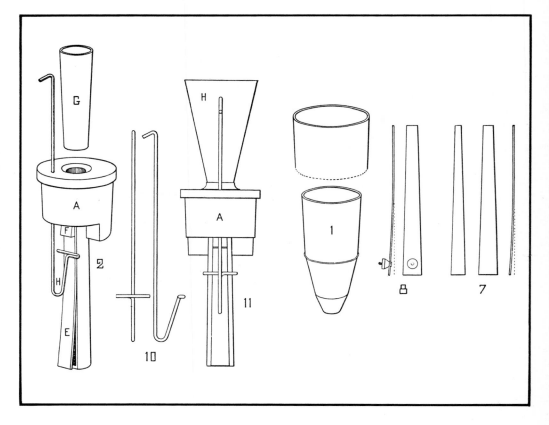

CELESTA. See chrysoglott.

CELESTE. A rank deliberately tuned slightly sharp (or occasionally flat) of a similar on-pitch rank, producing a pleasant wavering effect in the tone.

CHEST. The pressurized box on which organ pipes sit. Valves in the chest admit air pressure to the pipes, causing them to speak.

CHRYSOGLOTT. A percussion instrument with metal bars struck with soft hammers. From the Greek chryso, meaning golden, and the German glott, meaning voice. In organ terminology only, a synonym for celesta.

CLASSIC ORGAN. An organ designed to play classic literature, having a diapason chorus as its fundamental sound. Usually, but not always, largely straight and on lower wind pressures.

COMBINATION ACTION. A system for activating preselected groups of stops quickly. Usually the selected stops will move on or off as a group when a combination piston is pressed, except on a blind combination action.

COMBINATION PISTON. A piston which controls the combination action.

COMMON METAL. Metal for making organ pipes which is mostly lead.

CONCERT ORGAN. A term used to describe many instruments built in the era c. 1900-1930 which weren't theatre organs but which didn't play classical literature particularly well either. Not necessarily synonymous with orchestral organ or romantic organ.

CONE TUNING. A tuning procedure wherein the speaking length of the pipe is changed by altering the degree of flare at its top by means of striking the pipe with a pointed cone.

COUPLER. A device which connects one manual or division to another.

CRESCENDO PEDAL. See register crescendo.

CUTUP. The vertical distance between upper and lower lips, usually expressed as a fraction of mouth width.

DEATH RATTLE. The tendency of large reed and diaphone pipes to continue vibrating after their air supply has been cut off.

DIAPHRAGM REGULATOR. A pressure regulator whose primary moving part is a flat piece of wood surrounded on all sides by a canvas bag or diaphragm.

DIRECT ELECTRIC. A form of action wherein electrical magnetism, rather than air pressure, operates a device. In a direct electric chest, for example, an electromagnet opens the pipe valve directly with no assistance from air pressure. Direct Electric, a registered trademark of the Wicks Organ Company, seems destined to go into common generic usage as did cellophane and escalator.

DOUBLE LANGUID. A method of flue pipe voicing wherein a second lanquid is introduced inside the pipe immediately above the normal languid. This technique enables a high pressure pipe to have a lower cutup and to produce a tone as bright as a pipe eight notes smaller but with much more power and without sacrificing harmonic development.

These stopped brass pipes are part of a Tangley calliope. Note that the mouths are the entire circumference of the pipes. These pipes have tremendous carrying power when played outdoors.

Diaphragm regulators in the Atlantic City Convention Hall organ. This photograph was taken while the organ was under construction; four of the regulators have not yet been outfitted with springs.

DUCKBILL SHALLOT. 1) A shallot whose bottom is formed at a sharp angle to the shallot face. 2) A synonym for goosebill shallot.

DUPLEX. A rank of pipes controlled by exactly two stops, on the same or different divisions, at the same or different pitches.

EARS. Vanes attached to the sides of the mouths of flue pipes which help stabilize the speech of the pipes.

ECHO DIVISION. A portion of the organ placed at a distance from the main organ, usually at the other end of the room. This division usually consists of soft stops such as mild strings and flutes and almost invariably includes vox humana and chimes.

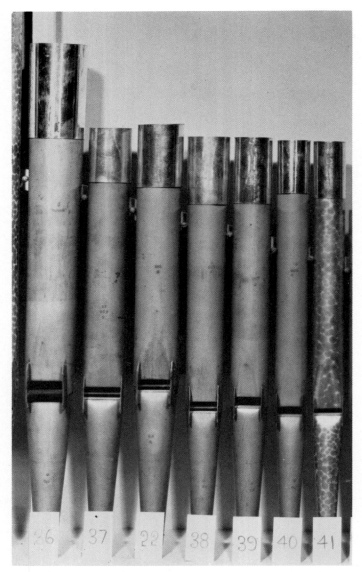

Sample pipes from the great diapason chorus in the Atlantic City Convention Hall organ. Numbers 37, 22 and 38 have double languids and are voiced on 20″ wind pressure. Number 36 has a beard and #41 is made of spotted metal.

(left) A Dennison kinura with a duckbill shallot. (right) A Moller post horn with a goosebill shallot. The post horn resonator has been removed in this photograph.

EFFECT. A non-musical sound effect such as a bird whistle or siren.

ELECTRIC ACTION. Any action wherein electricity plays a role, as opposed to tracker or tubular pneumatic actions which use no electricity.

ELECTRO-PNEUMATIC. An action wherein electricity conveys the signal but the actual work is performed by air pressure.

ENCLOSED. Inside a swell box.

ERECTING ROOM. That portion of a factory where the completed organ is assembled and often played prior to shipment.

FAN TREMOLO. A rotating vane above organ pipes which imparts a slight wavering to their tone.

FINISHING. See tonal finishing.

FLUE. The air slit between the languid and lower lip of a flue pipe.

FLUE PIPE. A pipe which has no vibrating parts other than its air stream. Synonym: labial pipe. Examples: diapasons, flutes, strings.

FOOT. The bottom of a pipe which conveys wind to the flue.

FOUNDATION. The tonal family which provides support for the rest of the organ ensemble. In classic organs the foundation stop is the diapason; in theatre organs it is the tibia clausa.

FREE REED. A metal tongue which vibrates through an aperture rather than against a shallot. The tone producing element in parlor reed organs.

FREIN. A sharp-edged beard placed at the mouth of a wooden violin pipe which stabilizes its speech.

FUNDAMENTAL. The first harmonic frequency of a pipe which determines its pitch.

GENERAL CANCEL. A combination piston which turns off all stops.

GENERAL PISTON. A combination piston affecting all stops in all divisions of an organ.

GOOSEBILL SHALLOT. A shallot whose bottom is rounded to a point similar to the bill of a goose. Used on bright, fiery ranks such as post horns.

HALVING RATIO. The rate at which the scales of the pipes in a rank change as they progress upward in pitch. For example, if one pipe of a rank is half the diameter of the pipe seventeen notes below it, the rank is said to possess seventeenth halving.

HARMONIC. 1) The process of making a pipe twice (or sometimes three times) its natural length in order to increase power in its lower harmonics. 2) One of the natural sound frequencies generated by a pipe which are whole number multiples of the fundamental frequency. The first harmonic is the fundamental frequency which determines the pitch of the pipe. Overtones are harmonics above the first. For example, the first overtone is the second harmonic, which is a frequency double the fundamental.

HARP. 1) Synonym for chrysoglott or celesta. 2. A single stroke marimba.

HASKELL BASS. A method of pipe construction invented by William E. Haskell which allows a pipe to be shorter than normal length and yet speak with all its natural harmonics.

HIGH PRESSURE. Generally, pressures above five to six inches. It's a matter of relativity, however; 5″ would be very high pressure for a tracker organ but would be considered low pressure in a theatre organ where the average pressure is 10″.

HOYT METAL. Lead which has been given a very thin coating of tin to give it a shiny appearance. Also called two-ply metal.

JUNCTION BOARD. A group of electrical connections where two or more cables are joined.

KEYDESK. 1) The base of a console on which the manuals are mounted. 2) An entire console.

LABIAL PIPE. A flue pipe.

LANGUID. The divider between the foot and body of a metal flue pipe which, opposite the lower lip, forms the flue.

LEATHERING. The process of applying leather or other airtight membranes to organ actions.

LINGUAL PIPE. A reed pipe.

LOW PRESSURE. See high pressure.

MANDOLIN. An attachment for a piano which creates a ″rinky-tink″ effect by having metal or wooden tabs come into contact with the piano strings.

MANUAL. A keyboard played with the hands.

MANUAL CHEST. A chest containing the smaller pipes of a rank which are usually no longer than 8′.

MARIMBA. A percussion instrument with wooden bars struck with soft hammers. Synonym: marimba harp. In Wurlitzer organs, marimba is the reiterating mode of this instrument whose single-stroke mode is referred to as harp.

MASTER XYLOPHONE. In an organ having more than one xylophone, the master xylophone is the louder one and is usually of larger scale and/or unenclosed.

MELODY COUPLER. A device which plays only the top note of a chord.

MIXTURE. A group of two or more ranks of higher pitched pipes which are drawn by one stop.

MOUTH. The area of a flue pipe between the upper and lower lips.

MUTATION. 1) Any pitch other than the unison or its octaves. 2) On Barton organs, a mixture unified from the tibia clausa, usually containing 3 1/5′, 2 2/3′ and 2 2/7′ pitches.

NEIGHBORHOOD THEATRE. A theatre in a suburban location as opposed to one in a downtown business center.

NICKING. Small notches applied to the languids and/or lower lips of flue pipes which make the pipes speak less percussively and with less harmonic development.

NUMERICAL DESIGNATION FOR AN ORGAN. A descriptive short cut using numbers to identify the size of

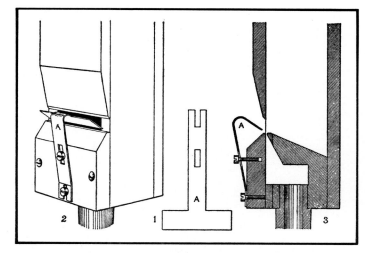

A wooden violin pipe showing the frein, A.

an organ. For example: 2/5, also written as 2m/5r, identifies an organ as having two manuals and five ranks.

OFFSET CHEST. A chest holding an octave or so of pipes which can't be accommodated on a manual chest.

OPUS NUMBER. The serial number assigned by an organ factory to a new organ. Some companies also assigned opus numbers to rebuilds, additions and parts sales.

ORCHESTRAL ORGAN. An instrument whose tonal design sought to be imitative of an orchestra.

ORCHESTRION. A self-contained automatic musical instrument incorporating several instruments and intended to be imitative of an orchestra.

OVERTONE. See harmonic.

PALLET. A flat valve, usually rectangular in shape.

PEDAL CHEST. A chest which contains pipes played by the pedal keyboard.

PERCUSSION. An instrument which produces a sound by being struck.

PERFECT PITCH. See absolute pitch.

PHOTOPLAYER. An instrument designed to accompany silent films whose basis is an upright piano, perhaps with one or two side cabinets containing percussions, effects and/or organ pipes operated via tubular pneumatic action from the piano keyboard and/or an auxiliary keyboard.

PIANO CONSOLE. An organ console consisting of a piano whose keys have been outfitted with electric contacts and to which has also been added an organ manual of 61 keys.

PISTON. A push button located near an organ manual. Usually operates the combination action but may perform any other function such as sounding an effect, signaling the projection booth, etc.

PITMAN CHEST. A form of straight chest pioneered by E. M. Skinner which features individual valves for every pipe and has air pressure in the chest at all times, unlike a ventil chest.

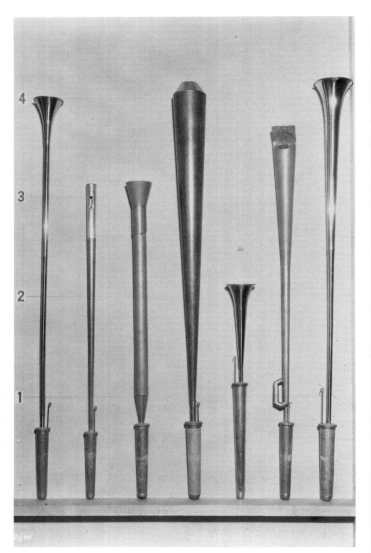

Reed resonators come in a wide variety of shapes and sizes. These samples are from Gallery IV of the Atlantic City Convention Hall organ. From left to right are the Egyptian horn, musette mirabilis, major clarinet, euphone, saxophone, major oboe and brass trumpet.

PIT ORGAN. An organ contained entirely in cabinets located in a theatre's orchestra pit. Usually does not include a piano, but if a piano is present, the organ must have electric action to be called a pit organ; otherwise, the instrument should be called a photoplayer.

PIZZICATO. An electrical device which activates a note only momentarily regardless of how long a key is depressed, creating a pizzicato effect.

PLAYER. A device which plays an instrument automatically.

PNEUMATIC. 1) An airtight pouch which performs a function by inflating or deflating. 2) A shortened form of tubular pneumatic.

PNEUMATIC STACK. A group of pneumatics which activate a piano action.

POUCHBOARD. A strip of wood containing round pouches which act as pipe valves in a chest.

PUSH-UP PLAYER. See vorsetzer.

RANK. A set of pipes of a given voice.

RECORDER BOARD. See setter board.

REED. 1) A reed pipe or set of reed pipes. 2) The vibrating tongue in a reed pipe.

REED PIPE. A pipe containing a vibrating metal tongue. Synonym: lingual pipe.

REEDLESS PIPE. A flue pipe voiced to imitate a reed.

REGISTER. 1) A stop. 2) To select stops. 3) A particular range of a rank, such as the bass register.

REGISTER CRESCENDO. A swell-type pedal which gradually activates stops from softest to loudest.

REGISTRATE. Slang for register.

REGISTRATION. Any selected combination of stops used to perform a piece of music or a portion thereof.

REGULATOR. See reservoir.

REITERATION. Repeating or vibrating action on a percussion instrument.

RELATIVE PITCH. The ability of some musicians to recognize a note, given a standard of reference. See absolute pitch.

RELAY. The electrical switching mechanism which connects keys to the correct chest notes in a unit organ.

REPRODUCING ORGAN. An automatic organ which recreates the playing of an organist via perforated paper rolls, including all notes, tempo changes, stop changes and swell shade movements (volume changes).

REPRODUCING PIANO. An automatic piano which recreates the playing of a pianist via perforated paper rolls, including all notes, tempo changes and the varying intensities with which the notes were struck by the recording pianist.

RESERVOIR. A bellows which maintains a constant pressure. Synonym: regulator.

RESONATOR. A tube containing a column of air which naturally amplifies the sound of a reed or percussion bar.

ROLL TOP. A cover for a console similar to a roll top desk.

ROMANTIC ORGAN. An organ designed to play music of a lush or sentimental character.

SCALE. 1) The size of a pipe. 2) A given progression of musical notes from lowest to highest.

SCROLL TUNING. The method of changing the length of a pipe, and hence its pitch, by bending a flap cut into the pipe itself.

SETTER BOARD. A matrix of switches which selects which stops shall be turned on or off by a combination action. Synonym: recorder board.

SHALLOT. The tube against which the reed tongue of a reed pipe vibrates.

SINGLE STROKE. An action which strikes a percussion instrument only once regardless of how long a key is depressed.

SOCKET. 1) The collar on a reed block into which fits a removable resonator. 2) Synonym for boot.

SOSTENUTO. A device which keeps a note playing after

a key is released.

SPOTTED METAL. An alloy of tin and lead which forms blotches or spots as it cools from its molten state. Used in higher quality organ pipes.

STOP. 1) A stop key or draw knob. 2) A rank of pipes. 3) Several ranks of pipes which are always activated together by one stop, such as a mixture.

STRAIGHT. A set of pipes playing at only one pitch on only one keyboard.

SWELL BOX. A soundproof enclosure allowing the volume of the pipes therein to be controlled by swell shades.

SWELL SHADES. Movable louvres which vary the volume of sound from a division.

SWELL SHOE. The pedal which controls the swell shades.

SWITCHSTACK. A group of electrical switches controlled by the stops of a unit organ which connect the proper chest notes to the proper keys for each stop. Synonym: switchboard.

SYNTHETIC. Usually found only on smaller organs, a synthetic stop seeks to synthesize the sound of a missing rank by combining pitches of two or more other ranks. The most common synthetic stop, for example, is obtained by activating 8' string and 2 2/3' flute pitches on one stop key engraved 'synthetic oboe.'

TENOR C. 1) The second C on a manual or pedal keyboard. 2) The C of 4' pitch in any rank of pipes. 3) An indication, often abbreviated TC, that a stop begins playing on the second C of a keyboard, there being no pipes for the first 12 keys.

TERTIARY ACTION. A feature of some percussion actions which contain both a primary and a secondary valve in addition to the power pneumatic which actually strikes the instrument.

THEATRE ORGAN. 1) An organ designed to play popular music, having as its foundational voice a tibia clausa. 2) Any organ installed in a theatre. See "What Is A Theatre Organ?" on page 16 of this book.

TIBIA. A large scale flute with a penetrating, hooty quality which is the foundational voice of the theatre organ.

TOE. The opening at the bottom of a pipe foot.

TOE PISTON. A push button operated by the foot. Synonym: toe stud.

TONAL FINISHING. The process of adjusting the volume, timbre and speech characteristics of each pipe in an organ to achieve optimal musical results in the room into which the organ speaks.

TRACKER. 1) A form of action wherein the pipe valves in the chests are opened by direct mechanical linkages to the keys. 2) One of the mechanical linkages in a tracker organ.

TRAP. A percussion instrument which does not produce a musical note. Examples: snare drum, Chinese block, tambourine, cymbal.

TREMULANT. A device for imparting a periodic unsteadiness to the tone of organ pipes at a rate of around five beats per second. Synonym: tremolo.

TRICK COUPLER. A coupler of mutation pitch such as 6 2/5' or 4 4/7'.

TRIPLE HARMONIC. Pipes which are three times their normal length in order to increase the power of their lower harmonics.

TRIPPER COMBINATION ACTION. A type of combination action wherein the stops are set into the system's memory by pushing and holding the piston while physically moving the stops to be changed.

TUBULAR. Short for tubular pneumatic.

TUBULAR PNEUMATIC. A form of action wherein signals are conveyed between keys and chests via pneumatic tubes. This type of action enjoyed a brief popularity in the late nineteenth and early twentieth centuries but was soon superseded by electro-pneumatic action.

TUNING SPRING. The sliding member of a reed which tunes the pipe by varying the vibrating length of the reed tongue. Synonym: tuning wire.

UNENCLOSED. Not enclosed in a swell box and hence not under expression.

UNIFICATION, UNIFIED. The process of making a rank of pipes play from more than one keyboard and/or at more than one pitch.

UNIT ORCHESTRA. A unit organ designed to simulate an orchestra. Wurlitzer tried but failed to register this term as a trademark and thus it was also used by Kimball and by a few other builders.

UNIT ORGAN. An organ whose ranks are unified.

VENTIL CHEST. A straight chest having one valve per pipe wherein the ranks are turned off by shutting off their supplies of air pressure.

VIBRAPHONE. A chrysoglott having rotating vanes in its resonators, producing a tremolo effect. Synonym: vibraharp.

VOICER. A person who takes raw pipes from the pipe shop and adjusts them to speak at the proper volume, pitch and timbre.

VORSETZER. (in German, 'that which sits in front') A device which pushes up to a keyboard and depresses its keys mechanically. Synonym: push-up player.

WILLIS WEIGHT. A round brass button screwed to the end of a reed tongue, thereby increasing its mass and reducing the harmonic content of its speech.

WIND CHEST. See chest.

WINKER. 1). A hinged pneumatic provided with a spring which helps stabilize wind pressure. Synonym: concussion bellows. 2) A pressure regulator consisting of a hinged pneumatic and a control valve.

WURLITZER. The world's largest builder of theatre organs. In the 1920s and to a certain extent today, the name Wurlitzer became a generic synonym for theatre organ in much the same way that Victrola became a synonym for phonograph.

INDEX

Costello Theatre, New York, NY, 301
coupler, 423
Courboin, Charles, 388
Cove Theatre, Glen Cove, NY, 318
Cowham, Bernard, 58-60
Cozatt, 103-104
Cramers, Howard, 388
Crandall, H. M., 210
Crane, C. Howard, 210
Crawford, Jesse, 16, 214, 226, 286
Crawford Automobile Company, 346
crescendo pedal, 423
Cronin, Francis J., 176
Crook, Charles, 182
cutup, 423

Dagmar automobile, 346, 347
Daniels, Peter Moller, 11-13, 347, 387, 390
Daniels, Riley, 209, 214, 347, 383, 388
Dargis, C., 327
Davey, Lloyd, 214, 223, 233
Davis, John A., 389
Deagan company, 171, 177, 211, 235, 244
death rattle, 423
Decorators Supply Company, 193
Deerpath Theatre, Lake Forest, IL, 139, 140
Delft Theatre, Marquette, MI, 298
DeMello, John, 98
Dennison company, 55, 65, 68, 71, 73, 84, 182, 195, 197, 290, 309, 397, 424
Derrick, Silas, 132
Derrick & Felgemaker, 132, 345
Des Moines Theatre, Des Moines, IA, 211
Dewar, Robert, 316
Diapason, The, 11, 12, 174, 421
diaphragm regulator, 321, 335, 337, 422
direct electric, 423
Discus blower, 386
divided manual, 60, 61
Doerr, Nicholas, 105
double languid, 321, 325, 331, 423, 424
Douglas, R., 327
Dowling, Leonard, 31
Dreamland Ballroom, Chicago, IL, 70, 73
Dream Theatre, Seattle, WA, 119
Duci Bella, Joseph, 11
duckbill shallot, 423, 424
Dudley Theatre, Boston, MA, 116
Dunstedter, Eddie, 185
duplex, 423
Dupont, Dorothy, 14
Durst, Val, 147
Durst, Boegle & Co., 55, 147, 261, 262

ear, 422, 423
Earle Theatre, Philadelphia, PA, 243, 249
Eastman, George, 42
Eastman School of Music, Rochester, NY, 41-45
echo organ, 220, 227, 423
Edgewater Beach Hotel, Chicago, IL, 371
effect, 424
Egyptian Theatre, Milwaukee, WI, 69
Ehrhardt, Alfred, 11, 154
Eilers Music Company, 49, 286
electric action, 424
electro-pneumatic, 424
Elgar, Charles, 70
Elliot, R. P., 22, 24, 33, 49, 156, 208, 209, 214, 223, 229, 233, 234, 348, 371, 421
Elliott, Walter V., 316
Elm Skating Club, Elmhurst, IL, 142
Ely, Augustus C., 28
Elysee delivery car, 347
Emerson, Ralph, 62, 70
Empress Theatre, Anchorage, AK, 210, 212
Empress Theatre, Cordova, AK, 210
enclosed, 424
Encyclopedia of Automatic Musical Instruments, 10, 12, 421
Endres, Anthony, 83
Engle, William, 33
erecting room, 424

Erie Reed Pipe Company, 147, 195
Essex Institute, 174
Essex Theatre, New York, NY, 317
Estey company, 20, 105-132, 137, 153, 316, 337
Evans, Roscoe, 332
Everett Piano Company, 378
Exeter Street Theatre, Boston, MA, 117

Fabry, G., 327
Fairchild Aviation, 400
Fair Park Auditorium, Dallas, TX, 64, 65, 68
fan tremolo, 35, 36, 424
Fargo Theatre, Geneva, IL, 137, 138
Fargo Theatre, Sycamore, IL, 137
Farrand, William R., 132
Farrand Organ Company, 22, 132
Farrand & Votey, 16, 22, 33, 132, 208, 322
Federlein, Gottfried, 28
Feiereisen, Chris, 11, 18
Felgemaker, A. B., 102, 132, 133, 145
Fenton, Arthur, 101
Fenton Organ Co., 101
Ferris & Stuart, 315
56th Street Theatre, Philadelphia, PA, 226
Fine Arts Theatre, Monmouth, IL, 104
finishing, 424
Fischer, J. & C., 206
Fischer Theatre, Fond du Lac, WI, 69
Five Boro automobile, 347
Flaherty, Charles A., 179
Floyd, C. B., 155
Floyd, Clifford, 155
flue, 424
flue pipe, 424
Foort, Reginald, 381, 386, 388, 421
Foort Moller organ, 346, 365, 382-388, 390, 399
foot, 424
Forster, Paul, 301
45th Streeet Theatre, Seattle, WA, 226
Forum Theatre, Los Angeles, CA, 210, 214, 216, 218-222, 230, 243
Fotoplayer, 16, 51
foundation, 424
Fountain Square Theatre, Indianapolis, IN, 299
four-poster lift, 65, 69, 190, 300
Fox, William, 348, 350, 371
Fox Theatre, Atlanta, GA, 192, 360, 362, 375-377
Fox Theatre, Aurora, IL, 170
Fox Theatre, Detroit, MI, 15, 374
Fox (Orpheum) Theatre, Oakland, CA, 368
Fox Theatre, Philadelphia, PA, 351
Fox Theatre, St. Louis, MO, 374
Fox Theatre, San Francisco, CA, 374
Fox Wilshire Theatre, Beverly Hills, CA, 108, 287
Frazee, H. Norman, 134
Frazee, Leslie, 132, 134
Frazee, Roy, 134
Frazee Organ Company, 134-136
free reed, 424
frein, 424, 425
Fruttchey, Frank, 162
Fuller, Frederick, 83
fundamental, 424
Funkhouser, J. O., 388

Gaiety Theatre, Trenton, NJ, 373
Garden Theatre, Greenfield, MA, 302
Gautschi, Alfred, 169
general cancel, 424
general piston, 424
General Precision Engineering, 270
Geneva Organ Company, 20, 137-144, 177, 178
Gerrard, C. P., 145
Gilbert, Robert, 11
Gillett, Don, 378
glass crash effect, 228
Glazer, Irvin, 11
Gleason, Harold, 42
Glen Theatre, Glen Ellyn, IL, 72
Goldthwaite, Chandler, 223

Gollnick, Walter, 58, 59
gong, Chinese, 235
Good Hope Lutheran Church, Bucyrus, OH, 207
Goodrich, William M., 174
Goodwill Theatre, Johnson City, NY, 91
goosebill shallot, 145, 333, 423, 424
Gordon, F., 327
Gordon's Olympia Theatre, Brockton, MA, 176
Gottfried, Anton, 145, 147, 150, 151, 330
Gottfried, Henry, 147
Gottfried Co., 20, 49, 51, 55, 69, 71, 83, 84, 137, 138, 145-152, 169, 176, 178, 265, 315, 397
Gould, C., 327
Grace Cathedral, San Francisco, CA, 12
Granada Theatre, Malden, MA, 134
Granada Theatre, Patchogue, NY, 319
Grand Theatre, Norristown, PA, 228
Grand Theatre, Wausau, WI, 184, 185, 190
Grant Union High School, Sacramento, CA, 51, 52
Gratian, 153, 154
Great States Theatres, 62
Green, W. S. "Stu", 11
Greenbrier Hotel, White Sulphur Springs, WV, 371
Gregory, S. J., 62, 66, 77
Griffith-Beach, 154
Griffith Piano Company, 154
Gutfleisch & Schopp, 145, 159

Hagerstown Trust Company, 346
Hagstrom, Oscar, 207, 214, 223
Haldeman, Clarence, 31, 32
Hall, Ben, 421
Hall, Harry, 155, 156
Hall, Thomas, 315
Hall Organ Company, 20, 155-157
Haltnorth Theatre, Cleveland, OH, 265, 268-270
halving ratio, 383, 424
Hampton, Hope, 296, 297
Hanrahan, J., 327
Hanson, Eddie, 60
Hardy, Walter, 208, 223
Harmon, Paddy, 70, 73, 77
harmonic, 424
harp, 424, 425
Harrah, Allen, 11
Harris, David, 196
Harris, Edward "Ted", 92
Harris, Murray M.—see *Encyclopedia of the American Theatre Organ*, Volume II
Harrison, G. Donald, 107, 365
Harrison & Harrison, 365
Haskell, C. E., 157
Haskell, Charles S., 157, 158, 264
Haskell, William E., 105, 107, 157, 337, 425
Haskell basses, 107, 109, 127, 425
Hastings, Anna C., 174
Hastings, Francis H., 174
Hedgeland, Frederic, 207
Hedges, Edwin, 145
Heinz Auditorium, Pittsburgh, PA, 232
Hess, Max, 182
Highland Theatre, Chicago, IL, 66, 70, 83
Highland Theatre, Ft. Thomas, KY, 90
high pressure, 425
Hill, John, 139
Hillgreen, Alfred, 159
Hillgreen, Robert Jr., 11, 159, 160
Hillgreen, Robert Sr., 159
Hillgreen, Lane & Co., 20, 159-168
Hillstreet Theatre, Los Angeles, CA, 370
Hillstrom, Nils W., 22
Hillstrom Reed Organ Company, 159
Hinners, Arthur, 169, 172
Hinners, John L., 169, 172
Hinners & Albertsen, 169
Hinners Organ Co., 20, 31, 32, 95, 103, 169-173
Hippodrome Theatre, Alton, IL, 153
Hippodrome Theatre, Los Angeles, CA, 371
Hogans, Henry, 137
Hollingsworth, Mr., 94, 95